The Powered PARAGLIDING Bible

Jeff Goin

Air Head Creations

Copyright © 2005 Jeff Goin, All Rights Reserved
Published by Airhead Creations

ISBN: 0-9770966-0-2
Library of Congress Control Number: 2005908312

Edited by
Dennis Pagen

Photographs by Jeff Goin except where noted.

For related materials, please visit
www.FootFlyer.com.

Naperville, Illinois, USA

Email jeffgoin@airheadcreations.com

The information is accurate to the best of our knowledge but inaccuracies may occur. This material is protected by U.S. and International copyright laws. No part may be reproduced or transmitted in any form or by any means, electronic or mechanical without written permission from the publisher.

The reader acknowledges that powered paragliding and related activities carry significant risk including dismemberment and death. You take this risk completely of your own volition and understand that neither Jeff Goin, nor Dennis Pagen nor any other participants assume any liability in connection with this book or other material related to it.

Printed in Canada

Table of Contents

Foreword viii
How to Use This Book viii
Thanks To ix
Preface x

Section I: First Flight

    Ratings 2
    What it Takes Physically 2

Chapter 1 The Training Process
    Finding an Instructor 3
    The School 4
    Different Methods of Instructing 5
    Certification 7
    Training Aids 7
    Getting to that First Flight 10
    Progression 10

Chapter 2 Gearing Up
    The Wing 13
    The Risers 15
    The Harness 16
    The Motor 19
    Instruments 20
    Accessories 21

Chapter 3 Handling the Wing
    Deflating the Wing 24
    Brake Positions/Pressures 24
    Preparing Yourself 25
    Preparing the Wing 26
    Forward And Reverse Launch 26
    Light Winds (Forward Inflation) 26
    Wind Over 6 mph (Reverse Inflation) 29
    Storing the Wing 35

Chapter 4 Preparing For First Flight
    Adjusting the Motor 37
    Fueling 38
    Preflight Inspection 39
    Starting the Motor 41
    Have a Plan: Patterns, Areas and Altitudes. 42
    Taking Instructions Via Radio 43
    Handling Emergencies 44

Chapter 5 The Flight
    Launch 51
    Flying Around 57
    Landing 59
    After Landing 62

Chapter 6 Trike Flying
    Setup 64
    Launch 64
    Flying 66
    Landing 66

Table of Contents

Section II: Spreading Your Wings

Chapter 7 Weather Basics
- The Perfect Day 69
- Thermals & The Daily Cycle 70
- Indications of Turbulence 70
- Thunderstorms 71
- Mountains 72
- Beach 72
- Whenever There's Wind 73
- Acquiring Aviation Weather 75
- Other Weather Sources 76

Chapter 8 Common Sense & The Law
- Regulations 78
- Case Law & Other Issues 79
- Commercial Use 81
- If I Violate the Rules? 82

Chapter 9 Airspace
- Airspace Types 84
- The ABC's of Airspace 84
- Reading The Charts 89
- The Airspace Test 92
- Other Uses for the charts 95

Chapter 10 Flying From Anywhere
- Choosing the site 98
- Site Permission 99
- High Elevation Fields 99
- Flying At or Near Airports 100
- Places to Look 103
- Safe Havens 104
- Telling Wind Direction From Flight Path 104

Chapter 11 Flying From Controlled Airports
- Telephone 105
- Aircraft Radio 106
- Letter of Agreement 110

Chapter 12 Setup & Maintenance
- Harness 111
- Motor 114
- Reduction Drive 117
- Clutch 118
- Propeller 118
- Propeller Repair 120
- The Wing 123
- Emergency Tool Kit 126
- Reserve 127

Chapter 13 Flying Cross Country
- Basic Tips 129
- Fuel & Range 131
- Getting Lost 131
- Navigation 132
- Pilotage 134
- Altitudes 136
- Using a GPS 136

Table of Contents

Chapter 14 Flying With Others
- Courtesy 137
- Risks 138
- Rescuing a pilot 139
- Communications 140
- Formation Flying 140

Section III: Mastering The Sport

Chapter 15 Advanced Ground Handling
- Upside down kiting to clean out cells 143
- Kiting Without a Harness 144
- High wind techniques 146
- Light Wind Techniques 151
- Inflation Issues 152

Chapter 16 Precision Flying
- Brakes—The Feel Position 155
- Straight Lines—Pendular Precision 156
- Balance of Power 158
- Low Flying 160
- Hitting Suspended Targets 161
- Formation 161
- Active Flying in Turbulence 162
- The Perfect Touchdown 163

Chapter 17 Challenging Sites
- The Horror of Hot, High, and Humid 165
- Tight Spaces 168

Chapter 18 Advanced Maneuvers
- Weight Shift Turns 174
- Speedbar Usage 175
- SIV Course 175
- Descent Techniques 176
- Wing Malfunctions 179
- Pendular Control 181
- Stabilo Line Pull 182

Chapter 19 Risk Management
- Probability and Severity 183
- Energy and Injury 184
- Getting Away With It 185
- Where the Risk Is 185
- Adding Safety Equipment 191
- Combining Risks 191
- Handling Situational Emergencies 192

Chapter 20 Competition
- How Good Do I Need To Be? 200
- Ground Precision 200
- Flight Precision (Navigation) 204
- Fuel Limited Tasks 204
- Endurance 205
- Kiting 205

Chapter 21 Free Flight Transition
- Transition to Thrust: Becoming a Power Pilot 207
- Transition to Free Flight: Going Soaring 211

Table of Contents

Section IV: Theory & Understanding

Chapter 22 Aerodynamics
- Balance of Forces ...217
- Stability ...219
- Glide & Drag ...220
- Center of Lift and Drag ...221
- Sink Rate ...221
- Speed ...221
- Efficiency Under Power ...222
- Wing ...222

Chapter 23 Motor & Propeller
- Thrust & Horsepower ...227
- 2 And 4-Stroke Motors ...228
- Propeller & Reduction Drives ...233
- Balance ...236
- Twisting Forces At Work ...237

Chapter 24 Weather & Wind
- Using Forecasts ...241
- Principles ...242
- Standard Atmosphere ...242
- Daily Cycles ...243
- Yearly Cycle ...245
- All About Thermals ...245
- Clouds ...247
- Fronts ...248
- Getting Weather Info ...249
- Turbulence from Wind ...249

Chapter 25 Roots: Our History
- Parasailing ...251
- Hang Gliding & Ultralighting ...251
- Sport Parachuting ...252
- Lost Lineage ...252
- Performance Improvements over time ...254

Section V: Choosing Gear

Chapter 26 The Wing
- Ease of Launch ...257
- Size ...258
- Glide and Sink Rate ...258
- Stability ...258
- Handling ...259
- Speed ...259
- Certification ...260
- Risers ...261

Chapter 27 The Motor Unit
- Weight ...264
- Comfort ...264
- Thrust ...264
- Quality ...265
- Powerplant Considerations ...265
- Ease of Launch ...267
- Ease of Maintenance ...268
- Fuel Storage—Above, Below, or in the Frame ...268
- Propeller Size and Style ...268
- Attachment Points & Separation Bars ...269

Table of Contents

    Weight Shift 270
    Transportability 271
    Support—Parts and Expertise 271
    Safety 272

Chapter 28 Accessories
    Reserve 273
    Trike 274
    Helmet, Hearing Protection, Communications 274
    Tachometer 275
    Wind Indicators 276
    EGT, CHT 276
    Altimeter/Variometer 277
    GPS 277
    Emergency Kit 277
    Cold Weather Gear 278

Chapter 29 Home Building
    Building Your Own Design 280
    Building From Plans (Scratch) 281
    Building From A Kit 281
    Testing & Changes 282

Section VI: Getting the Most Out of PPG

Chapter 30: Other Uses
    Using PPG for Transportation 285
    Flags & Banners 286
    Cattle Herding 287
    Search and Rescue 288
    Finding Model Aircraft 288
    Public Relations & Exhibition 288

Chapter 31 Traveling With Gear
    Shipping 289
    Transporting via Road 291
    Customs 292

Chapter 32 Photography
    Still Photography Basics 293
    Video 297

Chapter 33 Organizing Fly-Ins
    Preparation 299
    What to Include 300
    Sharing 300

Appendix - Checklists

Appendix - Resources
        Fuel/Oil Mix Chart 302
        Repair 302
        Instruction 302
        Welding 302

Appendix - FAR 103

Glossary

Page vii

Foreword

The easy travel inherent in my "day job" has let me learn from many of our sport's greatest pilots and teachers; people who have gone far beyond just succeeding. They have different styles, to be sure, and even different disciplines within the sport, but they share a desire for excellence in their respective realm. This book is an opportunity to share that wealth of knowledge.

Our instructors remain our greatest resource; I hope this material serves as an additional tool for them, for those coming into the sport, and those aspiring to master it.

No book can instill a skill. What we hope to show is not only how to do a task, but what *practice* will turn the task into a skill along with ways to minimize risk in the process. There is no way to learn a kinematic "feel" from reading, but knowing which exercises develop what skills will go a long way towards gaining that feel.

Is it Risky?

Flight always involves risk. What limited statistics there are suggest that our odds for survival are better than flying small airplanes or ultralights but we are more likely to suffer minor injuries. Our primary advantage is low speed.

It's certainly not as safe as watching others experience life through TV but is a whole lot more fulfilling!

As Wilbur Wright observed in response to the many naysayers: "If you are looking for perfect safety, you will do well to sit on a fence and watch the birds." But, of course, even that can be dangerous.

How to Use This Book

It is imperative that this book **not be used for self training!** That risky undertaking is fortunately no longer required given the presence of many qualified instructors. Absolutely nothing contained here should be tried without getting good instruction first.

Our craft is a wonder of simplicity—graceful and capable in the air but ungainly and challenging on the ground. You can, however, overcome a surprising amount of ungainliness with a small investment in instruction.

Read Section I to prepare for initial training and become familiar with the terminology. Read further sections as your interest dictates, but they'll be more meaningful later on. Section I gets you through the first few directed solo flights. It assumes that the instructor will take responsibility for determining appropriate gear, conditions, location and all the other things that go into choosing flight. It covers what most schools call the "Solo Course."

Section II covers the basic knowledge needed to head out on your own. Some schools include it in their solo course. Your instructor can help make the material more relevant to your particular location and situation. For example, if you live near a big city, ask about charts and airspace. If you live in mountainous terrain, dig more deeply into mountain weather.

Read Section III if you aspire to master the finer points of flying the craft accurately. The degree of control available to those who are willing to learn it is truly amazing. There are many nuances.

Every pilot should eventually read Section IV to build a more complete understanding of what's going on around them, especially the chapter on Aerodynamics. Among other things, it dispels myths that continue to circulate.

If you're an experienced pilot buying gear, read Section V first. New pilots should always choose an instructor rather then gear, but there is a lot of benefit to understanding the tradeoffs. It may help avoid shysters who would try to fit their round-pegged gear into your square-holed needs.

Section VI offers suggestions on "what now?" Some of it is just plain fun, but hey, that's what this sport is about.

Companion Web Site:

Updated and supplemental information to this book will be placed on **www.FootFlyer.com**. Videos and other material will also be placed there, geared toward you, the reader.

Thanks To

Many have contributed to my earliest and fondest memories of this sport and my flying; I am thankful for them all. Here are just a few.

Mom: "It's a passing fad, you'll get over it." —Words that my 13 year old ears just wouldn't accept. Fortunately she not only relented, but eventually encouraged and even joined my quest for flight. And Dad, who tolerated all this with aplomb.

Eric Dufour: "Don't look at the wing—it won't tell you anything you can't feel." At my first fly-in, I watched this man really *control* the craft and found out what *could* be done with it.

Michelle Daniele: "It's a fly-in, if anyone gets mad at you for launching early, have them see me!" —After asking if it would be ok to launch at dawn during their first Balloon Fiesta fly-in.

Nick Scholtes: "I thought you weren't interested" —After introducing me to the sport, I disappeared. The next time we met I had gotten training, purchased gear and couldn't get enough. We proceeded to gorge ourselves on airtime over the next few years.

Mark Sorenson: "Power up to go up." —Words of my first PPG Instructor that I wish I would have heeded more. Sorry it took so long.

Jerry Daniele: "We fly at the pleasure of the people; tick them off and eventually we won't fly anymore." —Wisdom that has driven many of my early efforts and some current ones (including this book).

Chris Bowles: "Uh oh, it's on." Words that ended the first USPPA officer meeting after recognizing that soarable conditions had developed at his Moore Mountain home.

Alex Varv: "This is my baby, every now and then I like to come out and just admire it" —Referring to his newly updated machine equipped with more gauges then some airplanes. And he knew what they all meant.

Rob Sutter: "Jeff, you gotta check this out. You wanna to go in with me on one of these powered paraglider things?" —The fellow who enticed me into that first fateful look at powered paragliding. He never did get into it.

Alan Chuculate: "Just lean back and go for it!" —One of many admonishments from the instructor who *really* taught me kiting.

Jeff Williams: "You might even like the soaring." —My first paraglider instructor whose patient wisdom guided me beyond the basics to a love for free flight. Yes, Jeff, I understand now, you *can* soar the heights without a variometer.

The Brothers Casaudemecq, Jose & Javier: "It'll fly you just fine at that weight" —The two gentlemen who gave me advice on a used motor that would be my first and longest lasting. They were oh so right.

Elizabeth Guerin: "Oh, you were the one that was never on the ground." —After my first fly-in when we met up several months later.

Bruce Brown: "Wanna go play in the road?" —an enticement that preceded a remarkable low-level romp around the New Mexican desert floor at my first fly-in.

Phil Russman: "Is it over?" Gifted crafter of content who always challenged me to excel. Yes, it's over.

And also...

Mom, again—A wonderful human, a picky editor, an English Major, newspaper woman, a flier of other things, creative wordsmith and *brutal*.
Dennis Pagen—For getting me to do it in the first place, refining it, tolerating all of my non-standardness and making it work. Brutal, too!
Tim Kaiser—Editing, photo victim and "Enterprise" captain whose many miles at the helm enabled many pages of work. And he survived being my first student. Thankfully, he was mercifully easy.

And to those who helped with material—they've improved this book *enormously*:

Mark Andrews . . . . . . .Maneuvers	Chris Lee . . . . .Aerial Photography
Bob Armond . . . . .Kiting, Setup, Emergencies	David McWhinnie . . . .Shipping
Chad Bastian . . . . . . .Maneuvers, Emergencies	Wayne Mitchler . . . . . .Handling The Wing, Setup, Trikes
Jeff Baumgartener . . .Homebuilding	Mike Nowland . . . . . . .Cross Country, Motors, Wings
Steve Boser . . . . .Propellers	Dana Hague . . . . .Aerodynamics, Motors
Bill Briley . . . . .Maneuvers	Steve Mayer . . . . .My "Paraglider Encyclopedia"
Chris Bowles . . . . .History, Engines, Setup	Scott MacMurray . . . .Line Tangles
Stu Caruk . . . . .Towing information, Airspace	Dennis Pagen . . . . . . .Everything
Alan Chuculate . . . . . .Wing Maintenance, Kiting, & Situational Emergencies	Phil Russman . . . . . . .Aerial Videography
	Nick Scholtes . . . . . . .Motors, Trikes, Precision flying
Francesco DeSantis . .History, Homebuilding	Tom Scott . . . . .Composite Propeller Repair
Eric Dufour . . . . .History, Glossary	Mo Sheldon . . . . .Trikes, Glossary, Propellers
Betty Pfeiffer . . . . .Reserves	Geoff Soden . . . . .History
Bill Heaner . . . . .Glossary	Alex Varv . . . . .Setup, Motor Maintenance

Page ix

Preface

When my friend, Rob Sutter, first suggested this sport I thought he was nuts. "You want to do what?" I asked him. He knew that I was a flying nut. That wasn't hard—I lived on an airport with a hangar in my back yard. He figured me an an easy mark, wanting us go in together on something I'd never heard of, yet another flying contraption. My first thoughts went to the guy who loosed himself over Los Angeles in a lawn chair with weather balloons. Not me. But Rob insisted, saying it was more refined and he wanted someone to share it with. So I went for a look.

What I found was astounding—revealing refinement and control that I could hardly believe. I first expected that it must be more *influenced* than flown; but after much browsing, and many questions, it came to light that they *could* be finely controlled. *That* got me fired up—it seemed almost too good to be true. Being free of regular airplane rules was even more exciting. I've spent my aeronautical life adhering to those necessary regulations and this looked like a way out, or at least partway out.

My mind raced—scooting around the surrounding fields at an airborne whim ignited desire. You mean I could wander at my leisure, flitting from point to point, in any direction, exploring in three dimensions? "There's got to be a catch" I thought. The idea of running into the air was cooler still—stirring me like no other flying ever had. And I was already flying airplanes for work, airplanes for fun and, most recently had just gotten my helicopter license. That was certainly all great but the paramotor seemed so much more intriguing. After all, I could take it *with* me.

I contacted Nick Scholtes who was already flying in the area. He was incredibly welcoming and answered my many questions, even hanging me in his little DK motor unit from some contraption he had sitting around his shop (a tip of his iceberg, I eventually learned). We watched videos, talked endlessly and he allayed my fears. I worried needlessly about plummeting to my demise from the least little bump. Yes, there is risk, but it appeared to be less than other risks I willingly accepted.

That visit sealed my fate. Unfortunately this all came about during our Chicagoland deep freeze—there would be no flying here and I wanted to start my training now! The recommended instructor, Alan Chuculate, was not available so I stumbled onto another gem, Jeff Williams. After eight days, spanning two trips to his home area in California, I earned my USHGA P2 paraglider rating (for motorless flight), an experience that re-ignited a long-held fascination with soaring flight (I had my glider license at 16 years old). Then I went in search of propulsion. After a few calls, Aerolight in Miami satisfied my thirst for thrust as instructor Mark Sorenson sold me a little direct drive unit that he had modified. Aerolight's Jose & Javier had just taken over the Fly line and were extremely helpful. Mark agreed to include training for which I am eternally thankful.

A week later it was at my house: the wing, the motor, the helmet, everything was there. I was captivated. The prospect of trotting down to the end of my little road and launching from 50 feet of grass was amazing. The summer of 1999 I flew every single day the weather cooperated, sometimes going both morning and evening. First the local area, then on to more distant locales, then on to 15-plus mile cross-country jaunts in whatever direction suited me.

It was a freedom that I could not get enough of, a pent-up longing to fly like nothing else ever had. It so invigorated me that I started writing about it—something I'd never had any interest in doing. Ask any of my high school teachers to peg the writers and I wouldn't have even made the long list. But write I did, flights of fancy spilled into PPG newsgroups and eventually magazines, letting me relive these unbelievable experiences.

The passion flourished, filling many aspects of my life and revealing new ones. The simplicity, the freedom, the minimal regulation, it appealed to me more than any other form of flight, including the helicopter. I wanted to help preserve it, to give our sport a voice, to help develop good training programs and to encourage others to embrace it in a sustainable way. This book is the culmination of that desire.

The PPG Bible: A Complete Guide and Reference

Section I

First Flight

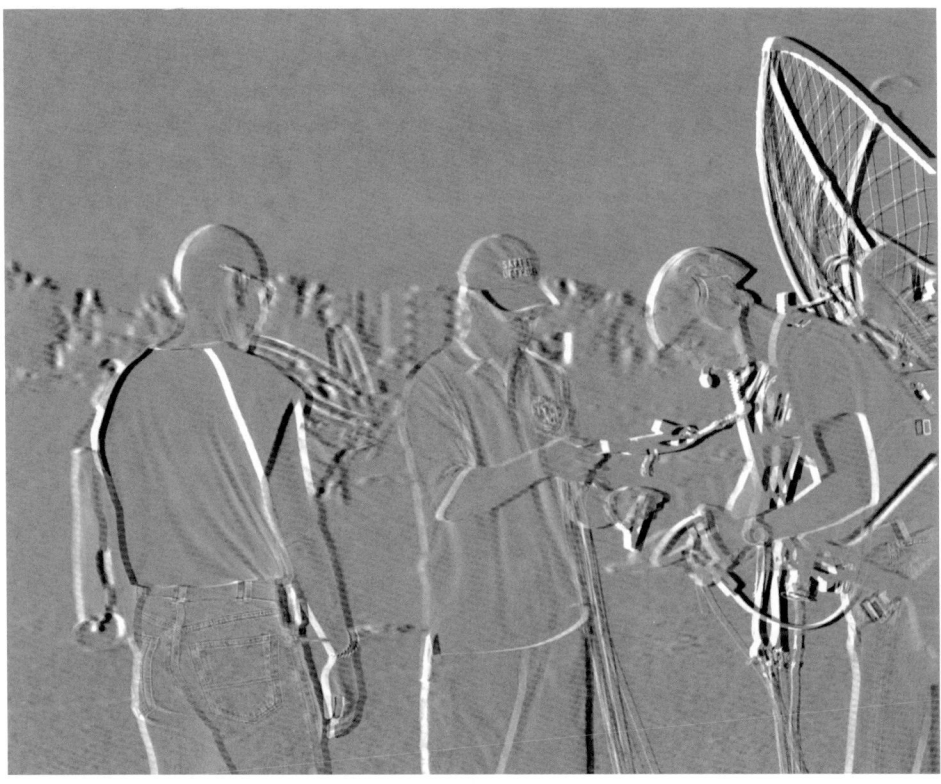

Section I

For many who take it up, powered paragliding is the apex of personal flying. Unprecedented freedom and simplicity combine with surprising safety and low cost. There is no runway needed, no radio, no trailer; just pull up to the launch site and be airborne in as little as 10 minutes.

A dedicated student can learn the basics in three days under the guidance of an experienced Instructor. This section is intended to help with the knowledge required to solo; to get that first flight. To be a pilot, flying comfortably on your own, expect five to eight days of training and practice. Continued practice, training, and reading will build a confident autonomy within a year.

Ratings

For solo paramotor pilots in the U.S. there is no requirement for a license or rating (although many other countries do require them), but there *are* requirements for tandem (two seater) flying. However, solo pilots will find that acquiring ratings gives a meaningful way to measure personal accomplishment and progress. Ratings can also provide milestones during the learning process that will help assure thorough, methodical training.

We in the U.S. are blessed with the simplest path to flight of any aviation segment in the world, and it is up to us, as responsible citizens, *to keep it that way!*

What it Takes Physically

You don't have to be an athlete; you don't even have to be in stellar condition, but it does take some exertion—especially while learning. Flying itself is almost relaxing, once airborne, but the early stages will produce some sweat.

Fortunately, as skills improve it gets *much* easier. Even after just a few sessions, newly recruited muscles adapt to their strange purpose and brute force gives way to finesse. A skilled "kiter," for example, can go for an hour with minimal exertion whereas the neophyte will be winded in a few minutes.

Expect to be a bit sore on the first few days—it diminishes quickly though. It is a soreness to be relished!

The instructor, Chris Bowles, makes final checks before launching a student on his first powered paragliding flight.

The Training Process

CHAPTER 1

No, a license is not required, but don't think that means no skill is required. Although powered paragliding may epitomize aerial simplicity, without proper training it can be most vexing. A good instructor will guide you carefully through many milestones while the under-trained pilot faces a horrible and dangerous experience.

Skimping on training can easily cost more in equipment repair and/or medical expense than is saved on instruction—many just give up without proper training.

Additionally, flying in the national airspace system is not a trivial matter. Considering world events and societal fears, heading into the blue without knowing the legalities is just irresponsible folly. Fortunately you've taken a huge step by using this book—the instructor will bring it to life.

Finding an Instructor

We do this because its fun and the training should be too. Try to find an instructor you can get along with, who is thorough and has access to a decent place to fly. Be mindful that training is a lot of work for both of you; don't expect to be pampered, but you should expect to be treated with respect. If you're willing to immerse yourself into the program then you will probably get along with just about anyone out there. Most instructors teach because they love the sport, certainly not for the fame and fortune! Even with decent profit margins on the gear there is not enough volume to make it big business. Instructors are Powered Paragliding's (PPG's) national treasure.

The best resource for choosing a school is personal recommendation by a trusted pilot. Try to find someone in the community with nothing to sell who you can talk

The PPG Bible: A Complete Guide and Reference

Some schools use wheeled tandem craft for an introduction to flight. It allows the student to taste control as well as delight in the experience. Eric Sansli (in back) is letting a new pilot get the feel of flying.

to. If possible, visit potential instructors, talk with them and watch them train—you'll learn a lot about their demeanor and style.

If you have no direct knowledge of an instructor or school, at least make sure they are certified for PPG, not just other ultralight types like powered parachutes (PPC's). While certification is not required by the government (except for tandem), it does show them to have minimum knowledge and skill along with demonstrated teaching ability. Not only do they meet standards established by a national organization but they enjoy the training resources of that organization.

Be wary of anyone who's only been flying for a year or so themselves—they will not be well versed in the intricacies of student issues. Just about any pilot can explain how it's done but experience gives the instructor a depth of understanding to better recognize and correct student problems.

Ask if the instructor uses a thorough syllabus, preferably one approved by a national organization. Such guidance will help insure that important details are not skipped.

Don't worry too much about equipment and don't buy into the sales pitches. When you start hearing that this or that is "best," step back and look around. Like most aspects of aviation, there are trade-offs. It is most important that you get matched up with appropriate gear for your size, weight and intended take-off elevation (flying at Albuquerque's 5000 foot elevation requires different choices then flying at sea level). A reputable instructor will do this matching within the line of gear he is authorized to sell. It turns out that your success in the sport has far more to do with your attitude and choice of instructor then your choice of gear.

The School

A school is not better because it is bigger but there are advantages. Larger schools are almost always full-time which makes scheduling easier. You'll be able to spend three to five days in a row—a concentrated environment that allows rapid progression. You'll have to travel, though, and support will largely be by mail and phone.

Smaller schools, usually one-person affairs, can offer equally good training but it will probably spread out over more time. They may have to schedule you on weekends. But if they're local, that is beneficial since you'll enjoy close support for training, equipment, places to fly and probably a ready community of other pilots. If you have a local instructor and he's qualified, be thankful, most don't.

Some instructors will come to you, but find out what expenses you'll be paying, it could wind up being less of a value. Also consider how you'll get service after they

> ⚠ **Caution!**
> Never, ever have someone pull you up with a rope (even by hand) or tie yourself to a stationary object while hooked into your glider. There are dynamics that make this incredibly dangerous. Unsuspecting flyers have died trying these things since it looks so easy. One of several maladies can whip the wing off sideways and down, dragging you along for the whack. Once it gets started, the controls are insufficient to recover—there is no stopping the inevitable.

leave. The benefit is that they'll be able to help you pick out local sites, identify local weather patterns and airspace issues.

Any school should have access to a sufficiently open area to fly that they have permission to use. They should also have a simulator, ground school materials, and examples of the various equipment available to buy. It is expected that they will prefer only a few types of wings and motors which is OK; they have figured out how to train on that gear and should be able to support it.

Schools that offers training on their equipment do so with the understanding that damage will be paid for by the student. They usually require a deposit. A few schools require that the equipment be purchased in advance.

If the school offers tandem introductory flights, try one to see if it's for you or not. You can also watch how the instructor and school operate with minimal commitment. Another good option is to find a school that will train you on their gear through first solo, then decide what to do. Be mindful that you are nowhere near ready to set out on your own after such an introduction.

Different Methods of Instructing

There are many different ways to learn and certainly one size does not fit all. Some instructors are very laid back, some are up tight. Some are more aggressive and some very conservative. Drill sergeant types use the military approach and have a very serious demeanor but can still be very effective.

Instructor Brad Weiss works with a student on high-wind kiting skills. Like many ocean beaches, this one serves up consistent on-shore breezes, ideal for learning to handle the wing. The bulging free-flight harness is for back protection—common on soaring harnesses.

Schools that have mountains available will probably teach free-flying first. That is fun in its own right and will expose you to a different type of flying; it was the approach I took. But it takes more work in many ways since the weather must fit a narrower window. You will come to understand "parawaiting:" what pilots do while perched atop some launch site awaiting better winds.

Flatland schools will more likely teach motor flying only. Their methods may incorporate towing or tandem although a few don't offer either—the student's first time aloft is his first motor flight. That is not ideal but, with strong guidance, proper practice on the simulator, and a huge open field it can be done with reasonable safety.

Towing Types

Several tow methods can safely loft pilots to various heights. They all include proper tow line, a release mechanism for the pilot, a way to control line tension by the tow operator, a weak link and a way to cut the line in case of emergency. The pilot should have (and rehearse using) a quick-release as well as a hook knife for a last resort line cut.

Special procedures help make the operation safer including visual signals and a well thought-out process. Radio communications are the norm, but pilot response usually comes from kicking (signals yes) or waving (signals no) his legs. Above all the tow operator must be trained to operate the rig safely and handle emergencies.

Most schools use the *scooter tow*, a modified motor scooter whose rear wheel has been replaced by a drum containing tow line. These systems are relatively inexpensive, stationary, and can be run by the instructor (although ideally there is a separate tow operator). The operator has a way to chop the line quickly in case of emergency. High tows are typically up to around 800 feet although higher altitudes are possible with more line and a stiffer breeze. A *turnaround pulley* can be used which has the line go out 1000' or so, through a pulley and back to the tow rig. This allows the student to start right from where the instructor is, allowing easy conversation during preparation and close supervision of the launch. Low tows are commonly used and are somewhat safer; you only get up to about 20 feet during these.

You may encounter *step towing*. The pilot is pulled upwind towards the winch as with scooter towing. At the normal release point, the winch clutch is released and he turns downwind to fly away from the winch, pulling line out as he goes. Then he turns around back towards the winch as it powers up to pull higher yet—"stepping" to more altitude than possible with regular towing. However, if the line catches on something as the pilot is flying away, it could plunge him to the ground. This very risky method is obviously not used for training.

Truck towing with a payout winch is another way to net higher altitudes (over 2000 feet depending on line and conditions). It requires a longer run and another person—besides the driver, there must be a winch operator. The truck starts off rolling and pulling the pilot aloft while the payout winch lets out line at a controlled tension. The truck may be moving 30 mph but the payout is letting line out at 15 mph so the effective pull is 15 mph. The line length increases as the truck progresses. If the glider is rocketing up at a steep angle (happens only with a breeze) then the payout may need to reel out so fast that the pilot is not even moving forward over the ground—just climbing like mad. This is where experienced tow operators must call on their expertise to prevent excess climb by metering payout rate and keeping line tension within limits. Gliders and tow bridles can be overstressed with these operations. Having a guillotine to chop the line is more important here because if the payout stops, the line suddenly starts moving at the same speed as the truck—a potential catastrophe.

Boat towing typically gets the highest tows—over 3000' is possible in good conditions. Expect to pay more owing to the need for a powerful winch-equipped boat. It's normally reserved for getting pilots high enough to practice aerobatics or learn to handle wing malfunctions at *maneuvers clinics*. It is like truck towing except the pilot launches from shore and flies mostly over water. Extra precautions, such as flotation, must be in place for safety in case the pilot goes swimming.

All methods can be effective although not all will be ideal for each student's learning style. The best instructors adapt somewhat to how each student learns but some adapting is left for the student too.

There is a balance to pacing your progress through training. For example, if you (or the instructor) pushes too hard, its real easy to skip necessary information or rehearsals, overlooking critical steps. On the other hand, training can bog down and require lessons to be relearned; it's easy to then become disenchanted—frustrated by the apparent lack of progress. There is a difference between rapidly paced and carelessness; with proper precautions, the quicker schedule can be accomplished with reasonable safety. For example, there is benefit to working with higher wind in order to be prepared for it.

The first flight is but a beginning. Much more remains to be learned and practiced, and much of that with the instructor's guidance. We are given a lot of leeway both in regulation and training required. The regulations are not intended to protect the pilot—only the non-participating public. So it is entirely incumbent on the student to continue his learning—not only for self preservation but also to understand the national airspace system in which we operate.

Like all freedoms, PPG flying requires responsibility. We will either accept that responsibility or we will lose the freedom.

Certification

Look for instructors certified by an organization with a thorough Paraglider or Powered Paraglider program. Anyone can hang a shingle out and call themselves an instructor but not everyone can demonstrate the skills and knowledge. While there may be good instructors who are *not* certified, the onus falls on the student to find out about them. Visit www.USPPA.org for a list of schools and their certification level.

Beware that requirements for getting certified vary dramatically; some organizations have done little more than "stamp" instructors based on non-PPG skills. Check out what minimums apply and what skills have to be shown to get their rating. If a pilot cannot demonstrate skills, it sure will be hard for them to teach those skills.

No ratings program is perfect; they all rely on human instructors and, regardless of the organization, there will be variety. This same diversity dogs government certification programs, too.

Training Aids

Training aids for paramotoring are simple and effective. Most important is the *simulator* which can be nothing more then a place to hang by your hook-in (attachment) points; all reputable schools use some form of it. Other aids help in various ways and degrees but, of course, not all aids will be used by all schools.

One valuable training aid is a method to get airborne, even if only for short unpowered flights, before that first powered solo. This can help alleviate first-flight anxieties and their attendant problems. If your school does not offer a method to do this (towing, hill launch or tandem), it is advisable to get at least one dual training flight in whatever craft is available. Even flying a powered parachute or ultralight would be better than plunging into the sky with no prior piloting experience; the fewer sensory firsts, the better.

Towing

Towing involves having an experienced operator pull you up like a kite—once airborne, you pull a release and glide down for landing. After a few low tows to get a basic feel for handling the

Towing in the right hands is a great training aid. Done casually or by inexperienced tow operators, it can be deadly.

1. Bill Briley controls a direct *scooter* tow using its throttle while talking to the student via radio. It's called that because it's built from a scooter whose rear wheel has been replaced by the line drum. It is anchored stationary as it reels in line.

2. Bruce Brown uses a *turnaround pulley* where the tow line goes out to a pulley and back to where both the student and tow operator can talk.

glider, you may progress to higher flights (depending on the school—some only do low tows).

It is also used for lofting free flyers high enough to catch rising air currents (thermals) and soar without power. They get towed up on very long lines and usually release above 1000 feet. Under the right conditions they can fly for hours this way. Soaring requires different, more advanced skills owing to the turbulent conditions associated with thermals. It invokes higher risk but offers its own reward.

Kyra Busque is getting an early start on wing handling. Her dad, Kyle, is showing her kiting without the risers. The wing is sized for him (larger) so she'll have to work pretty hard. There are no age limits for powered paragliding but parents must use good judgement. As a guide, student sailplane pilots can solo at age 14 in the U.S.

Tow operators must know what they are doing—preferably they are certified although it is not technically required. Some schools only do "low" tows which are generally safer than high tows but still require extreme care since the pilot is continuously low to the ground.

With some breeze (5-10 mph), hand towing is possible with appropriate precautions. It gives some minimal feel for the wing, flying, and landing flare. It takes a breeze and surprisingly hefty pull by two people who must know what they're doing. Like other towing, it can quickly go awry if not done properly.

Hills

"Bunny" hills are just large enough to allow a ground-skimming free flight. You can practice launching, flying briefly and landing before ever strapping on the motor—a nice benefit. A light-weight harness is used so trudging up the hill isn't that bad. This is how most students learn to paraglide (without the motor)—launching from shallow hills at first then progressing up to elevations where soaring flights are possible given the right conditions.

The slope of the hill should be about 4 to 1, meaning that it drops 1 foot for every 4 feet forward. That simplifies launch and allows the glider to pull away from the hill once in flight. Your flight time (and height) can be metered by how far up you start. In the right conditions this is ideal but does require the wind to be either calm or coming up the slope. Most schools in hilly areas will have several sites to choose from so they can find a hill with the right wind.

Tandems

Tandem foot launched instruction is very demanding of the pilot since he must carry a motor powerful enough for the combined weight of both occupants. (1) Jarrod Bottonelli launches from 5000 feet elevation in Albuquerque, NM. (2) Francesco DeSantis and Dawn Pistocci cruise Florida's West Coast.

Tandems allow you to get airborne with an experienced pilot at the helm of a two-place unit. They are frequently done in a two-place trike but sometimes are done foot launched—a far more challenging task for the pilot. They offer an opportunity to feel flight, gain a basic understanding of the craft's handling and give the instructor an opportunity to gauge your reactions to flight.

In the U.S. and most other countries the tandem pilot must hold a special pilot rating or certificate to give these flights and must follow special rules governing them. In the U.S., ultralights are legally limited to solo flight and may only be flown tandem under an exemption (see www.FootFlyer.com) and for the purpose of training.

Tandem training can be highly valuable although control feel is quite different from a solo wing, but the principles and directions are the same. The tandem rig will be much heavier on the controls, won't climb nearly as well and probably won't turn so crisply.

Simulator

This may well be the most important piece of equipment used by any instructor: It provides a place for the pilot to sit in the motor unit by its intended hook-ins. It can be as simple as straps around a tree limb or an elaborate device with brake lines, bungees, and special riser spreaders.

Critical aspects of flying will be rehearsed from this simple setup. Besides certain normal flight drills, you will rehearse emergencies whose solution is not always obvious and must be practiced.

You will learn to react to instructor directives on the radio while coping with a flood of strange sensations. On that first flight, you'll be glad you paid attention in the simulator.

Throttle simulator

This is a throttle handle that behaves just like its connected cousin but with a cable that goes nowhere. It seems silly until you get to the point of standing there with all this stuff in each hand. Practicing with the throttle simulator early on helps smooth the way to wearing the full motor.

Weighted Frame

A few schools use a motor frame (no motor) for early training then progressively add weight as you improve. It lets you learn kiting with the bulky motor on but without the full burden of its weight.

Multimedia

You'll hopefully get to see some videos. *Risk and Reward* is a must-see followed by *Instability II* and probably others. Some are just humorous, fun and add to the enjoyment.

Keep in mind, these are just tools. Like this book, they are not intended to replace thorough instruction, but to supplement it.

Radios

Ours is a solo craft and that makes communication essential. Good radios allow the instructor to give directions while you learn launching, flying and landing. If something goes wrong, or conditions change, the instructor can provide guidance. You'll either have to purchase or be provided with a helmet that works with the radio that your instructor uses.

1. Airlines realize the value of training aids. This $16 million dollar 737 model lets Southwest pilots master skills for situations that they will never likely encounter.

2. Bruce Brown has a student practice taking radio directions while experiencing the noise and feeling of full power. This invaluable rehearsal helps insure responses are swift and correct when it really counts. Emergency procedures should be rehearsed either with the motor running, or other distractions until the response is automatic.

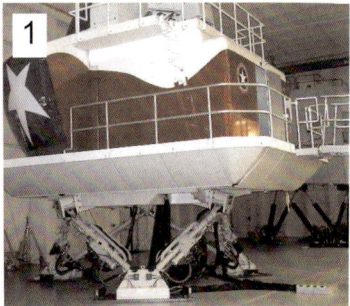

The PPG Bible: A Complete Guide and Reference

A must-see video is "Risk & Reward." It shows where the risk is and how to avoid it. If there is one video you purchase, this should be it.

Ideally, you'll watch it several times including once with your instructor. Ask about anything that's not clear. And far more important than watching is rehearsing!

The video was commissioned by the USPPA. Producer/PPG Pilot Phil Russman (pictured hanging on a simulator built for the production), myself, and others put hundreds of hours into it.

William Shatner, who appears several times in the video, got instruction in California and achieved 12 flights. Several years later he asked for help flying into a Chicagoland charity event. As a certified airplane pilot he knew the importance of training, recency and personal limitations. Nick Scholtes agreed to be the instructor and we all worked together to make it happen safely. The larger picture shows Mr. Shatner flying East over the Northern Illinois landscape, accompanied by Nick (on the right), myself (shooting the picture) and several other Illinois pilots. The mission was a success. Score one for the Federation.

Getting to that First Flight

As with all training, your attitude will largely determine your success, enjoyment and safety. Listening to the instructor and reacting properly to his directives is paramount. It's not always easy; new pilots have difficulty processing the instructions during the noise and sensation overload of those first few flights. Having the right attitude and simulator rehearsal will help a lot—the instructor wants to see you succeed but must be able to work with you. Come to the lessons with that understanding. Even if the training seems almost harsh at times, it's because of the critical necessity of following directions properly. In all likelihood you will cement a relationship with your instructor that will be enjoyed for years.

How long it will take

Duration of training is tough to call since there are so many variables with weather topping the list. If flyable conditions prevail, expect to solo with 2-5 days of training. A solo flight, with assistance, can be done quite early when extra precautions and preparations are taken but that is still very early in the learning process.

Much will depend on your stamina. Being able to handle the wing on the ground (kiting) is the most important skill for launching—that takes some effort. Newly minted muscles will make their presence known after day one.

Learning is way more demanding than actually flying. Once equipped with the necessary skills, you'll only bear the motor's weight for a minute or so before launch transforms it into your magic chair. But gaining even the rudimentary skill for wing handling will take several hours of practice and improvement will come for years.

Weather Dependent

One of the most desirable flying conditions is still air—the perfect calm of paramotoring nirvana. Unfortunately for early training, a 6 to 12 mph wind is ideal. The gusty conditions of mid-day are as undesirable for training as they are for flying. Beaches serve up the best conditions with their moderate "sea breeze" coming in almost every warm afternoon.

Winter weather presents both challenges and opportunities. Low sun means the typically stronger winds are smoother—good for kiting. It's mellow longer into the day too.

Progression

If you must travel to a distant school then try to schedule at least 3 consecutive days—5 is better. This improves the odds for getting acceptable weather. Depending on the location and time of year, that can be a challenge. You're one of a lucky few if the school is within daily driving range but be prepared to be cancelled due to weather—call first.

When you arrive on the first day, you'll be introduced to the people, the school, and yes, the paperwork. Have a full pen and strong reading glasses—the forms are many and their print is fine. There is indeed risk involved, but don't be scared off by the ubiquitous and dreadful sounding waivers—the sport has proven far less dangerous than they would lead you to believe.

Depending on what the school provides, expect to buy a few things even if your big purchases have been made. A kiting harness and helmet are common first purchases. It is far better not to buy gear in advance unless requested to do so by the school—each instructor has reasons for using what they do. Frequently it is compatibility with their training style or gear. Hopefully you can decide on a motor and wing by the time training has completed. All motors and most modern wings are just as good for flying as they are for training—so your best bet is to purchase the gear on which you learn. Then after gaining a year or so of experience you are better equipped to judge other brands.

Expect to be kiting on your first day if conditions cooperate. Mid-day may be used for simulator and ground work as this is usually a good time to hang in the simulator to make harness adjustments. It will be important to practice this essential skill. Being able to kite on your own would be beneficial but get at least some rudimentary training first.

After gaining proficiency with wing handling using just a small harness (15 - 25 hours is considered ideal), you'll graduate to doing it with the motor on, but not running. Then more practice in the simulator with the instructor on radio, probably with the motor running.

The big day for your first flight will probably include some dress rehearsal and review of emergency procedures before actually going aloft. The solo may be "assisted," which can get you airborne earlier but in a less-prepared state. There is nothing wrong with it as long as you remain committed to further training.

For those able to do training in stages, learning to kite in an early visit is valuable so that you can then go home and practice. Mind the cautions given by your instructor—dangers lurk whenever you're hooked into the wing.

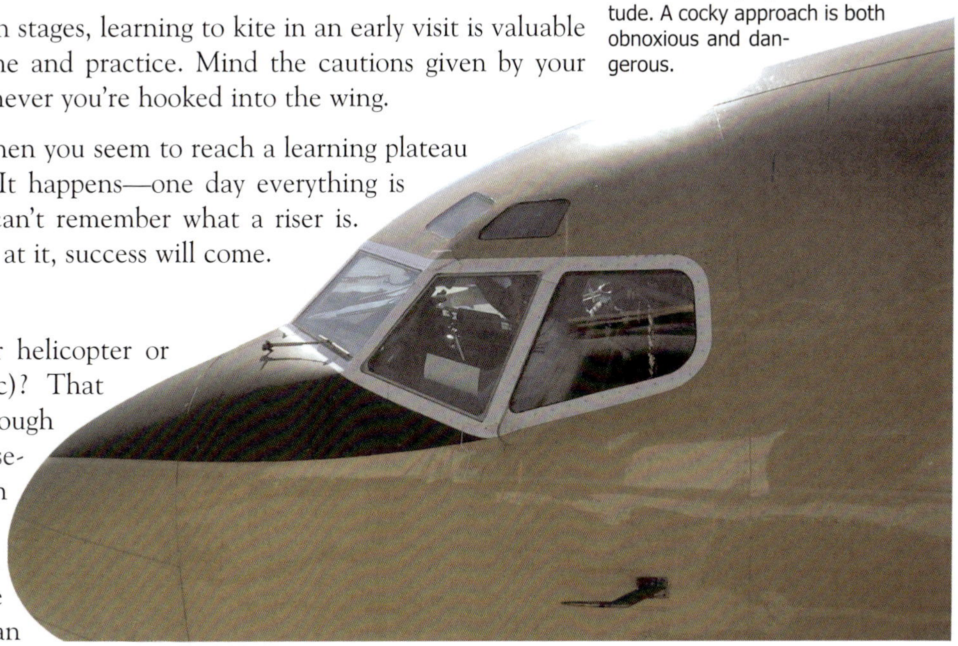

Regardless of past experience, treat this sport with great respect. Safety is almost entirely up to the pilots attitude. A cocky approach is both obnoxious and dangerous.

One common frustration is when you seem to reach a learning plateau or, worse yet, go backwards. It happens—one day everything is great and the next day you can't remember what a riser is. Maddening, but normal. Keep at it, success will come.

Previous Experience

So you're an airline pilot (or helicopter or sailplane or hang glider, etc)? That won't help you much here although the knowledge will prove useful—you already have an understanding of airspace, general aerodynamics, and other relevant bits. But for the physical aspect, this sport can make a mockery of previous experience.

We have found that previous experience in other flying machines has amazing irrelevance to learning powered paragliding. The critical maneuvering responses are vastly different than anything you've likely experienced. While not difficult, they certainly require the same attention and respect that your first "V1 cuts" (or auto-rotations, or spot landings or burner failures or whatever) did.

This warning is even more true for sky divers. Don't be tempted to think of the canopy as just an efficient version of what you jumped with. Some of the maneuvers done by good sky divers are nothing short of deadly in a paraglider. One experienced sky-diver turned PPG instructor tells how he nearly killed himself with this attitude; he tried to treat the paraglider like his free-fall canopy. It is likely that the flying will be easier but un-learning certain behaviors will be harder. Pay close attention to the limits of brake pull and low, steep maneuvering risks—give the craft much respect until you are very experienced.

The worst thing the pilot of another craft can do is to short-change his training based on perceived existing capability. Such arrogance has preceded the demise of many who take this "superior" approach.

The training process will be like many—frustrating yet invigorating. It will have highs and lows but the end result will be an experience like none other, whose value will far exceed the effort.

Attending fly-ins is another way to watch, learn and get help from a variety of experienced pilots. Pilot and safety officer Steve Boser (in yellow shirt) is offering John Coulter advice on a challenging launch towards the inland buildings.

Eric Dufour (inset wearing hat) works with the History Channel's Josh Bernstien. The outdoor adventurist wanted to learn powered paragliding both for fun and to use on his show. The larger shot is Josh enjoying the fruits of their combined labors.

Josh had the right attitude, he listened intently to his mentor and excelled. After the five-day session he had nearly 10 flights under his belt.

Gearing Up

CHAPTER

2

If only the Wright Brothers could see our stuff now.

This overview covers the strange collection of gear that gets us airborne. It is only for basic understanding—details on choosing are found in Section V and information for adjustment, care and repair are found in Chapter 12.

The Wing

The paraglider is your most important component. While strong and resilient—it is able to suffer any number of individual failures and still fly—it is also the most likely to degrade with time and use. When a wing wears out or fails an inspection, it must be replaced.

During flight, air is forced into the leading edge (front) openings and through internal holes to create a very slight internal pressure that keeps the shape against tension in the lines.

We share almost identical technology with soaring (free flight) paraglider pilots who fly off hills with the same wings. Of course, some models are indeed purpose-built for motoring; they usually have thicker lines.

Fabric

Most modern gliders use a coated ripstop nylon that is nearly airtight. Additional coatings help protect the fabric at some expense in weight and launch ease. With the right care, a wing will last for 300-500 hours but abuse or marginal care can easily cut that in half.

Wings don't like heat, sun, dampness, most chemicals or sharp objects. They easi-

The PPG Bible: A Complete Guide and Reference

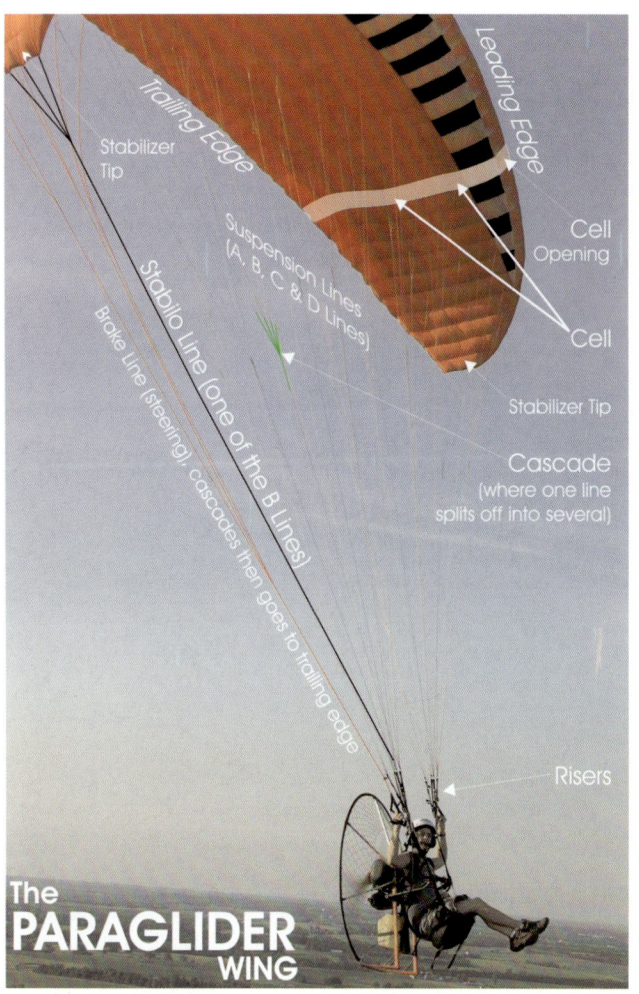

ly succumb to sharp rocks, sticks, nails or other protrusions. "Ripstop" just means that tears don't spread easily but they will still spread.

Ultraviolet radiation causes nearly invisible degradation that can weaken the fabric dramatically. It becomes porous and loses strength—keep wings out of the sun as much as possible. Many manufacturers say that 300 hours of direct UV is the maximum recommended lifetime exposure. Limiting sun time to early morning or late afternoon lowers total UV so it is possible to get more hours then that.

Lines

Lines from the risers form a wing's primary airfoil shape by virtue of their position and length. The forward row of lines, the "A's", bear most of the weight, followed by the next row (the "B's") and so on. Some wings have 3 rows of lines and some have 4 rows. Newer soaring gliders tend to have fewer and thinner lines to reduce drag. All but the oldest wings have relatively few lines down at the risers that *cascade* into many lines up at the wing—a method to reduce drag.

Each line actually carries relatively little weight but must be strong enough to handle sudden "pops" in case the wing collapses partially and then "pops" back to shape.

Most gliders have small loops sewn into the wing where the lines attach; this makes for easier line replacement. A very few models have the lines sewn right into the wing—not a good arrangement when lines need to be replaced.

Each line (except brake lines) is a strong bundle of finely spun material sheathed in a thin protective outer weave. This is very strong in the stretch direction (high tensile strength) but degrades quickly if bent sharply or heated too much. Avoid walking on or hooking lines in a way that could bend them sharply.

> ⚠️ **Caution!**
>
> It is possible for a line to break inside the protective outer sheath such that the damage is not visible. Sharp bending after trying to extract a wing stuck on something is the likely culprit. The break can be felt by running the line between your fingers and feeling for a "lip" where the inside Kevlar has separated.
>
> This would render the line useless—it would appear intact but be unable to bear any significant load.

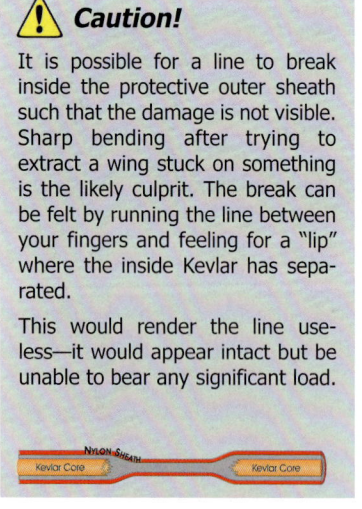

Brake Lines:

These *steering* lines run from the trailing edge (back of wing), down through a brake pulley (or sometimes a metal ring) and into *toggles* held by the pilot. They are made of a more flexible material than main lines so they can handle all the bending at the pulley. Brake lines require less tensile strength than regular lines since they carry no flight load.

They work by pulling one side of the trailing edge down which slows that side of the glider in order to affect a turn. The pilot swings in the opposite direction and pendulum action causes the bank.

Page 14 — Section I: First Flight

The Risers

These strap-like assemblies attach to the wing lines and give a loop where a carabineer can be used to connect the wing to the harness—one on the left side and one on the right. Each one is made up of several individual risers lettered A through D. They spread the load out to individual rows of lines. They are usually color-coded but the color schemes vary by manufacturer—a red riser on one glider may be the green riser on another.

Wing lines are connected to the risers through Quick Links (also called Maillons). Risers can be separated easily from the lines, and therefore the glider, so as to install different risers. Because this changes the distance to each row of lines, it changes the wing's characteristics. Wings and risers are certified together so optional riser sets should only be installed after verifying compatibility. The most common reason to switch risers is when using a free-flight paraglider on a high hook-in motor. It's hard to reach the brakes and lines unless shorter risers are installed.

Trimmers

Most wings marketed for motoring have a strap-slider attached to each rear riser that, when extended in flight, grants a small airspeed increase. By letting the trimmers out the trailing edge rises up thus making the wing faster by about 10%. It also increases the sink rate or, if flying level under power, requires more thrust.

For most wings the trimmers are left in their shortest (slowest) setting. Letting them out can improve the launch behavior for some wings since it makes the wing come up faster. The trade is a longer, faster run before getting airborne.

Split A's

Some wings have Split A's where the outermost A line has its own riser. That makes it easier to reach up and pull down just those outer lines which collapses the wing tips. Doing so is called "pulling big ears" and is done to increase descent rate.

Quick Links

It is never good to connect nylon to nylon (lines right through riser material) so metal fittings connect lines to their respective risers. A rubber O-Ring keeps the lines tightly together. When lines are replaced they are removed from this fitting on the riser and the wing.

Speed System

A speed system comes with most wings. It has a line on each riser that is intended to connect to a harness-mounted, foot-activated speed bar. When the pilot pushes on the foot bar, it pulls the A lines down which speeds up the wing.

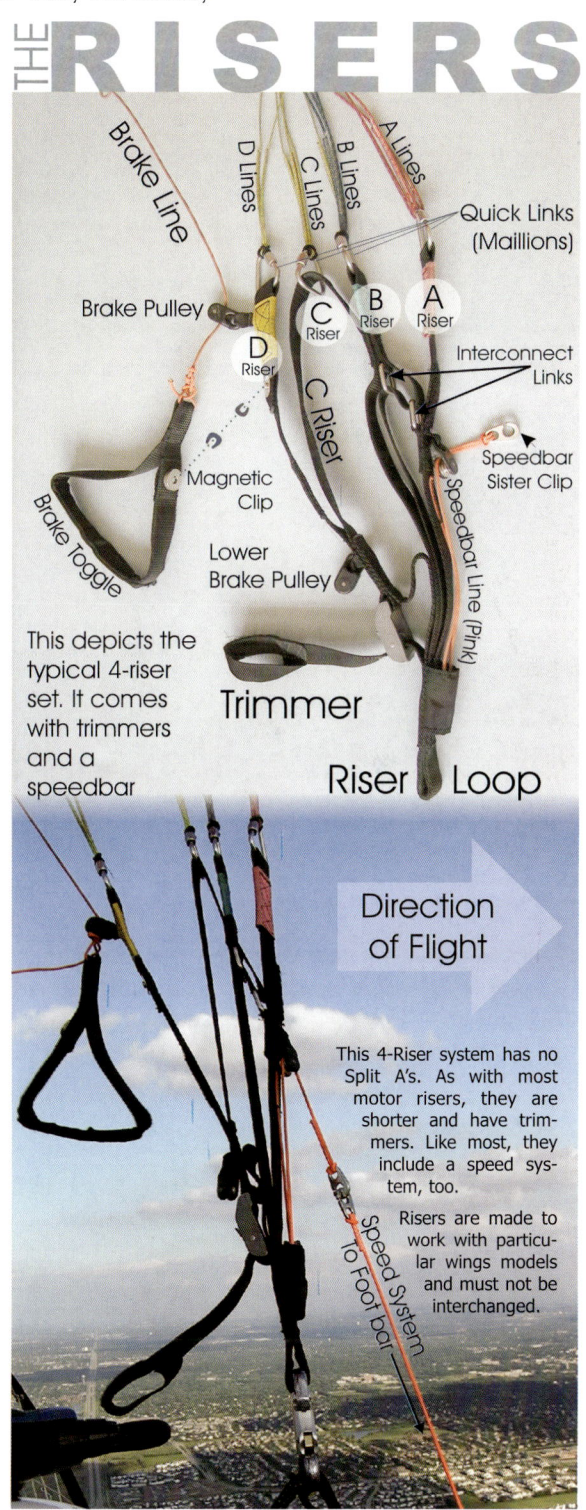

The PPG Bible: A Complete Guide and Reference

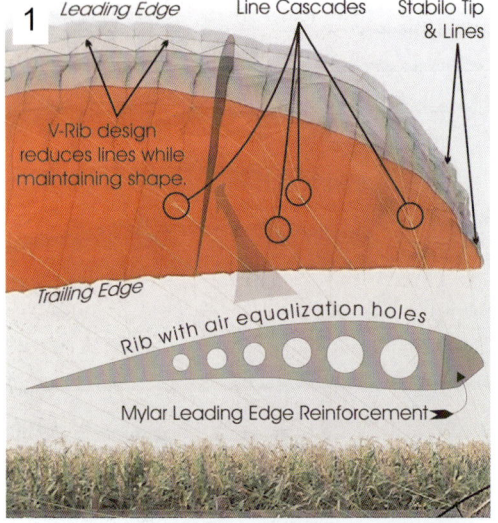

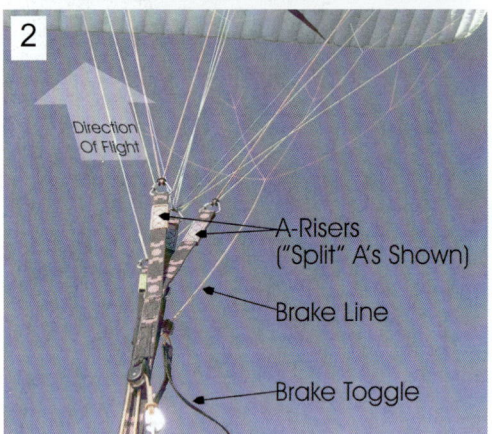

1. **Structure**: The wing's top surface is held to the bottom surface using *ribs* that keep the airfoil shape. The space between ribs is a cell. More cells make for a better airfoil shape but add weight, expense and confer slightly different flight characteristics.

Air enters at the leading edge openings and flows through internal holes between cells. This helps the wing re-inflate quickly after a deflation (collapse or "fold").

V-Rib construction reduces the number of lines (lessen drag) and Mylar rib reinforcements (on the front most part of the rib) improve low-wind inflation characteristics. Higher performance wings typically have more cells.

2. **Split A Risers** make it easy to pull down the outer line (right one), useful for "pulling big ears."

Interconnecting lines also pull the B's and C's down some to keep the airfoil shape.

The wing portion of the speed system connects to the harness portion through "sister clips" that are made to be easily attached/detached.

A speed system works similar to trimmers (which raise the wing's rear instead of lowering its front) but is more effective. It also has the advantage that it can be released immediately by letting off the considerable foot pressure but does require continuous push to keep it engaged (trimmers you can set and forget). It is best to avoid speedbar use with trimmers out (set for fast) or while in turbulence—doing so increases the chance for a "front tuck" (see Chapter 18).

Most systems have 2 pulleys which are used like block and tackle to give mechanical leverage. It takes more speedbar travel than on one-pulley systems but is quite a bit easier to push.

Speedbar systems are less common on motor units and so not all motor harness are equipped with the necessary footbar connection points and pulleys. Even if it is equipped, most schools will not have it hooked up for the early flights.

The Harness

The harness supports you and your motor in flight. Almost all motors come with one specifically designed for that brand and model. The simplest harness is a seat with leg loops, waist belt, with a place to hook the motor and wing.

A harness is generally way overbuilt with webbing capable of supporting many times what it will ever carry. A steep turn or turbulence, however, can bring it much closer to its design limits so it must be kept in good shape.

When you launch, the wing first lifts the motor's weight, then lifts you by the leg loops which are part of the harness. Once airborne, you kick or push a seat out and remain seated until ready for landing. The harness must be adjusted properly and be reasonably comfortable—that's not just for enjoyment either, leg circulation can get blocked leaving it numb.

Numerous adjustments (see Chapter 12) are made on the harness to fit your weight, height, and desires so expect your instructor to spend some time getting you situated with it. Among other things, adjustments determine how your motor will hang, how it will handle torque, where the brakes will be and how to best get into the seat (not always a simple matter). These adjustments are critical—failure to do them properly could yield a dangerous or un-flyable machine.

A few brands are intended to have the pilot put the harness on first then hook the motor to it (like the one worn by the girl at right).

Page 16 — Section I: First Flight

The PPG Bible: A Complete Guide and Reference

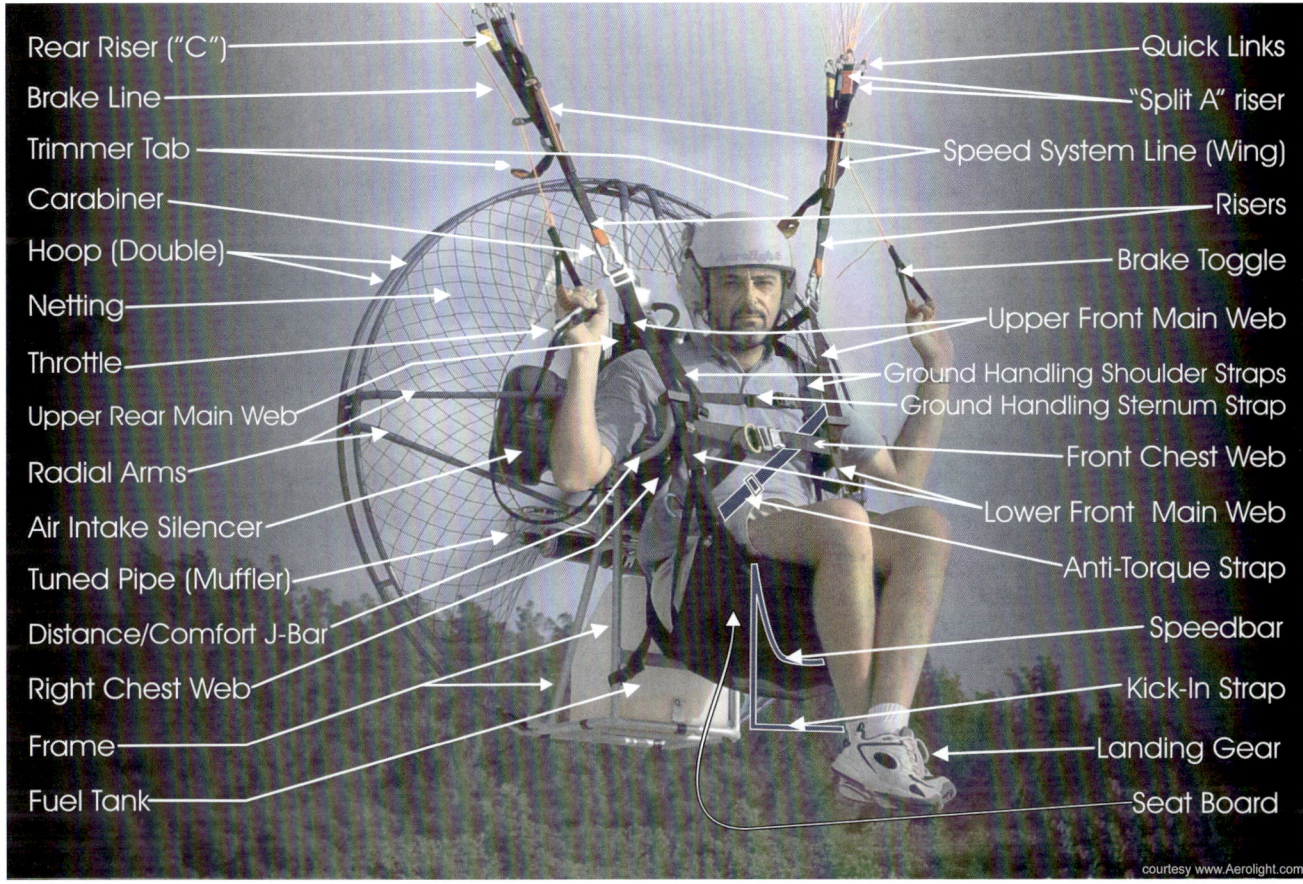

courtesy www.Aerolight.com

Diagonal Anti-Torque Strap

Torque is the root cause of several different turning tendencies opposite the direction of prop spin—it can be significant. Some harnesses add a strap that transfers pull from one side to the other to help even things out. It goes from down near one leg across the chest strap diagonally and up to the other side. Machines with *weight shift* (shifting one riser up and the other down to cause a shallow turn) do not use this strap because the weight shift feature can counteract torque.

These straps only reduce one element of torque and so have very limited authority, especially on machines adjusted with significant lean-back. See chapter 23 for a thorough discussion of torque's various causes.

Ground Handling Straps

Also known as *carry straps*, these are made to better carry the motor around on the ground. They bear no flying loads. Some ground handling straps include a chest

Not all motors have all features but these are quite common. This machine has fairly high hook-in points and uses *underarm*, also called *comfort* bars, to keep the harness webbing away from the pilot's body.

Webbing is the term used for the large load-bearing straps.

> **Digging Deeper**
>
> Several older designs started out with J-bars to balance the heavier weight of the motors in use at the time. Big motors were required to get the inefficient early wings airborne. That's not surprising since it was improvement in wing design that made our sport possible in the first place—the earliest wings would have required heavier motors than anyone could reasonably heft on foot.
>
> But as pilots sought better-performing soaring wings they unwittingly carved an opportunity for the birth our sport.

strap (sternum strap) to better hold them together. Most are designed to be loosened easily once airborne which is usually more comfortable.

Shoulder J-Bars

Nearly all machines have a *spreader system*, some way to keep the forward harness webbing from pushing against the pilot while under thrust. Shoulder J-bars were an early solution and are still used, in a modified fashion, on many machines. They provide a metal piece over the pilot's shoulder into which the wing hooks. Two hang points, in front and behind the pilot, support all the weight through webbing. By having the wing hook-in up high it reduces turbulence-induced motion transferred to the pilot.

On many J-Bar units, the wing hooks up through a D shackle and then the J-bar attaches separately to a strap going down to the front of the seat. Since a failure of the bar or shackle could be catastrophic, a safety strap is frequently employed that connects the main harness to each riser in addition to the shackle.

Modern machines with J-Bars usually have a "floating" variety that allows enough movement to give some feel for the wing. This keeps the pilot hanging in the same way as regular J-bars but without being as stiff. They can also allow varying amounts of weight shift steering (see Chapter 18).

J-Bar machines are considered to be high-attachment systems since the wing attaches to them up above the pilot's shoulders.

Underarm or "Comfort" Bars

The simplest harness has the front straps coming from the leg loops right up the pilot's chest—not a very comfortable arrangement. Underarm bars, like J-bars, provide the necessary separation. They are positioned under the pilot's arms and, on some machines may swivel up and down to provide weight shift steering. At least one brand allows them to swivel outward for easier entry and exit of the machine (but they must not be allowed to swivel *inward!*)

On some systems, the carabiners attach right to the bar which provides low attachment points. Usually this is done to more closely mimic free-flight harnesses and mate better with soaring wings. Those with pivoting arms are usually set with low-enough attachments to allow effective weight shift steering. If the arms are fixed then the machine is probably *not* intended to have much weight shift capability.

Soft Harness

Some of the simplest machines have no separating bars at all and are generally suited only for smaller pilots; taller pilots would be pinched by the front and back straps. This style is found most commonly on older designs or direct drive (small, low power) machines.

The Buckles

The vast majority of harnesses have quick release buckles that are easy to use: pinch buttons on the side to release. They are not designed to be releasable while under tension.

Some older harnesses have a pair of rectangular metal fittings that serve as buckles. They're simple, cheap and effective but take some getting used to. The small rectangle goes through the larger one at an angle. Pulling it tight flattens the pieces

Germany has the unique requirement that, to be certified there, a paramotor must allow jettisoning the engine and fuel tank. That is why this German-built unit has pull rings on the harness hardware—they are quick releases. The feature is not required by any other country and is not used on other brands. It is intended that the pilot release the motor in case of fire or water landing or other unforeseen calamity.

The carry straps (also called ground-handling straps) are common on many models and are intended to make it more comfortable on the ground.

This particular arrangement of harness and fittings is called a *soft J-bar* system.

Pull Rings   Carry Straps

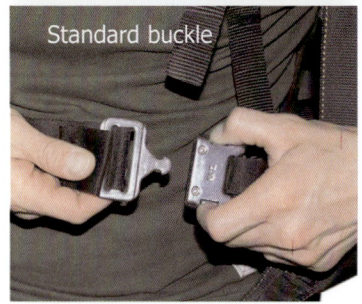

Standard buckle

together in a strong hold. These trade simplicity for convenience—they take a few more seconds to deal with and are difficult to disconnect in an emergency.

The leg loops should always be buckled first and unbuckled last. This habit may be a life-saver if you get into free flying where launching without the leg straps fastened is a serious mistake. Doing so with a motor could cause problems, but more likely is just embarrassing. Avoid walking around with just the chest strap buckled which makes forgetting the leg loops more likely.

Make sure the leg loops are properly fastened too—after clipping them together, try to pull the buckle apart. Not having them solidly fastened could let you fall out after takeoff. The chest mustn't be forgotten either lest it cause a distraction or allow the motor to fall backwards during launch (unlikely but possible during an abort).

A few brands are set up to help prevent the pilot from forgetting his leg straps. These "diaper" styles make the chest strap fasten into a center piece that comes up from between the legs. If the chest portion is fastened then the leg loops (at least one) are fastened too.

The Motor

Whether you provide your own or use the school's, the motor unit includes a harness that can be detached, sometimes easily enough to use for kiting practice.

Any good school will match the pilot to the motor based on his size, weight and expected launch elevation. See chapter 27 for details on choosing motors. In all likelihood, it will have a 2-stroke engine with between 100 and 210 cc's (cubic centimeters of piston displacement).

Success of training has little to do with the choice of brand as long as your instructor is familiar with it. If you bring your own gear then there may be a learning curve while the instructor figures out its nuances. If you bring unacceptable gear (too heavy, too little power, etc.) then the instructor may not be willing to train you on it.

Carabiners

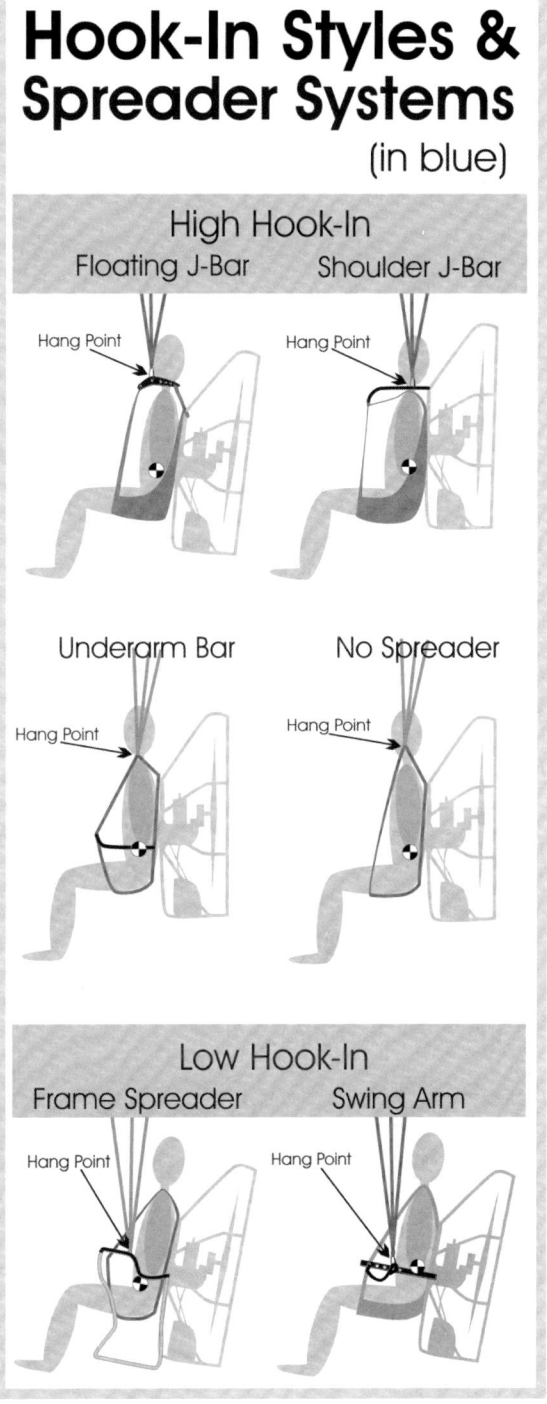

These are used to hook the wing's risers into the motor/harness. They are nearly identical to what mountain climbers use with one important exception: they have a locking gate that prevents accidental opening. Plus the majority allow one-handed operation—quite convenient.

The vast majority do not allow release under tension as a way to "cut away" from the wing like sport skydiving canopies. They must be deliberately unclipped. In fact, releasing from the wing while it's under tension is nearly impossible. The need to insure staying connected while flying far outweighs the advantage of a quick dis-

The PPG Bible: A Complete Guide and Reference

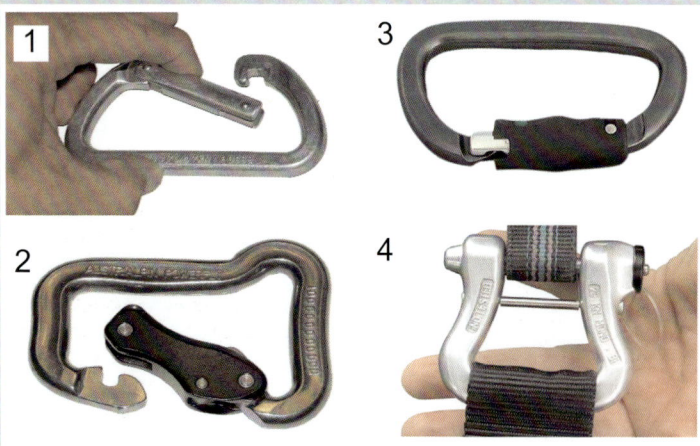

1. Non-locking carabiner. Use only for kiting practice since the gate can open easier by accident.

2. Press-gate carabiners have a self locking mechanism. This one is steel—it is heavier but stronger. This is the most common type since it can easily be operated by one hand. Pushing a button where the gate pivots both unlocks the gate and opens it (button is depressed in the picture).

3. Another locking gate style where you push the green button and twist the gate to open. Requires 2 hands.

4. A style that has not been widely adopted. Push the small button in the load pin to remove it. Requires 2 hands.

Most carabiners are made of aluminum with a strength of at least 18 Kilonewtons (KN). Steel ones (Mid photo), weighing slightly more, go up to 26 KN.

 This model can be opened while under load. That's a mixed blessing since it would be possible to open it in flight (albeit with difficulty). These are very uncommon for powered paragliding.

connect. Even after a reserve deployment, the pilot does not "cut away" from the paraglider as they do in skydiving.

The strongest carabiners are made of steel but most pilots use the lighter aluminum versions. Properly made, aluminum is quite sufficient. Strength is rated by how much force they can bear without deforming while the gate is closed; it is measured in Kilonewtons (KNs). One KN equates to about 225 pounds. 18 KN is the weakest that should be accepted but 22 KN is more desirable. Steel carabiners generally have ratings up to 28 KN. Some models may include a strength rating with the gate open and this number will be much lower—regardless of material or rating they should never be flown with the gate open.

Nearly invisible scratches and cracks can dramatically degrade the carrying capability aluminum carabiners so treat them with care.

Kiting Harness

A kiting harness is important for learning. Get a good one, you'll spend a lot of time in it. Given the importance of kiting skills, it should be convenient and comfortable to practice in. You can remove the harness from your motor and use it for kiting but, for some units, that's a pain. Plus, harnesses with high hook-in points will cause back strain after a short time.

The harness can be as simple as a strap tied in a special way or a full harness made for flying. Free flying varieties work great but are expensive and sometimes bulky.

Instruments

Simplicity is the sport's trademark but there are still some instruments that are useful in varying degrees. And human nature being what it is, if it can be carried, you'll find it on someone's machine. Be careful though, adding anything also adds weight, can get in the way of launch and/or controls, and, like other attachments, has a taste for propellers. Anything that *can* fall off, *will* go through the prop.

Much of what is really useful can be worn on your arm: a wrist altimeter. They are surprisingly accurate (given their small size) and not likely to fall off or be forgotten.

EGT or CHT

Exhaust Gas Temperature (EGT) is taken from the motor's exhaust stream (as opposed to the metal).

Tip: A mountain climbing harness, available from larger sporting goods stores, also works for kiting. It is a single and very strong waist strap plus leg loops that is light and fairly inexpensive. The carabiners must go around the waist strap and not the tool loops. Use those tool loops to keep the carabiners from sliding to the center.

It's nearly the hottest temperature inside the motor. Above-normal readings at this point are generally the first indication of a lean fuel-to-air mixture.

Cylinder Head Temperature (CHT) uses a probe at the spark plug to tell how hot the cylinder is. Since the metal has to heat up it does not respond quite as quickly as EGT but is useful for the same reason: telling whether the engine running too lean and if it is getting enough cooling air.

GPS

Common among drivers, hikers and cruise missiles, the GPS tells far more than direction to destination. Its most useful feature is displaying your speed and direction over the ground.

Airspeed Indicator

An airspeed indicator tells how fast you're flying through the air. They are rarely found on PPG's because it's difficult to mount them clear of the motor's interfering thrust field. Wind speed indicators (anemometers) can be hand-carried to give an indication, at least while the motor is idling.

Tachometer

Motor RPM is the most common measure of power since it's so easy to measure. Since the prop is fixed pitch (meaning the blade angle never changes), it works quite well. They measure the number of electronic pulses sent to the spark plug and displays that as an RPM.

Altimeter/Variometer

An altimeter tells your altitude using atmospheric pressure (also called barometric pressure). As you go up, the pressure decreases and the altimeter displays that as an altitude increase. Depending on how it is set, the displayed altitude is above mean sea level (MSL) or height above ground level (AGL).

Altimeter watches are generally accurate to within 20 feet and are quite sufficient for powered paragliding. Every pilot should have some kind of altimeter, especially if they fly in areas where restricted airspace overlies their flying area. The altimeter should be set to launch elevation before takeoff.

Accessories

So many gadgets and so few places to put them. Many goodies are available but remember, if you bring it, you've got to launch with it (and muck with it and keep it out of the prop, etc.). This list tries to stick with the more important basics.

Helmet

Most schools will require a helmet. Among other things, it guards against hitting the motor frame in a crash or getting hit by flying prop shards after a fall. It is especially beneficial for kiting where you can get tossed around near the ground. Full face helmets provide protection against the "face plant"—a non-impressive finish to be sure.

The ideal PPG helmet has quality hearing protection with audio and a microphone. The quietest designs avoid having the chin strap going through the ear cups. A push-to-talk (PTT) switch will either be on a coil that goes out to your

1. The Cylinder Head Temperature (CHT) has a wire going to its probe on the spark plug. That makes it painless to install.

2. A *tachometer* is mounted on the throttle. Just below that is a mirror for viewing the fuel level that would otherwise be difficult to see. It doubles as a check to insure the pilot still looks cool.

3. The *variometer* is a very sensitive altimeter and rate-of-climb (or descent) indicator. It helps determine if the flyer is in lift (rising air) or sink (descending air). Besides the readout, it beeps for lift or buzzes in sink so the pilot doesn't even have to look at it. The pitch of the sound tells the strength of the ascent or descent. It is used mostly by soaring pilots.

The PPG Bible: A Complete Guide and Reference

1. This purpose-built helmet for motoring is made to work with FRS radios. The plugs are far from standard. Some can even look alike but wind up being slightly different and not compatible. Your instructor will have compatible gear. In a few instances, the plugs can be identical but not work due to different electronics.

2. It's hard to cut yourself with a hook knife but easy to cut through harness webbing or lines in an emergency.

hand or on the helmet (usually an ear cup).

Most purpose-built helmets come with a built-in PTT but other helmets can be modified by the mechanically inclined.

Radios

In the U.S., most pilots use FRS (Family Radio Service) radios to talk with each other. Most instructors use them to talk with their students. These radios are, unfortunately, not very reliable. They are cheap and available which is why they've become so common. GMRS radios can be more powerful (on the lower 7 channels) but require an FCC license.

Some schools use the more reliable business band radios but they are more expensive and require a license (see chapter 28).

Aviation radios are the least frequently used but may be helpful later on. It's doubtful your trainer will use them. In the U.S., the frequency designed for air-to-air communications is 122.75 Mhz and for schools is 123.30 and 123.50 Mhz.

Boots

In most cases boots are helpful to prevent ankle injuries while running for launch or landing. They get more beneficial as the surface texture worsens. Good boots benefit free-flyers more since their launch is usually from sites that are strewn with the randomness of nature. Be careful to select ones that allow good running—in light winds, you'll be thankful. They should also have loops for their laces instead of hooks which can catch paraglider lines during inflation.

Hook Knife

It's incredibly unlikely a hook knife will be needed, but if you're getting dragged or pulled under water it may be the only way out. They are designed to slice quickly through lines and harness webbing with minimal risk to the user.

Reserve

The reserve parachute offers a last chance survival tool for major wing malfunctions or structural failures: events so rare that not all pilots use reserves. While they can be a lifesaver, without proper installation and understanding, they can add more risk then benefit (accidental deployment).

The reserve pouch is attached to the motor's frame and its bridles (risers) attach to the harness so as to avoid entanglement during deployment. The reserve bridles

Right: This is the only time a pilot ever wants to see his reserve outside its container.

Inset: A reserve can be a lifesaver, but it must be installed properly (see Chapter 12) and the pilot must know how to use it (See Chapter 19).

Your training rig may not have a reserve to avoid the possibility of deploying it accidentally.

connect to near the normal carabiners since that will offer sufficient strength during the opening shock and also give the best hang angle. The reserve's pouch has a handle with pins that must be installed and inspected to prevent accidental deployment, a very serious situation.

Section I: First Flight

Handling the Wing

CHAPTER 3

"But officer, I'm just flying my kite."

Ground handling the glider, or *kiting*, is getting the wing overhead and controlling it in a breeze. Fortunately it's fun, too, which is good since ground handling is our sport's seminal skill. It is also the most challenging one to really master.

The goal of kiting is to keep the wing overhead while standing mostly in one place. There are many fine points and to master kiting is to master launching—it will help you succeed, make you look good, and spare much costly aggravation.

There is no magic "feel," practice is king. Finesse and higher-wind handling skills come with practice. Happily this part of the learning curve is enjoyable and can be done in any open area with a smooth, steady breeze.

Kiting sites should be big, free of damaging ground objects that could tear fabric or kink lines and should not be in a wind shadow (downwind of a building or other obstruction). Have smooth terrain downwind too—it's easy to get dragged into and through objects if the wind picks up. The wing's pull will surprise you; at the hands of a brisk breeze or gust you can easily be picked up and dragged.

Use the instructor—he can save enormous frustration with sometimes important and seemingly trivial tips. But once the basics are down and you understand the limitations of when to kite, doing it on your own will hasten the training process dramatically. Repetition greases the wheels of progress.

Few students will want to attempt kiting in more than about a 10 mph breeze but it takes at least a 7 mph to practice effectively. As skill develops you may be able to handle winds as light as 5 mph and as much as 14 mph.

The PPG Bible: A Complete Guide and Reference

1. Beaches and their smooth on-shore winds are great places to practice kiting but deserve great respect. If the wing gets into the surf, even shallow surf, disconnect! Pilots have drowned after being dragged into moving water or surf, unable to disconnect due to the wing's water-driven pull.

2. To regain control over a wind-whipped wing, run around behind it then unclip.

Brake Positions/Pressures

References to hand position use the descriptions below. However, you should learn to equate them to brake *pressure*, not position. They will vary by glider; one glider's position 2 may do very little, while on another it quickly spills the glider into a spiral.

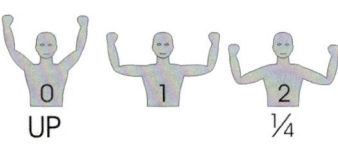

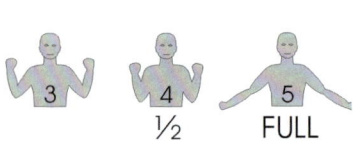

Deflating the Wing

A wing in a wind has a mighty power; before learning to control it, you should learn how to deflate it to minimize the consequence of a sudden wind increase.

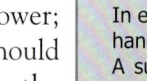 **Caution!**
In even moderate conditions, be ready to handle the wing as soon as you hook in. A sudden gust can quickly unravel your tenuous balance. Review methods to de-power the wing and rehearse them. Practice getting to your hook knife.

If you do wind up getting dragged, use whatever means you can to bring it down then aggressively run around behind it and unclip. Here are some ways to disable a wing:

1. The normal way is to pull both brakes hard. But don't do this in a stronger wind—it may add enough lift to loft you.

2. Pull only *one* brake hard. The wing will go over on its side, probably turning upside down. When it's pointed down, reduce both brakes.

3. Reach up and pull the C risers (3rd row back from the A's) as far as possible. Hold them. They may be hard to find while being dragged so rehearse doing it under more controllable conditions.

4. Reach up to grab any center line and keep pulling until you get to fabric. Beware that line burns are possible without gloves.

Brake Positions/Pressures

Throughout this book, references to brake positions are made using a fractional position or a number from 0 to 5. Zero is hands up and five is the maximum brake pull possible without stalling the wing (forward flight stops, dropping begins). Note that the forearm is kept vertical through number 4.

Think of control inputs as *pressures* more than positions. If it takes 5 pounds of pull (pressure) to get position 3, then use 5 pounds of pressure even if the brake moves more or less with that pressure. Every wing is different too, and lower hook-in motors will average lower positions than those with higher hook-ins. When trying a new model, be particularly careful about excessive brake pull. If possible, adjust your brake lines so the following positions work—they offer the most brake travel:

- Position 0: Hands up, no brake pull, the toggles are against the pulley.
- Position 1: Starting to feel brake pressure, around ½ pound.
- Position 2: Resting the weight of your arms. Your extended thumb would be about ear height on most configurations.
- Position 4: About shoulder height. Note the forearm is kept vertical through this position. It is the most brake pull that should ever be used for normal flight.
- Position 5: Anything beyond position 4 should only be used for landing flare or advanced maneuvering. Use only with extreme care.

These positions will depend on your glider's brake-line length but it should be adjusted so that these positions work. Beware that a glider *can* stall well before reaching position 5 under the right (or wrong!) conditions.

Section I: First Flight

Preparing Yourself

Besides the wing, you'll need a harness. Helmet and gloves are recommended, too.

Some harnesses, especially the mountain climbing and strap-only type, can be difficult to put on—make sure you understand how it's donned before taking it home from the seller or have good directions. Carabiners should go around the most structural part of the harness or in the loops intended for them. All gliders have a recommended riser separation width which is why kiting harnesses, unless built for flying, should not be flown.

Carabiners should open toward the center, facing each other. This helps standardize your operation and reduces the possibility for lines to snag on them or go through the carabiner gates accidentally.

Lightweight gloves can prevent line burns. If you're holding onto some lines when the air snatches a part of the wing, it will pull it through your fingers with skin searing force. Normally this is not a problem because you rarely hold the lines (you'll usually only be handling the risers) but some moves do require pulling lines. Plus just handling the glider and its lines can give reason for gloves.

If you're going to clip into the wing, have a helmet on—the most likely time to need one is while kiting. Pilots have been seriously hurt while clipped into a wing that got caught by a big gust. The only exception should be if somebody is just showing how to handle the lines *and* there is no wind.

Untangling Lines: Taming the Dips and Loops

Careful stowage prevents most tangles but if they do happen these steps can remedy most ills. Whatever you do, don't disconnect anything! Find a clear, open area and lay out the wing as in a forward launch. If able, kiting it between steps may reveal a solution.

1. Clip the brakes into their retainers and separate the risers as much as possible; pull them away from the trailing edge as far as the tangle allows and shake them to clear the easy stuff.
2. Make sure there are no *line overs* (middle picture). If so, bring them around (pull the wing through if necessary) so they are laying on top along with all the other lines.
3. Untwist the riser. It might be difficult to tell which way to do this in the early stages, but keep making sure they're untwisted as you proceed. Shaking the riser and try teasing the lines apart as you go.
4. Remove any obvious sticks and make sure no lines are caught in the riser pulleys or brake handles.
6. Look for and remove loops. Clearing just one loop (dip) may de-puzzle the whole mess.
7. Hold up the A riser so there's enough tension to bring the A's off the ground, there will be a bunch of lines on top of it. Pull the A-riser (start with just one A-line if necessary) through the maze until here are no lines between the quick link and leading edge. Once all the A lines are clear the remaining solution frequently becomes apparent.
8. Hold the cleared A's up with some tension to help sort out remaining tangles. Try tensioning the individual B, C, and D risers—if they are not separated, do so.
9. If none of this works, start from the wing. Find the innermost A and follow it to the carabiner. Do whatever it takes to get this A line clear to it's quick link. Then do the same for the next outer A and the next until finished. You will sometimes have to twist the risers around to get it to work.

Keep the risers separate from the rest of the wing.

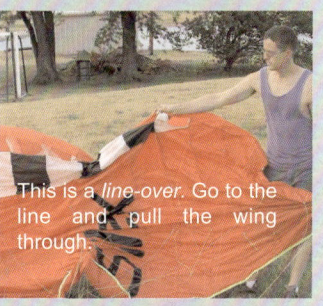

This is a *line-over*. Go to the line and pull the wing through.

Line overs can be difficult to detect, check from behind.

The PPG Bible: A Complete Guide and Reference

Preparing the Wing

Layout

Pull the wing out of its bag while keeping the riser loops together but separate from everything else. Lay it out as shown while preventing the riser loops from going through any lines, causing tangles. Determine which way the wind is blowing.

Hooking In for a Forward
(text on opposing page)

When you feel the wind directly in your face, that direction is upwind, lay out the wing on its back so that the lines are on top, the riser loops upwind and the cell openings (leading edge) downwind. In light winds, doing this carefully is the most important part of a successful launch.

Dan is pointing to the center cell, a dot near the trailing edge on this model. Most wings mark the center so you can easily make sure you're centered when getting ready.

Some pilots prefer a slight "U" or "V" shape (see frame 9, opposite page) where the center of the wing is positioned farther from the pilot. That helps it come up straighter but takes slightly longer to inflate.

Clearing The Lines

Any line tangle whatsoever will prevent success. Pick up each riser and make sure the lines are clear to the wing, especially the A's. There should be no loops or lines draped over the A's when you hold up the A riser. While holding the riser with one hand, leave the brake toggle clipped in place and pull the brake *line* just enough to tug at the trailing edge. That helps verify the brake line is not snagged on anything.

Forward And Reverse Launch

The terms inflation and launch are frequently used interchangeably although inflation is really just getting the wing overhead. A forward launch (or inflation) is where the pilot starts running with the wing behind him.

A *reverse* launch, used in winds over about 6 mph, is where the pilot faces the wing, pulls it up overhead, then turns around to launch. Technically it's a reverse inflation since, after you turn around, there is no difference from a forward launch.

Light Winds (Forward Inflation)

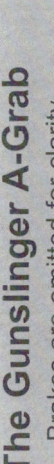

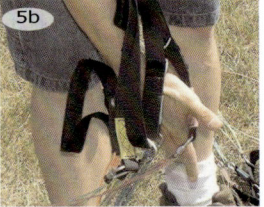
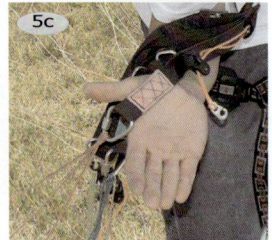

The Gunslinger A-Grab — Brakes are omitted for clarity

Calm winds are great for PPG *flying* but a challenge for launching. Unless you're at a beach, most early flights will probably be in light or calm winds. That means lots of forward launch practice—building a skill you'll be mighty thankful to have.

The basic technique is similar to what free flyers use and can be practiced at home with no motor. Other techniques use power to differing degrees.

Avoid forward launches in stronger winds. The breeze may topple you backwards as the wing catches air, snapping you back into the "turtle" position (lying on your back).

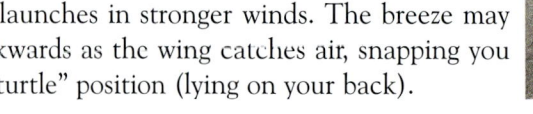

"Turtling"

Page 26 — Section I: First Flight

Hooking In

For this process, refer to the photo sequence beginning on the preceding page. Your wing should be laid out as shown (1) with the A risers up. Stand between the two risers facing away from the wing (2); if there's any breeze, it must be nearly direct on your face in this position. Step back towards the wing a few feet to prevent disturbing the wing's layout during the process.

Pick up the left riser and hold it up with the loop down and A's forward (3); think of how it will look in flight. Clip it to the carabiner and then let it fall forward and down (4). The rear riser will expose the brake toggle for easy grabbing. Repeat for the other riser.

With your left hand, follow the left riser down and unclip its brake. Do the same on the right. You should be able to move the brake handle outward and see its line moving freely through the pulley (or ring) without any kinks (5). Keep hold of the brake handles through the remainder of the process.

Now refer to frames 5a through 5c—the brakes are omitted for clarity. Starting with your right hand, point your index finger down and thumb up like you're making a gun (5a). Bring the "gun" forward towards the risers/lines and beside your body, catching the A riser with your thumb as it comes up (5b). Bring it up so the A riser is between your thumb and index finger as the "gun" points up at about 45° angle (5c). The other risers/lines will be draped down over the top of your arm but the A-lines go cleanly back to the wing with nothing on top of them. Repeat for the left side. This will feel mighty awkward with the brake toggles and A-Lines but it does come together as shown in (6).

You're now standing there, facing away from the wing, with a brake toggle in each hand (7) and the A risers resting between their respective thumb and forefinger. If your wing has "split A's" then only use the center one in each thumb. Stay close enough to the wing so that you do not pull the leading edge over on itself which would make it harder to launch. This might feel quite awkward—rest assured, it gets better. After you gain proficiency, the instructor may have you start holding a throttle simulator (not connected to anything) to get used to it.

It is critical that you are centered on the wing and facing straight away. The instructor is invaluable here and will help with the nuances of this routine, of which there are several. To help insure being centered, look where the center of the wing is and position your body there, then walk carefully forward until you *barely* feel tension in the A's but without pulling the wing's leading edge over. Move left or right so the tension is even—you're only feeling the weight of the lines to be centered here without actually pulling on them.

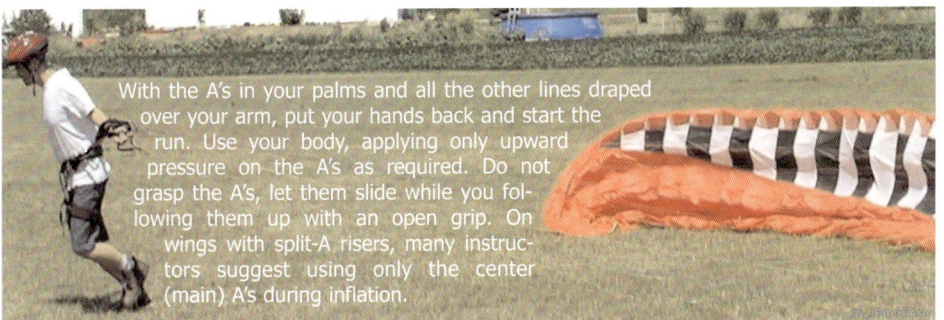

With the A's in your palms and all the other lines draped over your arm, put your hands back and start the run. Use your body, applying only upward pressure on the A's as required. Do not grasp the A's, let them slide while you following them up with an open grip. On wings with split-A risers, many instructors suggest using only the center (main) A's during inflation.

Forward inflation preparation should leave you like frame (7). You should be able to look back down the lines and have nothing draped over your A lines from the quick link to the wing (8) and see nothing draped over them.

It is important during the inflation that you do not *grasp* the A's, rather allow them to slide through your open palm as shown in the picture below left.

There are a very few exceptions (certain wings) where you must actually grasp and pull the A's but these will not generally be on beginner or solo wings. The instructor will let you know.

Below: "V" wing layout.

Take a step backwards toward the wing and rehearse the direction you'll start to run (directly away from the wing). Some pilots find a object to look at in that direction. You must be centered, perpendicular to the wing, and run straight for it to come up centered. Additionally, if there's any breeze at all, it must be nearly straight into your face. A very small crosswind component, up to 30° off provided it's less than about 2 mph. Any tailwind at all will torpedo the whole effort.

The Run

When you go for it, go hard! You will lunge away from the wing, quickly tensioning the lines as it fills with life. Pull hard through the resistance with your legs and exert upward pressure on the A's with your open palms—some require a lot more than others and some will "front tuck" (the leading edge folds downward) with just a bit too much pull. Your instructor will let you know.

Keep forging forward with your body, speed is life. Arms back, drive forward. If there's any wind, the wing will be pulling back fiercely as it arcs upward. As you think it's coming overhead, look up to verify that it is centered but keep moving!

You will learn to detect a subtle pull, left or right, from the tensioning lines. Go that way. If the wing starts pulling you to the left, go left enough to keep under it but keep driving forward. Looking up at the wing too early can tend to slow you down when speed is needed. You can also turn your head left or right to see if its centered instead of looking straight up.

Later on, when doing this with a motor, you'll be leaning back into the thrust, but for now you'll need to lean forward to get enough oomph. In completely calm wind, the initial run will feel like you're pulling a limp rag with little resistance. Keep driving forward, hard and fast—speed is success.

With even a couple mph breeze, the wing will snap to attention much faster then in a dead calm. It will try to stop your forward momentum then come up quickly and want to overfly you; be ready to pull on the brakes *briefly* to slow it down. But try to get moving as you let back off the brakes. The vast majority of blown forward inflations can be traced to insufficient speed or too much brake. Even having the wing come up crooked does not have to doom the effort, get some speed while getting under it. Use minimum brake (usually none) while getting under the wing.

Move Under the Wing

While running or forward kiting, you must move under the wing. If it goes right, you must go right; if it goes left, you must go left. Use minimal brake pull while gathering speed, then use just enough to steer and keep the wing from overflying you. This won't come easy, the wing will pull you to the left and you need to go left even more to get under it. Fight hard the instinct to pull against it: the wing goes left and you pull right; the wing always wins.

Through the inflation process you should keep the A's in your hand, pushing them up and forward to help the wing come overhead. On some models, you must stay on the As (keep applying pressure) until it comes fully overhead and your body is moving nicely forward. Then let off on the A's and go to the brakes but use minimal pull unless the wing wants to overfly you—it is much better to get moving quickly. Until you have some speed there is no point in doing much with the

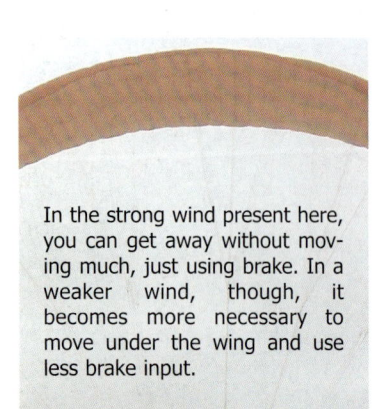

In the strong wind present here, you can get away without moving much, just using brake. In a weaker wind, though, it becomes more necessary to move under the wing and use less brake input.

Inflation or Launch?

The term inflation only describes the portion of a launch where the wing goes from the ground to overhead. But most pilots just label the launch according to the inflation method used.

brakes, they will only slow the wing and make it fall back. *Once* you are moving forward, do what it takes to steer the wing. Right brake to turn right and left brake to turn left.

With forward momentum established and the wing centered, the goal is to keep enough speed (airflow) to control it using brakes alone. If it goes left or right you may have to move with it, but only as much as needed. Turning towards it too much will send you quickly to the other side and start a zig-zag that worsens as you get out of sync with the wing—you run right to get under it but go too far and the wing goes left. These oscillations worsen until it swings you into a fall. Combine a bit of body turn with a bit of brake to the ease the wing back overhead. It is a fine dance that you'll just have to practice but it's oh so fun when done right.

Remember that, when you're doing this with a motor you'll need to stand up straight and let the motor push.

Forward Kiting

Most wings need at least 6 mph worth of air moving over them to start being controllable and more is better, up to about 12 mph. If there is no wind then you must generate all 6 mph by running, a maximum effort for most people. The benefit of a 3 mph breeze becomes painfully obvious after the first few tries dragging twenty (or more) square meters of wing overhead. It's good that you *can* practice it running as this is a very useful skill to master.

Forward kiting will reveal a critical behavior of the wing—if you move your body left, the wing goes right, and will continue to the right all the way to the ground. It reinforces why it's so important to stay centered under the wing. To move right by *your* choice you must first get the *wing* going right then follow it. As you near your desired track, apply left brake until the wing stops overhead as you move under it to the new position.

Always go with the wing. While reverse kiting, if the wing starts falling right, step right and pull right with your right hand like the pilot above. If the wing starts falling left, step left, pull left. If it tries to overfly, pull both brakes. If it wants to sag downward, let up the brakes and walk backwards to give it more airflow.

While forward kiting, if the wing is falling to your right, step to the right while applying some left brake.

Wind Over 6 mph (Reverse Inflation)

Much of your early learning will involve reverse kiting. You'll need at least 7 mph wind to do so. Some schools may teach how to kite the wing without the harness which can be quite useful and is covered later under advanced techniques.

Hooking In Reversed

Free flyers hook in forward then turn around while lifting one riser over their head. That method does not work well with a motor because of the cage.

Tip: Alternate Hook-In. Another method of hooking in reversed is to treat it almost like the more-obvious forward method. Free flyers transitioning to power may find this easier. Step up to the risers like a forward launch but beside instead of between them (as shown at left). Pick up both risers while remaining faced forward and lift them over your right shoulder. Hook the left riser to the left carabiner and the right to the right carabiner without twisting them. They'll be going around your right side but envision how they will be in flight and clip in like a forward.

The risers and lines drape around your right side. Once clipped-in, turn to the right and face the wing. After inflation, you'll turn the left. Reverse the directions if you normally turn to the right.

Reverse Hook-In: You should be facing the wing with its risers and lines laid out towards you, A risers up. Pick up the risers and put them together, keeping the A's up. Flip them over counterclockwise a half-turn so that the A's are now facing the ground. Separate them and clip each one into the nearest carabiner. The carabiner should open inward. This will leave you hooked in with the risers crossed, brakes on top and a half twist in the each riser. Move your right hand down the right riser and grab its brake. It may be covered by the other riser or it's lines, just reach under them, grab the brake and bring it towards you. There should be no twist in the brake line—it will go from the pulley to your hand. Do the same with your left hand, reach down to the riser attached to the left carabiner and grab its brake from the holder (magnetic or snap).

6. Pull the brakes off their clip. They should be free and clear to the pulley. You now have the correct brake in each hand.

7. Cross the risers up near your body, then grab each "A" riser as shown. One brake line will cross over.

8. There should be no lines (including brake lines) draped over the A's when this is done properly.

There are surprisingly many ways to hook in reversed but I'll describe one of the most common: you hook in while facing the wing in such a way that everything is sorted out after turning around to launch (steps shown on the next page).

It seems complicated but, when you pull the wing to life and turn around (you'll turn to the left using these instructions), it all sorts out magically. Your right hand will control the right brake and left hand the left brake.

After you're hooked in, make the two risers cross each other right up near the carabiners then, while holding a brake in each hand, grab the two A risers with your left hand. You now have a brake in your left hand along with the two A risers and a brake in your right hand. On wings with Split A's you may have four risers although some wings come up straighter when only the main A risers are used. Eventually you'll also have a throttle in that right hand (or left depending on the motor setup). This may be confusing at first but repetition will fix that. There are many ways to teach this and it is best to go with what your instructor is most familiar. You're now ready to build a "wall."

Construction: Building the Wall

Having the wing partially inflated while sitting on the ground in a moderate breeze (it needs about 8 mph) is called "building a wall." It helps control the wing while insuring that you're properly positioned so the wing comes up centered when you're ready to bring it overhead. Building a wall is the first thing to do after getting hooked in reversed as it improves the success rate for reverse launches. It is also a great exercise in handling the wing.

To build a wall, spread out the wing and hook in as described above. While holding the brakes, grab an A in each hand. Be prepared to pull brakes in case the wing tries to billow up before you're ready. Get some tension on the risers with your body, step forward once and then lurch backwards while applying some upward pressure on the A's. If there's enough wind, the wing will start to come up. Just as it leaves the ground, let go of the A's and pull the brakes to bring it back down but not too hard—you want to leave the wing standing there "at attention" with the leading edge a few feet above the ground. Do this several times—it will be confusing at first just finding the two A risers each time but practice really pays off.

Once the wall is built, you can modulate how tall it stands by spepping towards or away from it. Leveling the wall is done by stepping sideways toward the higher side. You can also practice holding both A's in your non-throttle hand to be ready for adding power. Get used to going for the A's, pulling the wing up mostly with your body, and then bringing it back down using brakes. Timing is a challenge, you want it to come just off the ground and then bring it right back down again—the trailing edge should never get more than a few feet high. Once you gained some experience you can do this without the trailing edge even leaving the ground.

Use your body, not the A's. Only help it with the A's; if the leading edge deforms, you're pulling them too hard. The wing must see pressure more evenly on the lines, especially if there's barely enough wind. On some wings, you do not need any pull on the A's at all which improves your feel for the wing's pull.

Reverse Inflation

Once the wall is leveled and looking good (if there's enough breeze for a wall), move forward a step to lower it slightly then be prepared to lurch backwards. When ready, take several steps backwards and let your body pull on the risers as your hands (or hand if using one hand) pulls *just enough* on the A's. This action should be more of a fast snatch or else you may wind up dragging the wing along the ground. Don't snatch it with *just* the A's—use your body.

With about 8 mph or more breeze you should build a *wall*. It allows a quick view of the wing to make sure there are no snags and helps get it square to the wind.

Once the wing inflates and starts up, keep pressure on the A's until it comes nearly overhead then let off. Be prepared with some brakes—you may need to prevent the wing from overshooting if it's coming up fast. You'll learn to feel this—if it's darting up quickly, let go of the A's earlier and be ready to pull brakes.

If it's lumbering up limply then you'll need to stay on the A's all the way up—in such a case you must wait until it is nearly overhead before even thinking about pulling on the brakes. You'll also probably have to be walking backwards to keep it coming overhead.

In a stronger wind it will want to come up quickly on its own and may even try dragging you downwind with it—be prepared. Shortly after it starts up you will not be able to avoid having it pull you through a few steps as you resist it. But do resist and be ready to stop an overshoot with brakes (called damping). If it lifts you when you brake to stop it, let up on the brakes until you get turned back around to control the wing and bring it down; hopefully you've rehearsed how to deflate it.

Reverse Kiting

Once the wing is happily overhead the fun is keeping it there. For the most part you will want to use as little brake pull as possible. We'll refine this process more later but, for now, the steps to successful reverse kiting are:

- Stay under the wing. If it moves left, walk left. If it moves right, walk right. And you must do so immediately.

- If it goes left, pull left (using the brake in your left hand), if it goes right, pull right (using the brake in your right hand). So if the wing drifts to the left, walk left, pull left. Pull only as much you need. Walk as little as you can get away with but be aggressive at first (with moving under it).

- Be light on the brakes, being heavy handed will tend to both over-correct and make the wing fall back down. In a light wind you must use *minimum* brakes—if it's sitting happily overhead, have little or no brake engaged at all. If the wing keeps falling back to the ground, and there's enough wind, use less brake pull. Use only enough brake pull to keep the wing from overflying you.

The goal is to be able to stand there, mostly using only the brakes (as little as possible) to kite it overhead. Move quickly if needed to prevent it falling over, but shoot for being able to just stand there.

Another benefit of having minimum brake is that you're less likely to get lifted. If the wing is hanging back and you've got the trailing edge deflected (as you will with pulled brakes), you are vulnerable. It's like sticking your hand out the window of a fast moving car—if the hand is angled up, the sudden slipstream will flick it upward and backward. But if it's streamlined, then there will be less effect.

In a light wind you may need to walk backwards. There must be decent airflow over the wing to have good control and if the wind isn't blowing enough, then you need to generate it. Airflow (airspeed over the wing) is life—the more of it, the better the control you have, up to a point.

If the wing tends to fly past you, apply both brakes, if it drops back ease up on the brakes. By modulating these inputs and movements you can become quite adept at making the wing stay where you want it.

This is the most common hold for reverse inflating a wing with a motor. He's got the A's in one hand and throttle in the other. Each hand also has a brake that was grabbed before anything else.

Holding all this feels very awkward at first—rest assured, it gets easier.

Practice kiting until it grows new brain stem connections—besides being fun to accomplish, the skill is the crux of becoming a skilled launcher.. It is what will determine the breadth of conditions you can handle, especially stronger winds. There are advanced kiting techniques covered later that will help dramatically with stronger winds but they are built on these basics.

Alternative Training-Only Method: Straight Risers

The normal way of kiting while reversed can be confusing at first; sorting out the brakes and A's each time the wing plops back down is time consuming. So some instructors use the straight-riser method to quickly get the student kiting and gaining a feel for the wing. But the regular method must eventually be learned.

This method forgoes a flight-ready hook-in and instead has the risers going straight out to the wing without crossing. The drawback is that brake input is backwards from what you'll eventually learn. It is quicker to master and still gives a good feel for kiting along with practicing how to stay centered under the wing.

It is simple: hook in without crossing the risers, A's face up. Grab the brake closest to each hand from the outside; there should be nothing crossed. With the brakes in your hands, reach up to hold the A's and inflate the wing as instructed above, using mostly your body but applying pressure to the A's.

As it comes overhead, be ready to dampen it to prevent overflying you. Then modulate the brakes to keep it there just like the other methods—in light wind you will generally have no brake pulled at all. If it wants to fall back, walk backwards to increase the wing's airflow. If the wing starts falling left, step left and pull some brake with the right hand and vice versa if it falls right. Only the brake pull is opposite to the flight-ready method (normally used and taught) of having the risers crossed.

Watch the trailing edge move and visualize it slowing down that side of the wing which is exactly what it is doing. That can make its behavior and response more clear.

Only do this method long enough to get a feel for the wing (if at all) since you will need to (re)learn the flight-ready method (walk left, pull with left hand) when you strap on a motor.

The Turn and Move

Once you are able to maintain the wing overhead, your next step is to turn around and kite it forward. You will turn left (counter-clockwise) if hooked in as described earlier.

While keeping the wing centered overhead, take a step backward (into the wind which is at your back) to get the wing moving, turn around quickly and *keep moving forward*. In light winds especially you must keep moving forward—lean if necessary but remember that, with a motor on, you will stand up straight and throttle up to keep moving.

You must turn and *move*—speed is life since the wing needs airflow for the brakes to be effective. The most common failure is the wing falling back or sideways—moving faster usually prevents this. Once you've got the wing under control and moving forward, you're doing forward kiting as described earlier.

Straight Riser Method

As a way to get students kiting quickly (as pictured), some instructors have them clip in directly, without any lines crossed. While this may get you kiting faster, don't do it for long since the control movements are backwards from what you'll need to launch.

Regardless of the kiting method used, always keep your body under the wing—and always be moving side to side until you get the feel for how much brake you can use without causing the wing to fall back.

The PPG Bible: A Complete Guide and Reference

Bringing the Wing Down

You could just let it flop down in a heap but that is both messy and inconvenient. Far better is to let it down so that it is either easy to re-inflate or easy to put away.

Turn around opposite the direction you turned to kite forward so that you're now facing it with risers crossed as if to launch. Once you're facing the wing, pull the brakes hard enough so that it falls back evenly. You can turn the other way but it's easier to habitually use the same direction every time so you're ready to re-inflate in the familiar manner.

Just before the wing touches down, take a step towards it so the leading edge lays back nicely. This makes it somewhat easier to re-inflate or fold up.

This *C-line deflation* disables the wing quickly. It is done by reaching up high on each C riser and pulling it down all the way. As the wing snakes onto the ground, let the C's go and pull the brakes far enough to keep it grounded.

If it's windy, you can bring the wing down on its side by pulling one brake more than the other; doing so reduces its tendency to re-inflate. A real strong blow can make it difficult to bring the wing down at all. One method is to get it way overhead (almost to the point of front-tucking) by squatting down and letting off the brakes, then with one quick motion, pulling the brakes hard as you stand up. When it goes through the "power band" (about 45°) you will get yanked a few steps towards it. Run around behind the wing so there is no tension on the lines and unclip right away.

A strong wind is also a good time to practice the *C-Line deflation*. You can use the B's or D's too with somewhat less effectiveness. Reach up with both hands as high as possible, grab the C risers (not the lines) and pull as far down as you can. If it comes down and remains a few feet above the ground, "snaking" about in the breeze, you'll have to run towards it; when it hits the ground, get around behind it. Running towards it may be the only way to get it all the way down. Don't let go of those B's until you do run around it!

Adding the Motor

The first thing to add is just a throttle simulator, if available; it's an assembly configured just like your motor with a spring back throttle and kill switch. You'll be surprised at how much this simple addition confounds nascent kiting skills—practicing with it can be quite valuable.

This description is for a right-handed throttle, if you use the left then you'll quickly see that the reverse inflation requires that you hold the A's in your right hand. Having a throttle on the right or left matters little—good arguments are made for both. If you have a reserve mounted on one side then the throttle should be on the other side though.

Learn where the kill switch is and practice pressing it—you'll want this reaction to be automatic when things turn ugly. There will be times where the wind has its way with you and being

> **Caution!**
> More serious injuries come from getting body parts into a spinning prop then any other cause. Use extreme care when handling a motor and do not start it until given specific instructions.

quick to the kill switch can save many shekels. While kiting with the throttle simulator, practice hitting (and holding) the kill switch whenever the wing differs markedly from your desire. At the first sign of trouble, hit the kill switch.

After proficiency is gained with the throttle simulator (this happens quickly), put the motor on and practice kiting. This will be tiring but you won't do it for long. Some schools use frames with weights to help the student build up to the full motor weight—not a bad way to handle it if available.

Learn the "turn and run" thoroughly—the instructor will pull or push you to simulate the motor thrust. You must be able to control the wing well with the motor pushing before considering flight. The motor has a lot of inertia so when you turn around it will tend to continue twisting—it's just a matter of feel to turn fast without letting it swing past forward.

With these skills reasonably in hand, you will start the motor (covered later—there are some significant "gotchyas" to know about) and go through these exercises with it running. Note that it is eminently possible for lines to go into the prop without due care.

Before hooking in, get used to the basic controls on the motor by running it up and feeling the range of power. Practice going for the kill switch.

Storing the Wing

Like film (a substrate used for chemically recording images, in case you forgot), wings want it cool, dry and dark. Heat or chemicals can degrade the material strength while dampness and its moldy cousin can rot holes in the nylon. UV from the sun makes the fabric weak and porous—all bad.

The wing has only so much life and most of it is measured in UV (sunlight) exposure. It costs about $8 per hour in replacement value (a $2400 wing typically lasts about 300 hours) to be exposed to sun. Whether lofting its owner into the joy of flight or basking unused in a field, it still costs the same.

Before putting the wing away, try to make sure there are no bugs inside. The best cure for this is to fold or stuff it right away. Grasshoppers and other critters will get trapped inside and put a hole in the wing one way or another; either by chewing their way out or by leaving their acidic little remains to do it later. If you notice crawling things already inside, find a reasonably bugless place and shake the trailing edge so that they fall out the leading edge. This can be done inside but you'll be amazed at how big the wing is. It can be helpful to leave half of it folded while you attend to the other half. Remember though, the ribs have big holes in them for the air to spread out, the bugs can do so also.

Rosette

When finished with the wing, put its risers together either with a clip or by inserting one into the other. Hold the riser pair with one hand while pulling the lines through in a bundle with the other and hand each length into the riser hand. Eventually the wing will look like a big flow or *rosette* at the line hand which makes it easy to carry.

The rosette (above) is a good way to carry the wing—throw it over your back like this. It is also the first thing to do before putting it in a stuff sack. Then make sure to keep the risers clear.

To make the rosette, slide one hand up the lines and loop the excess in your other hand.

> **Preservation**
>
> Some paraglider competition pilots, in an effort to preserve their gliders performance, make sure they never crinkle the mylar reinforcements that adorn modern gliders leading edges. They carefully put all the leading edges together and fold the wing in such a ways that they the mylar parts stay flat. For our purposes, such attention to performance detail will not likely yield noticeable benefit.

Stuffing

Stuffing is obviously easier and quicker. Open the stuff sack wide and plop in the wing. Keep the riser loops separate though; especially don't let them go through any lines. Some sacks have a riser pouch or you can use an old carabiner to clip the risers to the bag's handle. At least make sure they are placed on top of a wing fold where no lines will get mixed in.

Stuffing is not better or worse (for wing longevity) than folding although stuffing will leave more wrinkles.

Folding

Folding takes a bit more time because it goes into its more compact wing bag and must be done more carefully.

Methods abound for folding. This one is quick and easy to do with either one or two people. Whatever method you use, be loose with it—tight folding puts stress on stitching and will weaken the seams if done repeatedly. If you can keep from crinkling the leading edge cell Mylar it will help it stay crisp to better do its job.

Lay the wing out flat with the lines laid in the same position as for a forward launch (without any "V" of course). Pull the riser loops away from the trailing edge and lay them, A's up, on the ground then fold it as shown below.

Folding:
1. Layout like a forward.
2. Have the risers sticking out from the trailing edge to keep them separate. With two people, each one grabs a line while walking the tip.
3. Keep folding the tips to the center until it's about 1 foot wide then push the air out from the trailing edge towards the forward openings.
4. Roll or fold from the trailing edge. Loose folds are better for the wing especially the Mylar leading edge stiffener. Some pilots try to avoid getting folds in the Mylar to improve performance.

Preparing For First Flight

CHAPTER 4

Running into the air for the first time can be an overwhelming experience—a concoction of sensations and emotions that overpower normal reason. It is, for many, the zenith of their flight education. The steps described here, alongside a good instructor, will prevent it from becoming the nadir of that education.

Now that you know how to handle the wing, it is a matter of mating those skills with the addition of power to turn it all into an aircraft under control. Expect it to be somewhat awkward and tiring at first, but the results are well worth it.

Adjusting the Motor

Start by hanging in the simulator; your instructor will need to adjust the motor (harness) so that it hangs properly in flight (see Chapter 12). This is called the *hang check*. The propeller, when aligned vertically, should be tilted back no more than 15° (upper tip back); ideal is about 5°. The harness must be comfortable without any straps or J-bars pushing uncomfortably on any part of your body. If it has a kick-in strap you should be able to reach it while hanging there to get into the seat.

Getting into the seat is a surprisingly critical function. Harnesses are not designed for the pilot to hang from the leg straps for more than a few minutes—your legs may go numb after just a short while.

Practice getting into the seat while in the simulator and, if your equipment requires using a hand to do so, *Don't forget to let go of the brakes!* You must practice this process so that, in the heat of early flights, you don't make that potentially fatal mistake. Ideally, you can get in the seat by just moving into the seated position, second best is having a kick-in strap—it should be heavy enough to hang down in the slipstream.

Normal | Leaning Back | Upright

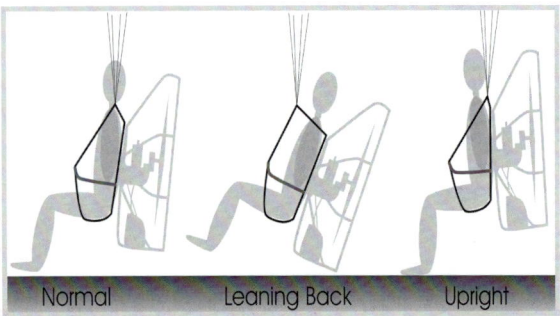

Nearly all harnesses have a way to move the hook-in position to accommodate differing pilot weights. A heavier pilot needs to move that point forward and lighter pilot needs to move it towards the motor. The results should be verified in a simulator.

The critical harness adjustment is covered more thoroughly in Chapter 12.

Fueling

Unless you're flying a four-stroke motor (very uncommon) then it will require a proper mix of gasoline and 2-stroke oil. You can mix it right in the motor's fuel tank, but most use a different container for convenience. Put the oil in first to improve mixing.

Plan to do your preflight inspection *after* refueling so as to catch an accidental missing fuel cap—this common mistake is incredibly dangerous. Don't put much more fuel than you're planning on using since you have to lift it (fuel weighs just under 7 pounds per gallon). In the early stages of learning, use no more than half fuel to reduce weight.

When pouring premix (mixed fuel and oil) into your motor, a long skinny funnel (like a transmission funnel) or a siphon hose is handy.

Unless otherwise specified by your owner's manual, mid-grade or higher automobile gasoline is sufficient. Aviation fuel (avgas) is recommended by some, but a few pilots have reported lead buildup; although avgas is called "low lead," it's actually heavily leaded by automotive standards. Those who use Avgas favor the constant formulation throughout the year (it varies in auto gas), lack of odor and cooler run. Avgas can be purchased at small airports where it is sold by Fixed Base Operators (FBO's) for about 30% more per gallon than auto gas. Tell them it's for your ultralight.

Fuel Selection and Storage

Fuel left exposed to the air over for over a week can degrade and may not run properly. Storing it in an airtight container (it hisses when you open the lid) helps keep it usable for several months although some instructors recommend using fresh fuel (less than a few weeks old) regardless of the container.

Use what the manufacturer recommends. Absent that information, regular autogas does seem to work fine but the higher grades can knocking, a premature rapid combustion that puts enormous stress on the piston.

Mixtures

There are two *mixtures* that get discussed: the fuel/oil mixture is how much oil you pour into each gallon of gas and the fuel/*air* mixture is how much fuel the carburetor doles out as the throttle is opened. The proper fuel/air mixture is managed through carburetor jets, orifices and needle valves. When you hear the term *lean*, it refers to not enough fuel in the fuel/air mix which can damage the motor by overheating.

Oil Selection & Mixing

2-Stroke motors derive all their lubrication from what gets mixed into the gas and it must be mixed in the correct proportion.

Modern 2-cycle oils work well with a ratio of gas to oil around 40:1 which means there are 40 units of gas for each 1 unit of oil. Lower ratios (more oil) are frequently specified for the first few hours of a motor's life (called the break-in period). The mix chart in the Appendix can be used to determine how much oil gets added to your any of fuel. Since many oils come delineated in metrics (liters or milliliters), they too are included in Appendix chart. Most 2-cycle oil has a chart printed on

⚠️ **Caution!**

When filling your can at a gas station, always place it on the ground first. Doing so avoids an explosion risk caused by static electricity.

the container for other ratios as well.

You'll hear nearly religious fervor when seeking advice on oil selection and ratio—go with the manufacturer's recommendation, if available, otherwise, make your selection based on the following priorities:

- Use two-cycle oil, never four-cycle oil such as that made for cars.
- Use two-cycle oil that is made for *air-cooled* motors. The marine stuff is made for cooler running outboards and may break down at our hotter temperatures.
- Use synthetics which are commonly recognized as having better characteristics at our higher RPMs and hotter temperatures. They also leave fewer deposits.
- Use oil that is dyed so that you can tell whether a particular batch of fuel is mixed. If using clear oil, develop a completely fool-proof way to keep track of what fuel is already mixed. A trail of seized motors follows clear-oil users who thought their fuel was mixed.

Avoid mixing synthetics with mineral oils. A very few brands may not mix well and could form gel-type clumps in the tank. This was more common when synthetics first appeared but is less likely now with modern oils.

Preflight Inspection

Any preflight inspection has three important elements: (1) Consistency—always start from the same place and do it the same way each time, (2) thoroughness—don't skip items, touching each item as you check it helps and (3) don't let interruptions stop you. If they do, go back to the beginning.

Motor

There's little reason to skimp here since it's so incredibly simple. On most machines a sufficiently thorough preflight can be completed in less than a minute. Resist the temptation to crank & go and **never, ever** start it without insuring the throttle linkage is at idle on the carburetor.

Start the preflight by pulling at the carabiners. That will bring out the harness webbing to make potential problems easier to see. Plus it allows better inspection of the carabiners and harness webbing—very critical elements since they will be holding you up. Check the webbing, fabric, straps and any attached connection hardware that must be free of tears, cuts, badly worn sections or other damage that could affect its integrity. Other things to check:

- Look for small cracks in the **carabiners**, such cracks could lead to a catastrophic in-flight failure, especially in some types of aluminum carabiners.
- Squeeze the **throttle** and watch the mechanism move at the carburetor. Besides

Siphoning Fuel

Siphoning is what happens when gravity pulls the fuel, through a hose, up over a ledge and down to a point below source fuel level. You have to get it started by filling the hose but, once started, it will continue until the source is empty (or below the source hose opening). The source fuel level must be higher than the paramotor's gas tank for it to work.

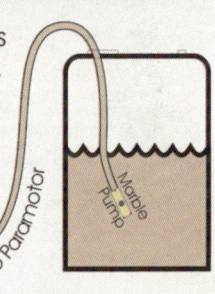

There are several ways to get the siphon going.
1. Submerging most of the hose in your fuel can. Cover up one end with your thumb and lift that end out while leaving the other end submerged. Put the thumb end in your paramotor tank. The hose should have stayed filled with fuel and when you release your thumb, the flow will begin.

2. Use the "wobble pump" as shown above. This ingenious little pump only requires that you wiggle it up and down for a few seconds to start the flow.

ensuring proper function, it prevents the harrowing possibility of suddenly going to full power upon start. Skipping this check causes more serious (and sometimes debilitating) injury than any other cause.

- Walk around the machine, moving parts for security and looking for loose bolts or other parts. Loose prop bolts, even one or two, can set up a vibration that allows the prop to come completely off its mount. This is neither good for the motor, the prop or the wallet.

- **Mufflers** cause many problems, look for cracks, loose or broken mountings and general security. Safety wire is best used on anything that can loosen.

- Check **redrive** belts for proper tension and position.

- Check **motor mounts and nuts** for security along with reduction drive bolts.

- **Spark plugs** loosen and fall off, especially on inverted engines. Check for general security.

- The **fuel system** needs a clear vent to allow air into the tank and a supply line running up to the carburetor. Check for tank security, line condition and turn on the appropriate valves. Some have an off valve for the vent—it must be open (on). If left closed, or the vent gets plugged, the engine will run for while until diminishing fuel lowers the tank pressure, possibly collapsing the tank. Eventually the fuel pump can't suck any more and the motor quits.

  Tighten the lid and vent (if removable)—forgetting this step is an unfortunately common, and extremely dangerous, omission.

- Check the **propeller** for condition—small nicks are generally OK but long splits must be repaired. Fortunately many prop maladies can be repaired in the field without removal (see Chapter 12).

- Align the prop vertically then push the top tip fore and aft. It should have less than about 1/16th inch (1.5 millimeters) of play. Flexing of the motor mounts is OK and they should be checked that they are secure and intact.

- If the prop has been removed since its last flight, check that it's not on backwards. This embarrassing mistake will be felt when the motor produces a third or so of its normal thrust. The curved surface faces forward (towards the direction of flight). Another way to remember is that the fatter part of the prop, the leading edge, faces forward.

- Check the **cage** for security and complete assembly. If the motor has a clutch (the propeller spins freely without the motor running), spin the prop around to insure sufficient clearance from the hoop and cage parts.

- Pull on all those added accessories and tuck loose straps out of harm's way. Nothing should be able to touch the exhaust or get into any moving parts. Close any zippered compartments.

- If equipped with a reserve, ensure the riser routing remains unobstructed, attached and the reserve pins are secured properly without being pushed all the way through.

---

1. The most important preflight action is to move the throttle while observing that the carburetor linkage returns to idle. The finger is pointing to the throttle arm on this unit. Float bowl carburetors hide the throttle mechanism inside a housing—on these machines, just make sure throttle freely moves to idle.

2. This style of prop mount has a center bolt. If there is any play in the prop (wiggling fore and aft), this bolt may be loose.

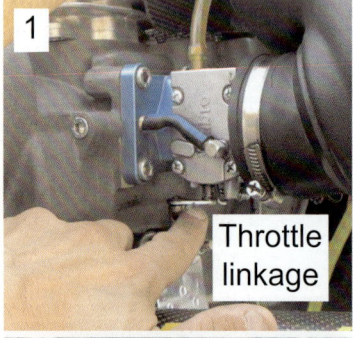

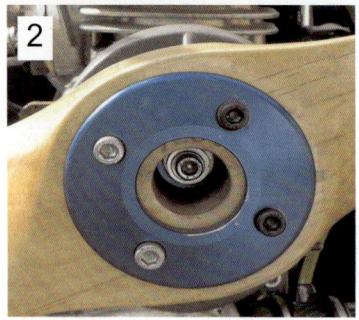

Wing

With a bit of breeze (6 mph), checking the wing is a lot easier. The most minimal preflight is to kite the wing up for a look. Always check that:

- Lines are connected, kink-free and sheathed (outer covering intact).
- The fabric has no tears or holes.
- The risers have no visible damage with trimmers set for takeoff, brakes are in their holders and the speedbar system is free.

A more thorough inspection should be done periodically (once every 25 flights or after any rough handling). Lay out the wing flat in a wind-shielded location and do the following:

- Field strength test; It should be done in several places on the most faded sections of the wing, which will usually be on the top surface. Pull the fabric taut with your hands, about 3 inches apart, and push your thumb into the fabric as if trying to poke a hole in it. It should hold with about 10 pounds of pressure.
- Run each line between your fingers from the quick-link to the wing (or cascade). Feel for thin spots—these indicate that the inside Kevlar is broken and that the line must be replaced; there is almost no strength in the outer sheathing which only protects its inner core. Having one line broken may not seem like a big deal, and usually isn't, but it stresses the remaining lines that much more, especially if it's an inner A or B line.
- Check overall condition of the risers, quick links, and brakes. Try to pull the risers apart at the stitching with about 20 pounds of pull.

If you leave something for later, you *will* forget it; maybe not this time, but eventually. A good example is the fuel cap—if you leave the machine, even for a moment, secure the cap. If you walk away from the motor, try to leave it in an airworthy condition. If unable to do so, use a reminder (like a wrench on the seat). Interruptions of a pilot's routine have caused serious accidents in everything from 747's to paramotors.

Starting the Motor

The most likely place to be seriously injured is starting the motor. Treat every motor like it will go to full power—that has happened all too frequently with sometimes-tragic results. Cages are only meant to keep paraglider lines, not hands, out of the prop. Advise bystanders to stand clear (keep them away from the propeller arc too) and shout "CLEAR PROP" before pulling/engaging. Starting without a cage is nearly suicidal. Again, make sure the throttle, at the carburetor, is at idle.

The motor and its propeller require extreme care for both the operator and those nearby. Wait for the instructor to work with you on the vagaries of a particular brand before trying to start it. More serious injuries befall pilots starting/running motors on the ground then any other cause (have we emphasized that enough?).

Kiting the wing by hand is a good way to inspect it before committing to flight. There are many ways to do so, but holding the risers apart lets you look at it like it will be flying. Look for line problems, holes, unusual wrinkles or anything else that just doesn't look right.

Setting Trimmers

Trimmers are used to make the wing fly slower (pull IN) or faster (let OUT). They will also affect launch and should be set properly and checked before inflating.

As shown below, pull tabs shorten or lengthen the rear risers to change the wing's shape. You can also cause a turn by setting them differentially. If you speed up only the right side (let out the right trimmer) you'll turn left. If you speed up only the left side, you'll turn right.

Each wing is different and the manual should be consulted but, in general, set the trimmers to neutral which is the slow (IN) position on most wings.

If the wing is difficult to inflate (doesn't come overhead easily), set them to half-fast. If it comes up OK but you have to run forever before liftoff, set them to their slowest setting or something in between.

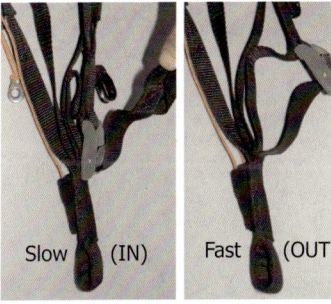

Slow (IN)   Fast (OUT)

The safest way to start almost any machine is with it on your back. That's not always the easiest but, if at all possible, is preferred. This is where a good electric starter is valuable. If using a pull starter, have another pilot pull it for you unless you can reach it with the motor on. The next safest way to start it is by securing the motor to something firm like a tree although those are hopefully scarce in your perfect PPG field. The least desirable and, unfortunately, the most common method is to start is by yourself while standing in front of it. There are some critical precautions to mind before pulling though.

Making it Go

Any gas motor requires fuel, air, spark and spin. An electric starter makes the spin easy but requires some extra care itself. Specific details of priming, choking, master switches and fuel/air valves will depend on your chosen model and will be described by your instructor or seller. If there's an owner's manual (be thankful), read it; many don't have a current manual.

If starting by yourself, put the throttle handle in a place where it cannot be activated accidentally but leaves the kill button accessible. One option is to hold the throttle stem and *not* the trigger. If the motor does go to power, it won't push the throttle into more power. Plus it keeps the kill button readily available. Brace the motor with your thumb hooked around a solid part of the frame and pretend that a gorilla is about to push on the propeller—they both have nasty bites. Position your body to be ready for accidental full power. It happens.

Starting the motor on your back is preferable but, if you have to do it yourself: hold the motor so that you keep quick access to the kill button and the throttle cannot be actuated accidentally. If the motor suddenly spools up to power, it could push your hand in a way that squeezes more throttle.

Always verify the throttle linkage at the carburetor is idle if you can see it.

Make sure the ground area is clear of loose objects (rocks, diamonds, sticks, cell phones, etc.) which get sucked into the prop. Loose straps or other things should not be able to reach the prop or exhaust. And be mindful of where the prop blast is going—even at idle it can disturb things nearby, especially a paraglider wing.

Don't let the motor idle for too long, carbon builds up on the spark plug, cylinder head and other parts (called *loading up*). After idling for more than a few minutes, run it up to 50% power for about 10 seconds—that's called *clearing* the motor.

Have a Plan: Patterns, Areas and Altitudes.

Before soloing you will have a plan, including signals, to use in case of radio failure. The USPPA has adopted a set of common ones but your instructor may have differences. You will fly a rectangular *pattern* (see Chapter 5) that helps judge landings, provides a known path that other pilots can easily search, and have a way to describe location.

All patterns are based on taking off and landing into the wind. It is simply a rectangular path around the field to position yourself for landing. After reaching a safe

> ⚠ **Caution!**
> Most propeller injuries happen just after firing up. Electric start reduces this risk as long as it's failure doesn't prompt an attempt at starting with the propeller.
> Most pull-start motors allow bracing against the impending thrust but a few older models have starter handles coming out the side. These were particularly dangerous since any unexpected thrust would quickly overpower the pilot's ability to stop it from falling forward. Hands can quickly dart into the propeller before realizing the extreme consequences.

> **Tip: Two Stroke Tuning:**
>
> There are many carburetors and many techniques for getting them to run just right. The owners manual, if available, is the best place to start. Chapter 12 contains a troubleshooting guide and chapter 27 explains adjusting the most common 2-stroke carburetors (*tuning*).
>
> Tuning is frequently required after big changes in temperature or elevation. But if the motor ran fine the last time, and there has not been any big change in temperature or elevation, then tuning will not likely solve anything.

altitude and getting into the seat you will turn left or right, to go crosswind and continue climbing. The next turn is downwind and positions you for landing back at the launch site in case of a motor-out. Even if you're not landing right away this is a good path to fly before heading out of the immediate area. As a new solo student you will continue climbing so as to fly the entire flight within gliding distance of the launch area.

Your instructor will tell you where to fly and what maneuvers to practice. If you have not gotten into the seat then he will direct you to come in for a landing. You cannot continue flying while hanging from the leg straps—it's too uncomfortable and may cut off the circulation to your legs. If everything is normal then you will just fly around and enjoy your accomplishment for a half hour or so. When you come back in, you will most likely enter the pattern (detailed in Chapter 5) for landing.

Taking Instructions Via Radio

You'll be up there alone but the instructor's voice will be right there, suggesting appropriate responses, filling in the blanks or insisting on immediate corrections. It can be difficult to concentrate amidst all the new sensations, but concentrate you must. This is why simulator practice is so valuable, especially with the motor running and controls in hand. Some instructors may prefer not to run the motor in the simulator (which involves some risk on its own), but should have you go through the drills while causing other distractions. It could save your life: *rehearsal is critical.*

You will be required to pull brakes, add power, reduce power, kick your legs in response to your instructor's directives (a front/back kicking motion means "yes" and a left/right scissor motion means "no.") Follow these instructions explicitly—you may not know why, but your instructor will. You must respond immediately in flight because the sooner control inputs are made, the less dramatic they need to be.

Rehearsing

If you have to think about a response, don't count on performing it correctly. Reactions must be rehearsed and be nearly automatic. For example, the reaction to a forward surging wing is applying some brake. The reaction to a wing falling back is to immediately reduce power and let up on the brakes while preparing to "catch" the impending surge. Throwing a reserve must be rehearsed—if it's needed, it probably won't be on a calm morning cruise.

Mostly you must rehearse taking instructions for the early flights then, as experience at those is gained, add other things. When you're getting tossed around, only rehearsed reactions will emerge through the chaos.

These are common hand signals used by many instructors and others. They supplement radio communications and can be effective in emergencies or when the radio fails.

Abort - Kill Engine
Clear To Launch
Cut Engine
Flare
Hands Up
Land Here
Pilot Negative Cofirmation
Pilot Positive Cofirmation
Start Engine
Turn to YOUR Left
Turn to YOUR Right
Wing Good - Go, Go, Go

courtesy Jerry Starbuck and USPPA.org

Power-Loss & Surge

No Input

Apply Brakes at power loss

"What do you do when the engine quits?" is a common question among the curious. "Not much" is pretty accurate if you're up high (200 feet or more). Applying brakes right when it quits helps reduce the surge, but even without doing so, the craft is entirely manageable. At low altitude, it's more critical to control the surge that follows a motor failure.

⚠️ **Caution!**

If you do not know what is happening:

"Hands up, power off, prepare to dampen the surge." Steer if a turn develops but remember that too much brake is the most common causes of in-flight mishaps.

After reducing brake pull, go back to position/pressure 2 for a good feel of the wing. Do this unless you *know* your action is correct.

Handling Emergencies

The vast majority of flights go without a hitch; but when "hitch" happens, you'll be glad you're prepared. These can be rehearsed in a simulator and some are best rehearsed with the motor running (or other artificial distractions). The flight environment is loud and foreign, but simulator practice will make it less so.

The distraction of an unusual situation can be worse than the actual problem. So when something does go pop, take a deep breath and deal with it in a methodical way.

Situational emergencies, where the pilot has more time to analyze and react, are covered in Chapter 19, Risk Management. That addresses important thought processes along with options that you might not think about.

Above All

Listening to your instructor's radio commands is the best defense, but a few common priorities apply to all emergencies:

- **Maintain Control**. Regardless of what happens—keep flying the craft. Remember "hands up, power off" in uncertain situations, but try to keep it flying straight with as little control input as possible. Avoid large movements—rash actions almost always cause more harm then good. Panic destroys the reason that can extricate you from nastiness and the only way to reduce panic is preparation. Fortunately, very few maladies require immediate action.

- To the extent possible, **get on a safe course and altitude**.

- Once control and flight path are established, **deal with the problem**. Look around at what you've got. Loud noises are rarely good and, in most cases, shutting off the motor and gliding back down to land is best.

- **Land Into the wind** and away from wind shadows (right behind an obstruction that blocks the wind) for best results. Obviously there are exceptions: a downwind beach landing would be better than an upwind water landing. An upwind water landing would be better than a downwind landing in boulders. Hopefully you were thinking about this before the motor quit and have an option in mind. Regardless of landing direction, make sure you're nearly level before touchdown. Don't land in a turn.

If facing two undesirable outcomes, pick the least objectionable one. For example, pick a field of low scrub over a tree landing.

Throttle Cable Caught

Example: after climbout and getting into the seat, you bring your hand back up and the throttle cable snags on something, stopping both it and your hand. Now the hand is stuck so that it can't reach for the brake. The throttle works but your hand is stuck.

Maintain control! This simple problem is a non-event, but pilots' rash actions have compounded it with inappropriate reactions. Fly the craft using normal brake input of the other hand (make shallow turns in that direction), look forward and keep climbing; you may be in a shallow torque turn. Once at a safe height with a safe flight path, move the throttle back, away from the motor and up. Make turns to stay near the launch site. It will probably be a simple matter of looking down to see the obvious solution then executing it.

If it remains snagged, plan on a power-off landing. Get over the landing area with plenty of height and shut off the motor. Then pull your hand out of the throttle and do a regular power-off landing.

Radio Failure

Your instructor's presence on the radio is very important but radios can quit. You must have a plan of action in mind. Usually this plan is to continue around the pattern, climb out above the field to get some feel for the machine then come in for a normal landing near the middle of the field. You'll hopefully have rehearsed this in the simulator and be able to recite it back to the instructor. It will be a detailed description of climbing up, getting into the seat (and the incredible importance of letting go of the brakes first!), pattern and landing.

Your instructor may have simple hand signals, if you've worked these out beforehand, maneuver so as to see him and respond accordingly.

Brake Line Failure or Tangle

If a brake line fails, gets cut off by the prop, tangles, or becomes disconnected, there is plenty of steering authority available using the rear risers.

As with all emergency situations, *fly the aircraft first*. Use the available control to steer while climbing to a safe altitude.

The most likely cause is a loop of brake line fouling the pulley. You may be able to undo this in flight but get up to a safe altitude first (300 feet or more). Remember, if the brake is stuck, it will still pull the rear riser but will take much more force and be much less effective.

Like any abnormal situation, don't do anything rash; this problem is normally benign. If possible, climb up higher than usual, carefully get into the seat (if able) and establish level or slightly climbing flight. Once on a safe course with plenty of altitude you can look up to deal with the problem.

It's usually obvious what needs to be done—reach up and fix it. You can safely land even without the brakes but it's obviously better to regain full use. If the brake line is missing then there is nothing to do but plan an approach and landing using the rear risers and throttle.

It's possible that you can use the brake line by reaching above its pulley and going right to the brake line. That may be difficult depending on the risers but give it a try—motor risers are more likely to be short enough.

If you cannot use normal brakes, plan on using the rear ris-

The pilot is pulling on D riser to achieve a rear-riser turn. This wing uses a 4-riser set designed for motoring. A soaring wing will have longer risers and may require a longer reach to grab the quick-link - just grab as high as you can. On a 3-riser set you would be pulling the C's.

It takes a lot of pull to affect even a small turn. This technique is used in the event of a brake line failure.

Embarrassment Avoided

While kibitzing with another pilot about the flight we just had, a couple cops showed up. They were fascinated by the craft and started asking questions. "Let me just show you!" I said.

Right after liftoff, it became obvious my right brake was stuck. The knot defied correction; too bad I didn't catch that one on preflight. Not wanting to look bad in front of our new observers, I came back around with power using only the left brake. On final, I shut off the motor and pulled the D's (rear risers) to flare. They had no idea that anything was amiss and I wasn't about to mention anything. "Wasn't that cool?" I asked while carefully fixing my brake.

"Here, I'll go again." They probably wondered why that flight was so much longer

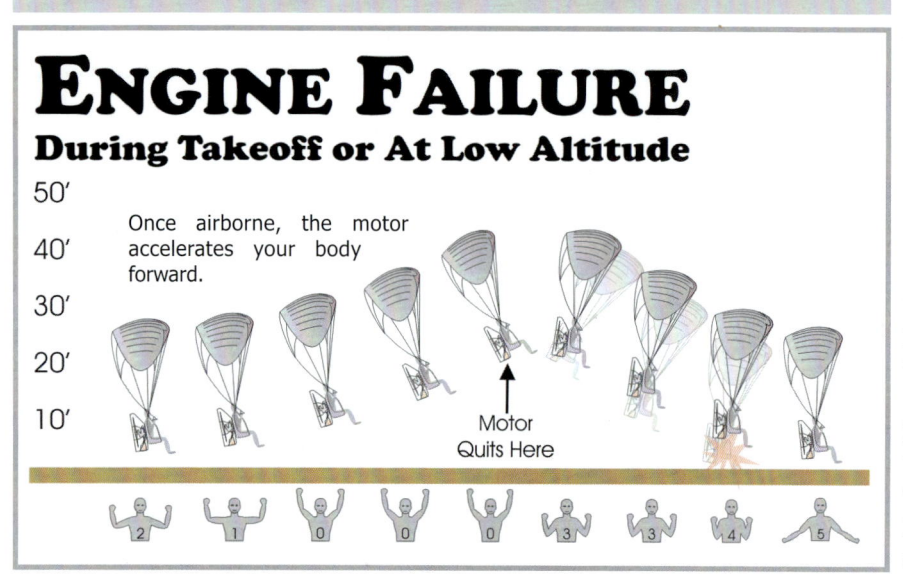

ENGINE FAILURE
During Takeoff or At Low Altitude

Once airborne, the motor accelerates your body forward.

Motor Quits Here

Liftoff is usually with some brake then easing off for the climbout. If the motor quits before reaching 30', go immediately to 1/4 brake (position 3), hold it and then flare just before touchdown.

Not doing anything after it quits will allow the wing to surge forward and dump you firmly during your swing back under it (as depicted with the faded flyer).

ers for steering and flare. It's better to use both rear risers (instead of one brake and one rear riser). Do some turns and practice getting the feel for how much pull it takes to effect a turn or slow-down.

The rear risers can also be used for landing but won't be nearly as effective as the brakes. At the point where you would normally use the brakes to flare, pull harder on both rear risers and be ready for a harder touchdown. It is best to do the landing without power to prevent damage and should still be soft enough to remain standing. With experience you can land with power but doing so adds risk in that the propeller will be spinning at a time when falling is more possible.

Avoid the temptation to pull too hard since the wing's response is dramatically slower. Limit pull to just what you need so there's less of a chance for parachutal stall.

Motor Failure

A motor failure is almost always a non-event; more of an inconvenience than an emergency unless you've wandered over bad terrain. Our slow speed means that losing power is nowhere near the bugaboo that it is with regular airplanes or even rigid other ultralights. Slow speed enables many landing options from all phases of flight. *Always* stay withing gliding range of safe landing options and be aware of the wind direction so that you can land into it.

The only time a quick response is needed after losing power is during the initial climb or while flying low (less than 100 feet). That is because a sudden power loss in climb will require a quick pull of the brakes to prevent the wing from surging way forward. The steeper the climb, the more pronounced the surge. A shallower climb reduces this risk.

> The proper action after a motor failure during climb is to immediately pull some brakes (about pressure 2) to control the surge then ease them up as the glide establishes or flare as necessary.

Rehearse responding to a motor failure so that it is automatic. You are most vulnerable during the takeoff phase: if the surge is allowed to go unchecked, the wing will shoot forward and you could pendulum right into the ground.

After that initial surge is controlled, the next action depends on altitude. If you're high enough, setting up for a normal flare is appropriate (brakes position 1 and then flare). But if less then 30 feet or so, the brakes should be held at position 2, ready to flare at the normal height. A flare from postilion 2 brakes will not be as effective but is better than coming off the brakes completely and being swung into the ground.

A motor failure from more than a hundred feet or so gives plenty of time to turn into the wind and set up a normal flare and landing. Don't do any steep turns but always turn so as to land into the wind. Only accept an off-wind landing if the terrain or obstructions for an into-the-wind landing are much worse. The stronger the wind, the more important it is to land directly into it.

If you have enough time (more than a couple hundred feet), get established in a landing pattern, then try to restart. Always attend to piloting before dealing with the motor. Try different throttles settings when attempting the restart. If you do get it started, maintain the same power setting until reaching a point where the normal power-off landing pattern can be flown. Plan the landing with no power even if you let it idle. Concentrate on landing below 200 feet.

Turbulence

If conditions turn bumpy, you want to hold increased brake pressure but use no more than pressure 2. Remember *pressure* is key, if a brake handle tries to yank upwards, let it do so while maintaining the same pressure. Same thing if it goes down—let it. When throttling off, hold at *least* position/pressure 2. When power off, slowing is better, but be careful—too much brake has proven to be way more dangerous than not enough.

Flying this way reduces the chance for various wing maladies including frontal collapses, where the leading edge tucks under causing a brief, but rapid descent.

If you must turn, use steady but minimal differential brake and hold it for 3 seconds. That will prevent getting into a left-right oscillation. You will bet getting swung around a fair amount but don't try to counteract—in almost all cases, beginning pilots who try to counteract oscillations only make them worse. And if you do start oscillating, let up on both brakes and hold them steady!

Small Asymmetric Wing Collapse

Small wing collapses (or folds) happen occasionally and the wing usually snaps back before the pilot even knows it occurred. Generally, just following the turbulence advice above will suffice. Small collapses that don't come out immediately can normally be cured with *gentle* pressure on that side's brake. If you simply do what it takes to steer straight, the wing will likely reform quickly.

Large Asymmetric Wing Collapse

A severe asymmetric collapse, covered more in Chapter 18, is where more then half of the wing tucks under. It is rare enough in powered paragliding that most pilots have never experienced it. The motor makes matters worse, though, since lines *could* get into the prop or wrap around a frame part. That is why flying in *big air* (turbulent conditions) should be avoided with a motor.

If you get a large collapse the initial reaction should be hands

The malfunction below was induced by the pilot but, even after all that, the wing recovered nicely on its own. A characteristic of beginner wings is that they recover quickly from most collapses with little turn. Of course it's possible for the weather to change which is why it's important to know how to handle them.

Real turbulence-induced collapses, while incredibly rare, can easily be worse than what is done intentionally by the pilot.

up, power off. Then carefully apply whatever brakes are needed to steer straight. Use the amount of pressure you normally feel at position 1 on the collapsed side (it will be limp). Be ready to let the brake come back up as its pressure builds. Nearly all PPG incidents that follow a collapse result from *too much* brake pulled by the pilot. If you're low to the ground or near an obstruction, do whatever it takes to steer clear even if that means a nearly immediate turn input.

Cravat

A cravat happens when part of a wing tip gets tangled in the lines and doesn't come out on its own. A small cravat is easy to deal with and, if you can steer easily, just come around to land. Sometimes a quick pump to pressure 2 will clear it. A large cravat could require quick action if a turn suddenly develops. Use minimum brakes at first, but *do what it takes to fly straight* (or as straight as you can).

There is a potential solution to this problem that you may learn later (Chapter 18), it is called the stabilo line pull. It involves reaching up and pulling the stabilo line (it goes up to the wing tip) in an effort to clear the cravat. This is something to rehearse under mellow conditions or while kiting since most simulators do not have a riser set attached.

Riser Twist

If you feel yourself starting to twist during launch, abort! Abort at the first sign of any uncontrollable turn. Before trying again, figure out why it's happened and find a cure. Details of various torque issues are covered in Chapter 23.

If you start twisting after launch, *immediately* **reduce power** and **reduce brake pressure**. Keep your hands up (no more than position/pressure 1) so the brakes don't get stuck in a pulled-down position (in the twisted risers). With the motor at idle and enough altitude, you will swing back around and be able to resume forward flight although at less power. The glider will actually fly quite fine, regardless of where you're facing as long as you stay off the power and brakes. Once facing forward, throttle up *gradually* if needed and only to what's necessary. An immediate landing into the wind may be appropriate if there's a safe landing option.

Get into the habit of fastening your leg straps first. If you ever take to free-flying, or launch your motor from a mountain, you'll avoid the possible catastrophe of launching with them undone.

Riser twist almost always happens on launch. If you don't reduce power quickly enough, you can spin around and hit quite hard. Even if you don't spin all the way around, pointing to the left means the thrust is pushing you left which causes a right bank. The solution is power reduction—pulling brake against this bank frequently leads to the glider spinning and a subsequent drop.

Kill Switch Failure

You probably won't know about this problem until it's time to land and you're instructed to shut off the motor. It's no big deal since you can land with the motor idling and have the instructor come shut it off using some other means. After landing, make sure to carefully turn around and bring the wing down so it won't get in the prop. You can also consider climbing up a bit and running it out of gas if you've got a lot of room, time, and don't mind doing a power-off landing.

Getting the throttle cable chopped off in the prop does two bad things. It can trap your throttle at a high setting *and* disable the kill switch. You may get stuck climbing. Hopefully, your motor has another pilot-accessible method of shutdown besides the kill switch; a choke or primer bulb works splendidly. Rehearse reaching for these in the simulator. What seems obvious while standing comfortably over the motor can be perplexing in the noisy adrenaline-pumped aftermath of a chopped throttle. See chapter 19 for more ideas on handling this situation.

One hapless pilot on a first solo had this happen without knowing how to kill the motor—she wound up circling into the chilly heights way above a large city, climbing through controlled airspace, until finally running out of fuel several thousand feet high. Fortunately her instructor guided her to a successful landing.

Unfastened Leg Straps

In free-flight paragliding, forgetting to buckle your leg straps can be tragic. It is equally dangerous for motor pilots if launching from a steep surface where the ground falls away quickly. And since many motor pilots eventually wind up free-flying, you shold get into the habit of buckling the legs first and unbuckling them last. Use the checklist in the Appendix *every time* to prevent this problem.

If you do forget one (or both) leg straps you'll feel it quickly on launch as the motor tries to lift off without you. If that happens, let off the power smoothly and abort. Swallow your pride and quietly buckle up before another try.

Reserve Deployment

The need for a reserve parachute in motoring is incredibly rare but they have scored some "saves;" mostly after botched aerobatics, very strong thermal turbulence or huge changes in wind. Free flyers are far more likely to "toss the laundry" in their search for strong lift or aerobatic exuberance.

Situations that warrant deploying your reserve must involve nearly complete or impending loss of control: a mid-air collision, a serious collapse that won't recover (probably a cravat), and wing malfunctions are a few. If you start to spiral, act fast—G-forces can build so quickly that you are not *able* to deploy the reserve. Very deliberately follow the steps below. You should be able to get the reserve out and tossed within 3 seconds.

1. Kill the motor, you don't want your last chance lines being chopped by the propeller. It is very possible you will be getting tossed around and, like all steps, this should be automatic.

2. Look at the handle—this avoids the wasted time of reaching endlessly for a handle that's not there. At least one pilot hit the ground while grasping wildly for the reserve handle on his right side—it was on the other sied.

3. Reach for the handle and grasp it. This seems obvious but rehearsing it this way helps when the "fur is flying".

4. Pull the handle out. The reserve sits at the end of a foot-long line—this is difficult to deal with if you've never tried it which is why rehearsing in the simulator adds such value.

5. Look for clear air. You don't want it to catch on anything, but remember, you want to get it out quickly.

6. Throw towards the clear air as much as possible. It will be like tossing a 5 pound

---

1. This pilot is doing a reserve clinic and was surprised that his first "toss" barely moved the reserve. By the third try (pictured) he was getting good distance into what would have been clear air in a real emergency. Throwing a reserve is much like throwing a 5 pound weight from the end of a 3 foot string.

2. A Save. The pilot's reserve sits to the left of his motor and the wing just below. After launching into air he wished he hadn't, the wing took a major collapse and his reserve was the only safe way out of it. It's never a guarantee, and the landing may be in a very bad location, but it sure beats the alternative.

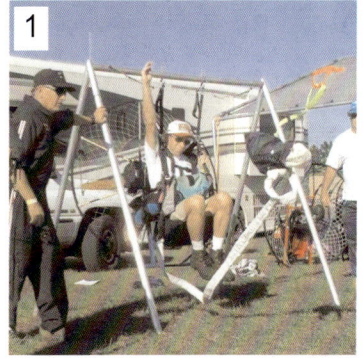

⚠️ **Caution!**

In any malady, do not accept an increasingly steep turn. After initially reducing brake pull, use whatever input it takes to prevent a spiral dive.

Parachute Landing Fall *by Dennis Pagen*

rock at the end of a cord. Yank on the bridle to help open the parachute if it doesn't deploy immediately.

The actions above must be a well rehearsed and performed with purpose. The procedure itself should be reviewed in advance and committed to memory: "Kill, Look, Reach, Pull, Look, Throw." Say that line over and over until it's automatic.

Parachute Landing Fall

Landing under a reserve will probably be pretty hard. Depending on your weight and reserve size, the descent rate at touchdown will be the equivalent of jumping off about a 4-foot table. The bigger the reserve, the softer the arrival.

Many years ago, military paratroopers devised a way to get their soldiers down with fewer injuries—the Parachute Landing Fall (PLF). It works well for landings under reserve or any hard landing.

The idea is to transfer vertical energy into horizontal energy. For a motor pilot, the frame will usually intervene before completing the fall which is desirable. Some instructors advocate lifting your legs and letting the frame take the impact. While that may work, be very mindful of protecting your spine. Success depends on your motor's frame bottom. Consider that a broken leg beats a broken back.

Once you recognize the need for a PLF, put your legs together with knees slightly bent. At touchdown roll in whatever direction is natural, absorbing some with the knees, then hips then the frame should take the rest. Allow yourself to roll it out and end up on your back (or frame, more likely) as depicted.

If you remember nothing else, make sure your legs are together with knees slightly bent and toes slightly down.

Once the reserve opens your next action depends on the situation. The paraglider will probably fall below you and may reinflate then fly out to the side, pulling you somewhat in one direction. If everything is stable, leave it. If you start to rotate it might be worth trying to pull the glider in to disable it but it can yank powerfully out of your hands, causing burns.

When approaching the ground, look at the horizon and prepare for the *Parachute Landing Fall* (PLF)—a tried and true method for absorbing high impact forces. Put your legs together with knees slightly bent. You'll hit hard but try to orient yourself such that you can roll to one side or the other. It should be feet, knee, hip then shoulder ending in a rolling motion. This may difficult with the motor on and it may be best to hit on the motor frame if it's below you. Protect the spine at all costs. If you us on your motor's frame to hit first, you may reduce the chance for leg injuries at the expense of increasing the chance for spine injuries. Use the frame (lift your legs) only if you *know* it will be below you and give sufficient protection.

Parachutal Stall

A wing goes parachutal when it stops flying forward and starts descending vertically like an old round parachute. After the wing falls back you'll notice no airflow past your face, but the wing is fully inflated. It can be caused by a number of factors including too much brake, power, turbulence or a combination thereof. Many of these turn into spins, where the glider rotates due to one side having slightly more drag (from brakes or turbulence).

Recovery is simple and must be done *immediately* upon feeling the wing start to go back: "**Hands up, power off, prepare to dampen the surge.**"

In the extremely unlikely chance that it's still not flying and you're above a hundred feet, then: reach for the A's, palms forward, thumbs down, and twist them down about 2 inches. This is called *tweaking the A's*.

This malady is far more common in motoring because the thrust will hold the paraglider a parachutal stall where it would otherwise recover on its own. Nearly every recorded parachutal stall accident involves the pilot hitting the ground at full power under a fully inflated wing.

Be aware that, during recovery, the wing surges forward and then you swing below it. If you're near the ground, recovering could be worse than landing from the parachutal stall. So if you're below about 60 feet, it's probably better to ride it down and prepare for the PLF.

The Flight

CHAPTER 5

Time to fly.

It's not always some momentous event, but rather a coming together of skills and conditions that leave you ready to take the lunge. You've learned rudimentary kiting skills, rehearsed the flight and know what to expect. After that it's a matter of practicing those skills until the right conditions find you ready.

This day's flight adds new and significant elements into what you've been trained for: sensation and adrenaline. This is where those hours of practice pay off! In the face of kinematic newness, don't expect to think things through—anything not rehearsed will likely be done wrong. Airlines have much experience with this undeniable human shortcoming and, like the airlines, PPG instructors have found that repetitive practice is the best preparation.

Launch

Variations in technique exist to accommodate differences in equipment, conditions, experience and simple preference; do what you've learned to minimize surprises. Listen intently to your instructor, be prepared to abort quickly and nothing gets fed to the propeller.

Unlike other forms of flight, launch is literally and figuratively, the biggest hurdle.

Do your pre-launch checklist (from memory) to cover the basics. Do just as you've rehearsed without the motor although everything will feel different with thrust. Your instructor may have you power up prior to starting your run. Machines with the most flexible cages can*not* support powering up right away (a powered forward inflation). Power assist improves the success rate while slightly increasing the

Below: Airlines use checklists for good reason: they work. Skipping them or omitting items has proven deadly.

While it takes 32 items to safely get a Boeing 737 into the air, our checklist is mercifully brief. It is no less important though. An easy-to-use set of checklists is included in the Appendix.

chance for line damage in the event of an aborted launch.

After the motor is on your back and warmed up, do a brief run-up to make sure it can smoothly reach maximum power.

Just before launch, determine wind direction. Your face is best suited for this if the prop isn't spinning (clutched machines), otherwise use whatever wind indicators are available. If the wind has turned significantly, you'll either need to wait or move. When it's light and variable, waiting may be the better course. As the day wears on, thermals increasingly come through and can change the wind direction dramatically. About the time you get it laid out into a new direction, a thermal comes by changing it again.

Before launch, do a brief runup to insure the machine can smoothly develop full power. Mind where the prop blast is going and keep the propeller plane away from bystanders.

Inflation—Light or Nil Wind

Launching in zero or light wind is probably our most challenging task. The technique described here has proven quite successful although your instructor may have good reason for using a different one. This *power forward* method uses partial power from the outset to help develop and build the all-important forward speed. Some instructors prefer going to full power right away but that carries additional risk from torque, cage flexing and the increased chance for a *face plant* (falling face-first.) Some prefer the initial inflation to be done with no power, especially if the cage is flexible and tends to get pulled into the prop.

Start with your wing laid out as described in Chapter 3, lines cleared, and aligned directly into any hint of wind. A good layout is critical.

You should be standing with a brake in each hand, arms out and an A riser in the "V" of each thumb (only the center A is necessary with split A's for most wings). All the risers and lines on each side should be draped over your biceps. Your throttle hand should have its A riser just in front of the throttle stem.

Back up a couple steps and insure that your run direction will be exactly perpendicular to the wing and check that your shoulders are square to the wing. Step left and right just enough to feel that the pull of the lines is centered being careful not to curl over the leading edge. Power up to about 30% thrust (if your machine allows), get it stabilized and then start the run aggressively. Keep your hands back and apply only minimal pressure to the A's. If there's much wind, don't be as aggressive.

1. Throttle to about 1/3 power, hold it for a second, then go for the run, holding 1/3rd power.

2. If the wing comes up too crooked, abort. Otherwise, keep driving forward to get it overhead and build speed.

3. As soon as you feel or see it going left or right, move that way. As the wing nears overhead and you're moving, let go of the A's.

4. When everything looks straight and the takeoff path is good, throttle up to full and pull about quarter brakes to ease lift off. Once established in the climb, ease up on the brake pressure.

Ready for inflation: With the A's and brakes in each hand, the other risers are draped over the forearm and the throttle trigger is free. It is important to be able to get to the kill switch immediately in case something goes awry.

Troubleshooting *Forward* Launch Problems

Calm air is a challenge. Some pilots don't even try to launch when it's calm which misses a wonderful opportunity. These solutions are for the most common launch problems but, as always, follow your instructor's advice—he can *see* what's going on.

Symptom: Wing comes up crooked.
1. You're not starting or continuing the run exactly centered and perpendicular to the wing.
2. If the wing always comes up to the left, make a conscious effort to always point slightly to the right before starting the run.
3. Make sure you're pointed exactly into the wind, if any.
4. Be more aggressive to build speed faster. This is easier with a relatively small wing.
5. Don't pull the A's too much or unevenly.

Symptom: The wing doesn't come all the way overhead, especially when there's no wind.
1. Stay on the A's longer and don't go to the brakes too early. In light winds, make sure you have a lot of speed before moving to the brakes. One technique is to let go of the A's then touch the risers (to make sure there's no brake pull) then go to the brakes.
2. You're pulling the A's too hard and curling over the leading edge. Feel the wing pull first then apply pressure to the A's.
3. Come up on the power earlier and use more of it.
4. Your initial run needs to be more aggressive.
5. Let the trimmers out (faster setting). This will require a faster launch run though.
6. Don't look up at the wing, look sideways and concentrate on driving forward.
7. Look up at the wing as you power up, this will encourage the correct upright posture while checking the wing to be centered.

Symptom: The wing tends to over-fly me then collapse.
1. Get off the A's earlier. If there's much wind, you'll need to release them earlier anyway.
2. Make sure the trimmers are in their slowest setting (pulled in).
3. If using power, only establish 1/3 throttle then start your inflation. The prop blast, on some wings, makes the wing shoot forward.

Symptom: I Can't get airborne in spite of running my fastest.
1. After initial inflation, stand up straight as you go to full power. Concentrate on letting the motor push you as fast as your legs will go with long strides before easing in some brake. You may need some brake to take off but then ease them up to nearly pressure 0.
2. Make sure the trimmers are in, motor is producing peak power (prop on forward), and you're into the wind.
3. Adjust your harness for the least amount of tilt-back possible so the wing's lift doesn't try to make you run leaning backwards.

Symptom: I tend to go side to side before lifting off.
1. Once you get the wing up overhead and moving, go to half power just to keep moving, steer the wing overhead straight, then go up to full power for lift off. Never takeoff in a pendulum swing.
2. Don't change running direction too much. Only correct half as much as you think.

Symptom: I tend to sink back down to the ground and land on my butt.
1. Keep running until you are churning air. Don't get in the seat until reaching at least 100 feet up.
2. Don't let off the brakes quickly after liftoff. Ease them up slowly to accelerate then it will climb.
3. Make sure the leg straps are somewhat loose to prevent the seat from kicking you into the air too early.

Symptom: I tend to lose my balance just as the wing starts lifting and fall down sometimes.
1. It's probably torque related. Make sure you stand straight up early in the launch run. If you're leaning forward when the wing lifts you, precession forces (see chapter 22) will make it want to twist as you straighten up and possibly lose your balance.
2. Adjust your harness to minimize torque affects (see Chapter 12), primarily decrease any tilt-back.

Symptom: Lines are catching on part of the cage rim as the wing comes up.
1. Hold your arms up higher when you start the run or shake your arms as the the wing comes up (the "A wiggle").
2. Install small hooks on the cage rim sides, like the system trike pilots use, to keep your lines from starting out below the rim.

If the wing comes up slowly, stay on the A's (pressure only) and keep driving hard—move under the wing if you feel it going to a side. Speed is success—keep moving. If the wing shoots overhead, falls to the side, or starts falling back, then abort! Some wings require more pull on the A's than others and some will front tuck with too much pull.

If there is more than a couple mph of wind, the wing may shoot up quickly; be ready to let go of the A's early and apply brakes as it nears the top. Pull the brakes to slow the wing *then let off* as you start moving forward. If you do nothing to prevent the wing from overflying, it can pass overhead then tuck right down into your spinning prop.

Once you're moving with the wing overhead, throttle up and stand up straight, letting the motor push you. Don't delay, there can be no hesitation and you may have to stay on the A's for some time in nil wind. *Once you are moving* it can be a good time to look up at the wing—doing so forces you into an upright posture.

Move left or right to stay under the wing but don't over-correct lest you set up an oscillation. That is where you go too far left and the wing goes right. Then you dart

The PPG Bible: A Complete Guide and Reference

This pilot is doing a no-power inflation. He gets the wing nearly overhead before throttling up. Another technique he employs is looking to the side to see where the wing is. As long as it doesn't slow you down, this can be a good way to see what the wing is doing before it gets overhead.

As he throttles up, he must stand up straight to let the motor push him.

Notice the arms are not pulling the A's, rather they are just applying pressure and following them up.

Applying too much pull on the A's results in the situation pictured below where the leading edge folds over (*frontals*) and prevents the wing from coming overhead.

The correct stance for reverse inflations: a brake in each hand, A's in your left and and throttle in your right hand. Reverse the hands for machines with left-handed throttles.

over to the right and the wing yanks to the left. Solution: consciously don't run so much towards it. Turn *some* and use *some* brakes.

Keep the speed up. Once everything is stable, *smoothly* go to full power and keep running. Pull some brake, no more then position/pressure 2, once you're moving quickly so as to reduce liftoff speed.

When you feel the wing lifting you, keep running! **Run until your feet are churning air**. A common mishap is when the pilot feels lift and tries to sit down too early. At best this is hard on the prop and cage. Stay on the throttle, too—letting off early in the climb will cause you to swing into the ground.

Inflation—Stronger conditions

Anytime you can stand there and kite the wing, do a reverse inflation.

You'll be facing the wing holding the brakes as described in Chapter 3 with the A's in one hand and throttle in the other. Build a wall, get it even and then lean a bit towards the wing. When ready, snap back using your *body* to pull the wing up. Get it stable overhead and moving into the wind before turning around. You want the wing to have some forward momentum before beginning the turn. Then as soon as you are facing forward, *move forward*. Turn and move. Throttle up to about 30% to help forward motion.

After you've turned forward, some instructors will rightfully want you to start walking forward and get the wing stable before throttling up. That reduces the chance of having the wing overfly you and collapsing into the prop. It's somewhat more difficult to walk forward without power, but you won't do it for long, just long enough to verify that the wing is under control and you're moving forward.

Another approach is to go strictly by feel. You turn around and throttle up while looking forward and moving. Be sensitive to the small left or right tugs given by the wing and respond with brake and course change. Obviously this takes practice.

If the wing tends to fall back you're either applying too much brake or aren't moving enough. When you get the wing overhead, raise the brakes all the way up as you move. Of course if the wing wants to overfly (come past your body) then you'll need some brake pressure to slow it.

It's important during the turnaround to have your hands mostly up to avoid engaging any brake. Plus, you must move forward immediately after turning around. Don't just stand there, get moving: it is the only way you'll have any control. Once moving and under control, it's just like a forward launch.

In all situations, be quick to abort if things aren't going well—turn around and kill the motor. Making another attempt is preferable to "parablending" your wing.

While running, you must take off going straight (wing overhead) and into the wind as much as possible. Steering should be minimal with just enough input to keep yourself going in the correct direction. Insure that you are pointed in a good climbout direction and under the wing before committing to takeoff. If it gets squirrely, or you feel yourself running side-to-side, abort.

Troubleshooting *Reverse* Launch Problems

The reverse launch can vary from easy to frustrating depending on conditions. Here are some possible causes and cures for troubles.

Symptom: Wing doesn't come up even when the wind should be strong enough.
1. Take one step toward the wing before moving backwards to build momentum when you back up.
2. Only barely pull on the A's until most of the fabric is mostly inflated, then pull primarily with your body.
3. If there is enough wind, building a "wall" helps make sure it comes up straight and quickly.

Symptom: The wing falls back when I turn around.
1. With the wing overhead, step backwards to get it moving, go hands UP, turn around and start moving forward immediately.
2. Throttle up during the turn so there is less delay in getting forward momentum.
3. Try to turn around only when the wing has forward momentum (into the wind).
4. Do a forward inflation.

Symptom: The wing falls over sideways when I turn around.
1. Insure the brakes are up when you turn and the wing is tracking straight in the same direction as your movement.
2. Avoid stepping significantly sideways as you turn. If you step left, the wing will fall to the right.

1. Building a wall is best, but when winds are light, it may not be possible. Your back must be to the wind.

2. Snap back hard with your body, applying pressure to the A's as they allow. Keep walking backwards, if necessary.

3. Use no brakes as the wing comes up except to slow it. Move left or right with the wing. Pull the A's *slightly* if it's rising slowly.

4 & 5. Use minimum or no brakes while turning around and throttling up. A quick transition to forward motion is key..

After abundant experience is gained you can steer more while running. Capable pilots can steer to most any direction desired including around obstacles and crosswind—this is an important skill for conquering challenging sites.

When everything looks good, you're running the right direction, the wing is essentially overhead, throttle up to full power and hold it. Stand up straight and let the motor push while taking increasingly large strides. Upward glances at the wing are OK, but most attention should be focused on the run and steering. If the wing tries to pull right, steer it back to the left with just enough brake. It will take practice and the instructor's input is invaluable.

Climbout

Use as little brake as possible while climbing out: "Hands up to go up" is a useful admonition. All motors *torque* (cause a turn) to one direction or another; use minimal brake to counteract it. If possible, let it turn in the direction it wants to go. If you feel any twisting in the risers, ease the power back immediately even if your climb rate will suffer. If you *must* turn against the torque, do so gingerly—turning hard against its can easily cause a spin.

If your body starts twisting one way but you are banking the other way, you are entering a *torque-induced lockout* and *must* reduce power.

With everything normal, climb up to at least 300 ft above the ground while keeping your landing area within gliding range. Altitude is your friend—it offers options in case of a motor failure and time to deal with anything else that might crop up. It's hard to hit an obstacle when you're up high.

Once up to safe altitude, reduce power. Avoid long-term use of full power, whenever possible. It's hard on the motor and makes it more likely to quit.

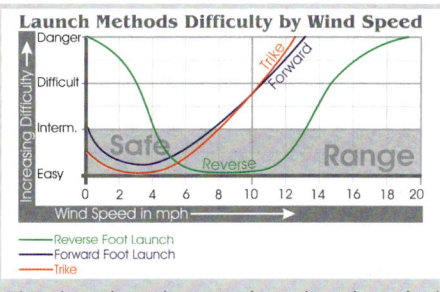

This chart shows how to select a launch method based on winds. Light wind reverses increase the chance for falling backwards while high wind forwards increase the chance for being pulled back into a "turtle" position. Trike flying is covered in the next chapter.

Getting Into the Seat

This action sounds simple but it *must* be done correctly!

After liftoff, you'll be hanging by the leg straps—a terribly uncomfortable position. If you cannot get into the seat easily, without letting go of the brakes, tough it out until at least 50 feet high or advised by your instructor. If it's easy to do *without* letting go of the brakes (may require a kick-in strap), you may get in the seat as soon as a safe climb is established. Some machines, when adjusted properly, require just a little wiggle to slip into.

If you *have* to reach down for the seat, be ready for a motor failure; new pilots sometimes hit the kill switch or get the throttle chopped off when it loops back towards the prop.

On some machines, if the leg straps are too loose, it may be impossible to get into the seat.

On machines equipped with a *kick-in strap* or bar, you can keep the brakes in your hands while using a foot to find the strap (or bar) and push it out. Some kick-in straps are hard to reach with just a foot; for those you will use the non-throttle hand to reach down and position the strap so your foot can reach it. Make sure to let go of the brake first.

The next best way to get into the seat is using one hand to push down on the back of the seatboard. Carefully release the non-throttle brake toggle, reach down with that hand and push down on the back of the seat board to pop it out. It may be possible (and is desirable) to put both brakes in your throttle hand before doing this.

The least desirable way (but unfortunately common) is using both hands to get into the seat. Let go of the brakes first! Make it two distinct steps: palms open to release the brakes slowly, and *then* go for the seat. Using your thumbs, grasp the forward outer part of the seatboard (where the front strap attaches) then push down and forward. On some machines, it's easier to push down on the *back* part of the seatboard and pop it "under center."

Kicking In

Rehearse getting seated in the simulator; it's not always easy, especially on some units.

Your instructor will know the technique for your particular machine, but however you do it: **Make sure not to pull brakes while getting into the seat!** Students have stalled their wings and plummeted to the ground by doing that.

Also be careful letting go of the brakes, especially on machines with lower hook-in points, since the toggles can flail into the prop and get chopped off or worse.

The best kick-in systems hang an aluminum bar down about 6 inches below the seat lip with elastic. It stretches out to 18 inches or so when needed. That keeps it out of your legs while maneuvering on the ground but within easy foot reach when needed.

> ⚠ **Caution**
>
> If you must reach down for the seat, let go of the brakes first!
>
> On some configurations it's possible for the brakes to flail into the prop especially if you're hanging low in the seat and having to wiggle a lot. Put the brake in its holder before letting go to prevent this possibility. On some units, you can also put both brakes in one hand.

Tightening the leg straps makes it easier to get into the seat (on most machines) but more difficult to run. Tighten them all the way, then loosen a couple inches. When setup properly, it's possible on some units to just lift your legs and wiggle into the seat. Get several successful launches under your belt before trying this though—the contortions can result in strange brake positions as a beginner.

If it proves too difficult to get into the seat (this *can* happen on some equipment), return to land. You need to be on the ground before your landing gear goes numb.

Rehearse getting into the seat while hanging in a simulator, preferably with the motor running for realism. Rehearse it until the action is automatic.

Flying Around

Now the reward—you're flying! Once up at altitude, everything gets much easier; its time to relax a bit and enjoy the view. Your instructor may have you try a few things after a bit. Normally the flight should last no more than about a half hour to make sure you have no numb or tired parts (like arms).

Having an Out

Your first flight will be a flood of emotions that drown out many normal thought processes—that is why having an instructor on the radio is so beneficial. But once you're up and the sensations ebb, here are some important considerations:

1. Where would I land if the motor quit? Allow plenty of altitude to get back and set up a pattern. Being high makes this easier since you can stay within glide range of the chosen landing spot. Always have an out, the engine *will* eventually quit when you least expect it.

2. What is the wind doing? Where are the wind shadows and rotors (see Chapter 7)? Staying abreast of wind direction makes planning for a normal or emergency landing easier. Since your emergency landing site is probably the launch site, wind is the most important part of having an out. Every landing decision, including an emergency, will be driven by a need to land into the wind. At our craft's slow speed, there is an enormous difference between landing downwind and upwind—enough to turn a no-brainer into a catastrophe.

3. Fuel remaining. In all likelihood you'll have plenty of fuel, but it's good to get into the habit of thinking about it. A small mirror is handy for looking at your fuel level—this is a good time try it. Even if you started with enough fuel, it is possible for a leak to dramatically reduce your flying time.

Turns

Before turning, "Look, Lean, then Turn." That means **Look** where you're about to turn (called *clearing the turn*), **lean** if you are using weight shift and then start the **turn** with brake input. This also indicates your intentions to others that may be nearby.

Turns are made by raising one brake while pulling down the other. Pull brake in the turn direction *slowly* and *hold* it for three seconds or longer as needed. Left brake to turn left and right brake to turn right. Start with position/pressure 1. Learn how much pressure it takes to get to position 1 and use that feeling (pressure) instead of position once you're familiar. When pulling the brake initially, you will swing out then swing back in to a stable shallow turn—don't try to counteract that swing—hold the brake for 3 seconds minimum. Don't try to dampen oscillations at this stage; just use measured, steady pressure and wait for the turn to develop.

Never leave yourself with no option if the motor quits. Always be happy with your answer to the question: "What if it quit right now.?" This pilot could have landed in the field below providing he could steer clear of the antenna and all its tower's guy wires. But it would be a challenge.

Make sure the plan keeps you able to land in an open area and clear of any wind shadows.

The "Bump Scale:"

Here is a common reference to help when relating "bumpiness" to other pilots:

0 Completely smooth

1 Getting jostled, no noticeable change in flight path.

2 Causes small changes in flight path. The most that new pilots should fly in.

3 Causes body swings of around 3 feet with no control input.

4 Causes moderate changes in flight path and body movements of around 5 ft. Causes significant surging/retreating and small tip collapses on high performance wings.

5 Very active air. Causes small tip collapses even on beginner wings.

6 Causes 50% collapses on high performance wings.

7 Causes 50% collapses even on beginner wings.

8-10 Increasing levels of dangerous air where 10 is completely uncontrollable.

To level out of the turn, let up the brake *slowly* (about 3 seconds). It needs to be released slower then the natural tendency of the glider to swing back and forth (it's natural pendulum period). Letting off too quickly can cause an oscillation as the canopy swings past level in decreasing little banks until level. Keeping your forearm vertical will naturally prevent over-braking.

Wake Turbulence

Planes and paragliders fly by pushing air down and out as they move through it. As they pass, little vortices swirl off each wing tip that spread slowly, drift with the wind, and settle at around 300 feet per minute (fpm).

If you do a 360° turn, you'll fly through your own wake, a potentially startling ripple in otherwise still air. The tighter the turn the more the wing is loaded by G forces and the more powerful will be the wake. Like a boat that sends a wake spreading away as a passes, an aircraft does the same thing only it spirals, spreading out and downward as well.

Altitudes

Having altitude means having options; going high keeps you out of obstacle's reach, leaves time to handle an engine out and increases the number of available landing sites.

Pattern altitude is about 300 feet above ground level (AGL), high enough to easily make it back to the landing site and avoid obstacles, without being too high to judge ground track.

Cruising is best done between 200 and 500 ft—below where most airplanes and helicopters fly. While a few aircraft fly that low (especially cropdusters and pipeline patrols), most stay up higher. If you're flying near an airport, learn the patterns and altitudes where airplanes normally fly (see Chapter 10 for airport patterns) so they can be avoided. It is legally *our* obligation to avoid all certified aircraft.

We can't ever fly with visibility less than 1 mile and require 3 miles visibility above 700 feet (1200 in some areas, see Chapter 9). Higher altitudes require better visibility to see and avoid the high speed airplanes likely flying there.

Glide Ratio & Wind

As a part of always keeping a landing option open, you must know how far you can glide. That is determined primarily by *glide ratio*, the horizontal distance traveled per unit of altitude lost. Our wings typically achieve about a 6:1 glide ratio (pronounced "six to one") meaning that you go 6 feet forward for every foot down.

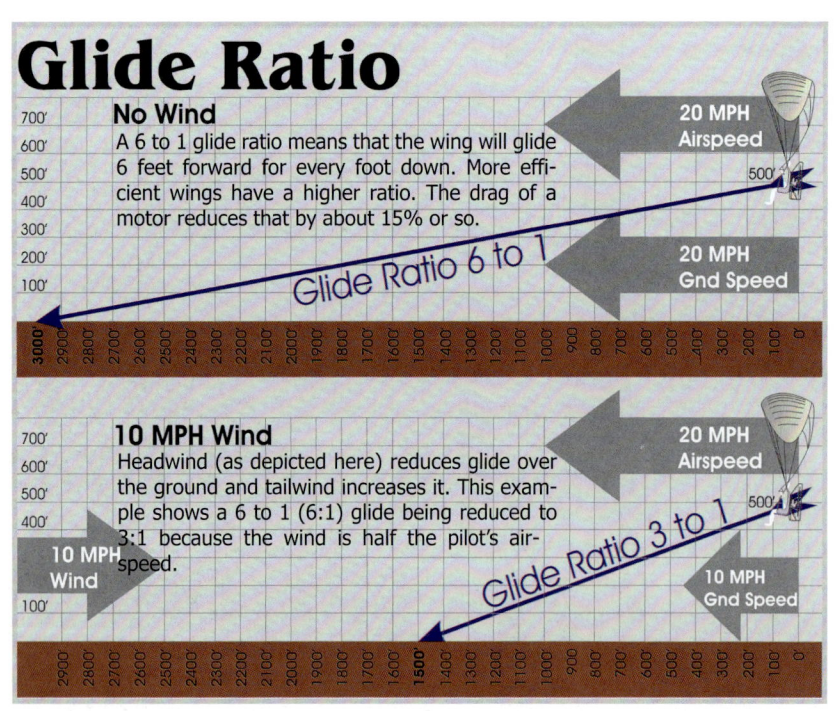

Glide Ratio

No Wind
A 6 to 1 glide ratio means that the wing will glide 6 feet forward for every foot down. More efficient wings have a higher ratio. The drag of a motor reduces that by about 15% or so.

Glide Ratio 6 to 1

20 MPH Airspeed
20 MPH Gnd Speed

10 MPH Wind
Headwind (as depicted here) reduces glide over the ground and tailwind increases it. This example shows a 6 to 1 (6:1) glide being reduced to 3:1 because the wind is half the pilot's airspeed.

10 MPH Wind

Glide Ratio 3 to 1

20 MPH Airspeed
10 MPH Gnd Speed

Wind has an important effect on glide. For example, a 10 mph headwind cuts the glide in half for craft that flies 20 mph. So you'd only glide 3 feet forward for every foot down or 3:1. Conversely, a tailwind helps your glide—that same 10 mph wind from behind means you're going 30 mph over the ground and dropping at the same rate for a glide ratio of 9:1 (9 feet forward for every foot down).

Think of your landing options in an upside-down cone with you being the pointy end up at altitude. The wind will tilt the cone downwind leaving more options downwind of you. Of course you need to allow room for the landing pattern too. As you go higher, the area of the cone at ground level gets bigger.

Ground Track

You may get aloft and notice that you're flying sideways after turning crosswind. That is because the wind is blowing you "downstream." The result is normal; your wing is still flying through the air like it always does, but the air is moving over the ground and so you are, in fact, drifting with the wind.

Ground track is the line your flight path draws over the ground—if the goal is to be flying right into the wind (as you will be on landing) then turn towards the "current", go into the wind, towards what's pushing you. So if you're drifting right (the ground is sliding by to the left), then gently turn left. Don't just pull the brake and release it, but hold enough to keep turning into the wind until you're going right into it—the drift will stop. Practicing this control when aloft so it doesn't surprise you on landing. You'll want to minimize sideways drift on landing.

Landing

Beyond the mechanics and concepts, landing is one thing the simulator and rehearsal cannot prepare you for as well. This is where you'll be thankful for any tow training or tandem flights. Something to remember: if you just land into the wind with quarter brake (position/pressure 2), you'll probably do no worse than slide to your knees—nothing should be damaged beyond your pants and pride. With just a bit of effort, though, landings can be completely and reliably smooth.

Always choose a specific landing spot where you want to touch down; something the size of a dinner plate. You won't get very close, at first, but always be trying. Eventually, with practice, good instruction and the techniques described later in this book, you'll be able to land on the spot most of the time. Leave the motor idling until told to shut it off (usually about 50 ft AGL).

The Landing Pattern

An orderly arrival into the landing area is helpful for several reasons. It:

- Helps plan the approach by giving common reference points,
- Allows you to scope out the landing field for wind and obstructions,
- Keeps the flow of traffic in one direction—very desirable for collision avoidance since you know where to

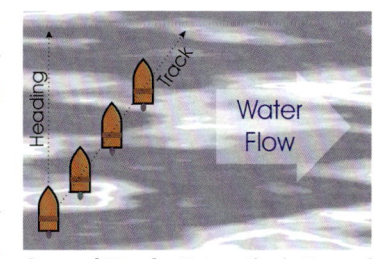

Ground Track: Picture the bottom of the river as ground, and the water is air. Relative to the water, you're just rowing straight forward. Relative to the river bottom, you're drifting downstream.

Energy & Injury

In an accident, energy and injury are powerfully intertwined. A fact of physics is that energy dissipated in a collision increases to the square of the speed, so a doubling of speed quadruples the energy (read damage).

Consider a mere 7 mph wind and a typical flying speed of 20 mph. Hitting something while flying into the wind is a 13 mph collision. Hitting it while flying downwind is a 27 mph whack: far more dramatic, having over twice the speed and more than four times the energy!

Landing patterns have proven to be a helpful staple of aviation for years. Almost all instructors will have their students fly some form of a pattern with variations based on location. Doing "S" turns on final is frequently done to lose altitude but should straitened out, into the wind, by 50 feet Above Ground Level (AGL).

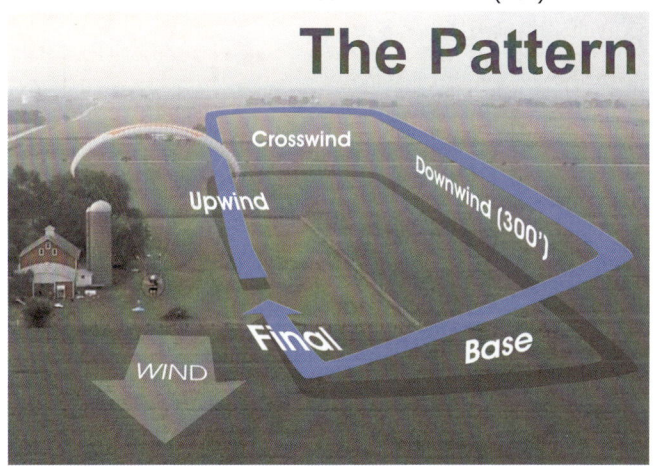

Landing: The Last 50 Feet No Wind

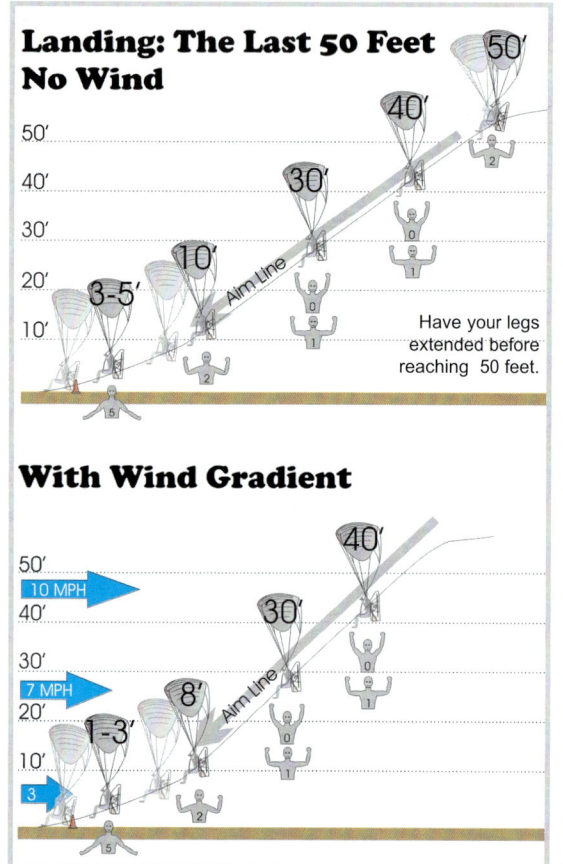

With a calm or steady wind, the spot that you're going to hit will not be changing angle, just getting bigger. That is your "aim line" and hopefully it's also your target.

By 50 ft be out of your seat and shut off the motor—the wing will surge forward slightly when you do and stabilize in a descent. Keep your hands mostly up, between pressure 0 and 1. At 10 feet, flare slightly. That will swing you out a bit (and the wing back), slowing both your forward speed and descent speed. At 3-5 feet do a full flare. Have one foot forward so you're ready to run. If there's a headwind, you can usually flare later and less. This technique varies somewhat by wing model and it's efficiencies.

If there's a wind then there's probably a wind gradient where wind speed slows near the ground. The descent angle is slightly steeper because the wing is losing airspeed in the descent and diving to compensate.

expect other pilots and avoid head-on encounters.

The initial pattern segments are named according to their relationship with the wind (see Landing Patterns graphic). The downwind leg is about 300 feet away from the runway and 300 feet high.

Patterns are either right or left according to the turn direction. A right pattern has all turns to the right and a left pattern to the left. Standard patterns are to the left but, for us, direction will more often be dictated by wind and terrain. The depicted pattern in the graphic is a right one.

Enter the pattern on the downwind leg, flying level at about 300 feet AGL. Pass beside the desired landing point (abeam) and continue until it is about 45° behind you then ease off the power and turn base leg. Here is where you will want to judge whether you are high or low. If it looks like you might not make the landing point (spot), turn towards it. If you're high, widen out away from the spot.

Don't do a 360° in the pattern and don't turn completely away from the landing spot—you can quickly become too low or not making it back directly into the wind. Also, losing eye contact with the desired spot can be disorienting for newer pilots.

Final Approach

Turn final and point yourself towards the landing spot then extend your legs so that you're hanging by the leg loops. The seat folds back to where it was on launch. Continue with small corrections to keep pointing at the spot. Don't over correct control inputs. Hold small steering inputs for 3 seconds, then ease up.

Once it's obvious that you'll make the landing area (not overshoot or undershoot), press and hold the kill switch. It takes a couple seconds to wind down completely and will fire back up if you let off the button early. Plan to have it shut off by around 100 feet up and no later than 50 feet.

Be mindful of drift—if you're drifting to the left it means a wind from the right is pushing you. Ease in enough right brake to correct to the right and hold for a few seconds or until the drift is almost stopped then *ease* off the brake. Look at your wind streamers to verify wind direction.

Below 100 Feet

When you get within about 100 feet of the ground, disregard the chosen spot and concentrate on landing into the wind and touchdown. But use minimum brakes! By 50 feet of altitude have your hands nearly all the way up (almost no brakes) in preparation for flare. you want to have maximum brake effectiveness (maximum speed) for the flare.

If you start to swing left and right (like a pendulum)—do *nothing*. At most, ease both

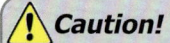

> **⚠ Caution!**
> Look at your desired flight path, not any nearby obstructions such as trees or buildings. A surprising number of accidents stem from *target fixation*, where a pilot looks at an obstruction that he wants to avoid, fixates on it, then flies into it.

Page 60 — Section I: First Flight

brakes to position/pressure 1. Trying to correct a pendulum at low altitude will almost guarantee a hard landing. Let the wing sort itself out—it is much better to land in a small pendulum than to try correcting, at least until you've gained significant experience.

If you notice a drift while flaring, beware of a nearly irresistible urge to put out the downwind hand as if to protect yourself from the impending fall. That's exactly the *wrong* thing to do! Practice correcting for drift—imagine yourself drifting left, pull a bit of right brake and hold for 3 seconds then ease up. Of course you cannot be aggressive on the brakes at this point but want to minimize drift, not pendulum—if it feels like a "swing" then don't do anything.

> **Troubleshooting Landing Problems**
> Landing is a given, style points are up for grabs. Here are some tips that may solve problems in the second most demanding task of our sport.
>
> **Symptom: My landings are consistently hard, making it difficult to stay on my feet.**
> 1. Start with your hands at position 0 to 1 above 50 feet AGL Start adding brake by 10 feet and wind up, just before reaching the ground, at position 5, maximum pull.
> 2. If you consistently slow down then drop to the ground, you're flaring too early. Also, make sure you're landing with the trimmers in (slow).
>
> **Symptom: My landings are fast and hard.**
> 1. You need to start the flare earlier.
> 2. Make sure you're exactly into the wind.
>
> **Symptom: I swing left/right a lot on final approach.**
> 1. Unless you have *mastered* damping these oscillations, do *not* try to correct them below about 50 feet.
> 2. Practice oscillation damping at altitude.
>
> **Symptom: Sometimes I land drifting sideways.**
> 1. Insure you're lined up into the wind on final. For example, if you're drifting right, turn left gradually but be level by touchdown.
> 2. Avoid steering input during the last 20 feet or so.

Flaring is the process of slowing your forward speed and sinking as you reach the ground. At about 10 feet pull very slight brakes—only a couple inches for most wings—to get your body swinging forward. That action will angle the wing up and round out your descent. At about 3 to 5 feet start pulling more brake. If done properly you will arrive at both the ground and full brake travel simultaneously. Run a few steps forward then turn around and pull both brakes to quickly get the wing on the ground. If it's windy, walk towards the wing and make sure it is fully deflated.

Before touchdown, your feet should be positioned for running—have one somewhat in front of the other. Touchdown with knees slightly bent, ready to absorb a potentially firm arrival. Fortunately our slow speeds and descent rates make this no big deal. In fact, going to your knees during the early landings is somewhat common.

Controlling Glide

The touchdown point can be predicted while gliding straight ahead. If it appears to be rising (you increasingly must look up) then you're going to be short. If it is falling below (you're increasingly looking lower) then you will pass over it. The stationary point is where you're gonna land. You've actually been doing this for years when walking or driving but in a horizontal direction: the stationary spot in your windshield or vision field is where you're headed, everything else slides by your periphery.

Glide is steeper (worse) when flying into a headwind and shallower when helped along by a tailwind. In a headwind you can steepen the descent by slowing down. Don't use more than about a quarter brake (position/pressure 2) though, until you're very familiar with the wing. If you do slow down, speed back up by 50 feet AGL so as to have enough speed left for an effective flare. As you let the brakes up, expect to drop 20 feet or so while regaining speed.

You can also do small S-turns to lose altitude and effectively shorten a glide. Keep them shallow, though, and get yourself steady back into the wind by 100 feet.

This pilot is gliding towards a clearing just to the right of some vehicles. With no wind, he'll make it just fine and will even have to do a couple S-turns (prior to reaching 50') to avoid landing long. If the wind were blowing 10 mph or so, he might only make about the point where his toe is.

When trying to stretch a glide *against* a wind, be hands up with trimmers out for more speed. Even with the higher sink rate, you'll cover more ground.

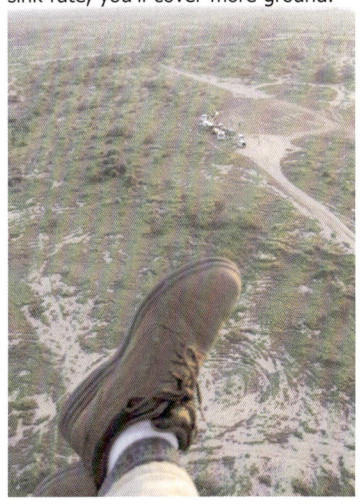

The PPG Bible: A Complete Guide and Reference

After Landing

Run out the landing just enough to keep the wing from overflying you; it should come down behind you. As you stop, turn around quickly and apply brakes so that the wing falls on its back. This makes bundling or folding easier, offers less chance for the lines to become tangled, and keeps them out off the motor.

Unclip quickly to avoid letting a gust catch the wing and pull you off balance. The motor makes this both more likely and more expensive.

Postflight

Get the wing covered—its lifetime hours get used whenever it's exposed to UV, even through clouds. Either fold, bundle, or put it in the shade and away from sandy, dusty or gravel areas.

Check out the motor and harness just like a preflight inspection—it is far better to find problems now than when you're getting ready to launch the next time out. Even if it was running fine when you landed, you may find loose parts or prop damage that can easily be corrected at home.

Cleaning

Cleaning the machine after each flight allows detection of cracks and other problems that can hide under a cloak of grime. For example, if you see a large increase in the amount of black goop squirting onto the prop, suspect problems; that's hard to detect with a dirty machine.

Gasoline, WD 40 and mineral spirits are good for wiping down parts. Carburetor cleaner is great on un-painted surfaces but is brutal on paint. Avoid getting citrus-based cleaners on aluminum. Fabric sprays that offer other protection work well and help preserve the gear but don't use them on wing fabric. If possible, cover the motor during transport to prevent UV damage to the harness—it fades pretty quickly when exposed to sunlight.

Clean the wing by draping the trailing edge over a clothes line hung high enough to keep the leading edge off the ground. Spray clean water (no solvents) on the outside and up into the cells. Dirt and debris will run out. Let it air dry, preferably out of the sun. Dust and sand abrade the fabric and shorten its life.

---

courtesy WalkerjetUSA

courtesy Christian Bultmann

Covering the motor is best although they sometimes get relegated to exposed outside travel.

The top picture shows a custom cover made specific for this particular model. The middle picture shows how easy it is to transport even with the smallest vehicle using a simple home-made carrier. The bottom picture shows a stock platform that plugs into a standard 2 inch trailer receiver.

Try to plan landings for a touchdown near your field's center spot without needing power. This pilot would have had to trudge through some crop had his motor quit. Be wary of corn, it's a complete nightmare to get your wing out of, let alone walk through with a motor. And it's surprisingly easy to get lost in. Plus, crops are expensive to produce—offer to compensate the farmer if you damage any.

Trike Flying

CHAPTER 6

Wheels add another dimension to the sport. Of course there are trade-offs too, but for those who prefer not to run, rolling can be a God-send. The typical arrangement is a three (or more) wheeled cart called a *trike*. It allows launching in a seated position from a reasonably smooth surface that is at least a couple hundred feet long. Converting a paramotor to use wheels normally involves just bolting your motor unit to the cart. Obviously there will be more weight on the wing (clip-in weight) so it will go faster, but wheels handle that nicely. Drag increases along with weight so don't expect a stellar climb rate.

There are some necessary techniques for these craft and different limitations apply, mostly regarding terrain and wind. In some ways it is easier to learn flying a trike because you don't have to carry the motor. In other ways though, it's more challenging: you can't move sideways to help control the wing and can't turn around to face the wing.

A trike requires more power since the motor thrust is all there is for inflation—no lunging pilot to help. You'll need a smoother surface for launch and landing too. Large, soft wheels act like shock absorbers and are preferred for rough surfaces such as grass. It is not desirable for the wheels to grab pavement, rather they should allow sliding to reduce the likelihood of rollover if you land with sideways drift. Tall, skinny wheels work well on hard packed surfaces and probably roll the best, but if they raise the center of gravity (CG), they are less stable.

Nil winds and high altitudes make the trike shine since wheels don't mind the extra groundspeed required. Trikes balk, however, at strong winds or crosswinds, since the wing can topple them or drag them backwards. As with foot-launching, increased skill allows greater capabilities. A good trike pilot can handle nearly as

Nick Scholtes pilots "Barney," his 2-place (tandem) trike. An introductory flight in one of these is a great way to try the sport while getting some early training. Foot-launched tandem is also possible but requires more skil. The pilot must heft a motor powerful enough for two people while managing a very large wing.

In most countries, including the US, certification is required for flying 2-place (tandem) craft whether wheeled or foot launched.

Trikes can be *turtled* too. It usually happens when there's *some* wind. The wing comes up fast, holding the cart almost stationary. As the wing passes overhead, the cart—freed of all that pull—accelerates rapidly under the now-limp lines. When the cart again gets in front of the wing and re-tensions its lines, the sudden force pulls the cart right onto its back. The hapless pilot is left staring skyward, spaceman style.

Some models offer the configuration below to minimize that undesirable outcome. It also helps reduce the chance for a sideways capsize by extending the wheel base. Those with 4 wheels instead of 3 also have more stability.

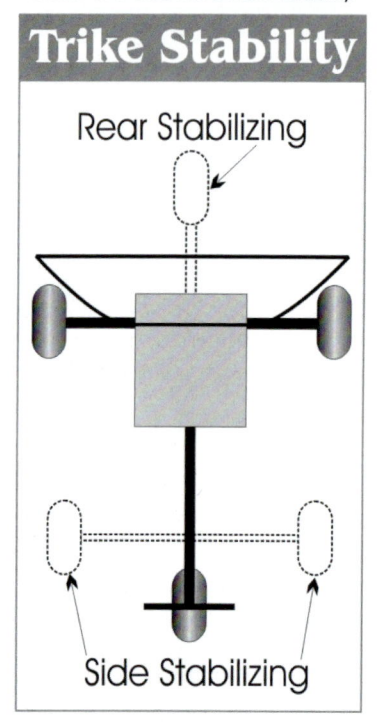

Trike Stability

Rear Stabilizing

Side Stabilizing

much crosswind as a good foot pilot with sufficient room. Regardless of skill, about 12 mph is the practical limit for trikes since the pilot cannot turn around to control the wing.

Tandem operations, which require more certification in most countries (including the U.S.), are far easier and probably safer with wheels. Tandem foot launching is quite demanding of the pilot and requires the passenger to actively participate, which is not necessary using a trike.

Setup

The weight distribution of a trike will affect how it hangs. Even more than foot launching, hang orientation must be checked before flying. It should hang so that the rear wheels are slightly lower than the nosewheel—a 10 to 20° nose-up angle is desirable. If the nosewheel hangs low, it will wheelbarrow on takeoff or landing, possibly causing a rollover.

Adjusting the clip-in points must be done each time a different pilot gets in since the pilot counterweights the motor. If a heavy pilot gets into the machine, it will be nose heavy (very bad) and vice versa for a light pilot (bad, but not as bad). All tandem, and many solo trikes come with a way to move the hang point and it's proper adjustment *is* critical.

Higher clip-in weights need larger wings. A strong cage is a must to keep tensioning wing lines from pulling the cage hoop into the prop. You should not be able to bend the cage to within an inch of the prop tips using hand force alone.

Launch

As with foot launching, layout is critical and is done just like a forward launch. The trike is carefully centered with the wing while suspension lines are draped in holders on the cage rim (if equipped) to prevent fouling the wheels. Once centered, move the cart back a foot or so to give it room to start rolling before tensioning the lines.

Most carts steer on the ground like old sleds: push the left pedal to right turn. It is mechanically simple but opposite to what airplane pilots are used to—anybody with much airplane or helicopter time will need practice. Fortunately just driving it around on the ground rehearses the appropriate skills.

After verifying throttle position at idle, start the motor, get in and buckle up. The thrust may ruffle the wing which is OK but having the thrustline point slightly

This is typical: hooks mounted on the cage rim keep lines out of the wheels. Cynthia is holding the A's in her hands as she powers up. Having a couple helpers pull you through initial inflation can help too, but make sure to brief them on what to hold and when to let go.

above the wing is helpful. Strap the throttle onto your hand, grab the brakes then put the A's between your thumb and palm. When ready, go to full power.

How much A's you hold depends on the wing. Most require some pressure, a few require a lot—so much so that it's hard to hold them forward enough. It also depends on the trike's seating arrangement and whether you can get a good hold of the A's. Some trikes are equipped with devices that exert pull on the A's (using a bungee cord) until the wing comes up overhead.

At full power, rolling will get the wing started up—stay on the A's. If it comes up quickly, be ready to let go of the A's and dampen the wing with brakes *briefly* (pull for a second, then let up). If the wing comes up slowly and crooked, avoid brake pressure but turn slightly towards the wing. Don't overdo the turn, though, lest you set up a flip-inducing oscillation.

Once the wing is mostly overhead and you're moving nicely, it can be very beneficial to reduce power while getting everything stabilized; when all is well, go back to full power. You should be able to easily taxi the trike/wing combo by applying brakes to steer the wing while steering the cart below. You'll need some airspeed to do this. It is imperative that the wing be centered and stabilized before accelerating into flight. Use minimum brakes to aid acceleration.

On thick grass or soft surface you may have to reapply brakes to pop it up then ease off the brakes to accelerate once in the air. The best rate of climb is almost always achieved with no brake pressure. At high density altitudes you may be un*able* to climb if holding too much brakes.

The most serious triking sin is lifting off in an oscillation. If the wing starts oscillating side-to-side, you must slow down and get it straightened out or abort. The dynamics of the cart aggravate this malady since the cart can accelerate quickly while the wing goes overhead towards the other side. As the wing lifts, the effective CG goes up, making the trike very easy to flip.

Crosswind Takeoff

Taking off in a crosswind is tricky. The wing must be tracking down the runway immediately overhead the trike, as always. But the wing will be angled (crabbing) into the wind and at liftoff the cart will twist to match the wing. That will put it just over the ground, moving quickly, while cocked slightly sideways, drifting with the wind. If it touches down this way, it could easily flip. That is why it is always preferrable to liftoff exactly into the wind.

If location limits you to taking off in a crosswind, gather plenty of speed while still rolling so that pulling the brakes gets you positively airborne with little chance of touching down again.

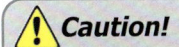

> ⚠ **Caution!**
> Launching a trike with the wing oscillating is the most likely cause for injury. Make sure the wing is overhead and stable before committing to flight. If the wing gets too far off, abort!

You may have to inflate into the wind and *then* turn the trike. Avoid inflating in a crosswind because the downwind part of the wing catches air first and wants to come up crooked. So get the wing overhead

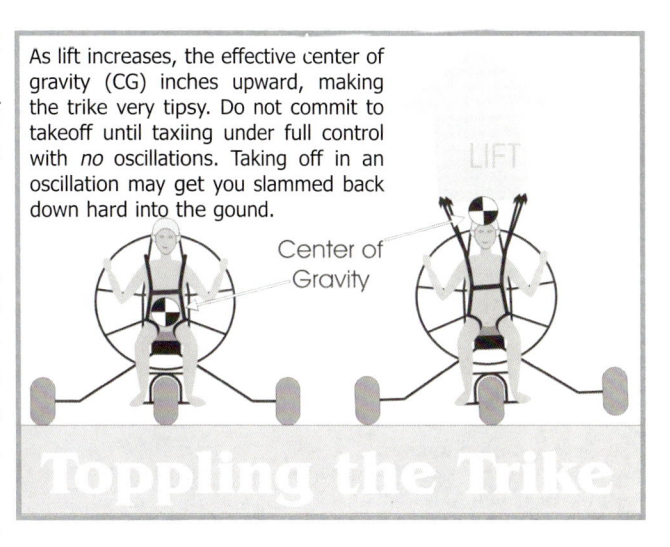

As lift increases, the effective center of gravity (CG) inches upward, making the trike very tipsy. Do not commit to takeoff until taxiing under full control with *no* oscillations. Taking off in an oscillation may get you slammed back down hard into the gound.

Toppling the Trike

1. Tipsy turvy: taxi first, get everything straight and smooth, *then* throttle up for for takeoff. This near-tip was staged for the "Risk & Reward" video.

2. A variety of wheels accomodate different surfaces. These skinny, tall ones do well on grass. The fat tundra tires do better on sand. Larger diameter, softer wheels handle bumps better than small, hard ones.

More than one pilot, and his mount, have been damaged after rolling over while racing around. And some tires (the plastic balloon types especially) are not designed to go much over about 25 mph—their bearings melt.

It is, however, good to practice steering which is done like an old sled: push the right side to go left.

Some pilots have a hard time leaving "man's best friend" behind. No tandem rating is required but be sure the pooch is perched securely—you never know when a stray cat could upset the cart. The dog pictured here, *Boots*, is quite used to this treatment.

and cart moving to get airflow over the wing then turn down the runway while keeping the wing centered above. Just "do what it takes" to keep tracking down the runway, don't worry that the wing is pointing slightly into the wind.

Flying

There is almost no difference in flying with a trike except for a slightly higher airspeed and heavier control, both resulting from the greater weight. There will also be some bobbling around because of the cart's higher mass which is spread farther away from the hang points. Torque will not likely be as much a factor because there is so much weight down low and the motor is usually vertical (not tilted bacl).

Low altitude maneuvering must be done very carefully—increased weight can really hamper climb from what you're used to. That weight also changes the pendulum period—the rate of its natural swing.

Landing options diminish since smoother terrain is required and more of it. It *can* be landed in the rough stuff or tall grass but doing so invites damage.

Landing

Landing is easy and not much different from landing on foot except that the pilot is lower. Being into the wind is more important because a sideways touchdown can flip it over. Approach speed will be a bit higher and the draggy cart makes glide a bit steeper. Landing with some power on makes landings much easier since you'll have a slower descent rate and be able to roll it on with minimal flare. You won't be running so it's not as critical to slow as much before touchdown.

As you roll out, try to get the wing to fall over sideways to de-power it. In breezy conditions, if the wing falls straight behind you, it could start pulling the cart backwards and end up tipping the trike onto its cage and rear wheels—the *turtle* position. With any wind at all, be ready to unbuckle, get out and secure the wing.

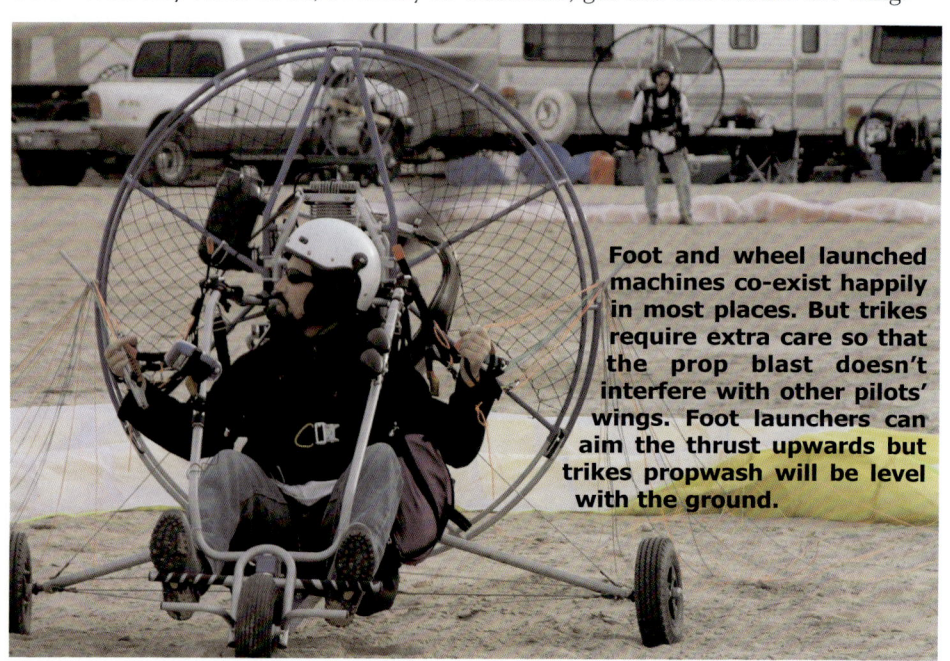

Foot and wheel launched machines co-exist happily in most places. But trikes require extra care so that the prop blast doesn't interfere with other pilots' wings. Foot launchers can aim the thrust upwards but trikes propwash will be level with the ground.

Section II

Spreading Your Wings

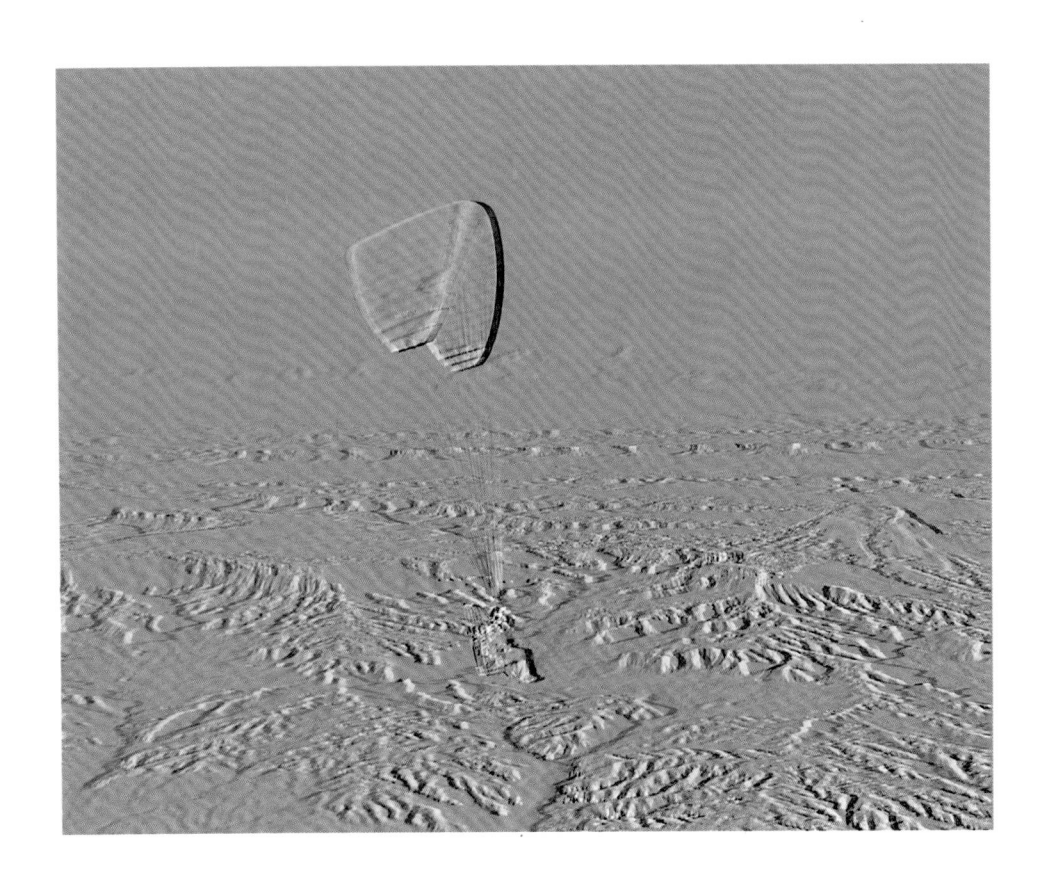

Section II

You've left training and plan to loose yourself on the world. Now what? Learning is far from over!

This Section covers what you'll need to know before heading out on your own. Remain under the instructor's watchful eye until these issues are well understood and, if at all possible, seek out other pilots to pick their brains. A willingness to learn from others is far more helpful than prideful distance. Be careful though, some input will be useful, some will be useless, and some may even be harmful. If something sounds fishy, get confirmation from your instructor or a trusted pilot before acting on it.

Ideally you will practice on your own for a while and then go back to your instructor. Bad habits may form or helpful techniques may be forgotten—by going back, these can be corrected while introducing more advanced techniques and refinements.

If ground schools or ratings clinics are held in your area, these are great ways to further your growth in the sport.

If you haven't seen the USPPA's "Risk & Reward," you should. it covers some of this material in an entertaining, easy-to-understand format.

Weather Basics

CHAPTER 7

Most of the weather information we need for safe flying is available on local TV or the Internet. This chapter will help make that information useful to your flying, especially for making the critical go/no-go decision. It is the bare minimum understanding to have prior to setting out alone. A more thorough treatment is found in Chapter 24.

It was good that he didn't fly. Soon after this picture was shot, a gust front blew through with 25+ mph winds.

One way to improve your understanding of local weather is by talking with other ultralight pilots who have been flying in the area for a while. they have probably formed some very useful observations on what to look out for.

The Perfect Day

In general, you want calm or steady light winds with little change expected during the time of flight. That leaves mornings and evenings during stable weather. It's easy to know when stable weather is expected; look at the forecast to see what it says about clouds, wind and rain.

Obviously rain is bad. Not only is it uncomfortable, but wetness hurts the wing's ability to recover from collapses and makes it more prone to parachutal stall (where it starts descending vertically like a parachute). Heavier rain can cause pooling in the trailing edge which makes the wing less able to recover from a stall. It's equally bad for the motor's metal parts and is hard to see in.

When rain *showers* are forecast, that frequently means they will fall from storm-type clouds and may harbor dangerous gusts.

Pay particular attention to the wind forecast because changes there mean something is amiss. A forecast calling for calm in the morning, 5 to 10 mph in the afternoon and then calm in the evening is perfect. Having the same winds all day, provided they're light (less than 10 mph), is almost as good.

The wind normally increases during the day, a good reason to limit flying to the first 3 and last 3 hours of daylight. Be leery of any wind forecast over 10 mph or a large change (speed or direction) during your planned flight. Wait until after the change so that you can assess its strength before taking off. You do not want to be surprised while aloft.

Thermals & The Daily Cycle

Every day the sun comes up and starts heating the ground, churning up rising air currents called thermals. They gather strength as the day heats up, peaking by around 2PM. They show up to paramotor pilots as bumpy air. Thermals are felt on the ground as gusts of wind during an otherwise calm day.

Under many conditions, the turbulence generated by thermals can become dangerous. Fortunately it builds predictably, and normally leaves mornings and evenings quite usable.

This daily cycle happens whether or not clouds are present but is diminished on an overcast day. Sometimes, a sunny afternoon will sprout cumulus clouds (fluffy white with a piled-up look) that mark thermal tops. If there is much wind aloft, these thermals will mix the fast-moving air above with the calm air below causing strong, gusty surface winds. Such conditions—thermals mixed with wind—can easily generate dangerous turbulence.

Indications of Turbulence

Turbulence lurks in many places, but fortunately, with a little knowledge, can usually be predicted. Clouds are an important clue although dangerous atmospheric shenanigans take place in the clear, too.

Cumulus

Cumulus clouds, typical of warm, summer days, indicate a tumultuous atmosphere. Soaring pilots use them to mark rising air so they can stay aloft. Cumulus clouds that get tall (lots of vertical development) have strong turbulence and warrant a wide birth.

Dust Devils

Dust devils are miniature tornados swirling near the surface. Created by strong thermals, they are the visible evidence of very dangerous air. While some are wide, slow twirlers, most are quickly rotating funnels of air. Dry climates see them more frequently because thermal action is stronger and there is a source of visible matter to pick up. You don't even want be clipped into a wing, let alone flying, when one of these devils slice through.

Testing conditions

If you have any doubt about conditions, spend 10 to 15 minutes at your launch site feeling what the winds are doing and how much change is happening. Sudden shifts in direction or speed portend a bumpy ride aloft.

1. Cumulus Clouds.

2. Cumulus Clouds gone bad. We don't even mess with these (thunderstorms) in a Boeing.

3. Dust devils, created by strong thermals, are deadly to paramotor pilots. Conditions strong enough to generate such turbulence are best avoided.

Another tool for testing is to kite your wing. You can use a harness or just use your hands (one reason the technique can be beneficial). Only clip into a harness if you're certain the conditions will remain benign. If you can steadily kite your wing, or there is never enough wind to kite it, then conditions are probably OK.

Be careful though, it *can* still be bumpy even when the surface air seems mellow, so don't use this test alone. It may be that gusts are simply farther apart than a 15 minute wait would reveal. Like dust devils that are sparsely spaced, you could be out there all day and never feel one. That is why simply avoiding the thermally mid-day time is best.

Thunderstorms

Thunderstorms are nature's most violent atmospheric production, especially when they spawn tornados.

Cumuli morph into cumulonimbus (rain producing cumulus) and get ugly in the process. Flying anywhere near them is almost suicidal. Pilots have died from getting sucked up to the heights and frozen. Even a small thunderhead is likely to go above 30,000 feet where the average temperature falls below -40°F (which also happens to be -40°C). Plus they can produce severe turbulence far beyond the capability of a paraglider to maneuver through.

Thunderstorms frequently produce gust fronts that precede the actual storm by up to 20 miles. The sudden wind change from such a gust front can be violent and impossible to outrun.

Don't be tempted to fly immediately after storms pass, either. It seems innocuous

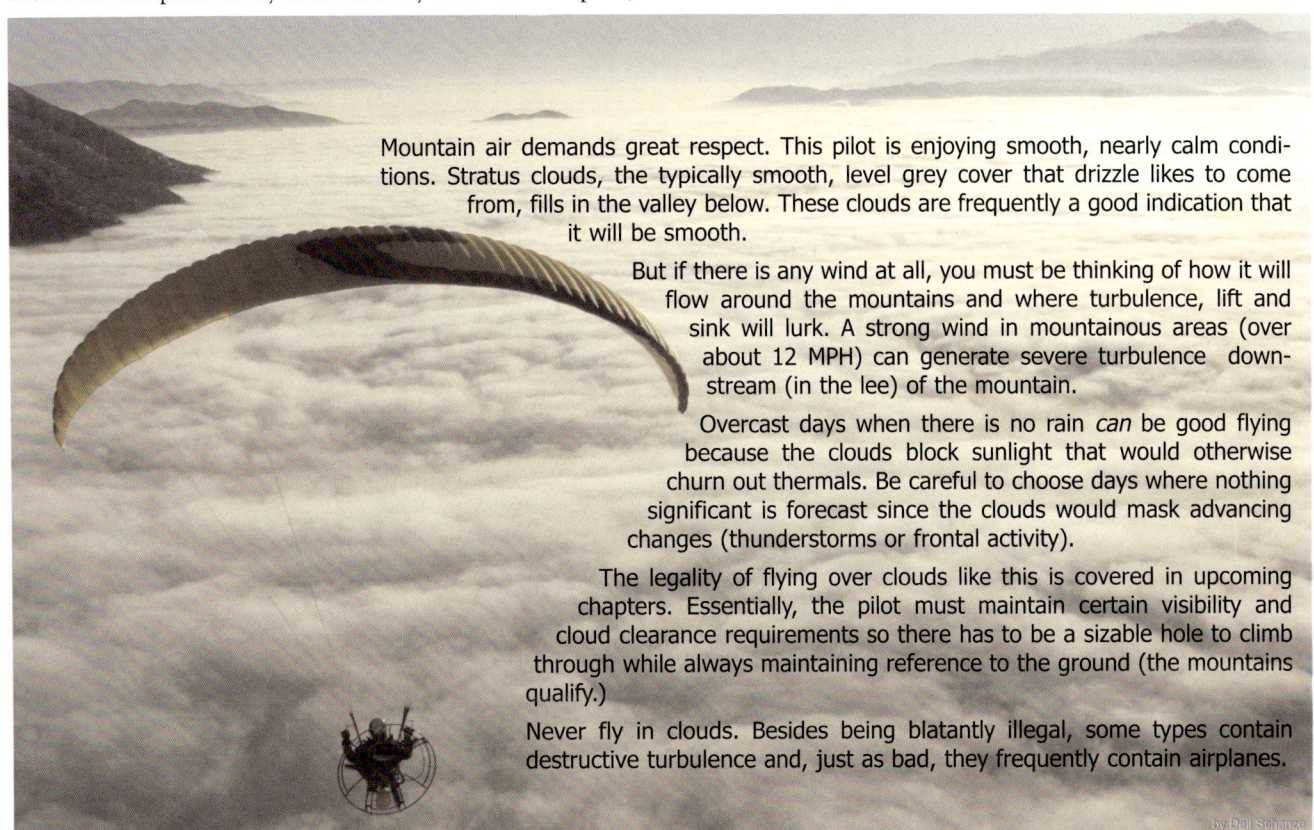

Mountain air demands great respect. This pilot is enjoying smooth, nearly calm conditions. Stratus clouds, the typically smooth, level grey cover that drizzle likes to come from, fills in the valley below. These clouds are frequently a good indication that it will be smooth.

But if there is any wind at all, you must be thinking of how it will flow around the mountains and where turbulence, lift and sink will lurk. A strong wind in mountainous areas (over about 12 MPH) can generate severe turbulence downstream (in the lee) of the mountain.

Overcast days when there is no rain *can* be good flying because the clouds block sunlight that would otherwise churn out thermals. Be careful to choose days where nothing significant is forecast since the clouds would mask advancing changes (thunderstorms or frontal activity).

The legality of flying over clouds like this is covered in upcoming chapters. Essentially, the pilot must maintain certain visibility and cloud clearance requirements so there has to be a sizable hole to climb through while always maintaining reference to the ground (the mountains qualify.)

Never fly in clouds. Besides being blatantly illegal, some types contain destructive turbulence and, just as bad, they frequently contain airplanes.

This beautifully illustrates how airflow around a mountain behaves just like water flow around a boat's bow. Whenever there's wind, this effect occurs, but the clouds make it visible. Smooth (laminar) airflow makes it more pronounced.

Soaring pilots will appreciate the rising portions of airflow well away from the source mountain. If you were eking out sustenance from this lift you would see that it extends well beyond the mountain itself. If you were motoring in this area you might wonder why your climb rate makes no sense (too high if in lift, too little if in sinking air).

An inversion is present here where the air aloft is warmer than the air below which is why the stratus clouds have formed in the first place. When the turbulent flow behind the mountain mixes up the two layers, a clear area forms. It reveals the nastiness that can be found downwind of obstructions. The stronger the flow, the more turbulent the rotor. This also shows how far away the effects of a large geographic shape can be felt.

The bigger the obstruction the bigger the turbulence and the farther downstream it reaches. A mountain this size can generate mammoth turbulence and sink well beyond our ability to handle it.

The red zone is the lee (downwind) and deserves a wide berth.

at times—the thunderstorm rages through, then a quiet calm settles in with benign-looking clouds. Don't fall for it. Give time for the wind to shift, call for weather and see what upwind stations are experiencing to insure there are no surprise wind shifts. A localized, individual cell that is not associated with a front may leave flyable conditions but you should still wait at least an hour.

If there is severe weather behind one set of storms, even if it is many miles behind, don't fly. The danger is that while it *may* indeed remain mellow enough to fly, we can't tell. Going up is a dreadful gamble in such conditions.

Mountains

Any wind in mountainous areas means turbulence in the lee (downwind) of the mountains. It can be completely calm at your launch site because of a wind shadow, but climb up a few hundred feet and the air becomes violent. A combination of local knowledge and forecasted winds aloft will keep you out of that air.

For example, if you're launching at 4000 ft in an area surrounded by mountains, and the winds aloft at 6000 ft are forecast to be over 20 knots, then it may be quite risky in certain areas. If winds are forecast to be westerly then make sure you're flying on the west side of the hills. If possible, it's hugely valuable to get to the top of a hill and see for yourself what the winds are up doing there.

Mountainous areas also have unique local conditions because of cool air flowing downhill and warmed air wicking up the sides (see Chapter 24).

Beach

The best air lives at the beach. On normal, sunny days, beach flying is hard to beat as heated land sucks in the smooth sea breeze, lasting past sunset. Unfettered by thermal heating, the air blows in steadily and consistently—making launch easy and flying easy. But when there is any forecast for the wind to be blowing out to sea, look out: that is a *very* dangerous condition to fly in.

Check the weather inland and make sure there is no off-shore flow there. If an inland site predicts an off-shore breeze (land-breeze—from land to sea) and it is currently blowing from sea to land, that could be trouble. There is some point where the winds meet and form a *convergence zone*. At best it will produce uncomfortable turbulence, at worst, the outflow (away from land) could win and blow you out to sea. These conditions are hard to forecast and can quickly turn a benign wind around. The turbulence of that turnaround is bad enough, but getting blown out to sea could be disastrous (see Chapter 19).

Whenever conditions diverge from normal—winds seem different, clouds are forming too early, temperatures are unseasonal, etc.—be suspicious.

Whenever There's Wind

Here are some common, significant phenomena that show up whenever the wind blows.

Mechanical Turbulence And Rotor

Just like a rock in a stream, whenever air blows past an obstruction it becomes turbulent (bumpy) downstream. More wind or bigger obstructions mean worse turbulence extending further past the obstruction and even *above* the obstruction. rotor, wind shadow and mechanical turbulence all have specific meanings (covered in Chapter 24); the latter two are mistakenly referred to simply as rotor.

Wind Gradient

Friction slows airflow as it rubs against the ground. In the morning, when cool air sits at the surface, it can be calm while only a few hundred feet above it's blowing 20 MPH. As the ground heats up in the morning, the fast moving air aloft (if present) mixes with the still air below and a surface wind develops.

A strong wind aloft on a sunny morning can quickly yield a bumpy blow an hour or or so later—be ready or be landed.

Wind Shear

A dramatic change in wind speed or direction from one altitude (or area) to another is wind shear. The transition is called a shear zone and will likely be quite turbulent. Wind shear associated with thunderstorms have brought down jet airplanes.

The forecast winds aloft give some indication of a shear's presence as do clouds moving in different directions at different altitudes. Days that are brewing thunderstorms can portend dramatic windshear in many directions, even without storms nearby.

Pilots experience it most often during climb; passing through some altitude you get strongly bounced around (hopefully that's all) and then notice that you're now drifting over the ground in a different direction, possibly even going backwards. Look for this when it's cooled a lot from the previous day's high temperature and the forecast winds aloft are strong (over about 15 mph).

1. Anything that sticks up into the wind will cause downwind turbulence—from mountains to trees and buildings to buses. Not only will there be turbulence on the lee (downwind) side, but there will be sink; descending air may make it impossible to stay level.

2. While away from your windsock, still water is one of several ways to tell wind direction. It will be calmer next to the shore on the upwind side.

3. Smoke, steam and blowing dust also work well for wind indicators. But if you see blowing dust, be ready for a ride. And don't fly through smoke plumes—they may harbor horrendous turbulence depending on their source.

1. You can never have too many wind indicators. Especially when the wind is light and variable, it's nice to see what's happening at the LZ. Surveyors tape or similar material make great streamers (also called "telltales").

2. It took 13 - 15 MPH to get this big flag waving.

3. Marketing flags are great for adding a feel of excitement. They're even better for wind indicators. Landing pilots are another good indication but they don't last long.

Telling Wind Direction

A windsock or streamers right at your launch site is best—both for launch and for when you come back. Wind direction will frequently have changed during your flight, sometimes dramatically. It's also good to keep tabs on the wind while you're up. Here are some clues to help:

- Lakes will be calm on the upwind side. Bigger waves overall mean more wind. Also, if boats are anchored off shore they will be pointing into the wind.

- Flags flap downwind of their pole but, be careful, big flags require a big wind to wave. What looks light on a big flag may be quite strong.

- Smoke is the most sensitive indicator. Plus it shows direction at different heights but, never, *ever*, fly in the updraft created by a large fire. The intensity, even up several thousand feet, can be extreme. Admittedly, the bump given off by small fires are not that bad but large or particularly hot fires can create severe turbulence even many thousands of feet high.

- Crops and weeds can show direction, intensity and gusts. It's quite interesting to watch a gust form on wheat or beans and spread across the field.

- Moving cloud shadows work but can only tell the wind at cloud height.

- In desert areas, blowing sand and tumbleweed show wind but if there is visible blowing sand, a strong, bumpy wind is brewing.

- Ground track (direction of slowest ground-speed) will reveal the wind speed and direction at your altitude (see Chapter 10).

Universal Time: Converting to Zulu

Aviation, and therefore aviation weather, has a standard clock and a standard time. It is called coordinated Universal Time. abbreviated UTC (oddly enough) and in pilot parlance is "Zulu Time."

It is the time in Greenwich, England and does not recognize daylight savings time (DST) so the conversion is different in summer and winter. DST runs from the first Sunday of April to the last Sunday in October.

Convert to Zulu time by adding the following hours to your local time.

Zulu is:	Pacific	Mountain	Central	Eastern
In Summer (DST)	Local+7	Local+6	Local+5	Local+4
In Winter (ST)	Local+8	Local+7	Local+6	Local+5

Lift & Sink

When air flows up over an obstruction it produces lift in front of the obstruction and sink behind it along with rotor and turbulence. The strength of each depends on the shape of the obstruction and strength of the wind. Soaring pilots make use of this lift (called ridge or

The Flight Service Station (FSS) Briefing Made Easy

Here is a sample briefing for an early morning flight using 1-800-WX-BRIEF (U.S. only). First you'll be offered a recording and a message. That may be all you need but if not, push 0 to get a briefer. It will go like this:

Pilot:
"Hi, I'm ultralight pilot Fred Flyer," (Briefer writes this down to record an activity). "I plan on flying locally in an field 8 miles northeast of Aurora Airport this morning at about 7AM local. I'll be up for an hour and would like a standard briefing?"

(You can also ask for an abbreviated briefing which just the current and forecast weather.)

Briefer:
"How high will you be flying?" (because I forgot to mention that)

Pilot:
"No more than 1000 ft AGL"

Briefer:
"OK, You've got high pressure over the area with a cold front well to the north...(describes an overview)"

"Currently Aurora is reporting sky clear, visibility 6 miles in haze, winds are 220 at 7 knots, altimeter setting is 29.92 and the temperature is 22 with a dewpoint of 14." (temperatures, even in the US, is given in Celsius)."

"The Aurora forecast calls for clear skies, winds light and variable until 1400 Z then becoming 230 at 10."

Pilot:
"what time is that local?" (if you don't know, ask, but it's better form to know the conversion before calling).

Briefer:
"That's 6pm local. Then after that they're forecast to be calm."

"The winds aloft in that area, Joliet, should be 280 at 16, temperature +12 at 3000 feet."

"There is a NOTAM for taxiway closures at Aurora (in following a standard format they have to include information that may not be of much use) and the VASI to runway 26 is out of service"

Pilot:
OK, thank you very much, that will do it for me.

1. Wind direction is always given as the direction it is *from*. Nearly all aviation reports and forecasts use the 360 degrees of a compass rose relative to true north. Magnetic north is where a compass points and true north is what lines on a map are drawn with.

So a south wind would be given as 180° and a West wind would be 270°.

2. Flight Service personnel have access to many tools that give them a more complete picture of the weather, notices about airspace and other issues affecting flyers. They are not meteorologists but can provide a wealth of information.

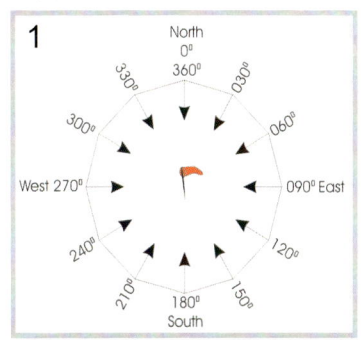

Orographic lift) to stay airborne but it must be given great respect—any lift powerful enough to keep a pilot aloft can also produce deadly turbulence if you wind up in the wrong place.

Acquiring Aviation Weather

There is great value in *aviation* forecasts—they tell winds at altitude, estimated times for frontal passages, wind shifts and other useful info. The same call can be used for finding out about airspace restrictions, too (see Chapter 9).

In the U.S., our Federal Aviation Administration (FAA) provides an valuable resource through Flight Service Stations (FSS). These facilities, contracted out to a private firm, give pilots a ready source for official aviation weather. Don't be daunted by the sound of that; it's not hard and they don't mind hearing from you (they helped edit this section).

Have the following info in hand before calling:

- Launch location relative to an and destination (if going cross country.) The FSS folks only have airports and navigation aids charted. For example, if you're 10 miles south of your city's airport, tell them that.

- Approximate Launch time and how long you'll be flying. Although they work with the worldwide standard time, Universal Coordinated Time (strangely, that's abbreviated UTC) they can translate to local; just be sure to say "local."

- Your planned maximum altitude above sea level (ASL). You can also use your height above ground level (AGL) but tell them that ("I'll be flying less than 500 ft AGL").

The clouds in this picture formed over the cool ocean then blew up against the mountains.

Mountainous air can be strange indeed, but weird weather comes out of the blue too—always check the forecasts!

Clear gust fronts will do just as much as those associated with clouds and they are frequently forecast in the aviation weather.

During the first major U.S. powered paraglider gathering, held in 2000, clues from the clouds went ignored. As pilots prepared to launch en-masse in search of a new record (number of pilots aloft), a line of sizable cumulus clouds was forming upwind. Some didn't like the looks of it and stayed put.

One pilot offered to call Flight Service on his cell phone. He was rebuffed—the clouds just didn't look that bad. After the first launch, lemmings soon followed. Ten minutes later, with 15 or so already airborne, a strong gust front came through.

A number of flyers didn't make it back to the field, landing in various places downwind. A few suffered minor injuries in the resulting high-wind landing and only one made it back to the launch area. They were *all* quite lucky.

What they missed by skipping that call to Flight Service, was a newly formed and very local cold front. The forecast (we called afterwards to see what it said) cautioned of a 20 knot wind shift at about the time launches began.

Be wary of changing conditions or incorrect current weather. If the forecast for right now is listed as winds south at 5 knots but the actual wind is northwest at 12 knots, be suspicious of the entire forecast. See what's coming by checking upstream stations (where the weather is coming from).

While on the phone, ask for another useful FSS product, the "VAD" (Velocity Azimuth Display) winds report. Winds are derived from special radar that uses airborne particulates to determine winds aloft over a wide area. VAD winds are helpful because they are actual winds and are given in thousand-foot increments (instead of 3000 feet for the regular winds aloft forecasts). Just ask if they have any VAD winds for your area.

Other Weather Sources

The Internet provides several great sources for weather information. Flight Service is good when you're out in the field (use a cell phone) or need to get NOTAMS, but consider looking at web sites that show surface winds throughout the day. Footflyer.com lists some good sources for both motor flying and soaring.

It is valuable to compare forecasts, though. Most of them get their data from the national weather service but may apply different interpretations. If one forecast calls for a big change in winds and another does not, one probably has old information. If there was no change in a forecast before, expect that the forecast containing the changes is probably newer.

Common Sense & The Law

CHAPTER 8

Our reality is that we operate at the pleasure of the people—a nervous and sound-sensitive people. It is all too easy for them to keep us grounded through laws on everything from sound to disturbing animals. Even where no law against flying exists, if you annoy enough of the right people, a law will be enacted.

It is a requirement of civilization that we collectively establish and enforce such laws. For example, we may not like the neighbor running his chain saw every morning by our window; preventing such behavior forms the basis for many noise regulations. Our impact is no different.

Aggravating people elicits a challenge from the disturbed ones and there are a lot more of them (non-flyers) than us. We must minimize aggravation, police ourselves and encourage others to also behave in a way that insures the sport's long-term survival.

Keeping a Low Profile

Avoid using any one area all the time. Don't buzz around the same location even if you have permission—it is better to launch and leave whenever possible.

Animals have people and vice versa. Annoying either can be downright expensive. For example, if you spook someone's million-dollar horse into to an injurious rampage, expect a visit from the riled owner and/or his lawyer; the possible loss of that flying site may be the least of your concerns.

Fly quietly. Stay high, use minimal thrust near civilization and make your machine as quiet as it can be—air intake silencers, mufflers, and big props all help in this regard.

Don't take the approach: "It's my land, I'll do what I want." That may be true but

---

Like any human interaction, treating law enforcement with respect will always make things better. You may be legal, but if they dislike your presence they'll find a way to make it difficult. Many encounters stem from simple curiosity about your strange flying machine

In one case, a cop showed up at a pilot's flying site and the pilot got all defensive. It turned out the cop was a fellow pilot who stopped in to watch his launch technique.

Being able to show law enforcement an air chart and how you were minding the rules can let them know you're trying to stay legal.

While the FAA (Federal Aviation Administration) governs U.S. Airspace, local police govern local launch sites.

The PPG Bible: A Complete Guide and Reference

only to a point—neighbors don't always need to be right next door to cause problems—they just have to convince the right people that you're either violating some existing law or they will try to enact a new law. Numerous laws have blossomed when existing ones didn't salve the irritated powers-that-be.

Regulations

In the U.S., a simple two-page Federal Aviation Regulation (FAR 103—see appendix) covers ultralights, defined as any powered aircraft weighing under 254 pounds, which easily includes PPG's. The most recent version can be found on the Internet (www.faa.gov). Other country's rules are probably equally accessible. FAR Part 103 was designed to let us risk only ourselves without endangering others. So every interpretation must conclude that the operation not endanger anyone else.

The absence of specific training requirements does not excuse ignorance of the law. Flying in any country's national airspace system is a privilege to be taken seriously. What a travesty it would be for someone to buy gear, train enough to get airborne, then crash into an airliner. Besides the obvious tragedy, public pressure to shut us down would extreme. We must not only learn the rules and follow them, but must help our fellow flyers do the same.

Perception is much of the battle: if you look like you're doing something dangerous, you'll draw undesirable attention. Steer clear of the law by not getting reported. Avoid *looking* like you're doing something bad; that tends to keep the operation safer, too, and you won't disturb people or their animals. "Showing off," chasing critters, and flying close to gatherings are all ways to get noticed in a potentially unwelcome manner. While we *can* fly close to objects, we must do so with discretion.

One common misconception is that we have to maintain 500 ft away from anything on the ground. While that is a good conservative approach, it is not the rule for us (as it is for most certified aircraft). That we can fly down a fence row at 5 feet is a wonderful freedom allowing us to interact with the land in amazing detail. Enjoy the freedom responsibly—don't endanger or annoy any humans.

Right of Way

All certified aircraft have the right of way. That means that if we see an airplane or helicopter, we have to stay clear or move, even if we're unpowered. Plus we must not create a collision hazard. Know where airplanes are likely to be and steer clear. Fortunately, we usually operate below their altitudes so it's easy, but near airports we have to be extra vigilant.

Among ultralights, the only rule is that powered craft must give way to unpowered ones. Common aviation practice, even though not regulatory, recommends:

- PPG's approaching head-on should each steer to the right.
- Overtake on the right.
- Landing pilots have the right of way although, when a field is crowded, landing pilots should let launchers go. Standing there while awaiting repeated touch-and-go's gets old quickly.
- The craft to the right has the right-of-way.

1. In the U.S., you can fly an additional 30 minutes before sunrise or beyond sunset provided you use a strobe that is visible for 3 miles. Plus, you must limit that additionall flying to class G airspace. Essentially that means staying below 700 ft AGL (1200 ft as charted).

2. Crossing fences and trespassing signs is bad enough, but crossing into this area would defy any definition of common sense. Not surprisingly, the area is near a military installation.

What is Congested?

It's the million dollar question. In the U.S., FAR 103.15 tells us "No person may operate an ultralight vehicle over any congested area of a city, town, or settlement, or over any open air assembly of persons." There is no altitude that allows overflight and no definition of congested—it's intentionally left to the eye of the enforcer. Some regional FAA offices consider even one house to constitute "congested," while others say that 6 houses qualifies and others have no set number.

The rule makers crafted a simple but broad wording and the term, *congested area*, has a cornucopia of interpretations. We will inject some practical experience into the interpretation that should be defensible by both the letter and intent of the law. Again, this is merely an interpretation, a *congested area* is:

- Any group of occupied buildings where there would not be enough room to easily launch or land. Remember, this defines the level of congestion, not the operational conduct. It should not be construed to allow flying over a congested area just because you have a good landing option available nearby. You can never fly *over* a congested area at any altitude. If it is not sparse enough to easily launch there, it is too congested for your particular operation.

- An open-air assembly of people is any gathering of two or more people. It includes golfers, beachgoers, sporting events, parties, and spectators (even at *fly-ins!*) Again, flying high enough avoids the problem in most cases because you don't appear threatening and the noise is tolerable.

- One interesting situation is roads. There is much precedence that suggests overflight of roads is OK, with caveats. There are fields with approved (by FAA control towers) ultralight flight patterns that go over major roads, even interstates. They usually specify some minimum altitude (300 feet is common). At major Fly-Ins there are ultralight flight patterns that go over well-traveled roads as well. But it requires reason: if you distract, annoy or endanger a motorist, then they may call the area congested. If there is enough traffic that something falling off your machine would likely hit a car and damage it, then it could be called congested. The best bet is to climb to at least 300 feet AGL before crossing roads and do not operate in a manner that disturbs the groundlings or brings undue attention.

Case Law & Other Issues

Verdicts that have been handed down to pilots who ran afoul of the law are most relevant. Even though U.S. flyers abide by Part 103, cases involving violations of other air regulations have been used as precedent for ultralight pilots. They have been used to impose fines (or other sanctions) by virtue of their definitions.

In one case, a definition of congested was given by saying that: "30 to 40 homes, located on relatively small and adjoining lots, constitutes a 'congested area' within the meaning of the regulation."

Even with the the houses, ultralights have been flying out of this field for years and have had no complaint by any FAA officials. Those white hangars belong to members of an ultralight club. Credit the responsible behavior of club pilots that it lasted well beyond the buildup of houses.

Flying over congested areas is prohibited at any altitude. In this case, the pilot, David McWhinnie, and I took off from a clear area adjacent to the beach and kept the flight out over Lake Michigan. The zoom was used to bring Chicago much closer than it actually was.

He is not flying directly over any houses but certainly an observer might think otherwise. The best practice is to stay well away from anybody you consider hostile to your presence.

Either be up high or make sure than nobody can prove you were over their house. Being higher does not allow overflight, but sure reduces your noise footprint.

Unfortunately no dimensions were given but little is left to the imagination and most suburban developments would qualify.

Another case is even less encouraging. It is a bit more complicated because it involved an agricultural airplane that operates under different regulations but is not allowed over congested areas. The judge labeled the following as congested: an area 0.6 miles long and 0.3 miles wide (about 115 acres) with 60 houses—pretty sparse by most definitions. That would equate to lot sizes of just over an acre. This definition was used to say a PPG pilot was flying over a congested area.

An FAA web site offers some relief regarding congested. It says that an operation (this was given for aerobatic pilots) can be done over an area as small as an acre, even if surrounded by houses. That means flying along a right of way, beside railroad tracks or a path that keeps you away from buildings would be allowable. Just don't fly over the nearby houses and, above all, don't do anything that would make people complain to authorities. It is worth reading and heeding these rules; each violation carries a fine usually exceeding $1000 and can get your equipment confiscated.

Endangerment & Dropping Objects

Anything you do that might endanger (or be perceived as endangering) another person would violate FAR 103.9(a), a catch-all regulation that says "No person may operate any ultralight vehicle in a manner that creates a hazard to other persons or property." Nearly every country has similar verbiage.

FAR 103.9(b) prohibits dropping things *if* they could be harmful. It says "No person may allow an object to be dropped from an ultralight vehicle if such action creates a hazard to other persons or property." That is why bean-bag dropping contests are legal.

What is "Flying Over?"

This all begs the question of when you are "over" some prohibited area and how far away you need to be. By one measure you are not over something unless you are directly over it. But if an observer thinks you are too close to something, then you will be labeled "flying over." For example, houses may be well to your right but, to an observer on your left, you may *appear* to be over them.

So here's a measure to use for keeping a reasonable distance horizontally from off-limits places: use the distance you would travel in 5 seconds of flying time. In our 20 mph craft we go about 30 feet per second; that would be 150 ft. Up higher that should be increased to maybe 10 seconds at 300 ft. So if you're flying alongside a road that is busy enough to worry about, stay at least 5 seconds of flying time horizontally away from it. Also, don't let the trajectory of potential falling parts endanger people.

Like so many aspects of life, attitude can be the difference between a lip lashing and enforcement action. If local authorities question your operation, be respectful and explain you were doing your best to follow the pertinent air regulation—they may not be aware of the specifics but don't assume that and certainly don't come across with arrogance, they may, in fact, be quite knowledgeable. Offer that you will avoid the area or fly where they suggest.

Have a copy of the regulations, an altimeter, an air map excerpt of the area (sectional chart in the U.S.) and know how to read it. If confronted, show them how you were trying to stay within the law. That may diffuse the situation.

If you wind up being investigated or have to answer a letter of investigation, be prompt, be honest, but be minimal. Your response to that letter may be what is used against you—it may be all they need and may be nearly all they have. The vast majority of FAA folks that I have encountered are not "out to get" pilots. They are trying to do their job with the least amount of effort possible. If you are belligerent with them though, expect that finding you guilty will *become* their mission—and there almost always is a way.

Digging Deeper

FAA Advisory Circular AC 103-7, dated 1/30/84, spells out many details under which FAR 103 was concocted and gives some interesting background. It offers detail on this subject and how incredibly limiting the interpretation is. The circular is available at www.faa.gov.

Commercial Use

Commercial use is prohibited in Part 103.

The FAA does not bother defining commercial use, rather it says our activity must be *only* for recreation or sport. This makes the stroke very broad and difficult to avoid. Don't confuse it with other rules such as those prohibiting private pilots from commercial activities—our rule is far more limiting. We are only allowed to fly for "recreation or sport." Flying for movies or photography missions are questionable even if no payment is made for the flying.

Regulators figured that, with no license given, there is little accountability and few safeguards to the public, so ultralight flying would not be inappropriate for commercial use.

Where the payment issue comes into play is when defending the "sport or recreational" nature of a flight. If you are getting paid then it becomes really difficult to justify that purpose.

The most common question is about aerial photography. The temptation is to say that you are not getting paid to fly but rather are selling a service and just happened to have pictures from your PPG. If you were out flying for sport, took a cool picture just for your own entertainment and later discovered it captured some unique scene, it would technically be valid to sell the picture. If you flew solely to get pictures then it's not even the selling that is illegal, it's that the purpose of the flight was not for sport or recreation.

So the rule is quite limiting. The people most likely to report your activity are those who legally and professionally offer up services, such as photography, video, or advertising using certified aircraft and pilots. They have a lot to lose if someone drains away their business with inexpensive, unregulated capabilities.

Instructing

The only way to get paid to fly is by giving tandem instruction. Experienced pilots can go through an approved program that allows them to fly students using two-seat craft. Such flights are done under a special exemption and are for instruction only. In the U.S., approved programs are run by several organizations and do not fall under the more-involved Sport Pilot regulation (an FAR for heavier aircraft).

You can also get paid to teach the sport if you do not fly—there is no restriction on teaching someone from the ground. Of course there are many pitfalls to

Tandem instruction is one way to get paid for flying; teaching flying in this case. You can give introductory flights too but must have some form of certification in nearly all countries including the U.S.

instructing which is why going through a thorough certification process is important.

Getting Someone Else to Pay

While you cannot get paid for flying, you can offset your flying costs by having a company buy your wing or motor for you. Their logo and text may be emblazoned all over it providing that they don't tell you when or where to fly it. It has nothing to do with getting paid—if you fly for the purpose of gaining exposure, it is a violation of the rule. If you're thinking that would be hard to enforce, you're right. But do something blatant where the purpose is obvious and you'll bring scrutiny.

Writing on the wing and having your sponsor buy the wing is about the only way to get someone else to help pay for your flying legally.

If I Violate the Rules?

Professional pilots have the most to lose: FAA officials will go after their certificates because it's the easiest and most effective course. A good aviation attorney is a must in that situation.

Generally the FAA is obliged to investigate any complaint and, once the wheels have started, there are many I's to dot and T's to cross; don't expect it to just go away. However, if handled amicably, the event may be settled with minimum fuss.

The first indication will usually be obvious: the police show up and take a report. They don't always contact the aviation authorities but will certainly do so if motivated. Be polite! And don't assume they're unaware of our rules. Be sensitive but it's possible they may accuse you of violating rules that don't apply. It can work in your favor if they cite you for a rule you don't fall under.

This is where flying with a copy of the regulations, air map and an altimeter can help show you're trying to be responsible. Don't be arrogant and don't offer the rules unless requested—they may find something else to use. Offering to show them the chart is a better approach.

Exemptions

It is possible to get exemptions from the rules as long as equivalent safety is maintained. For example, airshows commonly get pilots doing things that would otherwise be illegal but, by virtue of a waiver, are allowed to do them under certain guidelines aimed at protecting the public.

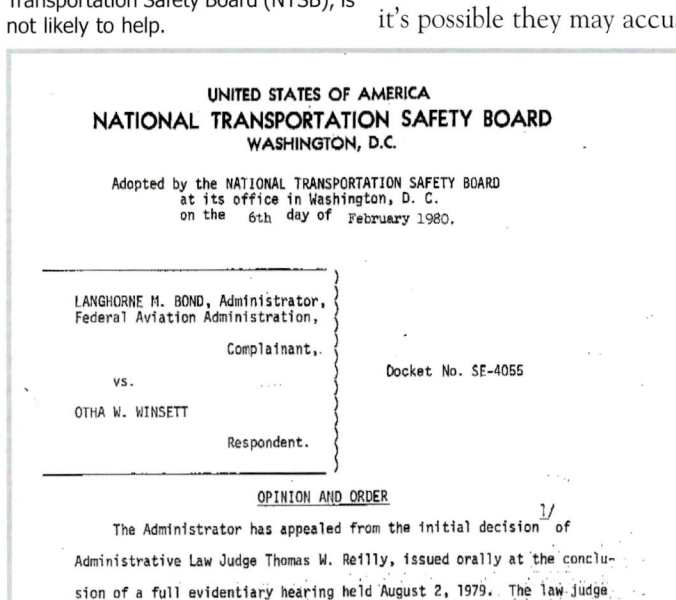

Our freedom is a double-edged sword that can *cut deeply.*

When one PPG pilot ran afoul of the local police, they contacted FAA officials. The case wound up going all the way to trial. FAA lawyers used case law (below) from many years prior that, and although not even about FAR 103, it did include a reference to *congested*.

The pilot was fined over $1000 in addition to his legal fees. There is, unfortunately, little recourse in such cases and the only one, the National Transportation Safety Board (NTSB), is not likely to help.

UNITED STATES OF AMERICA
NATIONAL TRANSPORTATION SAFETY BOARD
WASHINGTON, D.C.

Adopted by the NATIONAL TRANSPORTATION SAFETY BOARD
at its office in Washington, D. C.
on the 6th day of February 1980.

LANGHORNE M. BOND, Administrator,
Federal Aviation Administration,
  Complainant,
vs.
OTHA W. WINSETT
  Respondent.

Docket No. SE-4055

OPINION AND ORDER

The Administrator has appealed from the initial decision 1/ of Administrative Law Judge Thomas W. Reilly, issued orally at the conclusion of a full evidentiary hearing held August 2, 1979. The law judge concluded that a violation of section 91.9 of the Federal Aviation Regulations (FAR) occurred during the flight of a manned free balloon that took place Sunday, April 9, 1978, at around 8:00 a.m. The law judge deemed that the striking of the drainpipe on the garage of a residence (the Warren house) by the basket (gondola) attached to the

Airspace

CHAPTER 9

"Can I launch here?" you ask. Probably, but there are some things you must know.

In the U.S. our freedom is inspiring; we can fly just about anywhere with few restrictions. But, like all freedoms, that privilege carries great responsibility—knowing the airspace and adhering to its restrictions. Launching into a sky full of airliners without knowing the rules is pure folly; a risk for you, others, and ultimately, the entire sport. You don't need to become an expert on reading charts either—just understanding a fraction of what's available can prevent much peril.

A great resource for learning local airspace is the flying school at your nearest airport. Explain to them that you're an ultralight pilot and ask if they would share advice on where you can go and what you should avoid. In all likelihood they will appreciate your responsible approach.

Purchase and become familiar with the Aeronautical Sectional Chart for your flight area. These are packed with necessary airspace boundaries, among other things. Bigger cities have the more detailed VFR (Visual Flight Rules) Terminal Area Charts.

We will dispense with height limit descriptions (such as "up to but not including") and just use "above" or "below." The full U.S. air regulation, including cloud clearance minutia, is in the appendix.

There are two common sets of cloud clearance and visibility requirements that you should know. They are abbreviated here as follows:

- **5,1,2&3** means **500** feet below, **1000** feet above, **2000** feet horizontally away from the clouds and **3** miles visibility (most Class E airspace).

- **CoC&1** means "**Clear of Clouds**" and **1** mile vis. (most Class G airspace).

Sectional charts are available from most local airports (Fixed Base Operator or flight school), the Internet, and pilot shops. Charts come out every 6 months with the latest changes, although a call to Flight Service is the only way to be completely current.

The PPG Bible: A Complete Guide and Reference

Airspace Types

Air Traffic: Our first type of airspace concerns air traffic and helps keep controlled aircraft separated from those flying without control (ultralights and most private general aviation). This airspace is designated with the letters A through G (excluding F, which isn't used in the U.S.)

Security: These airspace areas keep air traffic away from nationally sensitive sites such as the Capitol, military installations, events with large crowds, politician's residences and others. They include Temporary Flight Restrictions (TFR's) that pop up whenever a dignitary swoops in, and can be issued with very little notice. Prohibited, Restricted and Alert areas are shown on charts but the temporary airspace information comes via Notices to Airmen (NOTAMs) which are accessed via computer or by calling a Flight Service Station (see Chapter 7).

Wilderness: National parks and other public preserves or monuments have altitude minimums for overflight. Even if you fly legally according to air regulations, disturbing wildlife may put you at odds with other rules. While it's true that the FAA governs airspace (in the U.S.), they don't pass judgement on what constitutes "disturbing" when it comes to animals.

Other: Special airspace restrictions can pop into being for a variety of reasons including tethered balloons, high powered rocket launches, and disaster areas.

The ABC's of Airspace

Airspace isn't as complex as it may seem. In the U.S., picture a 1200 ft. thick blanket of airspace covering the whole country known as G airspace. Above that is E airspace which goes up to 18,000 feet MSL. In populated areas or near airports, the "blanket" of G airspace is only 700 feet thick—these are called transition areas.

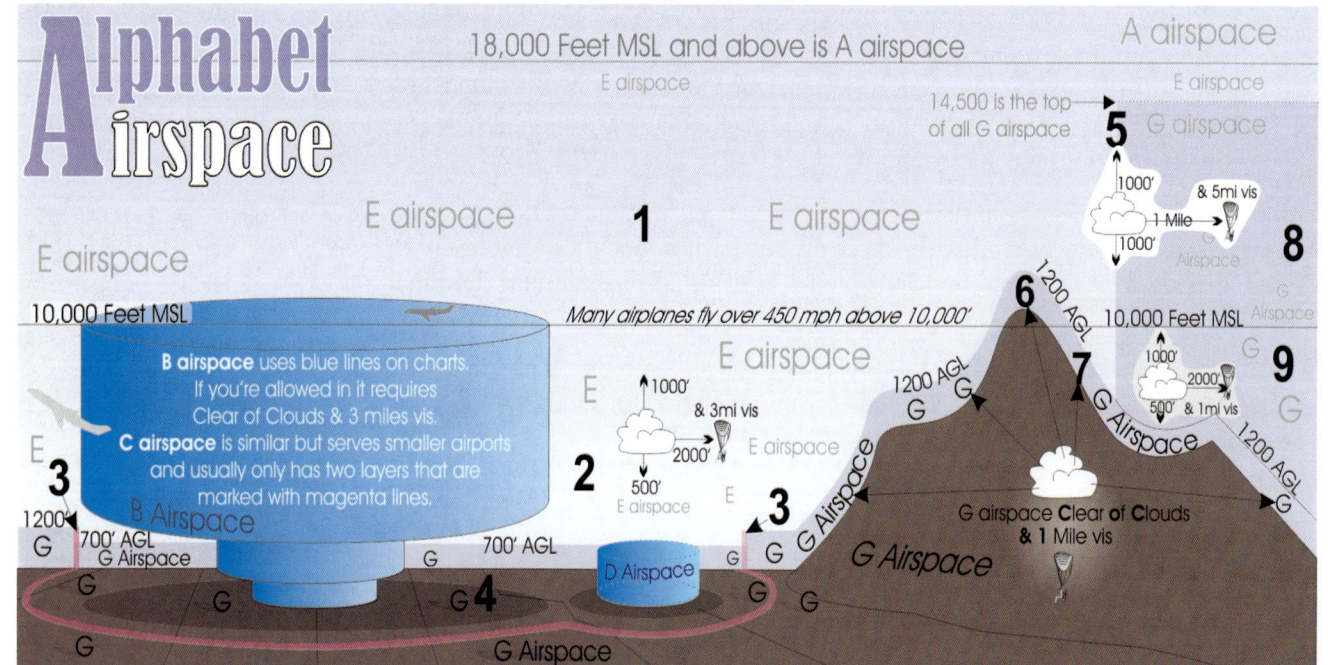

Altitude Abbreviations

Here are the common abbreviations when referring to airspace.

AGL is Above Ground Level.

MSL is above Mean Sea Level. It is used interchangeably with ASL, Above Sea Level.

The diagram below shows most airspace types with their associated cloud clearance and visibility requirements.

You can never fly with less than 1 mile visibility and must always stay clear of clouds. Above 1200 feet AGL the cloud clearance and visibility requirements increase and are even more stringent above 10,000 feet. We're not even allowed above 18,000 feet MSL.

Launching above 10,000 feet can be done with as little as 1 mile of visibility and clear of clouds provided you're within 1200 feet of the ground.

Positions 1 & 8, being above 10,000 feet, have identical minimums even though 1 is in E and 8 is in G airspace. Position 5 is the border of G airspace that goes up to 14,500 feet MSL with E airspace above; in the U.S. this occurs only in sparse areas—on charts it appears as a shaded blue line.

Position 2 is in E airspace.

Positions 4, 6 & 7 have the lower Class G minimums, being below 1200 feet AGL (700 feet for position 4).

You can fly at position 9 with only a mile visibility but need more cloud clearance. Position 8, being above 10,000 feet, requires much higher visibility. Position 3 points to a transition area where the floor of E drops from 1200 to 700 feet.

Class C is not shown but it's essentially a smaller version of B.

Alphabet Airspace

18,000 Feet MSL and above is A airspace

14,500 is the top of all G airspace

B airspace uses blue lines on charts. If you're allowed in it requires Clear of Clouds & 3 miles vis.

C airspace is similar but serves smaller airports and usually only has two layers that are marked with magenta lines.

Many airplanes fly over 450 mph above 10,000'

G airspace **C**lear of **C**louds & 1 Mile vis

Page 84 — Section II: Spreading Your Wings

Transition areas are marked on charts by a shaded magenta (purplish-pink) line. The idea is that, in areas with heavier airplane traffic, we must either stay down lower (below the planes) or must have better visibility up higher (above 700 feet) so we can see and avoid them.

Paramotor pilots fly, mostly unfettered, in class E and G airspace, which means the vast majority of airspace is open to us. The only difference between G and E airspace is the higher visibility and cloud clearance requirements in E; a design intended to give us a fighting chance at "see and avoid" up there.

If you live in a smaller city that has an airport but no control tower, there is probably no restriction on flying. Talk with those who run the airport and let them know you'll be flying in the area.

If you live near a city with more than about 50,000 people, there is probably a nearby airport with a control tower and its surrounding D airspace. Bigger cities have bigger airports and more restrictions.

The Lettered Meanings

In 1993 an international alphabet classification of airspace brought the US into world conformity. Reference the "Alphabet Airspace" diagram—the letters go down in severity of restriction as they go down the alphabet:

A airspace is above 18,000 feet MSL and off limits to us. Even if you could get up there it would be miserably cold (see Chapter 24) and probably have a howling wind.

Coverage: Entire Country and out 12 nm (nautical miles) from shore.
On Chart: Not depicted.

B airspace is associated with the biggest airports. Layered like an upside down wedding cake, it is marked on charts with solid blue lines and has tops around 10,000 feet MSL. We can fly below the layers but so too can everyone else—expect a lot of traffic and fly *well* below the bottoms.

Access: Authorization is required which will be very unlikely, even with an aircraft radio. You must maintain CoC (clear of Clouds) and 3 miles visibility.

On Chart: Solid blue lines with numbered altitudes for segment floors and ceilings. The altitudes are in hundreds of feet MSL (the last 2 zeros are omitted.) On the Chicagoland excerpt ORD is the inner area of a class B airspace area whose top is 10,000 feet.

Diagram: Blue layered cylinders.

C airspace is a mini version of B with less traffic. Some major, and many commuter, airliners fly into these airports along with business and private airplanes. The airspace typically extends 10 nm from the airport and goes up to about 4000 feet MSL.

Access: By permission only which is unlikely. You'll probably need an aircraft radio. Requires 5,1,2&3 (500 below, 1000 above, 2000 to the side of clouds and 3 miles visibility).

On Chart: Similar to B airspace markings but with solid magenta lines. On the Chicagoland excerpt, MDW is the inner area of its class C airspace.

D airspace surrounds most airports with an operating control tower (see Chapter 11), typically extending 5 miles out and 2500

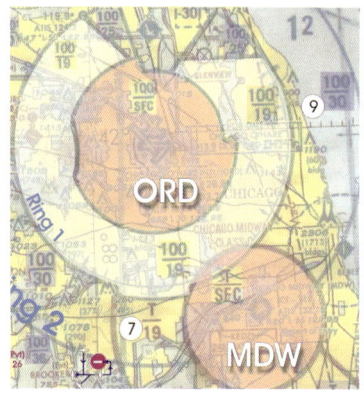

ORD is O'hare International, Chicago's big airport. It's rings of Class B airspace radiate outward with increasingly higher bottoms. Beyond the center (red shaded here but not on the chart) you can legally launch and fly below 1900 feet MSL. The ground is around 600, leaving 1300 feet to play with. Finding an uncongested area in this morass will be a far bigger problem. As you get farther out, you can fly higher.

Midway (MDW), Chicago's 2nd busiest airport, is just Southeast of O'hare and sports the smaller Class C airspace. You can't launch in the center (red shaded part) but you could launch under the outer ring. It happens to be the same floor as O'hare's first ring, 1900 feet MSL.

However, these areas will be extremely congested with air traffic operating below the main airspace. If you found a field and only flew over it below 500 feet AGL, you would probably be ok. Otherwise it would be extremely unwise.

All things considered, it is best to avoid big cities.

Digging Deeper:
The Nautical Mile (nm)

Aviation's standard measure of distance is the nautical mile. It is one minute of one degree of the earth's circumference. There are 360 degrees, 60 minutes and 60 seconds in the coordinate system popularized by GPS receivers.

That means that lines of latitude on sectional charts can be used to measure nautical miles. Lines of longitude get closer together at the poles so they only work for that purpose on the equator.

One nautical mile equals 1.15 statute (regular) miles.

Nearly all the U.S., like all of this chart, is covered with class G airspace. The overlying E airspace starts at 1200 feet AGL except for inside the magenta circles where it starts at 700 feet AGL (also called Transition Areas).

The logic behind transition areas is to give airplanes a safe descent to the airport. They want to insure there is no traffic flying around with only 1 mile visibility unless that traffic is below where they'll be flying (below 700 feet).

Remember, airplanes (and all certified aircraft) always have the right of way over ultralights, even unpowered ultralights.

feet above the airport's center. If the control tower is not operating then it reverts to **E Surface Area** which still requires permission.

Although Class D airspace is normally associated with control towers, you *can* have a tower with no Class D. Such an exception appears on this chapter's cover. Kissimee airport, southwest of Orlando International, has a control tower but no dashed lines, meaning no D airspace—you could legally launch right next to the field without talking to anybody (it has since added the D airspace).

Access: By permission only and may require an aircraft radio. Requires 5,1,2&3.

On Chart: Dashed blue lines around blue airport symbol. Its ceiling is in hundreds of feet MSL in the blue square. On the Chicagoland chart DPA, ORD and MDW are all control-towered airports.

E Surface Area is usually found as an extension from Class D airspace and is where E airspace goes to the surface (instead of bottoming out as G airspace). Position 2 on the Thousand Oaks chart (below) is in such an extension. It is unusual in that certified airplanes don't need to be talking with anyone but ultralights are not allowed in without permission. Strangely, that means we can legally fly over the airport (above its class D) but not over these extensions.

Can I Launch Here?

Refer to the Thousand Oaks excerpt.

1. Yes, It's G airspace with E starting at 700 feet AGL. You must remain CoC&1 until above 700 feet AGL (E airspace) when you must have 5,1,2&3.

2. Requires Permission. It's Class E surface area. Must have 5,1,2&3 if permission is granted.

3, 4, 5, 6. Requires permission. It's D airspace. Must have 5,1,2&3 if permission is granted.

7. Yes, this ring denotes equipment required for airplanes. We don't need it (a Mode C Transponder allows the radar controllers to "see" airplanes better and know their altitude).

8. Yes, this is just like 1.

9. Yes, you'll launch in G airspace, climb into E at 700 feet AGL but must remain below 7000 feet MSL which is where this piece of LAX's class B airspace starts.

K. Same as J except that the class B airspace starts at 5000 feet MSL.

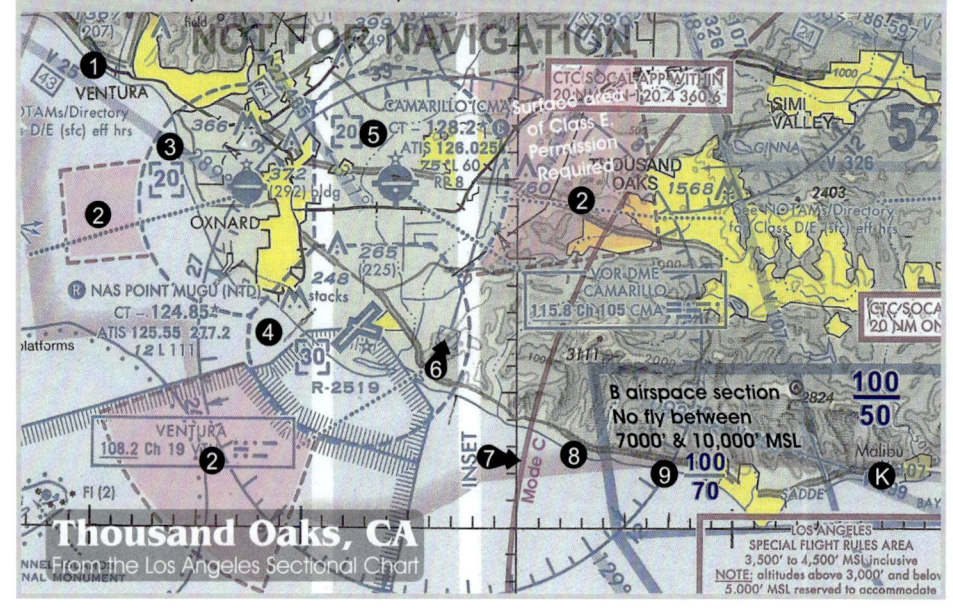

This is the airspace that FAR 103.17 calls the "surface area of Class E airspace designated for an airport."

- Access: By permission only, They may require an aircraft radio but usually not.
- On Chart: It is denoted on the charts by dashed magenta lines—just like the blue dashed lines around control tower airports, but magenta. On the Chicagoland chart the number 4 is in such an extension (just the squared-off extension, not the whole circle). The Danville excerpt has an unusual airport at the number 5 where the entire space is class E at the surface.

E airspace overlies G airspace starting at 1200 feet AGL (or 700 feet in magenta shaded areas). It covers most of the country except some sparsely populated areas.

- Access: Access allowed. Requires 5,1,2&3 for cloud clearance and visibility while below 10,000 feet MSL.
- On Chart: No designation except in very sparse areas. A blue shaded line means no E airspace at all on the sharp side of the line—class G goes up to 14,500 feet. A shaded magenta line denotes the floor of E drops to 700 feet on the fuzzy side of the line. The entire area of both chart excerpts have E airspace overhead starting at either 700 or 1200 feet AGL.

G airspace is what's there if no other airspace is depicted. It's where we launch. Most of the country, including sparsely populated areas, are covered with G airspace. It goes from the surface up to the overlying E airspace or, in a few sparsely populated areas, all the way up to 14,500 feet MSL.

- Access: Access allowed, requires at least CoC&1 below 1200 AGL (clear of clouds and 1 mile visibility).
- On Chart: No specific designation. If there is nothing on the chart, G airspace is assumed.

Security Airspace

The many flavors of military airspace are mostly off-limits to us. Some of it allows flight during a specified time range or between certain altitudes and some of it is just advisory. "Military operating areas" (MOAs) are advisory—they don't use it enough to close the airspace but want pilots to know of their possible presence.

Air Defense Identification Zones (ADIZ), previously surrounding only national borders, now keep traffic out of Capitol cities (including the U.S.) and a few other extremely sensitive sites. Flying in such a zone could get you shot at.

Visual and Instrument military routes (VR and IR) depict courses the military uses for practice and transit. While we're not prohibited, these thin, gray lines on sectional charts should encourage lively eyes—aircraft are frequently flying along them very low and very fast (up to 270 mph). Avoiding them would be wise.

Prohibited and Restricted areas keep airspace closed during certain published times as depicted on the sectional charts. The times of operation are frequently variable and require a call to the controlling agency, whose number is, unfortunately, not listed. To find out the "hot" times (when they're active) call Flight Service and explain your need (see Chapter 7 on calling).

Alert areas, Controlled Firing areas and MOA's do not actually prohibit flight, rather they serve as a warning that military operations will be conducted and pilots should "look out." Keep in mind that some military training involves low-altitude flying (called "nap-of-the-earth") where they follow the terrain, staying below a couple hundred feet AGL—in the middle of our favorite altitudes. We must avoid

---

Several websites offer graphical depictions of current Temporary Flight Restrictions (TFR's). The most reliable way to get them is a briefing from flight service. These areas can pop up with little notice.

Many require special aircraft radio equipment (avionics) and a filed flight plan to fly into and out of the area.

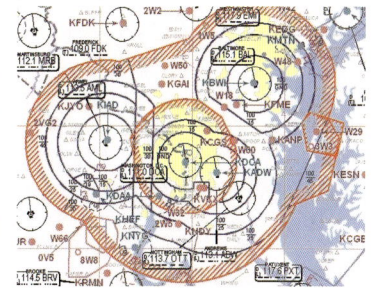

Digging Deeper: What is "Mode C"

Around most of the busy class B airspace areas there is a 30 mile ring that says "Mode C". This has no bearing on our ability to fly inside that ring.

The mode C "veil" pertains only to certified aircraft with an electrical system and requires them to have a transponder with altitude encoding. That equipment transmits lets radar controllers see the aircraft's altitude along with other information. We, as ultralights, are exempt from this requirement.

them—you can be sure these pilots won't be scanning for stray paramotorists!

Temporary Flight Restrictions (TFR's) are put up anywhere various government agencies deem them necessary. Some have been up for years while others pop up whenever the President or his people appear. Some pop up with no warning—don't be surprised when dignitaries soon show up. They also appear during or after disasters.

Regulations prohibit flying near large events. For example, in the U.S., pilots are not allowed to fly near major sporting events, conventions and many other public gatherings. Some facilities that might be considered terrorist targets are off limits. Even when there are no specific restrictions, verbiage in the regulation admonishes pilots not to "loiter" at sensitive sites. Such loitering may garner a special reception, possibly by helicopter, at your return.

Knowing the rules is important but common sense is helpful too—if it looks like it might be considered a sensitive site from the security eyes, either find out first or avoid it altogether.

Wilderness Areas

Many public parks, like the Grand Canyon, have areas preserved for their natural, quiet, separation from civilization. Some are protected by special rules prohibiting launch and even overflight. In most cases these areas are not strictly prohibited but pilots are admonished to avoid overflight below 2000 AGL.

Wilderness areas are indicated on charts by a blue dotted line. Some (like the Grand Canyon) have special restrictions outlined in Special Federal Aviation Regulations (SFARs) while other are covered in Notices To Airman (NOTAMs). Before flying in a popular park or famous site, contact the FSS and ask if they know of any restrictions. There may also be some local restrictions that apply—check with the Park administrators for that. Ask about overflight rules too.

NOTAMs

Whenever airspace is put off-limits, the FAA informs pilots through Notices to Airmen (NOTAMs). Adherence to these is critical; it may be for natural disasters, dignitaries, military needs, rocket launches or many other reasons. It could be a small area or, as on September 11, 2001, an entire country.

The NOTAM's location is usually referenced to a navigation station, such as a VOR, with direction (radial) and distance from the station. These are clearly marked on charts and have a convenient compass rose around them. Air traffic controllers have them on their radar maps, too.

NOTAM information can be obtained from FSS's in the same way as a weather briefing (see Chapter 7). If not offered, ask for any pertinent NOTAMs in the area.

Wilderness & Restricted Areas

Ocotillo airport is a popular ultralight field nestled amidst a charted wilderness area. The 2000 foot AGL minimum request applies there. Don't take this lightly, they can issue expensive fines for violating noise ordinances or disturbing habitat.

More important are Restricted areas just a few miles Southeast. The whole area with the blue hash marks is R-2510A. It goes from the surface to 15,000 feet. R-2510B sits atop the northern half of R-2510A, going from 15,000 feet up to 40,000.

The magenta Kane West MOA outlines a Military Operating Area that we can legally fly in but must understand the extra risk involved.

The details for all these areas are printed in the margin of the LAX sectional chart pictured above.

Here's an example (reference "Digging Deeper" at right): a truck carrying propane explodes on the highway northeast of Vermillion, IL. The highway is closed as a rescue and firefighting operation gets underway complete with helicopters. FAA managers, at the behest of local officials, close the airspace over the area by issuing a NOTAM—prohibiting overflight below 2000 and within 2nm of the DNV 042 at 12.5nm. In this example, the closed TFR area is shaded red for clarity. It is expected that, once receiving this NOTAM, you will get your chart and plot it out. Locate the DNV VOR (Danville VOR, what #3 is pointing to) then follow its 042° radial (the line at #4) northeast out 12.5 nm.

The same or similar method will be used to alert pilots when a dignitary's presence closes off airspace. This is taken extremely seriously—there may be patrols both in the air and on the ground.

Visibility & Cloud Clearance

Besides knowing *if* we can fly in an area, we need to know what visibility and cloud clearance is required to fly there. The *least* we can ever have is 1 mile visibility and clear of clouds. Those low minimums apply only down low while in G airspace.

As we fly higher (above 700 feet or more), the chance of mixing with airplanes increases and so do the minimums—see the Alphabet Airspace diagram. This makes enormous sense since we need more time to see an airplane that may be going 300 mph; that's 440 feet per *second*. At that speed, an approaching airplane that you spot a half-mile away is only 6 seconds from colliding—precious little time to recognize it, figure out that it's closing, do the right thing, and actually get out of the way in time. At that point, realistically, you're probably in for a collision. Better visibility provides more time for you or the airplane pilot to react.

Above 10,000 feet MSL airplanes go as fast as they want (they are limited to 250 knots below that) and so the visibility and cloud clearances minimums are the highest. That makes sense—with jets commonly going over 400 mph, they need a lot of room to see and react to a PPG pilot. Beware that they punch through those innocuous looking cumulus clouds, too, which is why the horizontal cloud clearance requirement goes up to a mile. Even then, a jet popping out of a cloud from a mile away has only 9 seconds to sort things out and maneuver away.

Reading The Charts

There is an information treasure trove crammed into these charts. For example, airports show the runway orientation (paved only), enabling better prediction of where to expect airplane traffic. Runways are numbered in the direction of takeoff so that runway 27 means the pilot is taking off to the west (270° Magnetic).

The charts also reveal that relatively few areas are closed to us. In the Danville, IL excerpt above, the only off-limits places are shaded red: spots 5, 10 and the TFR. Even those may be available with permission.

Danville, IL

Lets consider this chart excerpt with an eye to launching.

Position 1: Ignore that it's pointing to the 0° radial; you want to launch from the arrow's tip.

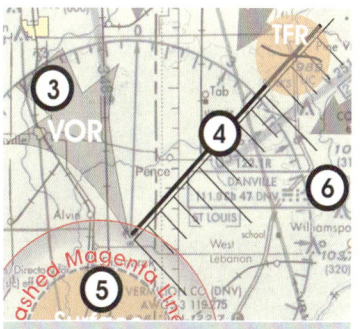

Digging Deeper: VOR

The VHF Omnidirectional Range (VOR) is a special navigation transmitter for aviation. An airplane's receiver can tell the pilot what "radial" he is on from the VOR—i.e. what direction he is from the VOR. A radial is a magnetic direction from 0° to 360° where 0° or 360° is north and 180° is south. That's obviously useful for navigation although GPS has largely supplanted it for primary navigation.

Why do we care? Those stations are used as reference points for airspace and notices to airmen (NOTAMs). Their prominent placement on sectionals makes it easy to plot these areas using a radial, distance and diameter.

The station name and its frequency is given in a blue box. In the excerpt above, the Danville VOR is on 111.0 Mhz (just left of spot 4 above).

Another reason they are of interest is that VOR's tend to concentrate airplane traffic overhead. It is best to avoid flying close to them, especially above about 800 feet. Most airplanes now use GPS's for navigation but still practice using VOR's.

Marking Position: VOR

This excerpt from the Chicago sectional chart shows how *radials* emanate from a VOR. A compass rose around the Danville VOR (position 3 points to the VOR) makes it easy to visualize them. A line (under position 4) is drawn out the 043° radial towards a temporary flight restriction (TFR) centered 12.5 nautical miles out. Cardinal degrees (0, 30, 60, 90, etc.) from the VOR are marked on the compass rose (positions 1, 2, and 7) so radials are easier to find. Position 7, for example, points to the 60° radial.

Hack marks going out the 042° radial line (under position 4) are nautical miles; they were added to show that they're the same as the hack marks going up lines of longitude (see position 11). That works because a nautical mile also happens to be 1/60th of one degree of latitude. Since lines of latitude are marked along each line of longitude (vertical line above the 87° at the chart's lower right), mileage is easy to figure, even without a special ruler. Mileage is also given along the bottom of each chart. Only use the hack marks on vertical lines, the ones made on horizontal lines (of latitude) get closer together as you near the earth's poles.

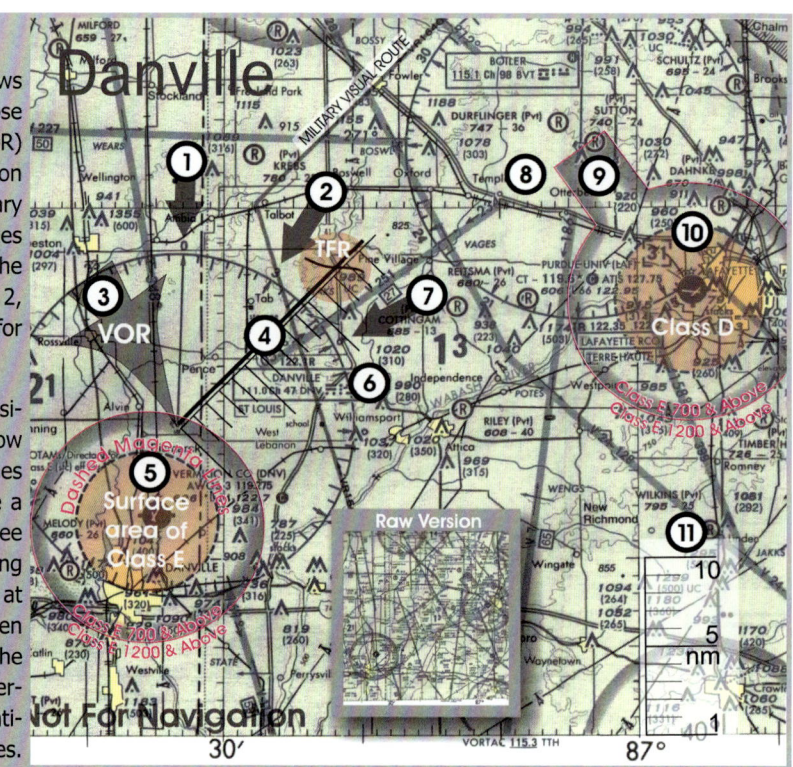

This VOR (VHF Omni Directional Range) in Southern Indiana also served as a turnpoint during the U.S. Nationals in 2004. Don't launch or land here—trespassing or affecting its operation is quite the federal sin.

Launch? Yes, you're in G airspace with E airspace starting at 1200 feet AGL.
Need: CoC&1 (clear of clouds and 1 mile visibility) until climbing above 1200 feet AGL then it goes to 5,1,2&3 (500 below, 1000 above, 2000 horizontally from the clouds and 3 miles visibility).

The Danville VOR (what position 3 is pointing to): Notice it's just inside a shaded magenta line. That means the E Airspace floor dropped to 700 feet AGL as opposed to 1200 feet AGL outside that shaded line.

Launch? Yes, you're in G airspace with E starting at 700 feet (that's what the shaded magenta does—lower class E from 1200 to 700 feet AGL).
Require: CoC&1 up to 700 feet AGL above which you must have 5,1,2&3.

Position 5 is just inside the "Surface area of Class E" which is off limits to us at any altitude without permission from air traffic control (ATC). The authority is usually an Approach Control or ARTCC facility ("Center") for that region.

Launch? No, unless you have permission. Call FSS for that since this is one of the few places in the country where an airport has class E at the surface that is not associated with a control tower airport.
Require: If you *do* get permission it would require 5,1,2&3.

TFR: The NOTAM that creates the TFR will give other information as to altitudes, restrictions and times of effectiveness.

Launch? No unless specified in the NOTAM verbiage.
Require: Specified in the NOTAM.

The Boiler VOR (a mile northwest of position 9): Purdue University, a control tower airport, is 8 nm southeast of here. We should be vigilant for airplanes flying instrument approaches from the VOR into Purdue airport—they may be down low.

Launch? Yes, you're in G airspace with E airspace starting at 700 feet AGL.
Require: CoC&1 up to 700 feet AGL above which you must have 5,1,2&3.

Position 10 is just inside a dashed blue line that represents the Purdue University airport's control tower airport.
Launch? No, unless you have permission. Have an aircraft radio but first call the control tower via telephone to explain your intentions. It's class D airspace.
Require: If you get permission, you must have 5,1,2&3.

> **Tip: Getting Permission**
>
> You can sometimes get permission to fly into control tower airports but only if the airport is reporting 3 miles visibility or more.

Chicagoland, IL

This chart excerpt (with ORD and MDW) is busier but follows all the same rules. The red areas were added to this chart for clarity to show surface area that is off-limits without permission. You can't climb up into the B airspace, either, and there are many congested areas to avoid. It is always far, far better to head out into the country to avoid potential conflict with people or other aircraft.

Position 1 is just outside the outer ring of ORD's class B airspace.
Launch? Yes, you're in G airspace with E airspace starting at 700 feet AGL. You can climb as high as you want legally. There is no shaded magenta line showing a transition from a 700 foot to a 1200 foot Class E floor. That's because the *entire area* has the Class E floor at 700 feet—common in heavily populated areas with a high concentration of airports.
Require: CoC&1 then 5,1,2&3 if you climb above 700 feet AGL..

Position 2 is just inside the outer ring of ORD class B airspace. The label to its right shows the B airspace "shelf" goes from 4000 feet to 10,000 feet MSL and we can't fly there between those altitudes.
Launch? Yes, you're in G airspace with E airspace starting at 700 feet.
Require: CoC&1 then 5,1,2&3 if you climb above 700 feet AGL.
Concerns: Aircraft funnel through this area so they don't have to talk to O'hare. Expect heavy air traffic above about 600 feet AGL.

Position 3 This is just inside ring 2 of ORD class B airspace. The label to its right shows the B airspace "shelf" goes from 3000 feet to 10,000 feet MSL and we can't fly there between those altitudes.
Launch? Yes, you're in G airspace with E airspace starting at 700 feet AGL.
Require: CoC&1 then 5,1,2&3 if you climb above 700 feet AGL.

Position 4: This magenta dashed line, just beyond ARR's Class D airspace, outlines an extension that takes class E airspace to the surface. The blue dashed line outlines Aurora's Class D airspace associated with their control tower.
Launch? No, unless you have permission from Aurora tower. The tower frequency is 120.6 (you can only see the 0.6 on the excerpt).
Require: If you get permission, you must have 5,1,2&3.

Chicagoland Excerpt

Airspace-wise, we can launch everywhere but the shaded red areas. Notice that airport symbols show the runway direction and relative length. That can help you know where to expect airplanes to fly when nearby.

Landing patterns have been drawn in at certain airports like Brookeridge, just southwest of position 7. It's good to know where aircraft patterns are.

Note that a pilot could fly along the lake shore (position 9) from the surface up to 3000 feet MSL and remain below ORD's class B airspace. Be careful of Temporary Flight Restrictions, though, some big cities have them around prominent buildings.

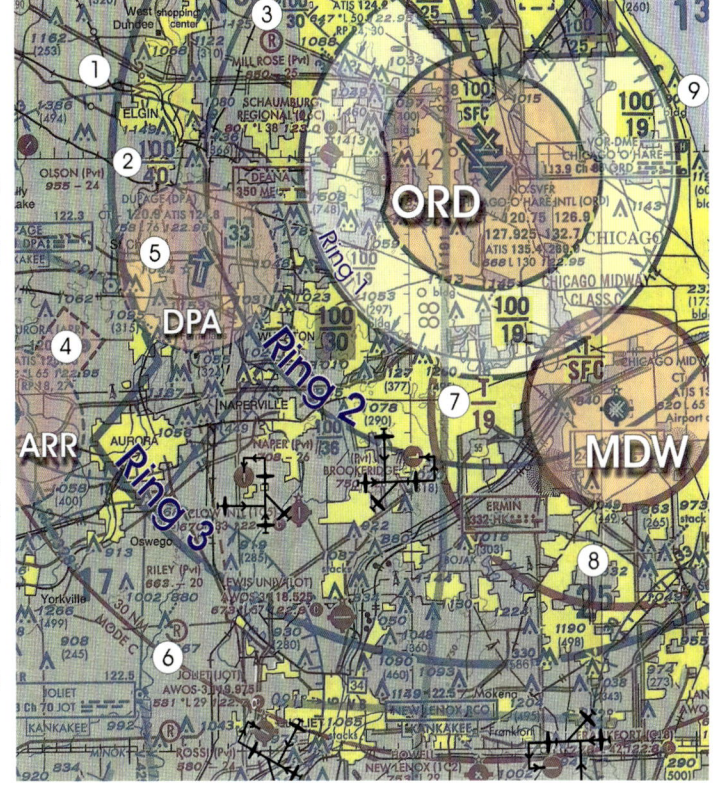

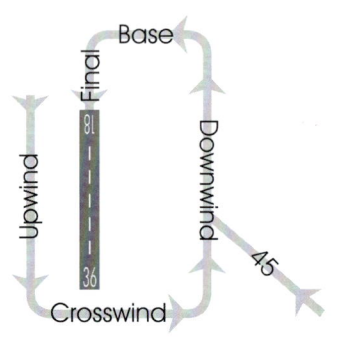

The PPG Bible: A Complete Guide and Reference

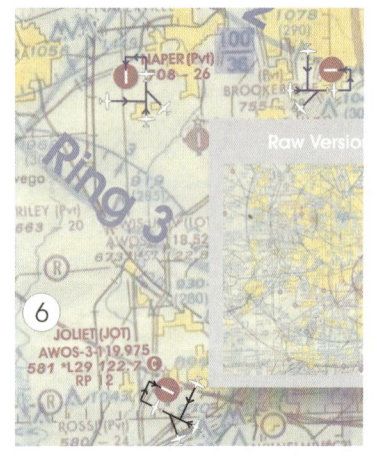

Position 5 is inside DPA's (DuPage) Class D airspace.
    Launch?   No, unless you have permission from DuPage tower. The tower frequency is 120.9 (that is on the airport information block above position 5.)
    Require: If you get permission, you must have 5,1,2&3.
    Notes: Airspace-wise you could fly above DPA's Class D (top at 3300 feet MSL) and below ORD's Class B (base at 4000 feet MSL) without talking to anybody. In the U.S., doing so would probably violate FAR 103.13(b) that forbids us from creating a "collision hazard with respect to any aircraft."

Position 6 is outside of the B airspace overlay and on the "Mode C" ring which doesn't apply to us. It is also just northeast of the Joliet VOR.
    Launch?   Yes, you're in G airspace with E airspace 700 feet above.
    Require: You must have CoC&1 then 5,1,2&3 if climbing above 700 feet AGL.
    Notes: Expect more airplane traffic related to the Joliet VOR above about 800 feet AGL. You can climb as high as you want but there will be Jet and other traffic shuttling into the side of both ORD and MDW's airspace.

Positions 7 & 8 are below MDW's C airspace which starts at 1900 feet MSL and goes up into the overlying ORD B airspace (that's why the "T" for Top instead of an altitude). Obviously most of this airspace is off-limits due to being congested.
    Launch?   Yes, you're in G airspace with E airspace 700 feet above.
    Require: You must have CoC&1 then 5,1,2&3 if climbing above 700 feet AGL.
    Notes: Expect high density airplane traffic to be skirting underneath and around MDW's airspace. This is a bad place to be more than about 500 hundred feet in a PPG. Helicopters are another threat and they operate close to our altitudes—they can be found cruising especially near the highways.

The Airspace Test

Think of this as a test. Look at the letters on the following pages and answer the questions yourself about launching from each point. What would you need to know and what are the concerns? To reduce page turning, the chart excerpts are split as PHX1 & PHX2.

First you have to know where you are on the chart. A GPS is great if you can translate the latitude and longitude (lat/long) coordinates. Sectional charts have lines of latitude (35° in the sample at left) and longitude (118°) clearly marked. The tick marks are *minutes* on lines of latitude and longitude. *Seconds* are 1/60th of a *minute*.

Point **A**: The 4₉ is a Maximum Elevation Figure (MEF) for that *quadrangle* (30 minutes of lat/long per side) meaning that the highest obstacle or terrain is 4900 feet MSL.
    Launch?   Yes, It's G airspace with E airspace 700 feet above. Requires CoC&1 then 5,1,2&3 if you climb above 700 feet AGL. Stay below the B airspace which starts at 6000 feet MSL.
    Notes: This launch site sits on a Victor Airway (V95) which is the 185° *radial* from PHX VOR. You can expect increased airplane traffic above about 800 feet AGL.

Point **B** is also below the B airspace. The floor of the "upside down wedding cake" (B-airspace) is 4000 feet MSL and it goes up to 10,000. Point B is just south of some high obstructions (top at 3047). Note that, except for MEF numbers, eleva-

---

It's easier to anticipate where planes will be flying if you can visualize this pattern. Overlay it on the chart as done below according to what pattern is being flown.

All patterns are to the left unless "RP" is listed by beside a runway number. At Joliet, for example, it says RP 12. That means a right pattern is used for runway 12 (depicted below).

North of Joliet, at Naper Aero, there is no such verbiage and so all patterns are to the left. If planes are landing on runway 18 (landing to the south), then expect them to be flying the depicted pattern (shown above).

The PPG Bible: A Complete Guide and Reference

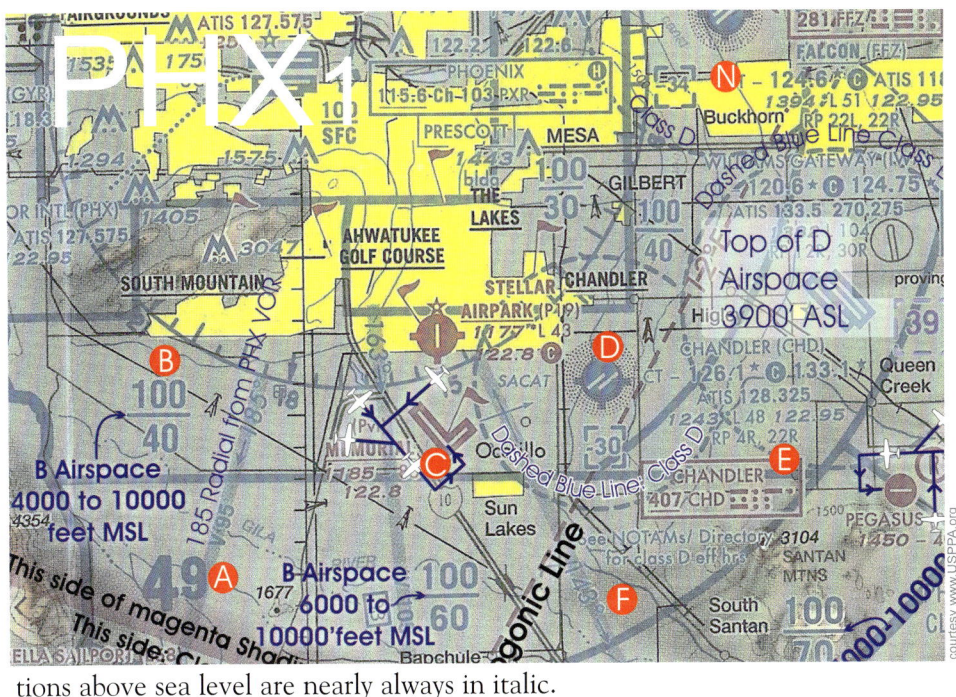

tions above sea level are nearly always in italic.

> Launch? Yes, It's G airspace with E airspace 700 feet above. Requires CoC&1 then 5,1,2&3 if you climb above 700 feet AGL. Stay below 4000 feet ASL (B airspace).
>
> Notes: It's just west of the airway V95 so again, be vigilant for airplane traffic above 800 feet AGL or so.
>
> The little magenta flag to the north (above South Mountain) means that it is a *reporting point* for aircraft flying into PHX. Although they may fly right over it, more often they'll just report their position referencing it such as "2 miles west of South Mountain," but do watch for traffic near these.

Point C: You can launch from here, it's got the same airspace situation as A and B but has an airport (Memorial) just northeast of it. You'll want to be familiar with that airport's traffic patterns to stay out the way and know where to look for airplanes. The depicted pattern, added for clarity, applies if airplanes are landing to the northwest. Since there's no "RP" in the airport information text, expect lefthand traffic patterns on runway 30 (headed 300° magnetic).

> Launch? Yes, It's G airspace with E airspace 700 feet above. Requires CoC&1 then 5,1,2&3 above 700 feet AGL. Stay below 4000 feet MSL to stay below Phoenix's B airspace.
>
> Notes: If you fly just a mile south, notice the B airspace floor goes up to 6000 feet MSL. If you have a hand-held aircraft radio, aircraft will be communicating on *122.8* Mhz as shown on the Memorial airport information text.

Point D is a control tower field, Chandler (CHD), with surrounding Class D airspace up to 3000 feet MSL—the last two 0's are dropped from the 3000.

> Launch? No, unless you have permission from Chandler tower. If you do get that permission, you'll need 5,1,2&3 and must stay below 4000 feet MSL to avoid the B airspace.

Point E: This line is the edge of Williams Gateway's Class D airspace. South of it you can launch without talking to anybody but if you want to fly north, you'll need permission. The magenta box with **407 CHD** is a navigation station that we

Tip: Quick Weather

Some airports have Automatic Weather Observation Systems (AWOS) that broadcast their current weather continuously on the listed frequency. Tune your aviation radio or scanner to the AWOS frequency listed on the chart. For example, at Joliet (spot 6 on the Chicagoland excerpt), the AWOS is on 119.975.

They also usually have a telephone number where you can call and get their weather recording. Call the regular airport phone number to get its weather number.

Chapter 9: Airspace *Page 93*

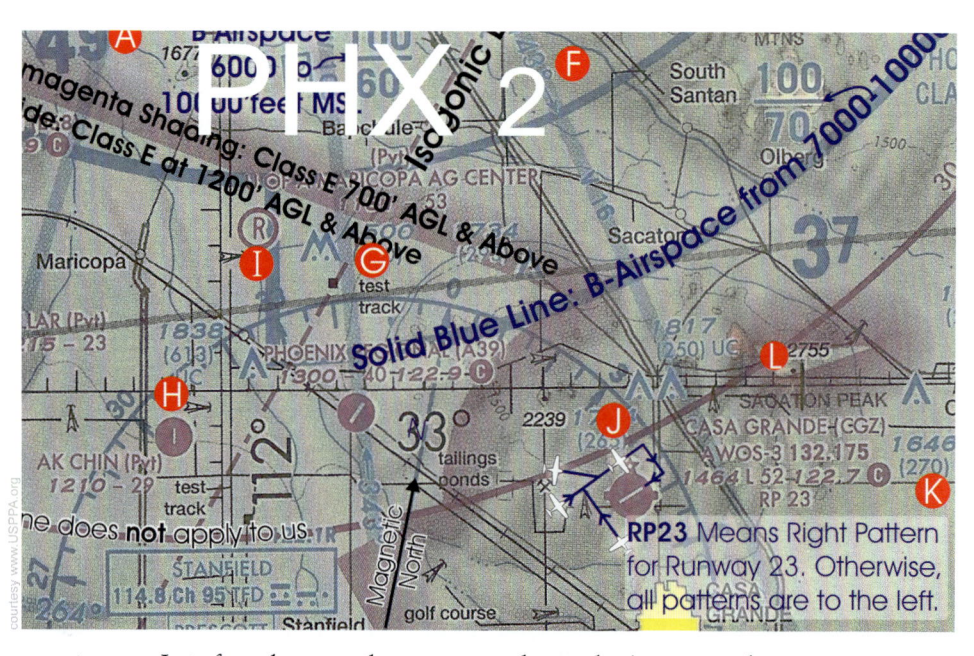

can ignore. It is for a beacon that even airplanes don't use much anymore.

    Launch?   Yes, if you are south of the dashed line which is G airspace with E airspace 700 feet above. Requires CoC&1 then 5,1,2&3 above 700 feet AGL.

Point F: This is well below the B airspace floor of 6000 feet MSL.

    Launch?   Yes, It's G airspace with E airspace 700 feet above. Requires CoC&1 then 5,1,2&3 above 700 feet AGL.

    Notes: The dashed magenta line to the left (running northeast to southwest) is an *isogonic* line showing there is 12° (the 12 is on PHX1) East variation between True North and Magnetic North (see Chapter 13). So if you are pointing True North, your compass will read 348°.

        There's a Victor Airway (V16) that goes out the 143° radial from PHX VOR so you should expect heavier aircraft traffic above about 800 feet AGL.

Point G (reference PHX2) is well below the PHX B airspace who's floor is 7000 feet MSL here.

    Launch?   Yes, It's G airspace with E airspace above 1200 feet. Requires CoC&1 then 5,1,2&3 above 1200 feet AGL.

    Notes: It's just east of an airway (V105) so expect more airplane traffic transiting the Stanfield VOR to the South. Airways present no restriction to us.

Point H: This little private airport, Ak Chin, has a paved runway, as indicated by the runway depiction, and might be a good site. It's elevation is *1210* feet MSL and the runway is 2900 feet long. Patterns would be left since there's no "RP" mentioned for any runway.

    Launch?   Yes, It's G airspace with E airspace 1200 feet above. Requires CoC&1 then 5,1,2&3 if you climb above 1200 feet AGL. You can climb as high as you want (up to 18,000 feet anyway).

    Notes: If you have an aircraft radio, the airplanes will be using 122.9 Mhz to announce their position; that is the standard frequency for fields where no frequency is listed.

        A few miles to the east is a high tower. The heights are shown just above the letter H. *1838* is the MSL elevation and (613) is its height above the ground. Expect some healthy guy wires spilling from its top.

South Mountain (Point A) is a high point just south of Phoenix. Being festooned with towers makes it a great landmark and check on altitude. The chart shows the towers to be 3047 MSL and 387' AGL. You can set your altimeter to that.

Point **I**: This grass or gravel strip (as indicated by the open circle) is private but might be a good place to ask for permission.

    Launch?   Yes, It's G airspace with E airspace 1200 feet above. Requires CoC&1 then 5,1,2&3 if you climb above 1200 feet AGL.

    Notes: If you have an aircraft radio, the airplanes will be using 22.9 Mhz.

Point **J** is only a couple miles north of Casa Grande airport and warrants close attention to their airport pattern which is depicted for clarity (only runway 23).

    Launch?   Yes, It's G airspace with E airspace 700 feet above. Requires CoC&1 then 5,1,2&3 if you climb above 700 feet AGL.

    Notes: Notice the RP23 under Casa Grande's airport data block. That means that airplanes using runway 23 will be making right turns (shown) instead of the standard left turns. Stay well away from the pattern, especially the departure/arrival corridors. Typical aircraft pattern altitudes range from 800 to 1500 feet (lower for helicopters). The airport is at *1464* feet MSL (call it 500) so you would expect the pattern to be from 1300 to 2000 feet MSL.

There's a tower just to the northeast (obscured a bit by the J) that tops out at *1794* MSL which is 265 feet tall.

Point **K**: This is an open area well clear of any airspace issues.

    Launch?   Yes, It's G airspace with E airspace 700 feet above. Requires CoC&1 then 5,1,2&3 if you climb above 700 feet AGL..

    Notes: If you fly towards Casa Grande and have an aircraft radio, the airplanes will be using Unicom on 122.7 Mhz and you can listen to their recorded *Automated Weather Observation System* (AWOS) on 132.175 Mhz.

Point **L**: This little sliver of airspace is different from Point J in that the floor of E airspace is 1200 feet. Owing to the vagaries of how transition areas (where the E floor lowers to 700 feet) are created, this area allows you to climb up to 1200 feet with only a mile visibility.

    Launch?   Yes, It's G airspace with E airspace 1200 feet above. Requires CoC&1 then 5,1,2&3 if you climb above 1200 feet AGL.

    Notes: The little mountains that stick up around there reach 2755 feet MSL just to the southeast.

Point **N**: (reference PHX1) This is within the D Airspace surrounding a control towered airport.

    Launch?   No, unless you have permission. The airport info is not shown (it's off the excerpt). If you get permission, you'll need 5,1,2&3.

    Notes: The yellow area roughly equates to what light patterns pilots would see at night. They do *not* denote "congested area" although they probably are.

Always have fresh charts. The previous version of this one had Casa Grande as a non-paved airport. Plus, occasionally control towers are added with their surrounding D airspace—you do *not* want to go blundering into someone's newly minted controlled airspace.

An interesting aside: some charted features can be quite inconspicuous. Note the mine symbol just west of Casa Grande airport. It doesn't look like much on the chart, but the bottom picture reveals how "grande" it really is. Besides mountains, this abandoned copper mine is the most prominent landmark within 20 miles.

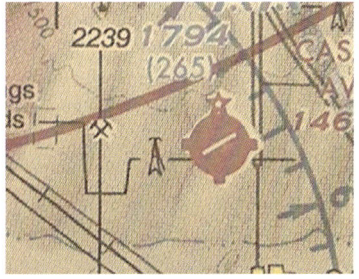

Other Uses for the charts

What's available on the internet now eclipses what these charts present, but paper versions are still handier in most situations. And they're a lot easier to carry. Online versions may be more current.

Topographical

One of the more useful elements is elevation. Not only do airports list elevation, but so do obstructions. Each tower gives the MSL top but also frequently the AGL height. Subtract the two for ground elevation. You can set your altimeter to that.

1. Josh Bernstein took a break from his History Channel show to learn powered paragliding. He is captured here flying above the Phoenix Regional Airport. At the time, this airport was very welcoming of PPG pilots.

It always pays to ask and then follow the rules. Although we may not need airports to launch, they are painlessly easy to find and usually offer plentiful wide open space. Pay particular attention to traffic patterns though, airplane pilots and airport managers are not very forgiving of ignorance.

2. Most chart questions can be answered using the legend that comes with it. About a third of the information is not very useful to us but that still leaves a lot of value.

The Terminal Area Chart legend for Phoenix is shown below. It is more detailed than the more-common Sectional Chart which covers a far wider area.

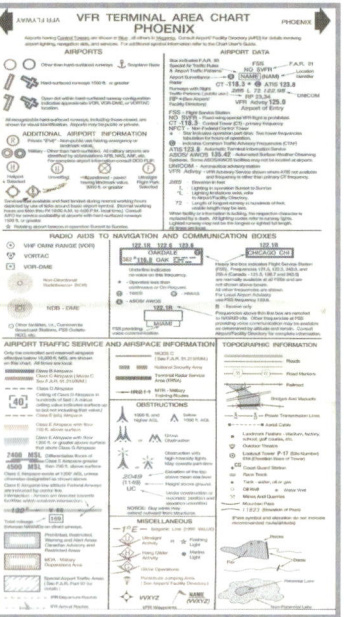

Contours give elevations in 500 foot (sometimes 250) increments—not terribly precise but good for general knowledge. You can generally estimate your height visually to within a couple hundred feet. Of course if you used the GPS to locate yourself on the chart then it will undoubtedly also give your altitude within a few feet.

Finding Sites

Ultralight strips and soaring sites that might be friendly to our operations are frequently listed on charts. Some private airports will allow us to fly there so it may be worth asking, especially if sites are scarce. Sky diving airports are usually pretty welcoming too; they're already used to seeing canopies although they're not so used to them going back up. Sky diving airports are marked by a little parachute symbol. On the chart, sailplane operations show a sailplane symbol with a G and hang glider sites show the sailplane with an H. Sorry, there's no symbol for paragliders.

Things Look Different Out West

Charts are colored by elevation which accounts for the browns. It's also far less populated so vast areas have the E airspace floor at 1200 feet AGL and some areas have *no* overlying E airspace. For example, west of spot J the floor of E airspace is 1200 feet AGL while East of spot J there is no E airspace. Spot K has the E airspace floor at 1200 feet AGL, Spot L has no overlying E airspace.

Here are some highlights on the listed spots.

Spot 1 is in G airspace with E at 1200 feet AGL. That's a pretty healthy ridge, be careful in any significant wind. Spot 2 is in G airspace and just below a gliderport (the airport). You could launch there if they let you. Spot 3 is pointing to an "airway" where airplanes are likely to be flying. Spot 4 is in G airspace with E starting 1200 feet above.

Spot 5 is the D airspace around Jackson Hole airport. You need permission from the control tower to fly in there. Spot 6 is inside the dashed blue lines that outline the D. The several spot 7's point to where the Class E floor goes from 700 feet AGL inside, to 1200 feet AGL outside the line.

Spot 8 points to a nature preserve of some sorts where you must stay above 2000 feet AGL while inside the area. Spot 9 is the DNW VOR, a navigational station used by airplanes.

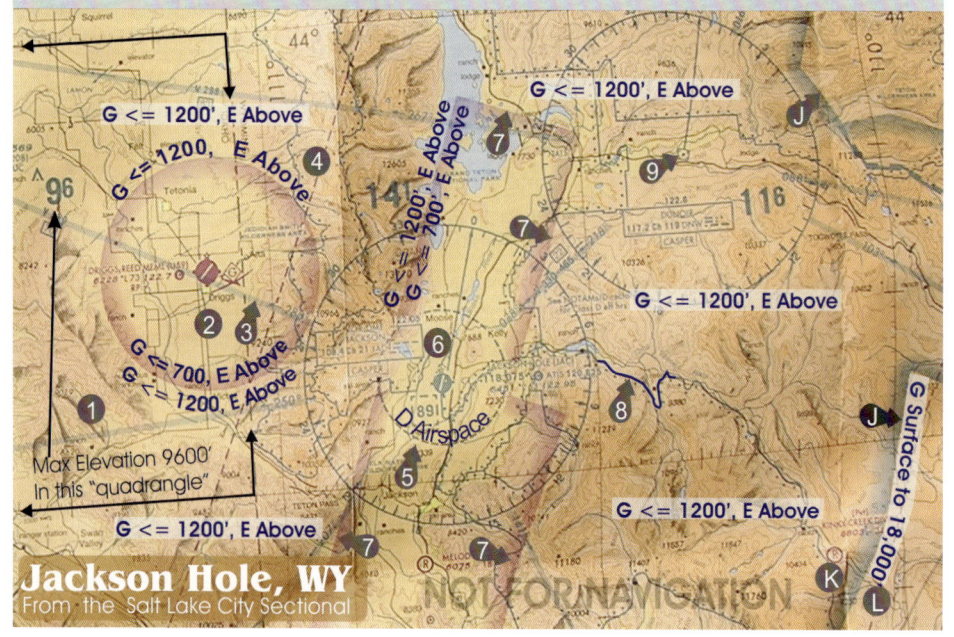

Flying From Anywhere

CHAPTER 10

What a treat—running aloft from the most unlikely places and taking reality for a ride that rivals our imagination. Launching from such places is one of our sport's greatest appeals as well as its greatest challenges.

Choosing a suitable launch site is crucial to safety and success; heeding a few basic rules can prevent catastrophe whether the site is a wide-open prairie airport or a tight little mountain clearing.

Being *able* to launch from anywhere doesn't mean that you *should*. Both safety and permission can be show stoppers. There's nothing worse than being all fired up, standing there with idling motor and wing laid out behind, only to have someone come put the kibosh on it. Searching out that perfect launch area is both a joy and a curse; in a country brimming with great sites, permission to use them can be elusive.

Any prospective site must first be in legal airspace, and second, must match your skill level. Additionally it should not require trampling through crops, climbing fences or going beyond any "No Trespassing" signs. Public property, such as state or federal lands, frequently prohibit any kind of flying. Parks are notoriously difficult because they usually have specific prohibitions plus the staff to enforce them. Flying from most state or national parks is illegal.

The need to always have an emergency landing site puts many forested areas out of reach; same with swamps. Even in these areas, though, if you can find a sufficient clearing to launch from, it is fun to just climb up high over the landing zone (LZ) and check things out. Many otherwise boring views sprawl into gorgeous panoramas with a bit of altitude.

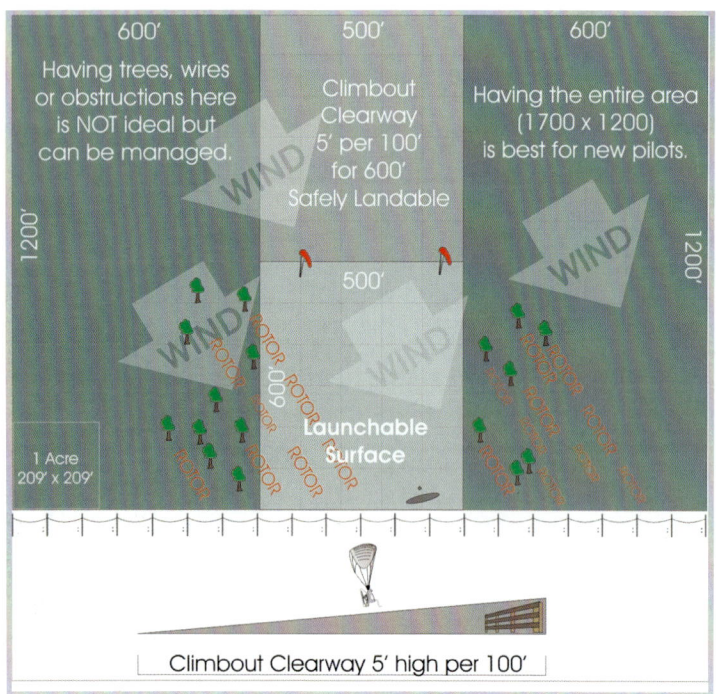

Figure labels (left diagram):
- 600' Having trees, wires or obstructions here is NOT ideal but can be managed.
- 500' Climbout Clearway 5' per 100' for 600' Safely Landable
- 600' Having the entire area (1700 x 1200) is best for new pilots.
- 1200'
- 1 Acre 209' x 209'
- Launchable Surface
- Climbout Clearway 5' high per 100'

Caption (left): Choose a launch site with plenty of room that is appropriate for your skill level. Small sites have been the downfall of those who pushed it. Know your limits by measuring your regular field and comparing any new locations to that. Pacing the edges works well enough.

Caption (lower left): It looked good from the road but didn't measure up. The pilot nearly impaled himself on a fence post trying to launch from here. Pace off potential sites and be conservative about launch distance estimates.

Choosing the site

Size Matters

Bigger is always better. Depending on your skills and the conditions, a congested site with trees or wires can be deadly. Your early unsupervised flights require more space. For one thing, you probably have little experience telling field size, knowing climb angle etc. Another factor that determines whether a field is acceptable is your climb technique; a relatively new pilot should make sure the field allows a straight-out climb (requires no turns.)

The sizes shown at left seem large but, when launching in still air, distance goes by quickly. Don't launch anywhere that *requires* turning below 100 feet above ground level (AGL). Past incidents have shown that new pilots need more time after launch to get their bearings.

Don't be fooled by training experience where you got airborne in a hundred feet—launch distances can double or triple under hot, high or calm conditions and it's easy to underestimate distance requirements.

One way to size up a field is to pace it off. Find your stride's length by walking a known distance such as a measured 10 yards then figure whether you step longer then a yard or shorter. Adjust from that.

Avoid the temptation to merely guess at a site's appropriateness when obstructions are involved. Wires, trees and buildings have all proven terribly unforgiving and the distance from them is hard to judge. Pace it off when in doubt.

A small field is OK providing the obstructions would let you plow through them harmlessly if things go awry (beans, wheat, tall grass, etc.) As experience gives you solid directional control during the run and after liftoff, then you can decrease the field size, especially the width (always minding mechanical turbulence, mentioned below).

A skilled pilot can launch in any spot long enough to get airborne and circle over. The most important requirement is that it be big enough to allow recovery from a motor failure at any point. Be aware, though, that wind can make a small, obstructed site dangerous at *any* skill level.

Mechanical Turbulence and Obstructions

Whenever wind blows by an obstruction it disturbs the downwind air flow, creating various forms of *mechanical turbulence* (covered in Chapter 7).

Some locations work well for certain wind directions only. For example, a big turbulence-causing building to the west is no problem in an easterly breeze (the wind is coming *from* the east). A light wind (less then 5 mph) makes minimal mechanical turbulence; it will be present but should be manageable. Look out, though, if the wind picks up—that light breeze at sunrise can turn nasty a couple hours later. Look at the forecasted wind direction and speed when considering a site.

In a 10 mph wind the turbulence will extend many times the obstruction's height, and it gets worse as wind increases. Be very leery of tall obstructions in moderately strong winds.

Mechanical turbulence can cause large collapses or altitude loss at the worst possible time (when you're down low). Wind shadow, the calm area just behind an obstruction, must also be avoided.

Slope And Surface

Launching downhill is always best for two reasons: (1) you can run faster and (2) the downhill component means the wing is already trying to lift you that much more while you're running. Landing downhill, however, can be a challenge as it seems you glide forever.

Landing uphill is dangerous; it can result in very hard landings due to both the slope and sinking air. If the wind is coming down the hill, it may be better to land crosshill (and crosswind) to avoid flying into rising terrain.

Smooth surfaces are far better than rough ones. In fact, tall grass, soft sand, or a rutted surface can add so much leg drag (see Chapter 17) as to prevent a launch. They also make it far more likely that you will trip and fall.

Site Permission

"It's better to beg forgiveness then to ask for permission" is a well worn statement that can get us in trouble. Permission is always preferable! Even if you *think* a particular site is OK, at least mind these guidelines:

- Never climb a fence or cross a "No Trespassing" sign to get there. In some places doing so could get you shot.

- Never do any property damage in your effort to get to the site or while preparing. This is especially true for crops—destroying crops in your search for pleasure doesn't sit well with either the owner or his brother, the Sheriff.

- Never set up where somebody lives or has a presence. If there is somebody to ask, you must do so even at the risk of refusal.

- Never use a park or other facility where known rules prohibit flying. Almost all state and federal parks prohibit launching aircraft and ultralights except at airports. You can probably use the airport. Be mindful that many parks have a minimum altitude to fly over. Don't quibble over who controls the airspace, they'll get you for disturbing the animals if they want you.

- Avoid lingering. Launch then fly off so as to avoid attention from the surrounding communities or neighbors.

High Elevation Fields

At higher elevations you'll need larger launch areas and better climbout options. More power and a bigger wing may be necessary to let you launch *at all*. Smaller or faster wings may require so much groundspeed (to get the necessary airspeed) that they exceed your ability to run, even with full thrust.

Chapter 17 offers details on procedures and techniques to improve your success

Surfaces can be deceiving. It's beneficial to do a test run without your motor on. Make sure there is traction and that no surprises lurk just under the top layer. This type of surface can hide quick sand (that a big deal unless you're trying to launch).

rate. Make sure your site has an "out" that allows for an unexpectedly shallow climb over a route with neither obstructions nor hills. The worst case is having to climb over something; this is always a bad practice, but at higher elevations, is particularly dangerous. At least one climbout route must allow clawing your way to a safe altitude without having to traverse any obstructions, especially wires.

Unless there is some wind, the launch surface will need to be smooth. Ruts or tall growth can easily keep you from generating the requisite speed. Roads out in the boondocks are good as long they have no power lines. Beware of barbed wire fences which do surprising canopy damage. And don't park your car *on* the road.

Flying At or Near Airports

Uncontrolled airports (no control tower) can provide a perfect PPG playground. Unfortunately, getting permission to use them can be tough. Airports with control towers are usually too busy but *can* be used with the right equipment (see chapter 11).

General aviation (non-airline) un-controlled airports normally sit in G airspace with E airspace 700' above. Functionally that means you only need 1mile visibility to launch and must stay clear of clouds, with stricter requirements above that.

A popular misconception is that airports accepting federal funds have to let us use them. Unfortunately, that is not entirely true. They can, and frequently do, restrict or prohibit us based on perceived incompatibilities with other traffic. They can also impede access so much as to make it impractical for us.

Many licensed pilots and airport managers are quick to condemn any mixing with us; that's unfortunate since a knowledgeable, conscientious PPG pilot adds less

It doesn't look like much but this dirt road got us airborne. We planned it so as to turn well before the highway. This entire area is landable leaving plentiful engine-out options.

Obviously roads must be nearly abandoned, have no wires and the pilot capable of steering during his run. That is an advanced skill that is well worth mastering.

> **Right of Way**
>
> Remember, we've got to stay out of *their* way. It's quite clear (in the U.S.):
> FAR 103.13 Operation near aircraft; right-of-way rules.
> (a) Each person operating an ultralight vehicle shall maintain vigilance so as to see and avoid aircraft and shall yield the right-of-way to all aircraft.
> (b) No person may operate an ultralight vehicle in a manner that creates a collision hazard with respect to any aircraft.
>
> That essentially means that we have to avoid putting ourselves in areas with heavy concentrations of airplanes in a way that could interfere. Airports are obviously the most common but most major cities also have jet routes published on charts. These must be avoided too. Fortunately they're high up, almost always 3000 feet or above. Check with local pilots in your area.

risk than another general aviation airplane. Another reason for the occasional cold-shoulder (and probably a big one) is our lack of contribution. Airplanes based at the airport pay rent, buy fuel, charts, and other services; we generally don't.

It is simple for us to have little or no impact on airport operations, but we must work with management and other users. If possible, explain our capabilities (to those willing to listen) then follow through with consistently responsible flying. Launch away from airplane traffic and remain clear of their patterns.

The onus is on us to avoid becoming a collision hazard. Beyond complying with air regulations and local rules, we must not annoy people, create a hazard or even have the appearance of such.

If planning regular operations from an airport, contact the airport manager and find out the best places to operate. Explain how you plan to avoid conflicts with existing users. Ask what areas to avoid flying over. This will also reveal local requirements, noise sensitive areas and other location-specific needs.

About Runways & Patterns

You must know where the airplanes fly in order to avoid them. Fortunately their patterns are fairly well defined although they don't always follow them.

Understand runway numbers—they indicate the magnetic direction of aircraft taking off or landing with the ending "0" removed. So north is 0 or 360 (runway 36), east is 090 (runway 9), south is 180 (runway 18) and west is 270 (runway 27). So if the runway was aligned east/west then the *approach* end of the runway for aircraft landing west (270°) would be 27 whereas a pilot taking off or landing in the other direction (to the east) would be using runway 9.

Airplanes are flown from the left side and so standard traffic patterns for all runways are "left"—all turns are made to the left until final approach. Runway 27 in the diagram uses a left pattern. Runway 9, however, uses a right pattern.

Sometimes airport operators want certain runways to use a right pattern to keep noise away from a sensitive areas (called noise abatement). They may indicate pattern direction using a large, highly visible segmented circle near the runway complex. It has little "L"s oriented to the runways they depict. The short part of the leg represents the base leg and the long part of the L represents final approach to the runway. Looking at the letter L on a page would mean right traffic for runway 36

It's best to remain well clear of aircraft patterns. But with concurrence of the airport operator, there are ways to safely co-exist.

One technique for crossing runways is to fly over the middle of the runway, maybe slightly closer to the beginning, at around 400' AGL The PPG is depicted below doing just that: he takes off into the wind then gains 400 feet in a left turn before heading across the runway.

To keep your welcome open, make sure the airport management approves of your plans. Otherwise, don't cross any runways at all—go around the ends, down low and at least a mile away.

On a standard glide slope, airplanes will be approximately 300 feet high for every mile away from the runway. Some airport managements ask us to be *above* pattern altitude before crossing the runways.

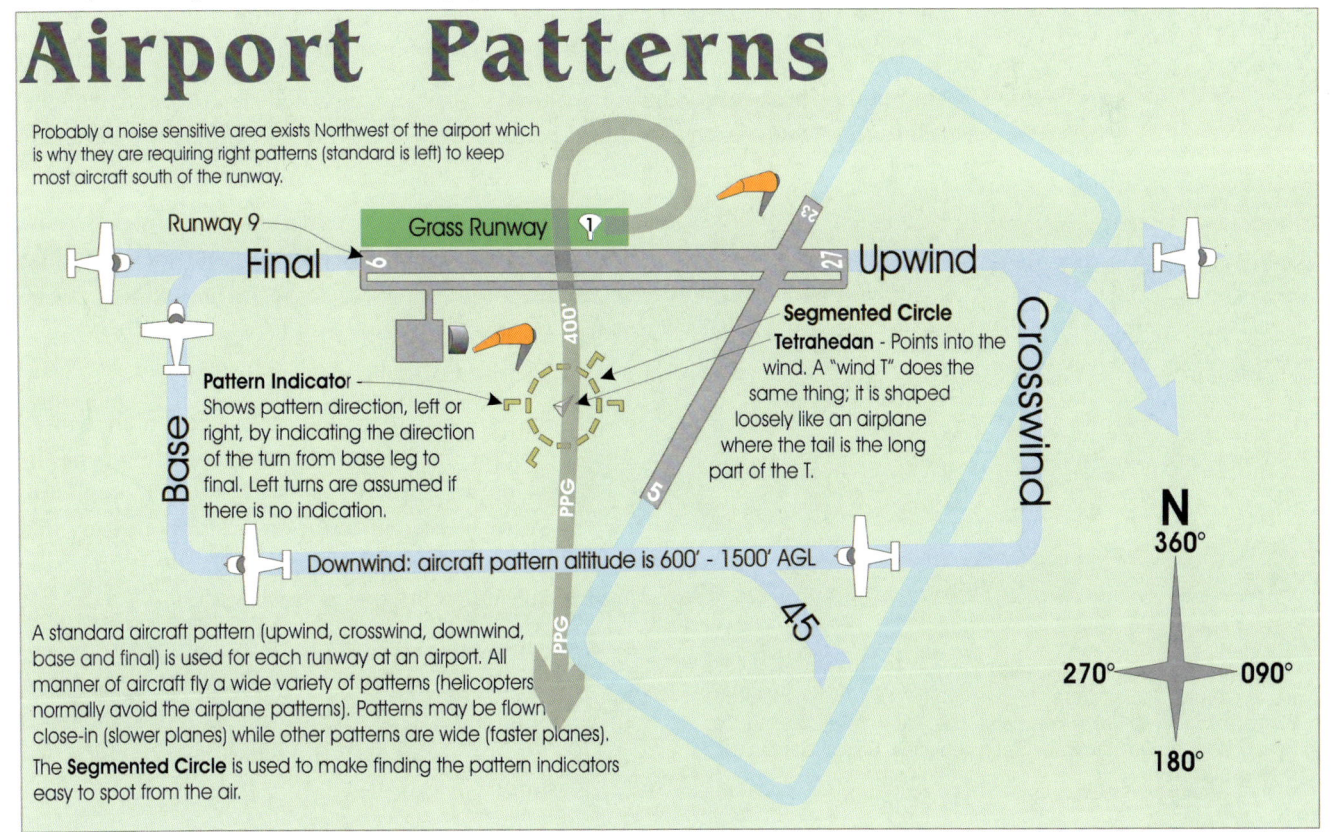

Airport Patterns

Probably a noise sensitive area exists Northwest of the airport which is why they are requiring right patterns (standard is left) to keep most aircraft south of the runway.

Runway 9 — Grass Runway
Final — Upwind

Segmented Circle
Tetrahedan - Points into the wind. A "wind T" does the same thing; it is shaped loosely like an airplane where the tail is the long part of the T.

Pattern Indicator - Shows pattern direction, left or right, by indicating the direction of the turn from base leg to final. Left turns are assumed if there is no indication.

Base — Crosswind

Downwind: aircraft pattern altitude is 600' - 1500' AGL

A standard aircraft pattern (upwind, crosswind, downwind, base and final) is used for each runway at an airport. All manner of aircraft fly a wide variety of patterns (helicopters normally avoid the airplane patterns). Patterns may be flown close-in (slower planes) while other patterns are wide (faster planes).
The **Segmented Circle** is used to make finding the pattern indicators easy to spot from the air.

N 360°
270° — 090°
180°

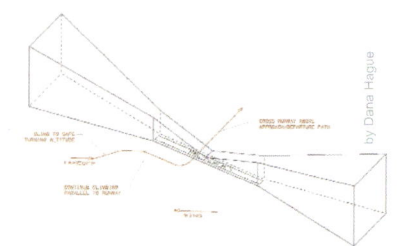

This depicts the typical corridors flown by aircraft as they arrive and depart runway surfaces. It is our job to avoid them.

(top of the page is north or 360°). You fly the base leg then turn right (the long vertical part) to join final. The segmented circle quickly shows what pattern direction is appropriate for each runway. If no indicator is present, airplane traffic is supposed to use left patterns.

Normal pattern altitude for airplanes ranges from 600 to 1500 feet AGL depending on aircraft type; jets and larger twins use the higher altitudes. The pattern size varies greatly based mostly on aircraft speed—faster aircraft typically fly larger, higher patterns. Jets may fly downwind leg over a mile away from the runway while slower aircraft may fly it less than a quarter mile away and other ultralights even closer. PPG patterns will be the closest to the runway (around 400 feet away and around 300-400 feet high).

Airport Status

You must know the airport's status—whether portions are closed, special operations are going on or there are any other unique situations. Ask the airport manager if there is anything you should be aware of. If that's not possible, call Flight Service (See Chapter 7). Tell them your name, that you will be flying an ultralight at airport such-and-such, and that you would like the NOTAMS.

Airplane pilots normally choose the runway based on wind but not always. Sometimes they'll do a long, straight-in final approach to a different runway even if it has a tailwind (for convenience). PPGers must be on the lookout for this—5 knots of tailwind isn't that big a deal to an airplane.

How to Mesh

Now that you have the airport information and know where the patterns are, it is fairly easy to stay out of the way. And indeed the most important practice is avoiding places where aircraft are likely to be. Fortunately that is pretty easy.

Your launch area should be away from the runways and their departure/arrival corridors. Your flight path should be planned so as to avoid runways, their extended centerlines, and any buildings.

Be vigilant to avoid noise sensitive areas: if the airport management gets noise complaints caused by you, your welcome may be brief. Staying clear of congested areas (required anyway) will frequently suffice.

Wake Turbulence

All aircraft produce wake turbulence (see chapter 22) but it can be severe when generated by an airplane. Slow-flying helicopters are worse. A helicopter in cruise is about the same as an airplane, but when slowed down, its wake turbulence increases significantly.

Always plan your flight path to be above or well beside an airplane or helicopter flight path. Remember that the turbulence sinks, spreads out and drifts with the wind, lasting up to two minutes.

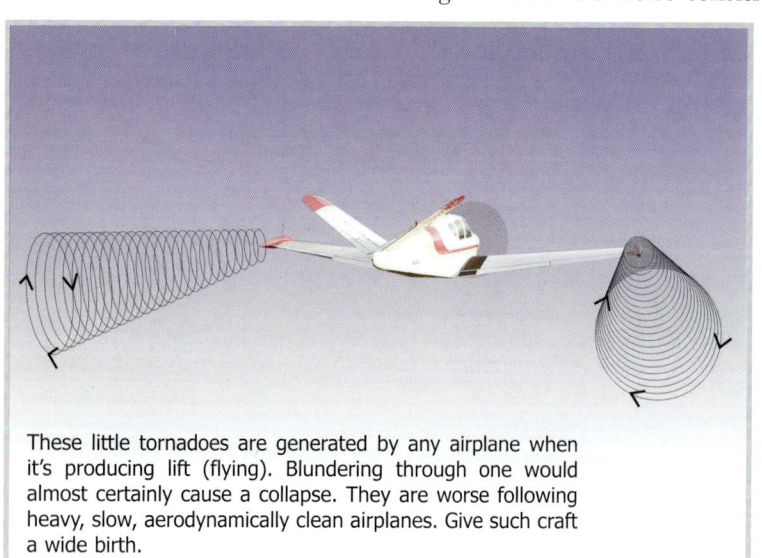

These little tornadoes are generated by any airplane when it's producing lift (flying). Blundering through one would almost certainly cause a collapse. They are worse following heavy, slow, aerodynamically clean airplanes. Give such craft a wide birth.

After Takeoff

When leaving the airport it is best to stay well below the aircraft traffic patterns; probably 400 ft. AGL or less (keep a safe landing option, though). If overflying a runway is absolutely necessary, go over the center, slightly closer to the beginning, at 400 ft. AGL. There is less likelihood an airplane will be flying there.

If climbout near the airport is necessary, climbout on the opposite side of any pattern in use. Note that some airplanes will overfly the airport at 500 feet above traffic pattern altitude to check things out before landing (a fairly common practice).

See and Be Seen

If you see an airplane that you suspect does not see you, *turn*. Not only will the motion make you more visible, but the changing aspect on the PPG wing will help as well.

The other obvious need is to keep a look out for others, especially when you're flying up where other air traffic may be. We have the best view in the world with nothing but a pair of risers between us and the visible planet—use it.

Be Heard

Aviation radios that can transmit and receive on the airport's frequency (called Unicom) are beneficial. Even a receive-only radio helps—you can hear where other radio-using traffic is. The airport frequency is found on air charts.

Keep any talk to a minimum but be listening for other traffic. When you're ready to go (if able to transmit), announce "Powered Paraglider launching from xyz and will be departing to the (state direction)."

Represent Us Well

We are the sport's ambassadors and, in the environment of an airport, a conscientious appearance does double duty. Our future access and acceptability will be based on our behavior. So, above all: be polite, don't annoy anybody, fly quiet and, by all means, fly safely.

While it's great that we can launch from so many places, always consider "what if." Besides the obvious engine-out plan, try to account for wind forecasts or trends. Launch sites that require an upslope wind, for example, may not allow a return if the wind shifts.

This site would is only feasible in a wind coming from the pilot's right.

Places to Look

It's strange that you sometimes have to go near cities to find launch sites. We don't want to be in the city, but near its perimeter. Humanity is always building things, which is good since they tend to clear the land before building on it. Many industrial areas have a long way to go before build-out and, in the meantime, tend to keep it nicely mowed for potential customers. This can be perfect for us!

Private farms with a co-located home can be good too. They frequently have nice, launchable grass areas and agreeable owners.

Safe Havens

One beauty of our sport's uniqueness is that its easy to make friends with others of like mind. The best places to fly are those already pioneered by a local pilot—somewhere that pilots commonly fly. Most PPG schools that their own have sites will let others fly there providing they respect the site and its surroundings. Some schools appropriately require a membership if you were not trained there.

Almost any site where pilots fly regularly has rules which, among other things, help keep their neighbors happy. Follow them closely or expect a brief welcome followed by a long unwelcome.

Telling Wind Direction From Flight Path

If you choose to alight somewhere that has no wind indicators, you'll need to know wind direction. Chapter 7 has tips on using ground features but, in the absence of those, here is one method to use while you're aloft. Descend to about 200 feet and do a slow 360° turn while watching the ground (or look at your GPS groundspeed). When you're moving the slowest over the ground, you're going directly into the wind. If there's much wind at all, you'll notice drift. If you're drifting left, the wind is from your right—turn into it until the drift stops and that's the wind direction.

The wind at the surface could possibly be completely different but this is a good start. In thermally conditions, of course, expect it to be variable and turbulent.

The owner of this palatial launch site discovered powered paragliding and shares it with friends. He keeps that lawn clear so that foot drags are possible for nearly the entire perimeter. Find out where the locals fly and respect their sites by adhering to any special requirements.

I've flown some unlikely lawns—you just never know until you ask.

Flying From Controlled Airports

CHAPTER 11

There are ultralight clubs that fly from controlled airports and their craft mix splendidly with others. Foot launching adds further challenge but can certainly be done with the same safety.

As learned in Chapter 9, airports with control towers have class D airspace around them and are off-limits without permission from the air traffic control (ATC). It's not hard to get that approval but generally it is easier if you have an aircraft radio; some control tower airports may require it.

See Chapter 10 for general information on flying from airports.

Telephone

If your launch site is within class D airspace, but not on the airport, you may be able to get permission via telephone. Even if you plan on using an aircraft radio, phoning first allows you to clearly explain your plans and accommodate any special needs they (ATC) may have. Explain what you are flying and what you want to do.

First, figure out where you'll launch relative to the airport. Get the sectional chart and plot it out as a bearing from and distance in nautical miles. If there is a VOR (see Chapter 9) nearby, you can plot it out as a radial and distance from the VOR. Make sure you have an idea what the airport's elevation is and where the runways are (available on the sectional chart). They will obviously not let you get in anybody's way. Also, come up with a route that will let you quickly (as much as we can do "quickly") exit and re-enter their airspace.

In the U.S. you can look up the tower's number under Government, Department

---

During my first summer of PPG there was no satiating the desire to take it new places and old. After years of arriving on these long concrete ribbons with a 150+ mph chirp, it was mesmerizing to now alight on one with my feet. Better yet was running down the first stripe and back into the air.

I had called the tower via telephone prior to the flight so they would know what to expect. That was exceedingly helpful. Of course I took my camera because it just seemed so unnatural.

The PPG Bible: A Complete Guide and Reference

of Transportation, FAA Control tower. They are not always listed, in which case you can call Flight Service (800 WX-BRIEF) to get the number.

Call and ask for the *Tower Chief*—if unable to reach the chief, you may be out of luck. Explain that you:

1. Would like to launch your "ultralight, a powered paraglider" (that may take some explanation) from location x. Provide your direction and distance such as 3 nautical miles (nm) northeast of the airport. 1 nm = 1.15 statute miles.

2. Will stay below 500 feet AGL (or some acceptable altitude) as you exit or enter their class D airspace.

3. Do or do not you have an aircraft transceiver.

4. Will be flying between certain times.

Ask if that would be OK and if they have any specially requests. This is one time where permission is *much* better than forgiveness!

If you do have a radio then find out what the tower frequency is (it's on the chart). If the airport has radar service they will likely still want you on the tower frequency, but ask to be sure.

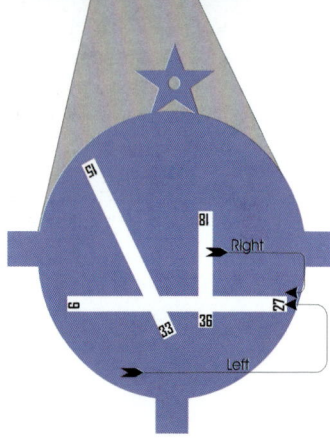

Aircraft Radio

If you fly from the towered field itself then you will probably have to have an aircraft radio. These hand-held transceivers can be had for a little more then the cost of a top-line helmet but must be used with a special headset. Most helmets don't work with aviation radios although some can be modified to do so. You may be able to make inexpensive helmets work with aviation headsets by carving out a line of foam under the helmet's shell.

Flying into a controlled field safely requires a working knowledge of runways, how they're numbered and traffic patterns (see Chapter 10).

Call the tower via telephone to see if they'll allow the flight and, if so, what special requirements may be imposed. You need to work out a launch location, flight pattern and acceptable times.

You'll want an easily understood, brief and descriptive call sign. "Ultralight Papa Golf" is good because its easy to say, easy to understand and conveys immediately that you're a relatively slow craft (ultralight). You may want to describe yourself on the radio (or telephone) as being a "foot-launched powered parachute."

ATIS

Most controlled airports have a one-minute or so continuously repeating recording of weather and airport information. This **A**utomatic **T**erminal **I**nformation Service (ATIS) is generally updated every hour (but repeats continuously) and includes the airport weather, runways in use and other relevant tidbits. To insure pilots have the latest information, each update is labeled with a different letter. So the first hour's recording may be information "Alpha" (A) and the second hour's would be "information Bravo" (B) and so on. The tower wants to know that you've listened to this recording and will expect you to let them know on an initial call.

The ATIS frequency appears on sectional charts under the airport's name and

---

Aurora airport's control tower is at 120.6 Mhz and the Automatic Terminal Information Service (ATIS) is broadcast on 125.85 Mhz.

The picture above was from a flight of three paramotor pilots who trekked into this Class D airport while one talked on the radio and the others followed.

We were instructed to make "Right Closed Traffic" for the grass North of runway 27 and remain east of runway 33. The enlarged airport above makes it clear what these instructions mean. We followed the right pattern, depicted above, meaning that our turns to final were to the right. Airplanes were using the standard left pattern.

Being instructed to remain East of 33 meant that we had to plan our climbout carefully to give that runway a wide berth. Airplane wake, just like our own wake, drifts with the wind and sinks. An encounter with that while down low could be messy.

control tower frequency (CT). Listen to this broadcast first then contact the tower via radio and mention it to them "…information Bravo" (if it's B).

Tower Talk: Launch

Communications is taken seriously, for good reason—woe to the pilot who hems and haws and gums up the frequency with slow, uncertain transmissions. Plan what you're going to say, press the transmit button and say it clearly and succinctly.

Your initial call to the tower should include the facility name, your call sign, the letter of the ATIS recording (if one is broadcast) and your request. When you're ready to launch, motor running, A's in hand then call the tower and radio that you're ready for launch. They will give you the winds, special instructions and clear you to launch. They will probably tell you to "proceed as requested" since technically you're not on any clearance.

When cleared, complete your launch and comply with any instructions. If you delay more than a half-minute or so they will probably cancel the clearance and ask you to call them back when you're ready. If the launch doesn't work out, explain that you needed to abort and will call back when ready in 8 minutes (or however long you need).

After you've launched and flown a few miles away the tower may offer a frequency change; just respond with your call sign and "roger". You are not required to ask for a frequency change when clear of their airspace.

Never do this at a time when there is any significant airplane traffic. Even one airplane in the pattern, with its higher speed, can make us a nuisance. At the first sign of conflict, it's better to bail and be able to come back another day.

Tower Talk: Landing

Before returning to land, listen to the airport's ATIS and note the letter (such as Alpha for A, Bravo for B, etc.).

Call the tower by saying its name, and the tell them that you "have information such and such" followed by your request for a landing. They will give instructions regarding patterns and runways. If you're coming into the airport you will need to tell them exactly where on the field you want to land.

Example Communications

Here is a sample communication for a paramotor pilot flying from Aurora airport near Chicago, IL. It's in Class D airspace at 600 ft MSL elevation (above mean sea level). Ideally you will have already talked with the tower by phone to explain your craft, it's capabilities and speeds, and established where on the field you will launch from. Have a name for the place such as "in front of GF Aviation" where "GF Aviation" is the name of a business on the field. Make sure you understand the airport's runway and taxiway layout along with its typical patterns.

In the examples, communications use this font and *ATC dialogue is italicized.*

Dial in the ATIS frequency—here is the sample ATIS:

"Aurora Tower information Charlie, time one four five three zulu weather, wind 040 at 5, visibility 6 haze, scattered 35 hundred, broken at 250, tem-

Tip: AWOS

Many non-tower airports also have recorded weather: remote equipment that monitors conditions and broadcasts it continuously. It updates every few minutes, broadcasting current info on the listed frequency.

These Automated Weather Observation Systems (AWOS) are noted on the sectional chart along with their frequency. They also sometimes have a phone number to allow retrieval that way.

In the example below, Casa Grande airport's recorded weather can be picked up on an aviation band radio using 132.175 Mhz.

perature 24, dew point 18, runway 9 in use, runway 33/15 closed, caution for crane operating 600 feet east of the tower up to 150 feet, taxiway Charlie closed, tower and ground combined on 120.6, advise on initial contact you have information Charlie"

The above tells you that the wind is from the northeast at 5 knots and runway 9 is in use (airplanes will be taking off and landing towards the East). The weather observation was made at 1453 zulu (the aviation standard time, see Chapter 7).

In our example, you are set up in the grass south of runway 9 near the GF Aviation building and plan to head south. Call the tower when you're ready to inflate.

"Aurora Tower, Ultralight Papa Gulf by GF Aviation is ready to launch, would like south departure."

"Ultralight Papa Gulf, remain clear of runway 9, southbound departure approved, proceed as requested, launch is at your own risk."

"Ultralight Papa Gulf, will remain clear of runway 9"

After launch, turn south and head out. If the tower has, or knows about traffic in your vicinity, they may call it out. Positions are given relative to your ground track using clock directions where 9 O'clock is off your left, 12 O'clock is in front of your flight path and 3 O'clock is to the right.

"Ultralight Papa Gulf, you have traffic at your 11 O'clock and a mile westbound at 1500 feet, he's on right downwind for runway 9"

Look for the traffic; it is given relative to sea level (not airport elevation) so 1500 feet means he's 900 feet above the ground. Stay below about 500 feet (airplane traffic patterns are nearly all 800 feet AGL or higher) and respond accordingly.

"Ultralight Papa Gulf, traffic in sight" *or, if you don't see it,* "Ultralight Papa Golf, looking for Traffic."

After you've flown out of the tower's airspace you are legal to change frequencies (no permission required). They may, however, offer the change.

"Ultralight Papa Gulf, clear of my area, frequency change approved."

"Ultralight Papa Gulf, Roger."

When returning to land, listen to the ATIS again (note the letter it gives—X in this case) to make sure there are no changes. Call the tower with your position and request. Since this is an initial request, precede it with the facility name.

"Aurora Tower, Ultralight Papa Gulf is 6 miles south, southeast, landing with 'X-Ray (the ATIS letter)'"

"Ultralight Papa Gulf, approach the field from due South, remain below 1200 feet call 2 miles out."

When reaching 2 miles out, report your position.

"Ultralight Papa Gulf is 2 miles out."

If there's no traffic, it's fun to do a touch and go on a runway. If a runway is not being used, you may be able to get permission.

"Ultralight Papa Gulf, if traffic permits, I'd like to do a touch and go on runway 36."

"Ultralight Papa Gulf, roger, can you keep your pattern south of runway 27?"

If you are absolutely certain, beyond the slightest shadow of a doubt, that you can

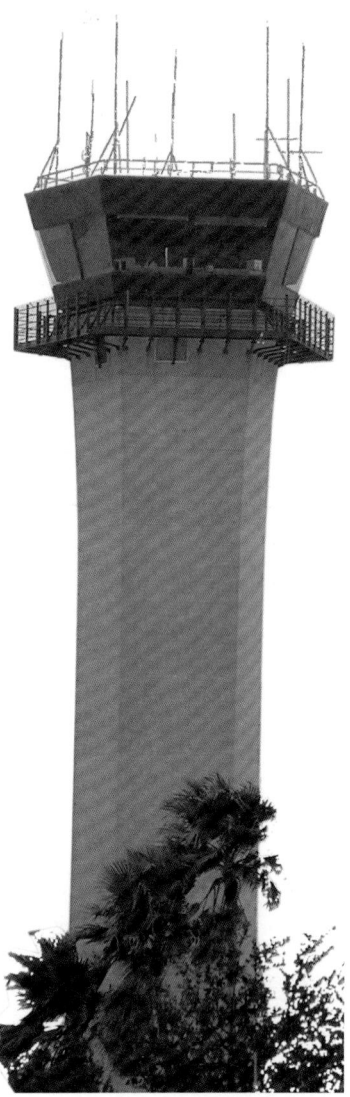

Tower controllers will not likely be familiar with our craft. It can help immensely to call them on the phone, introduce yourself, let them know what you want to do and describe the craft's limitations.

Ask when the slow periods are and how best to approach the field, if coming in from elsewhere.

safely comply with this request then respond with "affirmative." In this case, however, it would be wise not to accept such a clearance (say "negative"). Look at the airport diagram 3 pages back; there is very little of runway 36 south of runway 27. It would be tough to stay clear of 27. For this exercise, however, we'll assume there is plenty of room and that the tower is well south of runway 27.

> "Ultralight Papa Gulf, keep your pattern south of runway 27, make right traffic for runway 36, report abeam the tower."

When abeam the tower (the tower passes by perpendicular to your flight path), report.

> "Ultralight Papa Gulf is abeam the tower."

> "Ultralight Papa Gulf, cleared for the option runway 9 then make right traffic."

This means you are cleared to land and stop, do a touch and go, or do a flyby of the runway. If you land and stop the clearance ends (you cannot takeoff again until cleared for takeoff) but if you touch and go or fly by then make your pattern turns to the right while staying south of runway 27.

> "Ultralight Papa Gulf, cleared for the option runway 9, will make right traffic."

When you are ready to land back at your launch site:

> "Ultralight Papa Gulf is ready to land back in front of GF Aviation"

> "Ultralight Papa Gulf, remain south of runway 9, landing is your own risk, proceed."

You will only "cleared" to land or takeoff from a runway, not the adjoining grass or taxiways. Clearances, per se, are only issued when they involve the runway.

> "Ultralight Papa Gulf, roger."

Most instructions should be repeated (read back) to ensure you understand and will comply. All clearances relating to runways and taxiways *must* be read back. If you're only told to "proceed" then a full readback isn't really necessary; a simple

Digging Deeper: Phonetic Alphabet

Aviation radios are not known for high quality audio yet clear communications are obviously essential. So a special pronunciation alphabet was developed to reduce errors, especially with B's, C's, D's, T's and a few others. These words are used to represent each respective letter of the alphabet:

A	Alpha	B	Bravo	C			Charlie
D	Delta	E	Echo	F			Fox
G	Gulf	H	Hotel	I			India
J	Juliet (See R, someone had a sense of humor!)						
K	Kilo	L	Lima	M			Mike
N	November	O	Oscar	P			Papa
Q	Quebec	R	Romeo	S			Sierra
T	Tengo	U	Uniform	V			Victor
W	Whiskey (strange choice for aviation)						
X	X-Ray	Y	Yankee	Z			Zulu

Additionally, some numbers carry different pronunciations to prevent confusion with words in some languages:

3	Tree	5	Fife	9		Niner

This control tower was closed, leaving the surface area of E airspace. Permission is required and the pilots acquired it by contacting "Socal" (the Southern California Approach Control) by phone.

"roger" will do. If you are asked to maintain an altitude it will be MSL so have a reasonably accurate altimeter available—most of the wrist altimeters are OK but make sure to set it to the field elevation before departure.

Letter of Agreement

If you fly frequently from one location that sits within D airspace then you may benefit from working out an agreement with the controlling facility (almost always a control tower).

Set up an appointment with the ranking air traffic controller and have ready a map showing where you fly along with a picture of your craft.

If approved, then you will be issued a letter specifying boundaries, altitudes and times where you can fly without contacting them.

Every summer, the Oshkosh, Wisconsin control tower plays a part in the worlds largest airshow, the Experimental Aircraft Association's annual Fly-In. Ultralights (including PPG's), fly here without talking to the tower under a "letter of agreement." Owing to the extreme traffic density, they are under very strict flight patterns and are closely watched by "marshals."

The PPG Bible: A Complete Guide and Reference

Setup & Maintenance

CHAPTER 12

Our flying machines look so simple and, in most regards, they are. But proper setup and maintenance is critical beyond appearances. Manufacturer information is best, when available, followed by guidance from an instructor or dealer who is experienced with your particular brand. Improper adjustments, especially to the harness, can render a paramotor unflyable or dangerous.

Harness

The harness includes the critical liftweb, a series of thick straps (webbing) that hold you up, allow you to sit, and support the motor. It is the most important item of adjustment as it determines how you hang, how torque is handled, comfort and just about every other aspect of flight. Avoid exposing it to damaging UV rays, extreme heat, cuts and harmful chemicals.

Riser Spread

The harness must allow and maintain a riser separation of 17 to 20 inches (42 – 50 cm) across to keep most wings within certification. Your wing's manual may list other limits but few specify it. Be especially careful to avoid *less* than minimum separation which could lead to a very dangerous *riser twist*, where the pilot spins around under the wing.

Setup

Setup *must* be done while hanging from the carabiners in a simulator (see Chapter 1). You can hang it from a tree limb or rafter—anything high enough to get your feet off the ground. Use someone to help, preferably an instructor.

Below: The harness and frame mounting arrangement must keep the risers an appropriate distance apart. Being too wide hurts the wing's shape and being too close (2nd one pictured below) can allow a dangerous riser twist to develop where the pilot winds up facing backwards.

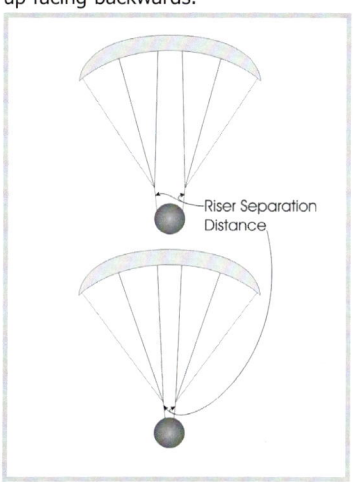

Chapter 12: Setup & Maintenance — Page 111

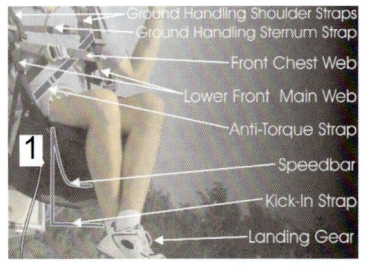

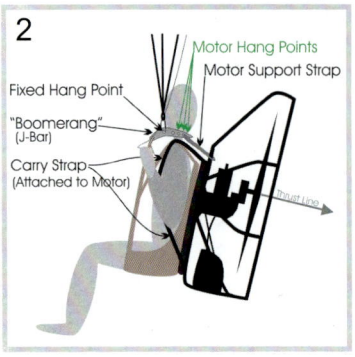

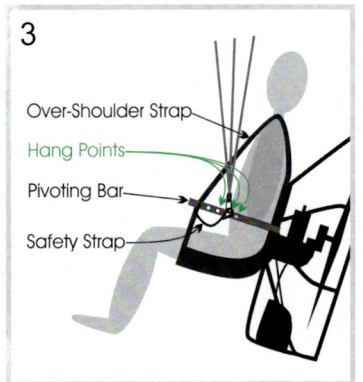

The PPG Bible: A Complete Guide and Reference

The primary goal is to make the thrust line point slightly downward (between 0° and 15°) from straight back. While the leaned-back posture is more comfortable, it makes takeoff and landing more difficult whereas sitting bolt upright is less comfortable but minimizes the twisting effect of torque.

Adjust the hang angle by moving the carabiner hook-in point. On many harnesses (the style depicted below) this is done by moving the carabiner loop along the upper front main web and then adjusting the upper rear main web (3) straps to allow enough slack so that it will not press against your body in flight. You should feel no (or very little) harness pressure on your body—the intent of the distance bar is to keep harness straps comfortably *away* from your chest and arms.

If the wing carabiners clip into a bar or frame (and multiple holes are provided), selecting the appropriate hole is critical. Moving to a hole more forward will make you tilt-back more. Light pilots typically use the more aft holes (those nearer the motor) to counteract the motor's weight. Its opposite for those models where the *motor* clips into a bar—holes farther back make the motor tilt back farther.

Leg straps should be snugged up tightly then let out a couple inches. If they're too tight makes it hard to run and, on most machines, if they're too loose it's difficult to get into the seat. A few models, however, are designed for the leg loops to be completely loose—check with the manufacturer.

The Anti-Torque strap, if equipped (see #1 at left), should be tightened until it's snug but without forcing the carabiners together. This reduces the effect of motor torque at the expense of weight shift. Machines *made* to weight shift won't likely have this strap since weight shift can be used to counteract some torque effects. This setup does not *prevent* torque turns, only reduces it somewhat.

On machines equipped with a seat lip adjustment strap, it should be left loose for launch and landing. Pull it tight while hanging in the simulator to get some feel for how much tightening it takes and then let it loose again.

The front chest web (figure 1 at left) keeps you from falling out forward and prevents the risers from spreading out too far. Being over-tight might bring the risers too close together and will also reduce weight shift authority (on machines so equipped). The chest strap should be just barely snug.

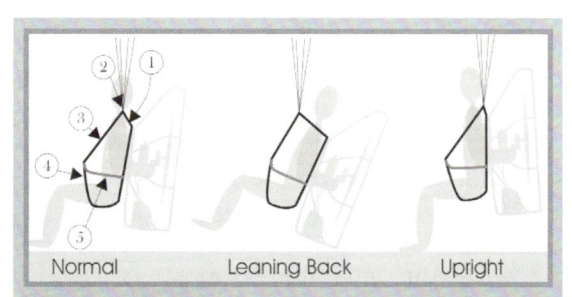

Ground Handling Straps

Ground Handling (or *carry*) straps (see figure 2 at left) help keep the motor "hiked up" while preparing for launch. On over-the-shoulder machines they keep the bars off your shoulder. They also make forward launch-

1. This excerpt from Chapter 2 shows the anti-torque strap, speedbar and kick-in bar which are not used on all machines.

2. This *soft j-bar* style adjusts the hang angle by changing which "boomerang" hole the motor hangs from. The last hole is typically used but moving to a more-forward hole gives a more upright hang position.

3. Low hook-in machines adjust the hang angle by choosing different holes in the weight shift bar (or rigid rail). Using a forward hole results in the motor hanging back farther. Motors with no carry strap are normally launched with the main strap (over-shoulder) tight and then it can be loosened in flight for comfort.

On both 2 and 3, throttling up will push the motor into a more vertical position. On fixed or *floating J-bars* the hang angle does not change appreciably with thrust.

Balancing the weight of the motor and pilot keeps the prop disk (area created by the spinning prop) nearly vertical or hanging back slightly. Many harness varieties exist; the example above shows a soft harness type where the high hook-in can be moved by lengthening the #1 distance. That moves the motor's weight farther aft causing the motor to tilt back more, vectoring (pointing) the thrust downward slightly. It may be more comfortable in flight but challenges the launch and landing. More tilt-back dramatically aggravates the twisting effect of torque.

A good compromise in comfort and safety is about a 5° tilt-back which means the thrust line is also correctly pointed about 5° down.

Section II: Spreading Your Wings

Repairs to the liftweb should be done by a certified parachute rigger or equally qualified professional. Other harness repairs can be made with any strong thread such as for leather or carpet. The hooked needle helps push through thick straps.

es easier by preventing the motor from "wallowing" around as much.

In flight they can be loosened to a more comfortable setting if they're bothersome. On those harnesses where these straps pass through a buckle, tie a knot at the end so it cannot come all they way out and wind up in the prop.

A sternum strap goes across your chest to keep the ground handling straps from slipping off your shoulder.

Machines without carry straps should have their main over-shoulder webbing cinched up very tightly. You can usually loosen them once in flight for comfort. Such machines will probably also provide a side strap tensioner that should be tightened for launch and loosened in flight if necessary for comfort.

Kick-In Bar

A kick-in bar (or rope) is used to aid getting into the seat on some machines. It should be heavy enough (like an aluminum bar) to hang down a bit and must not interfere with walking backwards (for reverse launches). Normally it should hang a little over halfway down to your foot while sitting in the simulator.

Speedbar

The speedbar (foot bar portion of the speed system) should be adjusted so as to ride just above the kick-in bar or about halfway down the back of your calf while seated. This provides a good compromise between easy access and full travel. Having it closer gives more travel at the expense of easy reach. Some harnesses have handy loops where the foot bar can be stowed during takeoff and landing.

Speedbar adjustment in a simulator requires that you attach the wing's risers and hold them up (like they're in flight) with the sister clips connected. Make sure the speedbar line is not so tight that it pulls the A's with*out* the bar being pushed out. When fully depressed, the two A-riser pulleys should nearly touch each other as pictured at left.

One way to adjust its length is to make the speedbar a bit longer than what the simulator suggests then go test fly it. While flying, pull the line up through it's rings (or pulleys, as equipped) until the bar just touches the harness. Mark that spot then readjust the speed system's line length.

Some speedbars come with two straps (no bar). One strap attaches to the speed system and the other attaches to the seatboard front as a kick-in strap. Some others have a second loop attached to the speedbar, these allow a two-stage activation of the speedbar. You push out on the first one to full leg extension then go to the closer bar for more travel.

Hard Point Hook-Ins

On machines with low hook-in points there are usually hard points that the carabiners attach too. Adjusting the hang angle is a compromise between keeping the risers forward enough for arm freedom and leaning back too far. These machines

Speedbar Attachment

Almost all speedbar lines hook together with *brummel hooks*, commonly called *sister clips* (Shown).

This is the simplest setup for a speedbar—a line goes from the foot bar, through one pulley (or ring) on each side of the harness and up to the wing's speed system.

The yellow bars are over-shoulder *floating J-bars,* considered a hardpoint hook-in since the carabiner attaches to a J-bar. It is floating because the J-bars can move up and down. Motor tilt-back angle is affected by where on the J-bar the carabiner attaches to: moving the carabiner back means you'll hang more upright.

J-bars spread the harness forward and away from your body while retaining a higher hook-in point. A back-up carabiner strap is frequently used in case the J-bar were to fail, retaining a load path through the harness's lift web. This type of J-Bars also forces a certain riser separation and prevents the motor from sliding around on the pilot's back. Fixed J-bar machines are typically only used on cart-launched machines.

A lightweight pilot flying a heavier machine, intended to power tandems. By hooking the carabiners to the farthest point aft, the pilot can be reasonably well balanced with about 5° tilt-back.

The carabiners, or straps to the carabiners, must go through the frame holes intended for them (on machines that have them). If they just go around the bars, the strap and attached risers could slide forward, allowing the motor to tilt way back and cause an immediate riser twist.

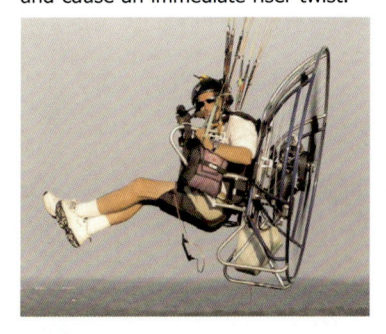

Torque Twist

As the wing lifted, the motor moved to the pilots right shoulder causing offset thrust and tilted way back inducing the horizontal component of torque. This put him into an uncontrollable twist. Had he continued, it would have quickly ended in a crash. Fortunately, he let off the throttle and aborted immediately after this picture was taken.

are designed to lean back farther to more closely mimic the free flight posture. Acceptable thrust line angles are between 10° and 20° on them but remember to expect more twisting and more challenge on launch with more tilt angle.

On over-shoulder J-Bar machines, the hang angle is decided by which hole the Carabiner attaches to. These machines typically have a shallower thrust line, pointing nearly level to about 5° back.

If the carabiners attach to a bar instead of the harness webbing, consider using a safety strap that goes from the riser loop to the harness. This is because a loose metal-to-metal contact point is slightly more susceptible to fatigue failure.

Reducing Torque

Torque tries to cause tilt and twist. Tilt is where one riser lowers like a weight shift turn and twist is where you swing the the left or right. Twist is worse since it redirects the thrust which can easily overpower the brakes' turn authority. The various effects of torque are worse in climb, but do cause some turning tendency in cruise, too. Here are some ways to mitigate the effects.

- Reduce the hang-back angle. This is the most serious cause of riser twist due to the horizontal component of torque. It is even more important with smaller pilots flying powerful motors—they should limit the lean angle to 8°.

- Make sure the motor cannot slide left or right on the harness. This is big since it can produce offset thrust and cause serious twisting. It's like having someone push on one of your shoulder blades with 100 or more pounds of push—you *will* twist. So if you tend to get twisted to the right, (motor pushing on left shoulder) secure the motor so that it is pushing more centered or slightly on your right shoulder.

- Insure that there is sufficient riser separation and the motor is held rigidly in place. Swinging arms, on machines so equipped, must not swing inward (outward is ok).

- Create a differential carabiner hang height. In other words, if the motor torque tilts you to the right (pulls down the right riser), make the left carabiner shorter. Doing so will make power-off glides want to turn you right slightly, like a weight shift turn, but you'll fly straight in cruise and torque less during climb. This works best on higher hang point motors because the motor's center of gravity (CG) is well below the hang points. It does not work well on machines with the lowest hook-in points.

- Move the hook-in point aft on one side (primarily for motors with hard point attachments). This does a slight thrust re-direction to help offset it's natural tendency. So if you tend to twist to the left (which makes your wing bank right), move the hook-in point aft on the left and vice-versa for right.

Motor

Getting into this sport means becoming, at least to some degree, a mechanic. Precious few shops—motocross and cart racing shops mostly—can work on the motor but may not if they know it's for flying (they worry about liability). Even if you find a local shop, it won't likely have parts—for that you'll need someone who

Two-Cycle Motor Troubleshooting Chart

Does the motor have compression when you pull/crank it

- **Yes** → continues to next decision
- **Too Much** → Remove the spark plug. If there is still too much resistance to pulling then it could be:
  - Siezure (piston partially melts against cylinder wall).
  - Bad Pull or Electric Starter.
  - Other Internal Problem.

  Otherwise it could be:
  - Clogged decompression hole (if equipped) - clean it out.
  - Bad decompression valve (if equipped). Clean or replace.

- **No** → The following could be the problem:
  - Spark Plug is Loose - tighten.
  - The piston has a hole in it - replace.
  - If it has a decompression valve this is normal.

Does the motor Start and continue to run?

- **Yes** → **Does it develop and keep full RPM?**
  - **Yes** → If full RPM does not deliver full thrust then it could be:
    - The prop is on backwards - the curved side always faces forward (towards the motor).
    - The belt or clutch (if equipped) is slipping.
  - **No** → **Does it go to full RPM then fade or does the power vary without changing the throttle setting?**
    - **Yes** → **Is it overheating?** A Cylinder Head Temp gauge is the best way to tell.
      - **Possibly** → (see Overheating below)
      - **No** → This common malady has many potential causes - some are not intuitive:
        - The prop is either too big or has too much pitch - "over propped".
        - The mixture may be changing as the motor heats up (even though it's not overheating. Tune Carb.
        - The cylinder and piston need to be de-carbonized.
        - Bad or broken tuned pipe. The damage is usually not visible. Try replacing the pipe if able.
        - There is an air leak into the cylinder or crankcase.
        - The throttle cable allows activation of the throttle without squeezing the trigger.
    - **No** → **Tune the Carburetor, Check the reed valve. Did that solve the problem?**
      - **Yes** → done
      - **No** → **Is properly-mixed fuel getting to the carburetor?** Try spraying starter fluid in the air intake. If it pops when cranked then fuel is *not* being delivered or is bad fuel.
        - **Yes** → (continue)
        - **No** → This may be caused by:
          - Air leak in a fuel line. Replace line. This can sometimes be seen as bubbles in the fuel line.
          - Blocked fuel filter.
          - Fuel tank air intake vent blocked. This will cause the motor to run for a while then become lean and quit.
          - Old fuel - it may last only a week if unsealed.
          - Improper fuel. Some machines don't like avgas or low octane fuel.

- **No** → **Does it fire at all?** Make sure it is not flooded: remove the spark plug, pull it through, then replace the plug. A wet plug may indicate flooding.
  - **Yes** → (continue - see fuel checks above)
  - **No** → **Is there spark?** Set the connected plug on the cylinder and look for a spark while pulling/cranking the motor. Don't touch!
    - **Yes** → Consider one of the following:
      - Hole in the piston.
      - Bad Reed Valve (if equipped).
      - Excess internal carbon deposits.
      - Bad ignition system. Even though it sparks the strength may be inadequate.
      - Exhaust is bad. Tuned pipes can make engines run rough if broken or improperly made.
    - **No** → Either the spark is not being generated or it is being shorted. It could be:
      - Bad spark plug - Try a new one.
      - Kill switch is shorted - disconnect it and see if it fires or use an ohm meter to verify the kill circuit is an "open" when not pushed.
      - The coil or magneto (if equipped) is bad. Most use a magnet and coil to generate the high voltage required of the spark plug.

Overheating has several possibilities:
- The fuel/air mixture is (or gets) too lean.
- Not enough oil is mixed in with the fuel. This should not be a problem up to 50:1 Fuel/Oil ratio.
- Bearings have seized.
- The Cylinder is scored.
- The piston ring(s) are stuck.

Safety Wire, Tools and Bolts

Aircraft safety wire is made to be twisted. Always consider which way the bolt or part is trying to unscrew or depart and make sure it can't do so. The springs on the muffler at right have been safetied so that if they break, they avoid an expensive trip through the prop. Such projectiles can damage bystanders, the wing or cage on their way out.

Safety wire comes in various sizes; thicker is better considering our machines' propensity to vibrate. 0.041 diameter is good.

Nearly all bolts on PPG's are metric. Allen wrenches sized 3 through 8 cover 95% of all requirements. Few bolts are made to accept safety wire and must be drilled through the head. Carrying basic tools with you, including a spark plug wrench and thin-nosed locking pliers can be salvation in the field.

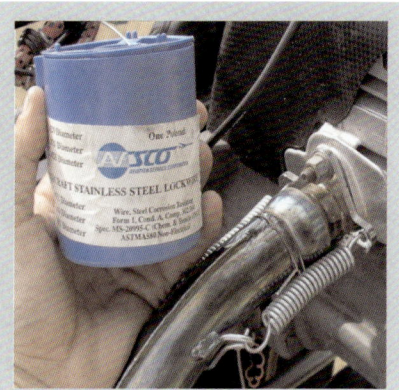

specializes on your particular brand. In all likelihood, you'll need to ship your broken unit to a shop that knows the brand. If you want it fixed quickly, you'll probably have to fix it yourself. There are some preventative measures that can help prevent problems from progressing to the point of needing repair.

Troubleshooting

All internal combustion motors need four elements, in the right proportion and at the right time: spark, fuel, air and compression. Make sure these elements are present and you'll likely solve the problem. Sometimes, cleaning the spark plug and setting the gap can also sometimes solve a problem. The flowchart will help diagnose most common problems.

Start with the simple and cheap then progress to the more involved. If you can't figure it out (or would rather not bother) then you'll have to find a small engine shop or someone who works on your particular model (especially the dealer).

Fortunately these machines are generally quite simple, fairly reliable and easy to work on. Many "mechanically challenged" pilots, when faced with being grounded have risen to the occasion.

Bolt Tightening and Force

When tightening bolts there is a universal way to describe how much: the Kilogram-Meter or Foot-Pound (imperial units list distance first). It is how much force and how far out on the handle to apply it.

If you hold the wrench way out on the handle, it doesn't take much force to get the bolt real tight. It's all about leverage. Torque is force times distance from the bolt's center.

Using the example at left, applying 10 pounds of pressure, 5 inches out on the wrench, is 50 inch-pounds of torque. Applying 5 pounds of force 10 inches out is also 50 inch-pounds of force. 1 Foot-Pound is 12 Inch-Pounds. Be careful with units: 50 foot-pounds is a lot more torque than 50 inch-pounds.

Over tightening bolts is worse than under tightening since they can easily strip out their threads, especially aluminum threads.

Preventative Maintenance

Spark Plugs may last as little as 10 hours before carbon deposits and other wear degrades performance. They should either be changed every 20 hours or at the first

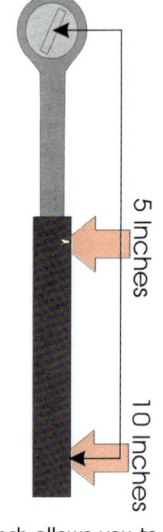

Torque

A torque wrench allows you to gauge how powerful you are twisting something. The farther out you push on the wrench, the more torque you exert. So 10 pounds of pressure at 10 inches produces the same torque that 20 pounds of pressure at 5 inches does— 100 inch-pounds.

sign of trouble—primarily because they are so cheap, easy to change and are so commonly the problem. Tighten spark plugs to about 6 ft-pounds which should be enough to flatten the washer that comes with most plugs. If you don't have a torque wrench, apply about 12 pounds of force 6 inches out on the handle (same as 6 pounds of force applied one foot out).

Fuel Lines harden over time, making them more likely to develop cracks or holes and should be replaced before becoming stiff. They should not be routed around sharp corners or allowed to touch sharp objects since chaffing may also form holes. The primary symptom of holes is bubbles in the fuel line—that will make the motor run rough, lean or not at all. Don't secure fuel lines with wire ties.

Exhaust system bolts, rivets and springs are always trying to vibrate off. This can be serious if exhaust parts either deform or drop onto the fuel tank. Although a fire is still incredibly unlikely, this area deserves close scrutiny. Exhaust components, whenever possible, should be safety wired. Putting heat tolerant sealant into the springs keeps can prevent failure from vibration.

Head bolts should be checked with an *inch*-pound torque wrench, especially when the machine is new. They tend to loosen up along with many other fasteners.

This is a common belt-drive arrangement. One good way to check belt tension is to see how much torque it takes to get the belt to slip. Put a torque wrench on the center nut as depicted, hold the prop still and try to tighten the nut. The nut should stay put but if the belt slips with less than 1.8 Kg-Meters (13 ft-lbs), then the belt is too loose. Tighten it and try again. The torque value may well be different on other models.

Reduction Drive

Most paramotors use a reduction drive to turn the motor's high-RPM into a propeller-friendly lower RPM. They either use a belt or gears.

Gear Drive

Most gear drives consist of: 2 gears, 4 bearings in a sealed grease-laden aluminum housing, and the output going to a clutch bell (geared systems usually have a clutch).

Normal maintenance requires insuring sufficient grease (or gear oil depending on make) and good bearings. They generally require very little attention; however, on rare occasion little bits of metal can play havoc and lock them up. In such cases, the case must be split open and gears inspected to remove the debris.

If you feel play in the prop, and it's not due to prop bolts, the bearings may be failing. Replacement requires splitting the redrive (gearbox) which is fortunately easy. Unscrew the bolts part-way then tap on the bolt heads (use something that won't deform the bolt heads). Once the halves are partway separated, use a gear puller or prying tool (chisel or something wide that won't scrape the metal)

Any mis-alignment of the pulleys will cause the belt to either come off or break well before its time. With proper adjustment and a light propeller, a belt should last 100 hours.

On average it should be tensioned so that there is about a 1/4" of play when pressed at spot 1 below.

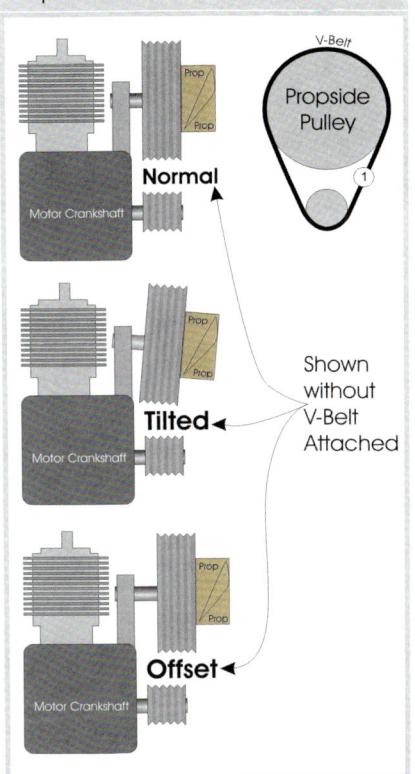

This is a gear reduction drive. The motor spins a small gear that drives the much larger propside gear at a lower RPM.

A clutch, shown below right, is attached to the motor's crankshaft and spins along with the motor. When throttled up, the two pads are thrown out against springs, contacting the clutch bell which spins the re-drive's small gear. At low RPM, the springs keep the the pads retracted so the prop does not turn.

The clutch pictured below has one broken spring so the two halves spread out against the clutch bell (left) causing the prop to spin, even at idle (which it should not do)

to finish the separation. If the gears are damaged you may need a gear puller. If the bearings are bad, you'll probably have to heat the case to get them out. Be sure to replace any sealer around the edges to prevent leaks.

Belt Drive

The primary adjustment on these units is belt tension. Too loose and it slips—a "chirping" noise may be the belt slipping at each power stroke. Too tight and it can bend the stand-off or stretch the belt. All motors have some way to adjust belt tension by changing the distance between pulleys You'll probably have to do so a few times soon after changing belts.

The two pulleys must be aligned properly as shown on the previous page.

The belt should not squeak during power up, that's too loose. A heavy propeller (especially where the mass is out towards the tips) will aggravate slipping and may dramatically shorten belt or redrive bearing life.

Clutch

A clutch allows starting and idling the motor without spinning its prop. They are found mostly on smaller motors because larger ones need the prop's mass to act as a flywheel.

It's just like a mini-bike; at idle, springs hold the clutch shoes in. As you throttle up, the faster spin moves the clutch shoes outward, rubbing against the clutch bell. The prop is attached to that bell and so starts spinning. The only maintenance is to insure that indeed the prop is free-wheeling (no rubbing) with the motor off and that the clutch shoes are not too worn which would then damage the bell.

If a clutch bell gets grooves worn in it or is pitted from rust, it will quickly eat up new clutches and should be replaced.

Propeller

The propeller must be mounted with the curved side (the fast part) facing forward and the bolts tightened evenly. The prop is held in place by friction with the plates, not the bolts. If there is torsional stress on the bolts, such as when they're too loose, they will break.

Do not drill extra holes in the prop hub to fit a different bolt pattern, the weakened wood could break, causing a catastrophic failure.

Use grade 8 bolts, or better, and check tightness periodically. They should be torqued to approximately 5 Foot-Pounds (0.7 KgN); the goal is not

The curved surface mounts towards the motor so that it faces the direction of flight. Putting a prop on backwards is embarrassing, trying to launch with it is even worse. It will produce thrust but certainly not enough to fly. Looking at a paramotor from behind you should always see the prop's flat side.

The 4 bolt holes go through the *hub* which mounts to a *flange* on the motor—usually a redrive.

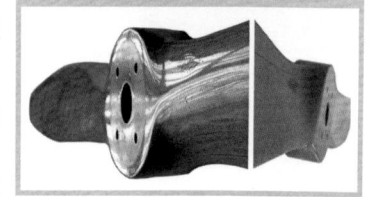

to deform the wood or dig into the flange. Tighten each bolt partway in succession, one at a time, on opposite sides, until getting to the desired torque just like a car wheel. Composite props can be torqued up to 7 foot pounds (1.0 KgN).

Rotate the prop vertical and try to move the tip fore and aft while watching the engine mounts. A broken or nearly failed mount may allow enough flex for the prop to hit a frame/cage part and must be replaced. If the prop wiggles, check the center nut (on those motors that use it) and tighten if loose.

Balancing Act

Vibration is a paramotor's mortal enemy and props can cause a lot of it. There are many methods for balancing props, but the most common, and fortunately the easiest, is static balancing. Less obvious is balancing out various aerodynamic maladies that can cause equally bad vibration.

Static Balance

The prop should balance exactly at the center of the hub. Special balancers can be purchased that will quickly reveal if the prop is heavier either spanwise (tip to tip) or chordwise (leading edge to trailing edge). They normally work by using a cylinder plug sized to fit snugly in the prop's center hole then either hanging or being suspended from a single point right in the middle. If one blade, or side, droops then it's out of balance. An lawnmower blade balancer works well too.

The cure is to put enough weight on the light side to bring it back to center. One method is to drill a hole opposite the heavy side and melt solder into it until balanced. Don't drill the hole all the way through so only one side has to be smoothed afterwards. Cover the hole with a glue and baking soda mix and sand to match the wood contour.

Carbon Fiber props are different since they're hollow. Drill a hole near the tip and add epoxy or, in more extreme cases, melt solder in it (usually only necessary after a significant repair on the opposite blade). Seal the solder with epoxy and sand to shape.

Minor corrections to fix an imbalance can be done by spraying clear varnish to the lighter side. Several coats will be necessary as much of the weight evaporates off.

Aerodynamic Balance

If one blade is pulling harder than the other blade, it will cause vibration; it is aerodynamically unbalanced. Possible causes are:

- The propeller has a chordwise offset, probably one or two bolts on one side is over-tightened which compresses the wood and/or rubber friction matte (if used).

- The propeller is warped. This is more likely if it has been significantly repaired.

- One blade is longer or fatter than the other, a relatively easy thing to correct if it's just shaving off length. One way to tell is to set shelf paper on the floor, put the prop on it and carefully outline one half. Then put the other half over the outline and see if it's close. If not, reshape the larger half to match.

You can measure the angle of each blade by first setting it on a smooth, flat floor. Go 75% out towards the tip, hold a straight edge against the prop's flat bottom and measure its angle to the floor with a protractor.

Anytime a prop is worked on or reshaped, it should be statically balanced.

Tracking

If one blade tip passes by the same point in space at a different spot (either fore or aft) than the other blade, the tracking is off. The prop could be warped, improperly mounted (bolts unevenly tightened) or it could have an aerodynamic imbalance which would be more difficult to detect.

The tracking can be off by up to a ¼ inch with little effect. Any more than that, though, should be corrected by tightening the bolts evenly. If the prop is not causing vibration, leave it alone.

All propeller blades flex and twist a bit when under power—causing either more or less lift as they do. If one blade does so more than the other, it will cause a vibration even though the prop balances statically. A vibration that worsens faster than what seems normal for a simple static imbalance may be caused by this. Poorly made props or those with large repairs are more likely to suffer from flexing differences or simply have one blade at a different angle than the other blade.

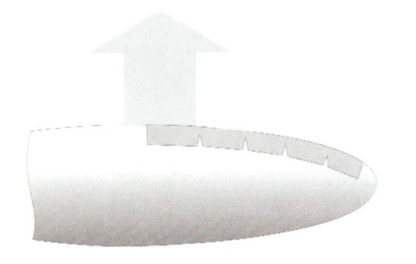

Prop Tape

Special tape can be applied to the prop's leading edge to protect it from minor dings but it extracts some performance. Also, if not adhering well, it can come off and cause an uncomfortable imbalance (it can generally be flown that way back to the destination).

Thin tape is better for going around the sometimes-difficult curves and tends not to hurt performance as much. Thick tape can sometimes be coaxed to work but may require small V-cuts or using a hair dryer to make it more malleable.

If prop tape does not adhere well to the curves, cut V's out as depicted here.

Propeller Repair

It is an unfortunate reality that props will be broken. They will find their way into cages, lines, departing parts and ground debris. Fortunately, however, many oops's are pretty easy to fix. They must be done correctly to avoid pieces flying off with

Cylinder Style Prop Balancing

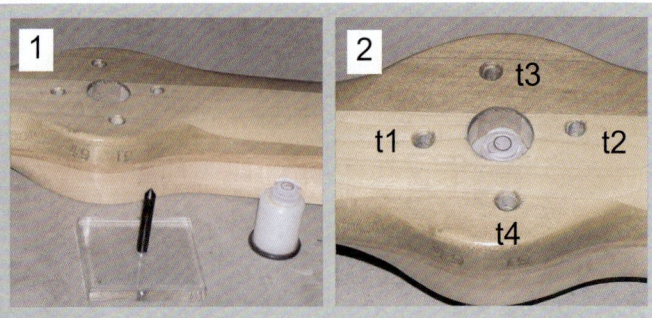

Here is a cylinder-style prop balancer in use. It allows balancing both lengthwise and widthwise.

The cylinder slides in the prop's center hole and then sits on the pointed stand. Any imbalance will cause the prop to tilt towards the heavy direction. On this prop, the bubble is down and left meaning that weight has to be added up and right.

The t1 through t4 is what order the bolts should be tightened when re-mounting the prop. Barely tighten t1 then t2 then t3 then t4 then go around again until they are appropriately tightened.

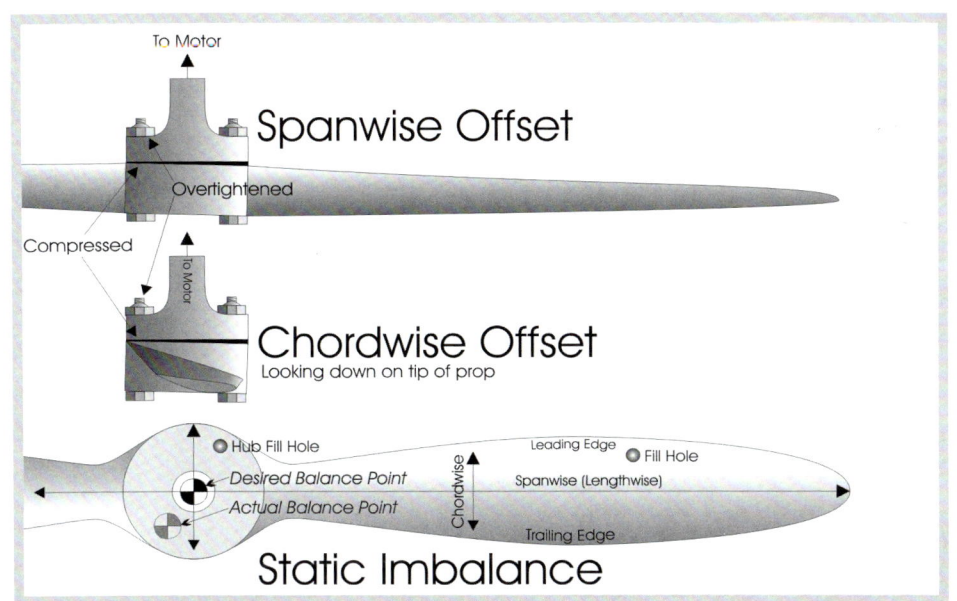

Spanwise Offset / Chordwise Offset / Static Imbalance

If a prop is not flat on the flange, the offset will cause some vibration. A chordwise offset is far worse because one blade has a higher angle of attack than the other: it will pull harder as it goes around even though the prop is statically balanced.

Static balancing can be done by drilling a shallow hole where weight is needed and melting solder into it. Put a layer of epoxy on top to hold it in place then sand and varnish. The prop above (Static Imbalance) shows that weight needs to added at the "Fill Hole" to counteract an actual balance point low and to the left. Use a fill hole on the hub when it is mostly a chordwise imbalance.

devastating consequence.

On all repairs, the surface should be clean and sanded. If two-part epoxy is used, it should be allowed to fully cure before sanding; use a hard sanding block to prevent airflow-ruining bumps.

Repairing Wood Props

The quickest repair for small divots is Super Glue (or equivalent) and baking soda. Micro balloons, available at hobby shops, can be used in place of baking soda—they are lighter and easier to sand. Layer on the glue and sprinkle in baking soda. In the right proportion the mix may smoke a bit but should harden quickly. Repeat until the damage is filled then sand to shape.

Somewhat bigger gouges can be filled with epoxy and baking soda (or micro balloons). Use tape to follow the prop's contour in a way that you can pour the mixed epoxy in. That reduces sanding. Use an equal amount of epoxy and baking soda (by volume) to help reduce weight and make it easier to sand.

After it hardens use a hard sanding block to reshape it. It must be well cured before sanding; 5-minute type epoxy should harden for several hours first.

Larger repairs, up to 30% of the length or width of one blade can be done with a variety of methods, one of which is depicted on the next page.

Repairing Carbon Fiber Props

Carbon Fiber props are less forgiving of damage. Even after being repaired, they may harbor invisible degradation that could separate later, without notice, throwing shards. They should only be used when no risk to bystanders is present.

> **⚠ Caution!**
>
> Poorly done repairs can leave props dangerously weakened. The repaired part could shoot off as a deadly missile.
>
> If uncertain about a damaged prop, send it to be professionally repaired. Beware that even professionally repaired props shed parts occasionally.

The PPG Bible: A Complete Guide and Reference

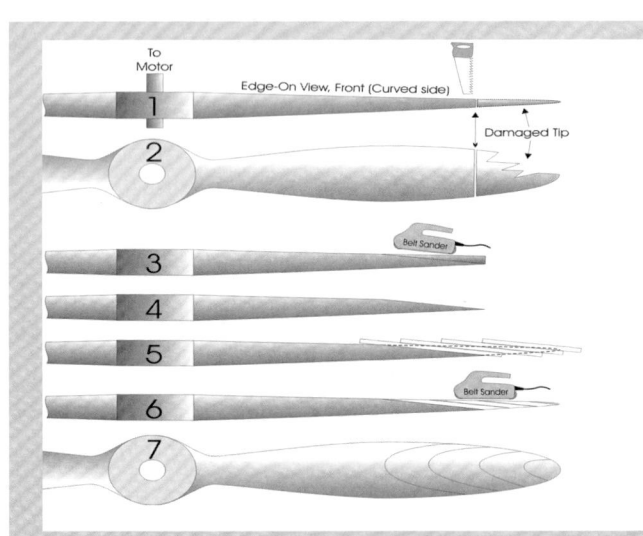

Surprisingly large repairs can be made on wooden props if done properly. A belt sander makes it easier but having a steady hand and some basic wood-working skill is a must.

Use a quality wood glue, spread evenly, on 1/4" thick slabs of poplar wood (step 5). Make sure they're completely flat against each other and clamp firmly for overnight drying before sanding.

Sand to shape then varnish, sand, varnish and finally balance.

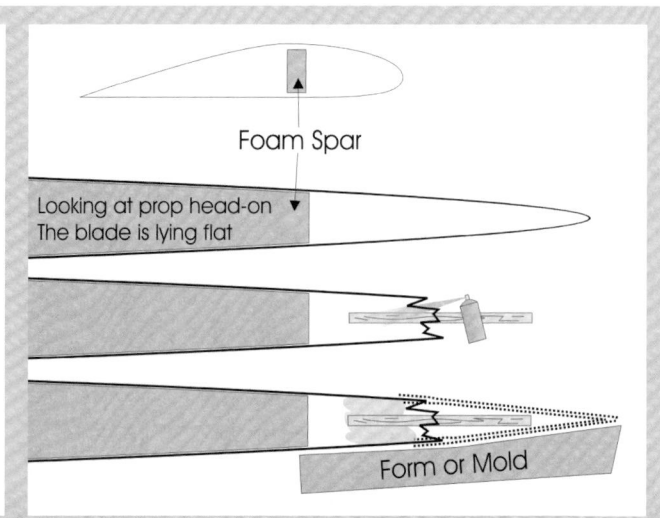

Small repairs can be filled without stiffening. Anything over about an inch across or deep needs more. Always wear a respirator and goggles whenever working with fiberglass resin or sanding the hardened result. Anything over 3 inches should be repaired professionally and some carbon fiber prop makers strongly recommend against trying to repair their products.

Fiberglass is heavier than carbon fiber so balancing after the repair is especially important.

Carbon fiber props are usually hollow with a ½" thick or so foam core to keep the halves spaced appropriately. Lighter, but much more expensive than wooden props, they are also more challenging to repair. Don't expect them to look perfect after being repaired because the fiberglass used in the above method needs to cover part of the top to have proper adhesion.

Simple cracks or holes aren't bad as they can be filled using epoxy. Force epoxy into the hole then use tape to form the prop's shape while the epoxy sets. Lay it so the epoxy puddles against the tape while curing. You can also use putty-type epoxy.

More severe damage, such as when more than about an inch of tip is missing, requires another technique. You'll need fiberglass cloth and resin (available at some hardware and most marine supply stores). See the diagram for clarification of these steps.

Clean and sand the area within two inches of the damage to have a good bonding surface for the resin.

Spray foam (insulating foam is sold at many hardware stores) into the tip void for support. With worse damage, embed some reinforcement material (wood or wire) into the foam such that it extends beyond the foam—it will be used to help hold the repair (next steps) in place. Let the repair set up overnight.

Trim the foam so that so it does not protrude into the repair area.

Mix the resin according to its directions. This step is finicky and warrants practicing once elsewhere, the mix must be just right. Cut up pieces of cloth, mix them into the resin then work the saturated pieces into the tip and around the mold. Longer pieces should overlap the prop's top and bottom upper and lower surfaces for the best bond.

Once hardened completely, sand to shape. A belt sander really helps to speed up the process but don't sand away where the fiberglass overlaps the existing prop—it won't look perfect, but is necessary for strength.

Balance the prop and expect to add weight in the other tip.

The Wing

Paraglider wings require attention in proportion to how they are stored and used. Age and water exposure result in line shrinkage so they must be stretched periodically. They can also get stretched due to overstress (aerobatics, B-Line Stalls, etc.) or weakened by heat or sharp bends (especially knots) and then must be replaced.

Fabric can tear, become porous, moldy or get chewed by insects and must be repaired. Most experienced pilots have found that beyond about 300 hours of strong UV time the wing has served its time. Here are some things that can help keep it airworthy and even extend its life.

Replacing Risers

Unless they get damaged, risers should outlast the rest of the wing; they are way over-built. When inspecting newly acquired risers, check general condition; especially check that the stitching is done correctly. At least one set was shipped with the riser loop only tack stitched—an incredibly dangerous flaw that will likely fail on the first flight.

Risers can be separated from the lines to accommodate either a different model or replacement. Mostly this is done to put *motor risers* (shorter) on soaring wings to use with motors having high attachment points. Otherwise the soaring wing's brake position can be too high. Risers on soaring wings are longer to go with typical free-flight harnesses which nearly always have low attachment points.

A different riser set can dramatically change the wing's flight characteristics and usually takes the wing out of certification. Only use riser sets recommended by the manufacturer. Even then the wing may be out of certification if it wasn't re-tested with those risers.

You can remove risers by taking the lines off at their *quick links*.

Complete one side before doing the other side, starting from the A's then proceeding back to the brakes. Put masking tape across a group of lines before detaching them and use a felt tip marker to note which side faces forward ("F" in the pictures) as well as what lines they are (A's, B's, etc.) including the split A, if equipped. Replacing the lines on one individual riser at a time is another good way to keep everything straight. Below is the method for replacing a riser in case you must do it all at once (such as sending a riser set away then getting it back for replacement).

Start by marking the brake line knot location with a felt tip pen. Untie the brake toggle it to pull its line through the brake pulley (or guide) then:

- If you have to cut away anything (such as the shrink wrap plastic used by some) always cut away from the fabric. Be careful while using any tools to avoid scratching the metal—that weakens it significantly.

Don't change risers unless the manufacturer approves of the new ones. Handling can change dramatically with different risers.

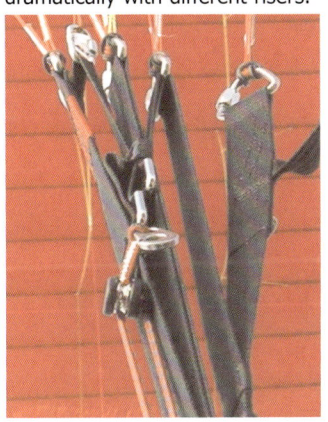

The PPG Bible: A Complete Guide and Reference

- Pull the lines off and inspect the rubber O-ring. It is best to replace them (plumbing supply outlets carry these) since they get brittle and break after a couple years. O-rings or plastic inserts keep lines from misaligning on the quick—link or from rubbing across the nut and threads.

- If hard plastic shrink wrap was used, replace with either electrical heat-shrink tubing (available at electronics supply stores) or electrical tape.

- Put the heat shrink tubing on the lines (if used), put the lines on the new riser, put the O-ring on with a figure 8 pattern (as shown) and then snug up the fastener.

- Snug to finger tight then go an 1/8th turn more with a tool.

When completed, kite the wing before flying to make sure everything appears in order and it handles as expected. Additionally, make sure the brake lines get adjusted before flying.

Adjusting Brake Lines

Brake line length is a critical dimension that should only be adjusted by, or under the guidance of, someone familiar with the procedure. Brake lines that are too short will deflect the trailing edge—an incredibly dangerous situation that could cause a parachutal stall (covered in Chapter 4). Excessively long brake lines might allow a brake toggles into the prop and will limit flare authority for landing.

When properly adjusted, with toggles at their pulley (flying hands-off), there should be some slack in the brake line with no trailing edge deflection. You'll see a slight arc in the line from its pulley up to the trailing edge. In flight, your hands should rest about position 2—that will leave enough flare authority while remaining comfortable. Having your arms hang lower may be more comfortable but sacrifices flare authority and control. Your bicep should be about horizontal when resting the weight of your arms in the brakes. Just a couple inches makes a big difference in comfort.

Many free flyers set their toggles lower since they can take *wraps* (wrap the excess line around their hands) to have full authority. The throttle makes that difficult for motor pilots.

On those few wings with two brake line pulleys to choose from, use the one that is most comfortable. Generally, with a low attachment motor, use the high pulley and for mid or high attachment motors use the low pulley.

Most wings come from the factory with the brakes set somewhat long to reduce the likelihood of a

This riser set is ready to have it's lines removed.

On triangular quick-links (inset), if you have to use a tool to remove the connector, it's bent. Don't use pliers to force it on. You're better off replacing a bent one than flying with a compromised part. Over or under-tightening can cause structural failure under load.

The black rubber grommet is used to keep lines together and positioned properly on the quick link. It prevents them from snagging on an edge. These grommets should be replaced with new ones if cracked. On the riser set above, the C lines (rear risers on this wing) are missing the grommet.

Brake Line Knots

The "8 Follow Through" is an ideal knot with low stress on the line. It is easy to tie since after looping through the brake toggle, it just follows itself back through the half-hitch.

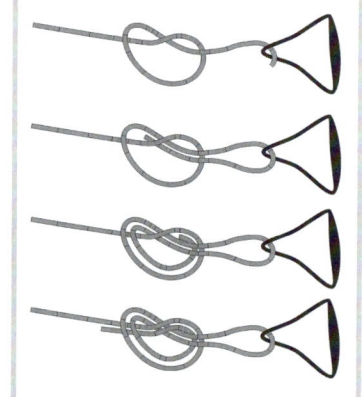

The Bowline (below) is commonly used for a quick tie but stresses the line more due to sharper bends and is not very secure.

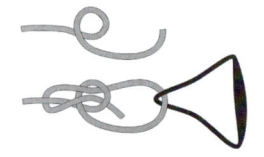

Whichever you choose, keep the brake toggle and knot close together to prevent the toggle from flapping about in the breeze.

Section II: Spreading Your Wings

new pilot stalling the wing. But that also limits control authority. To set the length, kite the wing and mark where the new knot should go. Untie the existing knot and retie it at the new location using the depicted brake line knot.

Repairing the Wing Fabric

Invariably you will tear the wing's fabric; either by pulling it too aggressively or mis—handling. Sometimes it's from having lines snagged on something in the ground. Fortunately there is a lot of resilience and this doesn't always have to be a grounding affair.

If the tear is structural then you'll have to bite the bullet and sent it in for a full repair. Structural is where there is significant stress on the material at that point. The best example is just about any seam or anywhere lines attach to fabric. If the loop pulls out of the wing you'll have to send the wing to a shop for repairs.

Anytime a wing and spinning prop mix, the wing should be inspected. Even the repair experts may not be able to put that mess back together. But a small tear, not located near an A line can be repaired. Obtain some self-adhesive repair material (repair tape) which comes in various colors and is similar to wing material. Cut it into an oval that covers the tear with about an inch of overlap. Make one for both sides of the fabric. Stretch the fabric out as much as possible, wipe it clean and dry then press the piece on top of it. Press hard. It is best to line the pattern of little squares up with the wing material's pattern. Repeat for the other side.

Inspection

After a couple years or 100 hours on a new wing it should be professionally inspected. After that, annual inspections should be done for hard core flyers and biennual inspections for casual flyers (less than 20 hours per year).

Don't be deluded by the high number of lines; a *cascade failure* is where one line breaks and transfers load to adjoining lines causing them to break in a cascade of many lines. It is extremely rare but does happen, especially on wings that are "ridden hard and put away wet." That includes those used in heavy maneuvering or aerobatics—such wings should double the inspection interval to catch problems before they cascade.

Line Stretching

Don't *ever* tie a broken line together, doing so not only halves the strength but leaves the line too short. The line *must* be replaced.

Lines shrink with time, especially if they get damp, losing up to a couple inches in length. Kevlar lines shrink less than Dyneema (or Spectra). Since the A's and B's bear more load, they tend to stretch back to their proper length during flight leaving just the C's and D's shrunk.

Given that line length determines the wing's shape, it is important to stretch them back to their proper length. A wing that is getting hard to inflate may be suffering from line shrinkage. Here's how to stretch lines.

1. Find out how long they are supposed to be using the wing's line chart which hopefully came with its user manual.
2. Locate a pulley, 6 feet of rope and a 40 pound weight (a 5 gallon water bucket or bag of rock salt works good). You'll need enough room to lay

1. The hole.

2. The Patch

3. Here is a typical inspection shop where gliders are tested and repaired. The porosity meter (being used at left) measures how quickly air can seep through the fabric. Strength testing of lines is done with a scale and repairs are done with the sewing machine at right. There's more to it than meets the eye.

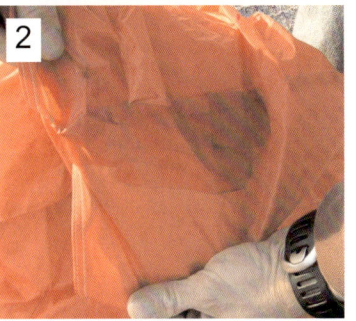

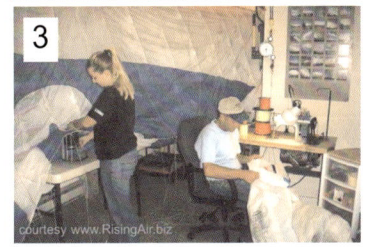

out your glider lines.

3. Affix the pulley to a door (or other structure). Run the rope through both risers, through the pulley and tie it to the weight. Use the tape measure to measure line length.

4. Stand behind the wing fabric and grab a D line (or cascaded lines that the D connects to) where it attaches to the wing. Pull hard enough to lift the weight up and hold for 20 seconds. Compare it with the same line on the other side to see how much it stretched—then stretch that other line. Repeat for each line.

5. As you do this, measure the line length periodically to see if they're getting to the prescribed length. If not, stretch again.

If you cannot get the lines to be within a 1/4 inch of their specified length, or they stretch too far, the offending lines need to be replaced. In all likelihood, that's a sign that all the lines should be replaced.

After An Ocean Dunking

It is universally accepted that dunking a wing in salt water is bad—finely abrasive salt crystals remain after the water evaporates, dramatically shortening the glider's life (both lines and fabric). But if you remove the salt water right away by hosing it down with fresh water, the damage can be avoided.

To best rinse a wing after it has been dunked, clip it along the trailing edge to a strong clothesline. Hoist it up high enough to get the cell openings above ground.

Spray it thoroughly with fresh water to clean out any remaining brine. Get up inside each cell opening to get it completely soaked. That should drain away or at least dilute the briny badness to a safe level. Then leave it on the line, out of direct sunlight, to dry.

At worst, just hose the wing down wherever it lays. This may be preferable to waiting but then go through the above method as soon as you can.

Whether fresh or salt water, take care when extricating a submersed wing—it becomes extremely heavy and will tear very easy if lifted with water in the cells. Pull it out *slowly* by the trailing edge.

Emergency Tool Kit

A lot can be fixed in the field with a few simple tools and parts that fit in your harness pouches. Mostly, you want to be able to tighten any bolt on the machine, tighten or replace the belt (if applicable) and replace the spark plug.

- Allen wrenches. Almost all engines use metric sizes 3, 4, 5 and 6mm.
- Screw drivers. Make sure you can adjust the carburetor.
- Lightweight spark plug wrench. The type with just the round hex fitting and a hole is good—your screw driver can be used through the hole to give leverage.
- Small Knife, small locking pliers, and small socket set (3, through 8mm sizes).
- Spark plug, wire ties and super glue (for the prop).

Alan Chuculate is repacking a reserve. It's not hard but must be done correctly. There's a lot more than just folding and stuffing. Some instructors give clinics and there are videos to teach repacking. Never rely on just a video though, do it with someone who knows how so they can make sure you're doing it right.

If you're not certain how, or haven't practiced, send it to a repacker. The manufacturer, your instructor, or FootFlyer.com can suggest a reputable shop.

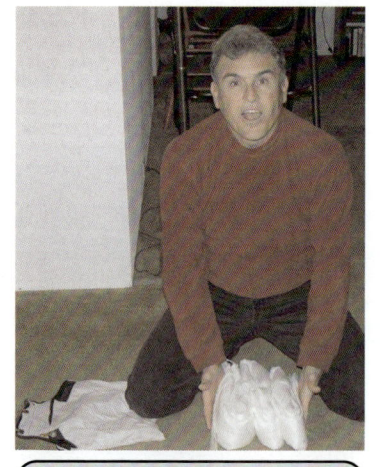

⚠ Caution!

Never put the wing in a washing machine or dryer. The stress and heat would be very damaging. If it gets wet, dry it immediately in an open area, preferably out of direct sunlight.

The PPG Bible: A Complete Guide and Reference

Reserve

Reserves generally come from the factory ready to install and deploy; most come with containers that easily clip onto your motor frame and harness but this *must* be done correctly. Installing it wrong may be worse than not having it at all.

There are several places where a reserve gets mounted: behind the head, on the side, in front of the pilot or under the seat. Each has advantages and disadvantages but most are mounted beside the pilot because it's usually the easiest to install. Some motors come with a reserve mount in the seat bottom, a nice arrangement because it is out of the way. Same thing for reserves mounted above and behind the pilot's head. For a machine to have the reserve mounted anywhere but on the side or in front, it generally must be *designed* for it.

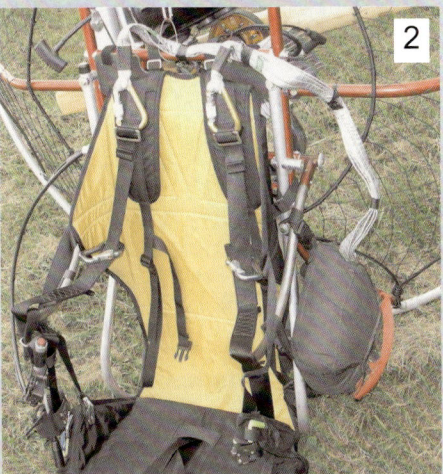

Setup

Mounting a reserve on your motor must be done with an eye on how it will deploy and how you will reach it. Make sure you can reach it quickly, have enough arm travel to pull it all the way out (over a foot of line pulls out before the reserve pouch itself), and be able to easily throw it in a clear direction.

Here are some considerations for mounting the reserve to your motor:

- Mount it opposite the throttle. Some suggest this to be your dominant hand but rehearsal can make either hand work. A front mount is acceptable but consider how the risers will pull on deployment. If your body gets between the risers and an inflating chute, you'll probably break.

- The reserve bridle should be routed along the harness or motor frame and remain clear of throttle cable, straps, speedbar or anything else that would get in the way during deployment. Use Velcro or very small wire ties that break loose with about 20 pounds of pull. This will prevent nuisance breaks during normal handling but allow the reserve to pull free when needed.

- Go through a deployment in your mind. Think about where the reserve will come out, catch air and where each reserve riser will be as it extends fully with you hanging below.

- Hook the reserve riser either to the same loops as the paraglider or as close as possible. Some consider it advantageous for the pilot to come down leaning back to let the motor absorb impact but most recommend the landing be on your feet with a parachute landing fall (PLF). That means the hang points for the reserve should be higher than for the paraglider. Of course if your harness comes equipped with reserve loops, use them—they will be designed for the opening shock.

1. On this installation, the pilot had two loops to choose from for his reserve bridle. The top ones would have been preferable but they were in use by the main carabiners. So he routed the reserve through the main carabiners to the lower "D" rings. When the reserve deploys, it will immediately scrunch these two carabiners together (should be ok but is not ideal).

2. This installation is preferred; the reserve risers go to the highest point on the harness meaning the pilot would land mostly upright after a deployment.

The wire ties/tape that keep the bridle (reserve risers) together must be able to break with only about 20 pounds of pull.

Insure the routing doesn't go through anything that would impede opening or cause injury.

Reserve Maintenance

Store the reserve as you would a paraglider—in a cool, dry place away from sunlight or chemicals. Of course, if it remains on your motor, be careful about where

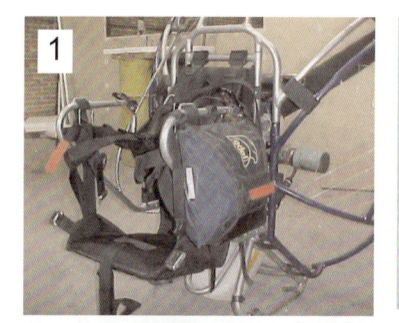

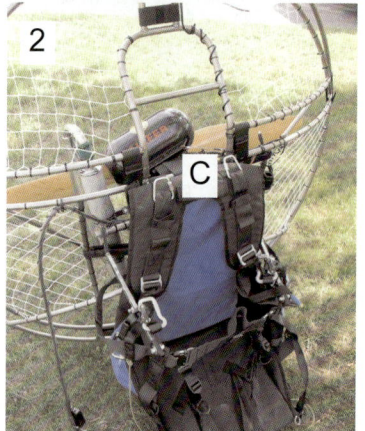

The PPG Bible: A Complete Guide and Reference

> **Skydiving Reserves**
>
> Paraglider reserves differ structurally from sport parachuting reserves and the two must not be interchanged. A paraglider reserve is designed to open immediately while the sky diving version opens more gradually to avoid injuring the high-speed free-faller.
>
> Terminal velocity (maximum fall speed) is over 120 MPH for a sky diver in free fall. Some paraglider reserves may not even hold together if thrown at that speed (a "terminal" open). A PPG reserve is more likely to be thrown below 50 MPH and a sky diving reserve might have difficulty opening at that lower speed.

1. This unit has a right-hand throttle so its reserve is on the pilot's left side. It must be secured both top and bottom so when the pilot pulls, he has full travel from the container. Some instructors recommend that the reserve be mounted on the side of your predominant hand so a right handed pilot would have a left-hand throttle.

Also note the hook-in style. Carabiners are attached to a strap that connects to the rails on either side of the pilot (what the reserve is mounted to). This is a fixed low hook-in style.

2. This one is made for an overhead mount. The two small metal carabiners on either side of the letter "C" (above the mains) are made for a reserve hook-in.

the motor goes. For example, getting the motor wet is no big deal, getting the reserve wet scores a repack.

Repacking should be done once a year or, for those left in proper storage, every other year. It is necessary because the fabric will eventually tighten into shapes that don't open quickly; plus, rubber bands holding the bridle array in proper shape become brittle and break. Repacking is a great time for the reserve to be inspected, too.

The preferable way to do a repack is to send it the factory that made it—they'll know it best and know what problems have come up on other similar models (fortunately they don't get tested a lot). You can also send it off to an experienced rigger who is familiar with the design—they will inspect it and replace anything as needed. Only do it yourself if you're certain about the procedure and have the requisite parts. It's not that difficult to repack, but the steps must be done correctly.

If liquid spills on the container or it goes in the water, it should be repacked.

Always use the repack as an opportunity to practice tossing the reserve. Hanging from a simulator is ideal but, if that's not possible, just sit in your harness and practice throwing it. Do so several times while rehearsing the steps (see Chapter 4).

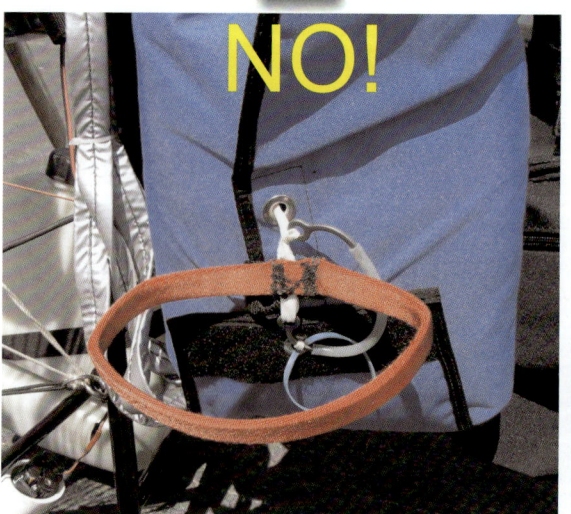

A pilot pulling on this reserve would be unsuccessful. The pin is completely through the loops and would likely not work. Make sure the hooks are through only halfway as shown below so they can pull out freely. Pulling the handle first lets the flaps open to reveal the deployment bag.

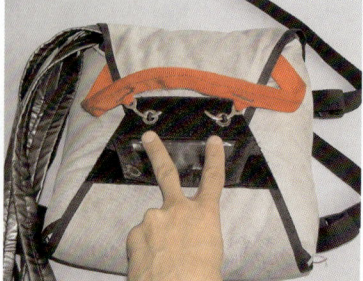

Section II: Spreading Your Wings

Flying Cross Country

CHAPTER 13

Heading out on a cross-country flight is premier—exploring new directions, going for miles to nowhere in particular, poking about the landscape from barely above — it is the freedom of flight that many have only dreamt about.

Obviously there are limits. Don't plan on commuting to work, although it's been done, and beware of small changes in weather that can lay waste to plans. Don't get out somewhere and *need* to get back—that could pressure you to fly when you otherwise wouldn't (and shouldn't). However, once armed with appropriate skills, gear and weather knowledge, cross country can be extremely rewarding: you launch from home, alight at some distant spot, relish the accomplishment, and then head back home via a different route.

The author found his mark. The pictured grass-runway airport was a target for the *Circle and 2 Lines* task of the U.S. Nationals in 2004. There were a lot of trees below which accounts for the high altitude.

Basic Tips

Whenever you fly farther than you're willing to walk, there are additional concerns. Some apply even to local flying but take on more importance with distance.

- Choose days where there are no weather changes anticipated anywhere near your flight times. Being away from your launch site when the weather turns sour is decidedly un-fun.

- Let somebody know that you will be flying and always take a cell phone if you've got one.

- If the wind shifts, try changing altitudes to improve penetration (groundspeed into a headwind). Wind is normally stronger up high but occasionally you can climb into a *weaker* wind. A GPS is invaluable for maximizing groundspeed—as you climb, just watch the groundspeed readout and note the best altitude.

Summer Escape

A warm summer afternoon beckoned and I rushed home. After gathering up my gear, I quickly slipped away before anyone could interfere: I had a mission. Fifteen miles south of my favorite launch site a new racetrack had just opened up—I wanted to go see it. Quick calculations suggested about 3 hours of flight time. I'd have to find thermals if I wanted to loiter anywhere since that was about my endurance. It was probably not going to be a complete round trip but, with this craft, landing out isn't that big a deal.

Off I went, running into the sky, then climbing on course, veering left and right as interesting targets appeared. Occasionally something came into view that warranted a closer look, and if it was next to a field, or otherwise open, I just went down and checked it out. A motocross track appeared—and there was nobody on it. Yeah! I went down and cruised along it's hilly meanders, a few feet high, trying to stay over the curvy course; playing. This is the *ultimate* off-road vehicle!

Then back up I went, like a migrating bird, heading south towards a place I'd never been. This was so delicious. I had just flown over the area in a Boeing 737 but was now commanding 28 square meters of nylon, searching for lift. Thermals were plentiful and well marked by capping cumulus clouds. I circled in the stronger updrafts, quickly getting above 3000 feet. Warmth below gave way to a chill up there. Sitting in my chair, overlooking the tiny sprawl of civilization below was amazing. Of course I've been up this high thousands of times—3 times just that day—but certainly never suspended by fabric and sitting in a tiny little seat listening to my favorite music.

Finding the racetrack was brainless from such altitude. Nobody was there so it was fun to power off and go low, cruising the outer perimeter from 100 feet, then again from 10 feet. Wow. After thoroughly scoping out the track, I pressed onward, westward, exploring. Landing at the Joliet airport let me really feel my new capability—actually *travelling* in the PPG. Here I was, many miles from home, having explored, gone to the heights and now just stood there for a moment, basking in the moment. I doffed the motor and checked the tank—lift had stretched my endurance and it looked like I might have just enough fuel—probably 45 minutes worth. But, after launching, a friend appeared below, waving wildly. It was Nick, my flyin' buddy—I *had* to stop. Of course that maneuvering spent whatever reserve fuel remained. Oh but how I enjoyed being able to do that—coming back around, alighting, chatting, and relaunching. Soon I was back on course. When I turned the GPS on it had bad news—with 15 miles to go, I was now making only 12 MPH. That didn't add up. Oh well—I figured I'd go as far as I could.

The GPS was indeed right and it became obvious that I would, in fact, land short. Using thermals (slowing down in lift, speeding up in sink, circling in the stronger ones) let me get closer, but alas, 4 miles or so shy of my starting point, Mr. Motor sputtered his last—I went on glide. Good fortune let me slip into a paramotor field where I could stash my gear and grab a ride back. What an incredible treat!

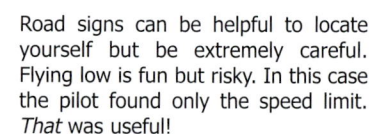

Road signs can be helpful to locate yourself but be extremely careful. Flying low is fun but risky. In this case the pilot found only the speed limit. *That* was useful!

Also, make sure there are no cars that could be distracted by your presence.

- Avoid flying low, but if you must, do so only while headed into the wind (see chapter 16). Staying above 200 feet AGL is dramatically safer since it keeps humanity's protrusions (especially wires) below you.

- Cross power lines at the supports (poles or towers), at least twice their height and at an angle. Judging wire height is surprisingly difficult unless you're over those supports. Cross them at an angle so you easily turn away if the motor quits.

- Check the airspace if it's a new area.

- After takeoff, look back and see what the launch area looks like for your return. Find a prominent landmark since the sun angle or clouds may change appearances. It can be hard to recognize your home site the first time out.

- Take a map or GPS if the area is not familiar or you plan on a long trip. It's value comes as much from the groundspeed readout as the distance and direction.

- Don't ever let yourself get squeezed into night time. Besides being illegal, finding your way safely to the ground can be tough. Do carry a small flashlight though. Even if you land before darkness settles, it would be handy to see what you're doing on the ground.

- Carry basic tools.

- Consider taking a small amount of two-stroke oil in case you wind up in someone's yard and they have only gas for their lawn mower. (Yes, I've benefited from this exact advice).

As with all flying, stay within gliding distance of safe landing areas, favoring those that are downwind of you since they'll be easier to reach. Stay close to roads to make egress much easier (unless you don't mind walking).

Fuel & Range

When choosing a route, start off into the wind. It's no fun being airborne, trying to get back and fighting a headwind, especially when you're ready to be on the ground. Plus it makes fuel planning easier to go upwind for half of your endurance and then turn around. It's a conservative approach that is convenient and more fun. For one thing, when you've had enough, it's nice that you can get back relatively quickly.

If there is little or no wind, only fly 1/3 of your endurance before turning around, just to leave some margin for error. If the route is a triangle, plan the flight's last leg to be going downwind.

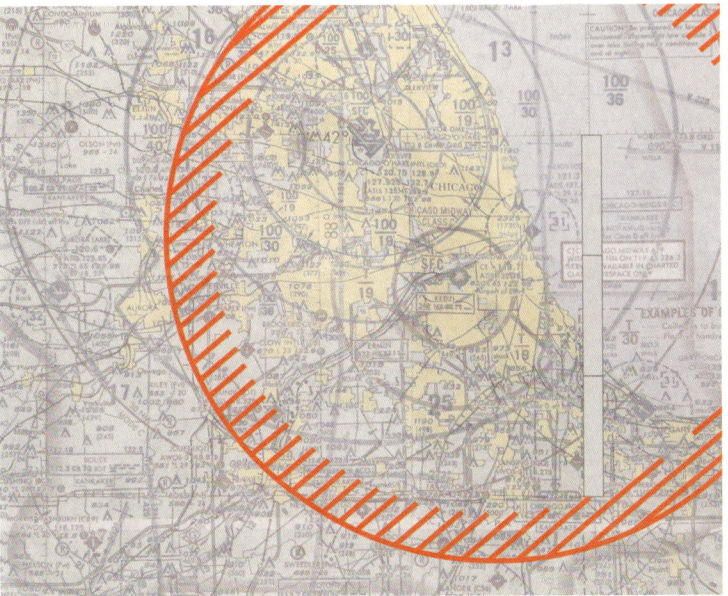

You should have a very good idea of how long you can fly before setting out. Also have an in-flight way to check fuel remaining (a mirror).

If you're carrying oil, sometimes it's possible to land near a gas station and refuel. It feels funny—walking up to the pump with your weird looking tank, filling it and knowing you'll be using it to run off into the sky. Strange and amazing.

Is the airspace where you're going legal *today*?

Chicagoland pilots had this surprise one day when the President dropped into town. They closed airspace within 30 miles—including many popular PPG destinations.

When flying to or through new areas we must be especially vigilant about airspace issues.

Getting Lost

In most areas of the country, getting lost is an inconvenience at worst and only possible for those not carrying a GPS. It may be embarrassing when you land to ask for directions but, given the ability to land about anywhere, there is little to really worry about unless you're out in the boondocks. But before getting to that dreadful state of affairs, there are ways to keep yourself oriented.

- After takeoff, look back towards your launch area. Do this first a mile out, then a few miles out. Remember what you saw so, on the way back, you will better recognize it.
- Climb up higher. As long as airspace and clouds allow, you may get a better perspective.
- Use Roads and other prominent landmarks. Think of major roads, rivers, or railroad tracks in your area and whether you've crossed them or not. For example, if a major highway carves northward and it is west of your launch site, but you haven't yet crossed it, then you know you're east of it.
- Use road Signs. Find a nice, landable field along a road with signs and scoot down to read it. Only with a PPG! Don't get below wire height, though, and always maintain safe landing options. This could be quite risky if you're not careful and is only an option in the most open areas.

Vector Diagram

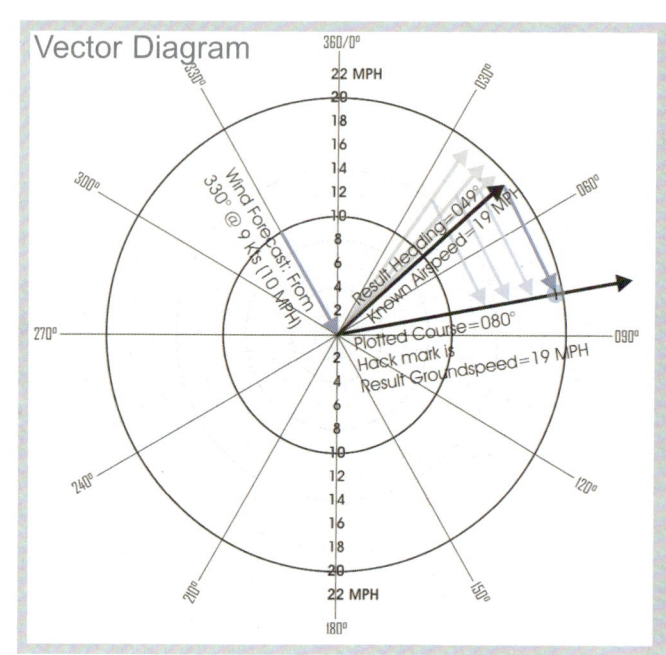

The latest blank version of this chart is provided at www.FootFlyer.com

Calculating Ground Track & Groundspeed

Once you know the desired ground track (plotted course) and how fast you fly (airspeed), you can use this chart to derive heading and resulting groundspeed:

1. Draw your plotted course (080°) from the center all the way outward.

2. Draw your forecast wind (blue line above) as the direction the wind is forecast from and long enough to represent the windspeed with the arrow head touching center.

3. You'll need two strips of paper. One should be marked as the wind arrow that represents the wind speed (mark an arrowhead to clarify wind direction) and mark the other piece's edge with your airspeed.

4. Keep the wind arrow parallel with the wind direction while sliding its arrowhead along the plotted course. At the same time, have the airspeed piece go from the center and stay in contact with the wind arrow. When the tail of the wind arrow touches the airspeed's marking, you've got a wind triangle. The airspeed arrow points to the heading-to-fly and the wind arrow is pointing at the groundspeed.

The example shows a plotted course of 080° (true course, without magnetic correction). The quartering tailwind turns out not to have any effect on groundspeed. The pilot will fly a 049° to maintain his 080° ground track.

Navigation

The following tools are not *necessary* to enjoy cross-country flight but they can be fun to master. In fact, they are the basis for an entirely different skill set: *pilotage* and *dead reckoning*. These have been (and continue to be) a staple of regular airplane pilot training.

Dead reckoning is the process of using a plotted course, a calculated groundspeed and heading to navigate and predict your future whereabouts. Using forecast winds, a map and compass you can come up with the heading to fly that should keep you on course. *pilotage* is the process of reading the map in flight and adjust-

Magnetism, Truth & Courses

Aviation charts are laid out in grids of longitude and latitude with respect to true north. Compasses, however, point to magnetic north. The difference between true and magnetic north is shown on charts as lines of variation called Isogonic lines. For example, on this chart, the dashed line pointed to by #1 means that the difference is 14° east.

Magnetic course (MC) is derived by subtracting east ("east is least") variation and adding west variation to the true course (TC). So, in this case, the TC was 80°. After subtracting 14° of variation (use the closest isogonic line), you get a magnetic course of 66°. So if you used your compass to walk a 66° heading, you'd walk along the plotted line.

But our sea of air is usually moving, so we must account for wind drift. The result of doing so is magnetic heading (MH)—the compass heading you fly to stay on course—theoretically.

Jackson Chart

ing heading to stay on the line. Manual navigation is a combination of these skills.

Even though we don't *need* all this, understanding it can be helpful. Mostly it can be a fun exercise—planning, then executing the plan accurately with just a map, compass and watch. International competition pilots get good at this since it makes up to 33% of their score.

The purpose of all navigation is to fly a desired track over the ground and arrive at the destination at an estimated time. Using the navigation log below, do the following (details on each step are provided below):

- Draw a line on the map representing your desired ground track. Mark the line at easily identifiable checkpoints along the way and measure the distances between each mark. These get entered as checkpoints on your PPG navlog.
- Measure the true course of each straight segment, then apply *variation* to come up with a magnetic course for that segment.
- Calculate the magnetic heading that corrects for wind and tells what the planned groundspeed will be (using the wind calculator described below)
- Build a navigation log to be used in flight or just for reference.
- Go fly the course using pilotage.

Plotting the Course and Heading

Chartmakers simplify matters by including vertical lines of longitude and horizontal lines of latitude on the charts. Point 1 on the Jackson Chart shows how it labels variation as E or W—in this case showing 14° east variation along the dashed *isogonic line* (a line that shows the magnetic variation in that area).

Remember this saying: "west is best, east is least." That means west variation is added to true course and east variation is subtracted from it. So if you want to go *true* east, which would be along a line of longitude or 090°, subtract the variation. So 90° minus 14° gives a magnetic course of 076°. In other words, flying a magnetic course of 76° would yield a 090° true course (not accounting for wind yet).

Draw a course line on the chart representing your desired ground track from launch to landing and measure its degrees relative to true north. This can be done using a protractor and measuring from either a longitude or latitude line. With this true course in hand, add (for west) or subtract (for east) the variation to get a magnetic course. That is the magnetic heading you would fly with no wind. Add a correction for wind (covered below) to get the initial heading after launch.

Choose checkpoints along the route that will be easy to identify and easy to get a time measurement on. The best ones will be usable even if you're off-course. Rivers, power lines, highways or railroad tracks that cross perpendicular to your course are great. If they *angle* across your course, it is more difficult—you must know more accurately that you're on the course line when taking a time.

If you're writing out a navigation log, it can be filled in with the points, distances and magnetic courses. These are the

Digging Deeper:
Earth's Moving Magnetic North

The Earth's magnetic north moves slowly over the years. In fact, the rate of drift is measurable and some charts show not only the current variation, but how fast it's drifting.

The line of variation that shows where true and magnetic north are the same (lucky compass users there) is called the *Agonic Line*. In the U.S. this line goes through central Indiana—anywhere on that line and your compass reads both magnetic and true heading.

The most significant difference between true and magnetic courses in the U.S. is on the northernmost coasts. Both east and west coasts have a difference of up to 20 degrees.

This is an example of *drift*. The wind from your right is causing a left drift. The resultant path over the ground is ground track.

You must angle into the wind so that ground track is taking you to the destination.

most useful pieces of information along with the headings.

Wind Correction

Any wind will affect your groundspeed and track. Think of wind as a block of air with which you're drifting. When you're airborne, that motion is added to your own and must be accounted for to achieve a desired ground track. If you're trying to track due east and the wind is from the north (wind is always given in the direction it's *from*) then you'll need to hold a heading to the left—that is called *crabbing*. And with our slow speed, a little wind makes a lot of difference.

One way to figure this out is with a *vector diagram* as shown on the previous page—it represents speeds and directions visually. Vectors, in this case, are arrows, one for your in-flight speed and heading, and another for wind speed and direction. Follow the diagram's directions for "Calculating Ground Track & groundspeed."

Note that if you're flying a round trip or any other course that end up back at the landing site, any wind at all will always *increase* your total flying time. Also, direct crosswinds slow you down. If any wind is present, it must have some tailwind component to keep groundspeed equal to or better than airspeed.

Pilotage

This is the process of flying your planned route using a calculated heading, a map, and visual cues to stay on course. It's the fun part and is amazingly easy in a PPG given our unobstructed view.

Planning tells you what the ground track will be and offers an initial heading that corrects for wind (*crabbing* into the wind). It will be as accurate as the wind forecast. After launch, take up that heading until you can find some of the checkpoints and see what kind of correction it *really* takes to stay on track.

The goal is to maintain a ground track: if there's any crosswind, don't just point at the next checkpoint when it comes into view—that will result in an inefficient curved path. Your goal is a straight line *over the ground*. It's not necessarily intuitive since you're pointing upwind of the target. Force yourself to look at what your *ground track* is doing and make sure *that* is heading towards the target.

To see that you're tracking as desired, pick a close ground feature between you and the target and envision a line between the two; if you are drifting off of that line then adjust your heading accordingly.

Reading a map and associating ground features takes practice. Some things on the map are nearly worthless, small roads and populated areas, for example. The outlines of yellow that indicate populace (roughly equating to night illumination patterns as seen by satellite photos) have little resemblance to what you'll see—they're usually too dated.

Obvious features, such as highways, railroad tracks, landmarks and the like are best. Using a long, straight feature (like railroad tracks) requires some way to tell where you are along that feature.

Telling distances is tricky too, more so in some areas than others. The U.S. Midwest has conveniently placed roads at one-mile intervals that run N/S and E/W which helps a lot. There is no such order in other areas, especially hilly ones.

The most useful tools on a navigation log are the mileage and estimated groundspeeds. You can either fill in the actual numbers or just use the log for reference. Some navlogs (or electronic calculators) have time in minutes; they must be converted to tenths—every 6 seconds is one tenth so 8 minutes and 12 seconds is 8.2 minutes.

Calculating Groundspeed

With a stopwatch and map you can calculate your groundspeed and, knowing that you to can predict your position at some future point and time. If you also know your heading and airspeed, you can even tell what the winds are, although that starts getting into a lot of computational effort for someone piloting a paraglider.

Just because you *can* navigate direct doesn't mean it's wise to do so. Consider your retrieval options if a landing becomes necessary. In some areas, like the one pictured, following roads is protective wisdom.

Consider ravines, rivers or other difficult terrain when flying away from infrastructure or retrieval option.

This chart can be useful for quickly accounting for wind to determine heading and groundspeed without needing batteries.

Vector Diagram

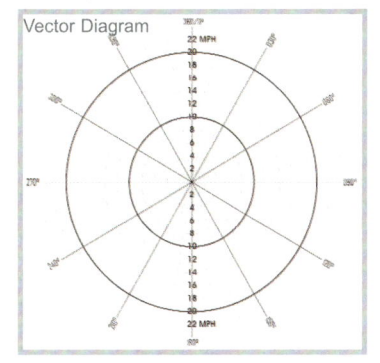

Charts presented on the next page allow these calculations to be done without any electronics. The charts can be taped to the same clipboard that you use use for your navlog for easy reference. Competition is about the only time you would use these tools.

Altitudes

Choosing altitudes is critical for maximizing performance—climbing or descending can yield free additional groundspeed if more favorable winds are found. Start with the winds aloft information (see Chapter 7) to get an idea of what to expect, but improve your mental wind-image by trying different altitudes. Generally, the higher you go, the stronger the winds blow, but not always. Be quick to try different altitudes, especially if groundspeed dwindles appreciably.

Most airplanes cruise over 1000 feet AGL. Above 3000 feet they tend to fly in 500 foot increments with the eastbounders using odd altitudes (3000, 3500, 5000, 5500, etc.) and the westbounders using even altitudes (4000, 4500, 6000, 6500 etc.). Knowing that may help you know where to look out for them.

Lingering above 10,000 feet is a very bad idea since jets travel at their fastest speeds up there but this is more of a concern within 60 miles or so of larger cities.

Using a GPS

The Global Positioning System (GPS) allows much useful information to come from hand-held *navigators*. Of course the moving maps with streets and restaurants and gas stations and so forth make using it brainless, but its most useful display is groundspeed and track. From that you can derive the winds pretty accurately.

If the GPS says you're tracking 120° (southeast) but you're pointed due east (090°) then you know the winds are out of the north, or have a significantly north component. If it says you're only going 15 mph and your normal airspeed is 25 mph then you have a 10 mph headwind component.

A GPS will also all tell how much time it will take to reach the next checkpoint, a valuable tidbit if you're fighting darkness and/or fuel exhaustion. Of course a few mph change can have a dramatic effect on flight time, especially if there is already a good headwind.

Mixing Units

As with all the charts in this chapter, different units can be used as long as speed and distance are compatible. For example, knots are nautical miles per hour. So if distance is in nautical miles, then speed must be knots.

If distance is regular (statute) miles, then speed must be in regular miles per hour.

U.S. air maps (*sectionals*) are marked in nautical miles so knots and nautical miles are a convenient combination.

Full resolution versions of these charts are available on FootFlyer.com.

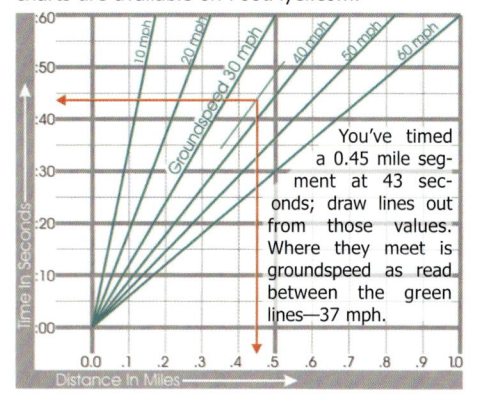

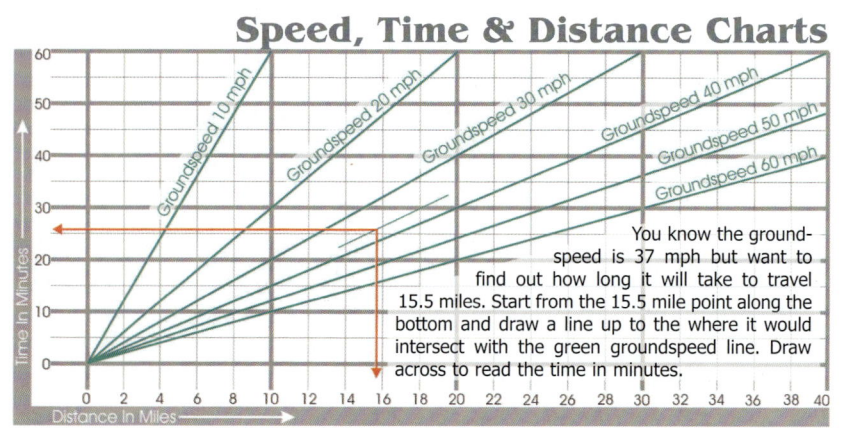

Speed, Time & Distance Charts

You've timed a 0.45 mile segment at 43 seconds; draw lines out from those values. Where they meet is groundspeed as read between the green lines—37 mph.

You know the groundspeed is 37 mph but want to find out how long it will take to travel 15.5 miles. Start from the 15.5 mile point along the bottom and draw a line up to the where it would intersect with the green groundspeed line. Draw across to read the time in minutes.

Flying With Others

CHAPTER 14

Eventually, most new pilots seek out like minded peers to share their flights with. It adds fun, education, and sometimes humor to the mix. It can also complicate matters in unusual ways; the more folks gather, the more complicated organization can get. Going to major events is the extreme case.

These three pilots are keeping an eye on each other over the Salton Sea. They are over land but the picture conveniently leaves that out of view below.

Courtesy

As with most issues of courtesy, a generous helping of common sense is essential. If an activity seems like it may be obnoxious, dangerous, or marginally safe—that's your common sense singing out "hmmm, maybe I should rethink this one." The folly of some actions, however, is less clear which is what these guidelines are for.

Where to Lay Out

If another pilot already has his wing laid out, avoid setting up in the way. It is best to set up behind him or well clear to the side. Even if you think you'll launch first stay clear of his path in case you get delayed. It is bad form to lay out your glider in a way that requires another pilot to steer around it. If your proximity is an issue, ask the affected pilot if it's OK. Better yet, if you think you have to ask, move farther away.

Look at where your run will take you and be sure that it's clear. Have a good climbout path that doesn't fly right over any spectators, campers or other pilots—doing so is illegal, rude and dangerous. An inopportune motor failure would put the others in danger. Even at official gatherings be mindful of your noise during climbout. If you can't figure out how to make a safe departure without getting close to people, don't launch.

While airborne, avoid buzzing about the launch area, especially in light winds. Your wake may linger for several minutes, making it even more difficult for those trying to takeoff. Plus, pilots in challenging conditions may be waiting for just the right puff of breeze and won't appreciate your annoying presence when it comes. Climb up at least 200 feet AGL after launch or go to another area so other pilots get their chance at clean air.

Prop Blast

Be mindful of your prop blast. Don't point it toward other people or their wings. Blowing someone's carefully positioned wing into a tangled mess will quickly sully your reputation. The same thing applies to fly-by's—be careful about where your prop blast goes. Even if nobody is preparing to launch, don't let wake or prop wash get to any laid-out wings. Flying near enough to roll up someone's wing is a sure sign of not being aware of your surroundings.

Keep the plane of the propeller clear so that if a prop were to come apart, the shards would miss those who might be in line with it.

After flying to a local airport, this group of pilots readies for their return. It is greatly appreciated when basic rules of courtesy are followed.

Plan the launch so as to let preceding wakes subside. Flying through that turbulence just after liftoff could get you dumped back to earth.

It is polite to offer assistance with spreading out a fellow pilot's wing but some are sensitive to setting it up in a particular way. Helping spread out their wing after a blown launch is almost always appreciated though.

Risks

There are additional risks to manage when flying with others. First, you must obviously be very vigilant about 1) your position, 2) the pattern and 3) keeping an active scan for other traffic. If you do not know where your other flying buddies are, you must carefully look around, including above and blow. Do shallow turns to make sure they are not directly above you. Don't make sudden changes in altitude until you know it is clear in the desired altitude. Don't turn until satisfied there is nobody coming from that direction.

Follow the turning rule without fail: "look, lean, turn." Besides weight shifting, the lean alerts other pilots of your impending turn.

Flying with one or two other pilots probably adds as much risk as flying with a hundred because we tend to drop our guard. A moment of distraction may be all it takes if your buddy comes up on you un-noticed.

Collision

One valuable tool for collision avoidance is your shadow. On sunny days you can find it quickly by noticing where the sun is and looking to where your shadow should be. The higher you are, the more blurry your shadow will be; the lower you are, the sharper your shadow will be. So even if you *do* see the shadow of another wing near yours, it's easy to tell whether it's pilot is above or below you—a handy trick in crowded air. If you do not see any other wings near your shadow, you're alone. If you see another wing shadow, and it's fuzzier than yours, then it's above you—descend while looking up towards the sun to find it.

Be wary of formation flying, especially with strangers but even with pilots you know (covered later).

Wake

Flying through a paramotor wake can be very rough. At best it will be startling; at worst it can partially collapse your wing. The motor, lines and wing all produce turbulence, but the swirling wing tip vortices are the strongest (see Chapter 22).

Wing wake tends to settle, spread out slowly and drift with the wind. Avoid heavier craft such as trikes, tandems, and even very heavy pilots, especially if they've just passed through. Also, flying through, but nearly parallel in another's wake is worse then crossing it and carries a greater chance for wing collapse.

Heavier machines like PPC's leave a violent wake that lingers longer—they must be given a wide berth. Smooth conditions allow a wake to last longer, too.

If you find yourself in a wake, treat it like any other turbulence—hold the brakes at pressure at pressure 2 and throttle for level flight. As always, if you feel the wing fall back, immediately go "hands up, power off, prepare to dampen the surge."

Fly *above* the path of preceding aircraft to avoid flying through their wake. Flying between the vortices is another bad idea—there is sinking air there. You may not have enough thrust to out-climb it if you're low.

Rescuing a pilot

If you fly with other pilots long enough you'll probably be faced with the need to help extricate someone from one of trouble's many forms.

What a Drag

Kiting or flying in strong winds means that, eventually, somebody gets dragged along the ground. If you see this happening, don't lunge on the pilot or his motor—stop the *wing*. A wind-whipped wing can overpower even several burly helpers. Run around behind it so the wing drapes around your leg (see Chapter 3). Grabbing a wing tip and running it upwind is also effective. Whatever you do, don't grab lines! They'll quickly leave painful burns.

Water

One of our biggest fears should be going in the water. Don't be fooled by stories of those who survive a dunking—other pilots have not. And it doesn't take much water to be deadly, especially if it's moving. One pilot even came to grief after landing *beside* moving water—his wing went into a drainage culvert and dragged him under before he could unclip.

If you must go out to help someone who landed in the water, get flotation—*good* flotation. A boat is obviously best, but use whatever else can be found quickly such as a surfboard, inflatable mattress or life jacket. Don't jump in the water yourself since the lines will try to snag you when nearing the pilot's gear. Probably the best thing to do is give the pilot something to hold on to so he can unstrap and relax for a moment. If he is submersed then your options dwindle. Leaving your flotation could easily put you in the same tangled dilemma as the victim.

Power Lines

Voltage is to electricity what pressure is to water and power lines have a lot of it. In the grip of such high voltage wires, your paraglider lines are conductive. They

1. The higher you are, the more blurry your shadow becomes in sunlight. It's a good way to tell whether someone is above or below you as this photo demonstrates. The photographer is higher so his shadow is more blurry.

2. After crunching down through some branches, this lucky pilot was only a few feet above the helping hands of his rescuers. This is one reason why flying with others is a good idea, so they can come fetch you from unplanned predicaments.

can make you a leak to ground (earth)—a small leak, to be sure, but with deadly pressure. The lowest voltage carried on poles is around 4000 and high-tension wires carry upwards of half a million volts. While it may be current that kills, it's this voltage that drives the current through our high-resistance bodies and lines.

So if a pilot lands in power lines and does not fall to the ground, leave him hanging! Do not reach up for him—that could cause current to flow through both of you. Rather contact the power company and wait until they shut the lines down.

Trapped By A Thrusting Motor

It can happen that a pilot's motor will unexpectedly go to full thrust, pinning him in the process. This is risky for the pilot but even more so for a rescuer. Before jumping into the fray, have a plan. Make sure the plan keeps you out of the prop *and* that the pilot sees you coming so he doesn't swing the revving motor your way. Also, know how you're going to douse the power in case the regular kill switch has failed. Don't think this so uncommon—a severed throttle cable usually disables the kill switch too.

Alternative kill methods are covered in Chapter 19. They include pulling the choke or covering the air intake. Pulling the spark plug off works but be prepared for a startling shock. Shutting off the master switch, if there is one, may not kill the motor—it primarily prevents inadvertent starter activation.

If you're flying with a buddy, it's a good idea to know how to shut off each others motors.

Communications

Flying with others gives added reason to have a radio, especially if it works through your helmet. Even if it doesn't, carry one so that if you go down, you can work out retrieval plans. Learn the *Bump Scale* (see Chapter 5) so you can communicate it to your flying friends.

Formation Flying

Formation flying is precision flying (covered in Chapter 16) and should be avoided until you're *experienced* at precision flying. Specifically you should be able to actively keep the wing where you want it, even in turbulence, without really thinking about it. Until that point, avoid flying within 5 wing spans of other pilots and always keep your distance from someone who angles away when approached. They are obviously not comfortable with your proximity.

Never accept a visibly fast closure rate. It could quickly yield a collision or last-minute control inputs that cause you to spin or stall. If it looks like your approaching someone quickly, turn away.

Tim Kaiser (red), Phil Russman (blue) and Michael Purdy (yellow) pose in this formation flight just west of the Salton Sea in California.

A midair collision or entanglement would likely be catastrophic. There is more to formation flying than meets the eye, make sure you're up to the task. Two of these pilots had already worked together while taping parts of Risk & Reward before flying this close.

Section III

Mastering The Sport

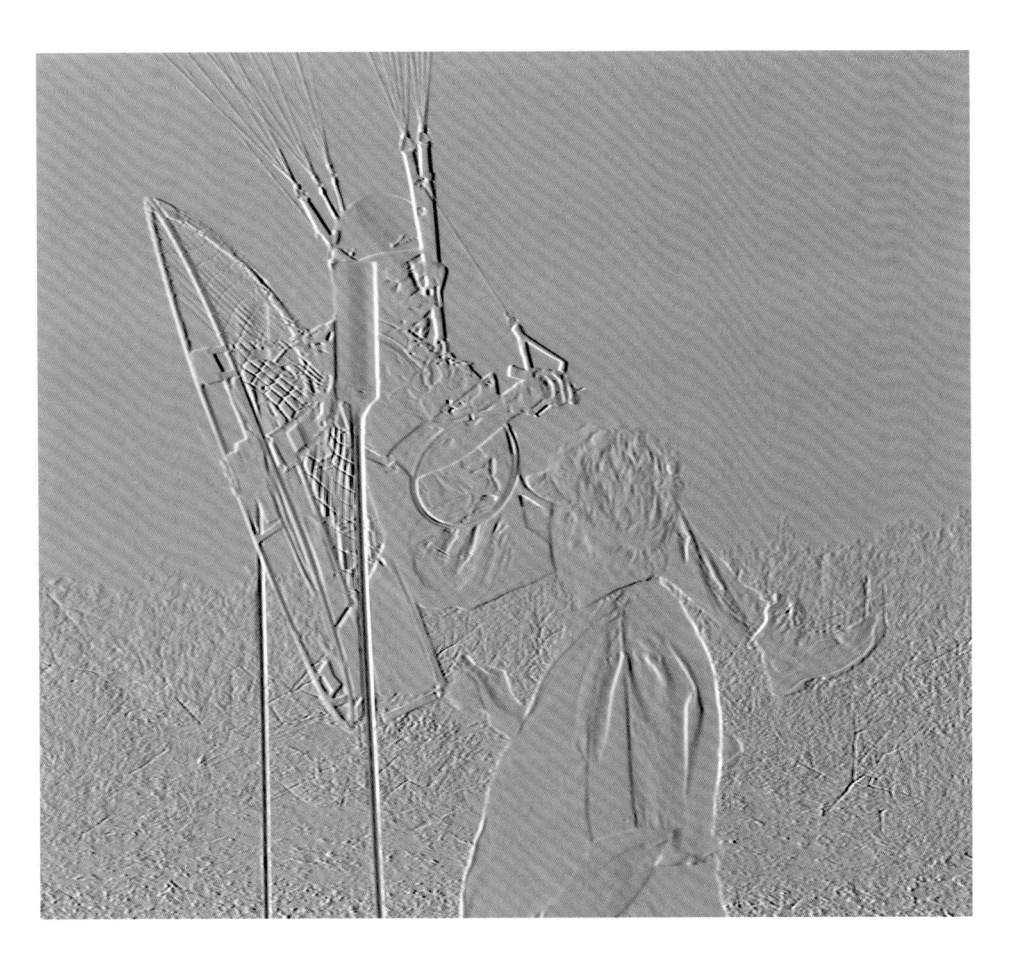

There's nothing wrong with having merely adequate skill. You can safely enjoy this sport without ever needing to go beyond basic launch, landing and flying skills as long as you stay within your boundaries, fly well-regarded, safe equipment from large fields and in good weather. In fact, getting to a high level of mastery involves *some* extra risk since you must venture closer to control's edge in the process.

This, however, is for those who want to go beyond flight's pure joy. It is for those who desire the thrill of surprisingly fine control, and who want to explore the limits of what our craft is capable of. It is, in fact, capable of a *lot*.

Section III is devoted to the endeavor of excellence. Here we will:

1. Show some of what's possible,
2. Explain the process to speed up learning,
3. Point out the risks, where appropriate and
4. Give methods to practice and to verify for yourself whether you've actually mastered the techniques involved.

Some of this practice is quite helpful to any pilot, but some must be left to the more risk-tolerant.

Section III

Mastering The Sport

"It's not how many flights you have,
It's what you've done with the flights you've had"

Advanced Ground Handling

CHAPTER 15

It's surprising what can be done with these wings when you know how. It's equally surprising how effortless the experts make it look and how advancement can be so vexing! Fortunately, most skills can be practiced in the privacy of your own field.

Of course, if you see someone doing something that you want to learn, go talk to them about it. Human nature means that they'll probably be happy to share the knowledge. And the best pilots almost always have the best ground handling skills.

Upside down kiting to clean out cells.

If you play with your wing on a beach, you will get sand in the cells. Other detritus, even from grassy sites, find their way in and can act like sand paper, shortening the life of your glider. You *can* hold up the trailing edge and shake the stuff out. While effective, that's slow and boring compared with kiting it upside down.

Find a smooth, clean surface (preferably grass) with the wind blowing from 7 to 12 mph. You can do this in the sand but, unless you're real good, it's tough to avoid picking up more than is emptied. Gloves are nice because you'll be handling brake lines, not the toggles, which could cause line burns in a strong wind.

A harness makes it easier but you can use only the risers. You'll want good control to prevent the wing from slamming down onto its leading edge—potentially popping out cell stitching (yes, we've see it happen). Hook into your kiting harness just like you were going to fly, then:

- Get the wing laying on it's back with the leading edge upwind as shown (next page). If there's not enough wind, just walk it into position.

- Grab the brake line closest to each hand above (beyond) the pulley as shown

Upside Down Kiting

1. Start from a regular reverse kiting position with the wing overhead. Or, build a wall and pull one tip A line just enough to get it turning over.

2. Keep pressure on the A line as the wing turns over. Walk with it until it turns but be prepared to pull on both brakes when it gets upside down.

3. As it comes over and down, pull on both brakes to cushion it's impact. Do *not* let it whack down hard on the leading edge which can blow out stitching.

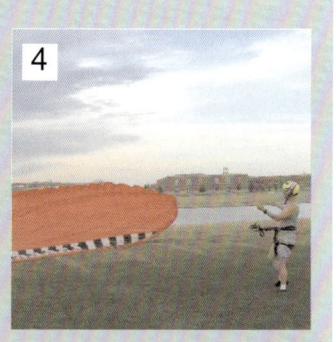

4. With the wing laid out upside down (or towards you if flat on the ground), grab the brake lines above their pulleys to kite it upside down.

One Hand Per Riser: Exactly where to hold the risers varies by wing. Experiment, but make sure you can rock your hands back and forth to pull more or less A's.

In light winds you may need to start out by holding both risers in one hand as Wayne Mitchler demonstrates in picture in 1. That allows you to pull the A's with one hand to help it up. Once overhead, holding them as shown in picture 2 (the swap can take some practice).

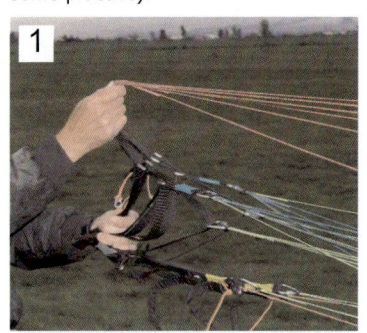

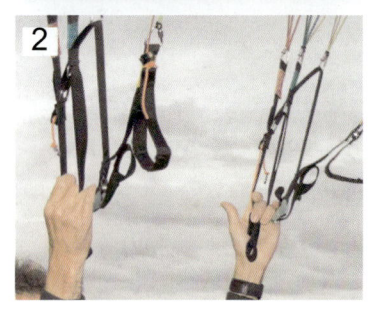

in picture 4 above. Treat the brake lines like the A's of regular kiting. Pull them *just enough* to get the wing to come up while snatching your *body* backwards. Once up, pull the brake lines back and forth to shake the stuff out. A satisfying show of falling debris means you did it right. Be careful to let the wing down gently on the leading edge.

If you're doing this in sand, the trick is to dump the debris as described then, just before the leading edge touches down, lean (or run) towards it. If you're fast enough, the cell openings will lay face-up with*out* scooping up more sand. Don't try to kite the glider back over—that almost always scoops up more sand. Instead, walk around it while holding the risers and bundle it up from downwind.

Kiting Without a Harness.

There are several reasons for kiting without a harness—it (1) is a great way to get some feel for the air, 2) spreads out the wing nicely, 3) lets you quickly check for tangles, 4) makes repositioning the wing easy, and 5) is fun. Plus it looks cool. There are many techniques, each with different advantages. We've picked a few that seem to work especially well.

Doing this with more than about 7 mph of wind is tiring and is dangerous if you let yourself get lifted. If that happens, let go of at least one riser immediately. That sounds ridiculous, but pilots have been injured when they held on too long and dropped 10 or more feet.

Regardless of the kiting method, you must move with the wing. If it goes left, go left with it. In fact, if you *want* it to go left, move right first, let the wing start falling left and follow it. To stop the wing, you must to walk (run) beyond it. This works on all the kiting methods.

One Hand Per Riser—Good For Higher Winds

The value of this technique is that, with each hand holding a riser, it offers more weight bearing capability—good for higher winds. Those who do summersaults while holding the risers usually do so with this method.

Face the wing and hold the risers as pictured at left. Some wings may need holding both the A's and B's in each hand. For most wings, hold the risers near where they split, the A's and B's go upwind with the C's and D's (if equipped) going out the back of your hand. If the wing doesn't want to come up, move your grip so as to pull more A's. If it wants to frontal or overfly you, then move the grip back so as to pull less on the A's.

Holding firmly, lurch backward as you would with a harness. When the wing comes overhead, decrease the pull or "rock" your hands back so as to pull the D's down. If the wing tries to overfly you, move backward while rocking your hands back. You have to be quick footed—moving quickly with the wing. Primary steering is done by pulling down one riser and letting up on the other. To go left, pull your left hand down and vice-versa with the right hand. To force the wing more overhead, or prevent it from falling back, tilt your hands so the A's are pulled down more.

You can re-grip but that's hard because of the wing's pull. If it is always trying to overfly you, let go of the risers briefly and grab them farther back. It's like letting go of a kite briefly while trying to catch the string in a different place.

There are several ways to bring the wing down: (1) walk towards it, steering it to the side so it falls over, 2) letting go of it (might make a mess though), 3) briefly letting go to re-grip back near the D riser or 4) put both risers in one hand and, with the free hand, reach back to pull the brake lines or rear risers.

A's and Brakes

This method offers the best control in light winds. Leave the brakes in their holders and grab both A's with your left hand and the brake lines (not the toggles) with your right hand as shown at right. Then:

- Inflate by pulling both A's *and* Brakes with just enough more A-pull to keep it coming up. It's important to feel pull in both the A's and brakes or else the leading edge will want to tuck over (frontal) and it won't come up as quick, if at all. You want it to initially inflate like a sailboat's spinnaker sail.

- This method makes inflation easy because you can modulate how much A's and brakes you pull. If the wing is jumping up quickly, pull more brakes with your right hand. If it's sluggish, walk backwards faster and let up on the brakes.

- Move left and right as necessary to keep under the wing. Steer with the brake hand, too—moving the hand right makes the wing fall left.

- If the wing wants to fall back, here are three ways to help bring it back up: (1) move backwards (into the wind), (2) pull more A's up to a point, and (3) ease both hands downward. After doing (3), when the wind picks back up, let your hands go up. Modulating like this can absorb small changes in wind speed that might otherwise require more moving around.

- If the wind increases and the wing wants to continually overfly you, either pull more brakes or walk downwind to reduce the relative airflow.

While you always want to move around as necessary, the *goal* is to control it well enough to stand still. That, of course, requires the finesse born of much practice.

To bring the wing down (deflate) in a stronger wind, get it to fly overhead, almost to the point where the leading edge tucks. Then aggressively pull the brakes while

1. As if kiting alone wasn't enough excitement, Jeff Thompson *barely* kept his head clear while performing this complete flip. It takes nerve, skill, and a strong wind to pull it off. It's also probably a good way to break your neck!

2. Here's an example of kiting with the A's & Brakes that works very well in light winds. You can move in every direction while tweaking the brakes too. If the wing falls back, step backwards and lower the risers—both moves help get it back overhead. It also allows your arms to absorb wind pulses by moving up and down.

The PPG Bible: A Complete Guide and Reference

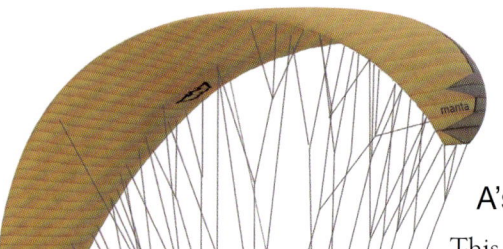

letting off the A's and walking towards the wing. Doing it this way snaps it down past the power band (angle of highest pull) quickly. If you try to bring it down while it is hanging back, the effort will be far greater and it will want to pull you with it.

A's and D's (or C's)

This is essentially identical to A's and Brakes but, since the D's aren't as effective at steering, it is not quite as sensitive. Instead of holding the brake lines with your right hand, hold the D's with your right hand. Its like what you learned in emergency handling when a brake line fails—the glider can be steered and slowed this way.

Loops and Brakes

This is where you hold the risers by the very ends (the loops) with one hand and reach behind to pull on one or both brakes with the other hand. The pilot at left demonstrates steering the wing by pulling the necessary brake line.

Loops & Brakes
Kiting with the loops requires holding both risers with one hand and using your free hand to control the brakes.

To inflate the wing, hold both risers at the loops with your left hand and the A's with your right hand. Pull primarily on the loops but help it come up by pulling the A's as necessary. Once it nears the top, let go of the A's and be ready to go for one or both brakes with your right hand.

High wind techniques

This can hurt—be careful!

Extra site precautions are necessary to make sure there is nothing downwind that would hurt if you got blown into (or strained through). Start learning these techniques in less than a 15 mph wind and, even then, only with someone else present in case you lose control of the glider; brief them on how to handle the situation. Namely, they should know that if you're being dragged, they should go grab a wing tip and run it upwind or get behind the wing and let it drape around them. They should not tackle you—the wing will potentially just pull the both of you.

Be prepared to deflate the wing as covered in Chapter 3.

Avoid doing this with the motor on—you are vulnerable to *turtling* onto the cage and getting dragged until you hit something. About the only way to stop such carnage is unbuckling from the harness, jumping out, and running after the remnants of your bouncing gear. It's much cheaper to master these skills with*out* the motor.

> ⚠ **Caution!**
> Exposing yourself to high winds with a paraglider is dangerous. If it's blowing hard enough to use these techniques then understand this increased risk and be ready to act the minute you clip in. Do not practice them until you have first worked with your instructor and know how to handle getting lifted or dragged.

Laying Out & Clipping In

Don't stretch the wing all the way out. Either leave it in a partial ball or lay it out at a 45° to 90° angle to the wind. The upwind wing tip may curl up and that's ok. Only spread the wing out

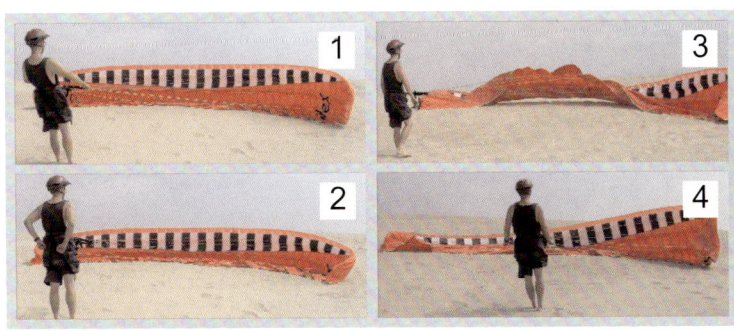

The Wall

1. Hold even brakes while pulling your body back against the wall to make it come up higher.

2. Step towards the wall to lower it and reduce it's tug.

3. If the tug gets too loose, wind may get under the trailing edge and cause it to flail upwards. If the tips want to come up, reach out to the brake lines and pull them in or get the wall high enough to prevent it in the first place.

4. This is Section III so you already know that this pilot needs to step right to bring down the high right side.

halfway with just the middle exposed. This becomes more important on smooth surfaces which allow the wing to slide with the wind.

Don't pull on the risers until you're ready to handle the wing. Initially, lay both risers within 10 feet of the wing's trailing edge. If you pull on the risers, even just a bit, a cell opening could catch the wind and start it inflating. Once that starts, it will want to inflate all the way with overwhelming power, dragging you along for the ride. So clip in close to the wing, get the correct brake in each hand and be ready to control it. Walk with it, if it starts getting blown downwind.

Controlling the Wall

Be ready on the brakes when bringing your glider to "attention." Step back to tension the A's, giving them a small tug if necessary. As soon as it starts to inflate, pull back on the brakes; it may be necessary to pull them *way* back. But if you pull too far, air gets under the trailing edge and may cause the wing to snake up out of control. Some wings may not need any A-pull at all—just step back and it will lurch to life. Again, be ready on the brakes to keep it down.

Some pilots have found that holding the wall down using the C-risers works well, too. Get a hold of them before letting the wing catch air, though.

In stronger conditions, pulling brakes alone may not be enough to keep the tips down, especially with longer brake lines. If that's the case, reach to the rear risers and pull them back while keeping hold of the brakes. You can hold both brake lines in one hand, behind your back, to free up the other hand. Be careful wrapping the brake lines around your hand (taking wraps) which could cause line burns and cuts in this strong of a wind.

Once you have a well formed wall, it may be bucking up and down. As you've already learned, backing away from the wing will raise it while pulling the brakes more, or leaning towards the wall, will lower it. If you let the wall get too high, its pull may be overpowering. If you pull the brakes too hard, the trailing edge may flail up into the breeze; there is a balance.

Done correctly, you'll be standing there with *lots* of brake pulled, controlling the wall's height by leaning towards it to lower, or leaning back (away) to raise it.

If You Get Lifted Off Your Feet

Getting lifted means you probably bit off more wind than you want to swallow. If you're hooked in reversed (as you should be) and get airborne, you'll untwist and end up facing forward after being deposited downwind somewhere. The *Alan Method*, described below, can keep you from getting turned forward after being lifted—you come back down while still reversed and under control. Once you get the

> **Tip: An Unwanted Turn**
>
> Here is another way (the Mayer Method) to prevent getting turned around while kiting in strong winds. You'll be leaning way back with the wing trying to lift you. Keep your hands on the brake toggles, but use one hand to grip where the risers cross. If you need the other hand, just switch which hand is holding the twist. This method will prevent them you from un-crossing but will not allow increasing your twist in the other direction.

wing down, pack up and thank your lucky stars you didn't go flying in this wind.

If you do get lifted, put your hands up and keep them there. Read that sentence again. Don't pull *any* brakes and the wing may well stay up there long enough to gather your wits and orientation. If you *do* pull brakes while facing forward, or with unsure footing, hang on. The wing will go back with vigor, first lifting then dragging you through whatever is downwind. Even just tapping the brakes in a strong blow can start this carnage—less brake is best.

Inflation

On a normal inflation you lean back, away from the wing, and pull just enough A's to help it come up. In high winds that may be difficult—the minute you reach for the A's, you reduce brake pull which may allow the wing to start inflating. Many wings will inflate at the tips which then come up and inward, leaving a mess. If that wants to happen, here are a some things to try.

- Pull the tips in. Start with the brake in your right hand which is going across to the opposite tip—pull it way back. Then reach out with your other hand and pull the tip in farther. Do the same for the other side so both tips are toward you. They may roll up a bit in the wind which is ok. Starting with the wing balled up, on horse-shoed slightly can prevent this from happening.

- Inflate the wing without pulling any A's at all. When ready, simultaneously reduce brake pull and step back. The wing will rocket upwards and pull you downwind—you'll need to run or slide towards it briefly. It can be tricky—the minute you let go of the brakes it will start coming up and want to yank you.

There is a balance in how much to resist the wing on its way up and how much to move with it. You must keep *some* resistance or it won't have any relative wind to work with. And you can't lock yourself in place (or try to) lest it shoot up and overfly you. That is why helpers, if used, must let you move some.

Sliding on your feet during inflation is perfect (and fun) albeit challenging. Done properly, you will slide (or run) about 5 to 10 feet, and stop the wing overhead. When you apply brakes to stop the wing it may lift you—be ready. By walking (or sliding) towards it while it's rising, there will be less chance of getting lifted. Once it stops overhead you *must* let up on the brakes

The Alan Method

One way to inflate and kite in high winds is to use the brake lines *above* their pulleys. Gloves are helpful since you'll be holding the brake *lines* (not the toggles) that could cause friction burns.

This gives deep control over the brake pull and, if you get lifted, allows you to remain reversed and in control which is hard while holding the brakes by their toggles. Once the risers start to un-cross, however, there is not enough leverage to prevent untwisting so keep yourself a little more twisted than exactly reversed.

Concentrate yes, but do pay attention to what's happening around you, too.

- Hook in reversed as if you were going to fly but do not grab the brake toggles.

- Inflate the wing by stepping back with your body and pulling on the A's as necessary. As the wing nears overhead, let go of the A's, reach back around the outside of the risers to grab the brake lines above their pulleys. Pull them enough to prevent the wing from overflying—the challenge is getting to those brake lines quickly.

- Steering is backwards from the normal crossed method (where each hand controls the opposite trailing edge). That takes some practice. One way to visualize what you're doing is by watching the trailing edge react to your pull. Control the wing surges and left-right tendencies by modulating the brake lines.

- Keep the risers crossed and touching each other. That means you'll be turned slightly beyond 180° from facing forward. Doing so allows you to remain reversed if you get lifted off your feet.

- Lean way back if it wants to lift you—you'll have more rotational inertial. That means greater resistance to getting swung around if you get lifted off your feet.

If you do get lifted, keep yourself reversed by opposing the turn with the brake lines while maintaining wing direction. It is entirely possible to actually fly this way (without a motor, obviously), but it can be confusing too. Pulling with your left hand will initiate a turn to the right (as viewed by a spectator). It needs to be practiced a lot before actually putting yourself in a situation where you'll be very high and flying backwards like this.

If conditions are light, when the wing falls back, you'll need to periodically let go of the brakes and pull on the A's to help it come back up. Going back and forth quickly between the brakes and the A's is the greatest challenge. Practice it during mellower conditions first since you'll need to be pretty fast-acting in stronger winds.

**The Alan Method
And Flying Backwards**

Kiting with the Alan Method (see text) this way allows you have far more control in strong winds than if you use the toggles. It also lets you oppose the untwisting force which allows you to remain facing the wing even after getting lifted.

You can actually fly backwards using this method (stay twisted). You'll be using the brake lines for two things: 1) to oppose the natural untwist tendency and 2) steering. Flying backwards this way is an extremely dangerous practice above any altitude from which you're willing to crash. And don't try it with a motor!

Steering is easy, look at the trailing edge and imagine how the deflected brake will slow that side down causing a turn. Envision it that way and it will be obvious. Kiting practice will make it second nature.

Preventing the untwist isn't hard either. If the risers want to swing you left to face forward, use your hands on the brake lines to oppose it. Yes, you'll necessarily be pulling some brake pressure on both lines. For example, if the risers are trying to swing you left, move both hands left to counteract it.

The hard part is combining the two—modulating counter-twist force while also steering. This is a skill that highly experienced paraglider pilots learn to help them control launches from higher wind situations.

Once mastered, you'll also find it allows kiting up vehicles and other obstructions.

Once mastered, this technique is good in other ways too. With very light winds it is a way to go from kiting with the A's to pulling brakes—an asset in light but thermally conditions.

Kiting Control

Minimize brake use in strong winds. Move left or right instead of pulling brakes. Lean way back so that getting lifted upwards a foot or so only angles your body up without losing traction. Keep your knees bent so that a quick gust only lifts you a few inches and will not scrap your balance.

While kiting reversed with crossed risers (the normal way), you can also control the wing using weight shift. Dip a hip toward the falling wing.

Kiting while facing forward gives an opportunity to learn a "feel" for the wing without looking at it. There is no magic, you'll feel it go left or right and, if your harness lets you see the risers, will see them move subtly left/right and forward/backward. Getting used to handling the wing like this can prove quite useful. A good test of your kiting skills is to be able to stand on the ground and kite while looking straight ahead at the horizon. It will take a fairly steady 8 mph wind or more to do so.

Assisted Inflation

In strong winds, assisted motor launches are dangerous, even if the assistants are familiar with flying; most risk is borne by them. Consider that, if you require assistance, it may be too strong even for kiting. In some ways, getting assistance makes it harder while adding risk to you *and* your helpers.

If you feel compelled to get help, make sure the helpers know to let you slide (on your feet hopefully) as the wing comes up. Do *not* have them try to hold you rigidly lest the wing dart up too quickly and overfly you. They should move with you as the wing comes up, resisting your motion with 30 or so pounds of pull. Doing so makes the inflation more manageable. It's important that your helper(s) not resist heavily until your motion has mostly stopped and *then* to try holding you in one place while allowing the left/right corrections necessary to kite. Instruct them that if you get lifted they should walk downwind while holding you. Emphatically instructor them to let go if they feel themselves start to get lifted (for their safety).

Having helpers assist during motor launches is very dangerous since they can get caught in parts of the harness and swung into the prop. That is why assistants should use short ropes (not long enough to get into moving parts) tied to a sturdy part of the frame—they pull on those ropes which are easy to let go of. Assistance is most often used when a large wing makes initial inflation difficult.

Handling smooth surfaces

High winds and smooth surfaces, like beaches, are a tough combination. The minute you lay the wing out it wants to go sliding away. To make the process easier, extract the wing so as to avoid the cell openings catching air. Here are two ways to get yourself clipped in.

---

1. If you use a helper, tell him to let you move initially as the wing comes overhead. Otherwise it may overshoot. The assist here is welcome because the pilot is inflating a large glider in strong conditions.

2. A strong, steady, beach breeze near Los Angeles, CA makes this possible. Even then it is high risk. Soft sand helps reduce the potential pain of a mistake but you should still never try to stand on objects higher than you're willing to fall—a front tuck could yank you over hard. Keep the power on and fly the wing while always maintaining some brake pressure.

3. You can do amazing things with the wing but be extremely careful—make sure that a loss of control won't cause injury.

Tip: Testing the Technique

You can easily see these techniques in action while kiting in a nice breeze. From a normal reverse hook-in, tug on the risers crooked and see what the wing does—it's a nice reinforcement.

1. If you normally stuff your wing, pull it out so that it's in a rosette but oriented properly to the wind. That's hard because some of the lines will be obscured, but if you always stowe the wing in the same way, this is easier.

2. Lay the wing out parallel with the wind and have someone hold the upwind tip. If you're alone, lay something heavy on the tip that won't damage the fabric. Sand works really well—just make sure it won't go in the cells. A slight tug on the downwind A's will bring the wing to life and it yank it around into position. Use brakes *immediately* to control the *wall*.

Regardless of the method used, be ready to get dragged! Have a plan and be somewhere with nothing nasty downwind to get strained through. And be ready to fly (get lifted) since, once the wing comes to life, it may be an ordeal to unclip.

The smooth surface will make the wing quicker to "snake" above the ground so you must hold the wall in a very narrow height range using the techniques described earlier. More than likely, you'll have to inflate it without using the A's—that's hard on some wings.

Light Wind Techniques

Normally, if it's too light to kite the wing overhead, a forward launch is easier and safer. But if you're ready to reverse when the wind dies, it's nice to have a method for launching without resetting into a forward.

Cross Armed

This method probably provides the most reliable method of reverse inflation in light winds since it imparts energy to the wing as you turn around. With fairly easy-inflating gliders, and practice, this can be done in no wind (see the video at www.FootFlyer.com). Our description is for a pilot hooked in reversed who will turn to the *left* after inflating.

Clip in normally and grab the appropriate brakes as usual for a reverse. While holding the brake toggles, slide your right hand down the right riser to its A riser which will probably be to your left. Grab that A and continue left and up—that A should have a clear path to the wing. With your left hand, reach *over* the other A and grab it as shown at right.

Pull your hands back towards you (arms are now crossed) to see that both A's are clear to the wing. When ready, lunge backwards with your body, pulling both A's as necessary. You can help a lagging side by pulling more A on that side. When the wing gets to about 60° overhead, turn to the left and throttle up. As you turn, your arms will uncross and move forward which provides some pull to the A's during the turn—very helpful in light winds. This method doesn't work as well on wings that tend to front tuck easily.

Kiting with the A's

This technique allows kiting in light to moderate winds while keeping the wing

Cross-Armed Method

Remember how the standard reverse hook-in was confusing? This is similar—don't worry about those crossed brake lines, just do the procedure and it will sort itself out when you turn around.

Kiting with the A's helps most in light winds. If one side sags, pull it's A more as you back up. This works well with the "Alan Method" since you can quickly go from the A's to the brakes. If the wind is blowing strong, you'll want to walk towards the wing as it's coming up to reduce the relative wind and therefore the power of its pull.

only a few feet above the ground. It is almost useless by itself but the skill developed helps handle nearly all other inflations. It's handy, too, for kiting wars—those who can do it have a distinct advantage over those who cannot.

Set up for a regular reverse but, like the "Alan Method," do *not* grab the brake toggles. Grab the A risers beyond where they cross as shown above.

Inflate the wing by stepping back and helping with the A's as usual. If the left side drops (as you're looking at it), pull more on the left A while stepping back. If the right side drops, pull the right A while stepping back. You may have to walk left and right to keep yourself centered as gusts come through.

Inflation Issues

In a perfect world, launch runs are always upwind, downhill, with a steady breeze and the sign on the sod farm driveway reads "PARAMOTOR PILOTS WELCOME." The following tips will prove useful in *our* world.

Fixing a Wall

Fixing a Wall: Your left hand holds the A line to an open part of the wing while your right hand holds it's brake line. Get some air into the open cells so it blows out the mess to the left.

An even layout is always best but sometimes the wing comes down in a heap after our abortive kiting efforts. One side sits lifeless while the other has some form. Here's a way to rescue mess quickly.

As long as some cells can get clear air, hold the A's going to those cells while holding their brake line in your other hand. Pull both sharply until they catch air. Done properly and with enough wind, it will billow out nicely. Too much A's will be ineffective. If a whole side is clear (as pictured at left), use the riser to that side. Always be careful when pulling on only one or a few lines, it's *far* easier to overstress the connection point or get line burns.

Salvaging Bad Inflations

In the beginning, an inflation that went this bad (above) had only two outcomes: abort or crash. Aborting is always the safest option, but if you are intimately familiar with your wing and willing to take the extra risk, you can salvage many launches with these tips. Be aware that pushing too hard on launch adds some unavoidable risk of munching your wing, lines or body parts.

- Keep forward motion. Powering up early, at least partially, makes doing so much easier.
- Turn towards the wing and keep pressure on the low side's A riser.
- Once you've got forward motion, use just enough brake pressure on the high side. The trick is using *just* enough—too much brings the entire wing back down.
- Do not accelerate or accept a liftoff until the wing is fully under control.

If it turns sour, be lightning fast on the kill switch.

Crooked Inflations

As learned in Section I, successful launches stem from a proper setups—everything must be lined up, especially in light-wind forward inflations. Lines must be clear, you must be centered on the wing, aligned straight into the wind and run exactly perpendicular to the wing.

The following factors can play havoc with your plans and lead to crooked inflations. Knowing crooked's cause will better enable it's cure.

- The wing always tends to come up *into* the breeze. So a wind coming from your right will make the wing come up and turn to the right. The left cells catch the air more directly and come up first.
- Not running perpendicular to the wing will pull up the tip opposite to your run direction. So if you start your run facing slightly right of perpendicular, then the left cells get pulled up first. It doesn't take much before the wing is too crooked to recover. The left side shoots up first and the wing arcs over sideways.
- If you're left or right of the wing's center when starting your run, the far side will come up first. So if you're off-centered to the right, the left side will come up first. This is worse than scenario #2 since you're not running even slightly to the right. The left side would come up first and carve over to the right before you knew what happened.

This started off badly. The pilot looked left to see the wing leaning heavily. He kept up the forward motion and turned towards it—you can see the prop blast off centered. He also kept slight pressure on the low A-riser and applied the slightest brake on the high side.

Thankfully, it worked, this time!

The PPG Bible: A Complete Guide and Reference

So if the wing "always comes up to the right", then point yourself slightly to the left. If you've mastered the hip shifting, no hands kiting, you can use your hips as you inflate the wing to make corrections (with a weight shiftable harness). If you suspect there is a problem with the wing, try kiting it in a steady breeze or, better yet, have an experienced pilot kite the wing to get another opinion. Just ask them to report unusual behaviors. If it really does come up consistently crooked then there may be a problem with the wing and it should be sent in for inspection or repair.

Handling Crosswinds

Turning slightly like this can counteract a natural tendency. If the wing always seems to come up to your right, angle yourself slightly left. The same is true for launching in a crosswind.

You can achieve the same result by slightly offsetting yourself from center. If the wing always seems to come up and go left, step a few inches to the right of centered.

Normally you always launch into the wind but, at some sites, especially long narrow ones, you may be forced to accept a crosswind (see Chapter 17). Also, the wind may shift after setting up—pretty common where thermals are budding.

The key is to use the previously mentioned inflation problems to your advantage. Use them intentionally to counter the crosswind effect by running or setting up off-center.

Lets say, for example, that you've set up pointing into a 1-2 mph breeze. But, just before your launch lunge, the wind shifts to your right. Simply driving hard may overcome it but the tendency will be for the wing to come up to the right—into the breeze. Point your launch run about 3° to the left. That will make the wing want to come up to the left and should offset the crosswind effect trying to make it come up to the right. Done correctly, the effects will cancel each other out.

A pilot pulls his wing up in a very light morning breeze. It's the perfect chance to check the air, inspect the wing and revel in your control of the craft.

Page 154 — Section III: Mastering The Sport

Scott Johnson lays down a long foot drag along Oregon's smooth, wide beach.

Chapter 16 Precision Flying

Just *flying* a powered paraglider is all the enjoyment many pilots need. And it can be done quite safely without ever learning to be super precise as long as you stay within your limits. A skilled pilot will indeed better handle the unexpected. Of course that benefit is forfeited if your superior skill is needed to counter inferior judgement.

For those who aspire to really *master* the machine, for whatever reason, this chapter is for you. You might be fooled into thinking that a paraglider's soft nature leaves its control loose or imprecise. The reality is blessedly more fun. In fact, *very* precise flight path control is available to those willing to work toward it.

Even in moderately bumpy air, a skilled pilot can craft a line within inches of his desired path. As you may imagine, such precision takes practice; especially since the pilot hangs so far below the wing. You must learn anticipation and a sense for how long it takes your *body* to feel results from control inputs—both vertically and laterally. You must learn the feel of input and resultant motion. But oh how sweet it is once mastered!

Brakes—The *Feel* Position

A lot of precision flight is done using minimum brake pull—not completely off, but just enough to affect minor corrections to the wing without giving up speed. This is the *feel* position, and is only about a pound of brake pressure on most wings which is about brake position/pressure 1. Hanging the weight of your arms is too much—while that amount gives *great* control feel, it also slows you down, giving up energy (speed) in the process. Find the feel position by pulling pressure, without looking at the wing, until you just *start* to notice a course or speed change.

Flying with *some* pressure is important when trying to fly super accurately, especially when flying right next to the ground. Of course you *can* fly with a lot more brake pressure than the feel position but that requires even more finesse in another area: thrust control.

Straight Lines—Pendular Precision

Hanging below the wing means you swing—fore/aft and left/right. Like any pendulum, there is a natural frequency to the swing called its *period*. Controlling the left/right oscillations is most challenging because the brake input is not intuitive—in fact, it is backwards from what the body feels. The fore/aft motion is easier to learn but has its own quirks.

Being able to stop oscillations precisely is a prerequisite to nearly every other aspect of fine control; it's what gives us rule over the inches. A telling test of whether you have this skill is being able to fly a straight line, within 3 to 6 inches, both vertically and laterally. Of course the only place to even recognize such precision is while flying a few feet above the ground. Features such as corn rows, tracks in the sand, or lines in a field are good for this. Such lines can be found, in some form, on nearly every piece of the planet. They don't even need to be straight lines but, if you're using curves, they must be fairly smooth and gentle.

The boundary between corn and soybean fields is another perfect place to practice. When the corn is 8 feet and beans are 3 feet tall, fly a track just over the corn row. If you hit sink, throttle up a bit and turn towards the beans—you'll instantly have an extra 5 feet of clearance.

This type of flying obviously requires extreme care! And only do it *into* the wind.

Left/Right Pendular Control

You can feel the pendular action of a PPG by getting into a turn then letting up on the brakes. It will recover past level, swinging back and forth in decreasing amounts until you are flying level again.

To fly precisely, these oscillations must be dampened. Wait until your body reaches a crest and just as it *starts* to swing back the other way, pull a quarter brake in the direction you're about to swing. Hold it for a second then ease up. Done correctly, you will have zero brake input as the wing levels.

This works both for preventing oscillations and for damping them once begun. If you have already started a swing (by a gust or your own action), let it crest, then, as soon as your body reverses direction, pull brake in that direction for a second and then release.

Timing is crucial—if turbulence or bank recovery has you swinging to the right, let it finish swinging to the right and then, just as it *starts* swinging to the left, pull a quarter *left* brake for a second and release. It may feel backwards at first—you start swinging left and have to pull a quarter left brake immediately. Don't hold it for too long or too hard lest you make it worse. The amount of correction should be proportional to the intensity of swing. It may feel unnatural at first but will become automatic with practice. And practice you must.

The best way to rehearse this is by doing mild wingovers (see Chapter 18) and

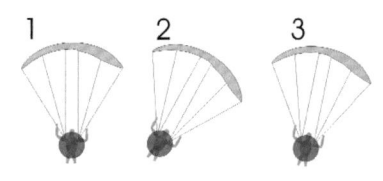

In a regular turn, you apply brake (1) and hold there (right brake depicted). The wing banks out to a maximum (2) then levels back to a lesser amount of bank (3) where it stays as long as you hold that brake. The rate at which it goes out and back is the pendular rate for your particular motor/wing combination.

Remember to avoid pulling more brake while the wing is returning from it's farthest bank (2) to the stable bank (3)—doing so can cause a spin.

Coordinated Turn

The goal here is to minimize diving and slipping which is where you briefly move sideways through the air. Looking for traffic first then:

1. weight shift (if able) to start the wing moving,

2. apply inside brake towards the turn, then

3. just after the wing starts responding, prevent a dive by adding a bit of power or pulling slight outside brake. The resulting turn is smooth and level.

It should be paced like this (when spoken aloud at a normal pace): "weight shift, one, brake inside, two, throttle up/add outside brake."

It will vary by wing since longer line lengths take longer to swing from side to side. Some glider tend to have more level turns anyway.

practicing returning to level flight with the least amount of oscillation. Fortunately, this skill can be mastered in the safety of altitude. You can also practice by getting into a bank, letting off the brakes, then dampening the resultant oscillation.

Flying a Line

Being able to closely follow a line on the ground requires mastery of the pendular tendency—you must catch it *before* you get swung. The previous explanation primarily covered how to stop it after it started—here is how to stop it before it even starts. This definitely takes practice. The problem is that you must feel even the slightest motions and then modulate the brake pull accordingly—stronger swing, more brake. Your reaction must be quick, too—any delay will only make it worse. The key to *preventing* oscillations is to apply brake in the direction of your body's movement *as soon as that movement starts*.

For example, you're flying along a line (like a corn row) and feel your body start swinging left (body left, wing right). You must immediately pull left brake then let it up. If you catch it before you've moved more than a foot or so, it will dampen the oscillation before it starts. If you wait too long, you'll aggravate it. Don't try to master this until you can dampen an established swing as described earlier.

Fore/Aft (Surge Control)

The wing always wants to maintain an equilibrium known as *trim speed*. That means if you pull some brakes to slow down, then release them, you'll dive a bit and accelerate back to your previous speed. Pulling trimmers to slow down sets a new and slower trim speed equilibrium.

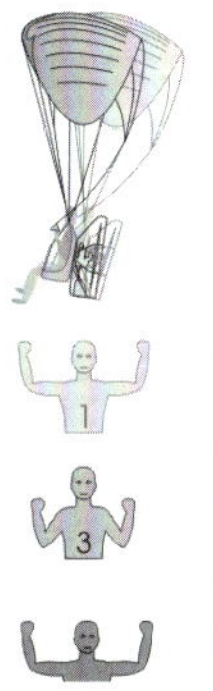

You're flying along with brakes at position/pressure 1 when the wing suddenly surges forward. Quickly go to pressure 3 for a second, then back to pressure 1. As you gain experience, you'll do this naturally and time it properly.

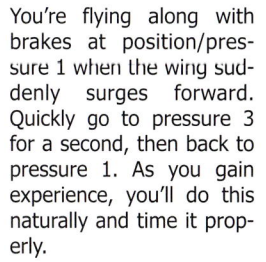

It's just like the left/right pendulum: give the input just as the wing *starts* to change direction. So if it goes forward, just as it *starts* to come back, let up on the pressure.

Controlling with pressure, not position, is critical in turbulence. Brake pressure 3 may happen at position 4 or more under some circumstances. Go to the pressure, not the position.

Digging Deeper

The reason pendular dampening seems backwards is that we are not exactly pendulums. When our body goes right the wing moves slightly left. We need to control the wing, not our bodies. Unfortunately we have to translate that kinetic feel into what the wing is doing. Additionally, during these oscillations, the wing is also turning slightly left and right which aggravates things. By pulling brake just as that turn would *begin*, we nullify it.

A sudden increase of headwind (like a gust from the front) immediately increases your *air*speed—you'll swing forward (the wing falls back), climb and lose forward momentum (groundspeed). With no further wind change, the glider would settle back to its trim speed and leave you moving slower over the ground and a few feet higher. A sudden decrease in headwind (or increase in tailwind) would cause the opposite: airspeed drops, the wing dives a bit and you accelerate over the ground. Once it stabilizes, you wind up at the same airspeed as before but going faster over the ground and a bit lower.

A brief gust is worse than a one-time change because it's a really two changes. For example, lets say you get a headwind gust. The wing surges back and you climb as the wing seeks its previous airspeed. Groundspeed (momentum) decreases, too. Then, when the gust subsides, the wing suddenly feels

Recognizing that the wing is surging can be difficult—the risers may angle forward only a half inch or so. Fortunately, the subtle recognition skill improves with practice. If you feel yourself tilt forward, rehearse immediately pulling some brake to catch it then let off as soon as it starts moving back. Alex Varv is pictured here damping a slight surge. Higher performance wings react more to turbulence and require more attention to keep them overhead.

The accuracy available is surprising given the minimal controls. Following the center of this gravel road requires a careful dance between throttle and brakes, fine inputs that yield a flight path measured in inches.

less airflow (less airspeed) and dives to get back to trim speed. This can be dramatic and cause large pitch changes where your body (and wing) angle skyward or groundward.

You can minimize all this with the brakes and power, keeping the wing overhead as much as possible. That's essential while maintaining altitude within a few inches of the ground where surges and drops are dangerous.

In the case of the wing surging forward, it will make you want to dive at the ground—you have to be quick with just enough brake to keep it right overhead. So when you sense the wing *begin* to go forward, you must immediately add some brakes but be prepared to let them off. As soon as you sense the surge has ended you must reduce brake pressure.

Keep the speed up through gusts (position/pressure 1)—it will help maintain brake authority so you can either add brakes to stop a descent or let them up to avoid a climb. That will require modulating the power, too. So if you get lifted and tilted back, ease up the brakes immediately, reduce power and be ready to come back in with both. You must be quick—as soon as you *start* swinging back down you'll need to be adding power to keep the speed up.

You must build skill through practice to really master the necessary reactions. This chapter may explain the principle but it's greatest contribution is describing what to practice and what to expect when you do.

Practice should start off in fairly smooth conditions, flying 10 feet over landable terrain, as always (sod farms, beaches or smooth desert floor are perfect. Try to hold altitude precisely. As you improve, go later in the morning (or earlier in the evening) when bumps appear but are not severe. You will build skill faster if practicing with *some* level of turbulence.

Balance of Power

In normal flight, you've learned that power controls altitude—add power to climb, reduce it to descend. It's somewhat different here. Throttle changes take a second or two to act—a luxury not available when you're only a few inches high. Brakes, on the other hand, effect an *immediate* change in climb or descent albeit in a limited, fleeting fashion. If you're cruising along at full speed and pull some brakes, you'll immediately climb and start to slow down. That immediacy can come in handy.

Energy State

Energy state is a term, fancied by fighter pilots, that describes the trade-off in speed or altitude that is best demonstrated by a roller coaster. When the coaster's cars go down a hill, they trade height (potential energy) for speed (kinetic energy).

> **⚠ Caution!**
>
> Doing steep maneuvers down low is incredibly dangerous Don't do anything down low that you haven't mastered up high and don't ever let any kind of vertical velocity develop. Competition pilots minimize their risk because the rules discourage maneuvers with a big vertical component (big dives, for example).
>
> Flying low and downwind sacrifices the inherent slow speed safety advantage of our craft. The higher speed makes it both harder to detect or avoid an obstacle and makes it hugely more damaging to hit something.

Climbing the next hill trades speed for height. The ever-present drag means that roller coaster cars are always slowing (losing energy) unless sufficient average decline, or thrust, is provided. A paraglider is no different. If you're going fast, you've got energy available to trade for height (briefly anyway). Likewise, you can let off the brakes and trade some height for an increase in airspeed. Adding power adds energy.

When flying low-level (a few feet above the ground), power is used to keep the speed up so pulling brakes causes a climb. If you're going fast and start to sink, you can pull brakes to arrest the descent. But that will also slow you down, limiting future brake effectiveness unless you power up to regain that lost speed. Speeding back up allows that, if you hit more sinking air, you can again use the brakes.

Slow Flight

Slow flight puts you close to a stall making it very risky! If you feel the wing start to go back unexpectedly, or the brakes start getting mushy, reduce brake pressure.

Get into level slow flight by reducing power then pulling enough brakes to prevent descending. Be ready on the throttle because you'll quickly need to add power once slowed down—in fact, it will take more power than before if you slow down very far. You must be 100% sure where the wing will stall and what it feels like. Don't go beyond brake position/pressure 4.

In slow flight, the roles of brake pressure and power reverse. Since brakes are already pulled, you can't count on them to quickly add height and must count almost exclusively on adding power. The good thing is that, with so much brake applied, the wing will respond very quickly to increased power. And since you'll be carrying plenty of power, the motor should respond quicker. Flying at *minimum* speed requires holding the wing near stall while controlling height with power. Practice this either up very high (and with a reserve) or within a few inches of the ground.

The least amount of power is required when flying at the glider's minimum sink configuration. That is normally with only slight brake input, trimmers set to slow and speedbar off.

Turns

Turns require adding power to prevent altitude loss since some of the wing's lift is spent pulling you around the turn. The steeper the turn, the more thrust is required. Competition pilots doing steep low turns are almost always at full power as they swing around pylons then completely let off the power as they level out. They convert the speed stored in the turn to altitude maintained.

When entering a turn, it can be helpful to reduce power briefly, start the turn, then come back in with power. That reduces the chance for spinning or stalling.

Eric Dufour picks up three cones cones in Albuquerque, NM. Make sure to drop them before landing, otherwise it's awfully hard to run.

Low Flying

For some, low flying is the single biggest reason they fly PPG—the ability to cruise about at any altitude and explore a three dimensional realm. Be wary though, it's also where most of the risk lurks.

As always, stay within reach of a safe landing spot, climbing if necessary. Down low that means flying over landable terrain the whole time. Flying 3 feet above grass is minimal risk, flying 3 feet above deep water or trees is folly.

Start out by flying relatively high, 10 feet or so and do gentle maneuvering. Note that any turn loses altitude and steep ones can lose a lot. You must build up to learning how much. Always keep in mind that you should never wind up deep in the brakes—they are your only control and, once pulled, there is nothing left to maneuver with. Like in the foot drag (covered below), if you notice that you're pulling high brake pressure, add power while easing your hands back up.

Foot Dragging

Its an amazing accomplishment to fly along while riding your feet on the ground, especially in mildly bumpy air (no more than 2 on the bump scale). You should first master a precise control of altitude, within a few inches, while also minding power, ground track and speed.

Always do this into the wind until you're extremely proficient—then doing it crosswind is possible. Crosswind foot-dragging is riskier since you'll be sliding somewhat sideways and will be far more susceptible to falling.

The safest stance for a foot-drag is with one foot out in front of the other so that you can be ready to run if necessary. Don't put much weight on the foot—drag can slow you down, forcing a run. Modulate the brakes and power to keep your cage from touching as much as possible. On wet, smooth ground you *can* get away with sliding the cage but risk a prop strike.

The idea is to keep the speed up using throttle and to control altitude with brakes. If you lose a few inches, immediately add enough brake to regain it and then add power to accelerate back to speed. Use about brake position/pressure 1 so you'll have control of both up and down. If you get lifted by a gust you can immediately reduce brake pressure and thrust just like you added pressure to catch a drop.

If you find yourself getting heavy in the brakes your airspeed is probably slowing down, too—get on the power immediately!

Picking Up Ground Objects

Start this slowly—first be able to do foot drags and control altitude within a few inches. Avoid descending towards an object—it's too easy to hit the ground while concentrating on getting the object and not powering up in time. It happens often that way and usually costs a prop and other damage.

Get down low, within a foot of the ground and be powered up for cruise; like a foot drag, your hands should be pulling no more than a quarter brake. That allows that when you grab the object with your feet, snapping a handful of brake will give an immediate climb while you get on the throttle. It is important to be stable while approaching the target so that you can concentrate more on what to do with your feet as you near it.

1. Eric Rys nabs a ball from an Illinois pasture. Before trying this, remind yourself to be extra vigilant about your surroundings—numerous pilots have hit their cages while trying this or lost track of nearby wires when concentrating on such tasks.

2. Foot draggin' Christy Damon squeezes throttle and pulls brakes after settling too much. But the motor takes a second to spin up and if there's not enough energy (speed) in the wing, it may not be enough.

Having a Motor Failure

When the motor quits while flying low, the immediate loss of push will make the wing swing forward into a descent. Unchecked, it could be quite the crash. But, if you're ready for the failure, and pull quarter brakes right away, the wing will not surge so far forward and you can minimize the effect.

If you're above about 50 feet you should be able to establish a normal glide (albeit very briefly) and have enough brake pull left for a normal flare.

Below about 30 feet you should not let off the brakes much because you're probably too low to regain all the speed. Hold pressure 1 until needing to flare.

Below about 10 feet there may be no way around a rough landing after the motor quits. You'll pull the brakes immediately to pressure 2 and hold them until flaring fully at 2 to 3 feet. There may be little flare authority, however, because of reduced brake authority.

The main point is to be especially ready for a motor failure while flying down low, especially below 30 feet or so and, since here won't be enough altitude to turn around, only do low flying into the wind.

Hitting Suspended Targets

Trying to hit something floating or falling through the air is a fun challenge. A good way to practice it is by inflating a helium balloon just enough to be buoyant and taking it up with you (tie it off with a short string to the front of the harness webbing for launch). If the balloon is neutrally buoyant, you won't have to keep climbing as you try hitting it.

As you approach the balloon, try to put it on the horizon so that it's at your altitude. Head straight for it—if there is no relative motion of the object with the horizon then you are dead-on. Make *small* adjustments as necessary.

Formation

It is fun to fly close with other pilots, but formation carries some surprising risks. Make sure each pilot knows that the other is approaching and have no more than one inexperienced pilot in the formation. Use radios and coordinate the formation while flight. Here are some additional guidelines:

1. Never, ever accept a high closure rate. If things are converging quickly, break it off and re-form. Approach unknown pilots slowly, from the front side and

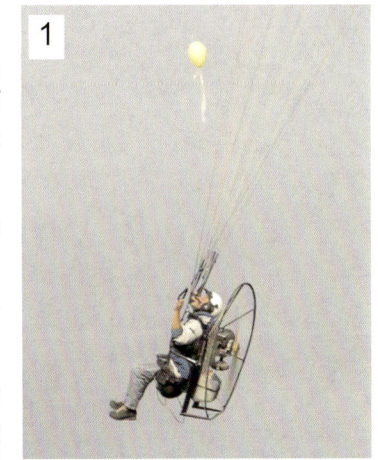

1. Randy Kester looks up at the balloon that he almost got. Only do this with something you're willing to get tangled in your lines.

Only do this above 300' so as to avoid hitting things while being distracted.

2. An Illinois gaggle heads for breakfast in loose formation at a couple hundred feet. While each pilot must be very aware of the others, they are not getting boxed in. Always allow for an engine failure that never risks those flying around you.

Move carefully and look in any direction (up, down, right, left,) before maneuvering. You can signal your intentions to other pilots by motioning a weight shift turn with your legs.

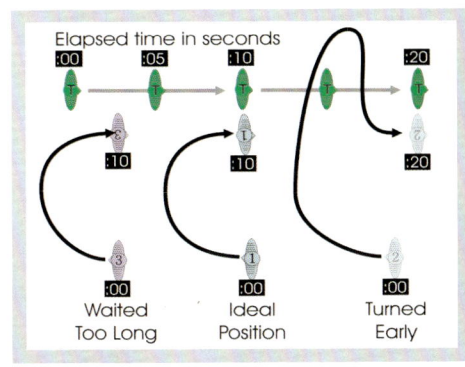

Intercepts: *Forming Up* On Someone

Forming up refers to joining another pilot in formation flight. Doing so with someone coming straight at you, or nearly so, is the most challenging version. When intercepting from head-on, you must start the turn quite early as shown by pilot 1 who starts when the target (T) is about 45° off his right.

It's better to start your intercept early rather than late. For example, pilot 2 started too early but still has the chance to join up with no need for excess speed. Whereas pilot 3 started late and winds up behind the target (T). His only option is to speed up which may be impossible.

Intercept from above so a mis-judgement won't cause a collision, then move down into position. This also keeps you out the interceptee's wake. Pilot 2 does his maneuvering above the target's wake then settles back down into a more side-by-side arrangement.

very near their altitude. Don't get any closer than about 5 wing-spans unless each pilot is looking at the other and the closure rate is slow. If another pilot starts turning away and you aren't sure of his desires, leave him be.

2. If you're closing on a pilot who doesn't know you're there, allow him enough clear air so that if he maneuvers, you can get out of his way.

3. Always keep both hands in the brake toggles. If taking pictures, at least have one hand in the brake toggle that turns you away from the other pilot.

4. The lead position is easy—fly steadily and don't do anything abrupt so your wingmen can react. It is better for the experienced pilots to follow others.

5. Always have an out. Look at your formation and plan an escape in case one of the pilots maneuvers or gets a collapse.

6. Never get in someone's wake. Think of where your wing is relative to their wake and keep it clear.

Intercepting

See the **Intercepts** diagram (preceding page). Joining up to fly alongside another pilot requires great care. It requires anticipation since speed is minimally adjustable. The most common error is not leading the intercept enough—you start late and wind up too far behind.

Turning

While turning in a side-by-side formation, the outside pilot must go faster than the insider which may make impossible. A solution is, during the turn, climb up and cross over to get on the other side. Another method is, before beginning the turn, climb up to get just behind and above the inside pilot. When leveling out, move back to the outside. Time right, it looks good.

Other Considerations

Don't even think about "walking" on another pilot's wing. The walker's disruption in airflow can cause the walked-on wing to collapse dramatically and snare the walker. It's happened. A reserve may not even help with the resulting carnage.

Active Flying in Turbulence

When flying in turbulent conditions the primary focus should be to keep the wing overhead. That means damping oscillations (left-right) and surges (fore-aft). The challenge is detecting changes and then giving correct input quickly.

Active flying is taking action to keep the wing directly overhead, rather than passive flying which is just allowing the wing to move around. You want the *least* amount of input necessary to keep the wing overhead. It's better to let it wander a little bit than to over-control while trying to dampen every little twitch. As you get better, you'll be able to make very small corrections before the wing gets very far out of position. Until you've mastered that, it's better to let the wing wander within a range.

For most wings, the best configuration in turbulence is: no speedbar, trimmers in (slow), brake pressure 2, and enough thrust to fly level. Lighter pilots on larger wings must be especially vigilant about parachutal stall (see Chapter 4) and be

---

Pole Standing

Only do this from something you're willing to fall from and over a surface you're willing to fall onto.

In a steady, strong wind, approach the poll from directly downwind and a foot or so below its height. Plan the touchdown to coincide with a flare to get yourself slowed as necessary. Once standing, modulate the power to keep from being pulled back and kite the wing straight overhead. Falling off is not that big a deal—continue concentrating on wing control as you walk down the pole or push away from it. Always keep brake pressure—if the wing front tucks or collapses, you will immediately fall off!

Most risk comes from getting caught on the pole after losing control of the wing or hitting the pole with your prop. You should be able to do this consistently on the ground before trying it on an object.

Footware:
Pilots feet have been saved by stout shoes or boots after getting a foot in the prop. Think twice before flying with this footware.

quick to reduce brake pressure and power at the first sign of slowing airspeed.

Becoming effective at active flying will take at least 50 flights and then only if you really work at it such as flying exactly straight lines within 100 feet of the ground in mildly bumpy air. While practicing, keep looking forward; use your kinetic sense to detect motion and then provide control inputs.

If at any time you start to "lose it" (not sure what to do), reduce brake pressure for 5 seconds. Let things settle down and *then* re-engage your corrections.

You must learn to interpret the small angular changes that get transferred to you through your harness as the wing moves around overhead. That takes practice.

Active flying requires applying the techniques covered earlier regarding pendular control. Remember, if your body swings left you must apply *left* brake as soon as the swing *starts*.

With repetition this will become automatic: it is best not to try damping oscillations for landing until it is automatic. During landing, your attention is so focused on the flare that your steering inputs could easily devolve into pilot induced oscillations (PIO's) that result in a crash.

The Perfect Touchdown

Among the numerous landing styles are two that have some practical value and are commonly employed to finesse the touchdown. The *slider* landing is good for fast touchdowns on smooth surfaces. The *one step* helps to minimize run-out when terrain is rough. Getting yourself to the target (spot landing) is covered in Chapter 17.

Sliding In, the *Scoop* Landing

Sliding in for a landing works better on higher performance wings (high glide ratio)—those that allow coming in for a power-off landing and have lots of flare authority in the brakes. You have such a wing if, on a power-off landing, you can flare and climb back up a few feet.

For a basic slider landing, start from a nearly hands-up glide at 50 feet. Reaching about 8 - 10 feet (wait until you're lower if there's with more wind) pull enough brakes (position/pressure 1 - 2) to get your body swinging forward then ease up on the brakes briefly. That initial pull gets your body swinging forward which pitches the wing up, nearly stopping your descent. Time it so the level-off happens right as your feet touch the ground. Practice will reveal how much pull, when and how long to hold it. As you level off, speed will quickly start bleeding off—apply more brakes to keep weight off your feet as long as possible. Done properly, you'll skid to a stop with full brakes.

This is useful when ground speed is high on landing and the surface is smooth. Even if you don't skid to a stop, the slide bleeds off a lot of speed so you don't have to run nearly as fast.

The *exaggerated* slider (see diagram) is fun but has little practical value. Practice it up high to get a feel for how much dive you get by letting off the brakes. If you start it too high on landing, you'll level out too high on the recovery. If you start it too late (low), you'll hit the ground while diving before it has a chance to recover. *Be*

Threading the goal posts at this vacant football field added some risk: hooking a line would have ruined his day but the zoom lens makes him look much closer. He was, in fact, just barely between the posts so there was virtually no risk of a line snag.

Pick your practice spots carefully and always allow for options should the engine quit. The tighter you squeeze your margins, the more certain you must be of your skills. Most accidents happen when the pilot pushes those margins just a bit too hard.

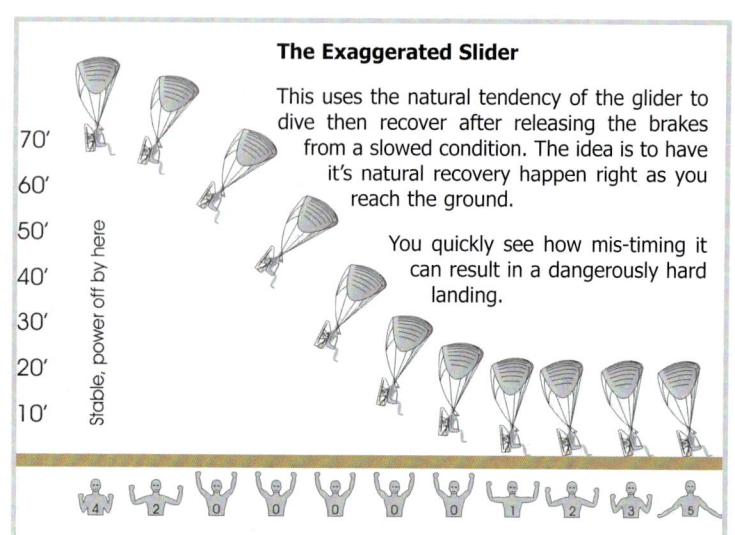

> **The Exaggerated Slider**
>
> This uses the natural tendency of the glider to dive then recover after releasing the brakes from a slowed condition. The idea is to have it's natural recovery happen right as you reach the ground.
>
> You quickly see how mis-timing it can result in a dangerously hard landing.

very careful, it could easily result in a broken leg, or worse, if mis-timed.

Even with high-altitude practice, start it slowly, doing only a little dive at first then increasing it as you gain familiarity.

You can also do an exaggerated slider by timing the landing to coincide with rolling out of a bank. This is dangerous since there is very little margin for error, it is surprisingly difficult to judge and terribly unforgiving of any misjudgment. Many sky divers have made it their final maneuver and it would be no different for us if timed improperly.

The One-Step

This is probably the most challenging type of landing to do well and the easiest to get hurt while trying.

Everything is normal down to the last 50 feet. Ease in the brakes to pressure 1 and hold, making steering inputs as necessary. Then at 4 to 8 feet, (depending on wing) go smoothly to pressure 4 so as to swing out and get down to minimum speed at touchdown. Go to full brake, pressure 5, just before touchdown. Your initial descent must use just enough brake pressure so that quickly pulling to pressure 4 won't swing you too far forward and back up into the air. The ensuing drop could hurt.

Timing must be right on—start the final brake pull so as to exhaust all speed just as you touchdown. Some wings, especially slow ones, will require starting this from a nearly no-brake position.

Be extremely careful—if you wind up having pulled all the brake too early, you'll plummet the vertical distance down to a *very* hard landing. A good place to practice this is onto soft sand. Like the exaggerated slider, errors are unforgiving.

> **Power-On Landing**
>
> Landing with power can make you look good. Yes, it's cheating, but it still takes skill. In turbulent conditions it gives you more options after being dumped by a gust and allows a go-around when things *really* go sour.
>
> One good technique for a power-on landing is to come in like any other approach but, during the last 50 feet or so, throttle up enough to reduce the descent rate by half. That will enable better timing of the flare since it's less critical and you'll have more time to finesse out any errors in judgement.
>
> Another technique that is fun and looks good, is to turn a foot-drag into a landing. Be prepared to bear weight when you're foot dragging in case of a gust—it's easy to fall if you're not ready for it.

Challenging Sites

CHAPTER 17

The fact that we *can* launch from such a wide variety of sites is impressive—it is a major draw to the sport. But some sites, under some conditions, and for some pilots may be impossible or dangerous to launch from. We must always make sure that our skills match the task at hand. The following tools will help you manage some of those challenges and, more importantly, recognize when to skip locations that are simply unsuitable.

The Horror of Hot, High, and Humid

The effect of high elevation on performance is dramatic. Gear that easily blasts you aloft at sea level may be downright doggy up at 5000 feet MSL. A machine that's weak at sea-level may not even get you airborne from that elevation—it takes more thrust to launch than to simply fly.

Everything works against you when at high elevations. The thinner air means less thrust, you get winded quicker, and yet you must run faster to get the same lift from less dense air. All told, launching from high elevations can be tricky, especially with no wind. Combining high with hot and humid makes the air thinner yet. Handling them all at once can render a launch impossible, especially with marginal thrust.

If you've ever been to a high-altitude gathering of pilots then you've likely witnessed (or fallen victim to) the struggle with still air. Occasionally pilots simply can't get airborne. Obviously more thrust would be handy but there are other possibilities.

- You may actually have a slight tailwind at 15 feet AGL, where the wing feels it but you don't. Try extending a telltale (small, very sensitive wind indicator) up high or just attempt launching the other way.

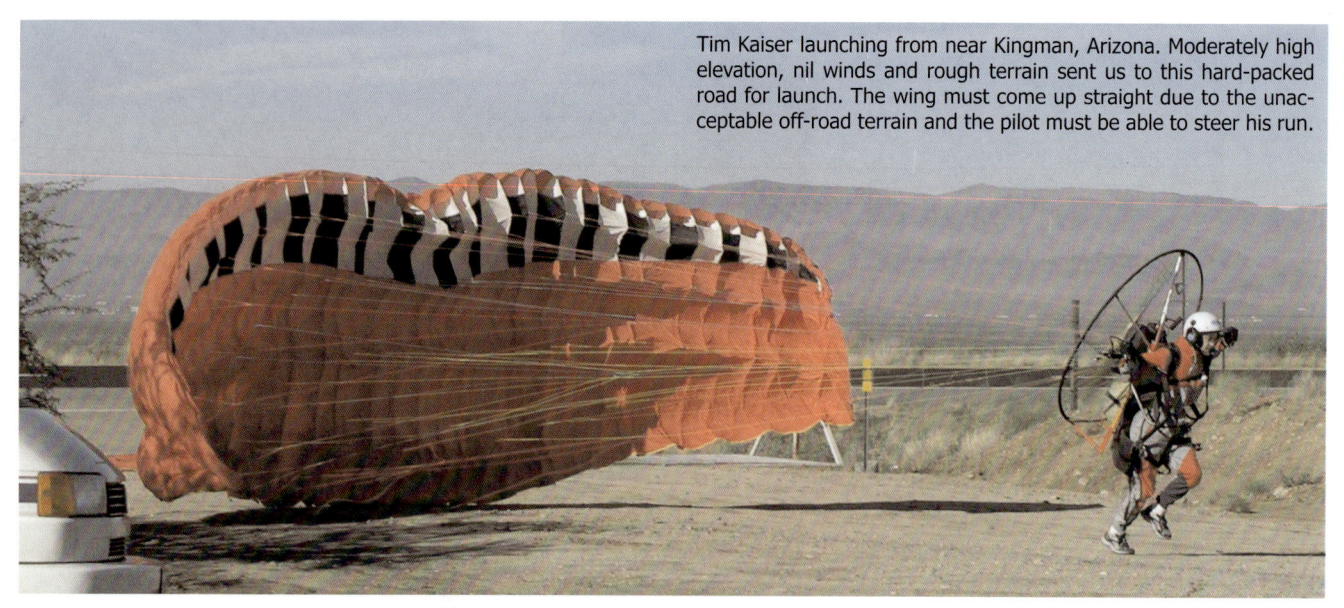

Tim Kaiser launching from near Kingman, Arizona. Moderately high elevation, nil winds and rough terrain sent us to this hard-packed road for launch. The wing must come up straight due to the unacceptable off-road terrain and the pilot must be able to steer his run.

• The motor is not putting out full thrust for that altitude. A quick check of max RPM will confirm it. Thrust will, of course, be diminished but the rpm should be close to its sea-level value if everything is setup correctly. Chapter 27 has a chart that equates sea level thrust with what you'll get at altitude.

Leg Drag

A more insidious cause of launch woe is the design of our landing gear. Encumbered with PPG gear, legs can only provide push at low speed. They're great for the initial inflation but, beyond about 4 mph, they represent only drag—the motor must do all the work. This is because the motor makes it difficult (and dangerous) to lean forward—your legs do little more than keep your cage off the ground. The effect of leg drag may be enough to prevent launch; the following factors make it worse:

• High density altitudes (see margin) which require more ground speed.

• No wind which requires more groundspeed.

• Limited thrust.

• Angled-back motor styles. Adjust the motor so that you sit more erect in flight. It won't be as comfortable while airborne but at least you'll *get* airborne.

• Rough or soft surface.

• Short steps instead of long strides as the wing lifts.

You must accelerate to get lift from the wing which then reduces leg drag. But if you can't accelerate enough to get enough lift to further accelerate, takeoff may be impossible. You may just have to wait for some wind. One way to increase wing lift is with brakes, but, pulling too much or too early may slow you down or cause the wing fall back. It's a fine line that requires experimentation while running.

Motors that force the pilot into a leaned-back posture in flight aggravate the problem. As soon as the wing starts lifting, it forces the pilot back. That is a difficult posture for running and slows you down if there is not enough thrust to overcome it. Machines with a vertical posture in flight minimize the leg-drag effect on takeoff.

Hot & High: Density Altitude

Density Altitude is elevation adjusted for atmospheric pressure and temperature. It's how high our equipment *feels* like it's operating at.

Humidity has a small effect on performance but a larger effect on our bodies. Hot, humid air makes it harder to cool off—we sweat but it doesn't evaporate. The effect can make us feel like we're wearing concrete shoes. High humidity also reduces thrust.

Atmospheric pressure has a small effect—100 feet per 0.1 inches of mercury (Hg). So a real high pressure area will lower the density altitude by a few hundred feet.

The big bugaboo is temperature. As a rule of thumb, every 10°F warmer than standard (59°F at sea level) increases density altitude by about 600 feet.

In a standard temperature (see Chapter 24) it is colder as you go up. At 5000 feet it's only 42°F. So on a 72°F day (30° warmer than standard), a 5000 foot elevation has about a 6800 foot density altitude.

The effect of density altitude is significant on our performance. At higher density altitudes you'll need to run faster and your motor won't push as hard.

Hot and High Solutions

Here are some helpful ideas to help succeed at high density altitude launches. Start with the smoothest surface available, downhill if possible. In a very light wind it may be better to launch crosswind from a smooth, firm surface then upwind through a soft or rutted surface. For example, soft sand can be impossible in still air whereas the nearby road, even if it is slightly crosswind, might be manageable. Never accept any downwind component—it will torpedo your effort. Here are some other preflight choices that will help:

- If you have a choice of wings, pick the slowest one; usually that means the largest size. It must also be easy enough to inflate.

- If you have a choice of motors or propellers, take the pushiest. This is a great time to have lots of thrust.

- If you don't need all the fuel, tools and accouterments in your harness—leave them behind. Lighter is better.

Here are some tips for when you're ready to launch:

- Do a power forward inflation or go to full power as early as possible. Keep pressure on the A's until the wing is nicely overhead and you're moving briskly.

- Once you've got speed and are no longer worried about the wing falling back, concentrate on staying erect and running as fast as you can with your hands up. Pretend the wing is not there and use the smallest steering inputs possible. It may *feel* like it's not there.

- On soft surfaces, or if you've reached maximum speed, start adding brake to get the wing lifting. That should relieve the weight from your legs. Don't add too much, though, and be ready to back off if you slow down. Add brake slowly to find the happy medium of wing lift and leg drag.

- Steer yourself to the smoothest, hardest surface possible or into the wind if you're not already pointed towards it.

Lord willing, this run will give way to long strides then to slapping the ground with your feet and finally, to flight. Once airborne, ease up the brakes *slowly* to avoid settling back down to the ground. The best climb is typically achieved with no (or very little) brake pressure.

If you do settle back down, be prepared to run and start the process again.

High And Dry

The place I picked was just outside New Mexico's Sky City at a 6000 foot elevation. It wasn't much, especially considering my underpowered motor (for that altitude) and the rutted surface. Plus, on this particular morning, there was nary a whiff of wind. I wasn't about to let that deter me—or so I thought.

After two tries at running my little legs off, I was exhausted. I simply could not generate the necessary speed in those ruts for the wing to lift enough so that I could accelerate—leg drag became more than a concept. More efforts would have eventually led to a fall so I sat down to wait for a puff of headwind.

Finally I felt it, and a smoke source confirmed it—the lightest little headwind, maybe 1 mph, was coming in. I stood up and went for it.

The wing came up sluggishly as I lurched over the ruts. Thankfully it came up straight. Running my hardest with hands up and motor screaming, I slowly gathered speed. Finally I felt fast enough and applied some brakes to unload my gyrating legs—too much brakes apparently—I slowed down. So I let them back up and concentrated only on speed. I got to a smoother surface and that made the difference. Again pulling a bit of brake gave enough lift to unload my legs—the pace quickened. More lift. More speed. Longer strides. And then finally—the magic smoothness of flight. I was skimming just inches above the ground as I eased off the brakes, accelerated and settled into a climb. Oh sweet rise!

Trials like these create an appreciation for *low* elevation launches. Admittedly, with enough power and an appropriate wing, it's not much of an issue, but with minimal power or a fast wing, you'll need some finesse to pull it off.

This high-elevation launch, northwest of Reno, Nevada, presented rough terrain except on the dirt road. Inflation was in a clearing, the run was through some rough terrain and then I had to accelerate down the road (black line) before getting enough speed to lift off.

The engine-out option was along the same dirt road until gaining enough height to land back at the launch site. It's not something to try unless you're able to reliably steer your launch run.

An engine failure immediately after launch here would have meant a swim. They used the grassy open area left of the water and had to circle up, gaining altitude while maintaining that field as an out. The water was shallow enough so that landing on its edge would have allowed standing. Going in the water would still involve falling forward—it's hard to stay upright in even shallow water. Wally Hines is seen on approach, staying between the two buildings.

Tight Spaces

Make no mistake, it's always risky to shoehorn your flight into sub-optimal spaces. But with skill, the right conditions and appropriate equipment, you *can* fly from surprisingly small areas.

Besides having sufficient room for running, a site must provide a clear path for climbout and departure. Make sure that if the motor quits at any point, you can either land safely along the departure, or be high enough to circle back.

Any site that doesn't allow inflating into the wind will be tougher (like roads) but it can be managed. The skills described in Chapter 15 will be valuable at such locations. Be incredibly leery of wind shadow—if the site is surrounded by high obstructions, you'll be hard pressed to tell what the winds are doing up higher and powerful turbulence may lurk in the transition.

Steering the launch

Being able to steer while running or walking with the wing overhead is a seminal skill for success in tight locations. It allows launch from places that require a turn before liftoff such as an L shaped or obstructed field. The skill is useful elsewhere since it allows you to safely avoid obstacles, like another flyer and his gear, without having to abort. It can also allow you to inflate into the wind, which is easier, then turn and finish the takeoff in a different direction (like a crosswind runway).

Steering with the wing overhead is easy to practice. Go out on a mildly breezy day and execute a launch but don't actually take off. You'll be powering forward while keeping the wing overhead and walking briskly (or slowly in a stronger wind). The goal is learning how to steer the wing without looking up at it.

> **Caution!**
> Never choose a site that requires the motor's continued operation to clear obstacles. Always insure that if it quits at any point, you can land.

After mastering straight steering, try making the wing go right or left, off the wind direction somewhat. Start with just a few degrees. Use steering inputs to make the wing go where you want then follow under it. Remember, the wing has momentum, too. If you and the wing are angling to the right and *you* stop, the wing will keep going right. You must lead it—while walking right, pull left brake to stop the wing; take a few more steps then *you* can stop.

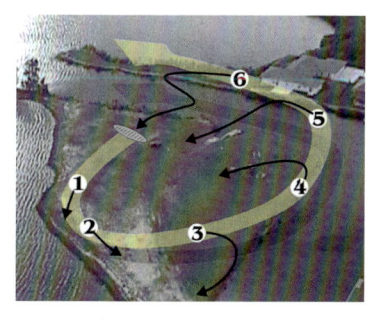

When you're facing forward, learn to *feel* where the wing is without looking at it. Do look at it, when necessary, while figuring out that feel. Walk forward enough to keep sufficient airspeed—you should feel the lines tugging just a bit. When the glider drifts off to one side use just enough brakes to bring it back overhead.

Always lead with the wing. To go left, get the wing going left first then follow it. The amount of lead depends on how rapidly you want to change direction. When you want to stop going left and get back into the wind, pull right while still walking left. When the wing gets slightly to your right, stop—momentum will carry the wing a few more feet.

The goal is to steer with only the brakes. Move left or right if it's *necessary* to keep the wing up, but strive to use only the brakes. That improves mastery of where your feet go which is beneficial in tight spaces.

Another skill that improves feel is controlling the wing with *only* your body (*no* brakes). It's quite difficult but will help you understand how the wing reacts to being offset. Walk left to get it going right, but not far lest it quickly fall.

As the wind gets lighter, these exercises get more challenging but are certainly doable. You can even practice in no wind but it's mighty tiring. It takes a lot of running to keep air flow over the wing for control.

Water is bad, every launch should be planned so as to stay out of it if the engine fails at the worst possible time.

This launch from a private park near Vero Beach, FL, shows how the pilot kept his options open. The numbered paths are where he would have gone in case it quit.

Climbing out

The climbout should always allow a return to the field until you're high enough to circle back. If the field is surrounded by obstructions, climb out on the inside edge so that a motor failure is handled easily by turning towards the field. Avoid high climb angles for the first 30 feet or so in case the motor quits and swings you into the ground.

If possible, plan turns in the motor's normal torque-turn direction.

Landing Pattern

Tight spaces sometimes require different landing patterns. It's always best to fly the pattern as you normally do, with a landing into the wind. But odd shapes can dictate odd patterns.

With an obstacle-lined field, your final descent will follow the contour of obstacles. For example, in a tree-lined, circular location, you would plan the descent just inside the trees to end with a short final into the wind (graphic at right).

This is obviously an emergency landing. Plan your approach to touch down as far as possible from rotor causing obstacles. You'll have to hug the edge of the field but don't get too close—hitting a tree up high is far worse than hitting rotor turbulence down low.

Dealing With Winds—Using Power

In turbulent conditions it is beneficial to keep the power on. Even if you need to get into a tight space, the value of having thrust available outweighs the chance of breaking a prop on landing. And it's not just to enable a go around—it can salvage what would otherwise be a very hard arrival.

Providing there is room, come up slightly on the power just before touchdown to shallow the descent. In a tight space, wait until you're within 10 feet of the ground or so. This will also "spool up" the motor enough to have instant throttle response if a sudden burst is necessary. That will leave you better prepared for a downward gust while landing.

If everything goes well and you do *not* get dumped, then do a normal flare and landing. Be quick to turn around as you kill the motor to get the wing down in strong conditions.

This is something to practice long before its needed. Become adept at making flawless power-on landings during smooth conditions then practice them when it's a bit rougher.

Without power, a gust that swings you forward (and possibly up) will make you bleed off speed followed by a drop into a possibly hard landing. Let off the brakes immediately if the wing goes back to minimize this possibility, but you'll still be swung out and have little speed with which to flare. Using a squirt of power just after the gust will regaining the lost speed and preserve brake authority for a normal flare.

Spot Landing

Next to steering the launch, this skill is what makes tight spaces manageable. You must be able to control your landing spot consistently—within 25 feet or so depending on the site. Practice and master it from a large area where there is no consequence to missing the target. Don't fly into a real confined space until you can consistently nail your target.

Come in with the motor idling but do *not* plan on using it. And don't fly over anything where a power loss would yield a crash—use turns if necessary to keep landable terrain available.

Fly a normal landing pattern to stay oriented and aware of altitudes but vary it, when necessary, to maintain safe landing options. The goal of the pattern is to deliver you to about a 200 foot final approach where you can accurately judge the crucial final glide. Use S-turns on final, if necessary, to bleed off excess altitude but not below 100 feet.

If the touchdown area is small and obstructed, consider using heavier brake application (pressure 3) to slow down and steepen the glide. Be *extremely* careful though—you'll be closer to a stall and have very little extra speed to maneuver with. Once the wing is slowed down there is little more you can do with those brakes beyond letting them up. Practice this first where a spot landing is not required. Be ready with the power to catch a big drop. More importantly, be ready

1. Bill Heaner is circling for a landing to this field near Salt Lake City. Staying legal is another challenge, you must be able to find a clear path that avoids congested areas. In this case it was at the bottom of the picture where a clear path to the mountains existed.

Launching required a well-planned run then circling over this small open area before heading out. With mountains behind, this site would be treacherous with strong winds blowing over them.

2. Alan Chuculate circles into a landing South of San Diego, CA. This small open area, next to a police station and along the beach required care but had a steady onshore wind that simplified matters. The beach is behind the photographer, in front of Alan.

to let up the brakes *immediately* if you feel yourself slowing down or the brakes getting limp—that could signal a stall or spin.

Judging glide is an important skill that must be mastered. Practice this judgment (or envision it) during your next approach in smooth air. Put a foot up so that it visually touches where you think your touchdown point will be. If the foot starts to pass over the spot then you're high, lift it up a bit to reflect the better glide. If your foot sinks below the spot then you're low and would land short. Move the foot down to reflect the steeper descent. Once the spot is no longer moving up or down, that is your aim line, it is where you'll touch down if nothing changes.

Glide is extended by letting the brakes up and steepened by pulling more brakes. If there's much headwind, you'll need to plan a much steeper approach. Be ever mindful of pulling too much brake—pilots have been seriously hurt when they were high and stalled or spun after pulling too much brake.

Once below about 100 feet avoid turns. Manage the aim line (glide angle) so that it stays on the target. Fortunately you can change your glide angle, but only so much.

Below about 50 feet, forget the spot and change your focus to touchdown quality (not location). Increase your speed (hands mostly up) to allow for a full flare. You'll briefly dive as the wing accelerates. As your skill improves, you'll be able to concentrate longer on making the spot—staying on the brakes longer when necessary. That will, however, sacrifice flare authority and must be timed *very* precisely. Flaring from more than about a half-brake glide will set you down hard—don't expect to be standing afterwards.

As the headwind increases, your glide worsens (all landings *are* into the wind, right?) Increasing airspeed improves glide in a headwind (penetration). If you're above 100 feet, let out the trimmers or push on the speedbar—you'll drop initial-

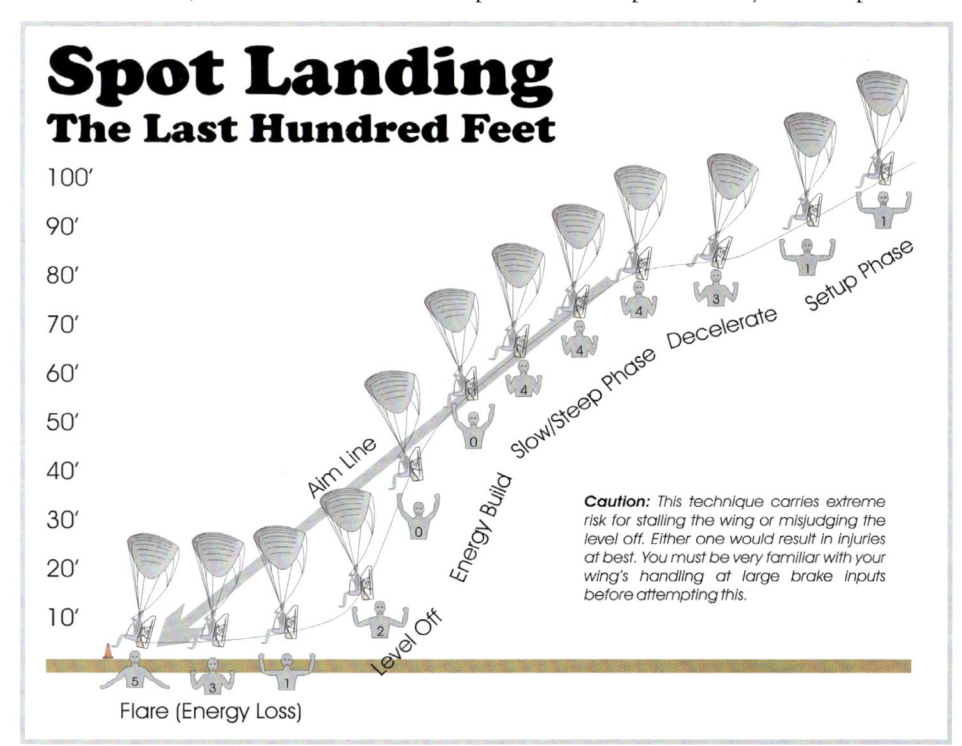

Spot Landing

This is a potentially technique for hitting an exact spot like a frisbee and is riskier than a normal landing. To make it safer, allow more room for error and avoid brake extremes.

If it's bumpy, don't use any more than brake pressure 3 or you'll risk hitting sink and having too little brake authority to arrest the drop.

The basic steps are:

1. Use a normal power-off landing pattern that is slightly high.

2. S-Turn on final to bleed off any excess height but plan the final glide with brakes around pressure 3.

3. Hands up to extend the glide if you get low, brakes to pressure 4 if you get high.

4. At about 50 feet, forget the spot and reduce brake pull to regain some speed for a normal flare and touchdown.

ly then the glide will improve. Avoid letting off the speedbar at the same time as letting off the brakes—that makes a front tuck more likely.

Slowing down steepens glide, especially in a headwind. Holding a lot of brake (be extremely careful of stall!) initially levels you off but then you'll settle into a steeper-angle glide. You *must* preserve enough altitude to re-build airspeed for the flare.

Flapping is a technique that some pilots use to fly real slowly for a steep descent without stalling. It is where the pilot repeatedly pulls a lot of brake then rapidly releases them in a "flapping" motion. It doesn't *prevent* a stall, it just insures that the wing sees some time without brake input. There appears to be no actual difference in steepness between flapping and simply holding steady brake pressure. Both carry a high risk of stall or spin but several skilled competition pilots feel that there is a benefit in the flapping technique.

Left: Launching on roads normally means the wing must be straight and leaves little room for left/right error. The road must obviously be sparsely traveled both legally and for safety. Plus it cannot have wires alongside. One good thing is the abundance of engine-out option as you climb out the landable length. Roads are obviously only tight spaces in one direction: width.

Below: This beautiful piece of New Mexico sits over 6000 feet high, giving these para-campers a challenging launch. Off the road, scrub brush and general roughness make the launch difficult. Some pilots found it easier to launch down the road instead of plodding through off-road vegetation.

Sometimes its better to accept a small crosswind on a smooth surface than going straight into the wind through difficult terrain.

Advanced Maneuvers

CHAPTER 18

Maneuvers serve various purposes in flight such as: losing altitude, changing flight path, skill enhancement, demonstration and others. The more extreme variations are very risky and should be learned only through a special *SIV* course (Simulation d'Incident en Vol - simulated incidence in flight). Do not try them on your own without such training since some can become un-recoverable. You can do an SIV course as soon as you're comfortable with basic launching and landing skills but it would mean more if you have at least 100 flights. You'll learn the latest methods for recovering your glider from unusual situations and, more importantly, get to practice them.

Techniques change with technology. What you read here, or even learn in a clinic, may become dated as knowledge and gear improves. Experts acknowledge that they are always learning better methods to fly and train. Ask instructors and respected pilots about the latest wrinkles.

Don't induce wing malfunctions outside of a clinic. Whenever doing maneuvers beyond normal flight or flying in turbulence, make sure you have a suitable reserve and know how to use it (see Chapter 12).

Aerobatics are maneuvers intended for show such as loops, rolls, helicopters, SAT's and such. Only the most risk-tolerant souls should consider attempting them and then only with the highest level of training—be ready for reserve rides!

Any advanced maneuver is best done first in a free flight harness to reduce the chance for getting lines tangled in the cage. A motor further complicates matters by adding twisting mass (possibly causing severe riser twists). If the extreme risk of a motor is to be accepted, at least have the propeller stopped before doing any type of maneuver.

> ⚠ **Caution!**
>
> These maneuvers have resulted in accidents. It is essential that pilots seek proper guidance from a qualified, experienced instructor before attempting any maneuver.

1. It's in the hips. The whole point of weight shift is to lower one riser while the other goes up. Low hook-in machines designed for weight shift (like this one) get results by the pilot throwing his body (and harness and motor) over to one side, similar to how it's done in free-flight harnesses. The pivoting bar actually moves for only a portion of the riser travel, tilting does the rest.

2. Machines with high hook-ins are weight-shifted by lowering a leg one the turn side. That pulls the harness webbing down which lowers the attached riser. On some units, pushing against the ground handling strap with one shoulder adds leverage and increases riser movement.

Weight Shift Turns

This isn't really an "advanced maneuver" but is included here because it's not intuitive on all machines. Weight shift steering is helpful in precision flying but is not necessary.

Motors with weight shift ability allow you to lean or shift in the harness such that one riser is lowered relative to the other. It causes a small amount of turn in the direction of the lowered riser. More importantly, it gets the wing banking in the desired turn direction so brake input in that direction is more effective. The whole goal is riser shift. Body contorting and leg swinging may look impressive, but if the risers don't shift, the wing won't react.

Use weight shift to begin a turn *then* apply brake—down pressure on the inside and ease up on the outside. As the bank increases, pull slight outside brake pressure to reduce diving tendency. This *coordinated turn* allows faster entry into banks since less total brake is required (more valuable if you're soaring or competing). Combining weight shift with medium brakes will induce a turn as quick as heavy brakes alone (with less risk for spinning).

High Hook-Ins

Many units with high hang points have good weight shift capability; they do so by using a pivoting (or floating) J-Bar or sliding straps in front of the J-bar. Pilot technique varies but the effect is the same: pulling one riser down while the other goes up.

On these systems, the pilot pushes one leg down to push that side of the seat down which lowers its attached webbing and riser—right leg down to turn right. Even more weight shift is achieved by using your shoulder—push up with your right shoulder while pushing down your right leg. The ground handling (or shoulder) straps must be adjusted tighter for this to work.

Your harness's chest strap and anti-torque strap (if equipped) should be fairly loose to achieve the best weight shift.

Low Hook-Ins

Units with low hang points use a different method of weight shift—the pilot tilts the entire machine left or right, more like a free flight harness. Pivoting bars provide about half the riser movement, the tilting machine the other half.

On these machines, you lean and throw your weight over to one side in such a way so the machine tilts. Since its center of gravity is so close to the attachment points, it's not too difficult.

If the low hook-in machine has no pivoting bars then it's probably not designed for significant weight shifting. These machines depend on having the pilot/motor's center of mass being very near the hook-in point. Even just a few inches higher sacrifices weight shift ability. So just because a machine has low hook-ins does not mean it readily weight-shifts. Check with the maker or an experienced pilot who knows the model.

Some pilots of low hook-in motors cross their the when turning. They put the high-side leg over the low-side leg which makes it easier to hold for a longer time, but it doesn't improve the turn. It can also serve as a signal to nearby pilots that you are about to turn which adds value to the "lean" in "look, lean, then turn").

Speedbar Usage

Although our craft is mostly a slow, one-speed affair, we can hasten it up with the speed system. It must be used carefully, though, since engaging it leaves the wing more susceptible to a front collapse (covered later). Apply it slowly and steadily while holding constant power. If combining speedbar with trimmers set to fast, let out the trimmers first, then apply speedbar—that keeps your hands on the brakes when going to this maximum speed configuration.

Most maneuvers have a far more severe reaction to wing maladies and recoveries at higher speed (trimmers fast, speedbar engaged). On some wings, especially the sporty handling ones, the results can be eye opening. Speedbar use should be avoided in bumpy air or less than about 100 feet AGL.

It takes significant leg-push to keep the speedbar engaged, an advantage in that it can be released quickly, restoring the wing to normal flight if rough air is encountered. Trimmers, however, take longer to get to and require that your hands release brake pressure in the process—not desirable in turbulence.

SIV Course

SIV clinics let you learn how your glider behaves in extreme situations and how to recover from them. Flights are almost always done over water, in smooth air after getting towed up a couple thousand feet high by boat. The tow operator and helpers must be extremely competent. Don't think the water will always cushion errors; it can be as hard and fatal as land for someone not taking the course seriously. Such courses are not intended to make you an aerobatic expert—pilots have died while trying the maneuvers on their own over land. Weather conditions play a big part, too; a recovery learned in smooth air may be go much differently in turbulence.

Proper and rapid recovery from many maladies requires decisive and correct reactions that, if done at the wrong time, can make the situation worse. Keep in mind that accident reports indicate that most control-related mishaps in paramotors are from *too much brake*. If in doubt, reduce brake input. Certified gliders are designed to return to normal flight with *no* input from the pilot.

Descent Techniques

As with all maneuvers, do these under the guidance of an instructor first!

Start the following descent methods with trimmers neutral, usually full slow, unless told otherwise. Power should be off with the propeller stopped or windmilling. Build up gradually, starting out shallow and building very, very slowly.

All of these techniques add stress to individual sets of lines. If done repeatedly, your glider may suffer increased degradation and should be inspected more regularly (no less than once per year).

Big Ears

This fairly benign descent technique about doubles your normal descent rate; even more when combined with speedbar (pull ears first, though). Steer with weight shift, if available, and avoid using power or brakes while in ears which increases the already higher risk of going parachutal. Stress increases on the center lines which support everything once the tips are pulled down. Forward speed stays about the same because, while wing area is reduced, drag is increased.

Descent rate: up to 800 FPM (4 m/s).

Entry: reach up with palms facing outward (thumbs down) and pull the outermost A lines down. Twist the hand inward so that your palm faces you when completed. It is easier if the wing is equipped with split A's.

Recovery: Let go of the A lines and do not pull any brake pressure—see if the tips open on their own. Higher aspect ratio wings tend to recover slower and may even need brake pressure 1 or 2.

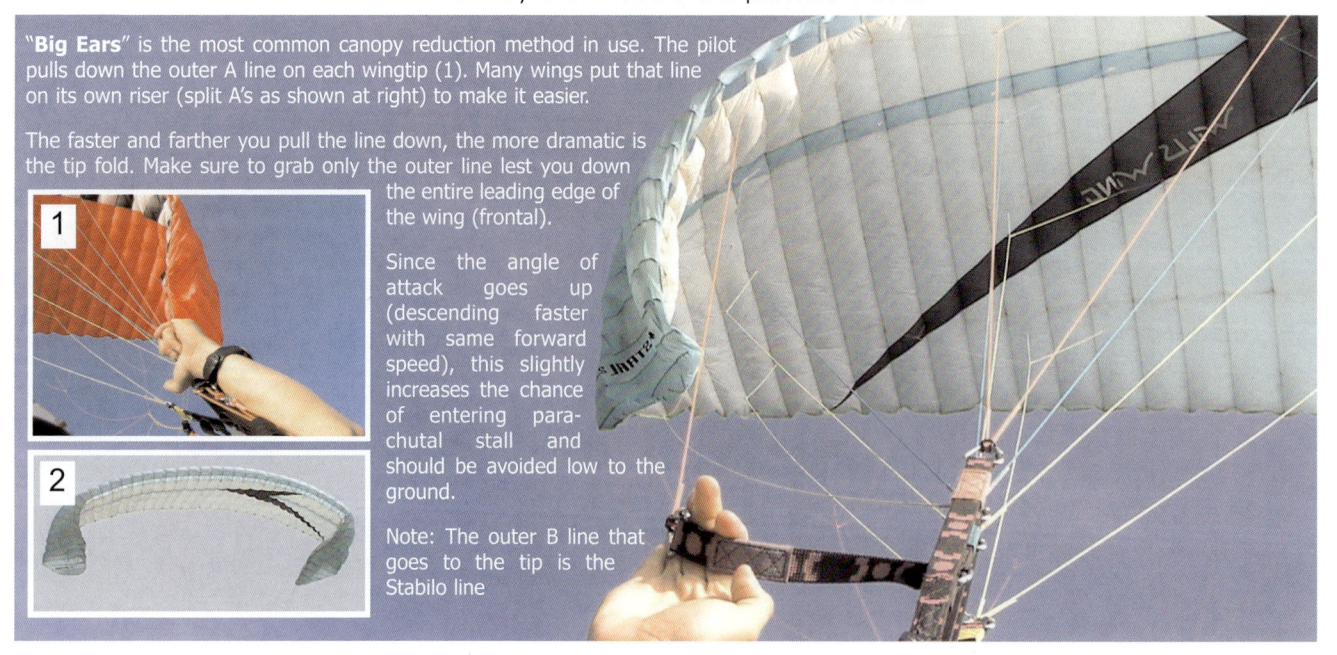

"**Big Ears**" is the most common canopy reduction method in use. The pilot pulls down the outer A line on each wingtip (1). Many wings put that line on its own riser (split A's as shown at right) to make it easier.

The faster and farther you pull the line down, the more dramatic is the tip fold. Make sure to grab only the outer line lest you down the entire leading edge of the wing (frontal).

Since the angle of attack goes up (descending faster with same forward speed), this slightly increases the chance of entering parachutal stall and should be avoided low to the ground.

Note: The outer B line that goes to the tip is the Stabilo line

B-Line Stall

This emergency descent technique causes the wing to stop flying forward while remaining nearly fully formed. Air spills equally around the leading and trailing edges. It puts added stress on the B line wing attachment points and so should not be done frequently. This maneuver is far more dramatic than big ears and should be mastered first at an SIV clinic. Excessive pull on the B lines can cause a front horseshoe which carries a large risk for cravat on exit.

Descent rate: up to 1600 FPM (8 m/s).

Entry: Reach up high on the B lines (just above the quick links or as high as possible) and pull them down to your shoulders with forearms upright. It will initially take a lot of force which decreases once established. The wing falls back (you swing forward) then settles overhead in a vertical descent. How far you pull depends on the wing and where you grabbed the B risers.

More pull gives more descent but too much pull may cause a front horseshoe where the tips fly forward into a U shape. If that happens, immediately let your hands up slightly.

Recovery: Let up on the B lines *quickly* and *evenly*. Letting up slowly may cause a parachutal stall and letting up unevenly may cause a spin. Also, let the wing get fully flying before applying any brakes—it will typically surge less than 45°. Some instructors recommend against letting go of them to reduce stress on the glider.

> ⚠️ **Caution!**
>
> When initially entering a turn, if pulling more brake does not cause more turn, do not pull more brake! Doing so may spin the glider. Also, once you start coming out of a steep turn, don't try to go back into it; let it fully recover first.
>
> While coming out of a steep turn, hold a bit of inside brake to reduce the aggressiveness of recovery. Letting it roll out too quickly can let the pilot swing forward and up enough for the lines go limp with very unpredictable results.

Steep Turns

In a normal turn, you pull a brake, to about pressure 2 and hold it there. The glider arcs into a bank then shallows out a bit, remaining in the turn as long as you hold that brake pressure. Sporty gliders respond quicker but exhibit the same behavior.

A steep turn is different. You pull a bit harder on the brake and hold it there until reaching the desired bank angle. As long as you hold that pressure, the bank *continues* to steepen (not coming back towards level). You'll feel pressed into your seat, G-forces building, as the bank increases. Brake responsiveness and pressure increase as the bank steepens. So a steep turn is where, once at the desired bank angle, you must reduce brake input to prevent careening into a spiral dive, the dangerous extreme of steep turns. Remember, start out slowly!

Any turn causes altitude loss (or requires more power) and gets dramatic at steeper angles. A 60° bank is pretty steep—you'll experience 2 times the pull of gravity (2 G's) and require probably half-again more thrust. Much steeper than that puts you in the spiral dive category.

Descent rate: up to 2000 FPM (10 m/s).

Entry: Initiate a turn and hold enough brake so that it gradually steepens to about 60° then modulate the brakes to hold it there. It looks about like frame 2 at right. Enter into the turn gradually to avoid pulling the wing into a spin.

Recovery: Enormous energy builds up during a steep turn and must be managed. Remove the turn input and the bank should start leveling out. Once it *starts* doing so, be ready to re-apply a bit of inside brake to slow the

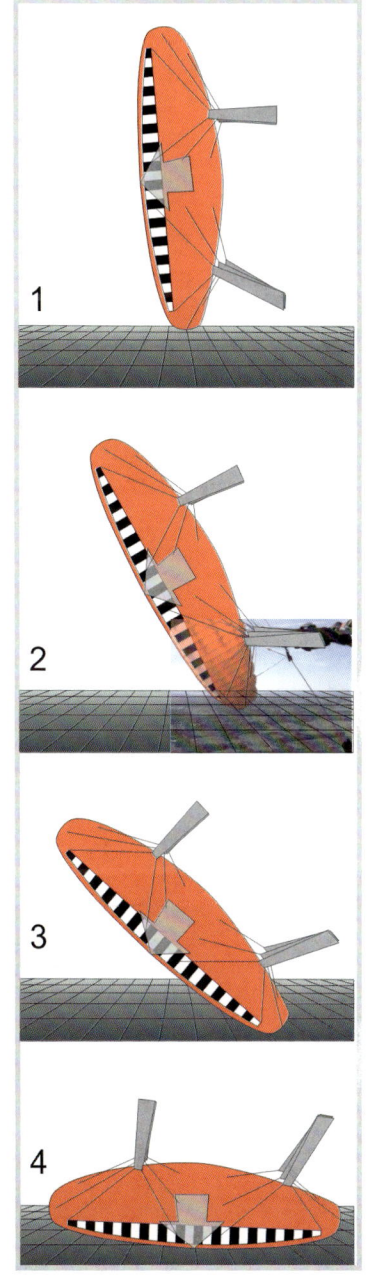

Banks 1 & 2 are steep turns, 3 would be considered a spiral dive. By the time a bank reaches 4, it may not be possible to recover. This "over-the-nose" spiral may inflict G-forces that prevent the pilot even getting to his reserve.

recovery. Much of the risk comes during this level-out—your body and motor are travelling far faster than the wing and want to swing up into a steep climb, possibly followed the lines going slack. That could result in severe collapses, cravats, or lines wrapping around the cage.

Spiral Dive

A Spiral Dive is a steep turn marked by very rapid descent (steeper than frame 2 on the preceding page) where letting up on the brakes may not initiate a recovery. They are dangerous beyond appearances. Even beginner wings may not recover from the steepest spirals. You can wind up "locked in" such that it takes strong opposite brake pressure to start the recover (possibly two hands).

Spiral Dive

When a bank gets this steep, it is perilously close to becoming an un-recoverable spiral dive. G-forces sky-rocket as the pilot plummets; disorientation or blackout is quite possible.

When the glider is pointed straight down, it is called an "over-the-nose" spiral. Getting to that point makes recovery even less certain.

Once established, the highly loaded wing is hyper-sensitive to brake input. You'll quickly get to 4 G's—enough to possibly cause a black out. It has happened numerous times where a pilot blacks out and spirals into the ground. Vertigo, where the pilot gets disoriented to the point of not knowing what brake to pull, is also a possibility. Proper recovery, as with the steep turn, is critical.

An **Asymmetric Spiral** is where one side of the circle is higher than the other. As long as the high side is not significantly higher, this can help avoid "locking into" a spiral dive. The G-load decreases on the high side and increases on the low side. This type of spiral requires high-end active piloting skills since the high-G's on the bottom makes it very sensitive to improper inputs and the pilot can quickly get slack lines on the high side if not careful.

Allowing a bank to steepen so much that the wing is pointing nearly straight down may not be recoverable. For one, this *over the nose* spiral is enormously disorienting. Your body is going to the left and the wing to the right (or vice-versa). It may be confusing as to which brake input will recover. Plus it can inflict G-loads that

1. Richard Good demonstrates a B-Line stall.

2. This is why full stalls should be left to SIV courses! Richard is thrown on his back violently and, although he controls this one, a line getting caught on some part of the motor or many other maladies could render the glider unflyable.

3. B-line stalls, frontal collapses and others can wind up with a frontal horseshoe. Pulling brake to position/pressure 3) normally brings order quickly. It is important to recover quickly to avoid the possibility of a cravat.

prevent deploying your reserve. A number of fatalities have resulted from pilots succumbing to these maladies, even on beginner wings.

Descent rate: up to 5000 FPM (25 m/s).

Entry: Weight shift (if able), then pull enough brake (probably will require pressure 3) to enter a turn and keep the bank increasing. Build slowly, taking an entire 360° turn to get into the spiral—too much brake can cause a spin.

Recovery: Remove any weight shift, put both hands up and let it start rolling out. If it doesn't start right away, pull both brakes some then opposite brake. As soon as it *starts* recovering, let up. If it's leveling off quickly, ease in some inside brake (in the direction you're turning) to dampen the recovery.

The steepest spirals may require weight shift and *heavy* opposite brake to start the recovery.

Think about the spiral in advance. Once banked up, with your body whistling earthward at breakneck speed and G's building, the recover may not be obvious. In a right spiral, for example, you will have used right brake to enter, then very little or no brake to stay in it and may need left brake to initiate the recovery. Although most modern beginner-type wings will roll out on their own, some may not.

Wing Malfunctions

Bad stuff happens, especially to those who challenge rough conditions or their skills. A maneuvers clinic is good preparation, but avoiding nasy conditions is better. Inducing any of these on your own can prove fatal without proper training and, even then, has proven risky. Parachutal Stall and Cravats are covered in Chapter 4 under Emergencies.

The standard emergency response is "hands up, power off" but, if you're near terrain, you must use just enough brake to steer away. Look up at the wing to see what has happened then look back at the horizon to stay oriented. Again, *too much* brake causes most recovery problems for motor pilots.

A full stall into soft sand. Entry and recovery varies by wing but it should never be done outside an SIV course. You can see the value of recovering well before if fully develops. Allowing a full stall to develop in flight by pulling this hard on the brakes has proven deadly. If you feel the brakes start to go "mushy," *immediately* reduce brake pressure, but if the wing has already fallen back, hold the brakes down for at least 3 seconds *then* recover.

Turbulence can play havoc on a recovery so, even if you've practiced, don't expect it to always go the same in rough air.

Full Stall

A full stall is probably the most violent maneuver with the least predictable outcome. Fortunately, it is rare, almost always resulting from excessive pull on the brakes, sometimes in combination with turbulence. It is the one maneuver where you must *not* use "hands up, power off" as the initial reaction. If you look up and see (or suspect) that the wing has full-stalled, you *must* hold the brakes down for several seconds to let the glider stabilize overhead before recovering. If you let up on the brakes when the wing is back, it will shoot forward and down, possibly pulling your flailing body into it.

A full stall's only practical value is as a last resort "paraglider reset." If you have an

Asymmetric Collapse

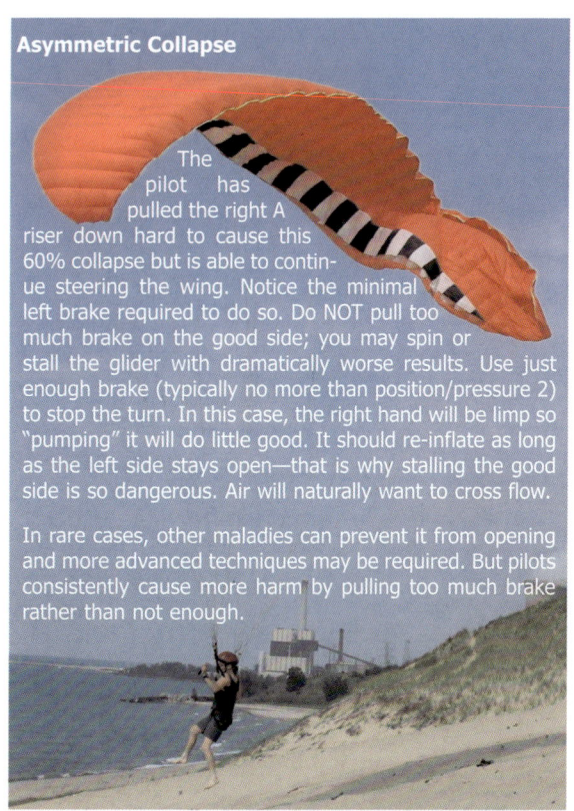

The pilot has pulled the right A riser down hard to cause this 60% collapse but is able to continue steering the wing. Notice the minimal left brake required to do so. Do NOT pull too much brake on the good side; you may spin or stall the glider with dramatically worse results. Use just enough brake (typically no more than position/pressure 2) to stop the turn. In this case, the right hand will be limp so "pumping" it will do little good. It should re-inflate as long as the left side stays open—that is why stalling the good side is so dangerous. Air will naturally want to cross flow.

In rare cases, other maladies can prevent it from opening and more advanced techniques may be required. But pilots consistently cause more harm by pulling too much brake rather than not enough.

un-recoverable malfunction, lots of altitude (1000 feet plus) and no reserve: take a couple wraps on the brakes and pull them down hard, below your seat for at least 3 seconds, then recover. Remember, this a last ditch effort with no guarantees.

Descent rate: over 2000 FPM (10 m/s).

Cause: Too much brake, probably beyond position/pressure 4 or hitting turbulence while pulling moderate brakes.

The wing will fall back and you'll feel like you've been pulled onto your back as you drop. If that happens, hold the brakes until the wing stabilizes overhead. It may be "bucking" about wildly but hold on for a couple seconds!

Recovery: Once the glider is reasonably overhead, let up the brakes smoothly, evenly and quickly (1 to 2 seconds) all the way. Hold that *pressure*. while the glider sorts itself out. While holding that pressure, your hands may move down a lot—let them. Don't try to control the surges unless you're absolutely certain of what you're doing. Recovery must be done properly lest you wind up cocooned in your glider—a usually short, one-time experience.

Spin

Spins are another malady caused by pilots pulling too much brake. If it's uneven pull, especially against the torque, part of the wing stalls while the rest keeps flying. The glider rotates nearly overhead as you descend. It can result in a riser twist as the pilot tries to catch up to the spin of his wing, potentially locking the brakes in place and preventing recovery.

If you feel any unusual slowing or turning, let up on the brakes! Most pilots will not detect the onset of a spin until it's already spun half way around so prevention is far better than correction.

Descent rate: around 1200 FPM (6 m/s).

Cause: Uneven heavy breaking, especially against the torque. Turbulence can also cause it but only if you're already heavy in the brake.

Recovery: Hands up, reduce power, prepare to dampen the surge. In a riser twist scenario, you may be able to reach above the twist and pull outward to forcefully untwist yourself. Be mindful of your remaining altitude and know where the reserve is—be ready to toss it.

Asymmetric Collapse

Remember that what nature doles out can be far worse than what you may induce. A big asymmetric may bank you violently, dropping you towards the collapsed side as it erupts into a turn (more collapse, more turn). Machines with low hook-in points that are intended for weight shift will feel more abrupt. Avoid pulling too much brake in the recovery but carefully do what it takes to prevent a spiral.

Descent rate: from 600 FPM (3 m/s) to 1000 FPM (5 m/s).

Cause: Turbulence. It can be simulated by reaching up high on one A riser (or both parts of a split A) and pulling down slowly. The faster (harder) you pull, the more wing collapses—be careful, a fast pull can cause a 70% fold. This can also result from a student grabbing a riser while trying to get into the seat—a big no-no.

Recovery: Steer using weight shift (if the machine allows it) and careful brake pressure on the open side to minimize turn. Pulling too much brake risks a stall or spin. Have the brake on the deflated side at about half but as soon as pressure builds (the collapse starts coming out), let that hand come up while keeping some pressure (about pressure 2). Older wings may require "pumping" the deflated side but be sure to steer first.

Most motor pilots usually cause worse problems by pulling too hard, be careful. Once tracking straight, if you do t"pump"

Frontal Collapse

Also called a *frontal* or *front tuck*, it results from the leading edge being forced downward, closing off the cells. You drop and the wing falls back, normally followed by quick recovery with no pilot input.

Descent rate: up to 1000 FPM (5 m/s).

Cause: A sudden and severe forward surge of the wing which can happen from a bad maneuver recovery, pilot action or turbulence, especially a strong downward gust.

Aggressively applying speedbar while at fast trim *and* letting off the throttle can also cause the wing to rocket forward enough to frontal. It is more likely when trimmed fast.

Recovery: Release the speedbar, if engaged, and "tap" the brakes if needed (to about pressure 2). Let it surge forward to get the glider flying before adding any brake which could cause a parachutal stall (also called constant stall). If it does go into parachutal stall, remember "hands up, power off" and be ready to "tweak" the A's—where you grab each A riser, palms forward and twist downward to lower the A a couple inches.

Pendular Control

Wingovers and surges are useful maneuvers to practice provided they're kept within your skill level. They are extremely risky if you get aggressive and should be done first with an advanced instructor on the radio.

Start off gently! Rehearse the reserve deployment sequence in your mind just in

A frontal collapse is induced by pulling down on the A's. Recovery is normally quick when the A's are released. Most wings come out on their own but some may require a tug (position/pressure 2) on the brakes. On some wings this can result in a front horseshoe where the wing tips come forward.

Wingovers

Wingovers, when done properly, will look like figure eights with the ends raised. Your heading changes a lot as you continually adjust the turn. Fine brake pressures are applied throughout the maneuver to keep yourself and wing going the same direction at all times.

1. Surge and retreats can be fun and a good skill builder but don't let them get too steep. Most importantly, practice and master how to dampen them quickly.

2. This is why it's so important to use brake *pressure* and not brake position. Kim Pearson is doing a steep wingover where the wing is nearly unloaded. He is only pulling *pressure* 2 but the trailing edge is heavily deflected (lots of brake *travel*). Without this, the wing would be far more susceptible to collapse (frontal or asymmetric).

As soon as the wing starts loading up, the brakes will want to come back up, let them! Keep the brake pressure on and your hands will return to a nearly full-up position. Holding them against an increasing pressure may lead to a stall or spin.

case things go awry.

Do wingovers and surges up high and never get so steep that the wing unloads (you feel light in the seat). Always have *some* brake pressure to reduce the likelihood of a front tuck or collapse. Once you've really mastered this level of control it will help you better handle turbulence too. As always, fly by brake pressure, not position. Let the brakes "float" at a given pressure instead of holding them rigidly regardless of pressure. Your hands may move a fair amount (lots of brake *travel*) even though the pressure is quite low, that is ok.

Wingovers

Wingovers are left and right turns done at the gliders natural pendular rate. Weight shift (if able) and pull left brake to pressure 2 for a second then let up. As soon as your body crests and *starts* coming back, pull right brake and hold for two seconds then release. The idea is to time it so that it gets a bigger swing each time. Just like a swing set, you don't pull *much* brake, but you pull it at just the right *time* to amplify the swing (or keep it going). Do the opposite to recover. This is a great exercise to grow skill in pendular control. Finesse requires using both brakes at times to prevent the tips from curling up or collapsing.

Fore/Aft Pendulums (Surge and Retreats)

Add power or pull brakes to pressure 2 (not both) for two seconds then let off. You'll swing out forward as the wing falls back. When your body starts swinging forward again, gingerly add power or pull brake for a second then let off. Like on a swing set, you'll gradually get the swings steeper and steeper. *Build slowly!* Practice stopping the maneuver quickly—like the swing, you want to build instinct in how to dampen these pendular actions.

Never get so steep that you feel near weightless in your seat—you'll be perilously close to unloading the lines and getting an unplanned reserve ride. And don't use both power and brakes until you're experienced—as always, start off slowly.

Stabilo Line Pull

The stabilo line (see Chapter 2) is the outermost B or C line that goes to the tip and is often a different color. Its importance lies in clearing cravats which is where a wingtip gets tangled in the lines (see Chapter 4).

While kiting, practice finding the stabilo line after inducing a tip collapse—it can be hard to locate with other lines draped around it and the practice will help. Then do the same in flight by pulling an outer A line down slowly (makes one "big ear") and watching what happens with the stabilo line so you'll know where it is when you need to use it.

Risk Management

CHAPTER 19

We're fortunate that most mistakes in paramotoring have already been made. We're even more fortunate that we know how to prevent their recurrence.

A lot can be learned from the airlines, which have amassed an amazing safety record by studying accidents and developing improvements to both hardware and procedure. They have turned an inherently dangerous operation (flying jet airplanes at ridiculous speeds) into the safest form of transportation ever devised. This chapter and, in fact, much of the book hopes to do the same for powered paragliding.

The familiar saying, "It's as safe as you make it," is especially true for us—nearly all risk comes from pilot action, not equipment failures or other peoples' actions. Enormous risk can be avoided through behavior changes that result from an intelligent application of knowledge. It's sad enough when tragedy comes to those taking known risks, but what a wasteful shame when it comes from ignorance.

During a demonstration flight, Igor Potapkin (from Russia) got his wing tip within grabbing distance of organizers. Getting to this point takes lots of experience, probably numerous crashes and the willingness to risk it all.

Unlike other segments of microlight aviation, a catastrophic equipment failure is incredibly rare, far less than even general aviation. Pilot behavior and questionable weather conditions are where the risk comes from.

Probability and Severity

Some things we do increase the *probability* of an accident and some things increase the *severity*. For example, foregoing maintenance on your motor, using really old fuel, or ignoring your fuel quantity, all increase the *probability* of a motor failure. Flying beyond reach of a safe landing site increases the *severity* if it does happen. Each probability has a related severity which changes throughout a flight.

Another good example is flying without a helmet. The probability of a mishap is no different than wearing the helmet but the severity sure is. The same is true of seat belts in a car—they don't prevent the accident, they just reduce the potentially horrible consequences.

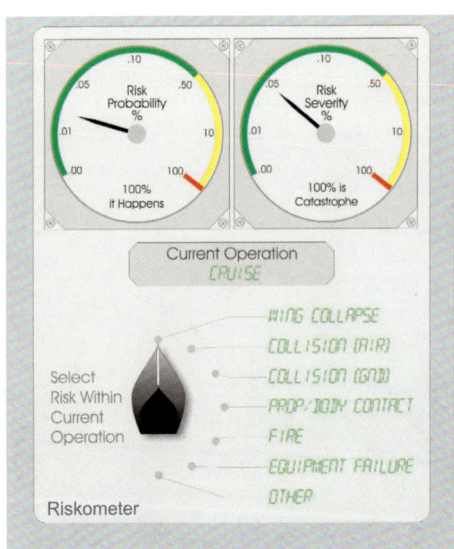

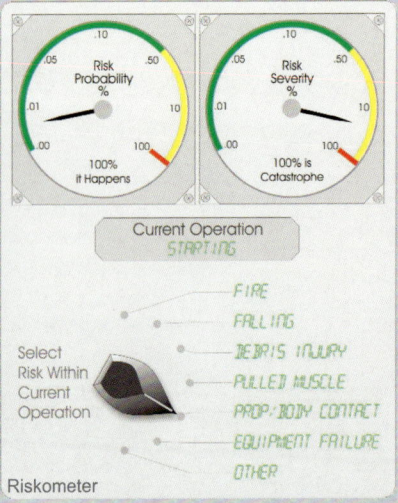

If we could put risk on gauges it might look something like these—a reading for probability and severity. The system would know the current operation (starting, takeoff, climb, cruise, etc.) and the risk type would get selected for display. Each operation has several risk types with related severities. For example, the probability of anything happening while flying along at 2000 feet AGL (in cruise) is incredibly low. Select "fire" and the probability gauge would read near zero with a high severity—although incredibly unlikely, a fire would be severe due to the time it would take to descend.

Sitting next to your paramotor, the current operation would read "preflight" and both needles will be 0. Starting the motor while standing in front of it moves both probability *and* severity needles way up—starting is a very risky phase. Once the motor is running and strapped on your back, both needles go back down to near zero—almost nobody gets hurt at this point.

Doing foot drags is interesting. Of course bad things can happen when doing them but, even when they do, the pilot doesn't have very far to fall. So, while the probability of a mishap is quite high (falling), the severity is low provided they're done into the wind. Doing them downwind or over rough surface increases probability slightly but the severity goes way up.

Both needles would frequently move in unison. For example, flying downwind, in the mechanical turbulence of large buildings or mountains increases both the probability and severity of a mishap. Stronger winds give higher readings.

Flying out of a tight field with corn yields a high probability (of hitting the corn) but low severity. If you run into the corn it's not that big of a deal (unless you do it downwind). Flying out of a tight tree-lined field is another matter, and far worse. The severity goes way up for that brief period of exposure while you climb over the trees. Flying over water, beyond gliding range of land does not increase the probability of an engine failure, but the severity skyrockets (drowning).

One common practice is to keep the severity reading low while letting the probability fluctuate. Maneuvers clinics (SIV courses) are this way. They intentionally make serious things happen (like wing collapses) so the pilot can learn proper reactions. But through careful preparation (rescue boat, pilot floatation, radio instructions, etc.) they keep the severity reasonably low. Frontal collapses, spins, asymmetric collapses and so forth are all induced over water, with a boat and safeguards in place to handle the worst.

Some things increase both probability and severity. Doing foot drags in deep water is a good example—the chance of a motor failure (water spray fouling the ignition) increases as does the severity (drowning). Shallow water (less than 6 inches) leaves the increased probability but severity becomes low.

Risks can frequently be more than additive—combining them may be way more risky than the two added together individually.

Energy and Injury

Our sport's overall safety stems mostly from its very low speed. Increasing the speed dramatically increases the injury potential, especially considering how exposed we are. Energy dissipated in a collision increases by the square of the speed so doubling the speed quadruples the energy (and injury). For example, hitting something at 30 mph carries four times more energy than does hitting it at 15 mph. The slow collision will hurt but the fast one may be lethal.

Anything that puts you in a high-energy state, especially near hard, immovable stuff dramatically ramps up the severity of a mishap.

Getting Away With It

Why do I need to use a helmet anyway? Personal choice is a valued freedom but *know* what you risk. The same is true of standard aviation safety practices that are eschewed by a few—helmets, patterns, footgear, preflights, reserves, checklists, etc.—are all layers that reduce the likelihood and/or severity of a mishap. Never accept the argument "such and such has never happened to me or anyone I konw."

A helmet, for example, reduces head injuries from exploding props and crashes where your head hits some part of the frame or ground. How often does it happen? Not often, but it *does* happen and has yielded fatal results. Quality footwear reduces the chance of injury from rough ground or prop strikes. At least one pilot avoided a prop-mangled foot by virtue his stout boots.

This sport is replete with examples of those who ignored common safety practices and it caught up with them. New people come in, forego collective wisdom or never learn it, succeed for a time and then consider the risk acceptable. In reality, they're just beating the odds.

The worst thing you can do is assume that past success will continue in the face of bad practice. Fortunately, accidents are rare, but when they do happen it's usually to those taking chances often. Relish the freedom to risk, but wield that freedom carefully.

Just because you've succeeded at a risky endeavor before doesn't make it safe. For example, you may fly low over wires many times, but if a problem, such as misjudgment or motor failure does happen, it carries potentially dire consequences.

Where the Risk Is

Here are some examples of risks along with ways to minimize them. The best counsel is to evaluate whether a planned activity is worth the possible consequence. What is the likelihood? How bad would it hurt and is the reward worth it?

Nobody launches expecting to crash. Analyze the operation: is it late? Is there questionable weather? Has someone suggested not flying? Am I going to fly low? Am I wearing appropriate safety gear?

Starting and Handling the Motor

It's the most dangerous part of our sport—starting and handling the motor. Serious and permanent injuries have befallen those who lost sight of this fact.

It happens, even to conscientious pilots who, in a brief moment of inattentiveness, let the motor get away from them. Then whack! The U.S. Powered Paragliding Association (USPPA) labels these incidents "Body contact with spinning propeller" and they are rarely forgiving. Heed the cautions in Section I and look at incident reports where available.

> Always, *always* inspect the throttle linkage before starting. *Do it every time*, insuring that the carburetor is at idle and throttle can't be increased accidentally.

Training

Inadequate training sets the stage for many injuries. Unfortunately, those who don't receive good training don't even know what's at risk. To have read these words and still skip quality, thorough training is to accept the highest levels of both probability and severity. Even with training, the early stages of learning involve risk on several fronts. While the probability for training mishaps is somewhat higher, the severity is usually minor—the same bruises and scrapes that come with many outdoor activities. Some simple precautions such as knee pads, decent boots and gloves can ease the pain.

The most serious risk comes during those first few flights. It can be nearly eliminated with a good instructor, thorough syllabus, simulator work, a methodical approach and appropriate location. Hopefully your instructor emphasized simulator rehearsal of emergency procedures—it's a great way to be prepared.

Intermediate Syndrome

Guard yourself against Intermediate Syndrome, a psychology that haunts moderately experienced pilots. As their skills improve they start taking chances that are just beyond their capability. Losing hurts.

Excelling at anything *will* put your skills to the test, but choose situations where the results of failure are tolerable. For example, taking on higher winds will improve your skills, but choose places where getting dragged won't cause injury or damage.

Inappropriate Gear

Inappropriate gear, or the wrong technique for the gear you have, adds risk. Most equipment-related trade-offs are covered in Section VI but here are some common risks associated with having inappropriate equipment.

- Excessive power for your weight increases the risk of riser twist and, to a lesser degree, makes falling more likely due to weight and torque. It can also increase the chance for a "face-plant."

- Insufficient power increases your risk of tripping during the extended run and will not allow quick climb over surprise obstructions. Plus, the slow climb adds vulnerability to even small downdrafts after takeoff.

- Flying an advanced wing without a mastery of active piloting increases risk, especially if flown in conditions other than calm.

- Too small of a wing increases speed which makes any accident worse and increase the takeoff run. Sportier handling can lead to a loss of control. It's easy to minimize handling since flying seems so simple, but sporty wings have contributed to numerous crashes due to mishandling.

- Too large of a wing increases the chance for parachutal stall and, being slower, may not allow penetration into a strong wind.

- Poorly designed equipment (structurally weak, dangerous attributes, etc.) is not appropriate for anyone. Lean toward models that embrace safety features over those using older, less-safe technology. It's always a trade off—sometimes safety features get traded for other attributes. Choose carefully by talking to respected pilots who have experience are familiar with various models.

Steep Maneuvering & Aerobatics

Steep maneuvers at low altitude, especially if they involve any vertical component, produce the sport's greatest lethality. While a prop strike is the most common serious injury, this is the most deadly. Of the few fatalities in paramotoring, this single

---

This is the single most likely time to be seriously injured with a paramotor. Most would be prevented if the pilot made sure the throttle was at idle and there was no way he could accidentally engage it.

What Is The Risk?

Foot launching a PPG carries about the same risk as moderately aggressive skiing. You may get a twisted ankle or similar type of injury during your flying career but it won't likely be fatal. The safety appears better than motorcycle riding based on the number of participants in both activities and the number of fatalities which, for paramotoring, is quite small even for the low number of participants.

Unlike motorcycles, paramotor pilots control their risk more. Making good choices can easily eliminate much of the risk whereas many other endeavors depend on the skill of other participants to keep from hitting you.

category represents over a quarter of them.

It's happens easily—after gaining some experience pilots get "braver," trying maneuvers beyond their skill and without instruction. Little banks graduate to steeper banks that become spiral dives. Little pendulums morph into wingovers. Given the need for our soft wing to always be loaded, these maneuvers can get ugly quickly. Plus, when the wing is heavily loaded (as in a steep turn), the controls become extremely sensitive—surprised pilots wind up with large excursions following small inputs. Steep maneuvering also adds enormous speed, too.

Allowing yourself to become weightless, or nearly so, is *really* asking for it—consider what happens when the lines quit holding the glider into its gliderly shape. Worse yet, those loose lines can now find things to wrap around (including pilot parts) before they reload with a bang.

If done without instruction or low to the ground, aerobatics are a terrible risk. Doing this stuff close to the ground has been the final ingredient in a dangerous cocktail of risk for pilots who pushed it too far.

Low Flying

You can't hit something if you're above it. Almost all the airborne injuries happen while cruising or maneuvering down low. Climbing to at least 200 feet eliminates most risk. Not only is mechanical turbulence more likely at low altitude, but there is less time to recover.

Simple misjudgments in turns are aggravated by low flying. The distraction of nearby ground objects contributes to this, especially with any downwind component.

Wire strikes, even at slow speeds, are a big risk. Most injury comes from the ensuing fall although electrocution is certainly possible. In most cases, the area was familiar to the pilot, but he either forgot about, or just didn't see, the lines—they can be essentially invisible.

Don't think wires will be stand out like they do from the ground. From below they are set against a plain sky, having contrast and uniqueness. But seen from above, they can blend completely into the background.

If you cannot resist the allure of the low, here are a few tips to mitigate *some* of the risk.

- Avoid flying *downwind* while low. With the higher ground speed, any miscalculation, unexpected obstruction, or motor failure would be far worse. The speed difference between a collision going downwind and one going into the wind is dramatic. Plus, higher ground speed leaves less time to notice and react to obstructions.

- Fly into an area above 200 feet AGL and scout for obstructions before descending into the danger zone. Look for poles or their shadows and be suspicious of any straight lines (road edges, field edges, etc.).

- As always, stay over landable terrain. This is even more

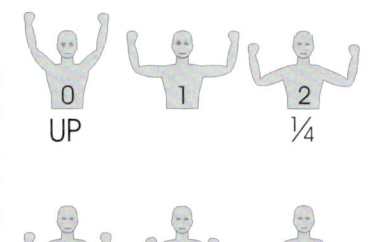

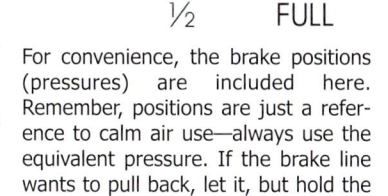

For convenience, the brake positions (pressures) are included here. Remember, positions are just a reference to calm air use—always use the equivalent pressure. If the brake line wants to pull back, let it, but hold the same pressure.

There's almost never any reason to go beyond position/pressure 4 except for landing.

In any situation that you do not know what is happening, reduce brake input first then steer carefully.

Think of position 0 and 1 as the "Green zone," Position 2 and 3 as the "Yellow caution zone," and position 4 or more as the "Red danger Zone."

Always approach wires at an angle so that you can quickly veer away if necessary. Fly over the poles since the wires are difficult to judge height over. Fly straight across only when clearly more than twice the pole height.

important when flying down low because you won't have time to maneuver after a power failure.

- Respect power lines and other obstructions. Don't ever plan a climb over something if a power loss would leave you without options.

Downwind Operations, The "Demon"

To the paraglider itself, flying downwind is no different than flying upwind. The same for turning from upwind to downwind—it's no different. But talk to enough pilots and you'll eventually hear of the dreaded "downwind demon." This myth incorrectly suggests that, when turning downwind, the air "hits the back of the wing, causing it to sink." It simply isn't so. Like a boat in a wide river, our craft operates in a fluid-like environment (the air) that is moving along over the ground. The best evidence is to go up high and do your turn. You'll see there is no difference whatsoever; in fact, it's hard to even know what the wind is doing up high. Look at the wake of a boat doing a nice, round 360° turn in the middle of a river—the whole circle is moving downstream but no part of the turn feels different to the boat driver.

There are, however, several very powerful *illusions*, and one real effect, that happen when turning from upwind to downwind—and they can easily fool the pilot into pulling too much brake. They are the real "downwind demons" and only happen near the ground.

Many of these problems arise from the fact that normally when you pull brakes, you go up, briefly anyway. Of course we know that to be a temporary sacrifice of speed, but the subconscious mind thinks, incorrectly, "pull brakes to climb."

The Climb Illusion: You take off into a 10 mph headwind, flying 20 mph and climbing at 200 fpm. The groundspeed is only 10 mph so that climb looks impressively steep. Now you turn downwind. Suddenly the *angle* drops way down even though the *rate* of climb remains unchanged. The ground is zinging by at 30 mph while you continue climbing at 200 fpm. The subconscious inclination is to pull more brake so that the climb looks the same as before, relative to the ground below.

Wind Gradient: This effect is no illusion. If you climb into an increasing headwind (wind gradient), the wing "sees" a bigger headwind and really does climb better as it seeks to get back to its trim airspeed. Your groundspeed is slowing down in the process. The reverse is true during a downwind climb in that gradient. You'll encounter an increasing tailwind that reduces climb as the wing *accelerates* to maintain airspeed. The stronger the gradient, the stronger the effect and it is usually most dramatic down low. Climbing upwind for the first 200 feet usually gets you above the gradient.

The Turn Illusion is usually a mild effect that,

Tip:

Remember, our wing flies in reference to the air, not the ground. All the "downwind demon" illusions happen when pilots look at the ground while maneuvering down low. It cases them to pull too much brake in certain situations. Use minimum brake and practice ignoring the illusions.

You can avoid *all* the "downwind demon" risk by climbing up to 200 feet, into the wind, before turning.

The Climb Illusion. Into the wind, your climb *angle* looks great since the ground speed is low. Turn downwind and, even though the climb *rate* is the same, the shallow angle can fool you into pulling more brake.

The Turn Illusion: When turning from upwind to downwind the turn rate is the same all the way around (number of degrees per second). But the ground speed picks up and the ground track shallows as you get pointed downwind. The inexperienced may succumb to the illusion and pull more brakes, potentially causing a stall.

like most, can become psychologically overpowering in moderately strong winds and lower altitudes.

Rate of turn depends only on bank angle and *airspeed*. If it takes you 2 minutes to turn all the way around when it's calm, it will take you 2 minutes to go all the way around in a strong wind. And the rate of turn is exactly the same going upwind as downwind. However, if you're looking at the *ground* track, the upwind portion describes a tight arc while the downwind portion has a shallow arc. If you're low, that shallow arc can *feel* like you're hardly turning.

A pilot in the throes of this illusion will subconsciously add more inside brake to steepen the turn so it looks the same as a no-wind or upwind turn. The bank can steepen severely before the pilot realizes it. Once banked up, the pilot dives into the ground, usually at high speed because it happens during the downwind portion.

You can avoid all these effects by climbing *into* the wind to 200 ft. before turning.

Distractions

Taking pictures, flying formation, and listening to or fiddling with music are among the many distractions that increase risk. They divert attention from the primary task of maintaining a safe flight path. Additionally, items can easily slip from your grasp and head for the prop.

Stuff hung around your neck holds the potential to slide back and catch on a moving motor part—not necessarily the propeller. Its strap could get pulled into the motor, bringing whatever it is connected to along. One pilot almost got decapitated when his camera strap went into the pull-start mechanism. Fortunately, the strap broke before his neck did.

Cinch neck straps so they cannot slide backwards into the motor area.

While unlikely, a mid-air would likely be catastrophic. Formation must be done with extreme care.

Formation

Flying near others adds a serious risk of collision or wing collapse due to wake turbulence. There are many nuances to formation flying (see Chapter 16) that should be learned gradually and first learned with large margins.

Before flying close formation, both pilots should be skilled with active flying and understand the severity of any mishap. What carnage remains after two wings get tangled up may not even allow tossing a reserve.

Watch This!

An interesting observation is that nearly half of all serious flying accidents have occurred with spectators watching or cameras rolling. Resist the urge to push it

> **Camera Encounter**
>
> At a major PPG event, an experienced pilot was doing close flybys while a video cameraman recorded the action. The experienced cameraman left it up to the experienced pilot to avoid contact. But the pilot wasn't so experienced with the higher elevation and slightly misjudged his pull-up. He wound up hitting the camera, leaving its operator with a walloping black eye. The cameraman was lucky.
>
> Cameras and flying continue proving their dysfunctional relationship—be extra vigilant when the two are combined.

A competitor slices through the start gate during a competition in Phoenix, Arizona. Any endeavor that pushes the limit of ability increases risk. Competitive tasks, however, are designed to minimize the severity of the risk.

under such conditions. It's very tempting. The term "Kodak Courage" is an apt epitaph for many pilots whose demise goes before a crowd and its cameras.

Note that professional airshow pilots practice their routines over and over again at high altitudes in order to perfect them. They also frequently practice them in the same locale where the airshow will take place. Then when they perform they do the exact same thing without exceeding their usual limits. "Show-Offs," however, tend to *exceed* their limits in front of eyes or lenses.

If you find yourself doing something steeper, lower, or wilder when folks are watching, conciously mellow out.

Terrain

Flying from flat land, with its more benign weather patterns and forgiving sites, adds safety. We give up a lot of that safety in mountainous terrain or by flying from confined sites. Other risky terrain features include water and congestion.

Flying mountainous regions also increases opportunity for weather related jams. Local knowledge is a good way to avoid surprises here.

Equipment Condition

Wings get porous, lines break, motors wear out, harnesses weaken, carabiners get scratched and other critical flight components degrade with time and use. These must be maintained properly and inspected regularly, especially the wing.

Carabiners are possibly the sport's only single-point where a failure would be catastrophic. Steel carabiners are stronger, but regardless of the material, make sure they have no scratches and the gates close properly.

The wing should command most of our attention as its degradation is most likely to cause problems. Having porous fabric or shortened or stretched lines dramatically increases the possibility of parachutal stall. Add some other factor, such as being too light for your wing or flying in turbulence, and a stall may be inevitable.

Don't neglect the motor—some failure modes involve the prop coming off and slicing into the tank. An engine failure, while relatively benign, can put you somewhere undesirable depending on where it happens.

Disintegrating props can send shards flying in all directions. Most of the time this mishap occurs when some piece of the machine vibrates loose and goes through the prop. Anything that can work loose should have lock nuts, safety wire, or other means to prevent ejection. Improperly repaired propellers, especially composites, are more susceptible to failure even with no prop strike.

Weather

A large accident category is weather related—pilots ignore weather warnings and fly anyway. One deception is that you can frequently get away with it—a success that leads to falsely thinking that the risk is small.

For example, and this is one of many, most thunderstorms don't actually cause problems until they're fairly close, but *occasionally* they cause horrendous winds from some distance—a gust front—and there's no warning.

Competition

This pursuit involves maneuvering low to the ground, sometimes at high speed, at the limits of pilot control and with distracting goals—obviously a riskier combination than regular flying.

A lot of risk, however, is mitigated by keeping pilots from getting high enough to develop dangerous *vertical* speed. They may fly low and fast but are rarely pointed at the ground. That's probably why competition has enjoyed a good safety record both in the U.S. and even Europe, where it's done a lot.

The way to minimize competition's higher risk is to be ever mindful of the fact that an injury will, at best, end an event with a low score. Fly within your ability and improve gradually instead of trying to do it all at once. A middling performer who safely completes all the tasks will beat the aggressive pilot who crashes in pursuit of perfection.

Adding Safety Equipment

Our choice of safety equipment depends on flying style and locale. If you fly over forests, a tree extraction kit is essential. If you fly over water then "Spare Air" (see Chapter 28) and floatation would be prudent. Certain items will help regardless of locale and style—a cell phone and hook knife are good examples.

Some safety gear reduces the odds of a mishap while some reduces the severity of it. Reserve parachutes are severity reducers. They won't decrease the probability of a malfunction but sure may improve the results. Flying in rowdy air makes a reserve that much more beneficial. Of course, it must be installed properly and its use rehearsed. There is some slight risk of accidental deployment.

Gloves are important for operating in windy conditions since ground handling the glider is where you're most likely to get line burns.

Boots can prevent ankle injuries and other foot-related maladies. Rough or rocky surfaces makes them even more valuable.

The helmet is probably the single most important safety element because, although unlikely, head injuries are so dire. They are essential for ground handling in strong conditions, too.

Combining Risks

Many risky behaviors, when combined, increase the chance of a mishap exponentially—way more then just adding them together. A perfect example is doing steep maneuvers down low. Both the *odds* of calamity and *severity of its outcome* skyrocket. The chances are far higher than just adding the two risks separately.

Another example is doing about anything in rowdy air. It increases the overall probability of an accident, especially during takeoff or landing.

By knowing what operations carry what risk, you can carefully pick and choose only those with sufficient reward to warrant their results. Knowing the risk will also help direct extra attention to where it is needed most.

Gusted

After a week of lousy weather and non-flight, I was anxious to get airborne. Lines of thunderstorms had been roiling through but the receding rumble of the last batch had quieted. Peering outside revealed a quiet calm. Hmmm...

The riled sky had mellowed, becoming almost strangely calm. I gathered my gear and headed out. A half-mile away, my field was nicely open—I could see to the horizon and noted darkness in the distance. Hmmm...

I waited about 5 minutes—the silence in that calm let me hear clearly. Soon I discerned a muted rumble. Uh oh, I thought, maybe this isn't such a good Idea. So I packed up and headed home. It wouldn't be fun anyway, knowing that this thing lurked in the distance and its nastiness could drop down on me unexpectedly.

Shortly after settling back at home into my project du jour, I heard it. Even before thunder signaled the storm's arrival—it was the unmistakable howl of a strong wind. A gust front had arrived. Within minutes, a destructive wind blew that would have been horrendous to anyone flying anything, let alone something with a 15 pound wing. I was thankful to be inside.

Handling Situational Emergencies

Dangerous situations may confront you while leaving time to make choices. These cannot be rehearsed in a simulator but rather require a cool, thinking head. Most are incredibly unlikely, especially during early training where the instructor keeps closer tabs on you. All of these can be avoided, but we're all human.

Each situation will normally have several options, not all will be included here. They should be considered with your particular skills and situation. What may be appropriate with one pilot in one situation may be a disaster for another. Weigh your choices and pick the least objectionable.

Be wary of absolutes and analyze your options before acting. Sometimes the first action that pops in your head isn't the best one. Having thought about options in advance (like reading this) can be helpful, but anything that requires a quick response must be rehearsed. The airlines have learned that reactionary physical skills, if not rehearsed, will likely be done wrong when they are really needed.

Never leave yourself in a position where a motor failure leads to a water landing. The outcome is far from guaranteed even when the procedures are followed. These three pilots are actually near shore which is just out of view below.

Landing In Water (Ditching)

To make the best of this very bad situation, undo your leg, chest and sternum straps, dispose of anything hanging around your neck (camera, radio, etc.) and prepare to jump out of the seat. Grab and extract your hook knife or, at least, practice reaching for it. Some instructors suggest leaving one leg strap connected (as long as it's a quick-release type) then undoing it after splashing in.

Approach with quarter brake (position/pressure 2) and flare only if you are absolutely certain where the water is—judging height above water can be deceptive. Consider landing crosswind so the wing blows away from you or slightly downwind (quartering tailwind) so it over-flies you. In a stronger wind (over about 5 mph), always land into it.

Take a full breath of air just before impact. As soon as your feet touch the water, exit and swim away from the gear. Do not try to estimate height and jump early—height has proven disastrously difficult to judge; one pilot died after jumping from too high. Once clear, do not swim back to your gear lest it entangle you, especially in moving water. The wing will probably float but the motor will sink once its cavities fill. The wing may hold the motor up for some time.

If you start getting entangled in lines, *immediately* start cutting them with your hook knife as much as necessary to swim away.

If your wing goes into ocean surf or a stream, *immediately* unclip as you walk toward it to prevent the wing from pulling you in. If it does start pulling, it will be nigh impossible to unclip; your only option may be start cutting with the hook knife. Pilots have landed on dry ground and then drowned when their wing fell into moving water. It seems so benign, but quickly becomes overpowering due to the waters incredible pull on the wing.

If landing in very shallow water (less than 3 feet) you will obviously not want to jump out. Unclip as described above but consider landing seated, with one or both legs forward, especially if there is no wind (high groundspeed). This will prevent you from "face planting" since it is impossible to run out a landing in even a foot of water.

Gust Front and Landing Backwards

Gust fronts occur on many scales, the worst being thunderstorms. Cold air plummets earthward, spreading out rapidly as it hits the ground in a deadly cauldron of turbulence. Gust fronts may be preceded by virga, a wall of dust, or debris, but not always. Your first indication may be nasty bumps or negative groundspeed—you are flying into the wind but moving backwards over the ground.

If you get caught in such a front, expect the ride to be wild with occasional wing collapses and extreme oscillations. Follow the turbulence penetration guidance in Chapter 4. Here are some things to consider regarding gust fronts:

- If you can land before it hits, do so! Don't let yourself get hit with during landing, though, that is worse than running downwind.

- If you don't think you can land before it reaches you, make a downwind dash to get as far downwind of the source as possible. Even if you can't outrun it, getting farther away may let the front expend itself into a weaker state. Consider going crosswind if that will keep you out of an advancing storm.

After the gust front passes and you are already in it, consider these options:

- If you are over a lake consider landing on the opposite shore before exhausting your fuel.

- If you suspect the wind will worsen, power off and land immediately. Accept a backward landing even if it means that you may get dragged. Aim for an area offering the most forgiving blowback zone and least mechanical turbulence (which will be wicked).

- Some gust fronts are short lived. If you can safely control the wing and expect the wind to subside quickly (i.e. it's not associated with major weather such as an approaching thunderstorm) you may be better off waiting it out. The same is true if landing options are unsatisfactory—consider riding it out.

- Typically, there is a gradient where winds diminish close to the ground. Going lower may allow upwind penetration but, be careful, it will also be more turbulent, possibly too much. Don't ever put yourself behind an obstruction that could cause severe rotor. Also consider that gust fronts can be limited, low-level affairs and climbing may help.

If you become committed to a high wind landing while drifting backward:

- Be thankful you thought to wear gloves!

- If it's smooth enough that you can momentarily let go of a brake or maybe hold both brakes in one hand, unclip from all but one leg strap to enable a rapid exit after landing. That will help if you are getting dragged and choose to try exiting the harness. Mentally rehearse going for that remaining buckle.

To ease your exodus from a machine with old style buckles (normally done like 1), fasten them as shown in picture 2. Simply pulling on the end will release it immediately.

- Locate your hook knife and be prepared to use it.
- While still airborne, find the C risers and prepare to pull them hard at touchdown. Even if you fall, keep pulling until you are able to get up and run around the wing. Unclip as soon as you're able.
- Kill the wing using one of the methods in Chapter 3. If you are getting dragged and cannot do so, use the hook knife to cut through the A risers or lines.

Consider finding a site where getting dragged back will be less injurious. Landing in front of a solid tree line, for example, will stop the wing when you get dragged to the trees. Be leery of small ridge-shaped obstructions, though, as the wing can pull you right up over the top.

Motor Stuck at Full or Partial Power

The most likely cause of this situation is having the throttle cable, and enclosed kill wire, go into the prop. There are several options available that depend on your situation. If conditions permit, you may be able to simply run it out of gas. Pulling big ears (with speedbar, if you've got it) or doing spirals will help prevent a climb. *Don't* do B-Line stalls since the recovery may not be possible with the motor at power. See Chapter 18 for information on these maneuvers.

If you decide to reach back and kill the motor, understand the extreme risk. On most units, you *can* get your hand into the prop. Hopefully you've rehearsed this in a simulator. Use the method requiring the least amount of reach. For example, if the air vent is right by your head, then plugging it is safer than reaching farther back for the spark plug.

After making sure you're over landable terrain, here are some ways to shut off the motor. Pick the easiest, most accessible one:

- If you have an alternate kill switch, relish your forethought and use it.
- If there's enough of the throttle left, try to work it down to idle.
- If you have a remote choke, pull it.
- If you can reach the fuel line, pinch it hard until it quits. This will take up to 20 seconds.
- If you can reach the air intake easily, cover it—it takes about 5 seconds for the motor to quit.
- If you have a primer bulb (or knob), squeeze it to flood out the motor.
- If you can yank the plug wire out or pry the spark plug cap off without touching it (you'll get shocked) then do so.
- If you can plug the fuel vent, do so. It may take several minutes until a vacuum forms from the fuel getting sucked out. With enough vacuum, the motor will die from a lean mixture. There's a chance this could seize the motor.
- If you cannot kill the motor safely, you'll have to run it out of gas.

Landing in a Tree

Trees only look soft from above. If there is no better option and you're going to

After landing in a strong and increasing wind, this pilot got lifted, dragged, and turtled but got it under control with the help of some fellow pilots.

wind up in a tree, go for its middle near the top and, as always, land into the wind. Grazing the branches may simply collapse the wing, sending you free-falling to the ground. Do a normal flare and keep your feet together, knees bent, and in front. Once motion stops, your ride may not be over. Grab a stout branch and hang on.

Getting Out of a Tree

If you fly where tree landing are a possibility then carry a tree rescue kit. It includes a roll of dental floss (or similar strong, light line) and a fishing weight. The weighted line is lowered down to a rescuer so that a strong rope can be pulled up.

Most injuries come from falling out of the tree after landing so remain in your harness while waiting for help. The wing may be the only thing preventing you from falling. If help is not likely or your status is precarious, try using the wing's lines to secure your harness to a solid part of the tree. Do that before trying to climb down.

If help comes with an adequate rope, lower a line to the rescuer. Pull the rope up and loop it over a strong branch. Secure the rope around your waist and have the rescuer wrap the rope around a strong, low branch for friction so he can lower you gently to the ground. If you're 50 feet up, you'll need probably 110 feet of rope.

If you have no rescue kit and time is critical (impending cold, weather, darkness, etc), consider using your reserve or glider lines to help lower yourself.

Getting Out of Power Lines

Paraglider lines can conduct current from even low voltage power lines. Power lines on poles are not insulated and carry a minimum of 4000 Volts. High tension lines have over 100,000 Volts. Do not allow yourself or rescuers to touch any part of the gear *and* the ground—they have been electrocuted just by getting close to a hung-up glider. Wait until the power company is alerted and the power removed. They will also have equipment that can reach up to allow for easy retrieval.

If you're low enough, jumping is an option but it's easy to misjudge height and get hurt. Awaiting rescue is still the best bet.

Cloud Suck

The vapor process that churns inside taller cumulus clouds (500 feet thick) creates powerful lift just below the base, called *cloud suck*. The effect can be dramatic in bigger clouds. Violent updrafts and downdrafts may exceed 3000 feet per minute (fpm) and may exist 500 or more feet below the cloud. Pilots have died from hypothermia and/or hypoxia after being taken into the upper atmosphere following such encounters. Do *not* throw your reserve—you could ride up and down in the cloud for a long time.

If you do inadvertently get sucked up into a cloud, there are a few things you can do—the earlier the better. Use one of the descent techniques listed in Chapter 18. Big ears are the safest but have the least descent rate. The B-line stall has a higher descent rate and is stable but involves possible exit problems.

A spiral dive offers the highest possible descent rate but must be considered as a last resort. You risk vertigo or blacking out from G forces and spiraling to the ground. The full stall, which plummets nicely, carries huge risk in the recovery. A botched recovery from either maneuver could "gift wrap" you in the glider.

1. This pilot was lucky that the small tree left him hanging close to the ground. Don't be too quick to leap out of your equipment, most injuries happen after the pilot has landed in the tree and tries to get down quickly.

2. Obviously, staying out of the wires is best. But if this happens, don't let yourself or anyone else touch the ground and gear simultaneously until you know the power is off. High voltage has a way of finding ground and both humans and lines work just fine if given the chance.

The PPG Bible: A Complete Guide and Reference

Out-Landing (Motor Failure)

The specifics of spot landings have been covered in Chapter 17, but when the motor quits away from your field, there are some other considerations.

If the motor is just running poorly, try to find a throttle range that improves power ("milking the throttle"). You may able to hobble back or, at least, reach a more favorable landing site.

If you feel a bad vibration, landing is probably best. Trying to nurse a shaking machine back home could result in the motor separating from the frame or prop shards shooting through the wing.

Once an out-landing is inevitable, here are some priorities. Remember that there is no hard and fast rule—choose the best option for the situation.

- You'll glide farther headed downwind but make sure you're pointed back into the wind by touchdown.
- **Land into the wind!** All things being equal, it's almost hard to get hurt if you follow this rule. Accept a crosswind or downwind option only if it's much better. For example, if the upwind option puts you in water or power lines and the downwind or crosswind option is smooth grass, choose the grass. Even then, try to get turned into the wind as much as possible while making sure to level by touchdown.
- Choose a rotor-free location. Avoid landing in a wind shadow or rotor.
- When presented with multiple safe landing options, consider retrieval difficulty or whether you can re-launch.
- Scout for wires on the way down. Any straight-line features or poles should raise suspicions that wires may be present. Plan your approach accordingly.
- Look for animals. A single cow in a field may be a bull.
- Consider where the wing will go if landing near water. Don't let it get into any moving water, including surf. If a water landing is inevitable, prepare for it.

If you're trying to reach spot that is upwind, you'll want to fly faster. The more headwind, the more speed you want. Anything over about a 10 mph headwind will call for maximum speed on most gliders, but only do that if it's fairly smooth.

With a tailwind, slowing to minimum sink speed gives the best glide. That means trimmers slow and brake pressure 1 or 2 on most gliders.

Regardless of wind, maximize glide by minimizing drag. Lift your legs and bring your arms in to present the smallest frontal area possible. Do turns using weight shift instead of brakes, if possible.

Fogged In

Besides being illegal, it is incredibly dangerous to fly without ground reference. Even though the craft is stable, an approach in the blind might hide wires or other surprises. So if you see fog forming or rolling in, *land while there is still enough visibility*, even if you are away

---

With no wind, your glide options are the same in all directions. With wind, you'll glide farther downwind than upwind so you'll have more landing options downwind.

The bottom frame illustrates a wind that's blowing as fast as you're flying. Groundspeed is 0 if you're pointed directly into it meaning that all your options are downwind.

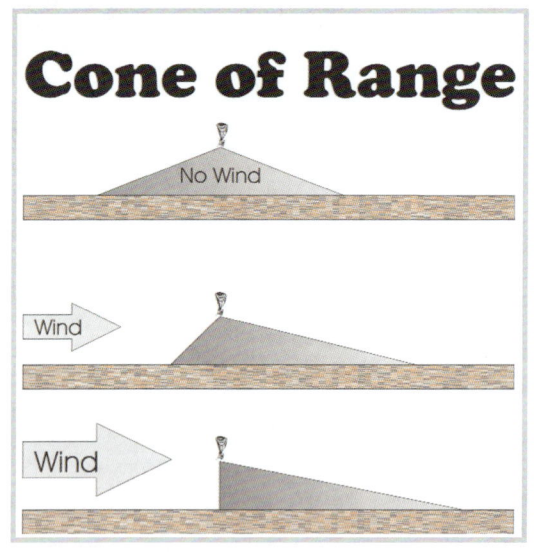

Cone of Range

from your launch site. Failing that, climb up above it, but do *not* put yourself in busy airspace. A PPG should be landed in the fog before taking on heavy airplane traffic. If you can fly to a fog-free location, do so.

Here are some considerations if you're faced with a landing in the fog:

- Note or recall the wind direction; you may need that later.
- Having a GPS in this situation is obviously helpful. Hopefully you've stored the launch site as a waypoint. If not, mark your current location and stay nearby. On many units you may be able to follow a plotted ground track back to your site.
- Consider circling above and waiting if you think the fog may move through. Use this option only if you're certain that wind drift won't take you somewhere undesirable (especially over water).

If you must land in the fog, use whatever means are available (compass, GPS, sunlight) to stay pointed into the wind. Leaving the motor run is probably best since it reduces the descent rate and allows going around if something unpleasant emerges. There is, however, some benefit to having prop stopped in case you hit something while blundering through the muck.

On final descent, go to quarter brake (pressure 2) and be ready for impact. Keep your feet angled down and forward, knees together, bent, and ready to absorb the energy of a collision or to run. Even in thick fog you should have enough visibility to flare—but beware of illusions that could spur a reactionary and inappropriate pull on the brakes.

Avoid any situation where the only landing option is through the fog. If the motor quits, it'll be impossible to see wires among other problems. Legally, you must always be able to see the ground and have at least one mile visibility. In the photo here, the pilot did have options to his right although they would have been tough.

Impending Aerial Collision

If you see a threatening aircraft, watch it for *just* long enough to know that it's really on a collision course, and then act decisively. If it's stationary relative to the horizon (not moving left/right/up/down) then it's on a collision course. For example, an airplane may be just above you but descending quickly. An aggressive descending spiral could put you in its path whereas doing nothing may let it pass.

If you're sure a collision is imminent, quickly enter as steep a spiral as you're comfortable with. Since you're so slow, this makes you more visible while also getting out of the way. If the other pilot suddenly sees you he will also see your downward motion and should pull up in response. Don't yank the glider into a spin and create another emergency.

Wing, Line, or Connection Failure

Be thankful you carry a reserve, this would not likely be survivable. You'll probably be thrust into a spiral with only a few seconds to get the reserve out before rapidly building G-forces prevent it. With no reserve, you'll be riding half the wing down in a high-speed spiral. Pulling brake may only worsen the spiral since most brakes act more towards the tip. The brake on the failed side will probably have ripped out of your hand but, if not, hold onto it as long as you're able.

Consider reaching up (if able) and trying to pull the inside rear riser line to oppose the turn direction. Pull just one line. Given the angle that you'll be dangling from, reaching it would be a long shot.

Quality carabiners and a back-up strap that goes from your harness webbing into the riser loop nearly eliminates the dreadful results of this extremely rare failure.

Kite Lines

A child's kite line can destroy your wing. Be careful when flying along the beach since kites are common and their lines nearly invisible. Even the cheap ones can destroy a paraglider—the line slides through, slicing as it goes.

If you're up fairly high and do contact a line, consider circling down to a landing so the string is not able to cut all the way through your wing. Once the kite is de-tensioned from its mooring (the child below), the damage may be reduced.

Accidental Reserve Deployment

Shut off the motor. In all likelihood there will not be time to react beyond this one action. As long as the reserve comes out properly, ride it down as described in Chapter 4. If it looks like you'll be set down somewhere undesirable, and your wing is still inflated, consider cutting away the reserve bridals with your hook knife or disabling it with your hands by pulling in some reserve lines (extremely difficult).

Grabbing the reserve on its way out is probably only possible if it gets snagged or malfunctions. Even then, having a hand full of reserve lines when it catches air may cause severe line burns as it snaps open.

Fire

There's little to do besides shut off the motor and land. Fire has been so rare that no established procedure has come forward but here are some things to consider:

- Spiral down to minimize your time aloft.
- If your motor has an ejection feature, this is the time to use it! Grab those tabs and pull outward just like you've rehearsed.
- Unclip from all but one leg strap and be ready to get away from the machine quickly. Rehearse going for that strap.
- Consider landing next to, or in, water so you can immerse yourself after getting free of the machine. Only land *in* water you know is very shallow.
- Roll in dirt, a blanket, tarp, or water as available to put out any remaining fire.
- Approach the motor with great caution. Although it's unlikely, certain failure modes can allow the tank to burst, spewing flaming fuel.

The Jolly Roger paraglider was no match for a $4 kid's kite line which easily sliced it asunder. Amazingly, the pilot was able to safely land the remains on the beach.

Competition

CHAPTER 20

It is human nature to see what we're capable of. Like all competition, when engaged with the right attitude, it is a healthy motivator to excellence.

Many aspects of competition carry more risk than just flying around—primarily the low-level tasks. Much risk, however, is mitigated by (1) avoiding tasks where pilots dive towards the ground, 2) experience requirements and 3) having rules that penalize dangerous maneuvers.

Eric Dufour puts his best foot forward during a practice run of the *cloverleaf*. Even while kicking the center stick he must be planning his next turn.

Those steep and low turns flown by competition pilots look riskier than they are. As long as the pilot knows how to keep them level (no diving), even touching the ground doesn't guarantee damage or injury. Of course it does mean zero points. A common question is "what happens if the motor quits during those turns?" Surprisingly, for an experienced pilot, the answer is: nothing. There's sufficient energy so that leveling off will allow the pilot to roll out and land on his feet—it has occurred a number of times.

Rules try to recognize skill in a fair manner, minimize risk, limit arbitrary factors, and keep the event flowing. Rarely is the simplest solution the most fair. Rules must be understood, too—knowing how a task is scored sometimes beats being talented. A few loser's last words were "I didn't know you could do that!"

Different sanctioning bodies have different flavors of the same basic tasks, so check rules closely. The Fédération Aéronautique Internationale (FAI) is the worldwide governing body for all competition and their International Microlight Commission (CIMA) handles microlight activities, including PPG. Most countries have national organizations that govern national competition and work with the FAI. Some countries have national organizations whose competition is run independently.

> **Unintended Consequences**
>
> At first it seemed simple, you get spot landing points for being within the rings around a center target (more points for closer rings) and none for landing beyond the outer ring. Then at one competition, an unexpected wind forced even the best pilots to land beyond the outer ring. Nobody got any points. That didn't seem fair because the closest pilot was a lot closer than the farthest. So the scoring was changed to reward pilots with distance points in addition to the ring points. Ahhh, that was better—it would make a portion of the score based on the farthest lander getting 0 and the closest getting 100 points (plus any ring points he got).
>
> Then at another competition, one pilot nailed the center and all but one of the other pilots landed close to the center. The one that who landed out was a *long* way out. By having him so far out it skewed the score. He took his 0 but all the other pilots got over 95% of the available distance points, wiping out much of the close-landing pilot's advantage. Back to the score designing drawing board.
>
> Even the best scoring system will not always seem completely fair.

How Good Do I Need To Be?

Everybody has to start somewhere. If you have 50 flights, can reliably launch and land within 100 feet of a target, then you can compete. Other minimums may be imposed but these qualifications are usually enough.

Being competitive is another matter but, if you've got the basic gear and a place to practice, you may be surprised at how well you do. Simply entering these events will improve and focus your skills.

If you've been refining your finesse, even just for the fun of it, then you're probably already competitive. To win you must indeed be a master of the craft—able to control your path within inches on a calm day and within a few feet in level 2 turbulence (see Chapter 5 for the Bump Scale). You should be able to prevent pendulum swings and generally keep yourself locked under the wing even with some bumps. Having the skills as described in Chapter 16 (Precision Flying) should be enough to earn a top 25 percent ranking.

Whether you're new to competition or a veteran, be ever mindful of personal limitations; there's no value in pushing so hard as to damage yourself or your gear. Many pilots have done quite well by being consistent and *finishing* each task, even with average points.

A common malady is when a good pilot pushes too hard and hits the ground, zeroing his points for a task. That really hurts in a close contest. Plus, the damage may prevent scoring on the next few tasks while repairs are affected.

Ground Precision

For many pilots, ground precision is the fun stuff. It can be intimidating, though—the key is to stay within your ability and build skill slowly.

The Cloverleaf

This is the mother of all precision flying tasks (see diagram for description). It mixes a number of skills: turning, power management, spatial orientation, adjusting constantly for the wind and planning ahead. Don't minimize spatial orientation—it is not as obvious as it seems. When you're down low, corning hard and

Competition adds several elements to the basic foot drag. You must not let the cage touch and you must steer through the gates while trying to be as *fast* as possible.

1. Tim Kaiser turning and dragging at a Chicago competition.

2. Bill Heaner speeds through the gate in Phoenix.

looking to the center, everything can appear the same, allowing confusion to cause a wrong turn. Wind plays havoc with the flight path, too.

There is a maximum height of 10 meters (33 feet) to keep pilots from diving and it is typically flown with less than 10 mph wind to avoid fast, downwind ground speeds. The best way to practice is:

- Be able to kick the center stick. You cannot win without doing this perfectly. So go out, find some small bush or other safe target, and practice kicking it from an approach in all directions. Of course, if you can set up a regulation-height stick, that is better.

- Practice level, fairly steep turns that require modulating power as you roll in and out. Practice rolling out on a heading by picking a distant spot on the horizon and finishing the rollout pointed at it.

- Make sure you know the order. Go out and fly the course from a couple hundred feet while looking down on it. Then go down to 50 feet and fly it; don't worry about the clock yet. Finally, go down low to within 30 feet and fly it.

- Before entering the course, mentally go over it. Look at the center then the left-far stick (1st one), look back to the center and across to the opposite stick, etc. until visualizing the last stick and finish. Great pilots have given up their great times by turning the wrong direction (which zeros points).

- After you can make all the sticks, minimizing time becomes the objective. Being fast on the wing helps but so too does minimizing distance. You want just your body to go around the corners (that's all the rules require). Being wide gives up distance and time. In the same vane, always plan your turns to finish with the least distance to the center and the next stick.

Power management is critical—as you go into each turn, throttle up enough to prevent settling. A steep bank will probably take all the power you've got. As soon as you *start* rolling out from the turn, relax the power—from a steep bank you will go completely to idle and still climb a bit. If you're using a speedbar, start applying it as you level out and modulate the power to keep from settling. Be careful using a speedbar on this task, it is difficult and makes it harder to kick the center stick since your feet are on the speedbar (or stirrup).

Being fast is good, to a point. Load up with fuel and (if permitted) ballast but it's certainly not worth being so heavy as to blow a launch. Setting the trimmers to fast seems most beneficial in spite of adding slightly to turn times.

The wind changes how the cloverleaf is flown quite a bit (see diagram). With wind, the basic idea is to always go upwind of the upwind sticks before turning. That minimizes the turn required to get back to the center and aim for the next stick. When flying downwind, anticipate the need to start turning earlier. Finish all turns with a crab into the wind so as to further minimize distance flown.

> ⚠ **Caution!** Using the speedbar, especially if its bumpy, could allow a front tuck. At low altitude, you would essentially just fall to the ground.

Cloverleaf

Kick the center each time; round the corners. Time goes from first kick to last kick.

Want to practice at home? 2-meter tall flexible poles are placed like a 5 die with 100 meter sides. The pilot can enter between any two corners. He must then kick the center, turn left and follow the pattern below, kicking the center pole each time.

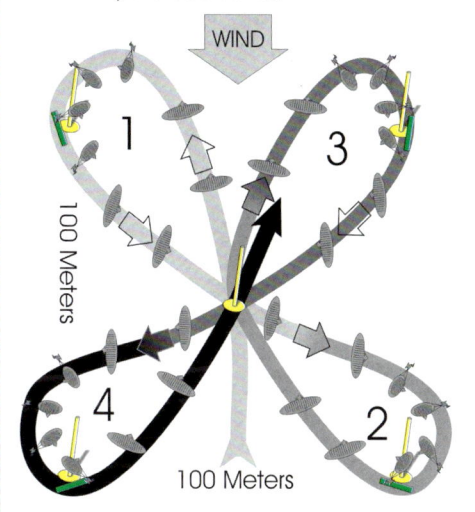

To fly the best time in a wind requires minimizing the distance flown. This pattern, where the pilot starts the turns upwind, does just that. Try to fly so that your body just barely clears the poles and flies along the green lines. With no wind it is a simple (to describe anyway) matter of getting as close to the poles as possible.

The PPG Bible: A Complete Guide and Reference

Foot Drag Course

The foot drag course does not involve a lot of turning but it's still a challenge when attending to everything else. The pilot is timed from start to finish and must drag at least one foot through the course. He can lift a foot or run but it costs points. Don't hit the polls or fall—both are bad for points.

The foot-drag is not typically done in European competitions.

Foot Drag

Once you've mastered the foot-drag basics described in Chapter 16, you can apply them to competition. Mostly you must learn how to do it fast (trimmers out), with some crosswind, and how to turn while dragging.

The course is a simple slalom of three gates where the center gate is offset. You drag at least one foot the whole distance through each of the gates. Faster is better and speed counts for about a fourth of the points. Passing all the gates with a foot on the ground is most important because lifting a foot or running reduces points significantly. Don't try too hard for speed, though, falling scores a 0.

The best stance is one foot out in front of the other so that you can be ready to run if necessary. Don't put much weight on the foot—drag will slow you down and leaves you vulnerable to a point-sapping run. But do run, if necessary, to avoid losing so much speed that the wing falls back—that's another 0.

Minimizing brake use is good for both points and options: if you slow down too much, the brakes will no longer be effective at quickly adding lift. If you wind up heavy in the brakes it means your airspeed is slowing down—add power immediately!

To be competitive, you'll need to fly with the trimmers out (fast) but only if you're willing to be dumped going fast. Dumping happens whenever you get a sudden tailwind or downward gust, thus losing lift and forcing a run or possibly a fall. Using the speedbar (one foot pushing the bar, the other dragging) is nearly impossible and, since touching any frame part on the ground zeros all points, it wouldn't be worth the risk of trying. Tying off the speed system so that it remains engaged is too risky—the wing is so much more susceptible to frontal collapse since the wing gets partially unloaded during the foot drag.

Slow Fast

This one is simple in description but challenging in execution. You fly through a straight course as slow as possible then go through the same course as fast as possible. To be competitive you must be comfortable using the speedbar, with trimmers fast, while close to the ground. With no wind, that's fast! The contestant must stay in a 5-meter wide lane, not touch the ground and stay below 2 meters.

1. Going through the *slow* course requires lots of brakes, lots of power and hopefully smooth air. If it gets bumpy, don't go so slow—you can't just pop up with the brakes because you've slowed down already. And adding power takes too much time to recover. Here the author is deep in the brakes, "hanging on the prop" during a Florida competition. Don't touch that cage!

2. Going fast is tough, too, when it's bumpy. You can't go above 2 meters and, at that speed, it's easy to get popped up. Tim Kaiser is pictured on full speedbar with trimmers out during a Chicago competition.

The slow part requires heavy brake pressure but, be careful, that will leave you vulnerable to getting dumped by sink or lifted above the height maximum. Altitude is controlled mostly by power since the brakes are already pulled about as far as they can go—adding more brake will just stall the wing.

The fast part should be flown with the trimmers out and, turbulence permitting, on full speedbar. You'll need to use brakes for finessing altitude but use them minimally. This is partially an equipment challenge given how some wings are faster, and have a broader speed range, than others.

Touch and Go

Doing a spot landing with power isn't terribly difficult so a challenge was added. Besides touching the spot, you must throttle up, taking exactly 10 steps then lift off again (touchdown plus 9). There is no need to put full weight on your legs during the run but the steps must be completed in a fairly short distance to preclude a fly-by with 10 foot ground taps.

Probably the best technique is to keep nearly flying speed so that your feet do not carry *much* weight. That way you can be ready to lift off quickly but within the limited distance. You'll still be fairly heavy in the brakes and need to power up on about step 7. At high elevations or with low power machines, you may need to be powering up well before reaching even step 7.

Spot Landing

Climb up to 300 feet, shut off the motor then glide down to land on a Frisbee-sized spot *and stop*. The point of landing is where you first touch.

It is the most useful task since a mastery can help in everyday flying. It also may be the riskiest for pilots who try too hard. The temptation is to shorten your glide by hauling in more brakes. That can result in stalling and falling, an embarrassingly painful ending with a no-point crash. Like most tasks, letting the cage simply *touch* the ground is disqualifying (an effort to discourage stalling and falling).

With practice, many pilots can touch the spot nearly every time. But arriving with minimum speed is another matter. Some scoring systems measure two distances (the USPPA's, for example): touchdown and traveled distance. The pilot who lands *and* stops on the spot will score better than the pilot who touches the spot but then takes a long time to stop. Regardless of scoring system, a pilot who first touches the target will always do better than a pilot who misses it.

The spot landing technique is covered in Chapter 17. If the scoring does *not* incorporate stopping distance then the *swoop* landing, where you come in fast and just touch the spot, is best.

If traveled distance counts then you'll modify the technique somewhat. It's tougher to hit the spot while keeping speed to a minimum at touchdown. However, it's never worth missing the target in pursuit of minimum traveled distance—hitting the center will always score more points just missing, even if you stop cold.

To minimize excessive runout moderate brakes nearly all the way down. Have just enough speed to flare hard and swing forward, stopping just as you touch. With too-little flare authority, this technique risks a point-sapping cage-touch.

Japanese Slalom
Kick 1, 2, 3 then Slalom 1, 2, 3 then Kick 1, 4, 3.
Time goes from first to last kick.

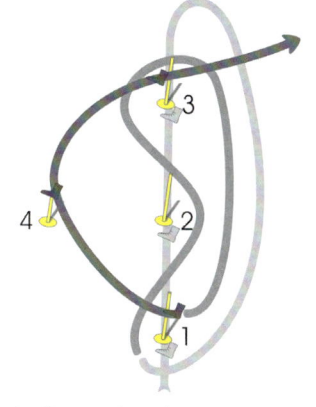

1. A pilot touches the center spot and runs it out for the Touch and Go.

2. The Japanesee Slalom is one of the FAI tasks done in Europe (as is the slow/fast and cloverleaf). They all involve the same basic skills but just employ different ways to express them.

Flight Precision (Navigation)

These tasks challenge a completely different type of piloting skill. You must be adept at planning, reading maps, pilotage and know your machine's fuel burn characteristics. Scoring involves flying with a covered GPS (so it can't be used for navigation) that will later be read by a computer to see what points you actually flew over and at what time. Other methods can be used for scoring where the pilot is given photographs that are used to identify (and write in a log) locations on the ground.

Competition directors will provide maps, pictures (if used) and instructions after which, pilots are given some time to do planning. This is where competition organizers spend a lot of time, getting all these things together. For the competitors, though, it can provide many hours of enjoyable flying. It is, in many ways, the relaxing part of competition. Of course that depends on your intensity—there is always *something* that motivated flyers can do to improve their odds or awareness—verifying position, studying the map for coming waypoints, determining wind, checking fuel, strategizing, etc.

Finding Points on a Map

One key skill is being able to correlate what is on the map or photograph with what you see on the ground—not necessarily an easy task. Some of the tasks require familiarity with your machine's fuel burn in various configurations.

Flying with a speedbar is a must since some of the tasks are almost pure speed. They'll give you unlimited fuel and limited time to go find as many points possible.

Planning

You must have some idea of the winds aloft and apply that to your planning (see Chapter 13) for flights. Understand the effect of wind gradient and try to maximize it. For example, if the winds at 1000 feet are south at 15 mph but at 500 feet they are west at 12 mph, plan accordingly.

Don't count on trying to do much writing in flight; organize the map and pictures to minimize moving things around. Some contestants have a larger map display on a kneeboard that is several pages wide so they don't have to flip pages.

Fuel Limited Tasks

A variety of fuel-limited tasks can be called that require optimization based on conditions. The idea is usually to cover the most amount of ground with the least amount of fuel burned. In no wind, fly at your glider's best L/D speed (usually trim

---

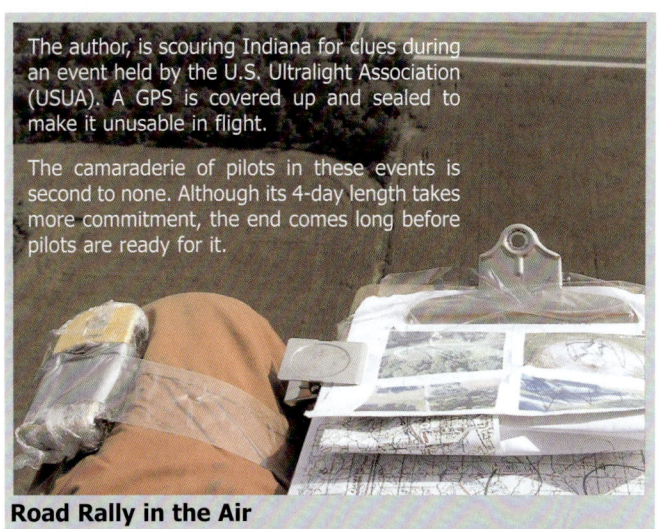

Road Rally in the Air

The author, is scouring Indiana for clues during an event held by the U.S. Ultralight Association (USUA). A GPS is covered up and sealed to make it unusable in flight.

The camaraderie of pilots in these events is second to none. Although its 4-day length takes more commitment, the end comes long before pilots are ready for it.

European style competitions involve a wide variety of navigation tasks. One good example is the fun-to-fly *Circle and Two Lines*.

The objective (from the FAI Rulebook) is: "To follow a circular track in the direction briefed, finding markers or identifying ground features from photographs and locating their positions on a map. It may be required to distinguish between on-track and off-track markers and ground features. Four markers or ground features will identify the points from which lines must be drawn. The task ends with an out landing at the point outside the circle where these lines intersect. Any route may be chosen from the airfield to the circle or from the circle to the out landing site."

Implementation is challenging and entertaining for both the flyer and the organizer (see diagram on next page).

The pilot gets a map with a circle drawn on it and a bunch of pictures. His mission is to fly the circle and put a hack mark each time he identifies one of the pictured points. Pictured points are sometimes a bit off the circle but the mark goes on the circle abeam where it is seen. Once all four marks have been made the pilot draws two lines that intersect those points. Where those two lines cross is the new destination. A judge awaits at that location for those who figure this out (while flying, I might add.)

It doesn't have to be a circle either—the same task is flown with other shapes using the same concept. If a possibility for ambiguity exists, the instructions will indicate the outlanding site's general direction.

Since it would be possible to fly the circle, miss only one point and therefore not be able to complete the task, an option is given. Just before takeoff, each pilot is given a sealed envelope. It contains the out landing site plotted on a map, just open the envelope and go find it. Of course, opening the envelope entails an enormous penalty but it's still better than not finding the site at all.

speed). Fly faster in a headwind and slower in a tailwind but never below minimum sink speed (see Chapter 22).

When flying between thermals, speed up in sink and slow down (or circle) in lift. That feels counter-intuitive since, in sink, you're already plummeting and speeding up seems to make it worse—but more importantly, speeding up gets you out of the sink faster and you'll end up higher. Depending on how the scoring is weighted, it may be beneficial to circle in thermals when going downwind and slow down in thermals when going upwind. The more that time counts, the less circling you want to do.

The FAI "Circle and Two Lines" navigation task is a fun challenge. Don't miss a point though, it forces you to open your sealed pre-launch envelope containing the destination.

Endurance

Endurance, also called *economy*, is a fuel-limited task that rewards those with soaring skills and efficient gear (motor and wing). It is normally flown just as thermals start heating up or later on when they're diminishing, but still present. Cloudy days, where little thermal action is available, primarily rewards the lightest pilots flying the smallest motors on the most efficient wings.

Pilots meet in a common area to ensure that tanks are empty (motors run out) and each one gets exactly 2 liters of fuel (or some other agreed-on amount) in their tank. They all must launch within a given time window and the longest one up, in minutes, wins.

One proven method is to climb to a couple hundred feet then throttle back just enough to hold altitude or climb slowly. Keep that power until you find a thermal then reduce power to about half of what it took to fly level. Circle in the thermal's lift, building a mental picture of where the strongest updraft is and trying to make that your circle's center. If lift is strong you may be able to shut off the motor (providing you can reliably restart it in flight). In weak lift, use *some* power to help you stay in the thermal.

Kiting

This simple competition is unique to the U.S. for scoring. It is a colorful spectator favorite too, evidenced by the many images of wings billowing to life that end up on videos and publications.

Competitors start off in the field, arrayed evenly within a boundary. When the judge calls "GO," they bring up their wings together and begin the battle. Kiters

This is, by far, the most physically demanding task of the competition. It is frequently brief for many pilots, but for those who stay up, it is very tiring. The winners deserve every point they get, especially since it's not worth that many points.

The PPG Bible: A Complete Guide and Reference

must stay within the designated area and keep their wing up for at least 2 minutes to score anything. They are allowed to maneuver so as to bring other wings down but cannot touch other competitors with their bodies. The last 3 wings up get 1st, 2nd and 3rd place according to who stays up the longest.

Tactically, the best way to bring down someone else's wing is to block their airflow with your wing. Advanced kiting skills are obviously a must, but even then, it's quite difficult. If a couple of wings get upwind of yours, it might be impossible to keep it lofted, especially if your route to clear air is blocked.

It is not necessary to wear a harness (you can hold the risers with just your hands) but, if there's much wind, your arms will tire quickly. Kiting with your arms only (no harness) may work better in a very light wind since you have more finesse—it's a judgement call based on conditions and your ability to riser-only kite.

The first point of strategy is to make sure you keep your wing inflated for at least two minutes—otherwise no points are earned. Avoid battles, if possible, but when it becomes inevitable, try to always stay upwind. You can turn and run forward but the lost time in turning may hurt. To be competitive you must be able to kite with the A's so that when someone gets your wing down low, you can grab the A's and keep it off the ground.

This task is worth only a few points but can make a difference in a close match.

As with all tasks, you must use the same wing you started with but are allowed to choose any kiting harness. In most permutations, it is acceptable to pull other pilots' *lines* as long as you don't touch the pilot. That, in itself is hard because it tends to bring their glider down on *yours*. The judges have a hard time telling who's wing hit first in that situation.

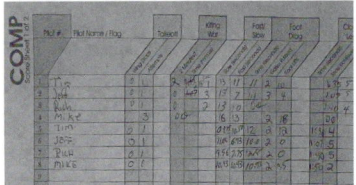

1. Pilots preparing for the real deal at a large gathering near Orlando, Florida.

2. Scoring is done on a computer but the judges (marshals) only write down times, distances and other raw data. They do no actual scoring on the field.

Each organization has a process to help insure fairness. They know it must be fair but also recognize that nobody is perfect and sometimes bad calls get made. Don't take it out on the volunteer judges, it probably won't do you any good and will make finding these valuable volunteers harder yet.

1. A large turnout came to see this kiting competition in Santo Domingo. Age is not much of an issue, 13 year old Benjamin (the photographer on this one) beat out several high-time pilots at a competition in the U.S. (including the author).

2. Dave Rogers prepares to cross the 1st gate in a Florida competition as judges Scott Adair and Sandy Good get the data right.

Section III: Mastering The Sport

Free Flight Transition

CHAPTER 21

When launching a free flight harness you lean forward with your hands back; with a motor you must stand up straight to let the motor push.

Free flying a paraglider is an adventure worthy of its own pursuit, an enjoyable use of many skills you've already learned. Paragliding first was my chosen path to PPG and soaring became an enjoyable staple. Free flying is worthy of much respect, too—mastering conditions strong enough to keep you aloft is a serious undertaking.

For free flyers, many find that power is a gratifying addition to their experience, but be ready to learn anew—there's more to it than standing up straight for launch.

Transition to Thrust: Becoming a Power Pilot

With power, the world becomes your play*sky*—allowing exploration of new launches, soaring sites and lift bands that were previously beyond reach. For example, rising air that coalesces well above its generation point becomes accessible, offering power-off soaring for hours. You can climb through the air to better understand it or use partial thrust to mimic high performance gliders, but that doesn't even touch what motor pilots relish—the ability to go almost anywhere.

Exploring terrain in the smooth morning air becomes a purpose unto its own. There are so many new angles to see things from and places and altitudes to fly. Portability and launch flexibility find their ultimate expression in this craft.

It's a completely different challenge. Fleecing the air of its lift gives way to precision control of flight path—control that is measured in inches. Of course you don't *have* to master it to that degree, but it's possible and the best motor flyers do it effortlessly. A pilot can be excellent at soaring without needing such precision just as a skilled motor pilot can be masterfully precise with little clue at coring a thermal. Fortunately the sports go wonderfully hand in hand.

If you're an accomplished paraglider pilot who is willing to adapt, then motor flying will come quickly. A very few points must be closely minded but then the transition will be easy. It's the same wing and behaves essentially the same regardless of propulsion.

Seek out an experienced power instructor whose best service will be to set up your equipment properly and instruct you on its nuances.

Launch Differences

Hefting the motor will seem awkward at first. A light motor, adjusted properly, speeds the process.

Don Jordan does the typical power reverse with one hand on the A's and the other hand working power.

Bottom: Jose Casaudemecq leans back into the power during a forward launch.

Reverse Inflation: Getting ready will be quite different—the normal method in paragliding is to hook in while facing forward then turn around as you pass one riser over your head. The motor's cage makes that difficult so you'll probably want to learn another procedure. One practice that may be easier is the alternate hook-in method described in Chapter 3 where you stand next to the risers facing forward.

Walking backwards can be a lot harder with some paramotors if your legs hit the cage. Avoid doing reverses in winds too light to kite the wing.

Another difference is the riser hold. You'll have the appropriate brake in each hand as normal with the risers crossed. One hand will have the throttle and you'll want to hold both A's in the other hand. If the wing comes up crooked towards the throttle side, then you can just pull the brake in the throttle hand. But if it comes up crooked to the other side, you can't use the non-throttle hand since it holding the A's. Instead, reach up with the throttle hand and pull the brake line above its pulley. This definitely takes some practice. Initially you're better off to abandon a crooked inflation and try again.

Forward Inflation: Hook-in is the same but the launch itself has one glaring difference—as the power comes up, you *must* stand up straight and lean back against the motor's push. The initial inflation is mostly the same—lean forward (but not as much), dig into it with hands back, pressing upwards on the A's. But once you start applying thrust, you must stand up straight. If you start with thrust right away, be standing up right away so the thrust does not drive you into the ground (a "face plant"). Remember: "stand up at throttle up." More than one free flyer has learned this lesson only after a mouthful of launch dirt.

The *power forward*, coming up to about 30% power prior to starting your run, gives the most consistent low-wind results. On reverse inflations, since you can't lean, you must be ready to throttle up as soon as you turn around. Turn and *move forward* under some power, then, when everything looks good, add power and launch.

The most common cause for failed motor launches by free-flight pilots is leaning forward. Thankfully, that's easy to fix.

All Launches: Learn to be quick on the motor's kill button; if the launch goes bad you must act fast to prevent parablending the lines or glider. If the wing gets nearly all the way up but you need to abort, quickly turn around to face it. Step backwards, if needed, to make sure the wing comes down away from the prop.

Some motors make it hard to see the wing because your helmet hits the cage. Get used to looking left or right to tell what the wing is doing.

Be mindful of staying on the power after lifting off. A common malady for free flyers is letting off the power after liftoff and settling back to the ground.

Climbout

Torque will be your next surprise: the more power, the more torque. It results in a surprising number of forces that conspire to cause a turn (see Chapter 23) but they can be dramatically reduced by proper setup (see Chapter 12). This is where a capable motor instructor will quickly earn his keep.

Depending on your motor model, the turning tendency can be so powerful that trying to counteract it with brakes alone (most machines have only limited weight shift capability) can cause a spin. If it wants to turn, let it. If it's still turning too much or in a bad direction, ease off on the power *then* correct the flight path. It is entirely possible for a powerful machine to spin you around into a riser twist—that won't have a happy ending. Reduce the power *smoothly*.

Maneuvering Differences

By virtue of adding weight and pushing so far below the wing, motor thrust tends to reduce the chance for collapses (slightly). And when they do happen they're typically shorter lived. The trade-off is that there is the potential to get lines wrapped around the motor or its propeller in wild air—that is one reason why such air is best avoided while powered. Plus, the motor adds a lot of twisting mass and offers less weight shift (very little on many units) so recovery from malfunctions can be more difficult.

Be sensitive to the wing falling back. Thrust can hold a glider into parachutal stall—a phenomenon that is almost unheard of in free-flight but *far* more common in motoring and frequently ends in a spin.

If you feel the wing go back, or your speed suddenly slow, *immediately* reduce power, reduce brake pull and be prepared to dampen the surge. Rehearse that action in normal flight so that it's automatic when it happens. Of course, if it feels like a full stall (*very* unlikely unless you were holding heavy brakes) then react accordingly.

Landing

Once you're experienced at landing with the motor (power off), it can be helpful to land power-on in turbulent conditions. Having some thrust (maybe 10% power) reduces your descent rate and may prevent an otherwise firm arrival if you hit a downdraft. You must be quick to add throttle when needed—if you get that sinking feeling, quickly squeeze on some thrust to regain airspeed so you can flare. If things look really bad, go around and try again. New pilots (including recently transitioned free-flyers) should land power-off since the chance for a fall increases with the extra weight of the motor and complexity of thrust.

Be ready to take on the motors weight after landing. Have your knees slightly bent

---

Torque and it's related effects can quickly derail the best launch. Be prepared to reduce throttle if you feel yourself twisting. You can twist all the way around into a spectacular crash.

Tip: Handling The Unknown

If something unusual is happening, remember: hands up, power off, and prepare to dampen the surge. There are certainly times where a skilled pilot can get better results by actively controlling the wing, but experience shows that far more damage is done by pulling too much brake rather than not enough. Also, be smooth on all power changes—abruptness makes matters worse.

and legs ready to run. A fast, smooth arrival can be skidded out. Most motors will allow sliding on the cage bottom (curved base skids) but that risks damage, it's always best to try landing on your feet.

Kiting

A good kiter will do well but there are some differences, especially since you can't lean forward as easily (lines go awkwardly around the cage hoop). The only way to safely kite while facing forward is with the motor pushing you. Trying to kite forward with*out* the motor's thrust is a bad idea—a gust can pull you back into the decidedly awkward *turtle* position (on your back with arms and legs flailing).

Reverse kiting is tougher on units with high hook-in points—you wind up using back muscles instead of body weight and it is quickly tiring. Plus, if you get lifted in a strong gust, the motor's inertia can make getting turned back forward difficult at best. If that happens, remember to keep flying the wing!

New Capabilities

The motor offers more options—keep them in mind as you fly. Primarily, if the wind picks up you may be able to reach a more favorable landing site, maybe even your original site. Consider going higher or lower to find less wind—obviously it will probably be weaker near the ground but so too will be the mechanical turbulence. At least there's never any reason to let yourself get blown into a bad rotor situation since you can power up and fly to a better location.

Landing in turbulence is easier with a motor. Once you're accustomed to the throttle and how it interacts with surges, you can essentially make every landing very predictable. However, as a beginner, it is far better to land power off until you gain skill at managing power.

If you're doing power-off soaring with the ability to restart in the air, you can let yourself get out of gliding distance from launch (but always in range of a safe landing option). This is a great way to explore an area's thermalscape—you can launch from nearly anywhere and land back there when you're ready.

Added Vulnerabilities

It's easy to become complacent about motor failure. Resist that temptation—if you fly long enough, it *will* fail. You must always be mindful of available options when it does, including while you're at full power right after takeoff. Be leery of steep climbouts. Having said that, be aware that an even bigger risk for newly transitioned free flyers: letting off the power abruptly just after takeoff and swinging into the ground. Until you're experienced, and as long as you're not twisting under the risers, keep full power until you've reached at least 100 feet. Then, as always, reduce it *gradually*.

Spinning propellers represent the sport's single most common cause of severe injuries. Most of them happen while starting or running up the motor when it is *not* on your back. A few have also resulted from pilots reaching back while in flight. Respect the prop on the ground and in flight.

Wires and obstructions become greater risks now that you can spend more time down low. Flying low *and* downwind is a dreadful risk because of the increased ground speed—escape time plummets and the results worsen.

You can soar with the motor but glide performance suffers by 20% or so due to the frame's draginess. Below, Thad Spencer powers up to cross a low spot on the ridge; weak lift would have otherwise dumped him to the beach.

Quiet beauty is a strong allure that brings many pilots into free-flight. Another is the challenge to match your own wits with nature to stay aloft and even go cross country. Eric Rys is pictured here enjoying smooth, easy lift that continued well past sunset—staying airborne was no worry whatsoever.

Soaring

You lose efficiency with the motor, a full point or more off your glide ratio, but you can still soar. The windmilling prop of a clutched unit creates more drag then a stopped prop. Don't even think of going without a cage, that is nearly suicidal—turbulence can angle the prop right into your lines. Pilots have been nearly beheaded when trying such folly.

Soaring with a motor is no different in technique than without it—you can run the motor at a constant throttle setting that equates to minimum sink (or less).

Noise

Possibly the biggest drawback to motoring is noise. The quickest way to lose sites or gain the ire of authorities is to buzz around the same locale. If people complain, you will get undesirable notice and people complain most about noise. Altitude is a wonderful buffer and distance is even better. Climb up and get away—adopy the philosophy "launch and leave." When returning, do so with minimal power.

Transition to Free Flight: Going Soaring

Free flight is a quiet realm that warrants preserving. Sites are limited with some teetering on extinction—they must be avoided with motors to keep the area quiet for both the free flyers and the surrounding property owners. Always respect the local's requests regarding where motoring is to be avoided.

The view alone from many launch sites is invigorating; it can be intimidating too. Running into the air from cliffs and mountains can be a thrill on its own right.

Your wing handling and flying skills will serve you well; a talented motor pilot will do fine flying a paraglider—the challenge will be soaring. Additionally, there are some skills that must be learned to handle potentially perilous sites that are far from flat and grassy. And thermal flying means conquering the turbulent air that comes with stronger conditions. Your early flights should be in relatively still air with less emphasis on soaring and more emphasis on getting used to the differences in feel and technique.

Free-flying adds risk in some areas while reducing it in others; most soaring risk comes from strong conditions and challenging sites. Even ridge soaring, which looks benign, requires significant skills and knowledge to do *safely*.

Basic Right-Of-Way

Free flight, especially on a ridge with limited lift, can concentrate traffic in a small area. So a few simple rules have been adopted to minimize conflict.

First and foremost is *see and avoid*. Prevent conflicts by using the rules whenever possible but always apply common sense. The rules don't work in every situation; obvious solutions are usually better. Don't forget when turning: Look, lean then turn.

For **thermaling** it's pretty easy—if there's already a pilot circling, go in the same direction. If another glider is below you, give way to him—he can't see you as well.

On the **ridge**:

1. Always turn away from the ridge. *Always*. This is a survival rule.

2. Overtake other gliders between them and the ridge. This allows them to turn away from you and be turning away from the ridge.

3. When head-on, the pilot with the ridge to his right has the right of way. "Ridge on your right, you're alright, stay in tight." If not head-on, give way to whoever is closer to the ridge.

So if you're flying along with the ridge on your left, move away from it to let oncoming traffic pass (the ridge is on their right). Exceptions to 3 are:

a. With the ridge on your left, when you turn around it could be confusing. Do what makes sense.

b. A lower pilot has the right of way—he's probably trying to "scratch" back up and needs to stay close to the ridge.

Ridge on the right, you're alright.

The best money you'll ever spend is to take a course from a free-flight instructor that offers transition training and seek out material on paragliding. What's covered here only scratches the surface. Dennis Pagen's "The Art of Paragliding" covers this subject in depth.

Free-flying in mellow mornings and evenings is not much different then motoring other than the requisite power-off landing. Conversely, flying in air buoyant enough to remain aloft requires far more attention. You must have, or develop, active flying skills (see Chapter 16) that let you keep the wing overhead without thinking about it. The adage "less brake and let it fly" applies here too. Just like in motoring, more pilots get into trouble by pulling too much brake rather than not enough. However, active flying is a far more important skill than in motoring. If you haven't mastered how to keep the wing overhead in rough air, avoid excessively turbulent conditions (thermally or gusty) like the plague.

An experienced motor pilot should devote from 1 to 3 full days of free-flight instruction before going on his own. Plus, many sites require ratings (such as those from the USHGA in the U.S.) and, in some countries, licenses to fly.

Weather at the typical mountain site is often unique; even rated pilots should seek out local expertise before flying a new site. Locals will have knowledge gained from sometimes bad experience—it's worth not repeating the experience.

Equipment

You'll love the harness. After being so nearly upright as with many motor models, the laid-back position of a soaring rig will feel downright dreamy. Almost all harnesses come with a reserve mount, speedbar accommodations and low hook-in points for comfort and weight shift authority.

Most include some form of back protection. Learn how that protection works because it may require proper setup. Airbag harnesses, for example, *must* be zipped properly (using the correct compartment) in order to have any effectiveness. Other styles have their own specifics.

Your motor helmet would work but, since you don't need the ear protection, a lightweight model is far more comfortable. Many free-flight sites use a different radio (2-meter FM in the U.S.) than what motor pilots use. They're more expensive but far more reliable (see Chapter 28).

Your motoring wing should work just fine as long as you follow the common practice of being heavy on the wing while motoring. If the wing was specifically made for motoring, than it may not be as efficient as those specifically made for soaring. A wing that takes a lot of power to fly level will take a lot of lift to stay up.

You'll want a reserve parachute even more so than with the motor. They have scored many saves for free-flyers who ran afoul of mean-spirited air. Good boots are helpful, too, especially in the mountains or other challenging terrain.

Launch Differences

Being able to deal with rough surfaces and a brisk wind is part and parcel of paragliding. Whether thermals are cranking up the hillside or stiff winds are making a ridge lifty, it is quite common to be launching in winds over 12 mph.

Bone up on the high-wind techniques covered Chapter 15 and practice them in

1. Tammy Bowles is departing Moore Mountain, North Carolina. It's common to need a *lot* of brakes when inflating on a slope. Not only are the hook-in points lower, but you actually do need more brake to keep the glider from overflying.

2. Alan Chuculate and Chris Bowles land simultaneously after a flight from Moore Mountain. More planning is required since there's no motor to count on. Fortunately, most free flight harnesses provide excellent back protection in case misjudgment yields a hard landing.

safe areas. You'll quickly warm up to kiting with a light-weight free-flight harness. Since free flying requires lift to stay aloft, pilots typically seek out wind blowing up hills. Although thermals thrive in a no-wind condition, they get good starts when forced up a mountain or some other land perturbation. The vast majority of sites are found atop ridges or mountains, facing the prevailing wind. Expect to deal with small obstructions (plants, rocks, etc) that are put there to snag wings and lines. They're usually very good at it.

As for technique, the main difference on launch is that, once committed, you must lean forward to run since there is no motor pushing. Whether the initial inflation was reversed or forward, once facing forward, lean over while putting your hands back and up to prevent engaging the brakes. Then run hard until you get lifted off the hill.

Doing no-wind forward launches is easier in some ways since the downward slope helps with your run and getting the wing to come to overhead. Be quick to damp it though, it will probably want to overfly you.

One situation that commands respect is launching from a cliff. Air carries great momentum and a vertical cliff will direct it up right in front of launch, leaving you in a difficult rotor. You may have to move back away from the edge just to get your wing in clear enough air.

Be mindful of the preflight check—forgetting to hook up properly can be disastrous when launching from a hill. Pilots have died after forgetting to buckle their leg loops—they wound up hanging by their arm pits for a time before falling out. Getting into the harness is nigh impossible from that situation although it *can* be done with some physical dexterity and the proper technique (covered in Pagen's "The Art of Paragliding"). One technique is to *never* unhook your leg straps without also unhooking the chest strap too. When it happens, it's usually after the pilot un-did his leg straps to walk. Modern harnesses incorporate buckle systems that reduce this possibility—buy one of those, if able.

The risers are almost always farther apart in free flight harnesses to allow more weight shift into the turn. Plus with low hang points, the pilot is essentially tilting on the balance point.

"Turbo" Bob Ryan swings back to head south on this Pacific Coast ridge.

Maneuvering Differences

The brakes behave the same, of course, but free flight harnesses add significant weight-shift capability. That becomes more important for several reasons:

- It's way more effective—the typical harness allows over 14 inches of up and down riser travel.
- It is more efficient than using brakes alone. When soaring, the goal is to minimize drag while staying in lift. That means flying near the minimum sink speed of the glider—usually only a few inches of brake pull, any more hurts sink rate.
- Recoveries from asymmetric wing malfunctions or spirals are enhanced.

Weight shifting is done differently in paragliding. Instead of shifting the whole motor or moving the thigh and shoulder, you use your hips. It's not what you do with your body, it's in the hips. Lower your right hip to turn right and left hip to turn left. Some pilots cross the high leg over the low one but do whatever it takes to maximize riser movement. Use the same coordinated turn technique as described in Chapter 16.

Big ears are easier to pull since the risers, and thus their A lines, are easier to reach. Plus, with better weight shift authority you can steer fairly effectively while holding big ears.

Free flying means you're usually seeking out lifting conditions and it's entirely possible to get into so much lift (on a mountain or ridge, especially) that you cannot come down at a desired location. Big ears provides one way to do that but there are other, more effective ways that warrant learning (see Chapter 18).

Kiting

There is little difference in basic kiting although, absent the motor, you can get lifted easier. Learning one of the advanced methods mentioned in Chapter 15 can be quite helpful since you will stay reversed and maintain better control if it happens.

New Capabilities

The best new capability is to fly soaring locations where motors are not allowed (soaring sites that are sensitive to noise). These treasured spots are gained by and maintained by dedicated volunteers and should be respected.

To realize these capabilities, most sites require free-flight ratings to insure some minimum skill level. Working towards these ratings will further advance your skills and is fun to boot.

Added Vulnerabilities

Without the motor there are some new concerns to deal with. The obvious lack of go-around capability must keep you even more focused on your landing options. Plus, unless you're willing to land away from your landing zone (and the ride home), you must keep getting closer to it as you descend. Pilots do frequently head out on cross-country adventures but they usually have a ride arranged.

You're far more likely to need a spot landing somewhere strange. Make sure your skills are up to par.

You will be inclined to fly in more turbulent conditions since, by nature, you need enough thermal strength or ridge lift to remain aloft. Most of the increased risk in free flying comes from this fact. Thermal turbulence in some areas, at some times of the day, and some locations can be disastrously strong, especially for pilots not adept at active piloting.

The wing is slightly more susceptible to collapse since it will be loaded lighter. It should also be less violent in the recovery but be ready to handle it or avoid stronger conditions altogether. You'll want to use more brakes in turbulence, about position/pressure 3.

For those who plan on venturing into the "biggest" (most turbulent) air, a maneuvers clinic is highly recommended (see Chapter 18). You will learn recovery and descent techniques that may serve be extremely beneficial, if not life saving.

A tandem paragliding lesson is a great for a site introduction. Choose your instructor carefully—this is not easy. The pilot must manage a huge wing in usually fairly strong conditions. When available, help is beneficial. Good tandem pilots know how to use helpers and aren't afraid to ask when they're available.

Above, Phil Russman is helping Alan Chuculate launch a tandem during strong conditions on the western Baja peninsula of mexico.

If you get recruited as a helper: never let yourself get lifted all the way off the ground while hanging on—let go immediately.

The PPG Bible: A Complete Guide and Reference

Section IV

Theory & Understanding

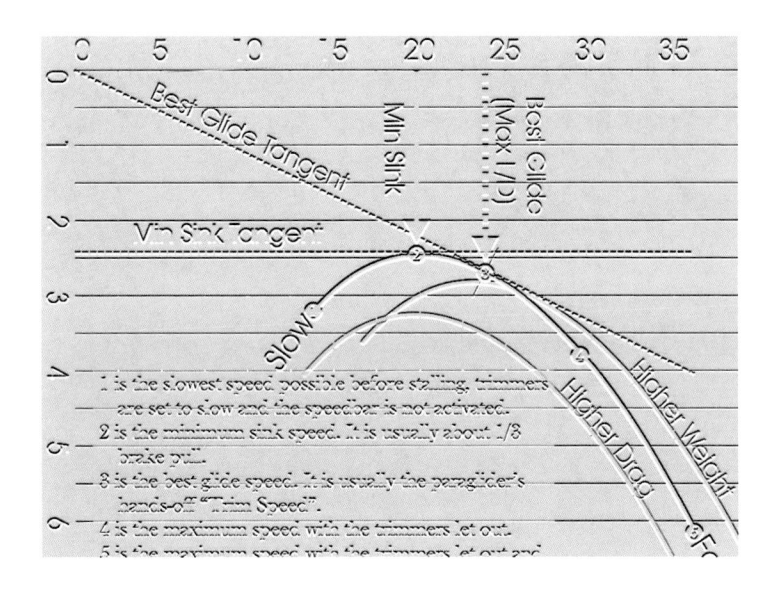

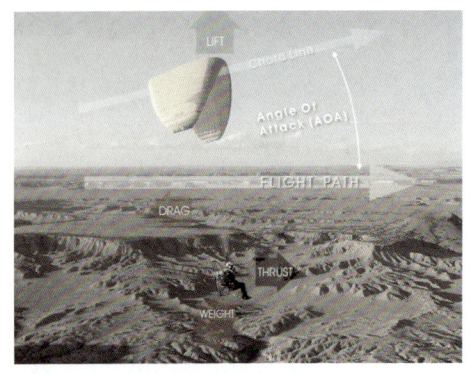

This Section builds an important foundation of understanding. Having a more comprehensive model of what's going on around you will improve decision making and make you a safer pilot. Besides, it's just plain interesting to know how things work. And for anyone aspiring to design the next generation of gear, it represents a good start at knowing what's involved. The simple PPG turns out to not as simple as it looks.

Pilots would be well served to learn this material gradually by reading, asking questions and improving understanding through experience. After gaining some flight time it would be enlightening to revisit the information. There's nothing like actual air time to grease the gears of understanding.

Section IV

Theory & Understanding

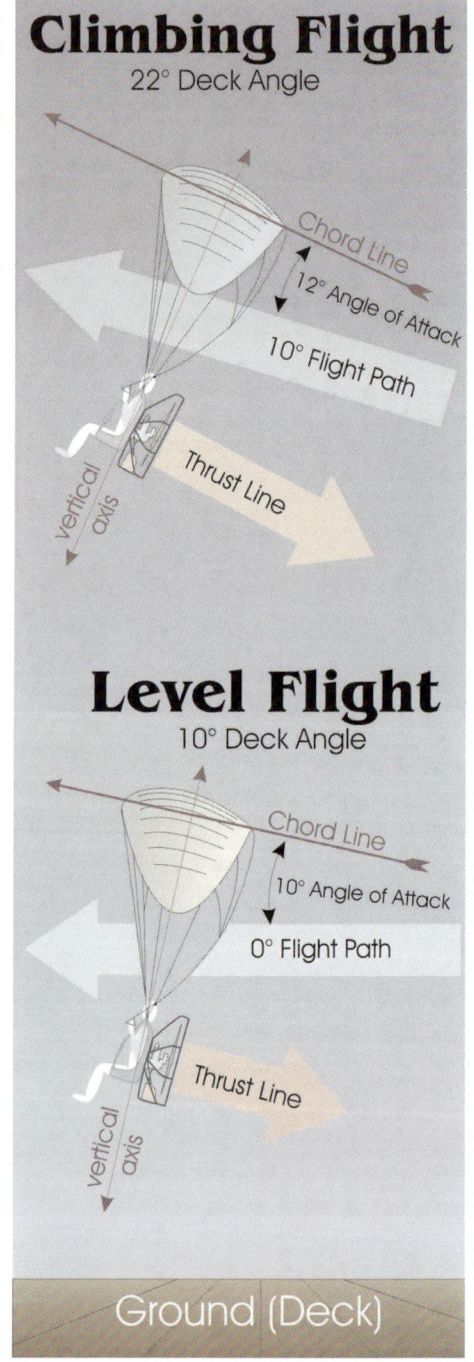

Climbing Flight
22° Deck Angle

- Chord Line
- 12° Angle of Attack
- 10° Flight Path
- Thrust Line
- vertical axis

Level Flight
10° Deck Angle

- Chord Line
- 10° Angle of Attack
- 0° Flight Path
- Thrust Line
- vertical axis

Ground (Deck)

Aerodynamics

CHAPTER 22

Flight is a fine dance of forces that must remain in step for you to stay aloft and in control. We follow the same aerodynamic rules as our fixed wing brethren, but with a few important differences.

- Thrust, weight, and drag all hang well below the wing. That gives great stability but imparts some different behavior, too.

- There is no tail which leaves very limited control of pitch and yaw (covered later).

- The soft wing and lines must always be under tension so weightlessness or negative G (like the top of a really big roller coaster) maneuvering is verboten.

Balance of Forces

You can learn most of what you need to know by sticking your hand out the window of a moving car. If it's flat and level with the air stream (or *relative wind*), there is no lift but it still gets pushed back a bit (drag). Angle the hand up slightly (increase the *angle of attack*) and it generates lift. Angle it up more and it gets more lift while pushing backwards more too—more drag. Angle it up too much and the lift stops altogether while drag skyrockets—that's a *stall*. If you keep the slight angle that produces lift, but drive faster, then lift and drag both go up.

Some dynamics of our pilot-on-a-string craft can be understood by imagining a small rock tied to a foot-long line hanging from your finger. Moving the finger around approximates how a pilot/motor will behave when the wing moves around in response to control inputs or turbulence.

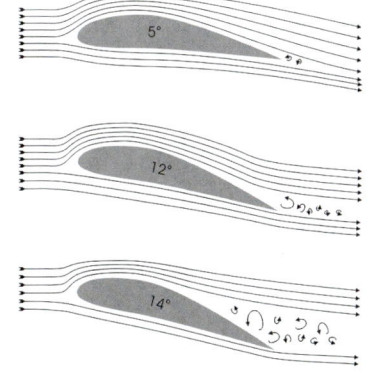

The air can only "stick" so much. Beyond a certain angle (the *critical" angle of attack*), it separates causing lift to plummet and drag to skyrocket. This is a stall.

Sum of Forces

- Lift = 100 kg
- Chord Line
- Deck Angle = 10°
- AOA: Angle of Attack = 10°
- Relative Wind / FLIGHT PATH
- Thrust = 20
- Drag = 20
- Weight 100 kg

Component Forces

All forces in kg

- Lift = 98 kg
- Wing Force = 99 kg
- LIFT from motor = 2 kg
- Induced Drag = 1 kg
- Parasite Drag = 19 kg
- Motor Push = 21 kg
- Weight = 100

Motor push contributes 19 Kg to thrust and 2 Kg to lift.

Steady Climb

All forces in kg

- Lift = 99 kg
- Chord Line
- Deck Angle = 15°
- AOA: Angle of Attack = 11°
- Relative Wind / FLIGHT PATH
- Thrust = 30
- Drag = 20
- Weight 100 kg

Climb comes from thrust in excess of what's required to maintain level flight. Airspeed slows down slightly in a powered climb.

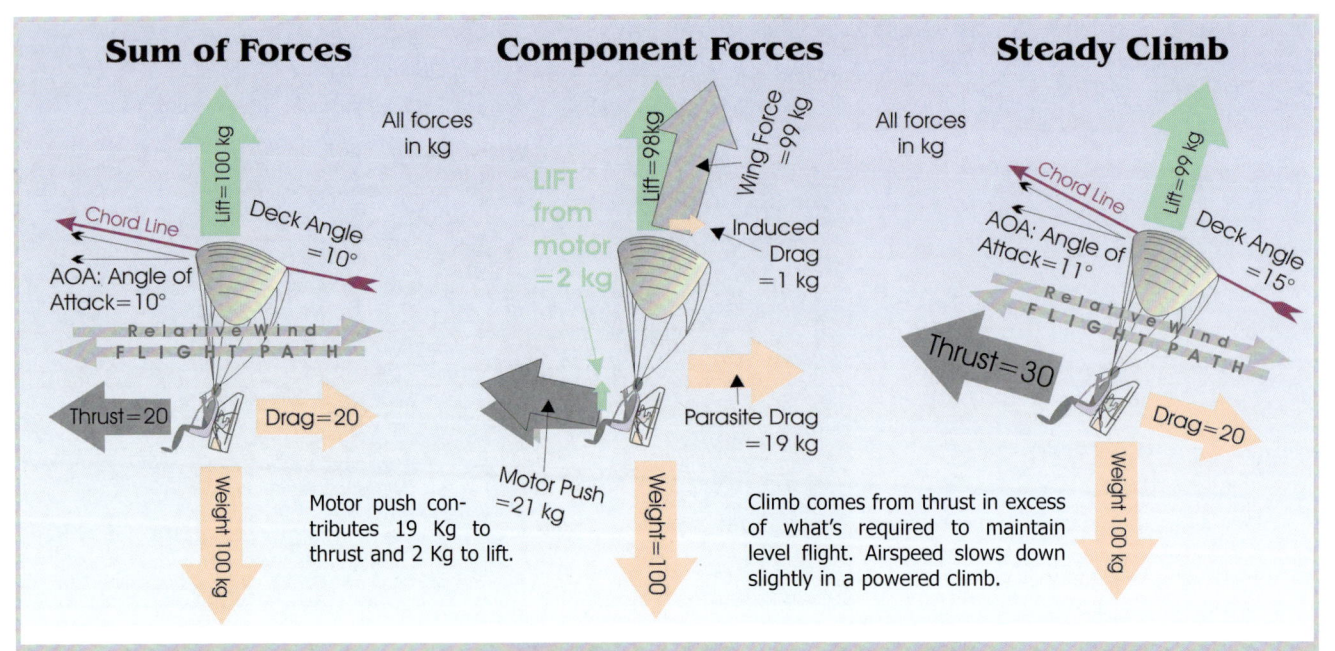

It's really kind of messy. The 4 forces are always described relative to flight path for simplicity, but they aren't actually lined up that way. Leaned-back motors, for example, make thrust contribute slightly to lift. Even the wing force is tilted back, adding drag (called induced drag). Each force can be represented as an arrow (vector), with direction and magnitude. In steady flight, they must all balance each other out as shown in the **Sum of Forces**.

Throttling up changes everything. After swinging forward then settling back into a steady climb, the flight path tilts up and the angle of attack (AoA) increases but only very slightly while lift decreases due to engine thrust lifting some weight. Speed slows down slightly and induced drag goes up a bit. Since weight is always pulling down to earth, thrust must keep air at speed *and* overcome gravity (just like going uphill). When under power, the wing is slightly more likely to enter a parachutal stall and far less likely to recover from it

Lift

There is no magic here, we fly by pushing air downward—just like your hand out the window pushes air downward. The nicely curved wing just does it much more efficiently. The motor provides forward speed while the wing redirects air downward. It's pure Newton: push enough air down and up we go.

To generate lift, any flat surface will work, including a plywood board. However, curving the surface is much more efficient—the air on top sticks enough to get redirected downward. With the board, airflow separates quite readily from the top surface into useless eddies. That would leave only lift from the bottom and boatloads of drag from disrupted flow on the top. Lift is good, drag is bad.

Drag

Our machines, with all those lines, frame, and distinctly un-aerodynamic pilot, have lots of drag. Shape has a lot to do with it—round tubes are terrible while the familiar teardrop shape is quite clean.

Drag comes in two forms: parasitic and induced. Parasitic drag is basic air resistance. Induced drag is a result of the wing force angling backwards from the flight path—it is a by-product of lift. Wingtip vortices are mostly to blame.

Put a symmetrical wing (curved the same on top and bottom) parallel with the slipstream and it produces no lift, only parasitic or *form* drag. Angle it up, like your hand out the car window, and it comes to life with lift. Induced drag goes up too

G Loads

Flying along in level flight, you feel your body weight in the seat, that's 1 G (force of Gravity). In a bank, as you swing around, it forces you against the seat and makes you feel heavier. When you steepen the bank to 60° it feels like you weigh twice your weight—2 G's.

Just like swinging a rock around on a string, the faster you swing it, the higher the G's.

since you had to angle it back slightly and part of the total wing force is rearward.

The *Center of Drag* is where the drag appears to act—for our craft it falls about halfway between the pilot and wing.

Speeding up increases drag dramatically, a doubling of speed quadruples the parasitic drag. That's why our abundant drag is less of a problem—we go so slow.

Thrust

Thrust overcomes drag. Whenever thrust exceeds drag, we get acceleration. In our case, having the thrust hang so low causes the pilot and motor to swing out in front of the wing. That in turn pitches the wing up, increasing the flight path and slightly increasing the angle of attack.

In level flight these forces are balanced; just enough lift counteracts the total weight and just enough thrust overcomes the total drag. Climbing flight obviously requires more thrust since the motor must overcome gravity *and* keep the airspeed.

Thrust is vectored—it will always push in the direction it's pointed and that is not necessarily the same as the direction you're flying. Serious problems can occur when the thrust line (which way the push is pointed) gets too far off kilter. Point the thrust to the right and the pilot will be pushed left—with potentially unpleasant consequences.

Weight

Weight is what lift overcomes—gravity pulling down on a mass. The center of mass is where an object theoretically balances—for a PPG, that's near the pilot's neck since there is so little mass (in spite of all the area up there) in the wing.

Stability

Stability is resistance to upset and the tendency to return to a previous steady state. By virtue of having the center of gravity (CG) so far below the center of lift our craft is inherently very stable. Unlike almost any other type of aircraft, if the pilot does nothing at all, it will tend to fly straight at it's *trim* speed (see below).

The term *stability* is also used frequently to describe a wing that resists collapses and recovers quickly. Further, it is stable when it resists fore/aft movements and returns quickly to steady flight. For example, a vertical gust of air will make the wing surge forward, then back, and continue back and forth in decreasing amounts. A stable wing will not surge as far forward, will not fall as far back and will settle into a steady state more quickly.

Motor units that mask wing movements to the pilot are frequently called "stable." This is a misnomer because it does not affect any actual stability but rather the sensation of stability. The higher the hook-in points are above the CG, the less the wing's bouncing around will wiggle the motor unit around. A motor with very low hook-in points will move more with the wing and feels "busier" in flight but it is not less stable.

Axis of Motion

Whether rocked by turbulence or control input, motion occurs around various axis as shown below. Pulling brakes makes you pitch around the lower latitudinal axis. Changing power makes you pitch around the upper latitudinal axis. Yaw is left-right twisting around the vertical axis) happens initially when pulling a brake. Roll (around the longitudinal axis) happens whenever you enter a bank.

Stability is like a rock on a finger. Move the finger and the rock swings in diminishing amounts until its still again.

Glide Ratio

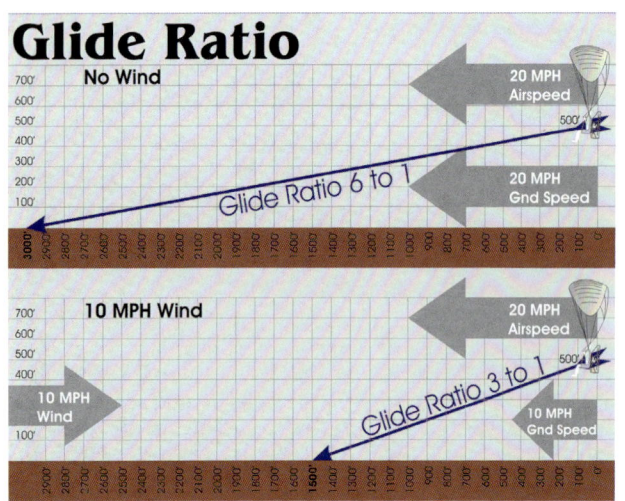

No Wind — Glide Ratio 6 to 1, 20 MPH Airspeed, 20 MPH Gnd Speed

10 MPH Wind — Glide Ratio 3 to 1, 20 MPH Airspeed, 10 MPH Gnd Speed

With a craft as slow as ours, glide ratio will be dramatically affected by wind. When trying to stretch glide into the wind, it is always best to speed up even though the overall sink rate is higher. You want to get through the sink faster. Picture the extreme: You're flying 20 mph in a 20 mph headwind. The glide ratio is 0, you're sinking over one spot on the ground. Speeding up makes you move forward although only by a few mph, but that's infinitely better than 0!

Measuring Your Glide

You need to have a GPS and variometer. An altimeter and watch works in place of the variometer.

Set up the GPS to display speed (it only measures groundspeed). Climb 1000' up into a smooth atmosphere and align yourself exactly into the wind, watching the ground to do so. Throttle off slowly and watch the ground speed as you keep yourself pointed into the wind. Note the sink rate (or calculate).

Do that for a half minute then climb back up to 1000' and turn exactly downwind. Throttle off and again watch the ground speed and sink rate. Average the two groundspeeds and sink rates. A 10 mph upwind speed and 30 mph downwind speed means your airspeed is 20 mph. Sink rate should be the same both ways.

Convert sink rate in feet per minute to miles per hour (fpm x 0.011) and divide the average airspeed by sink rate to get glide ratio.

Glide & Drag

Without power we glide, going downhill at a steepness defined by our *glide ratio*—the forward distance divided by the distance dropped. This primary measure of efficiency is also known as the Lift/Drag (L/D) ratio—how much lift versus how much drag is produced at any given speed. Lowering drag (friction) is the easiest way to improve glide since the wing planform and shape is fixed. Changes to the wing, such as adding brakes, trimmers, speedbar, or big ears, change the glide ratio.

A 6 to 1 glide ratio (or L/D) is said to be a glide ratio of 6. Bigger numbers are better—an 8:1 (pronounced "eight to one") wing will go further from the same altitude than a 6:1 wing. Another way to put it is that an 8:1 wing has 8 times as much lift as drag.

Glide ratio varies with speed and configuration. Each wing and motor combination will have a speed at which it is most efficient, the *best L/D speed.* Going faster or slower will steepen the glide (worsen it). For most wings, the speed for best glide occurs at *trim speed,* which is hands up, no speedbar, and trimmers neutral (usually the slowest setting). However, check your manual—there are exceptions.

Adding drag always hurts glide. Hanging a flag from your wing lines, for example, adds a lot of drag. In this case, speed stays the same while sink rate increases. Going faster with the extra drag dramatically increases sink rate.

Wing manufacturers advertise their glide ratio with*out* a motor to get the best number possible. They use a skinny pilot squeezed into a minimal free-flight harness holding his hands and feet inward. But a paramotor, with its hoop, netting and frame, make that number is a distant dream.

A windmilling prop has dramatically more drag than a stationary one. That is because the spinning keeps the blade's angle of a attack low enough for the air to stick to the back. A stopped prop, on the other hand, only represents the drag of its frontal area. A gyrocopter is a good example, it creates lift by having the air flow past it's spinning rotors. Stop the rotors and the area represented by the blades is woefully inadequate to stop its plummet. Expect a 10 to 20% decrease in glide performance with a windmilling prop (clutched units), 2 to 4% decrease with a stopped prop and no change for an idling prop (no clutch).

Good glide performance comes from:

- Large span wings. They reduce inefficiencies due to the tendency of air to flow spanwise around the tips rather than back and downward. The reason that soaring wings are long and skinny is to keep the total area the same but reduce these tip losses.

- Fewer and skinnier lines to reduce drag. The highest performance competition wings take this to an extreme—leaving off the protective sheath from lines to reduce their radius. They'll also have fewer lines by employing more cascades where one line goes up then splits into two which then splits and so on.

- A flatter profile—longer lines allow a flatter wing which improves efficiency but this factor must be weighed carefully against the increased line drag.

- More cells. More ribs mean a more precise airfoil shape. Closer spacing prevents each cell from billowing so far out of shape.

Interestingly, increasing the weight doesn't change the glide performance, it just increases the speed at which it occurs. *Sink Rate* will be higher, but the maximum glide ratio stays the same. This effect can be useful and, in fact, competition soaring pilots sometimes carry ballast to increase their cross country speeds. For example: a 150 pound pilot on an 8:1 glider may have a best glide speed of 20 mph. With a 200 pound pilot, that same glider still has a maximum 8:1 glide ratio but it will occur at 22 mph and will sink proportionally faster, too.

Center of Lift and Drag

The center of lift is an imaginary point on the wing where lift is said to act. The entire wing provides some lift but it is concentrated in the first 30% of the chord (front to back measurement). If you could attach a rope to this point the glider/pilot combination would balance from it.

The center of drag is the point in space, when looking at the pilot/wing coming straight towards you, where the drag is said to act. It will be somewhere between the pilot and wing. If you could attach a line to tow the glider from this point it would have no tendency to pitch or twist due to drag.

Sink Rate

How fast you descend is *sink rate*, commonly measured in meters per second (m/s) or feet per minute (fpm). Minimum sink rate is the lowest descent rate the glider is capable of. Minimum sink *speed* is where that minimum rate occurs. Going faster or slower than the minimum sink speed will always increase the descent rate. Unlike glide ratio, increasing weight always increases sink rate.

Wings with a good glide ratio usually have a low sink rate but not necessarily. For two gliders that fly at the same speed, the higher glide ratio wing will also have a lower sink rate. A fast glider could have a higher sink rate than a slow one.

Wing area, usually measured in square meters, is hugely important. More wing area means a better sink rate but at slower speed. A small, efficient (good glide ratio) wing will be fast and cover ground nicely, but will sink faster over time.

The *Polar Curve* (at the end of this chapter) shows these relationships. At each weight there is a speed that produces the minimum sink. For most gliders, that speed comes with about brake pressure 2 (one quarter).

Speed

Adding power does not add speed—it causes a climb along with a slight slow down. If you could move the motor thrust up to the center of drag then throttling up would indeed make you go faster.

Digging Deeper: Angle of Attack

Does adding power increase the AoA? Some say that only the flight path changes while other pilots argue that the AoA increases a fair amount. The truth appears to be in the middle. Experiments have shown that adding power mostly affects the flight path, but also *does* increase the angle of attack a small amount.

Parachutal stall has proven nettlesome for powered flyers far more than non-powered flyers. It nearly always happens at full or nearly full power, too. The thrust can help get the AoA to its critical stall value but, more importantly, will hold it there once stalled. Without power, most wings recover immediately on their own.

At extremely steep climb angles, the wing's weight will be trying to further pull it back. Imagine an extreme, nearly vertical climb: Line tension decreases, line drag, wing drag and the weight of it all would want to make the wing fall below the pilot—a decidedly unhealthy turn of events.

In level flight, deck angle is the same as angle of attack. Powering up will only push the pilot into a climb, not increase speed.

Level Flight
Deck Angle = Angle of Attack

Digging Deeper: Ground Effect
Ground effect happens when a wing gets within about a half-span of the ground. Lift increases while drag decreases because the tip vortices are reduced—air is prevented from circling around the wing tip.
Our wings benefit very little, if at all, from ground effect because the wing is too high over our head.

There *are* other ways to go faster, and they *do* always require more power. Anytime the speed goes up, more thrust is required to overcome the increased drag. Here are some ways to go faster with a PPG:

1. Smaller wings are faster then larger versions of the same wing. They take more running space to launch and require more power.
2. Higher weight will make any wing go faster (the other side of number 1).
3. Trimmer adjustments can increase speed by about 15%.
4. Speedbar activation increases speed by about 25%. Even more than trimmers, it increases the possibility of frontal collapse in turbulence.
5. Angling the thrust line upward (thrust vector downward) is like adding weight. You're leaning forward and down which isn't terribly comfortable but it slightly increases the speed just like adding weight does.

Efficiency Under Power

Thrust results from the propeller accelerating a mass of air from some speed to some new faster speed—pushing us in the opposite direction. How much thrust depends on how much air and how quickly it's accelerated. We can either accelerate a little bit of air a lot, or a lot of air a little. Jet engines burn copious amounts of fuel to accelerate a little bit of air (relatively) a lot. That's great for going hundreds of mph, but is terribly inefficient at low speeds. It's noisy, too. For slow craft—and we're about as slow as it gets—higher efficiency comes from accelerating a lot of air a little; i.e. using a big prop. That is, fortunately, also the quietest arrangement.

Efficiency can be spent either on improved fuel consumption or more thrust. In general, the larger the prop, the quieter and more "thrusty" the machine. Even jet engine makers have taken the large mass route, designing *high bypass* motors with huge fans that provide better takeoff power with less fuel use and less noise.

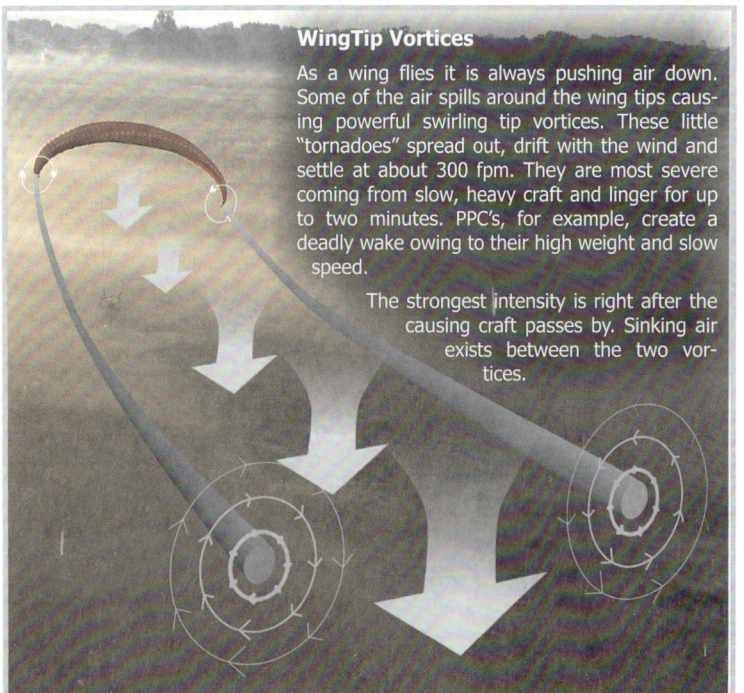

Wing

The airfoil shape is chosen by designers to optimize performance. Although, in principle, airfoil design is identical to rigid wings, softness dictates some special requirements.

Anhedral Curvature

That graceful arc carved by the wing's drooping tips is *anhedral curvature*, a concession to a support structure that can only pull. It must keep perpendicular pressure on the lines. Without that 90 degree pull angle, the fabric would deform. Higher performance wings minimize the curvature using longer lines at some expense in drag.

WingTip Vortices

As a wing flies it is always pushing air down. Some of the air spills around the wing tips causing powerful swirling tip vortices. These little "tornadoes" spread out, drift with the wind and settle at about 300 fpm. They are most severe coming from slow, heavy craft and linger for up to two minutes. PPC's, for example, create a deadly wake owing to their high weight and slow speed.

The strongest intensity is right after the causing craft passes by. Sinking air exists between the two vortices.

Tip Tornadoes

Tip vortices are a pair of surprisingly strong airflow spirals attached to the tips of any lifting wing. They represent the most dangerous element of wake turbulence which is left by an aircraft like a boat leaves a wake in water.

Wake turbulence is worse when the causing craft is heavy, slow and clean. You can see that heavy powered paragliders (tandems, for example) and powered parachutes meet two of the criteria, generating sometimes vicious turbulence that must be avoided for at least 2 minutes.

Aspect Ratio

When a wing is laid out flat on the ground, wingspan (tip to tip distance) divided by the chord (leading edge to trailing edge distance) is known as aspect ratio. A 32 foot wingspan with an 8 foot average chord means the aspect ratio is 4:1. Without knowing the average chord, you can also derive the aspect ratio using Span² divided by Area.

Long, skinny wings are more efficient (better L/D) than short fat ones because they minimize tip vortices but there are trade-offs. On a paraglider, the only way to have long, skinny wings is to put them on long lines which increases line drag. Long, skinny wings (high aspect ratio) also tend to suffer deflations easier and don't recover as well as short fat ones—that is why beginner wings frequently have low aspect ratios.

Airfoil Shape and Bernoulli

A plank will create lift but it won't be very efficient. A symmetrical wing, where the curve is the same on top and bottom, generates lift too (aerobatic airplanes frequently use them) but not as efficiently as one with different curvature. Bernoulli's law, which describes conservation of energy in fluid mediums, helps explain how air behaves around airfoils. It doesn't explain lift in the way old textbooks say it does, but that's only because the law was misused.

Much advanced science swirls around airfoil shape (also called wing cross-section) and some wings use different shapes at different points along the span but, generally, they will be flatter on the bottom than the top.

Soft wings give up performance due to their puffed-up cells—the deformations between ribs. Builders employ many tricks to minimize this through line cascades, internal bracing and different types of reinforcement, but losses are unavoidable. Higher performance wings typically have more cells to reduce this effect.

Shapes have trade-offs too. Some sacrifice stability for performance and vice-versa. The "reflex" (where the wing's aft 25% curves upward) feature of some motor wings is an effort to make it more stable at some expense in efficiency.

Angle of the Dangle

Air flowing past the pilot/wing combination is called the relative wind or slipstream. Angle of attack is the angle between the wing chord line and this relative wind. The climb or descent angle is the angle that your flight path makes to the ground. *Angle of incidence* is the angle the chord line makes to the C lines.

Deck angle is the angle made between the chord line and the ground.

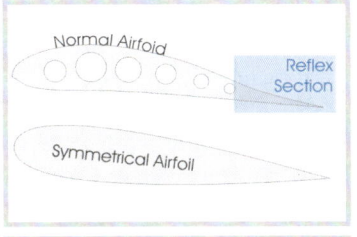

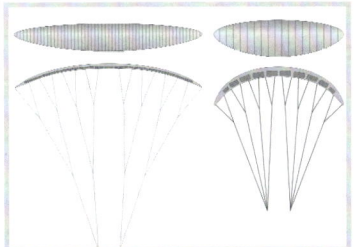

Top: A normal paraglider airfoil has more curved on the top than the bottom. A symmetrical airfoil is the same on both sides and is used for aircraft designed to fly upside down. They are not as efficient, but are way more efficient while upside down than a regular airfoil would be if *it* was flown upside down.

Given our craft's unlikely time in inverted flight, symmetrical airfoils are never used.

The *Reflex Section* is an upward tilt near the trailing edge that conveys some collapse resistance and allows a bit more speed. The price is a higher sink rate.

High aspect ratios, as shown above, are commonly found on high performance soaring wings.

Throttling Up
The Change of Power

A lot happens when you squeeze on some throttle. The pilot here was in level flight then powered up to full starting at circle 2. Here's what happens in the process:

AoA starts to increase as your body swings forward, increasing lift and accelerating you upwards.

You swing into a steep climb briefly, during which the AoA peaks (circle 4). When the wing surges forward, AoA decreases dramatically as the wing catches up (circle 6).

Finally, you settle into a steady climb (circle 7) with the AoA only slightly higher than when you started. You'll keep this condition as long as the power lasts.

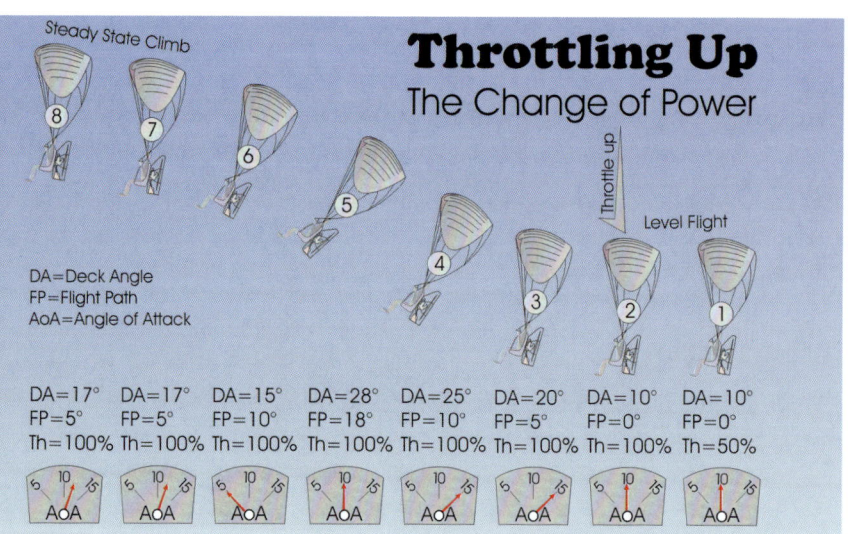

DA = Deck Angle
FP = Flight Path
AoA = Angle of Attack

Circle	8	7	6	5	4	3	2	1
DA	17°	17°	15°	28°	25°	20°	10°	10°
FP	5°	5°	10°	18°	10°	5°	0°	0°
Th	100%	100%	100%	100%	100%	100%	100%	50%

Increasing the angle of attack increases lift up to a point. That point is called the *critical angle of attack* beyond which airflow breaks off the wing's top causing lift to plummet while drag soars—it is called a *stall*.

When you add power, three things happen as thrust pushes you out in front of the wing: (1) the angle of attack (AoA) goes up which increases lift (and drag) momentarily, 2) the deck angle increases by the same amount, and 3) the climb angle goes up. Once you're in a climb, the AoA decreases to be just slightly higher than before.

In keeping the forces balanced, even though adding power increases drag through a higher AoA, thrust counteracts the extra drag so airspeed changes very little. Airspeed slows slightly with added power since the increased drag combined with overcoming gravity and outweighs the added thrust.

Angle of Incidence (AoI)

On airplanes, wings are bolted to the body (fuselage) at a fixed angle to the plane's longitudinal (nose to tail) axis—the *angle of incidence*. On paragliders, the angle is fixed by the line lengths. Letting out the trimmers decreases the AoI (faster) as does pressing on the speedbar.

Trimmers and speedbar change the wing in subtly different ways. The speedbar lowers the heavily loaded A's and B's whereas trimmers make a smaller difference by raising the rear risers. You'll feel the difference in how much pressure it takes to change each one. That's why the speedbar needs your feet—for leverage. It effects a much greater speed change at an increased susceptibility to frontal collapse.

Changing Angle of Attack (AoA)

Lift is a function of speed and AoA. More speed, more lift. More AoA, more lift. So changing the AoA will have a big effect. Adding or subtracting power gives a small change to AoA. It feels like a bigger change because the flight path also changes.

Pulling brakes increases the AoA by lowering the trailing edge which immediately tilts the chord line.

Turning

When you pull a brake, the trailing edge deflects downward, increasing lift and drag on that side. You might think the wing would bank opposite to brake pull since there is more lift on the braked side—much like how airplanes bank their wings with a downward deflected aileron. But, due to pendular stability, the wing primarily acts on the drag which slows down that side and causes it to turn. On many designs, the brake also pulls the wing sideways a bit in the direction of desired turn. That drag also slows down the overall airspeed, too, which will either require more power or, in a glide, will worsen glide performance.

A turn always increases sink rate since some of the wing's lift is now being spent pulling you around the turn.

Thrust Vectoring

Normally the thrust should be nearly perpendicular to the C line of the wing, pushing nearly straight backwards while in flight.

If the thrust line is angled upwards (thrust vector pushing you down slightly) then increasing power will increase down force on the wing, increasing speed slightly. If it is pointed downward (motor tilted back) it will have the opposite effect. Overall, this force is generally small enough to not be noticeable.

If the thrust line is off to the side (you're twisted) then it will cause a bank in the opposite direction. If the motor is pushing your body to the left then it will cause a bank to the right. In a very few cases, the wing and motor can interact in a way that causes a "wallowing" action back and forth. This was more common on the early vest-type machines but happens on others, too.

How a wing Collapses

A *collapse*, also called deflation, is where part of the wing folds under (it can't fold upwards) after getting pushed down by a vertical or horizontal gust. Usually it recovers before the pilot even knows it happened. A frontal collapse is where the leading edge tucks under while the rest of the wing remains mostly inflated or forms a "horseshoe" shape. There are two basic causes, **atmospheric turbulence** and **pilot inducement** (*see chapter 18*).

Atmospheric turbulence is what most fear, the proverbial "hand of God" swatting them out of the sky and it is surprisingly rare unless you seek out lively air. Usually it comes from flying through a vortex or swirl that hits the wing, blowing it down and out of shape. The slipstream pushes the now-loose fabric (with probably closed cells) back for a few seconds until internal pressure and line geometry sort things out. Pressure to stay inflated (or "open") comes both from the leading edge openings and from the exterior surface tensioning its lines.

One way to get a turbulence-induced collapse is to fly into a rapidly changing wind such as thermal. If you fly into a horizontal shear, it can "curl up" a wing tip as it tries to push the fabric in a different direction. Low G's, such as from a wingover where you feel light in the seat, makes a collapse more likely.

Stalling

A wing stalls when airflow over the top separates into a turbulent, random flow. It happens at the *critical angle of attack* and, although technically not related to speed,

The pilot is pulling his right A riser to collapse that side. You can see it trying to resist but soon it lets go and folds under. The remaining half of the wing, now carrying more load, speeds up and banks.

Drag increases mightily in a collapse situation, pushing the wing back (usually unevenly) and increasing the AoA on the inflated portion. Fortunately, that increase generally helps re-inflate the mess.

high angles of attack stem from heavy brakes and flying slow. If you're already flying slowly, it doesn't take much of a gust to cause a stall. A spin happens when only one part of the wing stalls and the flying part enters a rapid turn.

What is frequently called a full stall, when the pilot stuffs the brakes below his seat, is really more of an aerodynamic aberration than a stall—and far more violent, too. The wing does indeed go through the stall AoA, but then essentially becomes a luffing sail—flapping wildly in a hurricane force wind as you fall. Raising the brakes allows it to re-inflate, returning normal aerodynamics with an unpredictable bang (*see Chapter 18*) and surge.

The Polar Curve

A polar curve (see below) graphs a glider's sink rate plotted against flying speed. It is a great way to understand many relationships between control settings, speed, sink rate, glide ratio and endurance. The next chapter has a discussion of power vs thrust but know that *power* must take into account airspeed.

The polar curve shows sink rate as speed changes. At your slowest speed, just before stalling, the sink rate is quite high. As you speed up the sink rate improves until reaching the "Min Sink" speed. Then sink rate increases again as you speed up. The tangent line to the curve from 0,0 is the best L/D (glide). Where it touches the curve is the speed and its slope is the best glide ratio itself. Being heavy doesn't worsen the glide *ratio*; it just increases the speed and descent rate where it occurs.

Thrust Required

This graph shows how much thrust is required to hold level flight at various airspeeds. Each labeled point has some significance. The gray line represents the thrust required for a heavier pilot flying the same wing. You can see that a weak motor, with trimmers fast and on full speedbar may not have enough thrust to keep him level with trimmers out and full speedbar.

The point's significance:

1 is the slowest speed possible before stalling, trimmers are set to slow and the speedbar is not activated.

2 is the minimum thrust required point. On most wings it is the slowest trimmer setting and brake pressure 1.

3 is with the trimmers slow (or neutral) and no brakes which is normally very close to the best L/D speed.

4. is with the trimmers fast but no speedbar.

5. is with the trimmers fast and full speedbar.

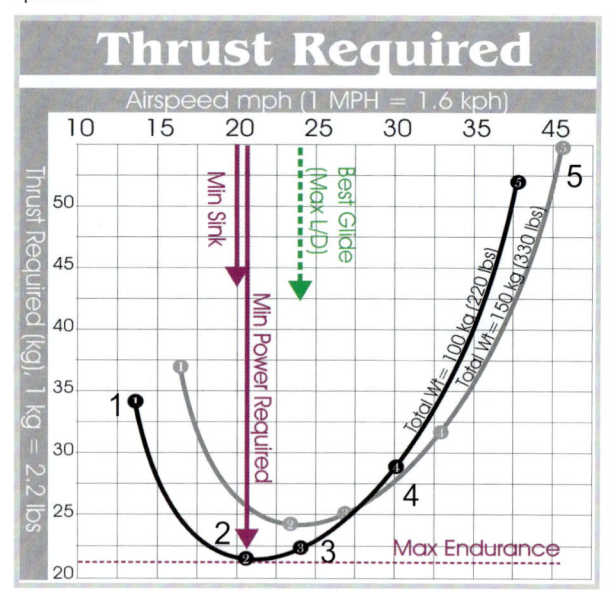

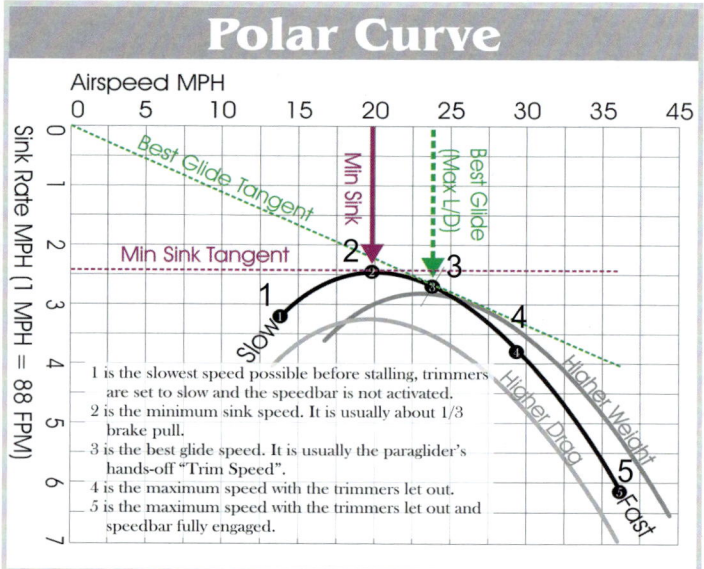

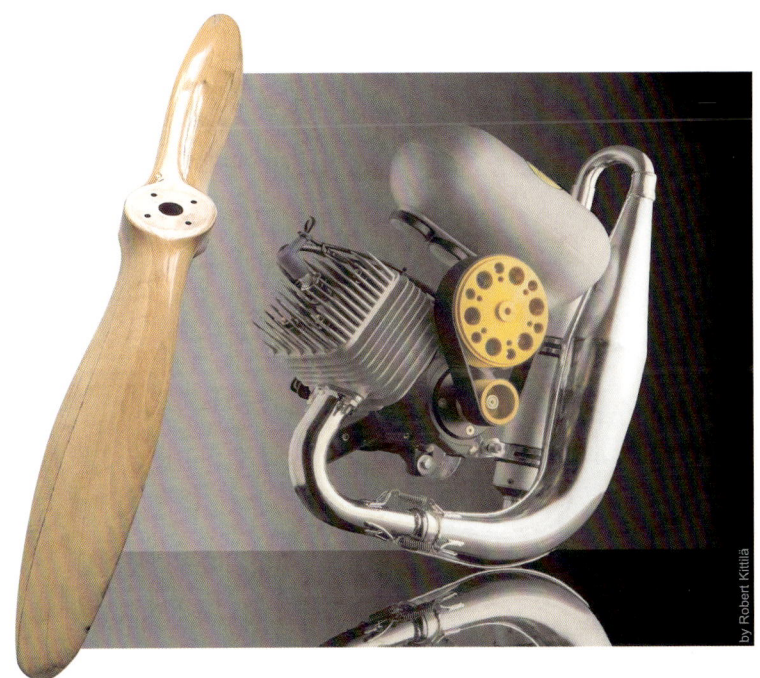

Motor & Propeller

CHAPTER 23

Thrust comes from pushing air with some sort of engine. Rockets would work but the fuel is hard to come by and it smells bad. Jet engines have lots of thrust but burn too much gas—plus they're expensive and loud. Electric motors would be great if not for their battery weight or long cords. Fuel cells will be perfect if they become affordable. Four stroke motors are reasonably quiet, fuel efficient and pollute less than 2-strokes—but they are heavier for the same power.

So that leaves the venerable 2-stroke—powerplant of choice for chain sawmen, go-cart racers and nearly all powered paraglider pilots.

Thrust & Horsepower

The only measure of power that we really care about is thrust—how hard will it push. The industry has never settled on a thrust testing standard and a few manufacturers make such ludicrous claims that they become meaningless. Independent tests, done at many fly-ins, are valuable since they use the same tester, under similar conditions, and with the interested parties mothering over the process. You can all but ignore the *absolute* thrust numbers since they vary due to external conditions and tester calibration but they are great for *comparison*.

Horsepower (HP) is a commonly used term to measure power, but it's not terribly useful for our purposes. A 30 HP motor is powerful for a PPG, but mated to the wrong prop, it can be woefully inadequate. A 30 HP motor spinning a plank, for example, will still put out 30 HP but provide no thrust. Mostly, HP tells what a motor is capable of doing given the right propeller and reduction ratio. Its value is in showing that most manufacturers try eking out the most thrust and wind up with similar efficiencies. By far, the thrust rating is far more useful information.

Expect a lot of variability in thrust. One motor that tests at 100 lbs. on one day may do 105 lbs. on the next day, even using the same tester. Plus, there are surprising variations within brand and propeller. Manufacturing vagaries will easily extract a 10% difference from the same model of paramotor and propeller. Wooden props can account for rpm differences up to 5%. Molded props, usually made from carbon fiber, have less of this effect.

2 And 4-Stroke Motors

"Suck, squeeze, bang, and blow" is the mantra of all internal combustion engines. The term "Two-Cycle" is interchangeable with "Two-Stroke" and means that a complete cycle of the piston takes only two strokes, up and down. It fires every time the piston reaches the top whereas a four stroke motor fires every *other* time. That's why 2-stroke motors get more power per pound than 4-strokes and why they tend to get hotter.

The four-stroke motor, which needs a better lubrication system to reach valves and cams, has crankcase oil whereas the two-stroke motor gets its lubrication from oil mixed in with the gas.

Understanding The Common 4-Stroke

The four cycle motor is what powers most cars, lawnmowers, snowblowers, etc. It is more complicated, having intake and exhaust valves in each cylinder's head (the uppermost part) that open and close in conjunction with the piston's travel. They control how the fuel/air mixture and exhaust gasses flow in four distinct strokes or *cycles*.

Valves, piston, camshaft, oil pump and the abundant moving parts add weight and complexity. Some small 4-strokes get by with just splashing the crankcase oil to needy parts.

Understanding the 2-Stroke

This marvel has come a long way since its inception over 50 years ago. Accumulated tweaks such as reed valves and tuned pipes are the big improvements but geometrics, electronics and materials have helped as well.

The two-cycle doubles up on tasks so that while the piston is being pushed down by burning fuel on top, it's also compressing the next fuel/air charge in the crankcase below.

A *tuned pipe*, specially shaped to optimize performance, is common. It works only through a narrow rpm range called the *power band*, improving efficiency that can be spent on either reduced fuel consumption or more power.

With a two-stroke motor, all the interesting stuff happens on the piston's bottom half of travel and a lot happens simultaneously. Here is a description of the process:

- As the piston rises, it sucks a new fuel/air charge through the carburetor and reed valve, into the crankcase below (**suck**).
- Above the rising piston, a fuel/air charge is being compressed (**squeeze**).
- When the piston nears its peak a spark ignites the compressed fuel/air mixture, powering the piston downward (**bang**).

This Bailey 4-stroke motor is one of the few to make it commercially as a powered paraglider motor. Although it is heavier for the amount of thrust produced, its efficiency allows carrying less weight in fuel which partially offsets the motor's weight disadvantage. It also pollutes less and tends to go longer between overhauls because of cooler operation and better lubrication.

Horse Power

In the 1800's, James Watt (yes, *that* Watt) was trying to sell his new steam engines. He needed a way to compare their output with the standard power plant then in use: the horse.

Mr. Watt determined that, on average, a horse could sustain 180 pounds of pull at 181 feet per minute—a pretty common workload in factories that used horses.

So the horsepower, 33,000 ft-lbs. per minute, was born. Like all measures of power, HP is work for some period of time. In this case, the power is measured as rpm x torque.

- On it's way down, the piston's bottom compresses a fuel/air charge in the crankcase (**very minor squeeze**).
- About halfway down the exhaust port is exposed, squirting the burned, high pressure gas out (**blow**). Some of the incoming fuel/air charge can escape out the exhaust, too, but a tuned pipe uses pressure waves to push it back in.
- As the piston continues down, a transfer port is exposed allowing the crankcase fuel/air charge to rush up around the piston and into the cylinder and the cycle repeats.

Besides producing power, the piston doubles as intake and exhaust valves. Fewer moving parts on a two-cycle makes it lighter and helps reliability. Unfortunately, minimal lubrication and heat (twice as many power strokes as a 4-stroke) sap some of that reliability which is why two-strokes tend to need more attention than four-strokes. Plus, lubrication relies on the proper type and amount of oil being mixed in with the fuel. Any malady that increases heat or decreases cooling can cause the motor to seize—a most unwelcome welding of the piston to its cylinder wall.

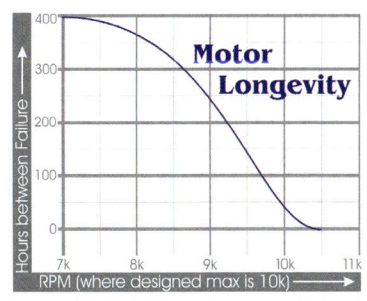

Longevity is better when rpm is kept relatively low. Wear increases significantly near a motor's maximum power output—you'll get more hours from a motor, lightly tasked, than one that spends much of its time screaming near maximum rpm.

Carburetors

A carburetor's job is feeding fuel and air, in just the right proportion, to the motor. It must maintain that ideal mixture throughout the throttle range. Piston action is always sucking air through the carburetor during intake pulses.

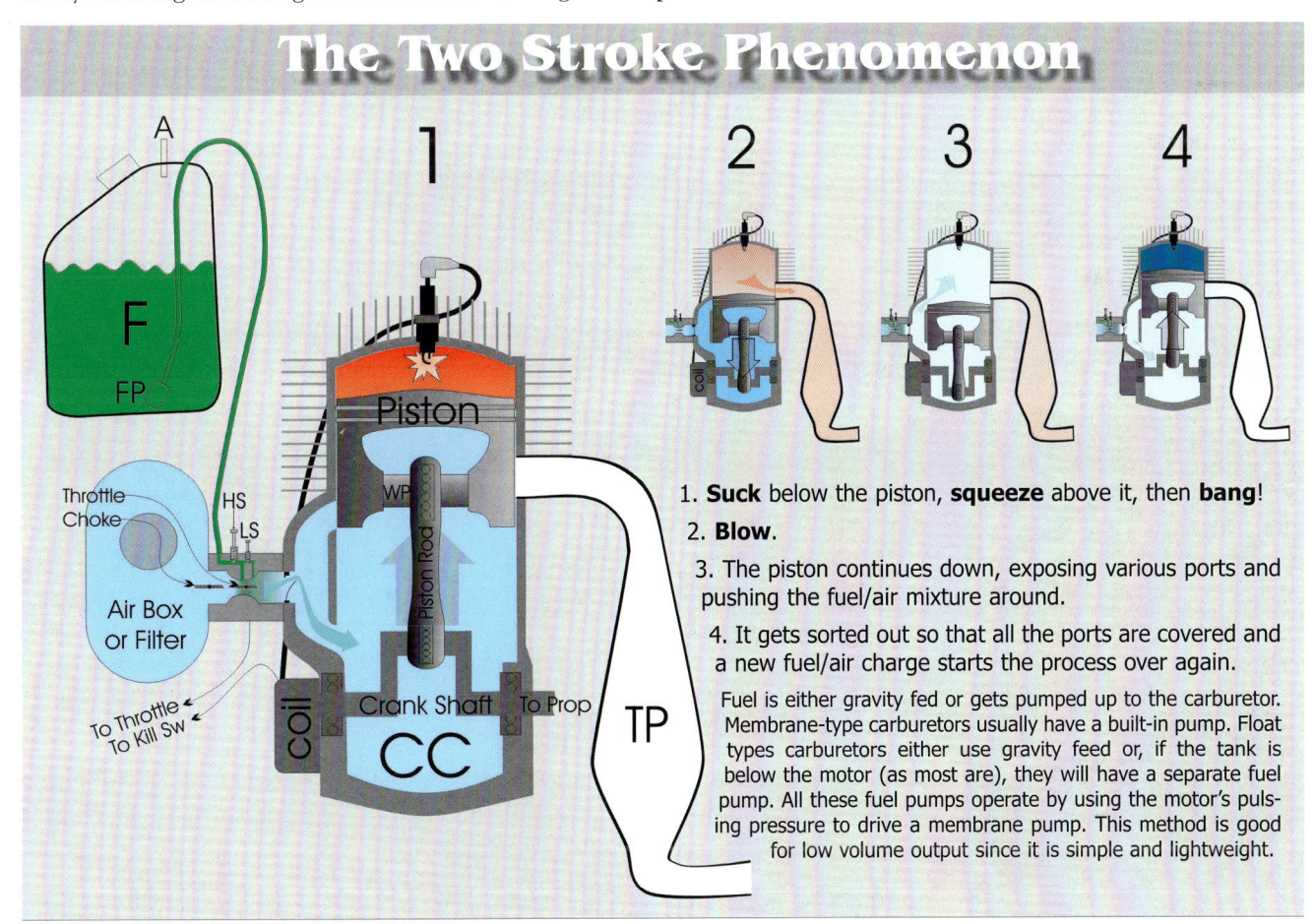

The Two Stroke Phenomenon

1. **Suck** below the piston, **squeeze** above it, then **bang**!
2. **Blow**.
3. The piston continues down, exposing various ports and pushing the fuel/air mixture around.
4. It gets sorted out so that all the ports are covered and a new fuel/air charge starts the process over again.

Fuel is either gravity fed or gets pumped up to the carburetor. Membrane-type carburetors usually have a built-in pump. Float types carburetors either use gravity feed or, if the tank is below the motor (as most are), they will have a separate fuel pump. All these fuel pumps operate by using the motor's pulsing pressure to drive a membrane pump. This method is good for low volume output since it is simple and lightweight.

Left: The back of a Top 80 motor reveals some common features employed on re-drive equipped machines. The clutch, in this case has 3 *shoes* that move out to engage the clutch bell with the centripetal force of increased engine rpm. The prop is attached through gears to the clutch.

Right: The other side, showing some basic parts of a fan-cooled motor with the cooling shroud removed. The fan wheel blows air upwards where the cooling shroud redirects it over the motor's cooling fins. If the fan breaks, the motor will overheat in just a few minutes.

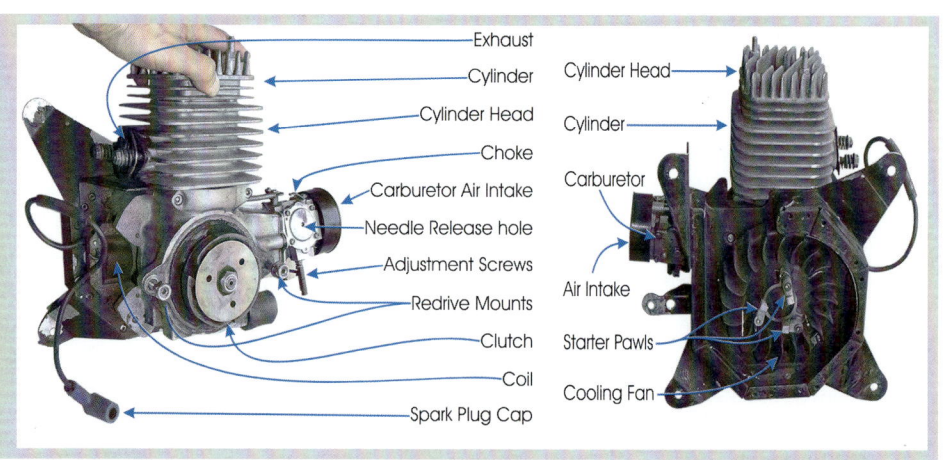

This pull starter assembly is what the starter pawls (see motor above) engage when you pull it. Springs hold them against the teeth, then when it starts, they ride over the back side of the teeth. At idle rpm, centripetal force pulls the pawls outward so they don't wear out riding on the teeth.

The primary structure of a carburetor is some sort of throttle valve that operates in a venturi, a constriction that lowers pressure to help suck fuel in as a fine mist (atomizing it). As the throttle valve is opened, more air gets sucked in, thus pulling in more fuel that gets mixed with it to speed up the motor. All carbs have various adjustments and/or interchangeable parts designed to optimize operation based on elevation and temperature.

Two types of carburetors are commonly used that differ in how they deliver fuel to the venturi: *float bowls* and *diaphragms*. As you can expect, each has advantages and disadvantages.

Float bowl carbs use a bowl and float just like those found in float bowl toilets. Fuel is delivered into the bowl through a valve. As the bowl fills up, a float inside rises to shut off incoming fuel which maintains a constant level. That offers a constant pressure at the pickup near the bowl's bottom. A higher float bowl level gives a slightly richer mixture and the converse for a lower level.

Fuel is sucked up from the bowl's bottom through the *main jet* (an orifice) into the venturi past a tapered needle. How far that needle goes into the jet determines how much fuel flows. The needle is attached to a *slider* that opens up the air passageway, exposing more of the venturi opening. Opening the throttle opens the air passage and, by lifting the needle, increases fuel flow. More fuel/air makes more power.

Once properly set up, float bowl carburetors generally proved a somewhat smoother throttle response with fewer adjustments except for big changes in elevation (more than a few thousand feet). When necessary, the *jets* (orifices really) can be changed to accommodate elevation changes—they change the opening through which fuel flows around the needle valve. Higher elevations require smaller jets since less fuel is needed to mix with the thinner air. Other minor adjustments can be available either by raising or lowering the needle position or changing fixed air inlets for idle.

Float bowl carbs must be oriented right side up lest the fuel run out of the bowl or the float not work. They must always maintain positive G-Loading, too, which isn't a problem given that, so too must your wing.

Membrane (or Diaphragm) carburetors work by filling a small expandable *metering chamber* with fuel then pulsing it into the venturi. This process uses changing crank case pressure and one-way valves within the carb. Fuel runs into the chamber when crank case pressure builds above a certain point, pushing against a needle valve held closed by spring pressure.

The design accomplishes its primary mission of working at any orientation as with chain saws. The membrane expands as fuel comes in through the inlet needle so it matters little whether the carburetor is right side up or sideways. The trade-off is a slightly more finicky nature. Small particles have myriad nooks to lodge in and the membranes, springs and other small parts can get worn or damaged although they're pretty robust given their small size and harsh environment.

Most of these carbs include a *high speed needle* and a *low speed needle* valve to allow fine mixture adjustments for their respective realm. These needle valves alter how much fuel passes by—unscrew the needle and it opening up for a richer mixture.

Tuning a Membrane Carburetor

If you have your motor's manual, or can get it, then that is your best information. Otherwise, this advice may help. If your motor strays too far from the recommended initial settings then there is probably a problem that tuning won't help. Consult the troubleshooting chart in chapter 12.

These basic guidelines apply to machines with membrane-type carbs having a low and a high mixture screw. The high screw primarily affects the mixture at high rpm while the low screw primarily affects the mixture at low rpm although they each have some affect throughout the throttle range.

First, a note about tuning. When a two-stroke motor is rich, it runs rough and sometimes fires every other stroke, that's called *4-cycling*. As you lean the mixture, it gets smoother and increases in rpm, eventually peaking then decreasing while remaining smooth. Further leaning makes it die. Whenever a needle controls fuel (as most do on membrane carburetors), screwing it in (turning clockwise) makes the fuel/air mixture leaner and unscrewing it makes the mixture richer.

Set the motor to its initial factory settings, strap it to something solid (tree, stout fence, stout friend, etc.) and start it. *Remember, more serious injuries occur from prop strikes than from flying.* It will start off lean and get richer as it warms up. After a minute or so, you're ready to begin the adjustments. Use increments of about an 1/8th of a turn when making changes.

Start by adjusting the low screw. Adjust it so the rpm peaks then unscrew it (enrichen) slowly until the rpm drops a bit. It should remain smooth. If the motor quits when throttle is applied, enrichen the low screw further. If it coughs or runs rough when throttle is applied, then lean it a bit.

Now to the high screw. Throttle up to full power. Just like before—you want to adjust the high screw until the rpm peaks, then back off (enrichen) a bit, about 50 rpm. This is called being slightly "rich of peak." It sacrifices higher fuel flow for cooler running—a good trade since a lean mixture can overheat and seize the motor. An excessively rich mixture makes carbon deposits on the cylinder head and spark plug. Better a little rich than lean!

With the high screw adjusted we need to recheck the throttle response. Try adding power quickly—if it runs rough, lean the high screw just a bit. If it dies, enrichen the high screw slightly. You may need to repeat this whole process once or twice.

Float Bowl Carb

The float-bowl carburetor doesn't need much tuning. But when you go to a significantly different altitude, you may have to screw in a different *jet,* an orifice that the needle (inset) slides into. A bigger jet lets in more fuel which richens the overall mixture. At higher altitudes, a smaller jet is required. They're made so that changing jets takes only a few minutes.

On this carb, the barrel slides up and down which also regulates the amount of air that flows through. The tapered needle, which is attached to the barrel, lets more fuel in as the barrel lets more air through. This generally gives a smoother throttle response since it provides a gradual but immediate increase in both fuel and air as the throttle opens. Besides changing jets, the only adjustments are for idle—a large screw (1) sets the idle stop up or down and a small screw (2) can change the amount of air let in; screwing it in decreases airflow, making the mixture richer.

Fuel comes up from the bowl that stays about 3/4 full to provide constant pressure to the orifice. A float valve keeps the level just like a float-bowl toilet keeps the tank at a constant level.

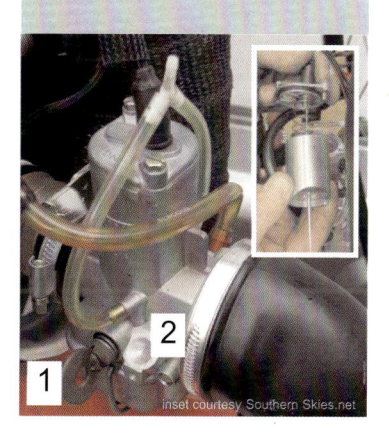

Membrane carburetors (left) are the most common type used for our motors. Their original use was for motors needing to operate in different positions such as chains saws. That also meant they needed to be lightweight—perfect for paramotors.

On this Walbro WG8 model the throttle is wide open and so is the choke. The choke is only closed for starting since a cold motor needs more fuel than air but only for a few seconds, then it's left open for normal operation.

The theory is that, as the throttle butterfly valve opens, airflow increases. It then sucks more fuel out of the jets (openings). As the throttle opens more, extra jets are exposed in an effort to provide the motor's ideal mixture through the entire throttle range.

Most membrane carburetors have two "circuits" that control the fuel/air mixture for high and low power. On the one shown here, there is only one circuit—for idle (1). Screwing it in leans the idle mixture. The other rod (2) is a throttle stop that controls how far open the throttle is at idle. Screwing it in increases idle by moving the throttle arm away.

The **reed valve** below, from a Black Devil motor, is simply a one-way valve that opens every time the piston draws in a new fuel/air charge. It's just like a heart valve.

The pointy part faces the cylinder and its reeds allow only inward airflow—they close if it tries to blow the other way.

The curved metal parts are strain relief—they make the reeds open around the curve thus preventing extra stress at the attachment points.

Higher elevations, above 3000 feet MSL, require leaning the mixtures. Once set, however, you should not have to adjust them until you change elevations again. Be especially careful to re-adjust them after going to a lower elevation because the mixture will be lean which risks overheating.

Anytime a nettlesome problem eludes you, consider replacing the carburetor whole. They are inexpensive, install easily, and can save many, many hours of headache. If that's not the problem, then you've got a spare carburetor on hand.

Pop-off Pressure and Other Membrane Carburetor Issues

The metering chamber is a membrane carburetor's version of the float bowl. An inlet needle reacts to incoming fuel pressure and vacuum in the venturi to keep the chamber nearly full of fuel, ready to deliver it to the various throttle circuits. *Pop off pressure* is how many pounds of air pressure it takes to lift the inlet needle against its spring.

If the inlet needle can't pop off the seat easily enough, the mixture will be too lean. If the spring is weak and the needle pops off too easily, excess fuel will make the motor run rich. Cutting the inlet needle's spring a bit shorter decreases the pop-off pressure and stretching it increases pop-off pressure. Only do this if you know exactly what you're doing, though.

Other little details can muck up the works too. Have a good fuel filter to keep unwanted debris from gumming things up. Carburetor rebuild kits are cheap and relatively easy to install. They usually replace the spring that determines pop-off pressure although that's rarely the problem. Rebuild kits will also replace the fuel pump membrane and a miscellany of gaskets and springs.

Reed Valves

Most modern two stroke motors employ reed valves (see sidebar at left) which increase efficiency. These stout one-way valves mount between the carburetor and motor. As the piston moves to compress the fuel/air mixture, the reed valve prevents that mixture from trying to go back into the carburetor. They do eventually wear out but are blessedly easy to replace.

Compression Release

Some motors come with a *compression release* (decompression) valve that makes pull starting easier. It works by venting the cylinder during compression. As soon as the motor fires, the valve closes. A few models have manual versions that must be reset after each start and others use just a small internal hole that goes from the cylinder head to the crankcase—these must be cleaned out about every 10 hours.

Propeller & Reduction Drives

A propeller is a rotating wing, pitched steeply at the center and flattening out to a skinny tip. Since the tip is moving very fast, it makes a shallow angle to the air. Strangely, the most efficient propeller would have only one blade since that blade would have the least amount of interference from the other blade's wake. The extreme imbalance would, of course, be problematic.

Propellers have a dramatic effect on a motor's performance. They are a case study in compromise. Matching the right prop to a motor is critical in harnessing the motor's power. Of the many compromises:

- Long, skinny blades are better for thrust but are harder to make strong. Plus the tips can't be allowed to go near supersonic due to noise and drag.

- Lighter is better for rpm acceleration but doesn't wear well in the presence of abrasives (beach sand and Illinois road gravel are good examples).

- Fewer blades are more efficient but more blades allow bigger motors to have a smaller prop diameter.

Tip Speed, Noise and Performance

The only thing that moves fast on a paramotor is propeller tips—and they move over 350 mph. That's more than half the speed of sound, also called Mach 0.5 where Mach 1 is the speed of sound. Any faster and supersonic shock waves start to form that are both noisy and draggy. Above Mach 0.6, (60% the speed of sound) the noise increases dramatically. When tip speed exceeds Mach 0.8, shock waves start adding drag in addition to the noise—more power gets used up overcoming the drag and creating noise.

High rpm is doubly bad for noise since, besides creating stronger sound waves, the waves come that much more frequently. Given the same tip speed, a small prop at high rpm will be louder than a large prop at low rpm.

The quietest combination for any motor is to spin the largest possible diameter prop (45 inches or more) at the slowest possible rpm. The large prop disk helps by having more clean air since it extends outward farther beyond the pilot's body.

Getting the RPM Right

Most two stroke motors get their best power at high rpm so a reduction drive lets designers extract maximum HP while keeping the prop at a more desirable (lower) rpm. Using gears or pulleys, a reduction drive lowers the output rpm to the prop by some ratio. If the input gear has three times as many teeth as the output gear then the ratio would be 3:1 (three to one). The motor would be spinning the small gear at 9000 rpm but the propeller, mounted to the large gear, would be going 3000 rpm. The extra weight and complexity of a reduction drive is well worth it.

Direct drive motors, where the prop is bolted to the crankshaft, are saddled with trying to balance the slower rpm needs of the prop with higher rpm needs of the motor. This noisy compromise offers small size in exchange

Reduction drives come in many ratios. The same housing is frequently used with different gears to give the user a choice. A larger ratio means the motor's high rpm will be converted to a lower prop rpm. The lower the prop rpm, the larger the prop can be.

The gears bathe continuously in gear oil. The prop is connected to the large gear in a ratio determined by the relative tooth count of each gear. This reduction drive utilizes four bearings, two for each gear, to keep things running smoothly.

for minimal thrust.

Since larger pistons typically get their horsepower at lower rpm, larger displacement motors have a better chance of working as direct drives but would give up enormous thrust potential. Larger pistons are heavier, though so most engines use a small piston that goes up and down *real* fast (high rpm). Small piston motors are lightweight but can't spin large props without a reduction drive.

For example, the Solo 210, a relatively large displacement motor (210 cc's), gets it's peak HP at around 6500 rpm. The Top 80, a small displacement motor (80 cc's), hits peak power at about 9500 rpm. The much-lighter Top 80, by virtue of its high rpm, can generate about 90% of the Solo's HP but there's no way the Top 80 could work as a direct drive.

Even for the slower spinning Solo 210, a direct drive arrangement doesn't work well. If you bolted a 48 inch prop directly to the solo and tried to get the motor running at 6500 rpm, the tip speed would be an impossible Mach 1.2. To get the tip speed manageable, a smaller prop must be used. Even with a 30 inch prop, the motor only spins up to about 5500 rpm—a noisy Mach .65 (noisy at that high an rpm). And it only gets about 80 pounds of thrust. That same motor, spinning a big prop through a reduction drive can easily put out a much-quieter 105 pounds of thrust.

One major prop maker recommends wooden PPG propeller tips never exceed Mach 0.75 and should remain under Mach 0.6 for quietness. Remember that Mach 0.6 at 3000 rpm will be far quieter than Mach 0.6 at 5000 rpm (smaller prop). And the quietest motors spin large props (48 inches or more) with tip speeds of less than Mach 0.5. On those machines the prop will likely be quieter then the motor, intake, redrive and exhaust.

Where the Thrust Is

Most thrust comes from outer half of the prop since it's moving the fastest and has the cleanest air. The blade gets thinner near it's tip which also makes it flex—mostly fore/aft but also some twist. Flexing forward does not affect thrust but could allow the prop to flex into the cage. A long prop will flex up to 2 inches (towards the cage) at full power. Twisting can reduce thrust and, if one blade twists more than the other, cause vibration since it will be pushing differently than the other blade(s).

The propeller *disk* is the area covered by its spinning prop. The pilot and harness disturbs the air passing into the prop which is part of why a large diameter propeller is more efficient—it sees more undisturbed (clean) air.

Pitch – A Bite of Air

A higher pitch equates to a higher angle of attack on the blades. Pitch is commonly described as how far the propeller would travel forward during one revolution if there was no slip. Propellers normally give two dimensions—length and pitch. So "48 by 23" means the prop is 48 inches long and would travel 23 inches forward during one revolution. Since the outer portions of the propeller travel a greater distance, the blade angle steadily decreases towards the tip but the *pitch* is the same. For various reasons, props are made with pitch that varies along the blade, but it's commonly measured 75% out towards the tip.

Calculating Tip Speed

If you're considering a different sized prop then you must take into account the ideal rpm and tip speed with respect to the speed of sound. Besides being loud, a lot of power is given up at high tip speeds.

Mach 1 is the speed of sound. It varies only by temperature and is faster in warmer air. At the standard temperature of 15°C (59°F) it is 761 mph.

To calculate tip speed as a mach number, use the following formula:

Tip Speed Mach = Prop rpm x prop diameter (in inches) / 256000. So a 48 inch prop spinning at 3000 rpm would have a tip speed of 0.56 Mach (56% the speed of sound).

Like a wing, more pitch means more lift (thrust) *up to a point*. Beyond that point it produces less thrust since the airflow separates early. But if the propeller is moving quickly forward, like on a fast airplane, then the angle of attack decreases. Some airplanes use *cruise* propellers which sacrifice slow speed thrust for more high-speed thrust. At paramotor speeds this effect is negligible—the difference between static thrust (no forward airspeed) and cruise thrust is too small to matter.

Prop angle of attack is highest when the pilot is just standing there. As he accelerates forward, the angle of attack decreases because now the air is hitting the prop with some speed. Props are designed with this in mind so that they actually produce slightly more thrust at 20 mph than they do with no speed although, for us, this difference is very small.

Some propellers have special hubs that let the pilot set the pitch to better match the motor. They have mechanisms for insuring that each blade gets the same angle. The greatest benefit of this arrangement is to determine the best prop pitch to combine with a particular motor and reduction drive.

Like wings, long skinny prop blades are generally more efficient but require more strength. That is why the more-expensive composite props enjoy some thrust advantage—they can be made skinnier while maintaining sufficient strength.

Tip shape affects noise—curves are quieter. Even the flat end should be rounded. Makers of higher speed props sometimes angle back (rake) the tips to reduce noise. Our props aren't fast enough to benefit from the technique.

Designing For Thrust and Quietness

When putting together design goals there are many options regarding propeller and redrive selection. **Lowest noise** means slow tip speeds and low rpm. **Maximum thrust** requires the most powerful motor you're willing to lift and the largest prop you can fit. The tips should spin fast but not more than about Mach .75 which is noisy but doesn't have too much sonic drag. The pitch can't be too high lest it lose efficiency. If you have more power than a two-blade prop can handle without over revving then you'll have to add more propeller blades. More blades can be quieter since the smaller diameter means the tips can go slower.

Left: These PPG props are getting ready for their final treatment by hand. Wood is well suited to this application although there is more variation in shape and strength than with carbon fiber props.

Chart: A lightweight prop is desirable because it spins up quicker. Weight towards the tips should be minimized the most.

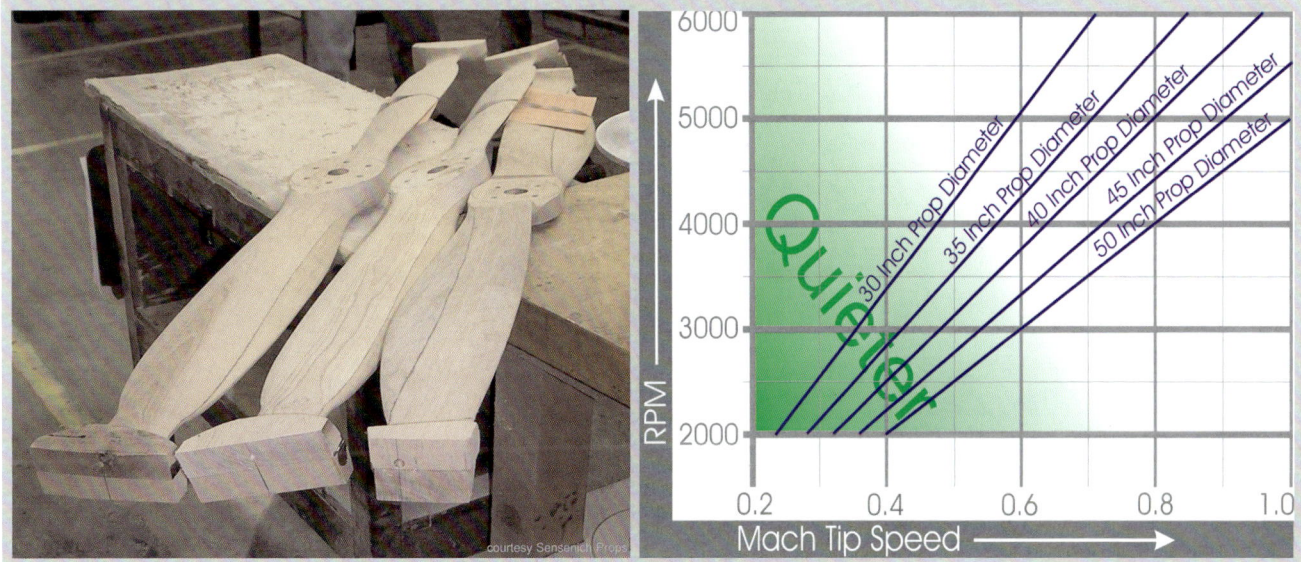

> **Horse Power Revisited**
>
> Your motor's horsepower turns torque into propulsion through the prop. In level flight, the resulting push can itself be measured as horsepower using the airspeed. HP = Thrust (lbs) x Airspeed (mph) / 375.
>
> For example, cruising at 30 mph with your motor pushing out 100 pounds of thrust, is 8 HP. The motor is probably putting 14 HP into the prop to achieve that. The difference is due to propeller inefficiency. Normally, cruise thrust is far lower but, with the trimmers out and speedbar engaged, it could easily require that much push.

Lets say, for example, that your motor turns out 25 hp at 8000 rpm and you're willing to heft a 48 inch propeller. For maximum thrust, you want the prop rpm to get the blade tips to hit Mach .75. Calculations (download the spreadsheet from www.FootFlyer.com/ppgbibleextras) show that the prop should spin at 3900 rpm which requires a reduction drive of about 2. At these tip speeds, it will be a screamer. Next you need to find a prop whose pitch allows the motor to accelerate to 8000. Too much pitch or too much prop area will bog down the motor without ever hitting 8000—that is called *over-propped*. Too little pitch and would *overrev*, probably causing internal motor damage. If you find that the pitch must be over about 26 inches, then you'll want more or bigger blades. Two-blade props are more efficient than 3 bladers which are more efficient than 4 but more blades are better than having too much pitch.

Materials: Rigidity and Strength

Propellers should be as light as they can be while being just strong enough to handle normal loads. That means they break easily when striking something other than air—a desirable construct for several reasons. When they hit things such as poorly designed cages, careless human parts or other undesirables, it is far better to sacrifice the propeller. That is why most PPG props are made of lightweight wood or carbon fiber material that shatters rather easily. Although the damage will *still* be severe, it will be minimized.

Frangible props also help prevent motor damage because, when hitting something, they transfer less energy to the crankshaft and other rotating parts. In certified aircraft, a prop strike requires an engine teardown and inspection.

Being lightweight also helps the prop spin up faster, especially if the weight is concentrated close to the hub. Rotational inertia is based on both weight and its distance from the center. Five pounds, centrally concentrated, will accelerate quicker than that same weight spread out near the tips.

Balance

CG, Hang Point and Thrust Line

The pilot/motor center of gravity (CG) is its balance point. It determines how the pilot hangs and whether he leans forward or backward in level flight. Machines with a heavy engine, or a light engine set far rearward, will have an aft CG that tends to tilt the pilot back. A lightweight pilot would also tend to make it lean back.

Center of Gravity is where the mass of the motor and pilot acts around. The motor pivots, however, around the hang points. If the thrust line pushes above the hook-in point then the motor will tend to tilt forward as you power up.

Although thrust always acts forward, you'll sometimes hear that "your thrust line is angled down" meaning that the air is blowing downward some amount.

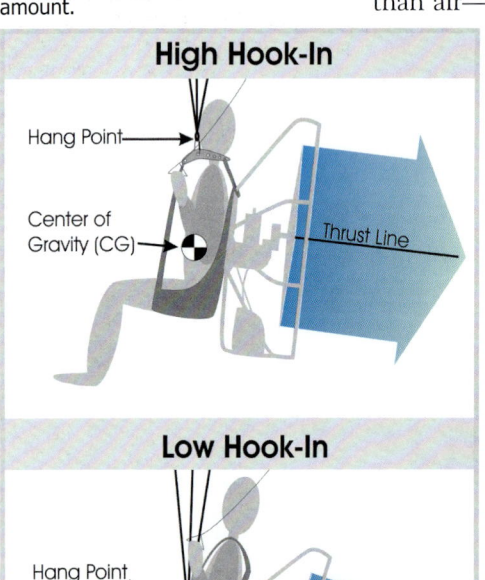

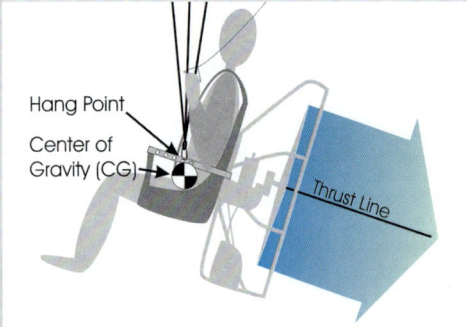

The hang point is where the carabiners connect to the harness (see Center of Gravity at right). Having the hang point well above the CG adds harness stability—the pilot will not move around as much in turbulence as with low hook-in points which are near the CG. This has no effect on wing stability.

Twisting Forces At Work

Several things conspire to cause turning when under power, most all are products of torque but other powerful ones exist. Techniques for overcoming these are covered elsewhere (mostly in Chapter 12) but one common cure is decreasing power. That will lessen (or eliminate) the tendency and solve most problems induced or aggravated by torque and its cousins.

There are serious misunderstandings of these forces that sometimes get fed by sales folks. Be wary of sellers who claim that one or another harness/feature solves all the problems—experience suggests otherwise. Chapter 12 describes methods to reduce twisting force and almost all paramotors can be adjusted to reduce it drastically.

Effects of Torque

Torque is the force that tries to twist the pilot around the propeller shaft in the opposite direction of propeller spin—nothing more. Just like turning a drill bit in wood—the drill and your hand want to turn opposite to the bit's spin. In flight, the paramotor is the drill and the propeller is the bit—it causes one riser to lower and the other to rise which induces a weight-shift type turn force. But that turns out to be very minor compared with the other effects.

Torque effects are always more pronounced with more powerful motors. The more thrust, the more torque, there is an incontrovertible physical relationship—it is why more power is not always better. The effects are:

Weight shift turn. This is the simplest and most common portion of torque. It gets wrongly blamed on most problems but is actually relatively benign. Even a full weight-shift turn on a motor moves the risers less than 6 inches (one goes up the other goes down) and this can be counteracted with medium brake. This force does *not* try to twist the pilot in the risers.

Offset thrust. This, in itself, is not a product of torque but torque can slide the motor into an offset position. The thrust line then starts pushing on a shoulder, causing your body (and the thrust line) to twist under the risers. It's just like having someone shove you on one shoulder on a swing set. As you twist, the thrust

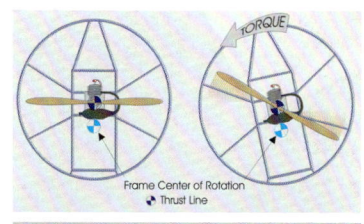

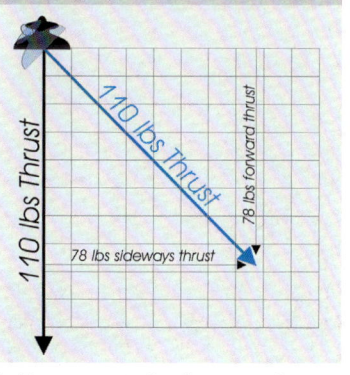

Off-Center Thrust

1. Torque can twist the motor into an offset position. It then pushes on the your shoulder, causing you to twist in the risers and re-direct the thrust line.

2. Once twisted, the thrust is no longer helping but rather spends itself pushing sideways into an ever-increasing bank. The only immediate solution is reducing power. This is the most powerful and common cause of power-related crashes. Chapter 12 covers adjustments that can nearly eliminate this problem.

The basic's of torque are simple enough - the prop spins in the air and tries to twist the pilot/motor in the opposite direction.

Torque can easily get skewed into trying to twist you under the risers. Riser tension is what prevents that. As you get into a steep climb, line tension decreases and you become more susceptible to riser twist. The only solution is immediately reducing power.

Many other factors, including wing selection, play a part in allowing torque to cause problems. In almost all cases, an experienced pilot or instructor can adjust out most twisting tendencies.

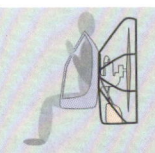

Weight Shift
With the motor perfectly upright, it pulls down the right riser when thrusting just like a right weight-shift turn. This effect is not terribly powerful and can usually be overcome with brake input alone on most machines.

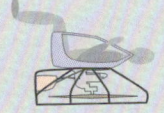

Horizontal Twist
This exaggeration of leaning back shows how the propeller spin would twist the pilot under the risers. The prop spins clockwise (when viewed from above) trying to spin the pilot/motor counter-clockwise.

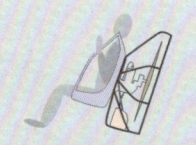

Mix
When mixed, the effect pulls down the right riser *and* twists left. The twisted thrust line pushes left which causes a right bank. The more angled back, the more pronounced the effect. It is the most common cause of pilots twisting under the risers.

Dangerous Torque

The most powerful and dangerous aspect of torque is that which acts around the vertical axis.

Whenever the motor is tilted back, part of the torque acts horizontally around the vertical axis—trying to spin you in the risers.

Your body twists left, the thrust pushes you left and the wing goes into a right bank. The bank gets steeper and the lines unload since you're not yet turning much. As the lines unload there is less resistance to riser twist which finishes the job as you helplessly whip around. Trying to stop the bank with brakes usually spins the glider.

The only solution when this happens in flight, is "Hands up, power off."

---

vector points more sideways, pushing you out into a potentially dramatic bank. Plus the thrust is no longer pushing your forward creating even more woe. It is possible to get twisted all the way around or get forced into a bank that brakes cannot counteract.

Vertical Axis torque. Also called the *horizontal component of torque*, this causes the vast majority of all problems and, on any motor that leans back, it tries to spin you around the vertical axis. The more lean, the more powerful the effect (see diagram above). It is best understood by envisioning a motor hanging so that the thrust line is straight down. The pilot is on his back, not sitting up. If he spins up the motor it will powerfully want to spin him in the risers. Now have the pilot start sitting more upright—there will still be an element of the torque that is acting in the same plane as the ground. If the pilot is sitting entirely erect (thrust line is exactly level with the ground) then this force does not exist.

Angled Thrust. If the motor hangs off the harness angled left or right then it will push sideways.

Many scenarios of torque-twist result in the pilot spinning the glider opposite to the direction of bank. Your body is pointed left, slowly twisting even more to the left while the wing is over to the right in a right turn. You don't want to go right and so you pull left brake which can stall the left wing and intimate a spin. The *only* solution for this is reducing power.

Gyroscopic Precession

This bizarre behavior of spin re-directs any force applied to a spinning mass 90° away in the direction of spin (See Precession Experiment, opposite page). This effect can be a factor during launch when you try to change the plane of the spinning prop, such as when you lean back at liftoff. Leaning back is the same thing as pushing backwards at the top of the prop plane—it will want to twist you right or left. If the prop spins clockwise (when viewed from the rear) then it will try to turn you right.

The force is proportional to the rotational mass and rpm. It's not a big factor for our craft but you can still feel it. Try it sometime—with the motor on your back, run it up and quickly lean forward. You'll feel it try to twist you some to the left or right depending on your propeller's direction of spin. But notice that, as soon as you're tilted, the force goes away, another reason why it has little real affect.

In flight, a very small amount of twist from this force could be felt due to uneven airflow on the propeller disk (see Transverse Flow below).

Rotational Mass Acceleration

If you've felt your car lean when stomping on the gas then you've noticed this effect. Any motor has a rotating mass—the crankshaft, flywheel, belts, propeller, etc. When that mass is accelerated, it wants to twist whatever it's attached to in the opposite direction. However, the effect goes completely away once the motor is up to speed—it is only present during rpm *acceleration*. On belt-driven machines the propeller spins in the same direction as the motor. On geared machines, the prop spins opposite to the motor's rotating mass so the effect is muted. Even then, the prop has far greater rotational inertia than the motor's rotating parts.

Sales people who claim that their gear-reduction product eliminates torque are engaged in hype or ignorance. The torque difference between geared and belted machines is *only* present during spin-up. In other words, that brief period where you go from idle to takeoff power. After that, torque is *identical* between belted and geared units (and in opposite directions). There is also some negligible difference in gyroscopic effects between the two types.

Transverse Flow or Uneven Thrust

Having part of the airflow blocked by the pilot/motor may induce a slight force left or right at the prop (up or down too but that would be less likely). The farther the prop disk is away from the hang points, the more pronounced the effect. Gyroscopic precession can aggravate this force by making thrust at the top act on the side, causing a twisting force.

Wing Enabled Riser Twist

Wing shape and lines play a large part in allowing or preventing riser twist. While the motor always *causes* the twisting force, the wing and lines work to prevent it. Short fat wings do better than others in this regard than long skinny ones.

It is quite simple: Angle the lines away from the pilot more and the wing will be more resistant to riser twist. Skinny wings (high aspect ratio) and long lines aggravate the problem. That leaves high-performance wings most susceptible since they are usually long and skinny with longer lines.

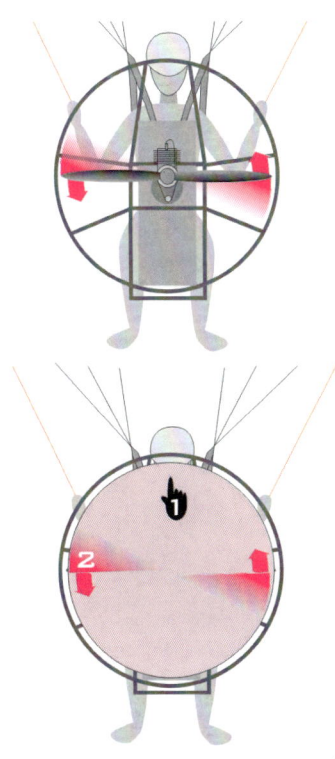

Gyroscopic precession happens only when the pilot tries to tilt such as when he leans for launch or goes back to vertical. Quickly tilting forward, for example, is like a force is pushing forward on the cage top (1). Precession causes that push to appear (be felt) 90° away (position 2) which would turn him to the right. It is brief and the strength depends on rpm, prop mass. and amount/speed of tilt.

Precession Experiment

Gyroscopic precession is the same force that keeps toy gyros from toppling over. As the gyro tries to fall over, the force keeps acting 90° away instead of actually falling over. More mass at more rpm makes the force stronger.

This experiment with a record shows the force in action.

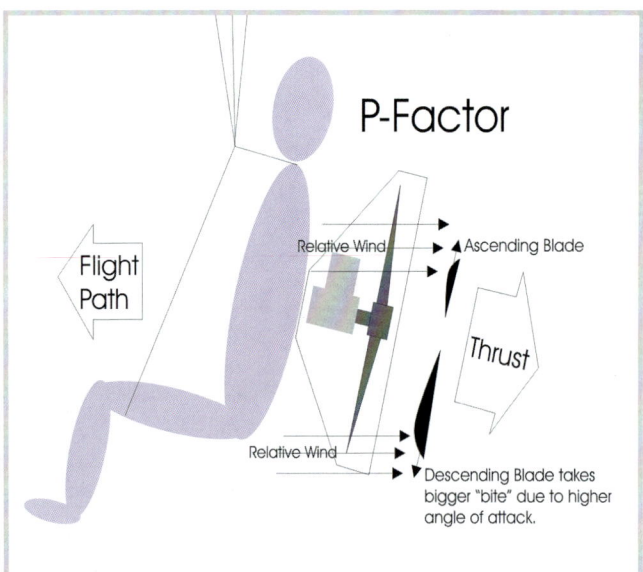

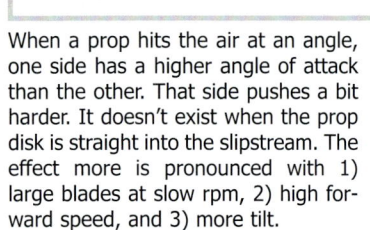

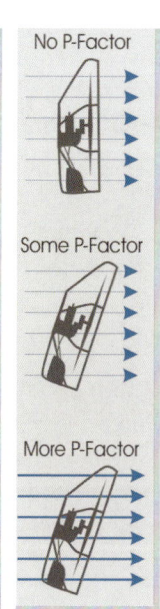

P-Factor

P-Factor, also called *Asymmetric Blade Thrust*, is what happens whenever the propeller disk is not hitting the air head-on. It results from one blade having more angle than the other due to the tilted relative wind. With the motor angled back (as is normal), the descending blade takes a bigger bite of air and pulls slightly harder.

Its effect is minor since it depends on the difference between forward airspeed and blade rpm. Our craft is too slow for it to be significant. The effect increases with more with more motor tilt or more airspeed but, even at it's worst, it pales when compared with the other twisting forces.

When a prop hits the air at an angle, one side has a higher angle of attack than the other. That side pushes a bit harder. It doesn't exist when the prop disk is straight into the slipstream. The effect more is pronounced with 1) large blades at slow rpm, 2) high forward speed, and 3) more tilt.

A few of these twisting forces are only present during your launch effort. Some show up as you stand up to accelerate, but the worst of them jumps to action when the wing lifts you into a leaned-back condition.

Weather & Wind

CHAPTER 24

You don't have to be a meteorologist to manage a useful understanding of weather. Grasping *micro*meteorology, however, is quite helpful and is our focus. Entire books are devoted to knowledge of atmospheric lore, a complicated puzzle that academia is still assembling. This chapter sticks to what is more useful to a powered paraglider pilot.

Most weather predictions revolve around the "big picture," stuff that can be left for the pros—frontal passage, strong winds, precipitation, etc. We're not interested in taking on such violence with our uniquely susceptible wings. However, on days where basically benign weather is forecast, knowledge of the little stuff will be invaluable. Some basics on the big stuff are provided for completeness. For more detail, see "Understanding the Sky" by Dennis Pagen.

Using Forecasts

You've learned the basics in Chapter 7 and should know how to get the forecasts. These extra details will help you interpret them and better understand what's going on. We can now delve deeper into the details: what happens around this one cumulus cloud, how does air behave in the presence of hills, what happens from the surface up to 100 feet and so on. Use professional weather people for the big picture and this knowledge for applying it to our smaller scale.

A forecast can be trusted more if what they expected earlier is becoming reality *right now*. It means the weather service grasps what's going on accurately. Otherwise their model is no longer valid—watch out. Did they expect a south wind and its actually from the northwest? If so, be suspicious of their remaining forecasts.

Sensing Weather

While out west one time, I was motoring along a 20 foot ridge that ran parallel and below a bigger mountain. I saw a chance to experiment; to see if my model of understanding the air worked.

Waning sunlight meant the ground was cooling, taking the adjacent air down with it. Indeed the bottom few feet was a good 4° to 5°F cooler than at 50 feet. The ridge had channels carved out where water drained to the lower level. I wondered—shouldn't the cool air try to drain down those channels and spill out at the bottom of the ridge?

It was otherwise calm so I should be a great little test. I flew parallel along the ridge's bottom where these culverts drained out and only a few feet high. Sure enough, as I passed along each one, there was a noticeable spill of air. It worked just as published!

Principles

Peeling the onion of atmospheric understanding can water the eyes. Deep physics underpins rules that can always lead to even more "whys." That stuff is beyond this book so the following basics are presented as some of our most important micrometeorology facts.

- Hot air rises.

- Cool air sinks and flows downhill to the lowest point, just like water.

- Air gets thinner with altitude. Pressure drops about 1 inch of mercury per 1000 feet. Sea level is the deepest reach in an ocean of air where, just like in deep water, pressure is greatest.

- *Radiant cooling* is the process whereby the earth looses heat into space just like a radiant heater can make your hands warm without warming the air. Solar heating is the warming part, where sunlight heats the land which then heats the air.

- *Conduction* is when terrain warms (or cools) the overlying air and *convection* is when heat is transferred by warm air moving into an area of cold air (or vice versa).

- The earth is always radiating its heat, day and night; much more so with clear skies since clouds reflect the earth's infrared energy back down. During the day the sun adds more heat than radiant cooling subtracts. When the sun comes up it starts heating the land and overcomes radiant cooling. Sun-facing hills or dark, dry spots warm up first.

- In a standard atmosphere (see below), air at higher altitudes is colder than at lower altitudes. The rate that it gets colder as you climb is the *lapse rate*.

- If you expand a parcel of air (increase its volume which also lowers its pressure), it cools. And it may so without external influence—that is what the term *adiabatic* means—no external exchange of heat. The reverse happens when you compress air like when it descends. Rising air that cools this way does so at the *Adiabatic Lapse Rate*. As it condenses into moisture, the rate at which it cools slows a bunch—that is the *Wet Adiabatic Lapse Rate*.

- Warm air can hold more water vapor (an invisible gas) then cold air. Further cooling of the air and its load of water vapor causes the water to change state (condense) into liquid as very fine droplets such as clouds or fog. The temperature where this occurs is called the *dew point*.

Standard Atmosphere

A standard atmosphere is what meteorologists use in order to have a common point of reference. It is also used by aircraft makers (and others) on which to base performance.

The International Standard Atmosphere (ISA) is 0% humidity, 59°F (15°C) and has a pressure of 29.92 inches of mercury (Hg) at sea level. For every 1000 feet of height, the temperature decreases by 3.5°F (2°C) which is the standard *lapse rate*, and the pressure falls by about 1 inch of mercury (Hg). So at 3000', you would expect the pressure to be 27.92 inches Hg and the temperature to be 10.5°F cooler or 48.5°F.

Daily Cycles

Depending on your local terrain there is an underlying daily cycle that represents the norm. Experienced local pilots know it best which is why they can provide such valuable input. This cycle can be as powerful as it is predictable—at some locations there are very specific places and times that flying is very dangerous owing to these daily cycles.

Since the cycle is driven by sunlight, clouds usually reduce its intensity, but clouds and pressure systems may point to some greater atmospheric change that will overpower the daily cycle; notch up your concern a bit at such times.

Radiation Cycle

Overnight, the ground radiates heat into space, cooling off the land. The land in turn, cools the air just above. That increasingly chilled (and therefore heavier) air tries to sink, finding its way into low spots. The cooling ground is like an ice cube—it just keeps cooling the air nearby. If the air cools enough, some of its water vapor condenses into fog or onto the cold surfaces as dew. This is why low spots get foggy first—cool air flows downhill. All this cooling inverts the normal atmospheric temperature gradient. Instead of being cooler aloft, a cooler layer along the ground forms so by morning the coldest air is at the surface. At some point up higher (maybe only a few hundred feet) there is a significant increase in temperature called the *inversion*. Above that, the normal temperature gradient of cooling with altitude resumes.

Sunrise is typically a very stable time—cool air sits in low places, with no desire to go anywhere. The sun starts heating the land right away while heat loss from radiation continues. Soon, around a half-hour past sunrise, the sun's heating wins out and temperatures begin to rise. Dry, dark spots heat up first and the air above those tries to rise. Hills that face sunward will heat up even more in the direct rays. Soon these warmer areas become the day's nascent thermals. They are joined by many others as the day wears on, mixing and warming the atmosphere.

As air rises, it expands and cools. As long as it stays warmer then the surrounding air, it will rise. Eventually the cooling due to expansion exceeds the atmosphere's normal lapse rate and the upward movement stops. With enough moisture present, it would form clouds when cooled to the dew point.

As the day wears on, thermals get stronger and go higher. Cloud bases go up too. Solar heating peaks at noon but this process peaks a couple hours later. Late afternoon's decreasing sun angle finally takes its toll and the process wanes although cloud bases keep rising. Thermal strength can easily be dangerous up to within a couple hours of sunset depending on location.

At sunrise, there is typically an inversion—warmer are just above the ground. The ground has cooled after giving up heat into space, cooling the adjacent air.

The sun starts heating it up, producing thermals that begin mixing.

By mid-day, the normal lapse rate exists where it is warmest at the surface. If enough moisture is present, cumulus clouds will form atop thermals.

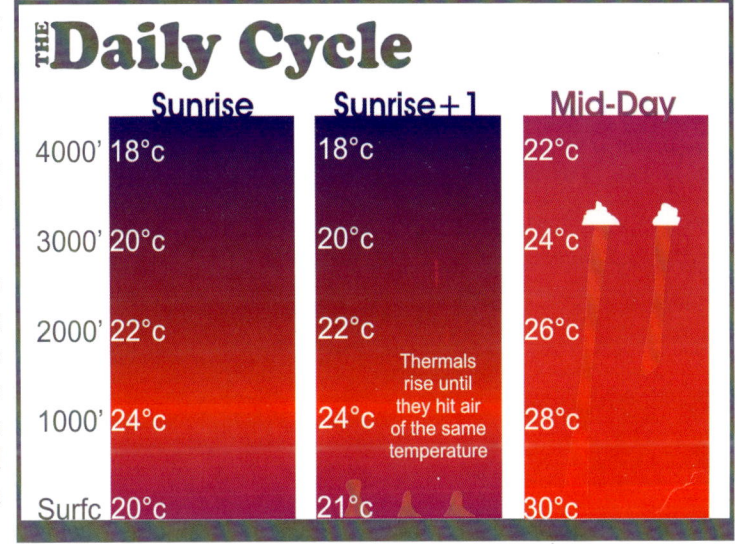

The Daily Cycle

	Sunrise	Sunrise+1	Mid-Day
4000'	18°c	18°c	22°c
3000'	20°c	20°c	24°c
2000'	22°c	22°c	26°c
1000'	24°c	24°c	28°c
Surfc	20°c	21°c	30°c

Thermals rise until they hit air of the same temperature

Flatland

In flat areas there is little beyond the daily cycle and large scale changes. Afternoons can be dangerously turbulent during periods of instability so stick with the first and last 3 hours of sunlight, especially in the summer.

Typical days start out smooth with nearly calm winds in the morning. These can be wonderful times to fly—smooth and pristine. The "dog days of summer" describe the flatlander's heyday—calm mornings and evenings with sultry afternoons of light breezes.

If the wind aloft is very strong, expect it to get bumpy quickly. Wind and thermals don't mix well. You'll know soon after launch what the wind is doing. In fact, it's not difficult to climb up into a perfectly smooth wind that matches or exceeds your airspeed. You wind up parked over one location (or moving backwards) while facing into the wind. It's strange and can happen pretty low. This is a wind gradient and the smoothness will be short lived once sunlight churns up the air.

Hilly

Surprisingly intense micro meteorology happens when air interacts with hills—even before the sun comes up. That's why flying in mountainous areas warrants so much attention. As air cools it tries to flow downhill, sometimes becoming a torrent. Like an avalanche, it gathers speed, causing rapid wind changes. Mountain passes, or anywhere that geographic constrictions squeeze the flow, adds intensity just like a wide, mellow river that narrows to rapids in tight places.

Hills also interfere with larger scale movements and mask winds. If the air is forced to go up or around a geographic protrusion you can expect turbulence in the lee (downwind of it). Be careful if launching in a valley with calm air but a known wind aloft—up near the level of the mountain tops could be a wild ride. And that turbulence *can* come down well below the peak's height.

Coastal

The beauty of a beach is in its smooth predictability. Usually by 11 AM the warmer land is sucking air in a steady *sea breeze* that makes launching painless. Free of thermal turbulence, this airflow from the water is usually very smooth. Most of the time the wind continues well past sunset. The cycle reverses at night when the land cools off and a *land breeze* sets in with wind blowing out to sea.

Digging Deeper: State Change

A significant impact on weather is the *state* change of water—going from ice to liquid to gas. Its lowest energy level is ice—if you add heat (energy) to ice it will warm up at a constant rate until it gets to the melting point (32°F). It will remain at that temperature while absorbing the heat until changing to the new state at which point it continues warming.

For example, put a 10°F block of ice in a 300°F oven and stick a thermometer in the ice. The ice will warm gradually until hits the melting point (32°F) where it momentarily stops warming as it changes from ice to water. The difference in energy between the two states is called *latent heat*. So immediately after changing from 32°F ice to 32°F water it is said to have gained some latent heat energy. The water will now continue warming at a steady rate until it reaches the boiling point (212°F) where it will again stop warming to change state from a liquid to a gas. Then the water vapor will continue warming.

Sublimation is where water vapor comes directly from ice. Evaporation is where liquid water changes to gas even though it's below the boiling point. As it evaporates, it cools the surface from which it evaporated. All evaporative coolant systems rely on this principal. The higher the temperatures, the more sublimation or evaporation happens.

The reverse happens during cooling. As water vapor cools, it does so evenly until becoming a liquid (like cloud). As it makes the change, it resists further cooling for a period of time until the state has fully changed.

These physics drive the formation of severe weather—giving teeth to a process that would otherwise peter out. It helps thunderstorms reach momentous heights and powers a hurricane's horrendous winds. If lifted air is cooled quickly, it would soon become the same temperature as the surrounding air and lose its buoyancy. The process would die out. But water vapor will hold it's temperature while rising because it needs to make that state change. Its buoyancy will remain as it slowly changes state from a vapor to liquid. This phenomenon happens on smaller scales, too, and pilots refer to it as *cloud suck*—where the cloud formation itself is driving the lift instead of the original thermal. Air mixing with the cooler surrounding air is what prevents it from shooting out of control.

One risk is when a prevailing off-shore wind gets overcome by the sea breeze. A few miles inland the wind is blowing out to sea but, on the beach it is coming on shore. Somewhere in the middle these two airflows meet in a potentially turbulent *convergence zone*. Besides turbulence, if the prevailing off-shore breeze wins the pushing contest, it will be trying to blow you over the water.

Desert

Deserts are beautiful in their own dry, rugged way. And they spawn the strongest, meanest thermals in the country—making for a wild daily cycle that can be much more dramatic than in wetter areas. It happens because the sun's rays don't get used up in evaporation—they go right into heating the ground.

One indicator of thermal strength is the difference in temperature from morning low to afternoon high—something deserts have to extreme.

These factors combine to make mid-day desert flying a spin of the roulette wheel.

Dust devils are the visible manifestation of a violent phenomenon that causes a rapid swirl of air as thermals surge upwards. These little tornadoes may also be occurring up high but would be invisible.

Flying the desert is beautiful in the mornings and evenings, but deserves great respect during mid-day.

Yearly Cycle

Many yearly cycles exist besides the obvious temperature swings: the monsoons of Tucson and Phoenix, the dry period of Portland, hurricane season, Santa Ana winds, etc. Some of these involve winds erupting with little warning. Long term local knowledge can be a life saver—if you don't know a local pilot, seek one out from the nearest airport. Most are happy to answer such questions as "I'm gonna be flying an ultralight in the local area, is there any significant seasonal weather I should know about?"

The most prevalent and relevant cycle, though, is thermal intensity. It follows the length of day where thermals are strongest in summer and weakest in winter. That makes sense—their driving force is sunshine and summer solstice packs many more heating hours and at a more direct angle than winter's shortest day.

The difference can be a dramatic. Long hours of direct sunlight heat up the ground, boiling its atmospheric soup into a sporty cauldron. The short days of winter get only a few hours of low-angle light leaving many smooth but chilly days to fly. Winter even tames the deserts enormously.

All About Thermals

A lot has been written on this topic but anyone who has watched a 1970's lava lamp (pictured at left) knows the process: sun-warmed patches of ground heat the air immediately above, making it want to rise. At some point this warm air blob pushes up through the overlying cooler air to begin its ascent. Air rushes in below to fill the vacated mass, now surging upward. Free flyers ride these rising currents to sometimes great heights. Most motor pilots typically avoid them and their related turbulence. Some

1. If you see this coming your way, unclip! Then pack up. If you're airborne, stay well away but land when your LZ is clear.

2. Brian Smith is chasing the swirling cauldron of a moderately strong but long-lasting dust devil in Albuquerque, NM with an anemometer. The overall winds that day were light but, even after several minutes, this was likely spinning air at over 30 MPH.

motor pilots use them for soaring and simply accept the increased risk.

Thriving thermals need the right type of atmosphere. Primarily that means a steady decrease in temperature with altitude (lapse rate), direct sunlight and a heatable surface. An overcast will douse the process dramatically which is why you can frequently fly safely all day long on cloudy days (as long as no rain is expected) even in the middle of summer.

Telling Thermal Intensity from the Ground

A good way to predict thermal turbulence from the ground is by wind gusts. Stand in one place or just be observant while setting up. Calm conditions on the ground portend calm air above while gusty conditions suggest lumpy air aloft. Sharp gusts, where the wind speed or direction changes rapidly, indicate sharper, more dangerous thermals.

Flying on a day with rapid gusts from 5-12 mph could be deadly where soft changes of the same magnitude might be manageable. Direction must be watched too—if it goes from east at 12 mph (the wind is coming from the east blowing to the west) and suddenly switches to west at 5—that is bad.

Thermals and strong wind don't mix. Gusts from mechanical turbulence add to energetic thermals to make potentially dangerous air.

Dust devils show that, even away from the swirl itself, the atmosphere is particularly turbulent. Any day brewing sufficiently vigorous turbulence to trigger dust devils is brewing nasty conditions.

Where Thermals Thrive

Cross country soaring pilots know where to find the "biggest air"—a description for powerful thermals that can carry pilots skyward at well over a 1000 fpm. Associated turbulence can play havoc on a paraglider. The immediate spiral that spurts from from such a collapse may require immediate and correct action or a reserve toss. Every year, it seems, at least one experienced free flyer succumbs to an unpleasant fate in "big air."

Dryer air breeds more dramatic thermals. Arid regions consistently give soaring pilots the highest altitude gains and longest soaring flights.

The *lifted index* is an atmospheric measurement that tells whether a parcel of lifted air will be warmer or colder than its surroundings after reaching a certain height. Negative numbers mean the parcel is warmer—it wants to accelerate upwards. That's unstable. It has to do with the atmosphere's lapse rate and moisture content. In an atmosphere that gets cold quickly as you climb, a lifted parcel of air would tend to remain warmer and therefore keep rising. Moist air rises more readily because water vapor is lighter than dry air. Lifted index charts can be found on the Internet although you'll need additional study to really know how to use them.

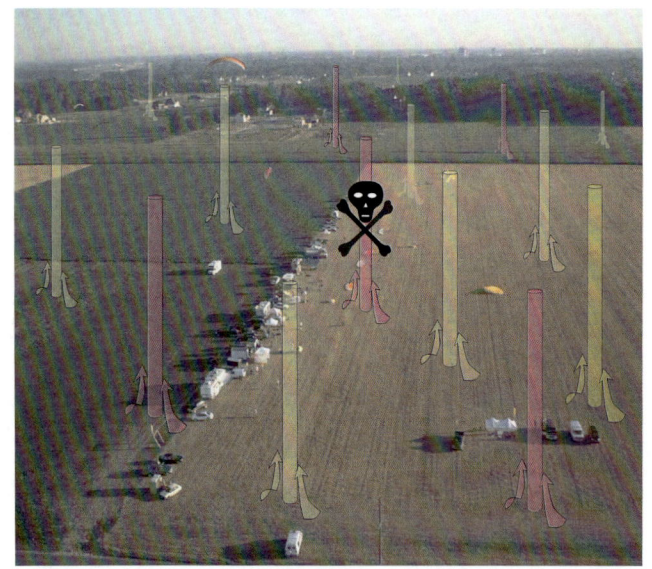

This illustrates the distribution of thermals on a bright, summer day. Yellow represents moderate thermals, red represents strong ones, and the skull represents dangerous versions that would make bad shapes of your paraglider. How many of these dangerous thermals exist depend on many factors, but the distribution is such that you could fly for a long time in mid-day and simply be lucky—not hitting one. Or you could hit one the first time out on such a day.

Summer afternoon's invisible fury should not to be treated lightly.

Clouds

The highest clouds, *cirrus* (or *cirriform*), are wispy affairs comprised of ice crystals. They form above 25,000 feet and can sometimes spread out from jet contrails. Mid-level clouds live between about 8000 and 25,000 feet. They're usually prefaced with the word *alto* (e.g. *altocumulus* and *altostratus*) and mostly only concern our micro view for their value in blocking out thermal-producing sunshine.

> ⚠ **Caution!**
> If a dust devil is present, don't even be hooked into your glider. Kiting is equally dangerous under such conditions.

Stratiform

Stratus clouds are the flat, boring clouds that form mostly on weekends. They generally indicate stable conditions with little vertical movement. If they drop rain, they're called nimbostratus.

Smooth and frequently layered, stratus clouds are usually associated with fairly benign weather although they *can* conceal significant ugliness. They frequently follow fronts and occupy large swaths of low pressure areas. The two worst worries of flying under stratus clouds are rain and imbedded thunderstorms. However, if neither is forecast, then all-day flying may be possible. By blocking the sun's most direct heating rays, they block most of the thermal-induced turbulence, leaving good, but bleak, motoring conditions (and lousy soaring conditions).

Stratus clouds must not be ignored when the forecast includes rain showers. It's hard to tell where the rain showers are and, with thicker clouds, its easy to get rained on by surprise. If you see a darkening in the sky then it's most likely because of embedded cumulus clouds which indicate coming trouble.

Stratus clouds that form around severe weather are particularly dangerous in that they conceal where the really bad weather is. That is why its important to know the forecast and only fly on forecasted dry days.

Cumuliform

When vertical development gets involved the term *cumulo* (having a heaped on appearance) gets appended or preppended to cloud names. Cumulus clouds that form mostly on nice summer afternoons cap thermals and indicate bumpy conditions. Any cloud with more then about 3000 feet of vertical development can produce rain. Once a cloud produces rain it earns the *nimbus* moniker: Cumulonimbus is the most violent example and is what thunderstorms come from.

The wispy beginnings of cumulus clouds typically form about 3 hours after sunrise and a few thousand feet high. If a steady breeze has picked up within a couple hours of sunrise *and* cumulus start popping, expect sporty air. Dry air could be just as sporty but without the cumulus clouds.

You must pay very careful attention to cumuliform clouds. What goes up must come down and thunderstorm sized cumulus clouds can cause strong downdrafts that spread well away from the ground in a *gust front (see below)*. Little ones are felt all the time, both from popping thermals

Stratiform clouds usually indicate benign conditions. Be sure you can see everything though, they sometimes hide cumulus clouds.

Christine Doughty is flying over a low scattered to broken layer in smooth air. She had good ground contact, good visibility and was able to stay clear of clouds. Had she been above 1200' AGL, she would have needed more cloud clearance (see Chapter 9 for all the airspace details).

Testing It Out

One summer afternoon, thunderstorms were coming through like waves. It had been a while since my last flight and I felt the need for air. So, just after a nasty storm passed by, I drove to my nearest field to see what conditions were like.

The air was perfectly still.

Unfortunately, there on the horizon was an early darkening of the western sky. Oh but it was so calm—and quiet. Alas, my sensible side prevailed and I decided against it.

By the time I got back inside, only 15 minutes later, an enormous gust front erupted—trees swayed and the house groaned.

It would not have been a good time to be aloft.

1. An old but appropriate axiom.
2. The zoom makes this menacing storm appear much closer then it actually is. However, thunderstorm wrath can extend tens of miles beyond the cloud itself.

sucking in air, and from sinking air spreading out. But bigger cumulus or lines of cumulus can cause gust fronts tens of miles away.

Be leery of wandering too close to large cumulus clouds. The cloud formation process itself generates extra lift which increases as you near the base. This *cloud suck* can easily overpower a paraglider pilot's ability to descend. Getting caught in such lift is a chilling experience which some pilots have not survived. Depending on the cloud's size, it can easily take you to heights where the temperature is well below freezing and the air is too thin to keep you conscious. And, of course, it's extremely violent.

Thunderstorms

Nature's fury is unleashed in the majestic and deadly thunderstorm. These mammoth storms, covered in Chapter 7, play havoc with winds over a broad area.

They come in two types: airmass and frontal. Airmass thunderstorms are usually scattered buildups on otherwise nice but muggy summer afternoons. They are typically not as severe. Normally airmass storms germinate in aging high pressure areas with lots of moisture and some instability in the air.

Frontal storms come in lines and are associated with fronts, usually cold fronts. They produce the worst weather including tornadoes.

When an atmosphere is unstable enough to produce thunderstorms it is no place for a paramotor. In most cases, two hours after a storm passes is enough to consider flying as long as there are no more storms (or cumulonimbus clouds) anticipated. First, find out what the weather is doing elsewhere before taking off.

Gust fronts are probably the thunderstorm's most dangerous fallout. Rain pulls cold air downward until it hits the ground and spreads out in a fast-moving, turbulent boil that can extend many miles from the storm. Although technically related only to thunderstorms, gust fronts happen in different degrees from other causes, too.

Fronts

These really belong to *macrometeorology* and are not covered in great detail. Fronts are the boundaries between air masses of different temperatures. They get moved around by high level winds, frequently swirling around low pressure areas. Low pressure areas arise from many causes including high level winds, called *jet streams*, which can suck air upwards under some conditions. Low-level air tries to flow inward to fill the low pressure and gets turned by Coriolis effect (the result of a spinning world)—thus the low spins, dragging fronts along with it.

Cold fronts are the most violent. Cold air wedges under a warm air mass ahead, lifting it quickly and creating lines of cumulonastiness. These fronts spawn the worst of all thunderstorms because they combine several powerful forces. Fortunately, they are usually fast moving; doing their damage and moving on.

Warm fronts ride over retreating cooler air and are more typically wet and mellow. Be careful for they do sometimes harbor thunderstorms in the stratiform mass of clouds. Unfortunately, they tend to linger and can muck up the weather for quite some time.

Lots of bad weather happens near fronts. If there is a forecast for frontal passage, even if no rain or clouds are present, be very wary of flying. Check out the wind forecast—there can easily be a dangerous and dry wind shift planned that you should avoid. If you're out on the field, unusual, especially sudden, temperature changes should lead to suspicion. For example, a day that gets to 80°F by noon but then forecasts a temperature drop to 70°F by afternoon would likely have a wind shift. That is a dry cold front—you would want to avoid flying until after the wind shifted since it could easily be violent.

Getting Weather Info

Chapter 7 covers acquiring weather through Flight Service. But a good way to improve your awareness of what's happening aloft is get the weather at locations around your site, especially upwind of it. It's not foolproof, and it doesn't work as well in mountainous regions, but it's a good start.

Be aware that the surface wind is not a good indication of where the weather is coming from. Look at the clouds and see which way they're moving. Different cloud layers may well be moving different directions; you're most interested in the low to mid-level layers (between 3000 and 10,000 feet).

TV is a reasonable source for weather information but the internet is much better; you can customize what you're looking for and probably get more detail on your particular area. Sites come and go but you can find links to good ones on www.FootFlyer.com.

Turbulence from Wind

There are some important differences in what pilots frequently lump into the term *rotor*. Knowing what those differences are could be a life-saver.

Mechanical turbulence is the general bumpiness that extends downwind from anything that sticks up into a wind, up to 20 times the obstacle's height. The resultant eddies drift with the wind and spread upward above the height of the causing obstacle. Turbulence extends further downstream as wind speed picks up. So, too, does intensity and quite dramatically—a 15 mph wind will have over double the intensity of a 10 mph wind.

Rotor itself is a stationary swirl of air that spins immediately downwind of the causing obstruction. It can be very powerful and produce incredibly strong shear since it's so well organized. Rotors don't always form—it depends on the obstruction's shape, wind speed and wind gradients.

Wind shadow is the calm that exists just downwind, and usually at the bottom, of an obstruction. Its what you feel when seeking shelter from the wind behind a building (or other obstruction). It extends about to the height of the obstruction. Picture your paraglider moving from that stillness out into the free airstream. That would be bumpy.

1. A localized front near Phoenix, AZ. Fortunately, the dust makes it quite visible. These happen on various scales from a few miles to over a hundred miles and the results are always dangerous.

2. Another type of localized front that was spawned by a line of cumulus clouds. Virga (rain that evaporates before reaching the ground) was an early indication of dangerous gusts that were soon to hit the ground.

Also, avoid dark bottomed clouds, they indicate there's a lot of vertical development above with potential turbulence.

In a light wind, less than about 5 mph, mechanical turbulence and rotor are almost non existent—flying next to obstructions poses little problem.

Mountain Waves

When a strong wind blows perpendicular to a mountain range, there may be mountain wave downwind of the range. It can extend many thousands of feet above the mountain but our real concern is what happens below the wave action—rotor. Besides the main rotor, powerful eddies cause turbulence that even sailplanes try to avoid—no place for a paraglider. It extends from just below the mountain's crest sometimes down to the surface.

Terrain and Flow

Whenever air is squeezed between two hills, the speed will pick up. It's just like where a river narrows, it speeds up. In a craft as slow as ours, that could stop all forward motion. Fortunately for power pilots, we have the option to throttle up and climb away from this *venturi effect*.

When air is forced up over obstructions it causes lift just upwind of the obstruction. Ridge lift, as its called, remains fairly smooth as long as there are no thermals in it and the pilot stays upwind or over the causing obstruction. The obstruction's shape determines the strength of the lift—a smooth, steep rise in the face of a steady wind creates the most lift. Terrain can also act like an airfoil where the air goes over the top then back down the back side, sticking to the surface and creating sink. For example, flying just downwind of a tree line can create enough sink to make climbing difficult or impossible.

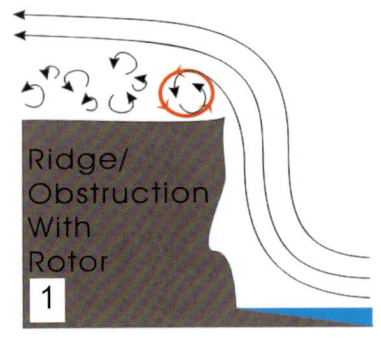

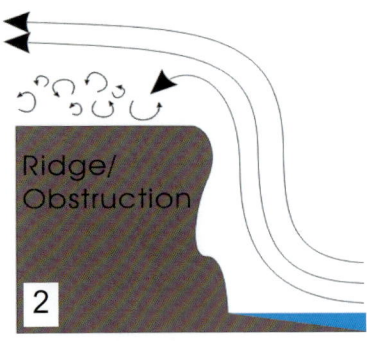

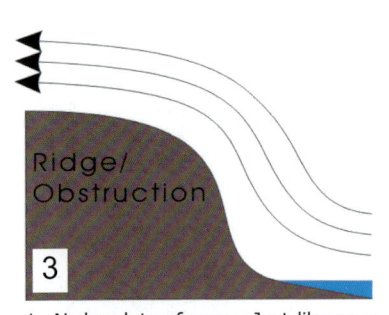

1. Air has lots of mass. Just like over an an airfoil, it won't make sharp bends. So when you envision the airflow past obstructions, expect turbulence and dramatic changes in the area of those bends. This shows that the air cannot stick and creates a standing rotor.

2. The lip of this ridge is sharp enough to create turbulence but not enough to create a standing rotor.

3. This smooth ridge would be perfect for soaring. If you stand near the lip of a sharp edge, you'll feel very little wind on your face. Setting up to launch there would be difficult at best. But on a curvy ridge, like #3, the wind flows steadily along the smoother surface—a much easier launch proposition.

Digging Deeper: Highs And Lows

Areas of high and low pressure resemble swells on the ocean but on a very, very large scale, spanning hundreds of miles. The troughs are low pressure and the peaks are high pressure. Air moves, in some ways, like a big slinky; piling up both vertically and horizontally. For example, it's possible to have the air pile up high in the atmosphere. It will, of course, start falling down but air has a lot of mass and that will take time.

Other forces act to lift air and pile it up in different ways. For example, the Jet stream has influence. It can start moving air upwards into the jet, creating a low pressure area.

A hurricane is a good example of another force that forms a low pressure area. Warm water feeds a group of thunderstorms that create enormous lifting force. They're like a bunch of vacuum cleaners, accelerating air upwards and spitting it out the top. Air flows into this continuous low pressure and gets turned by the Coriolis effect (like the marble that you roll inward on a rotating record). Rotation keeps pressure low because the air can't fill in the center low. That's why hurricanes cannot form on the equator—there's nothing that causes them to rotate. You get low pressure areas at the equator, but air is able to fill them in fairly quickly since it's not deflected into a spin.

Why do lows get the bad rap? Almost by definition, the air in a low is being sucked (or lifted) upwards. The motion is too slow to feel from the ground or even in flight, but is enough to cool the air which tends to form clouds. Air in a low winds up concentrating the forces since it's flowing inward and upward, even while spinning around the low. But high pressure air is generally descending and heading outward. Conservation of energy means that airflow decreases as it moves away from the center of pressure.

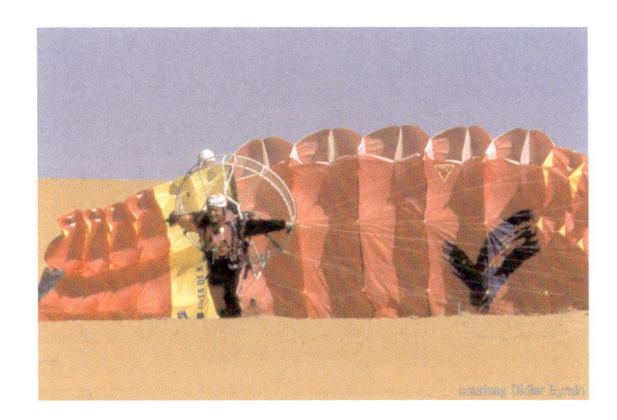

Roots: Our History

CHAPTER 25

Frenchman Didier Eymin has done photo work using a paramotor all over the world. He is here pictured taking off with one his first machines in the early 1990's.

It's a short history. Powered paragliding grew from the sport paragliding which itself has only been around since the 1980s. There are actually a number of roots, not all contributing to the same tree but growing in an underbrush of ultralight flying that prospered simultaneously.

Parasailing

You will soon tire of hearing your sport called parasailing. After all, you *ride* under a parasail; you *pilot* a PPG. Not that there is anything wrong with parasailing—it's a fun activity to be sure—but it is essentially a brainless amusement for the parasailer. A necessarily stable platform gives the rider almost no control—thus the ability to whisk unsuspecting tourists off the beach in reasonable safety. Try that with a powered paraglider!

Our sport has no origins in parasailing, a sport that branched from the round canopies of sport parachuting. They still use modified rounds because of their stability.

Hang Gliding & Ultralighting

Development of hang gliders started in earnest during the mid 1970's after a few enterprising individuals adopted Francis Rogallo's design, dreamt up way back in 1948. Rogallo was scheming to safely return spacecraft through the atmosphere. The 1970's earthmen used his designs to craft bamboo gliders. Eventually, professional manufacturers entered the fray with real soaring craft. Efficiency drove improvements into fixed wing variants. Motors were soon to follow. Strangely (and fortunately), the FAA did little about this grass roots effort as the pilots stayed mostly away from populated areas and only carried one person who bore the brunt of their significant risk. They remained, literally and figuratively, "below the radar."

As weight increased, wheels were added and Ultralighting was born. Flex wing Rogallos got longer, skinnier wings and became capable soaring craft. The proliferating rigid wing configurations all but took over the powered segment.

Sport Parachuting

Pilots used cloth to soften their intentional falls back in the late 1700's when balloons and buildings were the only way aloft. But until 1961 there was no control of the canopy—it just broke the fall and sometimes the legs. Then the Paracommander came along with holes in the back that streamed enough air backwards to gain minimal forward speed. Alas the parachutist could have some influence on his destiny. At about the same time, a Rogallo shaped parachute was devised but never really explored.

Alan Chuculate is braving the -20°F Alaskan air to try his 11-cell Harley. It was an English parascending canopy built in about 1987 to cary two people.

Efficiency has come a long way; it took Alan 500 feet of altitude loss to do one 360° turn.

The shape was not very distant from it's sport parachuting origins although it did have unsheathed lines that are now common on competition wings. But it had a *lot* of lines, far more than on modern gliders.

The big development came in 1964 with the square Ram-Air parachute. This design formed the underpinnings of modern paragliding.

These sport parachutists could fly almost like a glider but with very limited glide performance. French mountain climbers, who learned to launch their parachutes from the slopes, started using their canopies to descend from scaled heights. Others saw an opportunity and began to improve the wings, getting the sport well established in Europe by 1986. Modern paragliding came to Joe Public when manufacturers actually started producing wings for the masses.

Not long after efficiency gains earned it the name paragliding, enterprising European pilots started adding power. Large motors were required to overcome the drag penalty of early wings. These had necessarily high hang points to balance the heavy power units.

As wings became more efficient, the motors could get smaller and lighter, requiring less thrust. By 1989 the Pagojet, using a 3-cylinder radial engine, became the first production unit available to the public. Not that the masses flocked to it but at least they had the opportunity. By 1991 a number of European manufacturers were building machines and the US market was soon to follow.

Lost Lineage

An evolutionary aside to the paraglider story is that of David Barish, an airline pilot turned aeronautical engineer turned parachute designer. Like Rogallo, he was striving for a spacecraft re-entry method as the planet raced moonward in 1965. He and Rogallo only met once at NASA but their designs both shared some commonality—both sported about a 4 to 1 glide ratio and both were abandoned by the space agency.

But Barish, an avid and accomplished skier, took his single-surface paraglider to the slopes – scooting/flying down the hills at no more than about 30 feet high. He toured the country's finest ski sites in the summer of 1966, demonstrating his newfangled version of "downhill" with an apparently cool reception; it seems the public just wasn't ready yet.

The PPG Bible: A Complete Guide and Reference

Mike Byrne about to launch on a 5 minute flight with his home-grown, Konig-powered early paramotor in 1980. The rightmost picture was him flying the same wing but with wheels.

He could only fly that long because the 100-pound motor hung from him, not the harness. That got uncomfortable in a hurry!

He even tried using a motor with his creation but must not have found an adequate power system that he could lift; there is no record of any motorized flights with his wing.

Powering Up

Englishman Mike Byrne should probably be credited with first to foot launch a paramotor in the fall of 1979. By the summer of 1980 he was intriguing airshow and television audiences around England. The 95-pound home-built unit used a 3-cylinder Konig motor and hung from his back. It had no seat, limiting flight-time and probably limited appeal—about 5 minutes worth since the motor's weight hung from his back and he hung from the harness. Ouch. He was also probably the first to name the craft, along with his brother Johnny, calling it a paramotor.

It obviously didn't catch on and Mike moved on to bigger, faster craft, mostly with wheels. The privates could only stand so much.

Digging Deeper: Fan Man

James Miller had a passion for both flight and for freedom—paragliding gave his desire wings. He took to it quickly, learning from a friend before instruction was widely available. Residents of Juneau, Alaska spotted him frequently flying from Mt. Roberts near his home. He knew the value of training, though, and sought out advanced instruction in flying and towing. He went to Alan Chuculate, one of the sport's early instructors and certainly one of very few flying in Alaska.

Alan noted that besides "Having a lot of energy," James was enthusiastic, motivated and his previous experience made him an easy student. He earned his USHGA P2 paraglider and tow ratings in the fall of 1990 but he wanted to also explore the additional freedom of power. For that he would have to leave Alaska.

James' date with fate and fame was set when he traveled to Las Vegas in 1992. He hooked up with Patrick Sugrue who had recently started importing the LaMouette paramotor. After a few days of instruction he set out on his own flying with power.

Having flown for some time in Alaska, he found the desert conditions quite different. The dry, high-powered thermals caused frequent wing collapses and other maladies. Alan remembers getting a call from James with two questions: "How do I recover from collapses?" and "How do I thermal to stay up?"

The night before his famous flight, James called his brother Eric: "I'm going to do something big tomorrow," he said. Sure enough, two minutes into round 7 of the Evander Holyfield-Riddick Bowe heavyweight championship, James Miller landed his PPG in the ring. His mark was etched in history. It cost him a beating to unconsciousness by the crowd, 4 days in jail and a $4000 fine. A year later he made headlines again by landing on the roof of Buckingham Palace, naked.

His irreverence and free spirit bubbled up in English court just before being deported. On hearing the judge ban him permanently from England, he asked "How about my ashes, can they come back?" She said no.

He eventually gave his life back to the mountains he loved so much and had flown over. Health problems made the strapping 37 year old James Jarrett Miller unable to care for himself; in 2002 he took his own life in a wilderness area near his home.

Thanks to Mike Coppock of the Anchorage Press for information used in this story.

The powered parachute (PPC) came first. Although not really a part of our lineage, it is related. Wheels allowed sufficiently powerful, but heavy motors to push the early inefficient wings aloft. These square canopies have one major benefit—they are very stable. That ease-of-launch gave them great popularity.

Highly efficient wings have come along for these craft but they are more difficult to launch. Hybrid wings will likely become the norm as pilots seek performance gains at some extra requirement of skill.

The difference between PPC's and PPG's is mostly weight. A PPG trike is, by definition, a PPG with a trike attached. The essential difference is that the PPG trike is capable of being foot launched. Anything over about 120 pounds (trike and motor) was probably designed from the outset to be wheel launched. Some definitions try to dig into attachments and other minutia but the essence is that it was intended to be foot launched.

Most PPC's are dramatically heavier (over 200 lbs) and have proportionally more power. PPC's are usually steered by the pilots feet since line pressure is so high.

Interesting variations like the Flyke bike/trike combination (below) will continue to blur the lines though. They are machines with PPG handling but meant to be flown with wheels. Some even use PPG motors for thrust.

Barndt Bartig was another pioneer, foot launching from level ground in 1981. But he kept it secret until the first commercial paramotor, the German-built PagoJet, came out in 1987. It too, had a 3-cylinder Konig engine. Right behind him was Jet Pocket (also known as Air Plum), the first French company to manufacture and commercialize a foot launched paramotor starting in 1988, quickly followed by the Propulsar whose owner then joined up with Guy Leon Dufour of Adventure. There are several pilots in Italy who also started making personal units as early as 1987, including the past owner of Vitorazzi and Diego of Miniplane.

The U.S. saw its first paramotor when Patrick Sugrue flew one in 1988. He imported the LaMouette brand and his most notorious customer was James Miller.

Unfortunately, the real introduction of paramotoring to America came during a boxing re-match in November, 1993. Evander Holyfield was avenging his prior year loss to Riddick Bowe under an open-air arena in Las Vegas. Punches weren't the only thing flying. In the 7th round as James Miller descended with his paramotor into the ring, stopping the flight and then getting pummeled by an angry crowd.

Performance Improvements over time

Most of the technology has matured quite a bit, slowing the rate of improvement in both wings and motors. Gear gets better, knowledge improves, and training generally gets more available—all good progressions.

Technology advances come slowly but frequently in spurts when some new development lifts the entire sector. Manufactures employ various innovations and the good ones propagate to other gear. Copying is rampant because the sport's small size makes patent efforts unduly expensive and difficult to enforce.

Motor technology mostly comes from go-cart racing and motor scooters although purpose built motors have started to evolve. Economies of scale mean that development in other areas is more likely to drive innovation in our sport since paramotor production runs are way too small compared to the thousands built for larger industries. A few manufacturers do specialize in paramotors but improvements are incremental. Power to weight ratio, which measures power per pound, is the best measure of a new motor's performance.

It's hard for a company to invest heavy research into an endeavor with so small a payoff. Fortunately, enthusiasts come along periodically and pour themselves into the improvements without a need for large profits. We all benefit from their vision.

Our future is bright, with weight coming down, performance improving, and, even more importantly, with knowledge increasing. We have a lot to look forward to.

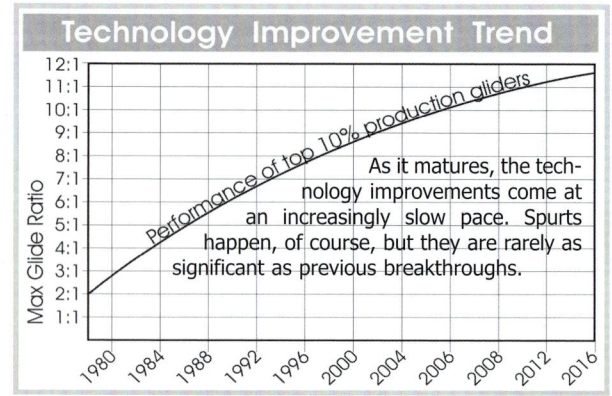

As it matures, the technology improvements come at an increasingly slow pace. Spurts happen, of course, but they are rarely as significant as previous breakthroughs.

Section V

Choosing Gear

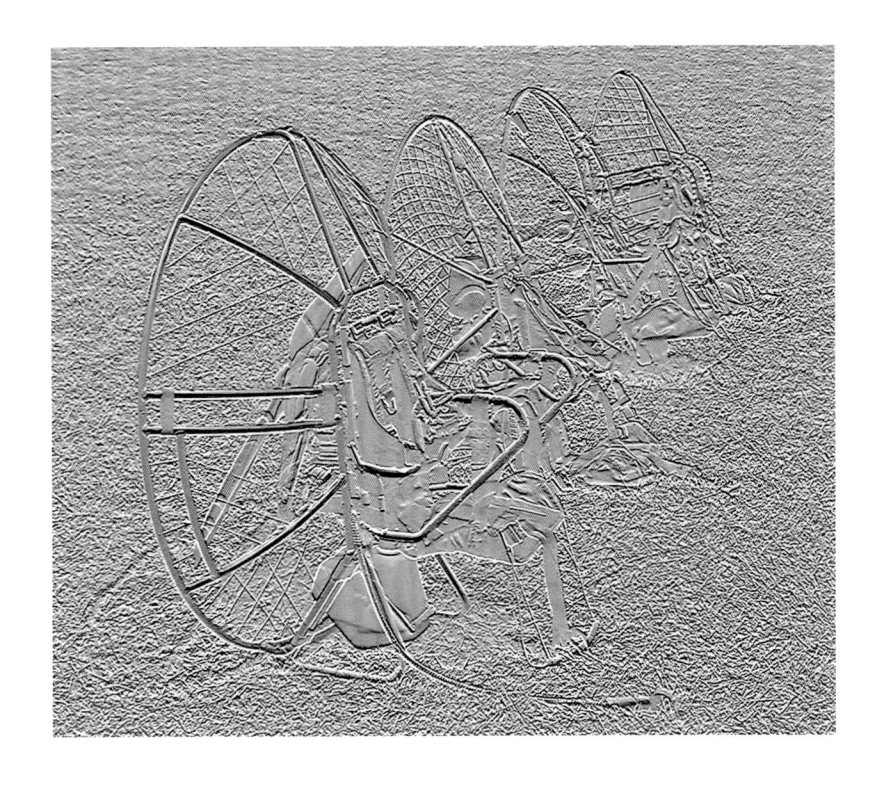

Section V

Choosing Gear

If you're just starting out, review Chapter 1 before even thinking about gear. Use your instructor's guidance to select the right wing and motor. If nobody is distributing your prospective purchase, you may be asking for trouble. Exceptions exist, mostly for newly introduced products by reputable companies, but those models must be purchased with extreme care and only by experienced, risk tolerant types with mechanical acumen.

Who to Talk to

The fact that you're reading this book is a great sign; you want to be informed. Hopefully these words get to you before some shady salesman does. The Internet is rife with them.

Your best resource is a trusted instructor, followed by experienced pilots who have nothing to sell. Seek out pilots who have flown a variety of wings and motors. A great approach is going to go to a fly-in to see what's out there. Not only will you *see* the various offerings, but you'll also see what people like and find out why. There will be a broad group of folks to talk with and pilots love talking about their gear!

Sales pitches are just that, pitches, and a few of them are out in left field. There is no perfect machine or wing, but rather many trade-offs.

Appearances

We all want stuff that looks good, but remember that your life depends on your choice—prioritize accordingly. The best looking gear on the ground pales next to anything that will get you airborne. If you can't fly it, looks won't count for much.

Cost

No, it's not cheap. While this is one of the least expensive ways into the air, it's still aviation. Requirements for lightweight reliability drive up the cost as do small sales volumes. It's necessary that sellers and instructors make profits. Their success is good for all of us and for the sport in general.

Cost will certainly be a factor for most people and you should know what you're getting into. Always price gear with any training packages that might be included.

If avoiding the middleman means skipping the local instructor or school, that's probably a bad trade-off. In the long run, local support can be worth way more than any dealer markup.

Realize, too, that costs will continue. Breaking a prop is not terribly uncommon and costs 3% and 6% of your motor's new purchase price. Wings wear out, too—after about 300 hours of sun time they should be replaced.

The Wing

CHAPTER 26

The correct choice of a wing will have the most profound effect on your safety, success and enjoyment of powered paragliding. It is not the place to skimp or buy on a whim.

Ease of Launch

A wing should be easy to launch. That means it should inflate fairly easily and tend to track straight. After all, if you can't get it airborne, it won't do you much good. If you fly only occasionally, then it's even more important since you'll be a bit rusty each time out, and may have a harder time with the wing. If you always fly in a steady breeze, like at the beach, then it's less important. A hard-inflating wing will be most difficult during the inland calm that morning makes so common.

If you're accomplished at launching or don't mind the steeper learning curve, then a more difficult wing should be a trade-off for some other redeeming quality. Some launch-challenged wings may actually be reasonably easy with the right technique, but you should find out before buying.

Wings with a high aspect ratio, usually higher performance soaring models, are more challenging in some ways. They tend to fall off to one side more, and their longer lines take more time to get overhead. They tend to over-fly you during windy inflations or gusts, and are "slippery" while kiting. Once they start sliding off to the side or yawing, it takes more effort to get them centered again.

Design is most important, but other attributes matter too. Physical weight of the wing plays a part; a thick, coated fabric will need more effort. Older versions of easy-inflating wings get harder to inflate due to line shrinkage and increasing porosity.

Wing Loading

Calculate placard wing loadings by dividing the maximum weight into the wing's projected wing area. Compare the different models to see which ones are already planned to be flown heavy.

The example models below represent three different wing loadings. The Compra would probably be a super high-performance glider (possibly not certified) and the Super Floater more geared to soaring. You wouldn't want to fly the Compra overweight since it's high wing loading suggests it will already be loaded.

Wing Model	Projected Area	Placard Max Wt.	Wing Loading
Compra (uncert)	20 m²	100 kg	6.82 kg/m²
Sportifly II	25 m²	100 kg	4.00 kg/m²
SuperFloater	28 m²	100 kg	3.57 kg/m²

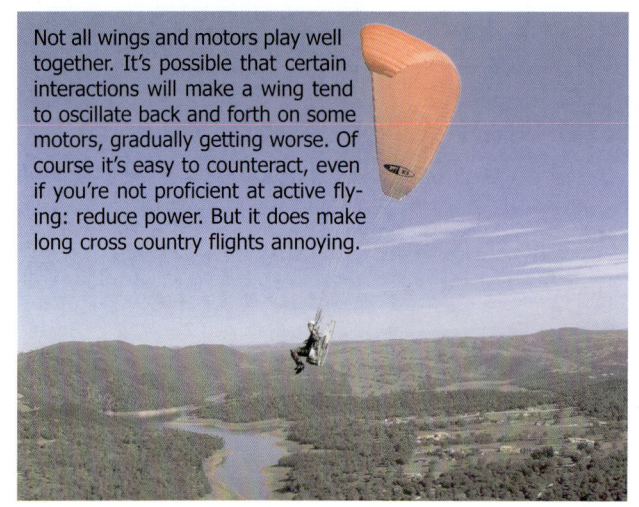

Not all wings and motors play well together. It's possible that certain interactions will make a wing tend to oscillate back and forth on some motors, gradually getting worse. Of course it's easy to counteract, even if you're not proficient at active flying: reduce power. But it does make long cross country flights annoying.

Size

Heavier pilot/motor combinations need bigger wings. They all have a recommended weight range (*placard weight*) and, except at higher elevation launches, it's generally better to be on the heavy side. Most instructors accept that being up to 10% overweight is beneficial. A heavier person can push through the inflation easier although running speed is faster at liftoff. The weight improves handling, making the wing more sporty, faster, less likely to enter Parachutal Stall, and is more resistant to collapses. On the other hand, being heavy means it will take slightly more power to fly level, sink rate will be faster, landing speeds will be higher and, if a collapse does happen, it will be more dramatic.

There are two methods of measuring size: flat or projected. Flat is the area of a wing when stretched out flat on the ground. Projected is the area made by an inflated wing's shadow—it will always be smaller. Most manufacturers list the flat size since it's bigger. On average the projected size is about 85% of the flat size.

Certified gliders are tested through their weight ranges but another important measurement is wing loading. You can tell whether the manufacturer is already loading it heavily if its maximum-weight wing loading is high. Being overweight on an already-heavy weight range may be excessive. Aerobatic wings are normally very heavily loaded.

For example, using the sample chart at left, the Compra's wing loading at 100 kg (it's max weight) is 6.82 Kg/m². That's a lot, as heavily loaded as aerobatic wings. The others are a more-normally 4 and below. Be extremely leery of loading a wing up past about 5 kg/m². Speeds are very high and handling can be extremely sensitive.

Glide and Sink Rate

The better the sink rate, the less power you'll need to stay up. A good glide ratio means you'll go further on a gallon of gas. Because the speed range is so small, there is minimal difference between a good glide ratio and a low sink rate.

Overall, a better glide ratio will be easier to land because you'll have more flare authority after the initial pull for landing. The glide ratio given on specifications should be taken with a grain of salt—there seems to be a lot of fudging on those numbers, especially on wings intended for motoring.

Stability

Stability, described in Chapter 22, usually means collapse resistance when talking about wings. Beginner-type certified wings are generally more collapse resistant as long as their flown within the placard weight range.

The tradeoff is that stable models may be boring for pilots who enjoy precise control while maneuvering. A few older-style beginner wings fall into this category.

Handling

Responsiveness to brake input is the biggest element of handling. Being heavy on a wing makes it will be more responsive. Several attributes affect handling:

- Brake travel—should be from a comfortable position and respond almost immediately to pressure. Full extension will result in a stall, which is only used just before your feet touch the ground. Wings that crumple the tip a bit will pull the wing over sideways in the direction of turn and be more responsive.

- Linearity—the response should be incremental throughout the range with no significant dead spots or unexpected reactions. A little pull does a little and more does proportionally more.

- Dive—all wings increase descent rate when banked, but some tend to dive more then others. Having short lines makes this more noticeable. It can be a dangerous characteristic in the hands of the ham-fisted. All wings can be turned flat, but some models require more pilot finesse to do so (see Chapter 16 on coordinated turns).

- Heaviness is how hard you must pull to achieve the result. Tandem wings flown with two people are going to feel heavy. Small wings will tend to have higher pressure, but are more responsive.

Some wings are "twitchy." If you're into active flying this may be OK. These will tend to also have sporty handling.

Speed

Some models advertise a high speed but that will depend hugely on weight. When they're advertising speed, it will always be done at the maximum certified weight so check to see how heavily loaded that would be. Fortunately, the makers of certified wings all do it the same way.

When comparing slow or speedy wings of about the same efficiency, fast models tend to require more fuel burn per hour than slow ones. So you won't stay up as long but will go the same distance (in less time).

Speedbar

The speedbar attachment is an arrangement of pulleys and lines that, when activated, lowers the forward rows of lines and speeds up the wing. Most motor pilots don't regularly hook it up. Almost all free-flight wings have a speed system and most free flyers use it since they frequently gravitate toward windier conditions.

Different arrangements exist for the pulleys that trade off foot pressure for travel. Since the speedbar pulls down the A's and B's, which have the most pressure, it is designed to give the pilot some mechanical advantage using pulleys. Having one pulley means the pilot does not have to press very *far* to get full travel, but must push *hard*. Having two pulleys lowers the foot pressure but increases the foot travel required.

Choices abound but handling is one area that almost everybody wants to be good. If you're the type that enjoys lots of precision maneuvering then it will be a primary concern. Fortunately, handling usually improves at the heavier wing loadings (see next page) and so too does speed.

Trimmers

You'll want trimmers. Fortunately, most motor wings have them. These adjustments can be let out to raise the C and D lines, which makes the wing go a bit faster.

Center Cell Visibility

Some instructors find that it's helpful see the center cell easily. It helps new pilots know if the wing is centered overhead. That is why many beginner wings have a distinctive mark on the underside's center.

Certification

Certification by a recognized body indicates how the wing will behave in certain defined circumstances. Wings go through both flight and strength testing. DHV, SHV, AFNOR and DULV are organizations that certify wings but only DULV certifies motor wings. CEN is a European standards organization which bases its testing on AFNOR's. Most wings do not go through motor testing since the larger free-flight market wants testing geared towards their use. Even DULV only flies through minimal maneuvers with the motor on.

Gliders can hide bad behaviors that testing will usually reveal. Nearly all glider makers have their wares tested and correct any handling deficiencies that cause a failed test.

You'll know it's certified if it has a label detailing the make, model, size, weight range (frequently in kilograms: 2.2 pounds per Kg) and certification level. Never buy a wing without this label unless you're an expert that can verify its behavior. The label is usually located on the wing tip or center cell and its absence likely means it has no certification.

Testing involves putting the glider into various maneuvers or collapses, and then letting it recover on its own with no pilot input. Time to recovery is measured, and fast recoveries get better grades (a lower number). Those that take a long time or require pilot input to recover get the worst grades (higher number). Gliders certified with trimmers must be tested at the slowest and fastest settings with and without speedbar. Many wings sold with motor risers are only certified in one setting, usually slow or neutral, you have to look at the test report to know.

DHV 1 and 1-2 (AFNOR Standard) gliders are good for all pilots and can have very good performance and handling. They are less likely to collapse and generally recover quickly on their own. You can still get into trouble on them, but it takes more turbulence or pilot buffoonery to do so. Motor pilots generally choose these wings since they don't need that last little bit of performance at the expense of safety. The motor also prevents some of the weight shifting that helps recover from problems more common on higher rated wings.

DHV 2 and 2-3 (AFNOR Performance) gliders are more likely to take a collapse and don't recover as fast. Pilots must be quick to dampen surges and pendulums. They are usually slightly more difficult to kite as they tend to fall off the side more, and are more likely to overfly the pilot. They require more attention but usually have better glide ratios (more efficient) and are frequently faster.

1. A design that allows immediate recognition of the glider's center. This is more common on beginner-type wings.

2. This wing is certified in the AFNOR Standard category—a beginner wing. Some manufacturers have the placards filled in with magic markers at the factory, an unfortunate practice that is leaves the placard hard to read after a few years.

The placard was on the center cell but most wings put it on one of the inside tips.

The PPG Bible: A Complete Guide and Reference

DHV/DULV	AFNOR/SHV/CEN	MEANING
1	Standard	Stable, resists collapses and recovers fairly quickly with no pilot input.
1-2		
2	Performance	Moderately stable, less collapse resistant, recovers slower but still with no pilot input.
2-3		
3	Competition	Collapses easiest, may not recover on it's own from malfunctions, requires very active flying.

There are many gliders with very desirable handling and great performance that are rated as class 1 or 1-2. There is little reason for paramotor pilots to choose less stable gliders. The relatively small increase in glide performance usually found in the higher classes offers minimal or no benefit to the motor pilot. The class 3 (competition) gliders generally sacrifice safety for glide performance for the most risk-tolerant soaring pilots.

DHV 3 (AFNOR Competition) gliders are the most demanding and dangerous gliders out there. They are prone to collapses without constant attention in turbulence. They may not recover readily on their own unless the pilot intervenes. These are generally flown by competition pilots wanting to eke out maximize performance while taking on increased risk.

Risers

Make sure the wing you're considering has its original risers, or that you know how the new risers will behave. Soaring wings are sometimes fitted with motor risers. These accommodate higher hang points, common on many motors, and have trimmers. Be aware that putting different risers on a wing takes it out of certification and should only be done with the wing manufacturer's approval.

Split A's

A lot of wings come with split A's to ease the application of *big ears*. Rarely is this descent technique required in motoring since pilots don't fly in the lifty, rowdy conditions that require it. Plus, it's easy to add a handle onto the tip A-line with a short length of clear tubing (see Big Ear Line at right) to make "ears" easier to pull. The hose acts as a stand-off to give you leverage.

Brake Holders

This may seem like a small issue but, if you fly an area with lots of iron in the sand or soil, it can render the magnetic brake holders useless unless they're cleaned. Many gliders come with these holders and, in most areas they are quite convenient, but not if they get clogged up. The magnetic field holds the sand in the hole such that the toggle won't stay. It may sound trivial but it's a real pain. Old fashioned snaps solve the problem nicely but can be more difficult to use with one hand.

Brake holders probably wouldn't be enough reason to abandon a glider model, but if you live in such an area it may be worth coming up with another way to retain the brakes, like velcro or snaps. It winds up being quite helpful to keep the brakes on their risers to prevent tangles.

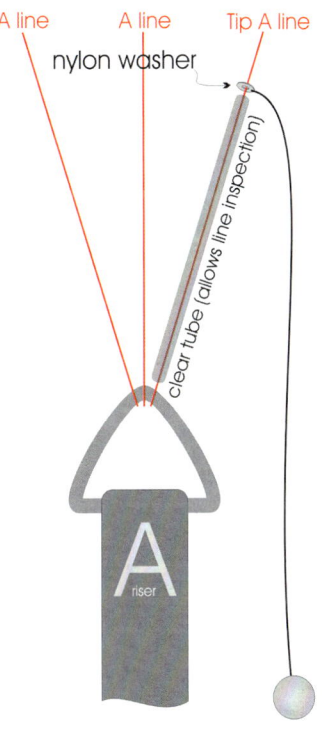

Above: A *Big Ear Line* is made to help those pilots who do not have split A's or cannot reach the tip A line for performing *big ears*.

Below: This complicated riser set goes well beyond just trimmers and a speedbar. It is festooned with more tabs and knobs than some airplanes, but it does not have split A's.

Chapter 26: The Wing

Kiting Only

There are many good deals to be had if you're just learning and want a wing for kiting only. While you must spend time learning the idiosyncrasies of your flight wing, having one to kite is nice since it takes the UV wear.

Smaller wings are better here because they'll be less effort to kite and can safely handle a higher wind range. Try to find one with good inflation, although such a glider will be more challenging to buy on the cheap. It can't be in too bad a shape, either, because you don't want it coming apart if you simply get lifted in a gust.

Don't be tempted to fly it; structural failure could easily be dire.

Some companies sell wings intended for kiting only and these are wonderful for that purpose. Unfortunately, they're also expensive. They can be used for practice in higher winds because they're normally less than half the size of a regular wing.

If you're buying a kiting-only wing, try to get the smallest size possible. It will allow you to kite in stronger winds safely. Use the wing loading chart presented earlier to tell the relative size—in this case you can be as far over the placard weight as you want—the more, the better (for kiting only!). Preferably it will have kiting characteristics similar to the wing you'll be flying but that's not terribly important unless you're learning on a difficult wing.

The Motor Unit

CHAPTER 27

The perfect machine for one person may be another person's nightmare. It depends on desires and dimensions. A petit pilot hefting a monster motor will be as miserable as a big bruiser trying to launch a petit pusher. Again, there is no "best" machine—manufacturers all make trade-offs and anyone unwilling to acknowledge that is mis-representing their equipment.

Some machines, admittedly, are relics, having long been replaced with better designs. They have no place in foot launched flying but their builders shamelessly market to unwitting marks, taken in by the slick brochure or website. For example, very few machines intended for foot-launched flight weigh over 70 pounds with prop and harness. Anything heavier than that is probably unsuitable.

Be careful thinking you're going to buy a powerful machine and take passengers up. In the U.S. and other countries that is either limited to instructors or regulated more closely than solo flying. It's harder, too; foot-launched tandem is probably the sport's most demanding skill. Trikes are much easier for tandem.

Be suspicious of advertised weights. Some companies do not include the weight of prop, harness or other necessary parts and say nothing about it. On a few models the harness is made to be detached after each flight, but companies should still make clear what is included in the weights. Harness and prop are obviously required for powered flight.

What follows are considerations for choosing your *second* motor. Your first one should have come from your instructor unless you have some very specific requirements. Even then you should choose an instructor who teaches on that gear..

This is one of the nicer looking machines, but it gives up some practicality for that appearance. Straight bars are easier to replace and easier to assemble. As with everything aviation, it's a trade-off.

Weight

For backpack units, intended to be foot launched, the dry weight (without fuel) of the motor should be on the lighter and more powerful side of the Thrust vs Motor Weight Graph below. Weight is noticeably greater on electric-start machines since they require both a starter motor and battery.

How the machine hangs is another major concern. If it hangs low and cannot be raised on your back, even a lightweight unit can feel awkward. If wearing the machine strains your stomach muscles after only a few minutes, it probably won't be comfortable on the ground.

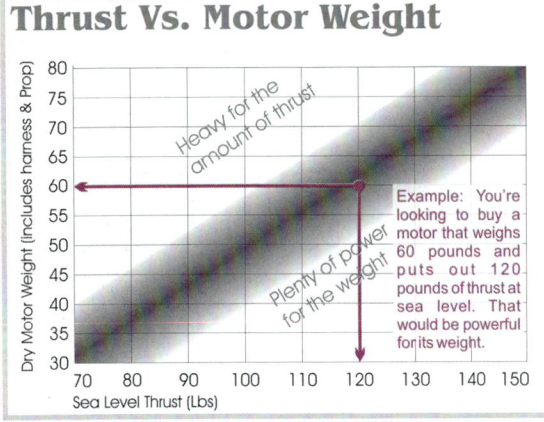

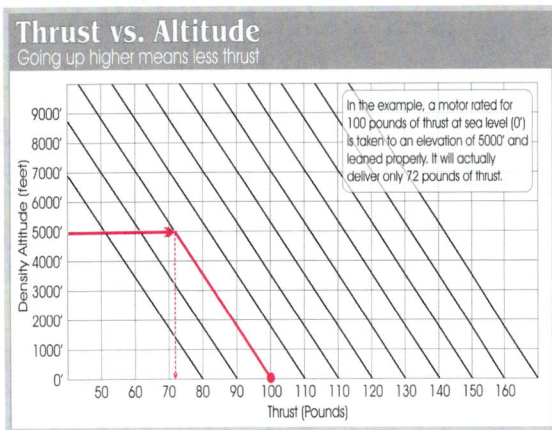

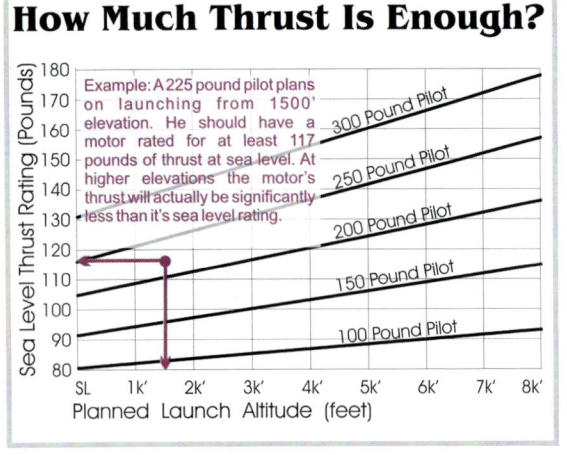

You'll hear justification for heavy or uncomfortable machines by saying you don't feel it for long since the wing will lift it off your back during launch. That's true for an experienced pilot, but until you've mastered the launch, though, it can make for a miserable experience. Plus, some pilots enjoy landing and taking off just for the fun of it.

Don't get an underpowered unit, though, in search of lightness. That can be equally frustrating.

The charts below can help determine desirable power and motor weight for your particular situation. When comparing manufacturer weights, be sure to find out if the prop and harness are included. Trike attachments will typically add between 30 and 45 pounds.

Thrust Vs. Motor Weight

Example: You're looking to buy a motor that weighs 60 pounds and puts out 120 pounds of thrust at sea level. That would be powerful for its weight.

Thrust vs. Altitude
Going up higher means less thrust

In the example, a motor rated for 100 pounds of thrust at sea level (0') is taken to an elevation of 5000' and leaned properly. It will actually deliver only 72 pounds of thrust.

How Much Thrust Is Enough?

Example: A 225 pound pilot plans on launching from 1500' elevation. He should have a motor rated for at least 117 pounds of thrust at sea level. At higher elevations the motor's thrust will actually be significantly less than it's sea level rating.

Comfort

There are a number of elements here. For one, it must be comfortable in flight. On some physiques, bars my get in the way of either visibility or movement—try it out. The motor should balance on your back, be comfortable, and not pull you backwards excessively.

As with many aspects, assess comfort only after adjustment by an instructor or other pilot who is intimately familiar with that model. Some machines will be completely underwhelming until the dealer explains how to adjust them.

It should be comfortable on the ground too. Can you get up with the machine? Do you sit on the ground? Again, talk to someone, preferably the dealer or instructor, about how it's intended to be used. Some motors can seem impossible to maneuver comfortably on the ground until you know the "trick."

Thrust

Generally, more thrust is better, up to a point. Beyond that point, too much thrust is dangerous. Thrust helps power through the inflation during a *power forward*, makes launch runs shorter, improves climb and allows flight at higher elevations. The downside is increased torque—some high thrust machines can be dangerous for light pilots unless they are experienced at handling the torque. A light pilot on a powerful machine may well wind up quickly twisting all the way around unless the machine is perfectly adjusted.

The chart at left gives a good indication of thrust required. All machines will advertise their sea-level thrust. Try to use numbers culled from published tests at fly-ins or by independent organizations. Balance them with advertised numbers and if there's a big discrepancy, ask why.

All motors lose thrust at higher elevations. If that's where you'll be flying, the sea level rated thrust must be greater. Add 2% per 1000 feet of elevation above sea level. A 200 lb. pilot flying in Albuquerque would be happiest with a motor whose sea-level thrust was at least 132 lbs.

Quality

Like anything else built by humans, some machines are better made than others; most call it the "fit and finish."

Quality can come in many forms. If things don't fit together well that is a sign of sloppy production. Well-made machines will interchange parts easily—the cage frame from one machine will fit fine on another like-model as long as neither has been damaged. It is rare, however, that a frame is not just a bit "tweaked" from even small falls or drops during handling.

The welds should look solid and be built to last without being overly heavy. Too much use of wire ties and hardware-store parts may be a bad sign although field-repairability is quite desirable. Hardware store parts are OK in places where they're not critical to structural integrity.

Powerplant Considerations

We want it to weigh nothing, be quiet, easy to start, have lots of thrust, linear throttle response, and sip cheap gas with no pollution. As long as we're dreaming, it should be maintenance free and be priced at a pittance. Waking up, we find that no, we can't have it all. So the trade-off begins.

Electric Start vs. Pull Start

It's handy to push the button and start it up. Doing do so while wearing the motor lessens your exposure to starting injuries, too, but as always, there are trade-offs.

Most models come with either electric or manual start but not both. Only a few models charge the batteries in flight and even those will probably require some minor modification.

Electric Start Pros: it's convenient, reduces some propeller/body contact risks associated with having to pull start, and enables easy in-flight restart for soaring or aborting a landing.

Electric Start Cons: having only electric start means that you'll likely be grounded if the battery or starter dies. Some can be "jumped" with a car if it's only a battery problem. It's heavier—the battery and starter generally weigh between 7 and 12 pounds. It costs more on most models, but not all, and may or may not require extra maintenance. Pull start assemblies are not maintenance free themselves.

Number of Cylinders & Displacement

Nearly all PPG motors have only one cylinder to minimize weight. Twin or multi

---

Reliability

"Why can't my paramotor be as reliable as my car?" you ask. You probably don't work on the car and it starts thousands of times with nary a snivel.

Two big reasons: Weight and mass production.

1. We have to carry the machine on our back so it must be exceptionally lightweight for the push that it produces. Parts are built out of lighter material and in the lightest manner possible. That narrows strength margins.

2. Even the best selling motors see fewer than a thousand units per year. They're all essentially hand-built. The most automation in most shops is usually the coffee maker. There's just not enough volume to enable investment in the mass production facility of an auto maker..

This unusual machine had an early Konig 3-cylinder radial mounted on it. Starting was unique—the pilot wrapped the pull cord around a protrusion at the prop hub and pulled. You hoped not to have to do that a lot.

cylinder motors may be smoother but will usually weigh more and offer more opportunity for mechanical problems.

Like motorcycles, displacement is measured in cubic centimeters and ranges from 80cc up to about 312cc. The larger sizes typically power tandem units, heavy pilots, trikes or those flying from high elevations.

Longevity & Reliability

Longevity is a measure of overall robustness. How many hours, how many cycles (start, fly, shut off) can you expect the motor to last with no problems? It is notoriously difficult to predict. For one thing, it depends on how hard the motor is run. A small motor run constantly near its maximum power will wear out quicker than a larger one that is minimally tasked. Aviation is rife with examples of this; motors run near their peak design limit have shorter recommended times between overhaul (TBO) than motors that are de-rated (maximum power is artificially reduced).

Another aspect of longevity is support for the brand after the purchase. One-offs or obscure motors may work fine while all the parts are intact but finding replacements could be challenging. There is a major benefit to using a motor that is common and enjoys good support.

Efficiency

Just like cars, small motors are more miserly with fuel. The 80cc machines have won competitions (frequently with small pilots) where efficiency matters. It means you don't have to carry as much gas or can fly longer on the normal amount.

Efficiency can be measured by how much fuel is burned per hour, *at a given thrust*. Bigger motors will burn more fuel at a given thrust to overcome their relatively greater internal drag.

Efficiency will also be impacted by the fuel/air mixture: running lean (less fuel per volume unit of air) will burn less fuel at the expense of higher temperatures. So any comparison should be done with the same relative fuel/air mixture.

Charging Ability

Some motors have the ability to output a current for charging batteries. This feature is nice if you plan to run other 12 volt accessories such as an aircraft strobe. Check to see that the voltage and current capability works for your device.

Air Cooled vs. Water Cooled

The vast majority of motors are air cooled—it's simpler and there's no water to leak out. Some water-cooled models use convection transfer to eliminate the water pump, but that doesn't cool as well as its more complicated pump-driven brethren.

Water Cooling: The ability of a motor is produce power is tied significantly its ability to dissipate heat; water does that well. The improved cooling can be used to either increase power or increase longevity by

1. European pilots frequently fly competition using 80cc machines like this Miniplane flown by David Sigier. It's because efficiency is a big part of their events and the small motors sip gas.

2. The water cooling on this rare unit has no pump, rather it relies on convection. The pilot must keep tabs on temperature because, like the loss of a cooling fan, a leak in any of the water system would soon cook it.

letting it run cooler. The main trade-offs are increased complexity, weight, and cost.

Air Cooling: Some air-cooled models, especially the smaller ones (80-125cc), generally use a fan to improve cooling efficiency. If the fan breaks, it's just like losing water: the motor is headed for a meltdown.

Two Stroke vs. Four Stroke

Relatively simple two-stroke motors power the vast bulk of our fleet. They are popular for the same reasons they are used on weed-eaters and such: lightweight power makes them easy to carry.

Four stroke motors are quieter, cleaner burning and more efficient than their two-stroke counterparts. You don't have to mix oil since the motor carries its oil inside, just like a car. But they are also heavier (for the power) and more complicated.

On average, a four-stroke motor will burn between 10 and 15% less fuel than a two-stroke at the same thrust. The two-stroke is consuming fairly expensive oil with each gallon of gas burned while the four-stroke uses almost no oil. The four-stroke typically weighs about 15-20% more than a comparably powerful two-stroke but efficiency means you'll require less fuel weight be carried.

Ease of Launch

The paramotor design can have a significant affect on how easy it is to launch. A number of factors come into play with varying importance based on your location and experience.

All other things being equal, more thrust will make it easier to launch, up to a point. More thrust also means more torque, which must be managed. Excessive torque effects probably stem from poor adjustments (see Chapter 12), but when actual thrust exceeds about 70% of the pilot's body weight, torque effects become more problematic. Of course the pilot can learn to not use all the power which would eliminate this risk, but that takes practice.

If a motor makes launching hard, it could be extremely frustrating. Flexible cages are a trade-off in launch ease since they require waiting until the wing is overhead before powering up.

On a forward launch, the lines should slide smoothly up the cage rim. If there's anything to snag on, it may sabotage the attempt.

Highly flexible cages make launch more difficult by preventing use of power during initial inflation. You must get the wing overhead by yourself before going to power—a technique recommended by some instructors regardless of cage type. It is generally easier to launch with power assist, if possible.

Hang style is likely the next most important element. A motor that sits higher on your back will be easier to manage and be less fatiguing while walking around with it. Motors that hang low tend to always pull your shoulders back.

Fuel Tank Position

1. By far, the most common fuel tank arrangement is below the motor. Care must be taken that the prop has sufficient clearance to reduce the possibility of it hitting the tank in a crash or fall.

2. Fuel is stored in the frame on this model which keeps the CG closer to the pilot. But fueling requires the machine be present (not just the tank) and a sight tube is needed to tell quantity. Be mighty careful if you have to weld the frame!

3. On this one, the fuel tank is on top primarily to gravity feed the motor (no fuel pump required). There is no more fire risk with this arrangement than in any other. Even if gas does leak on the hot motor is does not simply ignite—there must be a spark. This style has double hoops that help keep wing lines out the prop during aborted launches. Many brands offer a choice of units with one or two hoops. It's a trade-off of weight and simplicity for protection of the lines.

Ease of Maintenance

Complicated or proprietary shapes and pieces mean that repairs may be more difficult and expensive. What a shame it is to give up the simplicity of our machines with complicated access procedures.

Having pieces that can be readily replaced is valuable too, especially when you're out in the field. The more parts that can be replaced or repaired by readily available hardware, the better. Consider what "dinging" the cage (fairly common) will entail. It may be worthwhile to ask what each cage and part costs if it damaged.

Fuel Storage—Above, Below, or in the Frame

Almost all fuel tanks are made of a translucent white plastic that allows easy viewing of the level. Aluminum tanks are expensive, require a "sight tube" or other means to tell quantity and are more difficult to repair because they must be welded after thoroughly evacuating the tank.

History has shown that it doesn't matter a whit where the fuel is stored with regard to fire risk. Having the fuel tank above poses no extra risk for fire. Even on the rare occasions where fuel *has* dripped onto the motor it has not caused a fire.

Propeller Size and Style

In almost all cases, the largest prop will produce the most thrust with the least noise. But that might not be the most convenient for transport because it requires a proportionally large cage.

A three or four bladed prop is normally less efficient than a larger diameter two-blade prop. If the blades themselves are more efficiently shaped they will make more thrust. Carbon fiber or adjustable pitch props will be more expensive but tend to be more consistent. Powerful motors sometimes employ more blades to push out good thrust without needing a mammoth cage.

A few machines can accommodate a variety of prop sizes just by purchasing different cage pieces. This would be something to check on since, if you purchased it with the small prop but then needed more thrust, you could do so without buying a whole new machine. The trade-off is that such machines may not be ideally engineered for each size.

Attachment Points & Separation Bars

All motors try to keep the front portion of the harness from pressing against the pilot's chest, usually by incorporating some method of pushing the front webbing away from the back of the harness. J-Bars, distance bars or pivoting bars are different approaches to meeting the same objective.

A few machines have different options for hook-in points. At least one "floating J-Bar" machine has the ability to also use under-arm distance bars so the pilot can choose what suits him best.

Low

Most motors with low attachments are trying to mimic a free-flight harness. They appeal to pilots who also own free-flight harnesses which nearly always have low hook-ins points for maximum weight-shift. Soaring wings typically have longer risers that work on low attachment machines without needing to adjust the brakes.

Some models, those with the lowest hang points and pivoting bars, are able to achieve significant weight shift. They allow moving the risers differentially about 6-8 inches by tilting the entire pilot/motor combination and moving the bars.

Low attachment machines that have no pivoting bars are probably trying to avoid weight shift and the looser feeling it invokes.

The hook-in is almost always onto a metal part of the frame with some kind of safety strap as a back-up.

Mid

Mid-attachment points are an effort to simplify matters by having the carabiners hook directly to the harness webbing. Distance bars (underarm bars) of some sort, located beneath the pilot's arms, keep the front harness pushed away from the pilot. These machines are very much like their J-Bar brethren in stability since the hang point is still well above the center of gravity. In fact, in flight, the difference in hang point is actually quite negligible between these and J-bar units.

This type gets weight shift via pivoting distance bars or a sliding strap arrangement. Pivoting arm units have the front left and right web segments attached to a free-moving pivot arm. Sliding strap types allow the front web segments to slide through a cutout as the pilot moves a leg up or down in the seat—it does not move quite as freely as a pivot bar, but gives the same amount of weight shift.

This mid attachment winds up being just like a high attachment in flight. The forward pointing underarm bars keep the motor from pushing your body against the front harness webbing. Nearly all machines have some method that accomplishes the same thing.

High

High attachment points come on machines with some form of over-the-shoulder J-Bar. Since weight is so far below the hang point, they tend to reduce the amount of turbulence transferred to the pilot. The smoother ride comes at some sacrifice in feel. This is due to the fact that the J-bars dampen out uneven pull from the risers as each side of the wing flies through slightly different air currents. Otherwise this uneven pull is transferred to the seat board and the pilot feels it.

Some older designs have fixed J-bars, which give almost no feedback from the wing—most modern units that use high J-bars have them "float" in some way. They either pivot up or down or are connected by a harness-like strap.

If the ground handling straps are not properly adjusted on these machines, the J-bars can ride uncomfortably on the pilot's shoulders.

Hybrid

At least one model (like the one pictured above) starts with high hook-in points during launch then mechanically moves the hang points down and forward as the pilot pushes out on a bar. It gives a more laid-back posture in flight to more closely approximates free flight and improves weight shift at the expense of an increase in complexity and weight,

Weight Shift

The entire goal of allowing weight shift is to move one riser down while the other goes up (see Chapter 18). There are several ways to do this. Almost every design can achieve some weight shift, at least an inch, which is enough to effect very shallow turns.

Not everybody will like the active nature of the most weight-shiftable machines, especially the lowest hook-in styles. It gives a "busier" flight because you feel the wing's movement. Plus, those that hook in low on pivoting arms confer a fair amount of fore/aft tilting in turbulence in addition to the left/right motion.

Machines with good weight-shift will get over 6 inches of riser travel. Those that aren't designed for it will get less than two inches of travel with a fair amount of effort. Any fixed J-bar system with high hook-ins has almost none. Machines with low but fixed attachments will have some but not much.

Sliding strap

This system, described on the previous page, works well as long as it slides easily. Being able to weight shift is a by-product of the designs original goal which was to make getting in the seat easier.

---

1. This style has fairly high hang points with pivoting bars (called comfort bars) attached to the front harness webbing. They move up and down in response to pressure on the left or right side of the seat board, moving the risers in conjunction. The pivot is immediately above the "P" below.

Geared shifters work by forcing one comfort bar down when the other bar is lowered, improving the ease of weight shift.

2. Low hook-in with pivoting bars on this style tries to mimic the free-flight experience. The bars move and the motor tilts when the pilot leans. The trade-off is that it transfers wing movement to the pilot, giving a "busy" feel that takes a few flights to get used to

Whole-Machine Tilt

On machines with low enough hook-in points, the pilot can tilt the entire machine right and left to accomplish the riser movement (see picture 2 at left). Just having low hook-ins is not enough, they must be *very* low. If intended to have weight shift, this arrangement will invariably have pivot bars even though each bar generally moves only a few inches in flight. These types will get over 6 inches of riser travel and are closest to the way free-flyers achieve weight shift.

Having the CG this low tends to make the machine feel "loose" since its pivot point is so close to the center of gravity. They tend to swing around in turbulence both fore/aft and left/right. Pilots acclimate to this feel, though it can be disconcerting at first.

If the machine has no pivot bar, it was probably not intended to have significant weight shift and will only get an inch or two of travel.

Pivot Arm Only

Machines with high or mid hook-ins can get good weight shift using a pivoting arm. Even better are models where the action of one arm going up makes the other arm go down. These "Wally Shifters," named after the original designer, can get over 6 inches of riser travel. Picture 1 on the opposite page shows this style.

Transportability

There are different requirements for transportability. For example, if you want to haul your motor around on airlines or ship it places, you want it to break down easily to a very small size. Some are made for this purpose—both the cage and frame pull apart easily, usually with poles for radial arms that pull out. While great for boxing, they take longer to disassemble for car transport. It's another trade-off.

The pole-type takes about 5 minutes to prepare for transport in a car and about 10 minutes to re-assemble. They'll realistically take about an hour to squeeze into the suitcase and the same to reassemble fully. Of course an experienced dealer can do it in much less time because he does it all the time.

If the machine only rides in the back of a van then having the cage's top half pop off with Velcro may be better. These can be disassembled or reassembled for car transport in about 3 minutes, especially if they stand upright in the car. They do, however, require larger boxes for shipping. Packing time to prepare for shipping is about the same for most models—about an hour is pretty realistic.

The smallest models are direct drives. These loud little buggers have small props and cages so they can usually be carried in cars (or airplanes or helicopters) without *any* disassembly at all. It depends on how you'll need to transport it. The one pictured at left fits, even if barely, inside a small helicopter.

Support—Parts and Expertise

Make sure you can get parts. Unless mechanical pursuits are a hobby in their own right, you'll want support for your particular machine. Cages and frames, which can usually be fixed by local welding shops, aren't as critical as the engine itself.

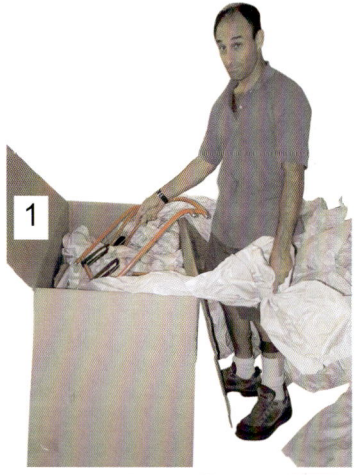

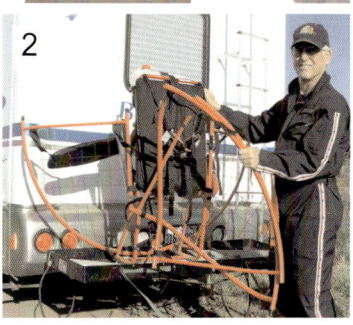

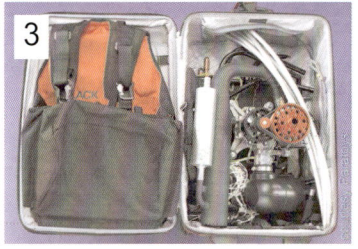

1. All motors can be shipped in boxes, some just need bigger boxes than others. They must be packed incredibly well to avoid damage.

2. Many motor's top cage half comes apart quickly. This may be more handy than having a style that breaks down farther but takes longer.

3. A motor that goes into a suitcase is great if you travel abroad a lot. Most airlines will not carry them as checked luggage so check before you go. But even for shipping, this is probably a safer way for transporting and certainly is the easiest to lug around.

After arriving at a North Carolina fly-in, Cory readied his machine and waits for the wind to mellow. Other pilots are preparing and a van-full of paragear awaits extrication. There are many styles that fit many preferences. Beware the salesman who claims any one model is "it." They are all trade-offs in weight, comfort, safety, convenience, feel, portability, and many others.

Buy your first motor from an instructor who you can work with. After learning the sport and gaining flight experience, then your second motor will be a more informed choice. Plus you will have established what features are important to you.

The motor and its attachments are the important pieces. You can have almost anything else fabricated. Sometimes companies will carry parts even though a model is no longer being sold. That can dramatically lengthen the life cycle of a particular brand.

Having a popular engine is valuable both in expertise and parts availability. With lots of a particular motor "out there", their biggest problems have probably been identified and fixes made. Even if the manufacturer doesn't have the fixes, the pilot community probably will. Having a common motor means more people are around to answer questions and there's a bigger market that allows dealers to stock parts. Inventory is expensive and they have to make a profit to stay in business.

If you have a local school or shop that can support what they sell, consider the enormous value of their proximity. It may well be worth several times what you pay for the gear in frustration avoided.

Safety

Hopefully equipment improvements will someday reduce our sport's biggest risk: the propeller. Getting a body part in the prop is the most common serious accident and many would be prevented with a well-designed cage system. The problem is that such a design imparts a small penalty in performance because it adds drag and weight.

Ideally, the cage should be able to hold back a human hand with any part of the cage, including the net, while producing full power. Both electric and pull start systems fall prey to this failing. The top half of the cage is most important. Almost no machine is able to do this.

Motor units should provide bottom protection in a hard landing. Fortunately, most do, but models where you sit on the ground will not provide as much. Having enough frame structure below the pilot's butt will help in case he pulls his legs up during a crash.

Safety is also reduced if the prop can easily hit the gas tank, or the cage can move forward into the risers, or the hook-ups can easily be done wrong, or the risers can come too close together, or the motor can move on the harness, or the user cannot easily see the throttle setting, or other things that make it easy for errors to be made. There is no perfectly safe machine, but some risks are painlessly easy to avoid.

> One of the worst injuries is when a body part goes into the prop. Of course it is entirely preventable with the correct procedure, but humans will be human, and if airline treatment of safety is any indication, we have to build our machines more pilot-proof.
>
> The curved blue bar on top is one idea to help make the netting strong enough to prevent a human hand (or other body part) from making it into the prop. Netting tightness and thickness should be strong enough so that a hand could hold the motor back from anywhere on the cage. The starter cord should be positioned so that the motor can be held even at full power. On most, if not all machines, trying to stop a thrusting motor by the cage or net will allow your hand to go in the prop.
>
> Pilots should always employ safe practices even with supposedly safe motors. For example, even with a super-strong cage, always check that the throttle arm is at idle before starting.

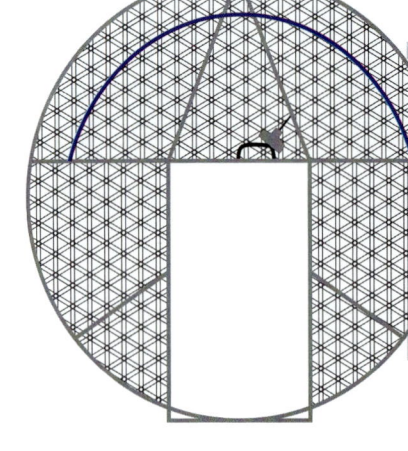

The PPG Bible: A complete Guide and Reference

Accessories

CHAPTER 28

We've covered the basic accessories in Chapter 2, but this serves up more detail on things that pilots typically add to a basic PPG package.

It's nice that you can accessorize with minimum fuss providing safety is minded. A lot can be attached, carried or used in conjunction with our craft but some goodies add more risk than utility. They cause distraction and yearn for the propeller. In fact, anything that can reach the prop eventually will. Accessorize carefully.

Reserve

A reserve (rescue) parachute can obviously be a lifesaver. This 10 pound accessory mounts on the machine, hooks in to the load bearing harness (see Chapter 12) and can be deployed successfully at very low altitudes (see Chapter 4). It is intended as a last resort for wing malfunctions that are unrecoverable.

The most popular reserve style is the *pulled apex* which achieves a slower descent rate on less diameter then the old round canopies. It deploys quickly and reliably. That quick deployment makes it completely unsuitable for use as a freefall canopy—paraglider reserves are not intended for terminal velocity openings where you reach terminal velocity after a few hundred feet of falling.

Bigger is better, to a point. Landing under a reserve is like jumping from a 3 to 6 foot ladder. How high do you want to jump from? The larger size equates to the 3 foot height.

The primary factors affecting choice are size, reli-

Chapter 28: Accessories Page 273

ability and opening speed. Sink rate will vary by size and you'll want to be within the weight range here. Unlike paragliders, where pilots frequently fly heavy on them, a reserve will not do it's job properly if improperly sized, especially if it's too small.

For any reserve to be used it must be mounted correctly. Improper mounting could make a situation worse than not having a reserve.

Trike

At it's simplest, the trike is a frame with three (or more) wheels and U-Bolt holes onto which you mount your motor. It is better to choose a trike that was made for your brand of motor—the mounts and balance will be optimized for its frame. At least make sure it has been successfully used with your motor.

Only a few bolts and you've got wheels. A trike does not fall under the U.S. *Sport Pilot* rule unless it has two seats or weighs 254 or more pounds.

The choice of wheels depends on where you plan to fly it. Balloon tires are great in sand and other soft surfaces but have more drag on the roll. Skinnier, larger diameter tires, more like a bicycle tires, work better on firmer surfaces but don't slide left and right as well which makes them slightly more prone to flipping on grippy surfaces.

Sitting close to the ground helps keeps the center of gravity low which helps resists toppling, but small wheels won't handle taller grass or rough ground.

Any trike should be able to provide reasonable protection to the pilot in the case of a flip-over or be light enough for it not to matter. On tandem trikes, look for protection of the front seat occupant. There should be some structure extending beyond the front person's legs so that the frame absorbs a head-on impact instead of the passenger.

A basic functional trike is not hard to build, but engineering it to safely endure a crash takes more thought. And make sure it will work with your motor, though simple, the hardware doesn't always match. Like most of this sport, there is more to it than meets the eye.

Helmet, Hearing Protection, Communications

A helmet does more than protect your internal computer from external damage. It can also come with ear protection and allow radio communications. If the helmet has no ear protection then at least use ear plugs with minimum 25 db noise reduction value to prevent permanent hearing loss. Even full face motorcycle helmets don't have near enough hearing protection. Plus, they limit your peripheral vision and ability to see the wing overhead.

Music

Portable music devices are miraculous in their universal use of an 1/8th inch jack. Everything from MP3 to cassette players work fine although many modern players will require amplification to be loud enough.

The helmet portion should have broad coverage, coming down on your neck since it also must protect from propeller shards.

Most pilots in the U.S. use Family Radio Service radios (FRS) and so radio helmets are usually made compatible with those. They have speak-

Helmet Types

1. Motorcycle helmets can be used and this one includes a radio communications apparatus designed for motorcyclists. It is voice activated so that when the pilot talks it transmits using FRS (Family Radio Service) channels. Be careful though, such setups rarely work for us due to our higher noise level. Motorcycles aren't as loud so these helmets have little hearing protection.

2. This helmet is purpose-built for our sport and includes a built-in music input and radio mixing circuit so that the user only needs to plug in the comm radio and music source. The transmit button is on the side of an ear cup as with many helmets.

3. This is the best protection, a full face helmet. It can prevent injury in the case of a face plant or other head-on mishap. This model is not designed for noise reduction so the wearer must wear ear plugs.

ers in the ear cups, a microphone and appropriate wires with jacks that (hopefully) fit your radio. Compatibility is always an issue so talk with the dealer about what it will work with. For example, a helmet designed to work with an FRS radio will not work with aviation radios. Some makers allow the customer to order their helmet with whatever plug they need and others have a *pigtail* where different plugs can be hooked into an in-line connecter. But even these can have compatibility issues.

Audio mixers can be had that allow music and radio communications to coexist. The music gets turned down when the radio sounds. Most ideal is having this capability built into the helmet. Another handy feature is *sidetone*. It pipes your own voice into the headset (you hear yourself transmit) which helps keep you from shouting and lets you know that your microphone is working.

The ignition circuit on a paramotor generates enormous electronic noise that interferes with radio reception or other electronics. It causes static that you'll hear change with motor rpm. This noise can be reduced using a resister spark plug or a resister plug cap, but never combine the two—it will affect the motor's operation. A braided wrap around the spark plug wire (shield) will also reduce the noise.

Tachometer

The Tachometer (tach) shows motor rpm and is your best indicator of power. Given that it's a fixed-pitch prop, if you're getting full rpm then you're getting full power. It's especially useful for peaking the motor and knowing how it's performing. Realize that propeller rpm will be less according to the reduction drive used. So a 9000 rpm indication through a 3:1 reduction drive means the propeller is spinning only 3000 rpm.

Almost all tachs used for paramotors work by counting sparks and you must have the right one for tour motor. Some motors fire two sparks per revolution and others fire only once. If your tach reads half or twice of what you expect, it's the wrong type. Of course it will work fine; you just need to adjust the reading mentally.

Installation is simple, run the detector wire up to the spark plug wire and wrap it around 4 times or according to the instructions. The ground wire should be

A tachometer is the single most useful instrument on a paramotor and the only one that many pilots carry. This battery-powered model has a wire that runs to the spark plug as its only required connection.

> ### Radios
>
> U.S. Free flight pilots use VHF radios on special designated channels. The hang glider association (USHGA) has worked with the Federal Communications Commission (FCC) to allow this. Membership in USHGA and passing a simple written test is all that is required. Visit www.USHGA.org for details.
>
> These radios are far more reliable, with better range and sound quality but cost more. The trick will be getting your flying buddies to use them.

hooked to a ground although most tachs work without it connected to anything.

Wind Indicators

You can be quite creative here with little more than a rod and a roll of surveyor's tape. Plastic plumbing pipe stuck together with connectors or a fishing pole work too. Inexpensive commercial windsocks, though, are certainly the easiest to use but make sure to get one that's sensitive to light winds.

Whatever you end up with, make sure it is discriminating in a light wind. If there's much breeze then it's not hard to tell direction but when winds are light and variable, you'll want sensitive sock.

Hand-held wind speed indicators (anemometers) are nice too, especially for learning to tell wind speed on the ground. With practice, you'll be able to estimate the winds within 10% or so.

EGT, CHT

Heat is the scourge of 2-stroke motors. Our application is brutal since we don't have much airflow around the motor and frequently spend longish periods at high power. Engine temperature gauges can tell whether or not you're toasting the top end.

An EGT registers the Exhaust Gas Temperature. It responds quickly to changes but is the most troublesome to install and maintain, requiring a probe be placed in the exhaust pipe. This is made more challenging on those machines with tuned pipes which must be changed carefully lest the power be affected. EGT probes, which endure some of the motor's hottest conditions, need periodic replacement.

No battery is required on analog dial types since the probe generates its own voltage to run the gauge. Anything with an LCD-type display will require batteries. Multipurpose models can come bundled with other indicators that combine temperature, sink rate, rpm and more.

The Cylinder Head Temperature (CHT) is far more common since it's so easy to install, just screw the spark plug over it. Plus it lasts longer since the element doesn't get anywhere near as hot as an EGT probe. It doesn't respond as quickly to temperature changes because the cylinder head must heat up so is not good for using to adjust the mixture.

Like the EGT, most CHT's generate their own voltage to move the needle (unless it is part of a digital readout).

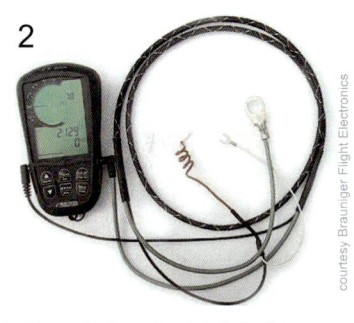

1. The wind sock at left is far more sensitive than the airport windsock to it's right. Fortunately, these are also the cheapest since they're not made for continuous use. Light wind indicators will not stand up to strong winds.

2. Soaring pilots will appreciate having a variometer. It shows instantaneous vertical speed which is useful for finding the the liftiest parts of thermals. This model also includes a tachometer and Cylinder Head Temperature (CHT) readout.

Altimeter/Variometer

For motoring, any of the popular altimeter watches are plenty accurate. They read atmospheric pressure as an altitude in feet. You set the field elevation before take-off and it will then accurately read your altitude above sea level as you fly.

Variometers, used mostly by soaring pilots, are very sensitive altimeters that give altitude along with its rate of change. They usually can be set to blurt out identifying "happy tones" for lift and "sad tones" for sink. Besides being accurate they are very rapid responding—just lifting it a foot or so off the table will elicit a happy tone (if set). The readout is either in feet per minute (fpm) or meters per second (m/s)

GPS

This useful tool can both navigate and provide altitude (on most). Technology has improved such that they are accurate to within about 50 feet of altitude and 10 feet of location—an amazing achievement given from how far away the signal emanates. The best choice is one that displays altitude, groundspeed and direction simultaneously. Some include a barometric altimeter but accuracy of the GPS-generated altitude is usually sufficient.

Emergency Kit

What you carry depends on where you'll be. A cell phone is the best defense in areas with coverage but consider a few things to help yourself. Besides the basic tools, lighter and knife, a tree rescue kit would be valuable for those flying over woodlands. The kit is little more then 80 feet of dental floss (or something similar) that is intended to allow retrieval of a rescuer's larger rope. It should be the length

Digging Deeper: Altimetry

We swim deep in an ocean of air. Just like liquid oceans, the pressure increases the deeper you go so. Conversely, it decreases as you go up. That is what altimeters measure; how much pressure the air exerts on a small *diaphragm* which they display as feet (or meters).

Almost all altimeters, including most of the wrist variety, have a way to set the current barometric pressure. It is called, appropriately, the altimeter setting. The advantage is that you don't have to know your elevation. By setting that barometric pressure, your altimeter will accurately display the altitude above sea level.

At sea level, the standard barometric pressure is 29.92 inches of mercury (abbreviated hg) and it decreases one inch for every 1000 ft altitude increase. Take a barometer that was reading 30.00 hg from it's sea level perch and drive it up to Atlanta, GA (about elevation 500 feet) and it will read 29.50 hg. When the weather men say the barometric pressure in Atlanta is 29.92, what they're really saying is that, *corrected for elevation,* the pressure is 29.92. The actual pressure is 29.42 but they account for the standard decrease of the higher elevation and call it 29.92 hg.

If you set an altimeter to the current field elevation and come back a few days later it will have changed, going up or down as the atmospheric pressure changes. A low pressure area will make it read higher and vice-versa for a high pressure area.

You may run into the terms QFE (Query Field Elevation) and QNH (Query Nautical Height). QFE is the pressure that results from setting your altimeter to zero. As you climb it reads height above field elevation. QNH is simply setting the barometric pressure. Your altimeter then reads altitude above sea level.

1. A wrist altimeter is is one of the most useful instruments you'll likely buy, after a tachometer. This version has a large display, with altimeter, vertical speed, compass and barometric pressure—it tells time, too.

The update rate is quick, registering an altitude change within a couple seconds, but the vertical speed is an average of the last 10 seconds—too slow for thermalling.

2. This very inexpensive GPS unit has all the necessary navigation functions and is well under the cost of a radio helmet.

3. Wearing GPS Nav on your wrist is convenient and they're just as accurate.

of the highest trees in your area.

If you're flying over water (beyond reach of shore) then there is a lot to carry. First off, the whole machine must have flotation affixed in a way that won't leave your head submerged, should you ditch. And *you* need flotation, preferably something that can be inflated just before going in the water (a CO^2 cartridge). Use common sense in equipping yourself for the mission and be prepared to handle the unexpected. Consider also, a small, portable breathing system like that pictured left.

Cold Weather Gear

There's no heater control and nothing saps the joy of flight quicker than being cold. In cold weather it takes more work to fly. Essential accessories include warm inside layers, a windproof outer layer, good gloves and face protection.

Full face motorcycle helmets with a visor are wonderful but make sure you can open the visor in flight to keep it from fogging up.

Every part of your body must be covered but scarves are a verboten—it's too easy to forget a loose end and have it stream prop-ward. Commercial flight suits are great but a cheaper option that also works are basic cold-weather overalls or snowmobile suits.

Big gloves are a necessary evil and a real pain to launch with—everything is difficult to feel. Some pilots have had luck with heated gloves and other garments but that entails more complexity. Chemical hand warmers, available from Walmart or sports stores, can also be helpful.

Home Building

CHAPTER 29

An entire organization, the Experimental Aircraft Association (EAA), has grown up around regular people building airplanes. There are, in fact, several thousand home-built airplanes plying the US skies at speeds upwards of 500 mph. Burt Rutan, pioneer of the first private ride into space, started off as a home builder. So building your own paramotor is a viable option for the some people.

Jeff Baumgartner flying a machine of his own making over Northern Illinois.

But it's certainly not for everybody.

There is a *whole* lot more to it than meets the eye. For one, there is enormous risk for anyone not taking it seriously—your life depends on sound design and execution. Very, very few people that set out to build a paramotor on their own, from scratch and without previous aircraft building experience, ever get to fly it. On the other hand, those who build from respectable kits usually do succeed in flying their creation. You can see a list of reputable kit makers on www.FootFlyer.com.

Don't build your *first* paramotor. For one thing, you'll be throwing away much of your ability to customize because you'll have no idea what you'll like. Buy an existing machine, learn on that, then build your masterpiece. It will allow forming ideas of what is *safe* to change along with what you'll *like* to change. The information in this book will help you know what *not* to change.

Build your own paramotor because you like to build—not because you want to save money. Building from even a well-implemented kit will take probably 50 hours minimum depending on what comes assembled. If you get one with little or no prefab, it may soak up to 4 times that many hours.

As with any machine, make sure you have an instructor that is sufficiently familiar to teach you on the gear. Most instructors will not mind as long as they feel the

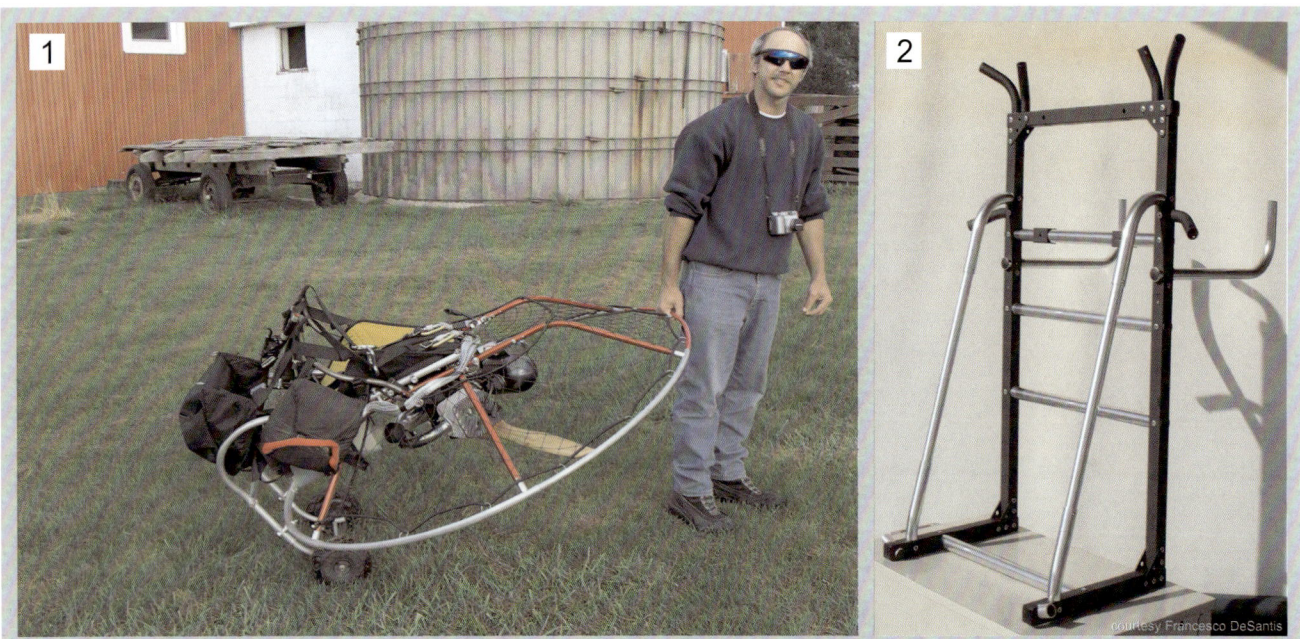

1. Welding aluminum is far more difficult than welding steel and is not something to be taken lightly. So almost all plans or kit machines do not require any welding. The machine above uses fittings wherever tubes meet or cross and a very clever key-ring-through-hoop idea to secure the netting. Wheels pop on and off easily for hauling machine, wing, helmet etc.

2. This kit frame uses rivets and gussets to fasten the pieces together. Nearly the same technology is used in regular aircraft; it works well provided it's done right and with plenty of rivets. These designs are both geared towards the home built market.

machine is reasonably appropriate for your weight and is safe. The worst possible combination would be a marginally trained pilot trying to fly an un-tested machine, whether kit-built or otherwise.

Don't be fooled by the time estimates. They may be accurate for someone who is familiar, but they don't include time for re-doing parts or multiple runs to the hardware store or any number of other surprises that invariably emerge.

Building Your Own Design

This is only for experienced paramotor pilots who are also dedicated do-it-yourselfer who understands the constructs, limitations and choices of the craft. There is so much more than casual observation can reveal—it takes flight experience on a number of different machines to understand the ramifications of each design feature. Even for an experienced builder of other things, these features will be foreign without expert help or extensive paramotor flying experience. And even expert designers get flummoxed when their great ideas don't pan out as expected. So don't be surprised when some super new feature you devised only makes the thing worse.

If you *do* have varied and significant experience, like to build, can work with simple tools and have time on your hands, then building your own design could be a very rewarding endeavor. The best approach is to model an existing machine as closely as possible. Find one that you like and learn why it is built the way it is. Look closely at how the harness attaches to the motor, where it hangs in a simulator and how the motor is mounted. Settle on the same type of motor too to keep it balanced. Keep the basic geometry unchanged.

Surprisingly small changes make big differences. For example, the weight shift bars common on mid hook-in machines must be positioned just right. It was found, early on, that positioning the pivot point just 2 inches back (towards the propeller) made them far more effective.

There are many, many factors that likely went into a tried and true design, one that people are actually flying. Change them at your peril. In the past, small changes to geometry or function have hobbled a machine to the point where it became unsafe. Be ready to deal with that and plan lots of testing in the simulator before taking it aloft.

After settling on a design, a time-consuming process that will probably involve many adjustments, the time and tools required to build it should be about the same as building from plans.

Building From Plans (Scratch)

If the plans are for a machine you've never seen fly, there's probably a reason. Find other plans where the machines are flying!

Buying plans from the back of a magazine or internet is a great money-toss into the wind unless you've talked to a respected individual who has built one or knows personally of its flying habits. Don't skip thorough research. Contact an experienced pilot whose opinion you trust and ask about your prospective purchase. It could save enormous heartache.

One of the biggest challenges will be acquiring all the parts. Harness, fuel tanks, throttle, aluminum, motor mounts, fuel line, motor, netting material, etc. Good plans will have a current source list. Make sure it's indeed current before purchase.

Tools: It will depend on the design but, in all likelihood, you will need to be able to weld aluminum (or have this done), bend tubes, cut thick aluminum (fine tooth jigsaw can be used), and fabricate various fittings. Anyone considering this should already have a normally-equipped shop with the skills to use it. Some plans don't require welding or they may sell any parts that do.

Expect to take from **100 – 500 hours** total building time from start to first flight. An enormous factor is how well the plans describe what's needed. If you want to build from plans, visit FootFlyer.com to see what kits are recommended. Nearly worthless plans have been foisted on unsuspecting buyers for years; buy something that comes recommended.

Building From A Kit

This is, by far, the best way to build a machine for those who want to do it on their own. Even so, it should only be done with a proven kit that has machines flying. Make sure you can watch or talk to pilots who have built the kit. Any reputable kit seller will offer a list of customers who you could talk to. Even if they cherry pick the list it would be preferable to having no other information.

Most kits will not require aluminum welding owing to its difficulty and the need for special welding gear. Instead, they will provide the welded pieces leaving only assembly up to the builder.

At least one kit makes extensive use of pop rivets and has no welded parts. The

1. As with all kits, the rivets and gussets of this machine must be done according to plan. In this case, it must be gusseted properly (the angled reinforcements).

2. Attaching cage netting is just as challenging for homebuilders as it is for manufacturers. On styles where the net is strung through frame members, it is cumbersome when a line breaks. The ingenious method shown below sidesteps that problem by riveting loops and having the netting line go through those. Restringing is a piece of cake.

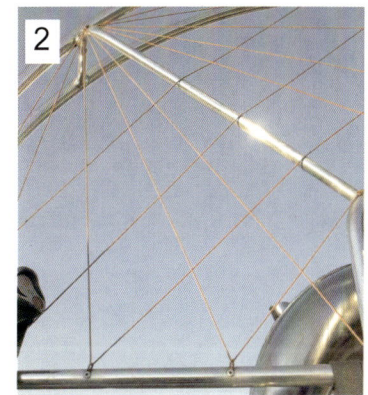

requisite rivet tool is inexpensive and, if done right, provides all the strength needed for a long life. Rivets work well provided no individual rivet supports too much load. By spreading the load across many of them, the same strength that is used in building airplanes can be brought to bear.

Tools: Generally you will already have what is needed: a drill, small hand tools, and a vice. The process is more assembly than fabrication which is especially good for the critical dimensions regarding motor mounting and frame alignment.

Time: Expect to take from **20 – 80 hours** total building time from start to flight. These times depend on the kit's level of completion.

Testing & Changes

There's always something. It may seem simple, but strange interactions and problems invariably show up during testing. Some are dangerous. Be ever mindful of the prop while going through the process. Some pilots (or would-be pilots) have been mangled after the briefest moment of inattentiveness.

Like any new machine, your preflight should make sure there's nothing within reach of the prop. The cage and prop must have good clearance and the fuel system has no leaks and a vent. These cautions go for the tinkerer who changes an existing design too. Have an experienced pilot check it out for you.

Consider what would happen in a crash. Will some component potentially skewer the pilot? Will the prop flex down enough to slice through the fuel tank, spraying fuel around and potentially igniting a fireball?

Will the change allow the risers to come together, causing riser-twist in flight? Will the cage come forward on the risers and allow the brakes to go through the prop? These things have all happened and many other possibilities exist.

Hang the system by its carabiners to make sure you can get in and out of the seat easily. Install a kick-in strap and practice until it's second nature. Have an alternative (besides the kill switch) way to shut off the motor that doesn't involve reaching too close to the prop. When everything checks out, run it up on the simulator and see if any problems creep up.

Keep those first few flights close to home and check the condition of everything carefully after each flight. This is no different than buying a new machine or one that has recently been apart. Postflight is always a great time inspect, but is even more important on a new machine or design.

Test your creation thoroughly. Hang it in a simulator where an instructor can go through the completed assembly. Make sure you can get in the seat, reach all the controls, etc.

Dan Kriseler is pictured above working with a student using an unusual but effective simulator. This would work well for trying out any new, machine.

Tinkering: Not all the bright ideas in paramotoring come from manufacturers; many of them, in fact, have come from users.

Tinkering pilots have devised both doozies and duds. Wally Hines' counteracting weight shift (where one bar's upward travel pulls the other bar down) was a doozy. It eventually morphed into a popular geared version designed by Jim Jackson.

Another Wally creation, pictured right, didn't go so far. While not a dud, this retractable foot rest never caught on.

It stowed for launch or landing and could be extended whilst cruising. He soon decided that the weight didn't quite justify the comfort. But it sure was comfy once airborne!

Section VI

Getting the Most Out of PPG

Section VI

Getting The Most Out of PPG

Now that you're flying an aircraft that can travel with you the list of possibilities is enormous. While a powered paraglider is wonderful for enjoying your *local* slice of good air, it offers so much more.

Being able to ship the gear frees you from the road; family vacations can become a whole different experience, business trips can become an excuse to explore from above and family visits can include "demonstrations." And, as you'll see, there are even more ways to enjoy this amazing craft.

Other Uses

Stefan Obenauer actually did launch with these skiis but it was also fun to cruise around. Of course, it's also easy to fall even as an accomplished skier!

What can be done with a paramotor is fun and surprising. They are certainly more amusing then they are useful but, who knows, one person's useless amusement may spawn another's useful application. Be mindful of the risks and expense, it's still an aircraft with that oh-so-effective spinning *fingerlator* on the back.

Using PPG for Transportation

The unfortunate catch phrase is: "Don't count on it," but exceptions may indeed allow using a paramotor to get somewhere. Fickle weather, limited conditions and slow speed generally conspire against us but, on those nice days, no locomotion scores higher on the intrigue scale.

Ideally, your launch is close to home (better yet, at home). The portability means that, after you get there, it can be folded up for the ride back. It's almost always much better as a one-way trip and even better yet with a tailwind.

If you've got an airplane (you'd be surprised how many paramotor pilots do), this can be a great way to get back and forth to pick it up from maintenance. The same is true for cars if your shop has a nearby field. You may even need to choose your shop differently now.

Be leery of planning a round tip, though. If the paramotor is your only ride home it will be extremely tempting to push the limits and fly when you would otherwise pass. "Get-home-itis" has been the fatal flaw in many general aviation flights where visual-only pilots take on conditions beyond them.

If you've got good sites at both ends of a planned trip, the PPG is a fun way to get there. As always, stay clear of congested areas.

Planes, Lanes and Helicopters

Before discovering PPG, I had a helicopter. It required yearly inspections at a shop some 35 miles away, an onerous drive through nasty traffic. I had an uncongested route from my house, and, of course, the shop had a helipad. The pad wasn't much, jutting out into a swamp and all, but it would do. So when the next inspection came due, I loaded my paragear into the helicopter and headed out. Flying there was quick. While helos are slow by aircraft standards, they're still a lot faster than driving! After landing, Darryl Oliver, the shop owner, spirited the helicopter away then got some friends to come out and my PPG launch. He thought I was nuts.

With the swamp before me, and the wing laid out carefully behind, I was ready. I was nervous, too, the climbout was over that decidedly un-appealing swamp. So I psyched up, powered up and went for it. The swamp's edge came quickly; I lifted off just before the water, held my feet just out of the swamp grass while easing off the brakes to accelerate. Whew! Climbing away from that was oh so satisfying. And so refreshing to be dry. Darryl later admitted that he half expected to fish me out of the muck. For some reason, the flight home was almost magical.

A couple weeks later I reversed the process—flying the PPG up to the helipad and flying everything home. Boy did that beat driving. Landing at the helipad seemed brainless compared with launching.

Another fun example of usefulness was retrieving a motorcycle after maintenance. How convenient it was that the shop had a field next door. I'm sure the employees got a kick out of that sight! And yes, a helmet *was* worn, both on the road and in the air.

Flags & Banners

Flags and banners can be fun to fly but do add some risk. Attaching anything to the wing adds drag which slightly increases the chance for parachutal stall and makes the wing that much more difficult to inflate. It may also impede recovery from malfunctions although the risk has proven minimal. Avoid excessive brake usage and follow the connection guide below.

When connecting a banner or flag, you want to minimize turning tendency, keep it out of the lines and make sure it flies fully.

There are several ways for attaching banners to the wing. Regardless of the method, put it near the center (to minimize turning pull) and, since it can't be exactly centered, on the opposite the side that your motor naturally torque turns. So if the motor makes you turn left, put the flag on the right side.

Use the most center brake line since it is the most rearward and will minimize turning tendency. You'll feel the flag flapping through your brake handle so some pilots will use a D-line (or C on 3-riser wings) instead.

You will have two lengths of 1/8" nylon strings that

are tied to the top and bottom of the banner's leading edge (2 & 3). The top line gets tied to where the brake line connects at the wing (1) and the bottom line connects where the brake line cascades from below (4). The length of each line, plus the flag's height should be slightly longer than the brake line distance between attach points. This will let the flag "bow" out without crumpling in the middle.

Put fishing clips (called snap swivels) on each end to make removing the flag easy.

Before launching, make sure the flag is on the ground and clear of the other lines. Generally just making sure it is on the ground and lines are on top of it is enough. After inflating (this is obvious during a reverse), make sure the flag is not hung up on anything before committing to flight.

Hanging Banner

Hanging the banner works well if you want to fly somewhere before deploying it or if no-wind conditions make the inflation difficult.

Tie a weight (3 pounds should suffice, more for a bigger banner) to the banner's leading edge bottom (6) then tie a line to the top and secure that to a Velcro strap. Attach the Velcro to a low-hanging part of the frame or to your foot (5). It should be attached in such a way that if it got snagged, it would peel off.

The pilot launches with it stowed and then, after reaching a safe altitude, throttles back and drops it. There is a possibility that it could foul the propeller so this must be done with extreme care. It is better done with the prop stopped. Be over landable terrain in case of problems.

While flying, avoid flying close enough to people below who could get hurt if it dropped accidentally. Be mindful of how low it hangs, even with the Velcro, getting hooked on something could be ugly.

Before landing, either drop it or stow it back in a bag.

Cattle Herding

Don't laugh, a paramotor "round-up" has been done and the rancher loved it. In fact, he asks the pilots to help out regularly. Of course you can't get paid but you may earn another flying site or at least a welcoming place to fly over.

Coordination is a must but it's mostly a matter of flying in such a way as to keep the cattle moving in a desired direction. Simply going out and finding strays helps a lot and the PPG, with its un-restricted view and slow speed, is perfect.

The coordination comes into play when two or more pilots are working one group of cattle. It also helps when working with people on the ground.

Be careful, it is quite easy to get distracted by the mission and fly right into the ground, wires or fences. It takes discipline to build a scan that regularly looks away from the "target" to ensure a clear flight path. Make no mistake, this adds risk; and doing it real low increases the risk dramatically.

Where cattle graze is usually landable terrain, but not everywhere. Be mindful of your engine-out option whenever spending attention away from flying. It's easy to get caught up in an activity and then be surprised by a motor failure. Surprise is decidedly unhelpful when only seconds exist before touchdown!

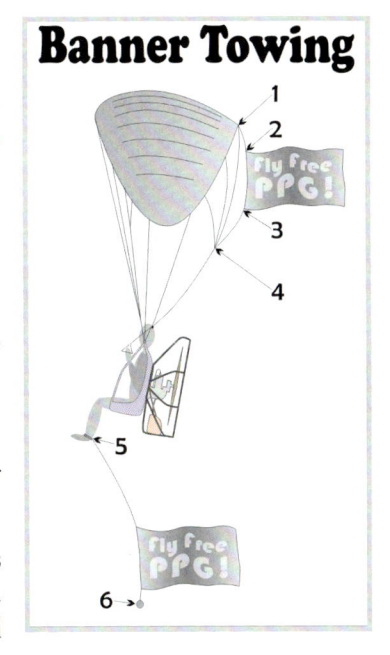

Top: This shows 2 ways to connect a banner, one on the wing and the other on your foot. Of course there are other ways, but these have proven reliable. The fishing tackle clip (middle) is a good way to fasten the banner line.

Above: The same New Mexico group that has pioneered rescue work has also been called on for cattle herding. This pilot is working a small band of separated cattle along the Rio Puerco, West of Albuquerque. Legally, these uses fall under allowed recreational use and there would probably be no question unless you were getting compensated in some way.

Search and Rescue

That unlimited view we enjoy can also be useful for search and rescue. Although cell phones and GPS's have reduced the amount of this work, people get lost in isolated areas. We're obviously not effective in wooded areas. This should only be pursued by experienced pilots who generally make launches on their first try.

Contact the state Search and Rescue director (if available) or the local fire and police departments to offer your services. It would be strictly on a volunteer basis but is a great show of community support.

Be up front with them about your capabilities and limitations. The worst thing to do is exaggerate what you can do and then wind up needing a rescue yourself. Most important, explain the limited weather conditions you need to operate in and time of day constraints—don't expect to do this mid-summer afternoons.

Finding Model Aircraft

A great way to become friends with the local Radio Control airplane club is offering your search services for their lost airplanes. Give them your telephone number and explain your capability.

When those planes go down they can be nearly impossible to find from the ground and they have quite a range. Tall grass is ideal to find planes by PPG—it's almost impossible to locate them on foot but is easy from above.

The flying is obviously simple: pick a pattern and fly it while scanning the ground. Pick different altitudes too. If the airplane is buried in deep grass, you might have to be nearly right over it. Going up high puts your farther away but provides the vertical angle that may enable a better view.

Once the plane is located, identify nearby landmarks that you can find from the road (or hack a GPS). It is best if you go out personally to get the plane because you know where it is. The nuance of location can get lost in a translation.

Public Relations & Exhibition

Flying in airshows can be difficult. You must get approved by the airshow management and work with the "Air Boss" who's in charge of all flight operations. There are frequently exemptions from certain rules that the organizer obtains. Among other things, all pilots that fly under that exemption must be specially qualified through the aviation authority (FAA in the U.S.). That can be a lengthy process.

At smaller gatherings, or even some airshows, it can be great public relations to have your craft out there with some basic information brochures. They may even let you fly since it would keep up the audience interest.

1 & 2. Looking for lost models can be tedious. There's no guarantee they are immediately visible and you must fly a search grid from different altitudes. I spotted this one from 500 feet or so. You can see how very close to the road this model was and how nearly impossible it would have been to see from the ground. From above, though, it was pretty obvious in spite of blending in with other yellow vegetation.

3. On another occasion, with a different model, the radio had quit working. The pilotless plane meandered almost a mile away before crashing here with little damage. It was another one that proved easy to spot from the air but impossibly hidden from the ground.

Motor Madness

The motor has turned up some surprising uses. First, they are the monster of all leaf blowers. Of course a regular leaf blower won't cut your arm off but for those willing to try it, there's no better way to move a big volume of air on very little gas. Only do this stuff wearing it on your back and don't let that cage near anything. The prop finds bystanders just as tasty as pilots. Be careful!

Traveling With Gear

CHAPTER 31

The ability to travel so readily with your aircraft is unique to powered paragliding. It's not always easy, but is almost always worth the effort. Taking just the wing and a harness for free-flying is even easier.

Shipping

A PPG is unique in its ability to be boxed and shipped around the world using common consumer freight carriers. However, you should know of certain precautions and tips that will minimize drama in the process.

Preparing the Motor

Clean the machine to remove anything that would create odors. If the harness smells bad, double bag it in plastic bags.

Make sure there is no fuel present. Nearly all carriers, whether ground or air, require this. Some may not check as carefully but, for everybody's same, don't risk it—drain the tank into a gas can then run the motor until it exhausts the last drop. That further insures that nothing remains in the carburetor (including fuel reservoirs) or fuel line. Remove and bag or replace the air filter, which inevitably smells of fuel. Dry the fuel tank completely. At the point where there is no fuel present it is legal for transport including on the airlines although, as covered later, they probably won't take it.

Remove as much from the motor as possible—muffler, reduction drive and air filter. If the motor can be removed from the frame easily, it should be. Usually only the throttle, fuel line and battery line remain connected to the frame. Being compact is better for motor shipping and probably a lot cheaper. Plus, keeping the motor separate reduces the chance that a careless drop will bend the frame.

Packaging

If you have a hard sided case then this is much easier. Pack so that it can survive a drop from several feet high—such a fate is not terribly uncommon. Firm foam of at least 2" should be used against the box with another softer layer next to the motor. Foam can be purchased from fabric shops in large sheets.

A few models break down enough to fit in a large but airline legal hard-side Samsonite suitcase—it looks just like any other luggage that you see being hefted across ticket counters. But all airline luggage is now screened in one way or another so, unless you know the carrier will accept it, have another contingency planned in case it gets turned away.

Cardboard boxes are adequate as long as they're well padded and taped securely. They must be large enough to allow sufficient packing; any hard piece that touches (or even gets close to) the side will likely be broken or bent. Pet carriers work well too.

Another option is forming foam—this material is made to form to your object (Great Stuff Foam is one brand) then harden. It can be re-used in new boxes as the old ones wear out.

Once the heavy pieces are secure then everything else can be added and packed in bubble wrap. Beware the weight of this box though; it is far, far better to have it be lighter. So don't just throw a bunch of stuff in it. A good idea, for example, is to wrap the muffler and gear box in plastic wrap and put them in with the wing that you will check. The lighter the motor box is, the less likely a drop will do damage. Having another box for the fragile frame pieces is ideal. Back them in light foam.

Propellers fit nicely in gun cases. Even the cheap ones from discount stores work well and accept two wooden props up to 50 inches long. *Puzzle props*, those that come apart at the hub, are great since they fit nicely into your other boxes, negating the need for a separate prop container.

It's quite convenient that the wing squishes into a sleeping-bag sized sack. How hard is that to pack! It can also be good for putting other things in since the wing serves as it's own packing material. Just be sure that nothing sharp protrudes and that no fuel or oil can get on it.

Airlines

Most airlines simply prohibit motors even though there is no federal regulation about it. There *are* regulations against carrying fuel and oil which are hazardous materials. These rules must be followed lest you wind up endangering lives and land in jail. You'd think that, since we don't have crankcase oil that our motors would be allowed. But they don't want to bother with differentiating types and simply say "no motors." Although some pilots have succeeded at getting motors on airlines, it's a gamble that the agent doesn't know their own rules. Non-U.S. carries have proven more tolerant.

If an airline *does* allow your motor, remember all baggage is subject to search and so it probably *will* be inspected. If they smell any fuel odor at all it will **not go**! Don't think that plastic wrap will solve the problem; they will probably open it up. You should have a contingency plan.

A better plan may be removing the engine from its frame and shipping it so that, when you go to the airport, you can check everything else on the airline. You'd end up with one largish box containing the motorless frame, clean gas tank, harness, muffler, prop, redrive and other miscellaneous stuff. The long props may need their own box. Larger frames with rigid cage pieces will probably need two boxes which should be fairly lightweight to minimize damage potential. You may have to pay an oversize or excess baggage fee.

This method allows using a very small box for the motor which is cheaper and safer anyway. It's an issue of convenience as to how much hassle you want to tolerate at the airport for the savings.

Freight Carriers

Hazardous material requirements still limit what cargo airlines can carry but they're more liberal. While the box is less likely to be opened, you must not take the chance of leaving fuel in it—doing so endangers all involved and is a federal offense.

Most all shipping companies work at varying prices. Some airlines have freight divisions but the cargo usually goes on passenger flights. If it's going to a foreign country, it must clear customs and may be delayed up to 3 weeks while incurring a steep customs fees (usually refundable once you take the gear back out of the country.) It can be quite the paper chase, too. These are reasons for taking the gear on your international passenger flight, if allowed.

Bus Lines

Some pilots have had good luck using commercial bus lines. You must drop the equipment off at the bus terminal and pick it up at a designated spot but sometimes arrangements can be made for delivery service. Check with the line but they don't seem to have any restrictions that prevent the shipment.

Transporting via Road

Bringing the gear by car is the most convenient option if you've got time to drive. Besides avoiding the teardown and restore process, you can fly along the way. Few experiences top being able to come upon some perfect piece of planet then exploring it from above.

Using the Platform

Taking apart the motor for transport by car is usually pretty simple, but even that can get tiresome after a while. The perfect solution is a platform attached to the vehicle's rear frame which almost any car can accommodate. The car must have a receiver that is made for towing. Instead of a trailer hitch, you buy a platform that slides into the receiver, making the perfect PPG perch. Most trailer outlets can sell and weld a 2 inch receiver to your car (or smaller 1 ¼ inch size). Your paramotor, fuel container and tools can all be strapped to it and secured with moving straps, bungee cords and a long bicycle lock.

No trailer lights are required because the platform doesn't extend very far back. It is very easy to remove, requiring only one pin to hold in place.

When securing your motor, use at least two straps and make sure that any one of them could fail or come loose without the motor falling off. If your motor has a clutch, the prop can spin in the breeze, putting wear on the bearings. Use a bungee cord or other method to prevent that.

Platforms come in many sizes. This one is wide enough to fit two motors but they must be positioned just right.

Bottom: Eric Sansli of Turkey totes it behind his motorcycle. A roadable trike negates the need for a trailer in his case. Quite handy.

The PPG Bible: A complete Guide and Reference

There I Was...

I'd had enough. Every morning and every afternoon I'd been flying. It was some of the country's prettiest scenery, including Meteor Crater and Flagstaff's volcanoes, but still, it was time for a break. Today would be that break—simply enjoying a nice scenic drive down to Phoenix. Just before going down the big hill out of Flagstaff I pulled off the highway to take in a scenic overlook. No flying, mind you, just admiring.

What a vista. I stood there reveling in it. My paramotorhome, the *Enterprise*, and it's flight gear rested. Passerby, though, were curious about the contraption on back and PPG signage festooned on the vehicle.

While soaking in the breathtaking expanse of colors, a family piled out of minivan next to me. The questions soon followed about my strange machine, "What is it? You don't really fly that do you?" etc. That got me going: "You can launch in no wind but would rather have a bit." I walked to a small open area and spread my hands as if to catch the breeze: "This is about right—5 to 7 mph" I continued. "You don't really need a lot of room but want an 'out' in case the motor quits." I walked to the edge and was surprised to see that it trailed down the hill with grass. That was it. "I'll tell you what, why don't I just show you!"

In a few steps I was off, climbing into the most spectacular meeting of landscape and sky to land on a retina. The area was a broad swath of sharp contrast in red hues and canyons and trees. Climbing higher allowed more landing options and I was able to explore. By the time I got back, the family was gone and I can only imagine the thoughts that flight inspired. Some, of course, were probably "crazy man" types. But I'll bet there had to be some wonderment at the incredible capability—running into the air.

I can make my own scenic overlook!

Be careful, gear gets damaged in transit more often than it gets damaged in flight for those who travel much. Plus, constant bouncing around is hard on it. If possible, put hard foam on the bottom to absorb some of the jostling.

Gas & Oil

When traveling by air, you won't be able take a gas container, so plan on buying one when you arrive. You won't be able to take it back with you, either, so just donate it to the pilot of your choice.

The oil available at gas stations is usually for boat outboards which is not ideal. Try to find oil that is at least made for air cooled motors. Motorcycle shops are good sources of quality oil and hardware stores carry 2-stroke oil for chain saws that will do in a pinch. Even if it's not what you normally use it should be OK since your motor will have been completely emptied and will be again before you travel.

Some experienced pilots recommend against mixing synthetic and mineral oils. Motorcycle or cart go-racing shops are your best bet at finding a wide variety of oils while you're away from home.

Customs

The problem here isn't fuel, it's taxes and tariffs. Registering your motor with an organization and having the documentation may help to show that it's yours. Some countries (not the US) require registration with the government. The border folks fear that you may be importing the motor for sale so it's more suspicious if you're traveling with more than one. They may also fear some nefarious use so having a picture of it in flight may be helpful.

Don't try sneaking one by customs, they can be very uncompromising. Admittedly, the only border this helicopter was enforcing belonged to the Albuquerque Balloon Fiesta.

If you're traveling with a group, it may be best to have the frame in a box with the prop separated. You'll attract less attention. Its not that it's illegal, it's that they don't know what to do with it.

The most appropriate declaration is "Sporting Equipment" or "Paragliding Equipment" for personal use. It is helpful if you have a local person there to help deal with issues especially if you don't speak the foreign language.

In the U.S. anti-terror laws do not allow individuals to ship using airline cargo services—you must go through a *freight forwarder* who ships using the cheapest means, most likely a freight airline for rapid delivery. Otherwise, you must be certified as a *known shipper*. Your dealer may have already acquired that status and be able to help.

The large freight companies can be used (Fedex & UPS) but are expensive depending on the destination. They do handle the customs issues but don't be surprised if there is a very large charge at the end. Some countries can be "creative" with charges which is why it's good to enlist the help of a local. Some charges verge on extortion.

In any case, some of the best advice you can get will come from other pilots who have already traveled to your intended destination. Seek them out on the internet and give a blessing to modern communications.

Photography

CHAPTER 32

We enjoy an amazing platform for capturing pictures and video. The unfettered view coupled with slow speed and stability make the paramotor nearly perfect for photography. In the U.S., as with many other countries, it must be for recreational purposes only (see Chapter 8), but you can certainly share your work with others.

Distraction is a major concern, requiring extra discipline to remain aware of your surroundings and insure a clear flight path. Concentrating too much on the photo elements, especially while flying low, ups risk dramatically.

Always attach the camera to something using a secure strap that's long enough to allow free range while staying out of the prop. Looping it through a front harness strap is better than around a part of your body. Hanging the camera strap around your neck could allow it to get caught in the propeller or other moving motor parts. This has happened with almost dire results. If you launch with anything around your neck make sure it is cinched up tight so it can't go behind you. Then once in flight, re-attach it to some part of the harness webbing.

Still Photography Basics

Photography merits its own book but these few tidbits will go a long way to help you get great shots, even ones worthy of magazine covers. It is geared towards digital technology owing to the cost, convenience and quality that has become standard. The basics are the same whether the recording medium is a chip or film.

Quality

If you're new to digital cameras, check out the Pixels and Pictures box on the next

The Killer Shot

Photog George Steinmetz has shared incredible views of the world through the pages of National Geographic Magazine. He's got an eye for the interesting and knows how to capture it. He is a photographer who flies.

His motorized paraglider has become a tool that sometimes has no equal. He winds up in remote corners of continents where no other way aloft makes sense. And he gains flying sites the same way most of us do—ask nicely for permission or, on occasion, forgiveness. He offers that being respectful is important and never be annoying—advice that has served him well.

When asked to share some wisdom with aspiring photographers, he offers: "I do a lot of research before I go, but always find interesting, unexpected things when I arrive. With close ground support, I can scout a lot by boat, car or camel, but it always looks different from above."

This shot of the Gobi Desert's "Empty Quarter" shows several principals at work. First, of course, you have to know it's there, you must then get to the right place with the right equipment, and finally, set up the shot. In this case, having the horizon in view adds greatly to the sense of size. Having an interesting foreground helps a lot too. Another helpful technique is to try getting shots during the low sun of morning and evening—fortunately, these are great times for flying, too.

courtesy www.GeorgeSteinmetz.com

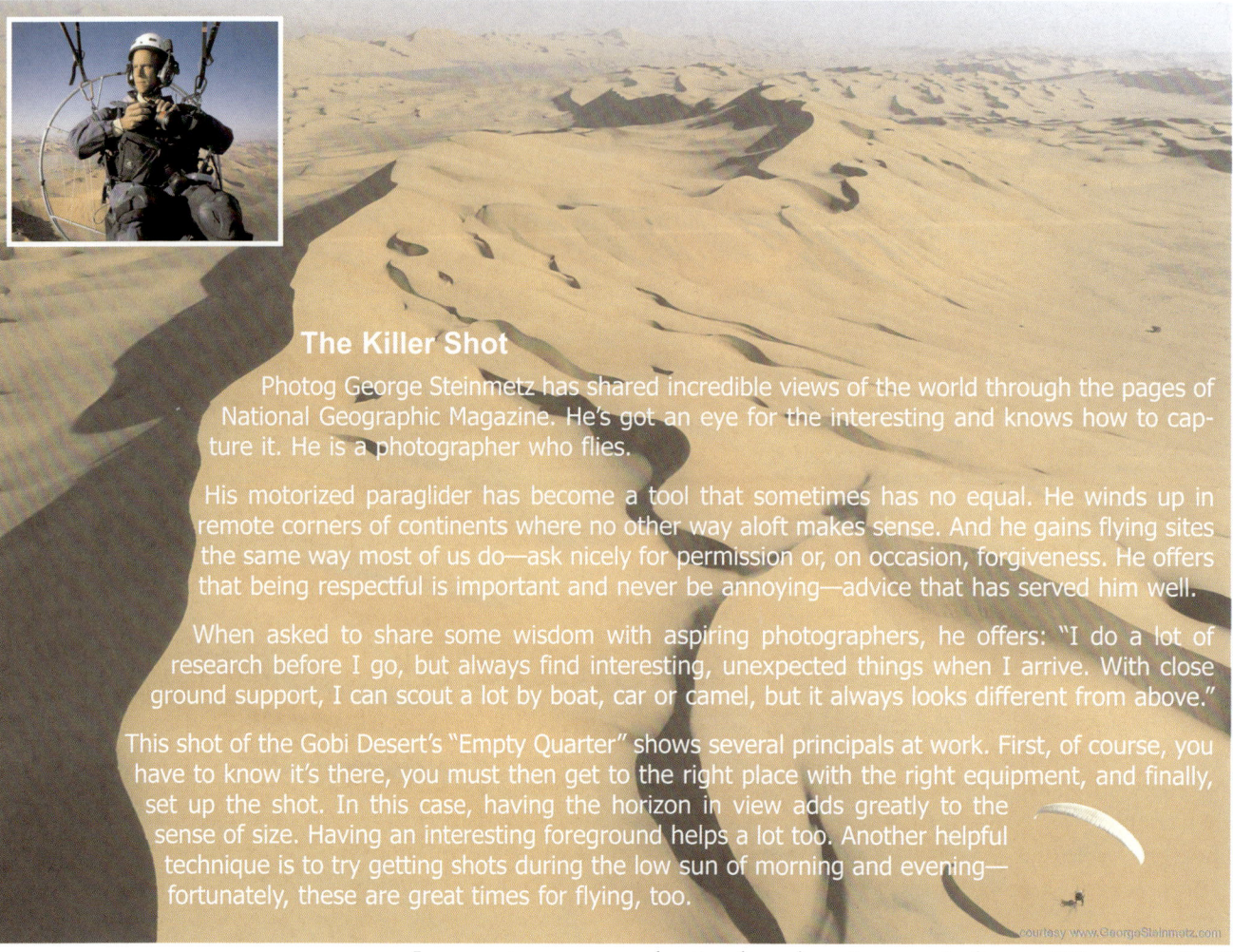

page. Inexpensive cameras, having less than 3 megapixels are OK, especially if you'll just be e-mailing pictures to friends or making small prints (3 x 5 inches) from them. Professional quality, however, requires at least 5 megapixels because printing is done at 300 dots per inch (DPI)—far more than what's required to look good on a computer screen. Another camera quality that you'll enjoy (and pay for) is a fast refresh rate—being able to take another shot quickly at the highest quality. A long shutter delay will make you miss some great shots in dynamic situations.

Photos take enormous space so most cameras default to storing a compressed version, usually JPEG (or JPG). These sacrifice some minor quality degradation (unnoticeable in most uses) for a significantly smaller file size. *Fineness* describes the level of compression—more *fine* means less compression.

If you plan to have your pictures go in a magazine or other published media, use the highest resolution and fineness available—you paid for the camera's highest quality, use it! You won't be able to take as many pictures but that just means transferring to another storage device sooner.

There's a lot more to quality than pixel count. For example, the image recording method, size of the capture area, storage and optics all play a big part. The best cameras usually have removable lenses and fast refresh rates, too.

Focus

Any picture is essentially worthless if the main subject is blurry. Most cameras have an autofocus that works well but it has limits, the worst of which is focusing on the wrong thing. Almost as bad is an autofocus system that increases shutter lag (how long it takes the camera to be ready for another picture). Such a system may "hunt" or pick up on something real close like your own risers or cage. As long as you're shooting with no zoom (the subject looks far away), you can set most cameras to remain on infinity, where everything farther than about 8 feet is in focus. There's nothing worse then discovering that your perfect shot of a spiraling pilot wound up as a perfectly focused shot of your leg.

In low light situations it gets harder for the camera to focus. On most models, holding the shutter down half-way makes the camera "calculate" the shot—setting shutter speed, focusing, and other parameters. Then when you press the button fully, it takes the picture right away. So if it won't focus on your subject, point it towards something with better contrast but the same distance, push the shutter button half-way, point it back to your subject and press the button all the way.

Sharp Subject, Blurry Background

Many times professional photographers use blurry backgrounds to make their subject stand out. There are two primary ways to do this:

1. **Panning**. Carefully track the moving subject so the background is zipping by, causing it to blur. The slower the shutter speed, the more dramatic the effect. Of course a slow shutter speed makes it harder to keep the subject sharp too.

2. Narrowing the **depth of field**. The distance range that is in focus is called *depth of field (DoF)*. A wide DoF means that most everything, distant and near, is in focus. A narrow DoF means that only objects at the focused distance are sharp, while closer or farther objects are blurry. Zooming in narrows the DoF; as you zoom

1. Depth of field blur. Zoom and an open aperture help create this.

2. Motion Blur. To get this effect, zoom a bit, pan the subject and use the slowest shutter speed possible.

Digging Deeper: Exposure, Getting the Light Right

Exposure tells a lot about a picture. As most know, under exposed means the picture comes out dark and over exposed means it is washed out or too light. There are three notable attributes affecting exposure:

ISO or film speed is the sensor's (or film's) sensitivity to light. The lower the ISO number the less the sensitivity. So ISO 100 is less sensitive than ISO 400. More sensitivity, however, means less quality to some degree. The highest sensitivities are "noisy" meaning they're splotchy or grainy when enlarged. But it's still better to have the sensitivity set high than it is to have the shot underexposed.

Shutter speed is how long the shutter stays open. Longer times mean more light. So 1/60th of a second allows more light to pass through than does 1/250th. That allows shooting in lower light but both the subject and the shooter must stay quite still at the slower settings (less than about 1/125th.

Aperture is how big the opening is where light comes through and is expressed as "f stop" where larger numbers mean a smaller opening. So an f-stop of f1.8 is wide open (many cameras can't go that big) and f5.6 is a small opening. The bigger the aperture, the more light can pass and so the less light you can shoot in.

Most cameras have an auto setting that analyzes the image and choose these values automatically when the shutter button is pressed halfway down. Almost all models beyond the most basic let you change one and have it adjust the other settings. For example if you want to "stop" the action in a shot, you choose a faster shutter speed and let the camera choose an optimum aperture (open it up to allow more light). ISO is set usually set by the user and not adjusted in the auto process.

Changing the ISO from 200 to ISO 400 makes the capture medium more sensitive (whether film or CCD) and allows shooting in lower light with acceptably fast shutter speeds. Most cameras produce slightly "grainy" pictures at their most sensitive (highest value) ISO settings.

The PPG Bible: A Complete Guide and Reference

Digging Deeper: Pixels and Pictures

A pixel is what digital pictures are made of—the little colored dots recorded by the camera and displayed on a monitor or printed on a page. Resolution is the number of pixels expressed as horizontal and vertical dots; more is better. For example, 1 megapixel is a million little colored dots which allows a resolution of about 1200 by 800 (1200 dots across and 800 dots down). Monitors have about 72 dots per inch (horizontally and vertically) so 1200 pixels across means the picture will fill up a monitor. Professionally printed material needs 300 or more dots per inch so that same 1200 by 800 shot will only serve up a 4-inch wide printed picture.

Your eye has amazing resolution—it would take a 25 megapixel camera to approach the quality available through an open human eyeball.

in on the subject its background gets more blurry. Opening up the aperture also narrows the DoF. The wide aperture (smaller f-numbers mean larger aperture) lets in a lot of light which means that shutter speed will be quite high. A camera with a large lens, and more importantly a large pickup area behind it, will be able to achieve a narrower DoF. More expensive cameras usually have a larger pickup area.

Other Settings & Tidbits

Fortunately the auto setting on most cameras does just fine in the bright light we usually get to work with. Using auto leaves you free you to frame and fly.

Remember to use the highest quality settings offered. You can always save lower resolution versions later but the bulk of your effort was getting the camera to its vantage point—don't waste the effort. Once the shutter is pressed any opportunity for better quality vanishes. That magazine cover shot that you're carefully framing needs to be at least 2700 x 3300 pixels.

Here is a summary of basic tips to help capture images from a PPG:

- Use the auto setting unless you really know what you're doing and the camera allows quick adjustments.

- Have sufficient light. Once the sun gets too low you must be very steady for pictures to be sharp. In poor light it might be a good trade-off to set the camera's *ISO* to a higher number (or use higher speed film if not using digital). This increases the sensitivity of the capture surface (just like film) at some expense in *noise*. Noise is to digital photography what *grainy* is to film.

- Fill the picture with the subject—at least 50% of the shot should be occupied by your subject and more is better. Of course if there is something equally interesting in the background then adjust accordingly.

- Be leery of zoom. Two things make it challenging. First, the autofocus confuses easily if you're not centered on the subject (depending on camera setting) and second, even slight movement of the camera will blur the shot.

- Use zoom. You'll have to have bright light for a high shutter speed, but it is much better to zoom now then to crop later in your photo editing software.

- **Skip** *digital zoom* where the camera simply makes the pixels bigger but has fewer of them. Cropping later does the same thing but gives you more control.

- Keep shooting. Take lots of pictures to increase the odds of getting it perfect. But if the shot is obviously boring, skip it. Later on you'll quickly tire of reviewing boring shots.

- Be close. This is extremely risky because you're not only flying close, but you're thinking about the camera. Keep flying the craft! Shots are far more interesting when they're close.

Including part of your own frame in the shot can add interest. It gives perspective while letting the viewer know what it was taken from.

Something to consider when buying a camera is the viewfinder. If you plan on doing air-to-air shots, a swiveling LCD display is valuable. If you are forced to look through a view finder, shots like the one below are difficult or impossible because you have to hold the camera out to clear your frame.

- Follow the usual camera rules about trying to keep your subject down sun from you.

- Pictures are frequently more interesting when you can see the pilot's face, especially if he's looking at you. There are exceptions, of course and experimenting with them is half the fun.

- Unless you have specific scenery in mind, try to get a human subject in the shot, especially another PPGer.

- Have something or someone of prominence in the foreground to add interest and scale.

Video

One of the hardest things to get while flying is good video. Start off with appropriate equipment—essentially as good a quality camera as you can afford. Quality has improved so that consumer equipment is only about 5 years behind its professional predecessor. Bigger is better for lenses, too, and make sure the camera can accept a wide-angle adapter. A wide-angle lens, about 0.5x, captures the pilot and glider in the same shot without being too far away.

Steady is king. The absolute worst thing you can do to your viewer is put them through a jittery video. Everything else is secondary. Technology that reduces jittery images may be helpful.

The camera can be hand held but it tends to shake—using two hands helps but that leaves little to mind the paraglider with. Weight shift steering helps here.

Helmet cams are great because your hands are free. For best results you need an eyesight for targeting, a steady head and a wide-angle lens. Phil Russman has the mother of wide angle lenses (1 and 3) while John Phillips makes good use of a helmet mounted consumer camera.

Occasionally, use the widest angle lens that you can afford. You must be ready to fly close, though, lest the subject appear too far away.

You'll eventually want a helmet mount with sighting viewfinder. Besides freeing your hands up to fly, it can yield reasonably steady shots. Wider angle is better to reduce jitter. Such a contraption is not difficult to make using Velcro and tape for the camera and a coat hangar for the sight. You can also buy small *lipstick cameras* that plug into your own camera which is then used for recording (make sure your model supports this). Still use a helmet-mounted framing device so you can see what you're framing—you don't want to be looking down at a display for obvious reasons. Also, skydiver accessory suppliers have helmets ready-made to accept a camera.

Hanging lipstick cameras from your wing or other locations can add great interest.

When flying close, as required with a wide-angle lens, be aware of the extreme risk for collision and include extra precautions. Plan to avoid wake turbulence, too, when working around another glider.

Here are some tips to improve your in-flight video recording:

- Be smooth. Smooth is king. If it wiggles, it will probably get tossed in any final production. Choose smooth air whenever possible.
- Be leery of zoom. Even more then still shots, video rarely looks good when zoomed because it's too jittery. Only zoom in with calm conditions if you can hold the camera extremely steady. Even then be ready for throw-away footage.
- Flying shots will usually benefit from the widest angle you can get as long as you can be close to the subject.
- Fill the lens with your subject. Little gliders, flying far away, drains the interest right out of most video.
- Vary the shot. Vary the angle, the zoom (oh so smoothly), the background, the subject, etc. After editing, shots should rarely last longer than 2 seconds.
- Try to always have something in the shot moving and have something else in the shot not moving much at all. For example, having the subject flying by from right to left may be more interesting if you don't follow him. Point the camera so that he flies into and out of frame where the background slides by at the same rate.

Some of the best PPG video is shot on the ground. It's not as much fun but the quality can be much better plus, it's a lot safer. Besides, launching and landing is frequently our sport's most entertaining endeavor. It can also be valuable to have someone record your own efforts for later review and critique.

Mounting the camera in different places is a great way to make unique pictures. Having the camera swivel all the way around can make for some amazing video. This was done for a newspaper that wanted a close shot of the pilot in flight. It's easier than flying formation and you never worry about where the camera pilot is.

Getting the cage in the shot made seeing Alex Varv bank it up below a bit more interesting. Having a camera with external display screen made this easier.

The coolest video usually comes from getting close. Unfortunately, that's also the riskiest way to get it. Phil is getting extremely close while Michael Purdy walks over a ledge. Notice how deep in the brakes Phil has to stay—be careful while doing something like this!

Organizing Fly-Ins

CHAPTER

33

Eventually you may want to host an event on your own turf. It can be little more than opening up your home site to a group of friends or putting on a major convention. Conducting it safely has priority and pilots should be made aware of the points in Chapter 14.

Your site is obviously worth protecting. Be mindful of the impact that lots of machines buzzing about is going to have. Sensitive places must be avoided although pilots will occasionally stray where they ought not, even after being asked not to. Some will forget, some will not get the word, some will, unfortunately, just not care. Consider this before opening up your own field.

Preparation

Your event doesn't have to be complicated. If you provide the field, basic guidance and a place to exhaust used food then the pilots will have fun. Just gathering is the single biggest draw, but some level of organization can add interest, especially for the non-flyers or those not *yet* flying.

Field Setup

The first priority is to keep observers away from running motors and flight operations. Children, pets and inattentive folks could quickly run afoul of a starting motor. The larger the event, the more important such segregation is.

There must be a clear area for launch and landing, commonly called the *flight line*. At some level of congestion it may be better to separate launching and landing traffic. Consider cutting the field half where the downwind half is for landing and the upwind half is for launchers. That prevents many conflicts. When the wind shifts enough, the halves can be reversed.

Pattern Design

You can't know what the wind will do so have a pattern picked out, in advance, for all possible wind combinations. Publish this pattern so that everybody can be completely clear about it. A critical collision avoidance feature is having pilots follow the designated pattern whenever they're close to the field. And don't have pilots flying where they would have no engine-out option.

This pattern is quite complicated only because the site is an active airport with a number of sensitive areas.

If your event allows heavier craft, arrange the pattern to avoid wake turbulence issues. The wake from a powered parachute, for example, can completely collapse a PPG wing.

Set reasonable pattern altitudes, usually from 300 - 500 fee, to keep the noise below neighbor annoyance levels and maintain better landing options.

What to Include

Informing The Flying Public

One day before your event starts, alert the flying public by doing the following:

Call 1 800 WX BRIEF and advise them that you would like to place a NOTAM. Use a sectional chart to locate your field relative to an airport or VOR (see Chapter 13). Give the distance in nautical miles and bearing from the closest VOR.

Lets say your event is 15 NM out on the 270 radial from STL (St. Louis) VOR from Dec 31, 2010 until Jan 01, 2011. We'll assume most flying will be within a 2 nautical mile (nm) radius or that spot from 30 minutes prior sunrise to 30 minutes after sunset.

The NOTAM would read: "INTENSE ULTRALIGHT ACTIVITY WITHIN 2 NM RADIUS STL 270 AT 15NM FROM THE SURFACE TO 800 FEET AGL. EFFECTIVE 10/12/31 UNTIL 11/01/01 FROM 30 MINUTES PRIOR TO SR TO 30 MINUTES AFTER SS". They will convert the times into Mean Greenwich Time (also called "Zulu") for you. The official name of "Zulu" time is Coordinated Universal Time; curiously, that's abbreviated UTC.

Details can get easily overlooked, here's a list of some things to think about when putting it all together.

- Set the location, dates, and times and costs. Get insurance, if required, along with scheduling porta potties (1 per 50 participants), trash cans, a tent, showers, hotel discounts, and other accommodations that you may provide. Publicize it using magazines or the Internet.
- Setup the field layout with all areas such as registration, parking, briefing, camping, etc. Establish patterns that can work with any wind direction.
- Line up the people who will help you pull it off. In addition to safety officers (at least 1 per 50 pilots), you'll need folks to help with registration, food (if any), transportation of downed pilots and the sundry unplanned tasks that crop up.
- Notify the nearest rescue folks and police about the event and provide some information on powered paragliding.
- Create and use a bullet-proof waiver. If the unthinkable happens, it will possibly be your only protection. Have verification that pilots signed the waiver such as a sticker they put on their helmet.

Sharing

Its in our nature to show others see what we find so fascinating about this sport and to be around those who share our passion. Having a fly-in, or helping someone else have one, is a great means to that end. Yes, it's a lot of work and no, you won't be a hero. But it will be rewarding in the long run. Who knows, maybe you will be the spark that ignites someone else's passion.

Now go enjoy some flying for yourself!

Appendix - Checklists

There are checklists for everything and they can easily include too much. One that is cumbersome will not be used. A well-designed checklist will be easy to remember, and therefore be fairly brief, covering only the most important stuff. After all, if it's not used, it's useless. These checklists have been designed to meet that goal. The "memory aid" is intended to be used in a sing-song fashion to aid recall.

It is helpful to copy the checklist and use the paper copy until you're thoroughly familiar with the routine. Refer back to the checklist after you've done a procedure to see if you've missed anything.

Items may be different based on your machine but these checklists give a good basic plan. If you do not recognize a part name then it probably doesn't apply to you. For the preflight, start with your carabiners and proceed around. Look for the most obvious: loose, missing or damaged parts, broken safety wire, etc. If a machine has just been assembled, give it a preflight just before flying in addition to a thorough look-over just after re-assembling. One minute is all it takes and you'll be surprised at what you'll find. Muffler parts are probably the most likely to have insidious failures—cracks, bolts working out of aluminum, sheared screws, etc.

When you're finish flying, it's extremely beneficial to do the preflight inspection so you have a chance to fix what problems you find before your next flying session.

These checklists are intended to help learn what to look for. Once you're familiar with the flow then the paper checklist can be used optionally.

Remember, more propeller-strike injuries happen while starting or test running a motor than in any other phase so treat the machine with enormous respect. Wearing a helmet can protect you in case of a disintegrating prop while also providing ear protection.

Preflight Inspection Checklist

Item	Action
Carabiners	Attached properly, no damage, in correct hole for pilot weight/loading
Lift web	No nicks, burns or other damage
Harness	Attached properly, no damage (lift at carabiners to shape for inspection)
Attachments	Pouches zipped, GPS/Instruments/strobe/etc secure
Reserve	Mounts secure, pin(s) in, bridle run properly
Kick-in strap & speedbar	Attached properly, no damage, stowed as needed
Distance/comfort/J bars	Attached properly to frame and lift web
Safety Strap (J-Bar)	Attached properly, no damage, motor release set (as installed)
Frame	General condition, velcro/fasteners in place
Cage	Netting General condition, velcro/fasteners in place, secure
Motor	Spark plug, muffler bolts, wires, head tightness, motor mounts secure
Air filter/box	Secure, free
Fuel Tank	Lid on, straps/bolts secure, vent free, fuel line in good condition
Propeller	Main bolts, does not wiggle fore/aft, (center bolt tight), no cracks
Redrive	Not loose, belt tensioned and on all groves
Throttle	Free, undamaged, **full travel at the carburetor** when moved
Battery	Secure, plugged in, master switch as required (on if about to start)

Before Start Checklist

Item	Action
Area	Look around to make sure the prop and blast area is clear
Fuel Valve	On
Choke or Prime	Set choke or Prime as required
Master Switch	Brace in case starter engages, then On
Throttle	Hold so that it is impossible to throttle up even if the motor pushes hard
Brace	**Brace in case of full power!** If possible, start it on your back.
Clear	Yell, Clear Pop (even if alone) to announce the impending start, wait for 2 seconds, then
Start	Pull or press the starter button until it starts

These basic checklists cover the most common problems that occur on launch or landing. For example, the helmet item "chin" may seem trivial, but numerous pilots have inflated their wing, reared up to look at it and had their unstrapped helmet fly through the prop. That's expensive.

Pre-Launch Checklist

Item	Action	Memory aid
Leg strap left	Fastened and adjusted.	Leg,
Leg strap right	Fastened and adjusted	Leg,
Chest straps	Fastened and adjusted.	Chest and
Helmet strap	Fastened and adjusted.	Chin;
Brakes	Correct hand, clear to pulley.	Brakes,
Carabiners	Closed, locked	'Biners,
Trimmers	Adjusted for takeoff.	Trimmers and
Straps, loose items	Secure and Zipped.	Zippers;
Launch path	Clear.	Path,
Run-up	Full power & kill switch test.	Power and go.

Pre-Landing Checklist

Item	Action	Memory aid
Harness Straps	Adjusted for landing	Harness
Trimmers	Slow (or as required)	Trimmers and
Pouches, loose items	Secure and Zipped.	Zippers;
Wind	Insure landing into it.	Wind
Pattern	Establish flight path	Path and
Gear	Legs (gear) extended	Legs

Appendix - Resources

Fuel/Oil Mix Chart

Consult your engine maker for recommended types of two-stroke oil and desired mixes. There are different requirements for for breaking in a motor (seating the rings properly) which is normally considered the first 5 hours.

For this many **gallons**	Add this many **ounces** of oil:		Or for this many **liters**	Add this many **milliliters** of oil:		
at 32:1	at 40:1	at 50:1	at 32:1	at 40:1	at 50:1	fuel:oil ratio
1 gal	4.0	3.2	2.6	118	95	76
2 gal	8.0	6.4	5.1	237	189	151
5 gal	20.0	16.0	12.8	591	473	379
1 ltr	1.1	0.8	0.7	31	25	20
2 ltr	2.1	1.7	1.4	63	50	40
5 ltr	5.3	4.2	3.4	156	125	100
10 ltr	10.6	8.5	6.8	313	250	200

Note the crazy English volume units: 1 US Gal = 4 quarts = 8 pints = 128 ounces = 3.785412 liters = 0.832 UK gallons
Metric units: 1 Liter = 1000 milliliters = 0.2641721 US gallon

Repair

The best resource for replacement or repair is the dealer where you bought the gear. It's likely that he/she knows where to look or what can be substituted. They will also know best whether or not replacement is necessary. Visit www.FootFlyer.com for updates to resources along with other new information relating to powered paragliding.

Instruction

A valuable resource is the www.USPPA.org web site where it lists all certified paramotor instructors. In the USA, there are solo pilot certification programs from the USPPA, USUA or USHGA. Tandem exemption programs are run by the USUA, EAA and ASC. Check with the organization for your country to find a similarly certified instructor.

Welding

Aluminum welding is very specialized and not all shops do it. Even fewer will do it if they know it's for a flying machine. Look in the yellow pages; even if they don't do aluminum they should know who to call.

When you do find someone to weld, avoid describing it's primary function; rather describe one of its auxiliary uses such glorified leaf blower, ski & skate power for the vertically challenged, etc.

Appendix - FAR 103

For convenience, here is the U.S. Federal Aviation Regulation (FAR) relating to Ultralights. The most recent version can be found at www.faa.gov using the title *FAR 103*. A related advisory circular (not included here) is AC 103-7 which details much of the process and intent of the regulation. Note that FAR 103.20 requires adherence to certain FAR part 91 rules that pertain mostly to airspace restrictions.

Subpart A—General

§ 103.1 Applicability.
This part prescribes rules governing the operation of ultralight vehicles in the United States. For the purposes of this part, an ultralight vehicle is a vehicle that:
(a) Is used or intended to be used for manned operation in the air by a single occupant;
(b) Is used or intended to be used for recreation or sport purposes only;
(c) Does not have any U.S. or foreign airworthiness certificate; and
(d) If unpowered, weighs less than 155 pounds; or
(e) If powered:
  (1) Weighs less than 254 pounds empty weight, excluding floats and safety devices which are intended for deployment in a potentially catastrophic situation;
  (2) Has a fuel capacity not exceeding 5 U.S. gallons;
  (3) Is not capable of more than 55 knots calibrated airspeed at full power in level flight; and
  (4) Has a power—off stall speed which does not exceed 24 knots calibrated airspeed.

§ 103.3 Inspection requirements.
(a) Any person operating an ultralight vehicle under this part shall, upon request, allow the Administrator, or his designee, to inspect the vehicle to determine the applicability of this part.
(b) The pilot or operator of an ultralight vehicle must, upon request of the Administrator, furnish satisfactory evidence that the vehicle is subject only to the provisions of this part.

§ 103.5 Waivers.
No person may conduct operations that require a deviation from this part except under a written waiver issued by the Administrator.

§ 103.7 Certification and registration.
(a) Notwithstanding any other section pertaining to certification of aircraft or their parts or equipment, ultralight vehicles and their component parts and equipment are not required to meet the airworthiness certification standards specified for aircraft or to have certificates of airworthiness.
(b) Notwithstanding any other section pertaining to airman certification, operators of ultralight vehicles are not required to meet any aeronautical knowledge, age, or experience requirements to operate those vehicles or to have airman or medical certificates.
(c) Notwithstanding any other section pertaining to registration and marking of aircraft, ultralight vehicles are not required to be registered or to bear markings of any type.

Subpart B—Operating Rules

§ 103.9 Hazardous operations.
(a) No person may operate any ultralight vehicle in a manner that creates a hazard to other persons or property.
(b) No person may allow an object to be dropped from an ultralight vehicle if such action creates a hazard to other persons or property.

§ 103.11 Daylight operations.
(a) No person may operate an ultralight vehicle except between the hours of sunrise and sunset.
(b) Notwithstanding paragraph (a) of this section, ultralight vehicles may be operated during the twilight periods 30 minutes before official sunrise and 30 minutes after official sunset or, in Alaska, during the period of civil twilight as defined in the Air Almanac, if:
  (1) The vehicle is equipped with an operating anticollision light visible for at least 3 statute miles; and
  (2) All operations are conducted in uncontrolled airspace.

§ 103.13 Operation near aircraft; right-o-way rules.
(a) Each person operating an ultralight vehicle shall maintain vigilance so as to see and avoid aircraft and shall yield the right—of—way to all aircraft.
(b) No person may operate an ultralight vehicle in a manner that creates a collision hazard with respect to any aircraft.
(c) Powered ultralights shall yield the right—of—way to unpowered ultralights.

Appendix - FAR 103

§ 103.15 Operations over congested areas.
No person may operate an ultralight vehicle over any congested area of a city, town, or settlement, or over any open air assembly of persons.

§ 103.17 Operations in certain airspace.
No person may operate an ultralight vehicle within Class A, Class B, Class C, or Class D airspace or within the lateral boundaries of the surface area of Class E airspace designated for an airport unless that person has prior authorization from the ATC facility having jurisdiction over that airspace.

§ 103.19 Operations in prohibited or restricted areas.
No person may operate an ultralight vehicle in prohibited or restricted areas unless that person has permission from the using or controlling agency, as appropriate.

§ 103.20 Flight restrictions in the proximity of certain areas designated by notice to airmen.
No person may operate an ultralight vehicle in areas designated in a Notice to Airmen under §91.137, §91.138, §91.141, §91.143 or §91.145 of this chapter, unless authorized by:
(a) Air Traffic Control (ATC); or
(b) A Flight Standards Certificate of Waiver or Authorization issued for the demonstration or event.
[Doc. No. FAA-2000-8274, 66 FR 47378, Sept. 11, 2001]

§ 103.21 Visual reference with the surface.
No person may operate an ultralight vehicle except by visual reference with the surface.

§ 103.23 Flight visibility and cloud clearance requirements.
No person may operate an ultralight vehicle when the flight visibility or distance from clouds is less than that in the table found below. All operations in Class A, Class B, Class C, and Class D airspace or Class E airspace designated for an airport must receive prior ATC authorization as required in §103.17 of this part.

Airspace	Visibility Required	Distance From Clouds
Class A:	Not applicable	Not Applicable.
Class B:	3 statute miles	Clear of Clouds.
Class C:	3 statute miles	500 feet below, 1000 feet above, 2,000 feet horizontal.
Class D:	3 statute miles.	500 feet below, 1000 feet above, 2,000 feet horizontal.
Class E:		
Less than 10,000 feet MSL	3 statute miles	500 feet below, 1000 feet above, 2000 feet horizontal.
10,000 feet or higher MSL	5 statute miles	1000 feet below, 1000 feet above, 1 statute mile horizontal.
Class G:		
1200 feet or less above the surface (regardless of MSL altitude)	1 statute mile	Clear of clouds.
More than 1200 feet above the surface but less than 10,000 feet MSL	1 statute mile	500 feet below, 1000 feet above, 2,000 feet horizontal.
More than 1200 above the surface and at or above 10,000 MSL	5 statute miles	1000 feet below, 1000 feet above, 1 statute mile horizontal.

[Amdt. 103-17, 56 FR 65662, Dec. 17, 1991] Last updated: February 18, 2004

Glossary

2-Stroke—A valveless motor with a power stroke every time the piston goes down.

4-Stroke—A valved motor with a power stroke ever other time the piston goes down.

A Lines—The first row of paraglider lines; they go from the A riser to the leading edge of the wing.

Accelerator—System used to accelerate the wing using a foot bar connected to the risers, through the harness. The pilot activates it by pushing the bar out with both feet. Also called Speedbar.

Active Flying—The fine control inputs required to keep the wing exactly overhead in turbulence or maneuvering, damping both left/right oscillations and fore/aft surges.

AGL—Above Ground Level.

ACPUL—Association des Constructeurs de Parapente Ultra Legers. European association that developed test standards for paragliders later adopted by AFNOR.

AFNOR—Association Française de Normalisation, French organization that does certification of paragliders (among many other things).

ASL—Above Sea Level.

ATC—Air Traffic Control which consists of Approach Controls, Control Towers and Air Route Traffic Control Centers (just called "Center").

Airspeed—Speed through the air. A GPS reads ground speed, the pilot feels airspeed.

Aspect Ratio—Ratio of the wingspan (projected) to the average chord.

Asymmetrical Collapse—When one side of the wing deflates and not the other. It is the most common paraglider malady that results from turbulence.

Asymmetric Blade Thrust—see P-Factor.

Asymmetric Spiral—A spiral dive where the bank on one side of the circle is shallower than the other.

B Lines—The second row of paraglider lines; they go from the B riser to the wing.

B Line Stall—A condition where the wing is stalled by virtue of the pilot pulling the B-lines down to his chest. Descent rate is usually about 4 times normal.

Big Ears—A maneuver where the pilot pulls the outer A lines such that the tips of the wing fold downward to increase descent rate.

Brake Lines—Lines that go from the brake toggles, through a pulley or loop on the rear riser and up to the trailing edge of the wing.

Brake Toggles—The handles used by the pilot to control the craft. They attach to the brake lines.

C Lines—The third row of lines; they go from the C riser to the wing.

Canopy—Another name for the wing.

Carabiners—Metal fasteners that attach the wing, through its riser loops, to the harness.

Cascade—The split in a wing's lines where it spreads from one line to several as it goes up to the wing. This design feature reduces the total line count and resulting drag.

Cart—see Trike.

Cells—A single sewn section of a wing containing air that makes up the airfoil shape.

CEN—European standards organization that does certification of paragliders (among other things).

CHT—Cylinder Head Temperature.

CIMA—International Microlight Commission of FAI.

Clip-In Weight—The pilot weight plus motor, fuel and any accessories necessary to fly. Aka *hook-in weight*.

Chord—The distance from the leading edge to trailing edge at any point along the span.

Collapse—What happens when part or all of the wing deforms (folds) due to turbulence or pilot input and looses lift.

Constant Stall—see Parachutal Stall.

Crab—Heading some amount into the wind to maintain a desired ground track.

Damping—The pilot action required to reduce any pendular or fore/aft oscillation.

Deck Angle—see Pitch.

Density Altitude—Altitude adjusted for pressure, temperature and humidity. Hot, humid air makes any aircraft perform as though it were at a higher altitude—it is said to be at a higher density altitude. Aircraft performance is based on density altitude, not the actual altitude as read on an altimeter.

DHV—German Hanggliding and Paragliding Federation "Deutcher Hangeleiter Verband." They certify free-flight paragliders, harnesses and related equipment in Germany. This is the most common service used to certify paragliders.

DULV—German Ultralight Flight organization that certifies paramotors and paramotor wings designed for paramotoring.

Downwind Demon—Series of illusions that frequently lead to a pilot pulling too much brake when low to the ground and turning downwind.

FAI—Fédération Aéronautique International. The world's Air Sports Federation. See also CIMA.

FAR—Federal Aviation Regulations; governing law for paramotor pilots in the USA.

Float Bowl Carburetor—A type of carburetor that uses a float to regulate fuel level in the bowl.

Fold—See collapse.

FPM—Feet Per Minute. A measure of climb or descent rate.

Full Stall—An extreme maneuver where the pilot pulls enough brake to deform the wing so much that slows dramatically and deforms the glider and is characterized with a very high descent rate.

Forward Inflation—Any inflation done while facing away from the wing and into the wind; usually done in light winds.

Front Tuck—see frontal.

Frontal—A wing deformation where the leading edge folds downward. Maintained in this state, the wing will descend about 3 times the normal rate.

Free Flyer—One who flies without a motor; a paraglider pilot. They generally seek out natural lift sources and launch from high places or get towed in aloft.

GA—General Aviation; all aviation that is not military, governmental or scheduled airlines.

Gyroscopic Precession—The characteristic of a any rotating mass whereby a force acting perpendicular to the direction of rotation will cause the reaction 90 degrees in the direction of rotation.

Harness—The combination of fabric and straps that holds the pilot up in flight through an attachment to the wing and also what the motor is attached to.

Glossary

Helicopter—One of several aerobatic maneuvers where the pilot is spinning around an axis other than the center of the wing.

Lateral Axis—An imaginary left/right line around which the PPG pitches up or down. The extended arms of a seated pilot represent the lateral axis direction but the axis itself is between the pilot and wing.

Leading Edge—Front of the wing where the cell openings are.

Longitudinal Axis—An imaginary front-to-back line around which the PPG rolls (banks).

Horseshoe—When referring to a paraglider, the wing deformation where the wing tips come forward and may touch each other. Descent rate is usually about 4 times normal.

Loop—A high energy aerobatic maneuver where the pilot uses speed from a steep spiral to fly over the top of the glider.

Maillon—see quick link.

Membrane Carburetor—A type of carburetor that uses a membrane to regulate fuel flow.

Mechanical Turbulence—Random swirls of air downwind of a solid object (building, hill, mountain, etc.).

MSL—Mean Sea Level—usually referred to as an altitude meaning above sea level. It is used interchangeably with ASL in many publications (not this one though).

NOTAM—Notice To Airmen. Information for pilots obtained by calling 800-WX-BRIEF.

Over-The-Nose Spiral—A spiral dive where the wing is pointed nearly straight down. Recovery can be difficult.

P-Factor—A force that results when the plane of a spinning propeller is hitting the air at an angle. The effective center of thrust will move towards the blade arc having the highest angle of attack.

Parablend—An expensive Nylon/Kevlar cocktail mixed by a spinning paramotor propeller, usually prepared just after an aborted launch.

Parachutage—see Parachutal Stall.

Parachutal Stall—A stall where the fully-formed wing stops flying forward and descends like an old round parachute.

Parasite—Location where powered paragliding takes place.

Pendulum—The left right swinging action that occurs whenever the glider is upset laterally.

Pitch—Motion around the PPG's latitudinal axis. The pilot is said to *Pitch up* when power is added.

PLF—Parachute Landing Fall.

PPG—Powered Paraglider

Pressure Altitude—True Altitude adjust for pressure difference from the standard atmosphere. See Density Altitude.

Propeller—The long skinny blade that provides propulsion.

Quick Link—The steel ring that connect the wing's A, B, C or D lines to their respective riser. Also called Maillon Rapide (primarily in Europe). The distinction is they use screw-together gates.

Rear Riser—The aftmost riser. On 3-riser wings, it is the C riser. On 4-riser wings it is the D riser.

Reverse Inflation—Any Inflation started while facing the wing instead of the wind. Usually done in stronger wind.

Riser Loops—The loops at the very bottom of each riser where the carabiner goes through.

Riser Set—The combination of individual A, B, C and D risers and their corresponding loop for each side of the wing that connect to the harness through a carabiner and lines through quick links.

Roll—Motion around the PPG's longitudinal axis. A pilot "rolls" into a bank.

Rotor—The swirling air that results from wind blowing around an obstacle.

S.A.T.—The "Safety Acrobatic Team's" maneuver of spinning where the glider and pilot appear to be rotating around each other.

SHV—A paraglider certifying agency created by the Swiss Hang gliding Association.

Speedbar—see Accelerator.

Spiral Dive—An extreme banked turn where the wing is angled towards the ground. See also "Over-The-Nose" spiral dive.

Stall—see Full Stall.

Surge—The characteristic of the wing to overfly the pilot under some conditions. It can be induced by pilot action or turbulence.

Stabilo Line—Line that goes to the very tip of the wing, usually a B line.

Tell Tale—A small wind indicator, usually a streamer of some sort.

Torque—The property of a motor/propeller that makes the motor, and its harnessed occupant, want to twist in the opposite direction of propeller spin.

Trailing Edge—The rearmost part of the wing when in flight.

Trike—An attachment of wheels that allows the pilot roll to launch his PPG motor on wheels. It is also called a cart.

Trimmers—Mechanism of some risers (usually on motoring wings) that allows changing the rear risers to increase speed. The pilot pulls a "Trim Tab" to effect the change.

Trim Speed—The speed that results when flying with no brakes applied, trimmers in their cruise setting and no speedbar.

True Airspeed—Actual speed through the air as opposed to what it feels like to the pilot. At high elevations, the pilot must move faster through the air to get the same feel as at lower elevations.

Tuned Exhaust—A specially designed exhaust that improves performance in 2-stroke motors.

Turtle—The occurrence when a pilot falls backwards such that he is lying on top of the motor, unable to move until un-clipping from the unit.

Vertical Axis—an imaginary top-to-bottom line around which the PPG yaws (twists left or right).

VOR—Very High Frequency (VHF) Omni Directional Range used for navigation by airplane pilots and as reference points on charts.

Windmilling—The spinning of a prop due solely to the relative wind blowing through it.

Wind Shadow—A calm that exists downwind of obstructions.

Wing—The means to our magic.

Wing Fold—see Collapse.

Wing Over—A series of turns in concert with the natural pendular bank rate of the glider.

Yaw—Motion around the PPG's vertical axis. If the PPG rotates to the left without banking it is said to yaw to the left.

Index

2-meter FM *212*
2-place. *See tandem*
2-stroke motor *228-232*

A

A wiggle *53*
accessories *40, 273-278*
active flying *162, 178, 212*
adiabatic lapse rate *242*
ADIZ *87*
adjusting, motor. *See harness, setup*
advertising *81*
aerobatic wings *258*
aerobatics *173*
AFNOR *260*
AGL *84*
agonic line *133*
air cooled, motor *266*
airbag *212*
airflow, mountain *72*
airfoil shape *222*
airline pilot *11*
airlines *183, 192*
airplane *58, 78, 85, 89, 92, 100-103, 132, 136, 285*
airport *58, 83, 85, 97, 99, 129*
airport, controlled *105-110*
airshow *190*
airspace *75, 78, 84-96, 130, 131*
airspeed *132, 157, 163, 172*
alert areas *84, 87*
allen wrenches *116*
alphabet, phonetic *109*
altimeter *20-21, 82, 277*
altimetry *277*
altitude *129, 136*
altitude abbreviations *84*
altitudes *58, 138*
aluminum *113, 116, 117*
anemometer
angle of attack (AoA) *217, 221*
angle of attack, prop *235*
angle of incidence (AoI) *223, 224*
angled-back *166*
anhedral *222*
animals *77, 78, 84*
anti-torque strap *17, 112, 174*
approach *59*
arrogance *12, 82*
ARTCC (center) *90*
ASC *302*
aspect ratio *223*
asymmetric spiral *178*
ATC *90, 105*
ATIS *106, 107, 108*
atmosphere *70*
atmospheric pressure *166*
attachment points *175, 269-270*
authorities *80*
aviation weather *75-76*
avisory circular AC 103-7 *81*
AWOS *107*
axis of motion *219*
  latitudinal (pitch) 219
  longitudinal (roll) 219
  vertical (yaw) 219

B

B Line Stall *177*
backwards flying *149*
balance, prop. *See static balance*
balloon *161*
bank *156, 189, 218, 219, 225*
banner. *See Flags*

Barish, David *252*
base leg, pattern *60, 101-103*
beach *155*
beach, weather *72*
bearings *117-118*
belt drive *117, 118*
  distance 118
  slipping 118
  tension 118
belt tension, checking *117*
Bernoulli *223*
Bernstien, Josh *12*
best L/D speed *220-221*
big air *214, 246*
big ear line *261*
big ears *176, 214*
B-line stall *194*
bolts *116*
brake line length *24*
brake lines *14, 124*
brake positions/pressures *24, 157*
brake pulley *14*
brakes, feel position *155*
brummel hooks. *See sister clips*
bubbles, fuel line *117*
bump scale *57, 140*
bundling the wing *35, 62*
burns, line *143, 148*
bus lines, transporting *291*
buzzing *138*

C

cage *40, 51, 64, 160, 173, 267*
  flex 52
capsize, trike *64, 65*
carabiner, *20*
carbon deposits *116*
carbon fiber prop *121*
carburetor cleaner *62*
carburetor tuning *231*
carburetors *229-232*
carry strap. *See Ground Handling Strap*
cart. *See trike*
cascade. *14*
cascade failure, lines *125*
cattle herding *287*
cell openings *26*
cell phone *277*
cells *143*
CEN *260*
center of lift *219, 221*
centered, forward inflation *27*
centripetal force *230*
certification *7, 63, 64*
certification, wing *111*
certified wings *176, 258, 260, 111*
CG *63, 65, 114, 175, 219, 236*
chart *82*
checklist *51, 301*
chest strap *174*
choosing a motor unit *263-272*
choosing the site *98-99*
chord line *223, 224*
CHT *20-21*
CIMA *199*
city *79, 136*
class A airspace *85*
class B airspace *85, 91, 92, 93, 94*
class C airspace *85*
class D airspace *85, 91, 92, 95, 96, 105, 107, 110*
class E airspace *83-96, 100-103*
class E surface area *86, 109*
class F airspace *84*

class G airspace *78, 83-96, 100-103*
cleaning *62, 143*
clearing the lines *26*
clearing the turn *57*
cliff, launching from *213*
climb *55, 139, 163, 167, 189*
  illusion 188
climb angle *98*
climbout *137, 168, 169*
C-line deflation *34*
clinics, SIV. *See SIV course*
clip-in weight *63*
cloud clearance *71, 83, 85, 89, 304*
cloud suck *244, 248*
clouds *89, 130, 131, 243, 247-248*
  as shear indicators 73
  cumuliform 247
  cumulonimbus 71
  cumulus 70, 76, 89, 130, 241
  from ocean 76
  indicating turbulence 70
  stratus 71, 72
  weather indicators 69
cloverleaf *199, 200*
clutch *117, 118, 230*
  bell 118
  pads 118
  shoes 118
  springs 118
clutch bell *118*
clutch, machines with *52*
clutched units *220-221*
coastal weather *244*
coatings *13-22*
cold fronts *76, 248-249*
collapse *47, 54, 69, 139, 162, 175*
  asymmetric 180
  frontal 181
collapse, how it happens *225*
collapses, large *99*
collision *59, 78, 89, 138, 140, 189*
collision hazard *100-103*
comfort bars. *See also J-bars*
commercial use *81*
common sense *77, 78, 79, 81, 137*
communications
communications, control tower *107, 109*
compass *132*
compass rose *75, 90*
compensation *81, 82*
competing *174*
competition *159-160, 172, 191, 199-206*
  circle and two lines 204
  cloverleaf 200
  endurance 205
  engine failure 199
  fair 200
  flight precision 204
  foot drag 202
  ground precision 200-203
  kiting war 205
  scoring 206
  speedbar 201
  spot landing 203
  touch and go 203
complaint *82*
compression *116-117*
compression release *232*
conduction *242*
congested *79, 82, 170*
control tower *85, 86, 87, 91, 93, 96, 105-110*

convergence zone *73, 245*
coordinated turn *174*
coordinates *92*
cost *256*
courtesy *137-138*
crabbing *65, 134*
crankshaft *118*
cravat *48, 177, 178, 179, 182*
critical angle of attack *217, 224, 225*
crops *62, 97, 99*
cross country *129-136*
cross-section *223*
crosswind *28, 59, 65, 134, 154, 160, 167*
cruising *58*
customs *292*

D

daylight *70*
daylight savings time *74*
dead reckoning *132*
deck angle *223*
decompression valve. *See compression release*
deflating *24, 34, 145*
demonstration *173, 183*
density altitude *65, 166, 167*
deploying *127, 179*
deposits, carbon *116*
de-rated *266*
descent techniques *176-179*
desert weather *245*
dewpoint *75, 242*
DHV *260*
diaphragm carburetor *230*
dips and loops *25*
direct drive *233, 271*
directional control *98*
disaster areas *84, 88*
disk, propeller *234*
distance bars *269-270*
distance, judging *98*
distraction *79, 138, 189, 293*
ditching *192, 278*
dog, as passenger *66*
downhill, launching *99*
downwind *72, 167*
downwind demon *188-189*
downwind leg *60, 102*
drag, aerodynamic *63, 176, 217-219*
  center of 219, 221
  form 218
  induced 218
  parasitic 218
drift *60, 61, 104*
dropping objects *80*
dry *70*
DULV *260*
dust devils *70, 245*
Dyneema *125*

E

E Surface Area. *See class E surface area*
EAA *279, 302*
efficiency *222*
EGT *20-21*
electric start *265*
electronic noise
emergencies *44-50, 56*
  brake line failure or tangle 45-50
  cravat 48-50
  kill switch failure 48-50

Page 307

Index

motor failure 46-50
parachutal stall 50
PLF 50
radio failure 45-50
reserve deployment 49-50
riser twist 48-50
severe asymmetric collapse 47-50
small wing collapse 47-50
throttle cable caught 44-50
unfastened leg straps 49-50
emergencies, situational 192-198
  accidental reserve deployment 198
  cloud suck 195
  engine failure 196
  fire 198
  fogged in 196
  gust front 193
  impending collision 197
  landing in power lines 194
  landing in water 192
  motor stuck at power 194
  toy kite lines 198
  wing or connection failure 197
emergency kit 277
emergency landing site 97
emergency tool kit 126
endanger 79
endurance 130
energy 158-159, 184
enforcement 80
engine failure 46-50, 98, 103, 130, 137, 163, 168, 169, 183, 184, 185
evaporation 244
exemption 81, 82
exhibition 288

F

FAA 75, 77-82, 84, 88, 251
face plant 52
FAI 199
Fan Man 253
FAR 103 78, 79, 303
FCC 22
federal funds, airport 100-103
federal lands 97
feel 169
final approach, pattern 101-103
fine, law enforcement 82
fire 117, 198
flag 220-221
flag, on wing 286-287
flapping 172
flare 124, 163
flat area (wing) 258
flight path 59, 218
float bowl carburetor 230, 231
floating J-bars 112, 113
fly-ins 79
fly-ins, organizing 299-300
folding 36, 62
foot drag 155, 160, 200-206
foot-launched. See tandem, foot launched
foot-pound 116
footware 162
footwear 185, 191
forces, balance 217-219
forecast 69
forested areas 97
formation 138, 140, 161-162, 189
forward inflation 26, 52-56
forward kiting 28, 29
free flight, learn motoring 207-208
free flight, learn paragliding 211-212

front horseshoe 178
front tuck (frontal) 28, 31, 53, 54, 145, 151, 175, 181
frontal, weather 71
fronts 248
FRS
FSS 76, 84, 87, 88, 90, 106
fuel 38-39, 131
  fueling 38
  mixture 38
  old 183
  preflight 40
  selection and storage 38
fuel lines 117

G

G force 177
gasoline. See fuel
gear, PPG 13-22
gear, reduction drive 117-118
general aviation 84, 100-103
glide 61-62, 66, 130, 170-172
glide ratio 58, 220-221, 226
gloves 25, 143, 148, 191, 278
GPS 85, 89, 92, 95, 129, 131, 136, 277
GPS groundspeed 104
gradient 129
grass 63, 65, 98, 99, 103, 129, 143
Greenwich, England 74
ground handling 23
ground effect 222
ground handling straps 17, 112, 113
ground track 59, 132, 133
groundspeed 129, 132, 135, 157, 166
G's 58, 218
gust 157-158, 164
gust front 71, 76, 247-248
gust front, handling 193
gusts 70
gyroscopic precession 238, 239

H

hand signals 43
handling the wing 23-36
hands up, power off 44, 50, 139, 179, 238. See collapse, assymetric
hang check 37
hang glider 11, 96
hang gliding 251
hang point. See compression release
hang-back angle 114
harness 16-19, 25, 37, 71, 111-114, 166, 173
  adjusting 16, 37, 166
  for kiting 20
  free flight 173, 174, 175
  height 16
  mountain climbing harness 20
  setup 111-114
heading 132
headset 106-110
headwind 61, 131, 136, 157, 171
helicopter 78, 88, 92, 102-103, 286, 292
helicopters 58
helicopters (maneuver) 173
helmet 21-22, 25, 106-110, 185, 191
high elevation 98, 99-100, 165-167, 168
high wind techniques 146-151
highway 100

hill, launching from 213
history of PPG 251-254
home building 279
hook in
  high 174
  low 175
hook knife 22, 192
hook-in 219
  adjusting hang angle 112
  hard point 113
  high 113
  low 113
  low, fixed 128
  thrust re-direction 114
hooking in, alternate 29
hooking in, forward 27
hooking in, reversed 29-35
horsepower (HP) 227-228. See compression release
horseshoe 225
hot conditions 98, 165-167
houses 79, 80
humid 165-167
humidity 166
hurricane 245

I

illusions
inch-pound 117
inflation 26, 31-32, 166, 167
  assisted 150
  crooked's cure 153
  high winds 148
  overfly 150
  power forward 167
  risk 150
  salvaging 153
  without a harness 144
inflation, stronger winds 54
inflation, trike 63
inspection 13-22, 154
inspection, postflight 62
inspection, wing 125
instructing, for pay 81
instruction 302
Instruments 20-21
intercepting 162
intermediate syndrome 186
introductory flight 63
inversion 72, 243
investigate 81, 82
IR, instrument route 87
ISA 242
isogonic line 132, 133

J

James Watt 228
J-bar 174
J-bars 17, 112, 113, 114
  comfort bars 18
  shoulder J-Bars 18
  underarm 18
jet 183
jets 89, 102-103, 136
jettison 18
judging distance 98

K

Kevlar 125
kick-in bar 112, 113
kick-in strap 56
kill switch 34, 48, 56, 60, 140
kit, building from 281
kiting 11, 23, 48, 139, 143

forward 29
high winds 146-151
light winds 151
reverse 32-35
straight riser reversed 33
upside down 143
wars 152
without a harness 144
kiting harness 25, 143
kiting war 205
kiting, the wing 51, 54
knot, brake line 125
Kodak Courage 190

L

landing 59-61, 99, 163, 170
  backwards 193
  crosshill 99
  crosswind 99
  flare 61
  in turbulence 170
  one step 164
  pattern 57, 59
  power on 164
  scoop 163
  slider 163
  spot 163
  troubleshooting 61
  uphill 99
landing, trike 63, 66
landmarks 131
lapse rate 242, 246
latent heat 244
latitude, line of 85, 90, 132, 133
launch 51-56, 98, 168
  distances 98
  roads 166, 172
  slope 99
  steering 168
launch, trike 63, 64-66
law, the 77-82
layout 26
layout, wing 52
leading edge 27, 31, 40, 144
lee, of obstruction 72
leg drag 99, 166
leg straps 112
letter of agreement 110
letter of investigation 81
lettering the wing 82
license 2, 81
licensed pilots 100-103
lift, aerodynamic 217-219
lift, atmospheric 74
lifted index 246
liftoff 98
liftoff, trike 65
liftweb 111, 113
line chart 125
line over 25
line stretching 125
lines, paraglider. See ultraviolet
loiter 88
longitude, line of 85, 90, 132, 133
loops 173
lost 131
low flying 160-161

M

mach. See compression release
macrometeorology 248
magnetic course 132
magnetic north 75, 133
maillon. See quick link
maintenance, motor 111-128

Index

flowchart 115
motor 114-117
troubleshooting 116
maintenance, wing 123-126
  adjusting brake lines 124
  brake line knot 123
  cascade 125
  fabric repair 125
  inspection 125
  ocean dunking 126
  replacing risers 123
  tape 125
  water exposure 123
maneuvers, advanced 173-182
mechanical turbulence 73, 98, 249
MEF 92
membrane carburetor 230, 232
Mercury, inches of 166
metal-to-metal 114
meteorologist 241
metric, bolts 116
micro balloons 121
microlight 199
micrometeorology 241
mid-air. *See collision*
mid-day 71
military 84, 87
Miller, James 253
minimum sink speed 226
minutes, degree 92
mirror 131
MOA's, airspace 87
mode C 87
model aircraft, finding 288
monsoons 245
motor failure 55, 56, 57, 58
motor mount 40
motor risers 260-261
motorcycle 291
mountain clearing 97
mountain weather 72, 76
mountains 170
MSL 84
muffler 40, 77, 116
music 189

N

nap-of-the-earth 87
nature preserve. *See wilderness areas*
nautical mile 85, 90, 136
navigation 132
negative G 217
neighbors 99
Newton, Isaac 218
night 130, 136
noise 77, 79, 80, 101-103, 137, 235. *See compression release*
nosewheel 64
NOTAM 75, 76, 90
NOTAM for fly-ins 300
NTSB 82

O

obstacle 92
obstacles 168, 169
obstructions 98, 99, 168
ocean 192
offset thrust 114, 237
oil 130, 302
  four-cycle 39
  mineral 39, 292
  mixing 38, 302
  selection 38
  synthetic 39, 292

two-cycle oil 39
oil, gear 117-118
open air assembly 79
orientation, trike 64
orographic lift 75
oscillation 29, 53, 58, 65, 156, 157, 162, 163
other uses 285-288
over the nose spiral 178
over-braking 58
overfly 28, 29, 32, 33, 53, 54, 62, 145, 148

P

parablending 53, 54
parachutal stall 50, 69, 162, 176, 286
parachute landing fall. *See PLF*
parachute rigger 113, 128
parachute, reserve 40, 173, 191
paraglider, high performance 163
paragliding 211-214
parasailing 251
parascending 252
park, state or federal 99
parks 84, 88, 97, 169
parts, availability 271-272
passenger 64
patch 125
pattern 42-43, 96, 101-103, 138, 169, 171
pattern, airplane 91, 92, 94
pattern, designing 300
pendular control 181
pendulum 14, 58, 60, 66, 156, 157, 163
penetration 171, 186
permission 99
P-factor 240
phonetic alphabet 109
photography 81, 293-298
  aperture 295
  depth of field 295
  exposure 295
  focus 295
  ISO 295
  noise 296
  panning 295
  resolution 296
pictures 293
pilotage 132, 134-136
pipeline patrols 58
piston rings 115
pitch 217
pitch, propeller 234
pivoting bar 174, 175
placard, wing 260
plans, building from 281
platform 291
play, in prop 117-118
PLF 50
polar curve 221, 226
pole standing 162
police 77
pop-off pressure 232
porosity 125
porous 190
postflight 62
posture 166
power 99, 158, 160, 167, 170, 175
power band 228-232
power forward 51, 52, 208-209, 264, 267
power to weight ratio 254
PPC 139, 254

precision flying 155-164, 174
preflight choices 167
preflight inspection 39-41, 301
  motor 39
  risers 41
  wing 41
premix. *See fueling*
preparing the wing 26
preservation, wing 36
preventative maintenance 116-117
private pilots 81
professional pilots 82
prohibited area 80
projected area (wing) 258
pronunciation, alphabet 109
prop blast 52, 66, 138
prop disk 112
prop tape 120
prop wash 138
propeller 37, 40, 118-120, 233-236, 268
  aerodynamic balance 119
  balancers 119
  chordwise offset 119, 121
  impbalance, offset 121
  larger repairs 121
  leading edge tape 120
  mounting 118
  static balance 119, 121
  static balance, solder 121
  torsional stress 118
  tracking 120
propeller efficiency 236
propeller plane 52, 138
propeller repair 120
  baking soda 121
  carbon fiber props 121
  caution 121
  fiberglass 122
  foam 122
  small divots 121
  wood props 121
property damage 99
public property 97
public relations 288
pull start 230, 265
pulled apex, reserve 124
pulley, brake 124
pulleys 113-114, 117, 118, 124-126
puzzle props 290

Q

QFE 277
QNH 277
quick links 15, 41, 124

R

radiant cooling 242
radio 9-10, 22, 43, 140, 161, 212, 276
radio, aviation 85, 86, 87, 91, 94, 95, 103, 105-110
rain 69
range 131
ratings 2, 68
ratio, fuel/oil 115
record, number aloft 76
recreation 81
reduction drive 117-118, 233-236
  propside gear 118
  small gear 118
reed valve 232
regulations 78-79, 82, 83
rehearse 28, 56
relative wind 217

reliability 265, 266
repair 116, 119, 122. *See propeller repair*
repair shops 114
rescuing 139
reserve. *See parachute, reserve deployment* 49
reserve parachute 22, 127-128
  bridle routing 127-128
  deployment bag 128
  installation 127
  maintenance 127-128
  mounting 127-128
  repacking 128
  setup 127-128
  skydiving reserves 128
retrieval 135
reverse inflation 29-35, 54, 55
rich fuel/air mixture 231
rich of peak 231
ridge lift. *See lift, atmospheric*
ridge rules 211
rigger, parachute 128
right of way 78, 100
right of way, soaring 211
ripstop nylon 13-22
riser separation 25
riser twist 53, 55, 111, 114
risers 15-16, 123, 124, 143, 261-262
  changing 123
  spread 111, 113
  Risk viii, 142, 153, 160, 161, 163, 245, 246, 293
Risk & Reward 9, 65, 68
risk management 183-198
risks 12, 138-139, 140
risky 159, 171, 173, 179
rivers 133
roads 79, 92, 100, 131, 133, 167, 172
rocket launches 84
Rogallo 252
rollover 63, 64
rolls 173
rosette the wing 35, 151
rotor 57, 72, 73, 74, 196, 249
rules, competition 199
runup 52
runway 89-92, 101-103, 129
rust 118

S

safety strap 114
safety wire 116
salt water 126
sand 99, 143, 156, **164**, 167
Santa Ana winds 245
SAT's 173
school viii, 4-5, 104
sea breeze 245
search and rescue 288
seat 56
seat, getting into 37
seatboard 56
seconds, degree 92
sectional chart 81, 82, 83, 85, 87, 89-92, 96, 105, 106, 136
security airspace 84, 87
see and be seen 103
segmented circle 101-103
seized 39, 115
self training viii
setup, trike 64
severe weather 72
shadow 138

Page 309

Index

Shatner, William 10
shear zone. *See wind shear*
sheath 14
shipping 289
shop, repair 114
showing off 78
SHV 260
sidetone
simulator 7, 9, 37, 43, 56, 111, 112, 113, 128
single-point failure 190
sink 72, 74, 99
sink rate 221
siphoning fuel 39
sister clips 113
sites 96, 97, 98-99, 103, 104, 168
    challenging 165-172
    tight 168-172
SIV course 173, 175-176, 184, 214
sky divers 12
sky diving reserves 128
slider 164
slipstream 37
slow 159
soaring 13-22, 72, 74, 96, 174, 211, 246
soft J-bar 112
span 220-221
spare air 191
spark 116
spark plug 40, 116, 126
sparsely populated 79, 80, 87
spectators 79, 137
Spectra 125
speed system 15, 113
speedbar 112, 113, 127, 162, 171, 220-221, 222, 226
speedbar use 175
spin 171, 172, 174, 180
spiral dive 178
split A's 15, 27, 52, 261-262
sport parachuting 251, 252
Sport Pilot regulation 81
sporting events 79
spot landing 170-172
    flare 171-172
    touchdown 170
springs, safety wiring 116
stability 219, 225
stability, trike 63, 64
stabilo line 48, 182
stall 171, 172
stall, aerodynamics of 217, 225
stall, full 179-180
stall, parachutal. *See parachutal stall*
standard atmosphere 242-243
standard temperature 166
starter, electric 42
starting 185
starting the motor 42
state change 244
state lands 97
statute mile 106, 136
steep descent 172
steep turns 177
steering lines. *See brake Lines*
steering, launch run 100
Steinmetz, George 294
sternum strap 113
storage, fuel. *See fueling*
storing the wing 35-36
straight riser kiting 33
straight-in, airports 102-103
stratiform 247

strength test, field 41
stretching, lines 125
strobe 78
stuffing the wing 36
S-Turn 171
sublimation 244
suitcase, packing into 290
summersaults 144, 145
sunrise 78, 98, 243
sunset 78
surf 196
surface area of Class E 87, 90
surfaces 99, 147, 163, 166, 167
    difficult 172
    smooth 147, 150
surge 149, 158, 162
    pendular control 181
suspended targets 161
swinging arms 114
symmetrical airfoil 218, 223

T

tachometer
tailwind 28, 61, 132, 157, 165
tandem 2, 5, 7, 8-9, 63, 64, 66, 81, 139, 214, 263
    foot-launched 263
tandem, foot launch 63, 64
tangled 25, 62, 138, 173
target fixation 60
TBO 266
telephone, permission 105
telltale 165
temperature 166
tensile strength. 14
Terminal Area Chart 83, 96
terminal velocity 128
terrain 99, 135, 179, 190
test, airspace 92
TFR 89-92
thermaling 211
thermals 52, 70, 104, 130, 154, 225, 243, 245
throttle 54, 64, 128, 139, 158
throttle simulator 27, 34
thrust 159-160, 165, 166, 167, 170
thrust line 64, 112, 114, 219, 222, 225
thrust required 226
thrust vs. horsepower 227-228
thrust, choosing 264
thunderstorm 71, 73, 248
time, universal 74
tip speed 234
toggle, brake 27, 162
toggles 14, 143, 148
tool kit, emergency 126
tools 116, 130, 167
topographical information 95
tornados 70, 71
torque 52, 55, 237-240, 264
torque wrench 116
torque, motor 112, 114
touchdown 50, 60-62, 163-164, 171
tow, boat 175
tower frequency 92
towing 6
town 79
traffic 59, 138
trailing edge 14, 31, 143
training 185
transition areas 84, 85, 86, 95
transmissions 107
transponder 87
transportability 271

transportation 285
traveling with gear 289-292
tree rescue kit 277
trees 98, 169
trespassing 97
trike 55, 63
trim speed 157, 220-221
trimmers 15, 157, 162, 171, 175, 220-221, 222, 226, 260
true course 132
true north 75
tundra tires 65
tuned pipe 228-232
turbulence 99, 104, 139, 156, 158, 162, 170, 173, 175, 179
    all clouds 71
    convergence
    cumulus clouds 70
    flying in
    from gust front 193
    landing in 170
    landing power-on 210
    mechanical turbulence 193
    obstructions 72, 74
    oscillations 193
    thermals 70
    thunderstorms 71
    turbulence 245
turning, aerodynamics of 225
turns 57, 98, 138, 159-160
turtle 55, 66
tweaking the A's 50

U

U.S. Nationals 129
ultralight 69, 78, 83, 84, 88, 96, 251, 304
un-controlled airports 100-103
underarm bars 17. *See also comfort bars*
unicom 95, 103
unstable atmosphere 246
untangling 25
updrafts. *See thermals*
USHGA 212, 253, 302
USPPA 7, 10, 68
USUA 204, 302
UTC 76. *See Zulu*
UV 14, 62

V

variation 132
variation, line of 94
variometer 277
vector diagram 134
venturi 230-232
VFR 83
vibration 117, 119, 120, 121
video 81, 293, 297
    f-stop 295
    lipstick cameras 297
    zoom 298
visibility 58, 71, 83-96, 304
VOR 88, 89, 90, 92, 96, 105
vortices. *See wake turbulence*
VR, visual route 87

W

waiver 11, 82, 300
wake turbulence 58, 102-103, 138, 139, 162, 223
wall 54, 144, 147, 151, 152
wall, building 30-31
warm fronts 249

water 139, 160, 169, 175, 192, 278
water cooled, motor 266
weather 69-76, 241-250
webbing, harness 16
weight 13, 14, 16, 18, 19, 20, 63, 263, 264
weight shift 57, 112, 114, 138, 174-175, 176, 212, 237, 270-271
welding 302
wheels 63
Wilbur Wright viii
wilderness 84, 88
wildlife 84
wind 52, 69, 99, 129-136, 241-250
    aloft 72, 73
    bow wave 72
    Coriolis effect 250
    direction 134
    drift 132, 134
    fronts 249
    gradient 73, 129-136, 188, 193
    high pressure area 250
    hurricane 250
    indicators 52, 60
    jet stream 250
    land-breeze 73
    low pressure area 250
    mechanical turbulence 249
    mountain wave 250
    ridge 250
    rotor 193, 249
    sea breeze 72
    shadow 57, 72, 99, 196, 249
    shear 73
    surface 73, 104
    telling direction 74, 104
    turbulent flow 72
    upslope 103
    VAD winds 76
    venturi effect 250
windmilling 176, 220-221
wing 99, 167
    area 221
    choosing 257-262
    fast 167
    loading 258
    overview 13-14
wingover 181, 225
wingtip vortices 218, 222, 223. *See also wake turbulence*
wire ties 117, 126, 127
wires 98, 130, 133, 140, 160, 185, 187
wraps 147
Wright Brothers 13
www.FootFlyer.com 76

XYZ

yaw 217
Zulu 74